Addiction: A Comprehensive Overview

Addiction: A Comprehensive Overview

Editor: London Stevens

MURPHY & MOORE
www.murphy-moorepublishing.com

www.murphy-moorepublishing.com

MURPHY & MOORE

Cataloging-in-Publication Data

Addiction : a comprehensive overview / edited by London Stevens.
p. cm.
Includes bibliographical references and index.
ISBN 978-1-63987-009-7
1. Substance abuse. 2. Psychology, Pathological. 3. Substance abuse--Treatment. I. Stevens, London.
RC564 .A33 2022
362.29--dc23

Murphy & Moore Publishing,
1 Rockefeller Plaza,
New York City, NY 10020, USA

ISBN 978-1-63987-009-7 (Hardback)

Contents

Preface

The disorder of the brain in which compulsive engagement in rewarding stimuli is observed even when it has negative consequences is termed as addiction. A few examples of behavioral and drug addictions are amphetamine addiction, chocolate addiction, nicotine addiction, alcoholism and marijuana addiction. The diagnosis of addiction can be done by studying physical dependence and withdrawal syndrome in relation to the addiction. A few symptoms of withdrawal are anxiety, body aches, nausea and hallucinations. Addiction can cause changes in the structure of the brain. Therefore, non-invasive neuroimaging scans can also be used to diagnose addiction. The treatment of addiction generally involves behavioral therapy and medications. This book elucidates the concepts and innovative models around prospective developments with respect to research on addiction. It presents researches and studies performed by experts across the globe. The book is appropriate for students seeking detailed information in this area as well as for experts.

This book is the end result of constructive efforts and intensive research done by experts in this field. The aim of this book is to enlighten the readers with recent information in this area of research. The information provided in this profound book would serve as a valuable reference to students and researchers in this field.

At the end, I would like to thank all the authors for devoting their precious time and providing their valuable contribution to this book. I would also like to express my gratitude to my fellow colleagues who encouraged me throughout the process.

Editor

1

Addiction and the brain-disease fallacy

Sally Satel*[1] *and Scott O. Lilienfeld*[2]

[1] *Yale University School of Medicine, New Haven, CT, USA*
[2] *Department of Psychology, Emory University, Atlanta, GA, USA*

Edited by:
Hanna Pickard, University of Oxford, UK

Reviewed by:
Serge H. Ahmed, Centre National de la Recherche Scientifique, France
Bennett Foddy, University of Oxford, UK

****Correspondence:***
Scott O. Lilienfeld, Department of Psychology, Emory University, 473 Psychology Building, 36 Eagle Row, Atlanta, GA 30322, USA
e-mail: slilien@emory.edu

The notion that addiction is a "brain disease" has become widespread and rarely challenged. The brain-disease model implies erroneously that the brain is necessarily the most important and useful level of analysis for understanding and treating addiction. This paper will explain the limits of over-medicalizing – while acknowledging a legitimate place for medication in the therapeutic repertoire – and why a broader perspective on the problems of the addicted person is essential to understanding addiction and to providing optimal care. In short, the brain-disease model obscures the dimension of choice in addiction, the capacity to respond to incentives, and also the essential fact people use drugs for reasons (as consistent with a self-medication hypothesis). The latter becomes obvious when patients become abstinent yet still struggle to assume rewarding lives in the realm of work and relationships. Thankfully, addicts can choose to recover and are not helpless victims of their own "hijacked brains."

Keywords: brain-disease fallacy, addiction, fMRI, Project HOPE, brain-disease model

INTRODUCTION

In 1970, high-grade heroin and opium flooded Southeast Asia. Military physicians in Vietnam estimated that nearly half of all U.S. Army enlisted men serving there had tried opium or heroin [(1), p. 1046], and between 10 and 25% of them were addicted. Deaths from overdoses soared. In May 1971, the crisis reached the front page of the *New York Times*: "G.I. Heroin Addiction Epidemic in Vietnam" (2). Fearful that the newly discharged veterans would join the ranks of junkies already bedeviling inner cities, President Richard Nixon commanded the military to begin drug testing. No one could board a plane home until he had passed a urine test. Those who failed could attend an army-sponsored detoxification program (3).

Operation Golden Flow, as the military called it, succeeded. As word of the new directive spread, most GIs stopped using narcotics. Almost all the soldiers who were detained passed the test on their second try (4). Once they were home, heroin lost its appeal. Opiates may have helped them endure a war's alternating bouts of boredom and terror, but stateside, civilian life took precedence. The sordid drug culture, the high price of heroin, and fears of arrest discouraged use, veterans told Lee Robins, the Washington University sociologist who evaluated the testing program from 1972 to 1974 (5).

Robins' findings were startling. Only 5% of the men who became addicted in Vietnam relapsed within 10 months after return, and just 12% relapsed briefly within 3 years. "This surprising rate of recovery even when re-exposed to narcotic drugs," wrote Robins, "ran counter to the conventional wisdom that heroin is a drug which causes addicts to suffer intolerable craving that rapidly leads to re-addiction if re-exposed to the drug"(1). Scholars hailed the results as "revolutionary" and "path-breaking" [(6), p. 215]. The fact that addicts could quit heroin and remain drug-free overturned the belief that "once an addict, always an addict."

Unfortunately, that lesson has faded into the past. By the mid-1990s, the truism "once an addict, always an addict" was back, repackaged with a new neurocentric twist: "Addiction is a chronic and relapsing brain disease" (7). It was promoted tirelessly by psychologist Alan I. Leshner, then the director of the National Institute on Drug Abuse (NIDA), the nation's premier addiction research body and part of the National Institutes of Health, and is now the dominant view of addiction in the field (8). The brain-disease model is a staple of medical school education and drug counselor training and even appears in the antidrug lectures given to high-school students (9). Rehab patients learn that they have a chronic brain disease. And the American Society of Addiction Medicine, the largest professional group of physicians specializing in drug problems, calls addiction "a primary, chronic disease of brain reward, motivation, memory and related circuitry" (10). Drug czars under Presidents Bill Clinton, George W. Bush, and Barack Obama have all endorsed the brain-disease framework at one time or another (11). From being featured in a major documentary on HBO, on talk shows and *Law and Order*, and on the covers of *Time* and *Newsweek*, the brain-disease model has become dogma – and like all articles of faith, it is typically believed without question (12–15).

That may be good public relations, but it is bad public education. We also argue that it is fundamentally bad science. The brain-disease model of addiction is not a trivial rebranding of an age-old human problem. It plays to the assumption that if biological roots can be identified, then a person has a "disease." And being afflicted means that the person cannot choose, control his or her life, or be held accountable. Now introduce brain imaging, which seems to serve up visual proof that addiction is a brain disease.

But neurobiology is not destiny: the disruptions in neural mechanisms associated with addiction do constrain a person's capacity for choice, but they do not destroy it. What's more, training the spotlight too intently on the workings of the addicted brain leaves the addicted person in the shadows, distracting clinicians, policy makers, and sometimes patients themselves from other powerful psychological and environmental forces that exert strong influence on them.

DISEASE, MIND, AND BRAIN

For over three centuries in the United States, physicians, legal scholars, politicians, and the public have debated the nature of addiction: is it a defect of the will or of the body? A moral or a medical problem? (16) Such polarization should by now have exhausted itself. After all, mountains of evidence attest to the fact that addiction entails both biological alterations in the brain and in personal agency. But given what is at stake in these debates – namely, our deep cultural beliefs about self-control and about deficits in personal responsibility paired with concerns about what society owes to addicts and what it can expect of them – we must be very careful not to ascribe too much influence to the addict's brain.

This is an opportune time to pause and clarify two potential sources of misunderstanding.

First, we do not address the question of whether addiction is a "disease." With the potential exception of certain organic brain syndromes, the field of psychiatry recognizes "disorders" or syndromes, rather than diseases because the etiologies of mental illness are not yet well understood. So, addiction fits the notion of disorder insofar as persistent craving and/or continued, excessive use leads to dysfunctional behavior. We are more concerned with the very different issue of whether addiction is best construed as a *brain* disease or *brain* disorder. Addiction is typically associated with brain changes, to be sure, but in contrast to conventional brain pathologies, such as Alzheimer's disease, those alterations rarely if ever preclude individuals' capacity to alter their behavior based on foreseeable consequences. The term "brain disease," which often implies a lack of control over behavior, obscures that crucial distinction. Moreover, although severe addictions are partly rooted in genetic predispositions that are themselves manifested in brain functioning, these conditions can be profitably understood at multiple levels of analysis (e.g., psychological, social, cultural) in addition to the neural level.

Second, our distinguishing between the addict's brain and his or her mind does not imply an endorsement of substance dualism. That is, we do not believe that the mind and the brain are independent of each other or composed of different physical substances with consciousness existing in a spiritual world separate from the body. Few scientifically literate persons do. But, speaking of literacy, there is indeed value in examining the language people use when talking about the relationship between the brain and the mind. To say that the brain and the mind are "different" does not necessarily mean that the two are *materially* separate domains. Every subjective experience, from the ache of nostalgia to the frisson of a Christmas morning, corresponds to physical events in the brain. The mind – the realm of feelings, desires, ideas, memories, intentions, and subjective experience – is produced by the action of neurons and brain circuits. How else could it work?

Yet the mind is not identical with the matter that produces it; one cannot use the physical rules from the cellular level to completely predict activity at the psychological or behavioral level. Put somewhat differently, there is a fundamental difference between substance dualism and property dualism: the latter acknowledges that everything mental is ultimately produced by physical matter but allows for the fact that certain mental phenomena have different properties than neural phenomena (just as molecules themselves are not alive, but complex configurations of certain molecules can produce life).

At this time, one cannot rely on the brain alone to predict or understand everything important about human subjectivity or behavior. This is because many psychological phenomena are emergent properties of lower-order constituents such as neural circuits, neurons, proteins, and genes. "Constitutive" reductionism – reducing complex entities to the sum of their component parts to facilitate study – is not controversial in the scientific community; nor do we take issue with it. In his 2006 book, *An Argument for Mind*, Harvard University psychologist Jerome Kagan notes that the appreciation of an impressionistic painting requires far more than the sum of its parts (17). As the viewer slowly approaches Claude Monet's painting of the Seine at Dawn, Kagan notes, there comes a moment when the scene dissolves into tiny patches of color. When we adopt the eliminative reductionist position, he writes, "the coherent psychological component vanishes" [(17), p. 213]. Some philosophers of mind take a different view. They speculate that such properties (the painting in full) will ultimately prove reducible to more basic elements (the paint) (18). They may prove correct. But for the foreseeable future, valuable information is often lost when descending from higher explanatory levels, such as mental states, to lower levels, such as neuronal systems.

The distinctions between substance and property dualism and between constitutive and greedy reductionism may appear arcane, but overlooking them can lead us to overestimate the explanatory power of neuroscientific findings. Take addiction, for example. The dominant view among researchers is that it is a "brain disease," plain and simple. Without a doubt, chronic drug exposure often changes the brain, but knowledge of the neural mechanisms underlying addiction typically has less relevance to the treatment of drug addiction and alcoholism than the psychological and social causes. To be sure, intervening directly on the brain, say with medications such as methadone, can sometimes be of value too. But understanding the brain of addicts gives us only partial insight into why they become addicted and how they recover.

ADDICTION AS A "BRAIN DISEASE"

So, what exactly makes addiction a brain disease? "That addiction is tied to changes in brain structure and function is what makes it, fundamentally, a brain disease," Leshner wrote in a now-landmark article in *Science* in 1997. But that can't be right. Every experience changes the brain – from learning a new language to navigating a new city. It is certainly true that not all brain changes are equal; learning French is not the same as acquiring a crack habit. In addiction, intense activation of certain systems in the brain makes it difficult for users to quit. Genetic factors influence the intensity and quality of the subjective effect of the drug, as well as the potency of craving and the severity of withdrawal symptoms (19).

The process of addiction unfolds partly through the action of dopamine, one of the brain's primary neurotransmitters. Normally, dopamine surges in the so-called reward pathway, or circuit, in the presence of food, sex, and other stimuli central to survival. Dopamine enhancement serves as a "learning signal" that prompts us to repeat eating, mating, and other pleasures. Over time, drugs come to mimic these natural stimuli. With every puff of a Marlboro, injection of heroin, or swig of Jim Beam, the learning signal in the reward pathway is strengthened, and in vulnerable users, these substances assume incentive properties reminiscent of food and sex.

"Salience" is the term that neuroscientists often use to describe the pull of substances on the addicted – it's more of a sense of wanting, even needing, than liking. The development of salience has been traced to the nerve pathways that mediate the experience as they emerge from the underside of the brain, in an area called the ventral tegmentum, and sweep out to regions such as the nucleus accumbens, hippocampus, and prefrontal cortex, which are associated with reward, motivation, memory, judgment, inhibition, and planning.

Other nerve fibers travel from the prefrontal cortex, a region involved in judgment and inhibition, to parts of the brain that control behavior. As one psychiatrist put it memorably, "The war on drugs is a war between the hijacked reward pathways that push the person to want to use, and the frontal lobes, which try to keep the beast at bay" (20). Note the word "hijacked." As shorthand for the usurpation of brain circuitry during the addiction process, it is a reasonable metaphor [(21), p. 1715].In the hands of brain-disease purists, though, "hijacking" has come to denote an all-or-nothing process, likened to a "switch in the brain" that, once flipped, affords no retreat for the addict (22). "It may start with the voluntary act of taking drugs," Leshner said, "but once you've got (addiction), you can't just tell the addict, 'Stop,' any more than you can tell the smoker 'Don't have emphysema'" (23).

The reward circuit is also intimately involved in "cue-induced" craving. Such craving is a special species of desire that manifests itself in a sudden, intrusive urge to use brought on by "cues" associated with use. The mere clink of a whiskey bottle, a whiff of cigarette smoke, or a glimpse of an old drug buddy on the corner can set off an unbidden rush of yearning, fueled by dopamine surges. For the addict who is trying to quit, this is a tense feeling, not pleasurable at all. Because the rush of desire seems to come out of the blue, users may feel blindsided, helpless, and confused (24).

In a very impressive display of brain technology, scientists have used PET and fMRI scans to observe the neural correlates of craving. In a typical demonstration, addicts watch videos of people handling a crack pipe or needle, causing their prefrontal cortices, amygdala, and other structures to bloom with activity (25) (videos of neutral content, such as landscapes, induce no such response). Even in users who quit several months previously, neuronal alterations may persist, leaving them vulnerable to sudden, strong urges to use. The familiar "This is your brain on drugs" is still with us [this slogan was created in 1987 by an American drug-prevention charity. To illustrate how drugs affect the brain, an egg (representing the brain) was cracked on a sizzling frying pan (representing drugs). Result: fried brain]. Nowadays, however, the brain itself often substitutes for the fried egg.

THE ADDICTION PARADOX

But that egg is not always sizzling. There is a surprising amount of lucid time in the daily life of addicts. In their classic 1969 study "Taking Care of Business: The Heroin User's Life on the Street," criminologists Preble and Casey (26) found that addicts spend only a small fraction of their days getting high. Most of their time is spent either working or hustling (27–29). The same is true for many cocaine addicts (30). We tend to think of them, at their worst, frantically gouging their skin with needles, jamming a new rock into a pipe every 15 min, or inhaling lines of powder. In the grip of such hunger, an addict cannot be expected blithely to get up and walk away.

These tumultuous states – with neuronal function severely disrupted – are the closest drug use comes to being beyond the user's restraint. But in the days between binges, cocaine users worry about a host of everyday matters: should I find a different job? Enroll my kid in a better school? Kick that freeloading cousin off the couch for good? Attend a Narcotics Anonymous meeting, enter treatment, or register at a public clinic? It is during these stretches of relative calm that many addicts could make the decision to get help or quit on their own – and many of them do. But the decision to quit can be long in coming, far too long for those who destroy their health, families, or careers in the meantime.

The paradox at the heart of addiction is this: How can the capacity for choice coexist with self-destructiveness? "I've never come across a single person that was addicted that wanted to be addicted," says neuroscientist Nora Volkow, who succeeded Leshner as director of NIDA in 2003 (31). Aristotle noted this paradox as well. He used the term Akrasia to denote an appetite or strong desire for pleasure that leads to actions that are harmful to our conscious wishes for our well-being (32). Hume spoke of "liberty" as being a "power of acting or not acting according to the determinations of the will" (33).

Indeed, how many of us have ever come across a heavy person who exercised his or her freedom expressly toward the goal of becoming fat? Many undesirable outcomes in life arrive incrementally. "We can imagine an addict choosing to get high each day, though not choosing to be an addict," says psychologist Gene Heyman. "Yet choosing to get high each day makes one an addict" (34).

Let's follow a typical trajectory to see how this dynamic plays out. In the early phase of addiction, drugs or alcohol become ever more appealing, while once-rewarding activities, such as relationships, work, or family, decline in value. The attraction of the drug starts to fade as consequences accrue – spending too much money, disappointing loved ones, attracting suspicion at work – but the drug still retains its allure because it blunts psychic pain, suppresses withdrawal symptoms, and douses intense craving [(35), p. 3]. Addicts find themselves torn between the reasons to use and reasons not to (36).

Sometimes a spasm of self-reproach or a flash of self-awareness tips the balance toward quitting. William S. Burroughs, an American novelist and heroin addict, calls this the "naked lunch" experience, "a frozen moment when everyone sees what is on the end of every fork" [(37), p. 199]. Lawford (38), himself in recovery from drugs and alcohol, edited a 2009 collection of essays called *Moments of Clarity* in which the actor Alec Baldwin, singer Judy Collins, and others recount the events that spurred their recoveries. Some quit on their own; others got professional help. A theme in each of their stories is a jolt to self-image: "This is not who I am, not who I want to be" (39). One recovered alcoholic describes the process: "You tear yourself apart, examine each individual piece, toss out the useless, rehabilitate the useful, and put your moral self back together again" (40). These are not the sentiments of people in helpless thrall to their diseased brains. Nor are these sentiments the luxury of memoirists. Patients have described similar experiences to us: "My God, I almost robbed someone!" "What kind of mother am I?" or "I swore I would never switch to the needle."

LONG-TERM ADDICTION IS THE EXCEPTION

And it turns out that quitting is the rule, not the exception – a fact worth acknowledging, given that the official NIDA formulation is that "addiction is a *chronic and relapsing* [italics added] brain disease." The Epidemiological Catchment Area Study, done in the early 1980s, surveyed 19,000 people. Among those who had become dependent on drugs by age 24, more than half later reported not a single drug-related symptom. By age 37, roughly 75% reported no drug symptom. The National Comorbidity Survey, conducted between 1990 and 1992 and again between 2001 and 2003 and the National Epidemiologic Survey on Alcohol and Related Conditions, done between 2001 and 2002 with more than 43,000 subjects, found that 77 and 86% of people who said they had once been addicted to drugs or alcohol reported no substance problems during the year before the survey (41).

By comparison, people who were addicted within the year before the survey were more likely to have concurrent psychiatric disorders. Additionally, NIDA estimates that relapse rates of treated drug-addicted patients run from 40 to 60% (42). In other words, they are not representative of the universe of addicts. They are the hard cases – the chronic and relapsing patients. Yet these patients often make the biggest impressions on clinicians and shape their views of addiction, if only because clinicians are especially likely to encounter them.

Researchers and medical professionals err in generalizing from the sickest subset of people to the overall population of patients. This caveat applies across the medical spectrum. Just as the clinician wrongly assumes that all addicts must be like the recalcitrant ones who keep stumbling through the clinic doors, psychiatrists sometimes view people with schizophrenia as doomed to a life of dysfunction on the basis of their frequent encounters with those whose delusions and hallucinations don't improve with treatment. The error of extrapolating liberally from these subsets of difficult patients is so common that statisticians Patricia and Jacob Cohen gave it a name: the "clinician's illusion" (43).

INTENDED BENEFITS OF THE BRAIN-DISEASE MODEL

Advocates of the brain-disease paradigm have good intentions. By placing addiction on an equal medical footing with more conventional brain disorders, such as Alzheimer's and Parkinson's, they want to create an image of addicts as victims of their own wayward neurochemistry. They hope that this portrayal will inspire insurance companies to expand coverage for addiction and politicians to allocate more funding for treatment [(44), p. 33]. And in the hands of Alan Leshner, the model has had real political utility (45). Before he was NIDA director, Leshner served as acting director of the National Institute of Mental Health. There, he saw how brain-disease "branding" could prompt Congress to act. "Mental health advocates started referring to schizophrenia as a 'brain disease' and showing brain scans to members of congress to get them to increase funding for research. It really worked," he said (46).

Many experts credit the brain-disease narrative with enhancing the profile of their field. The late Bob Schuster, head of NIDA from 1986 to 1991, admitted that although he did not think of addiction as a disease, he was "happy for it to be conceptualized that way for pragmatic reasons. . . for selling it to Congress"(47). For decades, addiction research had been a low-status field, disparaged by other researchers as a soft science that studied drunks and junkies. Now the field of neuroscience was taking greater notice. "People recognize that certain decision makers and others are very impressed with molecular biology," said Robert L. Balster, director of the Institute for Drug and Alcohol Studies at Virginia Commonwealth University (48).

Psychiatrist Jerome Jaffe, an eminent figure in the field and the first White House adviser on drugs (the precursor of the "drug czar"), sees the adoption of the brain-disease model as a tactical triumph and a scientific setback. "It was a useful way for particular agencies to convince Congress to raise the budgets (and) it has been very successful," he said. Indeed, neuroimaging, neurobiological research, and medication development consume over half of the NIDA research budget. In light of the agency's reach – it funds almost all substance-abuse research in the United States – it sets the national agenda regarding which research gets funded and therefore the nature of the data produced and the kinds of topics that investigators propose. But Jaffe argues that the brain-disease paradigm presents "a Faustian bargain – the price that one pays is that you don't see all the other factors that interact (in addiction)" (3).

Many proponents of the brain-disease concept were deeply committed to dispelling the stigma surrounding addiction. Medicalizing the condition was a powerful way, they hoped, to rehabilitate addicts' poor public image from the perception of undisciplined deadbeats to people struggling with an ailment. This approach had its roots in the world of mental health advocacy. Until the early 1980s, plenty of people blamed parents for their children's serious mental problems. Then advocates began to publicize neuroscientific discoveries, demonstrating, for example, that schizophrenia is associated with abnormalities of brain structure and function. In this effort, brain imaging has served sufferers well, helping legitimize their symptoms by representing visually the illness in their brains (49–53). The idea, of course, was that these benefits would extend to addicts. But it turns out that it's harder to destigmatize addiction.

SHORTCOMINGS OF THE NEUROCENTRIC VIEW OF ADDICTION

For all its benign aspirations, there are numerous problems with the brain-disease model. On its face, it implies that the brain is the most important and useful level of analysis for understanding and treating addiction. Sometimes the model even equates addiction with a neurological illness, plain, and simple (10). Such neurocentrism has clinical consequences, downplaying the underlying psychological and social reasons that drive drug use.

Recovery is a project of the heart and mind. The person, not his or her autonomous brain, is the agent of recovery. Notably, Alcoholics Anonymous, the institution perhaps most responsible for popularizing the idea that addiction is a disease, employs the term as a metaphor for loss of control. Its founders in the 1930s were leery of using the word "disease" because they thought that it discounted the profound importance of personal growth and the cultivation of honesty and humility in achieving sobriety (54).

The brain-disease narrative misappropriates language better used to describe such conditions as multiple sclerosis or schizophrenia – afflictions of the brain that are neither brought on by the sufferer nor modifiable by the desire to be well. It offers false hope that an addict's condition is completely amenable to a medical cure (much as pneumonia is to antibiotics). Finally, as we'll see, it threatens to obscure the vast role of personal agency in perpetuating the cycle of use and relapse.

Addicts embarking on recovery often need to find new clean and sober friends, travel new routes home from work to avoid passing near their dealer's street, or deposit their paycheck directly into a spouse's account to keep from squandering money on drugs. A teacher trying to quit cocaine switched from using a chalkboard – the powdery chalk was too similar to cocaine – and had a whiteboard installed instead. An investment banker who loved injecting speedballs – a cocktail of cocaine and heroin in the same syringe – made himself wear long-sleeved shirts to prevent glimpses of his bare and inviting arms. Former smokers who want to quit need to make many fine adjustments, from not lingering at the table after meals to ridding their homes of the ever-present smell of smoke, removing car lighters, and so on.

Thomas Schelling, a 2005 Nobel laureate in economics, refers to these purposeful practices as self-binding (55). The great self-binder of myth was Odysseus. To keep himself from heeding the overpowering song of the sea sirens – the half-woman, half-bird creatures whose beautiful voices lured sailors to their deaths – Odysseus instructed his men to tie him to the mast of his ship (56). The famous Romantic English poet Samuel Taylor Coleridge, an opium addict, is said to have hired men to prevent him from entering a pharmacy to purchase opium (57). Today, one can hire a firm that will provide binding services. It imposes surprise urine tests on the client, collects evidence of attendance at AA meetings or treatment sessions, and sends a monthly status report (with the good or bad news) to another person, such as a parent, spouse, or boss (58).

Some addicts devise their own self-binding strategies. Others need the help of therapists, who teach them to identify and anticipate cues that trigger craving. Beyond the classic triad of people, places, and things, they come to realize that internal states, such as stress, bad moods, and boredom, can prompt drug urges (59).

Managing craving matters mightily in recovery, but it usually is not enough. Another very important truth is that an addict uses drugs or alcohol because they serve a purpose. Caroline Knapp, in her powerful 1996 memoir *Drinking: A Love Story*, recounted why she spent two decades of her life as an alcoholic: "You drank to drown out fear, to dilute anxiety and doubt and self-loathing and painful memories" (60). Knapp doesn't describe an urge to drink so much as a need to drink. She was not manipulated by an alien desire but by something woven into her being. To say that Knapp's problem was merely the effect of heavy drinking on her brain is to miss the true threat to her well-being: the brilliant but tormented Knapp herself.

Heroin and speed helped screenwriter Jerry Stahl, author of *Permanent Midnight*, attain "the soothing hiss of oblivion." But when the drugs wore off, his vulnerabilities throbbed like a fresh surgical incision. In surveying his life, Stahl wrote, "Everything, bad or good, boil(ed) back to the decade on the needle, and the years before that imbibing everything from cocaine to Romilar, pot to percs, LSD to liquid meth and a pharmacy in between: a lifetime spent altering the single niggling fact that to be alive means being conscious" [(61), p. 3–6]. The negative states to which we refer are typically underlying problems with emotional distress, especially mood or anxiety. To be sure, repeated use of drugs such as alcohol and cocaine can exacerbate primary depressive and anxiety disorders in the long term (62), but in the short term, the user almost always feels relief. Given the common problem of "steep discounting" in addicts, it is not surprising that addicts will attend to the experiencing self at the expense of the future self.

Or take Lisa, a 37-year-old woman featured in an HBO documentary on addiction. When we meet her, Lisa is living in a rundown hotel room in Toronto and working as a prostitute. She sits on the bed and talks with the filmmaker behind the camera. Flipping her shiny brown hair and inspecting her well-kept nails, Lisa is animated as she boasts about how much she makes selling sex, how much she spends on cocaine, and the longed-for "oblivion" that drugs help her attain. When Lisa was filmed, she was healthy and engaging; she looked and talked like someone who had recently been abstinent but was back in the early stages of her next downward spiral. She had no interest in stopping things at this point. "Right now, I am in no position to go into recovery (this way of life) is working for me . . . I have money, drugs, business. I'm O.K." To say that Lisa's problem is the effect of cocaine on her brain is to miss the true threat to her well-being: Lisa herself. "I always use for a reason. It's repressing what needs to be repressed," she says (63). To be certain, not all drug use in the service of improving mood is dysfunctional. But Lisa, who had been in treatment several times, is representative of individuals whose drug use starts out as a controlled and effective attempt at self-soothing but eventually becomes all-consuming and interferes with her life.

These stories highlight one of the shortcomings of the neurocentric view of addiction. This perspective ignores the fact that many people are drawn to drugs because the substances temporarily quell their pain: persistent self-loathing, anxiety, alienation, deep-seated intolerance of stress or boredom, and pervasive loneliness. The brain-disease model is of little use here because it does not accommodate the emotional logic that triggers and sustains addiction (35, 64, 65).

THE POWER OF INCENTIVES AND ADDICTS AS CHOOSING BEINGS

In December 1966, Leroy Powell of Austin, TX, USA, was convicted of public intoxication and fined $20 in a municipal court. Powell appealed the conviction to county court, where his lawyer argued that he suffered from "the disease of chronic alcoholism." Powell's public display of inebriation therefore was "not of his own volition," and the fine constituted cruel and unusual punishment. A psychiatrist concurred, testifying that Powell was "powerless not to drink" (66).

Then Powell took the stand. On the morning of his trial, he had a drink at 8 a.m. that his lawyer gave to him, presumably to stave off morning tremors. Here is an excerpt from the cross-examination:

> Q: You took that one [drink] at eight o'clock [a.m.] because you wanted to drink?
> A: Yes, sir.
> Q: And you knew that if you drank it, you could keep on drinking and get drunk?
> A: Well, I was supposed to be here on trial, and I didn't take but that one drink.
> Q: You knew you had to be here this afternoon, but this morning you took one drink and then you knew that you couldn't afford to drink anymore and come to court; is that right?
> A: Yes, sir, that's right.
> Q: Because you knew what you would do if you kept drinking that you would finally pass out or be picked up?
> A: Yes, sir.
> Q: And you didn't want that to happen to you today?
> A: No, sir.
> Q: Not today?
> A: No, sir.
> Q: So you only had one drink today?
> A: Yes, sir (66).

The judge let stand Powell's conviction for public intoxication. A second appeal followed, this time to the U.S. Supreme Court. It, too, affirmed the constitutionality of punishment for public intoxication. "We are unable to conclude," said the court, "that chronic alcoholics in general, and Leroy Powell in particular, suffer from such an irresistible compulsion to drink and to get drunk in public that they are utterly unable to control their performance" (66).

For people like Powell who are not otherwise motivated to quit, consequences can play a powerful role in modifying behavior. Powell took only a single drink the morning of his trial because of foreseeable and meaningful consequences. Far from being unusual, his ability to curtail his drinking accords with a wealth of studies showing that people addicted to all kinds of drugs – nicotine, alcohol, cocaine, heroin, methamphetamines – can change in response to rewards or sanctions (67–69). Powell had surely experienced many alcohol-induced brain changes, but they did not keep him from making a choice that morning.

If Powell came before a judge today, his lawyer might well introduce a scan of his brain "craving" alcohol as evidence of his helplessness. If so, the judge would be wise to reject the scan as proof. After all, a judge, or anyone, can ponder scans of "addicted" brains all day, but he or she would never consider someone an addict unless that person behaves like one (70–73). As legal scholar Stephen Morse puts it, "actions speak louder than images" (74).

Consider the following fMRI experiment by researchers at Yale and Columbia. They found that the brains of smokers reporting a strong desire to smoke displayed enhanced activation of reward circuitry, as would be expected (75). But they also showed that subjects could reduce craving by considering the long-term consequences of smoking, such as cancer or emphysema, while observing videos depicting people smoking. When subjects did so, their brains displayed enhanced activity in areas of the prefrontal cortex associated with focusing, shifting attention, and controlling emotions. Simultaneously, activity in regions associated with reward, such as the ventral striatum, decreased (76).

Investigators at NIDA observed the same pattern when they asked cocaine users to inhibit their craving in response to cues. Subjects underwent PET scanning as they watched a video of people preparing drug paraphernalia and smoking crack cocaine. When researchers instructed the addicts to control their responses to the video, they observed inhibition of brain regions normally implicated in drug craving. When not deliberately suppressing their cravings, the addicts reported feeling their typical desire to use, and the PET scans revealed enhanced activation in brain regions that mediate craving (77).

These powerful findings illuminate the capacity for self-control in addicts. They also underscore the idea that addicts persist not because of an inability to control the desire to use but from a failure of motivation. Granted, summoning sustained motivation can be a great challenge: it takes a lot of energy and vigilance to resist craving, especially urges that ambush the addict unexpectedly. Studies on the regulation of craving also help distinguish behavior that people do not control from behavior that they cannot control. Imagine, by way of contrast, promising a reward to people with Alzheimer's if they can keep their dementia from worsening. That would be both pointless and cruel because the kinds of brain changes intrinsic to dementia leave the sufferer resistant to rewards or penalties.

What Powell's case showed was that even though he sustained brain changes, those changes did not prevent his behavior from being shaped by consequences. Contingency management – the technical term for the practice of adjusting consequences, including incentives – often succeeds with people who face serious losses, such as their livelihood, professional identity, or reputation. When addicted physicians come under the surveillance of their state medical boards and are subject to random urine testing, unannounced workplace visits, and frequent employer evaluations, they fare well: 70–90% are employed with their licenses intact 5 years later [(78), p. 165]. Likewise, scores of clinical trials show that addicts who know they will receive a reward, such as cash, gift certificates, or services, are nearly two to three times as likely to submit drug-free urine samples as addicts not offered rewards (79, 80).

Unfortunately, treatment programs are rarely in a position to offer cash or costly rewards. But the criminal justice system has an ample supply of incentives at its disposal and has been using such leverage for years. One of the most promising demonstrations of contingency management comes from Honolulu in the form of Project HOPE, Hawaii's Opportunity Probation with Enforcement.

Project HOPE includes frequent random drug testing of offenders on probation. Those who test positive are subject to immediate and brief incarceration. Sanctions are fair and transparent: all offenders are treated equally, and everyone knows what will happen in case of an infraction. The judges express a heartfelt faith in offenders' ability to succeed. These basic elements of HOPE's contingency administration – swiftness, sureness, transparency, and fairness combined with expectation for achievement – are a potent prescription for behavior change in just about anyone.

Indeed, after 1 year of enrollment in Project HOPE, participants fared considerably better than probationers in a group who served as a comparison. They were 55% less likely to be arrested for a new crime and 53% less likely to have had their probation revoked. These results are even more impressive in light of the participants' criminal histories and their heavy, chronic exposure to methamphetamine, which can impair aspects of cognitive function [on project HOPE, see (81); on the effects of methamphetamines, see (82–86)].

These findings join a vast body of experimental data attesting to the power of incentives to override the lure of drugs. Yet because the facts contradict the idea that addiction is analogous to Alzheimer's disease, some HOPE personnel objected to incentives, arguing that addicts couldn't be accountable for their behavior. Likewise, when researchers asked NIDA to consider reviewing HOPE in its formative years, the agency declined on the grounds that methamphetamine addicts are not capable of responding to incentives alone (87–91).

CAN MEDICINE "CURE" ADDICTION?

The brain-disease model leads us down a narrow clinical path. Because it states that addiction is a "chronic and relapsing" condition, it diverts attention from promising behavioral therapies that challenge the inevitability of relapse by holding patients accountable for their choices. At the same time, because the model implies that addicts cannot stop using drugs until their brain chemistry returns to normal, it overemphasizes the value of brain-level solutions, such as pharmaceutical intervention. In 1997, Leshner ranked the search for a medication to treat methamphetamine addiction as a "top priority (23). A decade later, Volkow predicted, "We will be treating addiction as a disease (by 2018), and that means with medicine" (15).

The search for a magic bullet is folly – and even NIDA has given up hope of finding a wonder drug – but the brain-disease narrative continues to inspire unrealistic goals. When British pop star Amy Winehouse succumbed to her high-profile alcoholism in the summer of 2011, a *Psychology Today* columnist asked, "Could neuroscience have helped Amy Winehouse?"(92). The author answered in the affirmative, suggesting a dopamine-altering medication of the future because addiction "may be a brain problem that science can eventually solve." Neuroscientist David Eagleman goes even further, asserting that "addiction can be reasonably viewed as a neurological problem that allows for medical solutions, just as pneumonia can be viewed as a lung problem" (93). But the analogy doesn't hold up. Changing a behavior like addiction requires addicts to work hard to change their patterns of thought and behavior. In contrast, antibiotic cures for pneumonia work even if the patient is in a coma.

The hope of a medical treatment is the logical outgrowth of placing the brain at the center of the addictive process. Overall, success to date has been genuine but modest. When motivated patients take medications – especially patients already armed with relapse-prevention strategies and the support of family and friends – they can sometimes vault into sustained recovery. Methadone, a long-acting synthetic opiate taken once a day to prevent opiate withdrawal, has played a major role in treating addiction to heroin and painkillers since the 1960s (94). Still, to their counselors' chagrin, up to half the patients in methadone clinics also fortify themselves with heroin, cocaine, or Valium-like tranquilizers called benzodiazepines, sold on the street (95). Despite three decades of effort, there is still no medication therapy for cocaine. Cocaine immunotherapy (popularly called a cocaine "vaccine") to prevent cocaine molecules from entering the brain is now in development, but previews do not look promising for wide-scale use (96). Other types of medications include blocking agents, such as naltrexone for opiate addiction, which occupy neuronal receptors and blunt a drug's effect (97). Aversive agents, such as Antabuse (disulfiram), cause people to feel nauseated and vomit when they ingest alcohol (98). They can be effective in some cases, although many individuals elect to stop taking them.

These medications are not the product of modern neuroscience; they were developed decades ago. Even a vaccine was sought in the 1970s, although today's techniques are vastly more sophisticated. More recently, neuroscientists have collaborated with pharmacologists to develop medications to reverse or compensate for the pathological effects of drugs on the brain. The premise is that different components of addiction can be targeted by different medications. These components are the "reward" circuit (which mediates a strong desire to use and preoccupation with imminent use) and the craving mechanism associated with conditioned cues. Thus far, success has been elusive. Anticraving agents have shown some promise for alcoholics, but treatments for cocaine addiction have been disappointing (99–102).

Traditionally, pharmacologists have approached the treatment of alcoholics and addicts in the same way they address most psychiatric diseases: as a matter of reversing or compensating for neuropathology – in this case, the neural alteration resulting from repeated use. This is a logical approach, but instead of focusing almost exclusively on what is wrong in the brain, perhaps they should also investigate the ways in which addicts recover. Addicts find non-drug sources of interests and gratification that generate their own outpourings of dopamine; they practice self-binding and mindfulness exercises that make the prefrontal cortex better at controlling impulses. Relinquishing drugs and alcohol is accompanied by a shift in the brain's valuation systems. How, and even whether, these dynamics will translate into pharmacotherapy is a complicated question, but perhaps the answer will spur discovery of more effective medications – not panaceas but helpful aids to hasten the process of recovery. Some proponents of the brain-disease model would say that emphasizing the role of choice in addiction is just another way to stigmatize addicts and justify penal responses over therapeutic ones. To this way of thinking, if we see the addict as a "chronic illness sufferer," we will no longer view him or her as a "bad person" (23, 103). This sentiment echoes throughout the addiction community. "We can continue playing the blame game," said Volkow in 2008 "Or we can parlay the transformative power of scientific discovery into a brighter future for addicted individuals" (104).

FALSE CHOICES: SICK OR BAD

Sick brain versus flawed character? Biological determinism versus bad choices? Why must these be our only options? This black-and-white framing sets a rhetorical trap that shames us into siding with the brain-disease camp lest we appear cruel or uncaring. The bind, of course, is that it is impossible to understand addiction if one glosses over the reality that addicts do possess the capacity for choice and an understanding of consequences. Forcing a choice between "sick or bad" adds confusion, not clarity, to the long-standing debate over just how much to hold addicts responsible in ways that are beneficial to them and to the rest of society.

Although it makes no sense to incarcerate people for minor drug crimes, exempting addicts from social norms does not ensure them a brighter future. Stigmatization is a normal part of social interaction – a potent force in shaping behavior. Author Susan Cheever, a former alcoholic, coined a new word, "drunkenfreude," to denote how the embarrassing antics of intoxicated friends and strangers keep her sober. "[Watching] other people get drunk helps me remember," Cheever writes. "I learn from seeing what I don't want and avoiding it" (105).

Too often, well-meaning family members and friends try to insulate individuals from the consequences of their behavior and thereby miss an important opportunity to help the addict quit. There is nothing unethical – and everything natural and socially adaptive – about condemning reckless and harmful acts. At the same time, because addicts are people who suffer, we must also provide effective care and support progressive approaches, such as Project HOPE. If we want to garner social and political support for addicts' plight, the best way to do that is to develop the most effective modes of rehabilitation possible – not to advance a reductive and one-dimensional version of addiction.

And what of the efforts to destigmatize addiction through medicalization? Results are mixed. In some surveys of the public, well over half of respondents saw addiction as a "moral weakness" or "character flaw." In others, over half to two-thirds classified it as a "disease." An Indiana University study asked over 600 people whether they viewed alcoholism as the result of a genetic problem or chemical imbalance (i.e., a "neurobiological conception") or as an outgrowth of "bad character" or "the way he or she was raised." Those endorsing a neurobiological explanation rose from 38% in 1996 to 47% in 2006; the proportion endorsing psychiatric treatment increased from 61 to 79% (106–112).

Another study revealed an unexpected pattern over the past few decades. As people accepted a biological explanation for mental illness and substance-abuse, their desire for social distance from the mentally ill and addicted increased. Biological explanations also appear to foster pessimism about the likelihood of recovery and the effectiveness of treatment (113–121). This finding may seem counterintuitive. One might think that a biological explanation would be good news to a patient – and to be sure, some people with mental illness do indeed find it a relief. But when the patient's affliction is addiction and there are no medical cures to restore an addict's disrupted brain, emphasizing the biological dimension seems misguided.

The authors of the chronic-brain-disease narrative were inspired by discoveries about the effects of drugs on the brain. The promise of finding powerful antiaddiction medications seemed great. The maturing science of addiction biology would mean that once and for all, the condition would be taken seriously as an illness – a condition that began with the explicit, voluntary decision to try drugs but transitioned into an involuntary and uncontrollable state. This knowledge, they hoped, would sensitize policy makers and the public to the needs of addicts, including access to public treatment and better private insurance coverage. A softening of puritanical attitudes and an easing of punitive law enforcement were also on the agenda.

The mission was worthy, but the outcome has been less salutary. The neurocentric perspective encourages unwarranted optimism regarding pharmaceutical cures and oversells the need for professional help. It labels as "chronic" a condition that typically remits in early adulthood. The brain-disease story gives short shrift to the reality that substances serve a purpose in addicts' lives and that neurobiological changes induced by alcohol and drugs can be overridden.

Like many misleading metaphors, the brain-disease model contains some truth. There is a genetic influence on alcoholism and other addictions, and prolonged substance-abuse often damages brain structures that mediate self-governance. Yet the problem with the brain-disease model is its misplaced emphasis on biology as the star feature of addiction and its relegation of psychological and behavioral elements to at best supporting roles. "If the brain is the core of the problem, attending to the brain needs to be a core part of the solution," as Leshner once put it (7). The clinical reality is just the opposite: The most effective interventions aim not at the brain but at the person. It's the *minds* of addicts that contain the stories of how addiction happens, why people continue to use drugs, and, if they decide to stop, how they manage to do so. This deeply personal history can't be understood exclusively by inspecting neural circuitry.

BEYOND THE BRAIN

In the end, the most useful definition of addiction is a descriptive one, such as this: Addiction is a behavior marked by repeated use despite destructive consequences and by difficulty quitting not withstanding the user's resolution to do so. This "definition" isn't theoretical; it explains nothing about why one "gets" addiction – and how could it offer a satisfying causal account when there are multiple levels at which the process can be understood? Our proposed definition merely states an observable fact about the behavior generally recognized as addiction. That's a good thing because a blank explanatory slate (unbiased by biological orientation or any other theoretical model) inspires broad-minded thinking about research, treatment, and policy. Is there room for neuroscience in this tableau? Of course. Brain research is yielding valuable information about the neural mechanisms associated with desire, compulsion, and self-control – discoveries that may one day be better harnessed for clinical use. But the daily work of recovery, whether or not it is abetted by medication, is a human process that is most effectively pursued in the idiom of purposeful action, meaning, choice, and consequence.

REFERENCES

1. Robins LN. Vietnam Veterans' rapid recovery from heroin: a fluke or normal expectation? *Addiction* (1993) 88:1041–54. doi:10.1111/j. 1360-0443.1993. tb02123.x
2. Schuster AM. *G.I. Heroin Addiction Epidemic in Vietnam*. New York: New York Times (1971).
3. Jaffe J. *Oral History Interviews with Substance Abuse Researchers: Jerry Jaffe," Record 16*. University of Michigan Substance Abuse Research Center (2007). Available from: http://sitemaker.umich. edu/substance.abuse.history/oral_ history_interviews
4. Massing M. *The Fix: Solving the Nation's Drug Problem*. New York: Simon and Schuster (1998). p. 86–131.
5. Robins LN, Helzer JE, Davis DH. Narcotic use in Southeast Asia and afterward. *Arch Gen Psychiatry* (1975) 32:955–61. doi:10.1001/archpsyc.1975. 01760260019001
6. Granfield R, Cloud W. *Com- ing Clean: Overcoming Addic- tion Without Treatment*. New York: New York University Press (1999).
7. Leshner A. Addiction is a brain disease, and it matters. *Science* (1997) 5335:45–7. doi:10.1126/ science.278.5335.45
8. Dentzer S. Substance abuse and other substantive matters. *Health Aff* (2011) 8:1398. doi:10.1377/ hlthaff.2011.0811
9. Koop CE. Drug addiction in america: challenges and opportunities. In: Jack E, Hen- ningfield P, Santora B, Warren B editors. *Addiction: Science and Treatment for the Twenty First Century*. Baltimore: Johns Hopkins University Press (2007). 13 p.
10. American Society of Addic- tion Medicine. *Public Policy Statement: Definition of Addic- tion* (2011). Available from: http://www.asam.org/advocacy/ find-a-policy-statement/view-policy-statement/public-policy-statements/2011/ 12/15/the-definition-of-addiction
11. Smith P. *Is Addiction a Brain Dis- ease? Biden Bill to Define It as Such Is Moving on Capitol Hill*. Drug War Chronicle (2007). Available from: http://stopthedrugwar.org/ chronicle/2007/aug/09/feature_ addiction_brain_disease
12. Massing M. *Seeing Drugs as a Choice or as a Brain Anomaly*. New York Times (2000). Available from: http://www.nytimes.com/2000/06/ 24/arts/seeing-drugs-as-a-choice- or-as-a-brain-anomaly.html? pagewanted=all&src=pm
13. Rose C,Volkow N. *The Charlie Rose Brain Series, Year 2." The Charlie Rose Show, PBS*. New York: Lexis- Nexis (2012).
14. Lemonick MD. *How We Get Addicted*. Time (2007). Available from: http:// www.time.com/time/ magazine/article/0,9171,1640436, 00.html.,
15. Interlandi J. *What Addicts Need. Newsweek* (2008). Available from: http:// www.newsweek.com/2008/ 02/23/what-addicts-need.html
16. Quenqua D. *Rethinking Addiction's Roots, and Its Treatment*. New York: New York Times (2011).
17. Kagan J. *An Argument for Mind*. New Haven: Yale University Press (2006).
18. Churchland PM. *Matter and Con- sciousness, Revised Edition*. Cam- bridge, MA: MIT Press (1988).
19. Robison AJ, Nestler EJ. Tran- scriptional and epigenetic mecha- nisms of addiction. *Nat Rev Neu- rosci* (2011) 12:623–37. doi:10. 1038/nrn3111
20. Fiore K. *Doctor's Orders: Brain's Wiring Makes Change Hard*. Med- Page Today (2010). Available from: http://www.medpagetoday. com/Psychiatry/ Addictions/18207
21. Henningfield JE, Schuh LM, Jarvik ME. Pathophysiology of tobacco dependence. In: Bloom FE, Kupfer DJ editors. *Neuropsychopharma- cology – The Fourth Generation of Progress*. New York: Raven Press (1995). p. 1715–29.
22. Schnabel J. *Flipping the Addic- tion Switch*. Dana Founda- tion (2008). Available from: http://www.dana.org/news/ features/detail.aspx?id=13120
23. Leshner A. Treatment: effects on the brain and body, *National Methamphetamine Drug Confer- ence* (1997).
24. Childress AR. Prelude to pas- sion: limbic activation by "unseen" drug and sexual cues. *PLoS ONE* (2008) 3(1):e1506. doi:10.1371/ journal.pone.0001506
25. Goldstein RY, Volkow ND. Drug addiction and its underlying neu- robiological basis: neuroimaging evidence for the involvement of the frontal cortex. *Am J Psychi- atry* (2002) 10:1642–52. doi:10. 1176/appi.ajp.159.10.1642
26. Preble E, Casey JJ. Taking care of business: the heroin user's life on the street. *Int J Addict* (1969) 1:1–24.
27. Hanson B. *Life with Heroin: Voices from the Inner City*. Lex- ington, MA: Lexington Books (1985).
28. Faupel CE, Klockars CB. Drugs- crime connections: elaborations from the life histories of hard-core heroin addicts. *Soc Prob* (1987) 1:54–68. doi:10.2307/800729
29. Agar M. *Ripping and Running: For- mal Ethnography of Urban Heroin Addicts*. Napier, NZ: Seminar Press (1973).
30. Bourgois P. *In Search of Respect: Selling Crack in El Barrio*. Cam- bridge: Cambridge University Press (2002).
31. Gugliotta G. *Revolutionary Thinker: Trotsky's Great- Granddaughter Is Following Her Own Path to Greatness*. Washington Post (2003).
32. Aristotle. *Nicomachean Ethics*. Trans. Bartlett RC, Collins SD. Chicago: University of Chicago Press (2011).
33. Hume D. Enquiry concern- ing human understanding. In: Selby-Bigge LA III, Nidditch PH editors. *Enquiries Concern- ing Human Understanding and Concerning the Principles of Moral*. Oxford: Clarendon Press (1975).
34. Hyman SE. The neurobiology of addiction: implications for volun- tary control of behaviour. In: Judy I, Sahakian BJ editors. *The Oxford Handbook of Neuroethics*. Oxford: Oxford University Press (2011). p. 203–18.
35. Heather N. A conceptual frame- work for explaining addiction. *J Psychopharmacol* (1998) 12:3–7. doi:10.1177/026988119801200101
36. Elster J. Rational choice history: a case of excessive ambition. *Am Polit Sci Rev* (2000) 3:685–95. doi: 10.2307/2585842
37. Burroughs WS. In: Grauerholz J, Miles B editors. *Naked Lunch: The Restored Text*. New York: Grove/Atlantic (2001).
38. Lawford CK. *Moments of Clar- ity: Voices from the Front Lines of Addiction and Recovery*. New York: HarperCollins (2009).
39. Richards K, Fox J. *Life*. New York: Little, Brown and Company (2010). 408 p.
40. Atkinson J. *Act of Faith*. New York Times (2009). Available from: http:// proof.blogs.nytimes. com/2009/01/26/act-of-faith/
41. Heyman GM. *Addiction: A Dis- order of Choice*. Cambridge, MA: Harvard University Press (2009). p. 67–83.
42. National Institute on Drug Abuse, National Institutes of Health, U.S. Department of Health and Human Service. *"Principles of Drug Addic- tion Treatment: A Research-Based Guide,"* 2nd ed. Rockville, MD: National Institute on Drug Abuse, National Institutes of Health (1999).
43. Cohen P, Cohen J. The clini- cian's illusion. *Arch Gen Psychiatry* (1984) 12:1178–82. doi:10.1001/ archpsyc.1984.01790230064010
44. Babor TF. Social, scientific, and medical issues in the definition of alcohol and drug dependence. In: Griffith E, Malcolm L editors. *The Nature of Drug Dependence*. Oxford: Oxford University Press (1990). p. 19–36.
45. Rosen BR, Savoy RL. fMRI at 20: has it changed the world? *Neu- roimage* (2012) 5:1316–24. doi:10. 1016/j.neuroimage.2012.03.004
46. Leshner AI. *Personal Communica- tion with Author* (2009).
47. Schuster CR. *Oral History Inter- views with Substance Abuse Researchers: C. Robert 'Bob' Schuster, Record 36*. University of Michigan Substance Abuse Research Center (2007). Available from: http://sitemaker.umich. edu/substance.abuse.history/oral_ history_interviews
48. Balster R. *Oral History Interviews with Substance Abuse Researchers: Robert Balster," Record 3*. Ann Arbor: University of Michi- gan Substance Abuse Research Center (2004). Available from: http://sitemaker.umich.edu/ substance.abuse.history/oral_ history_interviews
49. Goldstein B, Rosselli F. Etio- logical paradigms of depression: the relationship between perceived causes, empowerment, treatment preferences, and stigma. *J Ment Health* (2003) 12:551–63. doi:10. 1080/09638230310001627919
50. Phelan JC, Cruz-Rojas R, Reiff M. Genes and stigma: the connection between perceived genetic etiol- ogy and attitudes and beliefs about mental illness. *Psychiatr Reha- bil Skills* (2002) 6:159–85. doi:10. 1080/10973430208408431
51. Illes J, Lombera S, Rosenberg J, Arnow B. In the mind's eye: provider and patient attitudes on functional brain imaging. *J Psychi- atr Res* (2008) 43:107–14. doi:10. 1016/j.jpsychires.2008.02.008
52. Borgelt E, Buchman DZ, Illes J. This is why you've been suffering: reflections of providers on neu- roimaging in mental health care. *J Bioethic Inq* (2011) 1:15–25. doi: 10.1007/s11673-010-9271-1
53. Buchman DZ, Borgelt EL, White- ley L, Illes J. Neurobiological narratives: experiences of mood disorder through the lens of neuroimaging. *Sociol Health Illn* (2013) 1:66–81. doi:10.1111/j. 1467-9566.2012.01478.x
54. Kurtz E. *Alcoholics Anonymous and the Disease Concept of Addic- tion* (2000). Available from: http://ebookbrowse.com/ernie- kurtz-aa-the-disease-concept-of- alcoholism-pdf-d168865618
55. Schelling TC. The intimate con- test for self-command. *Publ Inter- est* (1980) 60:94–118.
56. Fagles R. trans. *The Odyssey of Homer*. New York: Penguin Books (1997). p. 272–3.

57. Clark D. *Historical Perspectives: Opium, Morphine, and Heroine, Wired into Recovery* (2003). Avail- able at: http://wiredintorecovery. org/articles/entry/8932/historical- perspectives-opium-morphine- and-heroin/
58. Southwest Associates. *How Inter- ventions Work* (0000). Available from: http://www.southworth associates.net/interventions/how- interventions-work
59. Khantzian EJ, Albanese MJ. *Under- standing Addiction as Self Medication:Finding Hope Behind the Pain*. Lanham, MD: Rowman and Little- field (2008).
60. Knapp C. *Drinking: A Love Story*. Dial Press (1997). 267 p.
61. Stahl J. *Permanent Midnight*. Los Angeles: Process (2005).
62. Lingford-Hughes A, Potokar J, Nutt D. Treating anxiety compli- cated by substance misuse. *Adv Psychiatr Treat* (2002) 8:107–16. doi:10.1192/apt.8.2.107
63. Perrier P. *Cracked Not Broken, DVD, Directed by Paul Perrier (HBO)* (2007).
64. Kalant H. What neurobiology can- not tell us about addiction. *Addic- tion* (2010) 5:780–9. doi:10.1111/j. 1360-0443.2009.02739.x
65. Hamill P. *A Drinking Life*. New York: Back Bay Books (1995).
66. Powell L. 392 U.S. 514 (1968). Available from: http: //bulk.resource.org/courts.gov/c/ US/392/392.US.514.405.html
67. Higgins ST, Silverman K, Heil SH editors. *Contingency Manage- ment in Substance Abuse Treat- ment*. New York: Guilford Press (2008).
68. Prendergast M, Podus D, Finney J, Greenwell L, Roll J. Contingency management for treatment of substance use disorders: a meta-analysis. *Addiction* (2006) 11:1546–60. doi:10.1111/j.1360- 0443.2006.01581.x
69. Volpp KG, Troxel AB, Pauly MV, Glick HA, Puig A, Asch DA, et al. A randomized, controlled trial of financial incentives for smoking cessation. *N Engl J Med* (2009) 360:699–709. doi:10.1056/ NEJMsa0806819
70. Kosten TR, Scanley BE, Tucker KA, Oliveto A, Prince C, Sinha R, et al. Cue-induced brain activity changes and relapse in cocaine-dependent patients. *Neuropsychophar- macology* (2006) 31:644–50. doi:10.1038/sj.npp.1300851
71. Heinz A, Wrase J, Kahnt T, Beck A, Bromand Z, Grüsser SM, et al. Brain activation elicited by affec- tively positive stimuli is associated with a lower risk of relapse in detoxified alcoholic subjects. *Alco- hol Clin Exp Res* (2007) 7:1138–47. doi:10.1111/j.1530-0277.2007. 00406.x
72. Janes AC, Pizzagalli DA, Richardt S, deB FrederickB, Chuzi S, Pachas G, et al. Brain reactivity to smoking cues prior to smok- ing cessation predicts ability to maintain tobacco abstinence. *Biol Psychiatry* (2010) 67:722–9. doi:10.1016/j.biopsych.2009.12. 034
73. Shapiro D. *Cited in Sally Satel and Frederick Goodwin, "Is Addiction a Brain Disease?* Ethics and Public Policy (1997). Available from: www.eppc.org/docLib/20030420_ DrugAddictionBrainDisease.pdf
74. Morse S. Actions speak louder than images. In: Bizzi E, Hyman SE, Raichle ME, Kanwisher N, Phelps EA, Morse SJ, Sinnott-Armstrong W, Rakoff JS, Greely HT, editors. *Using Imaging to Identify Deceit: Scientific and Ethical Questions*. Cambridge, MA: American Acad- emy of the Advancement of Sci- ence (2009). p. 23–34.
75. Westbrook C, Creswell JD, Tabib- nia G, Julson E, Kober H, Tindle HA. Mindful attention reduces neural and self-reported cue- induced craving in smokers. *Soc Cogn Affect Neurosci* (2011). doi:10.1093/scan/nsr076 Available from: http://scan.oxfordjournals. org/content/early/2011/11/22/ scan.nsr076.full,
76. Kober H, Mende-Siedlecki P, Kross EF, Weber J, Mischel W, Hart CL, et al. Prefrontostriatal path- way underlies cognitive regulation of craving. *Trends Cogn Neurosci* (2011) 3:132–9. doi:10.1073/pnas. 1007779107
77. Volkow ND, Fowler JS, Wang GJ, Telang F, Logan J, Jayne M, et al. Cognitive control of drug crav- ing inhibits brain reward regions in cocaine abusers. *Neuroimage* (2010) 49:2536–43. doi:10.1016/j. neuroimage.2009.10.088
78. DuPont RL, McLellan AT, White WL, Merlo LJ, Gold MS. Setting the standard for recovery: physi- cians' health programs. *J Subst Abuse Treat* (2009) 2:159–71. doi: 10.1016/j.jsat.2008.01.004
79. Stitzer M, Petry N. Contingency management for treatment of sub- stance abuse. *Annu Rev Clin Psy- chol* (2006) 2:411–34. doi:10.1146/ annurev.clinpsy.2.022305.095219
80. Vadhan NP, Hart CL, Haney M, van GorpWG, Foltin RW. Decision- making in long-term cocaine users: effects of a cash monetary con- tingency on gambling task per- formance. *Drug Alcohol Depend* (2009) 103:95–101. doi:10.1016/j. drugalcdep.2009.02.003
81. Hawken A, Kleiman M. *Man- aging Drug Involved Proba- tioners with Swift and Certain Sanctions: Evaluating Hawaii's HOPE* (2009). Available from: https://www.ncjrs.gov/pdffiles1/ nij/grants/229023.pdf
82. Kalechstein AD, Newton TF, Green M. Methamphetamine dependence is associated with neurocognitive impairment in the initial phases of abstinence. *J Neuropsychiatry Clin Neurosci* (2003) 15:215–20. doi:10.1176/ appi.neuropsych.15.2.215
83. Nordahl TE, Salo R, Leamon M. Neuropsychological effects of chronic methamphetamine use on neurotransmitters and cognition: a review. *J Neuropsychiatry Clin Neurosci* (2003) 15:317–25. doi:10. 1176/appi.neuropsych.15.3.317
84. Woicik PA, Moeller SJ, Alia- Klein N, Maloney T, Lukasik TM, Yeliosof O, et al. The neu- ropsychology of cocaine addiction: recent cocaine use masks impairment. *Neuropsychopharmacology* (2009) 5:1112–22. doi:10.1038/ npp.2008.60
85. Gold MS, Kobeissy FH, Wang KK, Merlo LJ, Bruijnzeel AW, Krasnova IN, et al. Methamphetamine- and trauma-induced brain injuries: comparative cellular and molecu- lar neurobiological substrates. *Biol Psychiatry* (2009) 2:118–27. doi: 10.1016/j.biopsych.2009.02.021
86. Hart CL, Marvin CB, Sil- ver R, Smith EE. Cognitive functioning impaired in metham- phetamine users? A critical review. *Neuropsychopharma- cology* (2012) 37:586–608. doi:10.1038/npp.2011.276
87. Kilmer B, Nicosia N, Heaton P, Midgette G. Efficacy of frequent monitoring with swift, certain, and modest sanctions for viola- tions: insights from South Dakota's 24/7 sobriety project. *Am J Pub- lic Health* (2013) 1:e37–43. doi:10. 2105/AJPH.2012.300989
88. Harrell A, Cavanagh S, Roma J. *Findings from the Evaluation of the D.C. Superior Court Drug Inter- vention Program*. Washington, DC: Urban Institute (1999).
89. Satel SL. *Drug Treatment: The Case for Coercion*. Washington, DC: AEI Press (1999).
90. Alm S. *Personal Communication with Authors* (2009).
91. Chezem LL. *Personal Communica- tion with Authors* (2009).
92. Greenberg M. *Could Neuro- science Have Helped Amy Wine- house?* Psychology Today (2011). Available from: http://www. psychologytoday.com/blog/the- mindful-self-express/201107/ could-neuroscience-have-helped-amy-winehouse
93. Eagleman DM, Correro MA, Sing J. Why neuroscience matters for rational drug policy. *Minn J Law Sci Technol* (2010) 1:7–26.
94. Musto DF. *The American Dis- ease: Origins of Narcotics Control*. Oxford: Oxford University Press (1999). p. 237–53.
95. Cone EJ. Oral fluid results com- pared to self-report of recent cocaine and heroin use by methadone maintenance patients. *Forensic Sci Int* (2012) 215:88–91. doi:10.1016/j.forsciint.2011.01. 046
96. Kosten T. *Shooting Down Addiction*. Scientist Daily (2011). Available from: http://the-scientist.com/2011/ 06/01/shooting-down-addiction/
97. Srisurapanont M, Jarusuraisin N. Opioid antagonists for alcohol dependence. *Cochrane Database Syst Rev* (2005) 1:CD001867.
98. National Institute on Drug Abuse. *Drugs, Brains and Behavior: The Science of Addiction*. Bethesda MD: National Institutes of Health (2007).
99. Koob GF, Lloyd GK, Mason BJ. The development of pharmacothera- pies for drug addiction: a rosetta stone approach. *Nat Rev Drug Dis- cov* (2009) 6:500–15. doi:10.1038/ nrd2828
100. Minozzi S, Amato L, Vecchi S, Davoli M, Kirchmayer U, and Ver- ster A. Oral naltrexone mainte- nance treatment for opiate depen- dence. *Cochrane Database Syst Rev* (2011) 2:CD001333.
101. Dodd ML, Klos KJ, Bower JH, Geda YE, Josephs KA, Ahlskog JE. Pathological gambling caused by drugs used to treat Parkin- son disease. *Arch Neurol* (2005) 9:1377–81. doi:10.1001/archneur. 62.9.noc50009
102. SAMHSA. *Acamprosate: A New Medication for Alcohol Use Dis- orders," Substance Abuse Treat- ment Advisory* (2005). Available from: http://kap.samhsa.gov/ products/manuals/advisory/pdfs/ Acamprosate-Advisory.pdf
103. Leshner A. Outlook, Described In Peggy Orenstein, "Staying Clean. New York Times Magazine (2002).
104. Volkow ND. *It's Time for Addiction Science to Supersede Stigma*. Wash- ington: ScienceNews (2008).
105. Cheever S. *Drunkenfreude*. New York Times (2008). Available from: http://proof.blogs.nytimes. com/2008/12/15/drunkenfreude/
106. Pescosolido BA, Martin JK, Long JS, Medina TR, Phelan JC, Link BG. A disease like any other? A decade of change in public reac- tions to schizophrenia, depression, and alcohol dependence. *Am J Psy- chiatry* (2010) 11:1321–30. doi:10. 1176/appi.ajp.2010.09121743
107. Rivlin A. *Views on Alcoholism & Treatment* (2005).
108. *USA Today Poll* (2006). Avail- able from: http://www.hbo. com/addiction/understanding_ addiction/17_usa_today_poll.html
109. Substance Abuse and Mental Health Services Administration. *National Poll Reveals Public Atti- tudes on Substance Abuse, Treat- ment and the Prospects of Recov- ery* (2006). Available from: http: //www.samhsa.gov/attitudes/

110. Hazelden. *National Study of Public Attitudes Towards Addic- tion* (2008). Available from: www.hazelden.org/web/public/ document/2008publicsurvey.pdf
111. *Open Society Institute Poll* (2009). Available from: www. facesandvoicesofrecovery.org/pdf/ OSI_LakeResearch_2009.pdf
112. Robert Wood Johnson Founda- tion. *What Does America Think About Addiction Prevention and Treatment? RWJF Research High- light* (2007). Available from: https://folio.iupui.edu/bitstream/ handle/10244/559/Research%20 Highlight%2024[3].pdf? sequence=2
113. Schomerus G, Schwahn C, Holzinger A, Corrigan PW, Grabe HJ, Carta MG, et al. Evolution of public attitudes about mental illness: a systematic review and meta-analysis. *Acta Psychiatr Scand* (2012) 6:440–52. doi:10. 1111/j.1600-0447.2012.01826.x
114. Lam DCK, Salkovskis P. An experi- mental investigation of the impact of biological and psychological causal explanations on anxious and depressed patients' perception of a person with panic disor- der. *Behav Res Ther* (2006) 45: 405–11. doi:10.1016/j.brat.2006. 03.005
115. Read J, Harré N. The role of biolog- ical and genetic causal beliefs in the stigmatisation of 'mental patients'. *J Ment Health* (2001) 10:223–35. doi:10.1080/09638230123129
116. Read J, Law A. THE relationship of causal beliefs and contact with users of mental health services to attitudes to the 'mentally ill'. *Int J Soc Psychiatry* (1999) 45: 216–29. doi:10.1177/ 002076409904500309
117. Mehta S, Farina A. Is being 'sick' really better? Effect of the disease view of mental disorder on stigma. *J Soc Clin Psychol* (1997) 4:405–19. doi:10.1007/ s00391-008-0569-0
118. Walker I, Read J. The Differ- ential effectiveness of psychoso- cial and biogenetic causal expla- nations in reducing negative atti- tudes toward 'mental illness'. *Psy- chiatry* (2002) 4:313–25. doi:10. 1521/psyc.65.4.313.20238
119. Deacon BJ, Baird GL. The chemical imbalance explanation of depression: reducing blame at what cost? *J Soc Clin Psychol* (2009) 4:415–35. doi:10.1521/jscp.2009.28.4.415
120. Angermeyer MC, Matschinger H. Labeling – stereotype – discrimination: an investiga- tion of the stigma process. *Soc Psychiatry Psychiatr Epidemiol* (2005) 40:391–5. doi:10.1007/s00127-005-0903-4
121. Haslam N. Genetic essen- tialism, neuroessentialism, and stigma: commentary on dar-nimrod and heine. *Psy- chol Bull* (2011) 137:819–24. doi:10.1037/a0022386

2

Addiction is not a brain disease (and it matters)

Neil Levy *

Florey Institute of Neuroscience and Mental Health, The University of Melbourne, Parkville, VIC, Australia

Edited by:
Hanna Pickard, University of Oxford, UK

Reviewed by:
Richard Holton, Massachusetts Institute of Technology, USA
Jerome C. Wakefield, New York University, USA

***Correspondence:**
Neil Levy, Florey Institute of Neuroscience and Mental Health, Royal Parade, The University of Melbourne, Parkville, VIC 3010, Australia.
e-mail: neil.levy@philosophy.ox.ac.uk

The claim that addiction is a brain disease is almost universally accepted among scientists who work on addiction. The claim's attraction rests on two grounds: the fact that addiction seems to be characterized by dysfunction in specific neural pathways and the fact that the claim seems to the compassionate response to people who are suffering. I argue that neural dysfunction is not sufficient for disease: something is a brain disease only when neural dysfunction is sufficient for impairment. I claim that the neural dysfunction that is characteristic of addiction is not sufficient for impairment, because people who suffer from that dysfunction are impaired, sufficiently to count as diseased, only given certain features of their context. Hence addiction is not a brain disease (though it is often a disease, and it may always involve brain dysfunction). I argue that accepting that addiction is not a brain disease does not entail a moralizing attitude toward people who suffer as a result of addiction; if anything, it allows for a more compassionate, and more effective, response to addiction.

Keywords: addiction, disease, well-being, agency, dysfunction

Neuroscientists and other scientists involved in the study of addiction rightly see their work not merely as objective science but also as a compassionate project. It aims not only to elucidate the neuropsychological causes and correlates of addiction, but also to provide knowledge that can be applied in the treatment of people who are suffering. Even those whose work is far removed from the clinical coalface – those working on animal models of addiction, for instance – take their findings and those of their peers to have important implications for how we ought to respond to addicts. The elucidation of the neural underpinnings of addiction show that addiction is a disease that must be treated, not something for which addicts can be blamed. As Leshner (1997) has said, addiction is a brain disease, and it matters.

In this paper, I will argue that the slogan is, at best, misleading. Addiction is not best understood as a brain disease, though it certainly involves pathological neuropsychological dysfunction. Addiction is a disorder of a person, embedded in a social context. The neuroscientists and their allies have mistaken some necessary conditions of the disorder with the disorder itself[1]. Notwithstanding this claim, there is, nevertheless, a strong case for saying that addiction is often a disease. Restoring addicts to their social contexts does not require us to accept the view of addiction to which the neuroscientists oppose themselves, the moral model. Rather, we can situate the addict in a social context, and even recognize that judgments about disorder are partially normative, without abandoning an entirely naturalistic framework.

Neuroscientists embrace the brain disease model of addiction for an obvious reason: because they have made great progress in elucidating neural mechanisms and neuroadaptations that are correlated with, and undoubtedly causally involved in, addiction. Neuroscientists have identified a range of such changes, including (but not limited to) the longterm depression of reward circuitry and increased activity in antireward circuitry (Koob and Le Moal, 1997, 2008); alterations in the midbrain dopamine system (Volkow and Li, 2004); and in frontal regions involved in impulse inhibition (Goldstein and Volkow, 2002). However, there are neural changes associated with and causally involved in *all* behaviors. Establishing that this is true with regard to addiction therefore does not establish that it is a brain disease.

What would it take to show that addiction is a brain disease? The details of the neural correlates of addiction matter: addiction is a brain disease if these correlates are pathological and if that pathology is sufficient for the person to have a disease, in almost any accessible environment (I will say more about this condition later in the paper). I will argue that though there is a case for saying that the correlates of addiction are pathological, these correlates are not sufficient for the person to have a disease in some accessible environments. Regardless of whether the correlates are themselves pathological, the person has a disease only insofar as their functioning as an agent is impaired, and in many environments the correlates of addiction are not sufficient for impairment. Further, I will suggest, judgments about impairment are normative judgments, where the norms in question are not norms of brain functioning. However, since a normative judgment need not be a non-naturalistic judgment – the protestations of many to the contrary – accepting that the judgment that addiction is a disease is partially normative does not require accepting the moral model of addiction, as that model is standardly conceived.

[1]It should be noted that Leshner (1997, p. 46) himself recognizes that addiction is not *just* a brain disease; rather he claims that it is "a brain disease for which the social contexts in which it has both developed and is expressed are critically important." For Leshner, addiction is a brain disease in a social context, just like (to cite his own examples) stroke, schizophrenia, and Alzheimer's disease. My claim is that addiction is *not* a brain disease like the other conditions Leshner cites; it has crucial features that make it different from stroke, schizophrenia, and Alzheimer's.

ARE THE NEURAL CORRELATES OF ADDICTION PATHOLOGICAL?

If the judgment that addiction is a disease is unashamedly normative, and the norms in question are not norms of brain function, then addiction is not a brain disease. Addiction is a brain disease only if pathological deviations from norms of brain function are (in almost any accessible environment) sufficient for being impaired. Whether addiction is caused by pathological brain dysfunction is not as obvious, however, as it apparently appears to many scientists. There are scientific accounts of addiction according to which it does not involve any brain pathology at all. On the theories I have in mind, explaining addiction requires us to postulate *non-pathological* brain mechanisms.

Consider a *mismatch* account of addiction (Durrant et al., 2009). Mismatch accounts focus on a mismatch between our evolved capacities and dispositions, on the one hand, and the environment in which many people find themselves today, on the other. This kind of hypothesis seems a plausible (partial) explanation of the current obesity epidemic. Roughly, the idea is as follows: in the environment of evolutionary adaptiveness, calories were relatively scarce. It was therefore adaptive to develop dispositions to consume as much as possible of high-calorie (sweet or fatty) foodstuffs when they were available, given that these foods couldn't be stored for long. Today, however, fatty and sugary foods are plentifully available, but we remain disposed to consume them beyond immediate and near-term need. Because we did not need to exercise self-control in the EEA with regard to these foods – just the opposite – we are reliant on limited, top-down, and domain-general mechanisms for self-control to resist overconsumption, and these mechanisms are relatively easily circumvented or exhausted. Hence the obesity epidemic. Just as in the absence of a domain specific reasoning mechanism for conditionals, we are required to use domain-general reasoning for their evaluation and we do predictably badly (Cosmides and Tooby, 1992), in the absence of substance-specific self-control mechanisms, we are thrown back onto our domain-general self-control mechanisms, and overconsumption is a likely result.

There have been attempts to develop mismatch accounts of mental illness. For instance, Murphy and Stich (2000) have hypothesized that depression might sometimes result from an overly (but not pathologically) sensitive relative status detector. Their proposal builds upon Nesse and Williams (1995) suggestion that depression may be an adaptive response to a fall in, or a failure to gain, status. Such failures trigger a disposition that focuses the individual inward (hence the rumination characteristic of depression) thereby encouraging them to identify unsuccessful social strategies and develop new ones, and causes them to withdraw from social contact which might trigger aggression on the part of dominant group members. Murphy and Stich propose that when the relevant social status detector is toward the more sensitive end of the normal distribution, it will be continually set off in contemporary societies in which we have constant opportunities to compare ourselves to high status individuals (celebrities, moguls, athletes, and so on) around the world. The result is the triggering of depression.

Consumption of mind-altering substances dates back thousands of years in human history, and very plausibly began in pre-history. Records of opium use date back nearly 6000 years (Booth, 1996); beer brewing dates back even further. However, it is unlikely that anyone had access to a sufficient quantity of such substances, over a sufficiently extended period of time, for these substances to generate serious problems until quite recently, when agriculture became widespread and humans became sedentary (Durrant et al., 2009); indeed, it is very likely that self-control with regard to them first came to be required only with the growth of cities. In these conditions, there was no selective pressure for human beings to develop a specific self-control mechanism with regard to these substances.

Today these substances are abundantly available, at least to some people and in some places (alcohol and tobacco for most people in developed nations; other substances for particular subgroups; addiction is correlated with lower socio-economic status, and addictive drugs tend to be more abundant in lower SES areas). Since we lack a substance-specific self-control mechanism, we are thrown back on domain-general self-control resources, and these resources are easily depletable (Baumeister and Vohs, 2007).

There is a salient difference between high-calorie food and drugs of addiction, though: it is plausible that evolution left us with dispositions to pursue the first but there is no evidence that we have innate dispositions to pursue the second (*pace* Sullivan and Hagen, 2002). However, the taste for drugs can be acquired; there is no reason why an acquired disposition need be weaker than an innate one. Moreover, even if the disposition to use drugs is less motivating, or motivates fewer individual actions, than the innate disposition to consume food, the harms associated with drugs accrue far more quickly, so a theory postulating a weaker disposition may explain the observed effects.

The mismatch theory does seem to go a long way to explaining the problems many people have with addictive substances. It also helps to explain why environmental factors that limit access to these substances are strongly protective. But the mismatch account clearly does not entail that addiction is a brain disease. The reason is simple: if the mismatch account explains (or, more plausibly, has a significant role in explaining) addiction, then it entails that addiction is explained by brain mechanisms *functioning as they are designed to* (Murphy and Stich, 2000). To the extent to which the mismatch account explains why addicts find it hard to resist addictive drugs, it entails that they are not suffering from a *brain* pathology at all.

If we are to show that addiction is a brain disease, we shall need to show that the underlying pathology is a pathology of the brain. We need to show that the brain is dysfunctional, in much the same way as medical scientists establish that an organ is diseased by showing that it is dysfunctional. The canonical example in medical science is heart disease: heart disease counts as a disease because it threatens to interfere with the function of the heart. The heart's functional role is pumping blood; because heart disease interferes with that role, it is a disease.

Dysfunction accounts come in two varieties, corresponding to the two competing philosophical analyses of function. On a *selectionist* account, expounded most influentially by Millikan (1984), a dysfunction occurs when something fails to play the role for which it was selected in the evolutionary history of the organism. On the *systemic* account, developed by Cummins (1975), it is not the role that something played in evolutionary history that gives it its function; rather, it is the role it (or its homologs) actually plays in a system. I do not intend to try to settle the debate between these accounts. Rather, I shall focus on what the accounts have in common, arguing that neither entails that addiction is brain disease.

There are plausible theories which (partially) explain addiction and entail that the addict's brain is dysfunctional. Suppose some kind of dopaminergic account of addiction is correct; suppose, that is, that addiction involves a pathology in the midbrain dopamine system. It is widely held that the midbrain dopaminergic system is a valuational system: it has the role of signaling the value of a resource to the organism and motivating the organism toward consumption of that resource. This view stems, in significant part, from important work of Schultz et al. In several experiments, Schultz et al. recorded the activity of midbrain dopamine neurons in monkeys performing various tasks that were rewarded with water or juice. In one experiment, monkeys learned that they would receive a reward if they pressed a particular lever, following a cue (Schultz et al., 1992). During the learning phase, the neurons responded strongly to the delivery of the reward, but once the task and the association between the cue and juice availability was learned, neurons responded when the cue was given, but not when the reward was delivered. Similarly, dopamine neurons in monkeys respond initially to the delivery of a reward predicted by a visual cue, but as the association between the cue and the reward comes to be learned, the response to the reward declines while the response to the cue predicting the reward increases (Sutton and Barto, 1998).

On the basis of this kind of evidence, many researchers have come to believe that the mesolimbic system is a reward prediction system (Montague et al., 1996; Schultz et al., 1997). It allows us to learn the value of a reward and the relationship between environmental cues and rewards. This function is obviously adaptive, since it plays a crucial role in guiding and motivating the organism in seeking out rewards, where "rewards" are goods needed for survival and reproduction.

However, addiction seems to involve dysregulation in this same midbrain dopamine system. Nearly all addictive drugs increase dopaminergic activity. Amphetamine, nicotine, cannabis, cocaine, and alcohol all either stimulate dopamine release or decrease dopamine reuptake. They thereby increase dopamine in the nucleus accumbens. Opioids increase dopamine indirectly, by influencing neurons that alter accumbal dopamine (Carter and Hall, 2012). Caffeine also increases extracellular dopamine in the nucleus accumbens (Solinas et al., 2002). The manner in which addictive drugs (and, in a very different way, gambling; see Ross et al., 2008) drive up the dopamine signal is widely thought to be central to explaining how addiction develops and why it is a chronic relapsing condition. For many addiction experts, addiction *is* a pathology of the dopaminergic system. In the common metaphor, addictive drugs "hijack" this system. That is, addiction crucially involves a *dysfunctional* mesolimbic system.

The reward prediction hypothesis seems to explain addiction by understanding it as a pathology of reinforcement learning. When the system is operating as it should, dopaminergic activation attenuates in response to *expected* reward. Dopamine response increases when the world is better than expected; when an expected reward is delivered, the world is exactly as expected and there ought to be no dopamine response. If drugs worked like natural rewards, we could expect them to trigger an initial dopamine response to consumption, but an attenuation of this response as consumption is repeated. At the same time, we ought to expect an increase in dopamine response to predictors of drug availability. Instead, what we find is dopamine response to predictors of drug availability *and* – because drugs of addiction drive up the dopamine response by their chemical action – continuing dopaminergic activity at consumption as well. In effect, the dopaminergic system responds to drugs with the signal that consumption is better than expected. It does so *every time* the drug is consumed. The addict cannot learn the reward value of the drug, because the system for reward value learning is dysfunctional. On every occasion the drug is consumed, the dopaminergic system reports that the drug is more rewarding than expected. The result is pathological learning; the system treats the drug as of ever increasing value.

It should be noted that there are rivals to the reward prediction interpretation of mesolimbic dopaminergic activity. Berridge, 2007 suggests that the role of dopamine is incentive salience, not learning. Berridge points out that learning about the relationship between a stimulus and a reward can occur without dopamine. In mice genetically engineered to be unable to synthesize dopamine, normal learning seems to occur. It also occurs in mice that have virtually no mesolimbic dopamine due to neurochemical lesioning. Further, activation in the ventral pallidum, downstream of the mesolimbic dopamine system, is stronger in response to a second, redundant, predictor of reward than in response to the first. Since the second predictor adds no new information, we ought to expect a smaller response to the second predictor than to the first if the dopamine system was itself a reward prediction system.

For Berridge (2007; Holton and Berridge, forthcoming) addiction is a pathology of incentive salience and not reward prediction. It does not involve pathological learning; rather it involves pathological "wanting." We can leave this dispute to one side. For our purposes what matters is what the researchers agree upon: that the dysfunction in the dopaminergic system either is, or is reflective of, a dysfunction of a system that evolved to play (or normally plays) a specific role in behavior, whether that is learning or incentive salience. On either story, we could understand the system that is awry, whether it is the midbrain dopamine system or something upstream of that system, as representing something about goods in the external world, such as how valuable they are to the organism. On either story, addiction causes a misrepresentation and for that reason it is a pathology. It is a pathology because the system was selected to play, or actually plays, a particular role in the psychology of animals like us, but it is no longer playing that role in addicts, at least in response to drugs and cues predictive of drug availability.

Both these dysfunction accounts, together with plausible hypotheses concerning the neural correlates of addiction, entail that addiction involves a neuropsychological dysfunction. However, neither account entails that addiction is a brain disease. I claimed earlier that addiction is a brain disease only if two conditions are satisfied: its neural correlates are pathological, and that pathology is sufficient for the person to be suffering from a disease in almost any accessible environment. This second condition is necessary to rule out conditions in which the appropriate response to suffering is to alter the environment and not to "treat" the person. Consider homosexuality. It remains an open question whether the neural correlates of homosexuality are adaptive. Wilson's (1975) conjecture, for instance, according to which homosexuality exists today due to frequency dependent selection maintaining the relevant genes at some low frequency in our ancestral population, might yet be proven correct. If this hypothesis, or another one that entails that homosexuality is adaptive (or at least not maladaptive) is false, however, it does not follow that homosexuality is a disease, not even if homosexuals suffer in homophobic societies. The conjunction of causation by dysfunction plus impairment is not sufficient for disorder, when the impairment is due to social conditions that can relatively easily be altered; that is, when the alterations necessary to remove the impairment are not alterations we have good reason to refuse to make (because they would impose significant costs on third parties, for instance)[2]. I express this claim by saying it is a necessary condition of a condition being a disease that it causes suffering in almost any accessible environment. If it is the case that there is an accessible environment – where accessibility is a function not merely of physical possibility, but also of the costs (economic, social, moral) of actually accessing that environment – in which a dysfunction does not cause an impairment, then the dysfunction is not sufficient for a disease.

Apparent counterexamples to this account are, I claim, only apparent. Consider peanut allergy[3]. It is certainly possible to alter the environment of sufferers such that they do not suffer any impairment. That fact entails that if such alterations are sufficiently cheap, peanut allergy is not a disease. This seems to be contrary to standard medical usage (ICD-10, for instance, has an appropriate category for peanut allergy). Standard medical use notwithstanding, however, I maintain that if it is true that there are accessible environments in which a peanut allergy does not cause any impairment, then it is not a disease (perhaps the intuition that it is a disease is partially due to the fact that avoiding peanuts is, right now, far from costless, since the burden is placed on individuals to carefully monitor their diet in an environment in which many products and dishes contain traces of nuts sufficient to trigger the allergic reaction). Compare a peanut allergy to dyslexia. Dyslexia may have a genetic basis, but it seems wrong to say that our hunter-gatherer ancestors suffered from dyslexia prior to the invention of writing. Rather, dyslexia seems to be a disease only in a society in which reading is sufficiently important for reading problems to count as a disability (Buchanan et al., 2000, p. 123). Now, if it is true that dyslexia was not a disease in the pre-literate past, because it did not cause an impairment in those who (in some attenuated sense) suffered from it, then it seems that if it were possible costlessly to alter the environment so that it did not cause an impairment in sufferers today, it would not count as a disease today. It would be analogous to homosexuality, inasmuch as it would be incumbent on us to eliminate the suffering it causes by altering the environment. The example of peanut allergy also seems to be closely analogous, and therefore I maintain that it does not constitute a counterexample to the account offered[4].

According to this account, addiction is not a brain disease, because it is sometimes not a disease at all. While the claim that the dopaminergic system is dysfunctional in addicts is plausible, a dysfunction of this kind is not sufficient for impairment in many accessible environments. The misrepresentation identified is at a subpersonal level, but an agent suffers from a pathology of the mind only when there is personal-level problem. Mental illness is quite plausibly identified with a defect of rationality of some kind (Graham, 2010), and a subpersonal misrepresentation is not a defect of rationality. It is quite possible for *mechanisms* to misrepresent while *agents* properly represent; once someone is acquainted with a particular visual illusion this might be true of her on future encounters with it. Of course, a subpersonal misrepresentation might in some cases straightforwardly cause a personal-level misrepresentation, but that doesn't seem to be – straightforwardly – the case in addiction. If agents accepted the valuation placed on the drugs to which they are addicted by subpersonal mechanisms, they would not want to give up, and a range of facts about them would be inexplicable (why they often, though not always, say they want to give up; why they expend significant resources in an apparent attempt to give up (Ross et al., 2008); why spontaneous recovery is so common).

On the Holton and Berridge (forthcoming) view, addiction involves intense cravings as well as misrepresentations; the midbrain dopamine system for them is the system that generates the cravings rather than itself a representational system. This addition to the account might go some way toward explaining how addiction is a personal-level defect: the agent experiences these cravings no matter how she judges, and is therefore motivated to act. However, even with this addition it seems that the hypothesized dysfunctions fall short of a pathology, because there are

[2]Suppose, however, that impairment is caused by a dysfunction plus social conditions we cannot alter, or altering which would be prohibitively costly, but those social conditions are unjust. Suppose, for instance, that some kind of biological dysfunction caused an impairment only because people were repulsed by it; would such a condition count as a disease (I thank Jerome Wakefield for raising this question)? I think we should count any dysfunction that causes impairment as a disease when the impairment cannot be (for practical purposes) avoided. This entailment of my account might strike some as counterintuitive; perhaps the impression might be softened by pointing out that in cases like this, we might owe sufferers from the impairment some special duty of recompense or compensation. Gillet and Huang (forthcoming) argue the case for such a view with regard to psychopathy.

[3]Thanks to Richard Holton for pressing me on this issue; the suggestion that peanut allergy is a counterexample to the account of disease offered here is due to him.

[4]The example of dyslexia well illustrates how "accessibility" is a partly normative notion: an environment counts as accessible if it is not merely physically possible for an individual suffers access it, or for a whole society to adopt its norms, but it is reasonable to expect the person or society to take these steps. There may continue to be extant cultures in which dyslexia does not cause an impairment, because literacy is not a benefit to members. However, for the vast majority of sufferers these cultures are extremely hard to access: barriers to entry to these cultures (learning a new language and a new way of life) are high, newcomers may not be easily accepted and people originally enculturated into a different way of life might find the new culture very unsatisfying. In addition, members of these cultures may be inadequately fed, may lack access to clean drinking water and to health care. These facts entail that it would be unreasonable to expect most dyslexics to avoid impairment by accessing these cultures, even if there is some sense in which some of them could do so; for closely analogous reasons, it would be unreasonable to expect developed societies to adopt the ways of life of such cultures. I thank Jerome Wakefield for pressing me on this issue.

accessible environments in which the agent will not suffer from any defect of rationality or impairment of agency. There are two reasons for this. The first is that the dysfunctions identified are not sufficient for the experience of cravings. Cravings for drugs are heavily cue-dependent, and the cues that trigger these cravings are avoidable (how easily the agent may avoid them will differ from person to person, depending on their learning history; in any case, for some agents with the relevant dysfunction, there will be accessible environments in which cues are avoidable).

Second, though cravings are unpleasant, experiencing them seems to fall very far short of any kind of mental illness or pathology. Subpersonal over-valuation of drugs plus intense cravings are not sufficient for the person to suffer from a defect of rationality. Nor are they sufficient for the person to suffer from a sufficiently serious impairment of agency or of their ability to pursue a worthwhile life. The neuroadaptations characteristic of addiction are longlasting; it is for this reason that the Alcoholics Anonymous slogan "once an alcoholic, always an alcoholic" has more than a grain of truth to it. Yet plainly the former heavy drinker or drug taker who has been abstinent for many years need not be suffering from any impairment (though she may have a vulnerability to suffering an impairment). All by itself, this fact shows that the neuropsychological dysfunction underlying addiction is not sufficient for disease. Indeed, with regard to some addictions some individuals who satisfy the dysfunction condition suffer no impairment despite continuing to take the drug. Whether this is true will vary depending on the drug, the consumption method, and (importantly) the ability of the agent to access the drug safely and reliably. Most people addicted to caffeine suffer no impairment. More controversially, some individuals addicted to benzodiazepines or to nicotine delivered by "e-cigarette" may suffer no impairment of rationality, of agency or of the capacity to pursue a worthwhile life. Even some heroin addicts, with the resources to obtain heroin from safe sources, may not suffer harms significant enough to plausibly constitute an impairment of their agency or their ability to pursue a good life.

It will not help the defender of the brain disease account to add the other neural correlates associated with addiction into the mix. Consider the chronic deviation from reward set point identified by Koob and Le Moal (2008). The allostatic state they postulate is the result of the brain adapting to drug ingestion. So long as the drug is reliably available, the person will suffer no ill-effects from this neuroadaptation[5]. Rather, the anhedonic state from which individuals suffer is associated with chronic abstinence. Identifying the pathology with this unpleasant state entails, counter-intuitively, that the abstinent addict suffers from a pathology but the addict who is using does not.

Other neuroadaptations characteristic of addiction are more plausible candidates for an agency-impairing pathology. Dysfunctions in mechanisms involved in self-control can be expected to impair agency under a range of conditions. However, in many environments and for many individuals, the defect is not so significant as to entail an impairment of agency or rationality. Rather, in supportive environments, where the agent is buffered from many demands by social support, this impairment is fully compatible with pursuing a good life.

If my claim that the neural correlates of addiction do not cause impairment in all accessible environments is true, addiction is *not* a brain disease in the way in which the other conditions Leshner (1997) cites are. Stroke, schizophrenia, and Alzheimer's disease cause significant defects of rationality and agency in almost any environment; though it might be possible to imagine environments in which some of these conditions did not cause impairment, such environments are not genuinely accessible (the costs of maintaining them would be prohibitive, to begin with). Addiction differs from paradigm brain diseases in that its correlates do not cause impairment across all, or nearly, accessible environments. For some conditions that cause suffering, neural correlates are sufficient to cause an impairment and for some they are not; only those which fit into the former class count as brain diseases. Addiction fits into the latter class because, with the possible exception of some deficits that are likely relatively minor (such as somewhat impaired self-control mechanisms), addiction only causes impairments in certain social environments, and social environments in which addiction would not cause any significant impairment are accessible.

These remarks suggest that if addiction is properly understood as a disease or pathology, it is not *just* because it involves neuropsychological dysfunction. Rather, capturing the manner in which it is pathological requires that we adopt an explicitly normative account of pathology, according to which someone suffers from a pathology when and only when they are subject to significant impairments of agency and consequently of the ability to pursue a good life. In the absence of such impairment, the person who ingests drugs and undergoes the neural changes associated with longterm drug use does not suffer from a disease.

The forgoing remarks ought not to come as a surprise: they amount to nothing more than the claim that addiction must fit the influential two-stage model of disease or disorder. On the two-stage model, an individual suffers from a disorder only if they experience a biological dysfunction and that dysfunction is harmful, where the judgment of harm is made by reference to social norms of flourishing (Wakefield, 1992; Murphy, 2006). Biological dysfunction may be a necessary condition of being a disorder. But this necessary condition is not a sufficient condition, and addiction is not a brain disease. Rather, *when* it is a disease, it is a disease that essentially involves brain dysfunction.

WHY IT MATTERS THAT ADDICTION IS NOT A BRAIN DISEASE

The claim that mental illness partially, but essentially, involves some deviation from norms does not entail accepting the moral model. It does not entail that addicts are to blame for their addiction. This ought to be obvious, since the account emphasizes that addiction may not count as a disease because the suffering it causes is very largely due to social conditions that are, in some sense, optional; clearly the addict is not herself responsible for these

[5] Because reliable availability of the drug enables the addict to maintain homeostatic equilibrium, addiction seems to be a counterexample to Roe and Murphy's (2011) claim that it is a necessary condition of having a disorder that the mechanisms designed to maintain homeostasis be disordered. An addict may suffer an impairment, caused by a dysfunction of the dopaminergic system, and yet be able to maintain homeostasis.

conditions. Nor does the account entail that addiction is not real, or that the suffering involved is not genuine. There may be a fact of the matter whether and when addicts suffer from a genuine impairment of agency. There are a variety of realist accounts of what constitutes a good life. Addiction may be a normative failing but if these accounts are correct it is not a normative failing *rather* than a naturalistically explicable disorder. Rather, it is a normative failing *because* of the kind of naturalistically explicable disorder it is.

The forgoing remarks are important, because they help us to recognize that the insistence that addiction is a brain disease is merely one way we can avoid both the crass moralism of those who blame addicts and a facile relativism about disorders. Addiction is not a brain disease, but there is a good case for saying that it is, nevertheless, a disorder which may require treatment (which may be medical or psychiatric, though other kinds of treatment may be appropriate in addition or instead), for which the sufferer is not to blame and the sufferer from which is an appropriate recipient of compassion.

To that extent, my claim that addiction is not a brain disease may seem to change nothing, compared to the situation that would prevail were the scientists' claim that it is a brain disease to be accepted. Though the overlap between the two accounts is important, there are some important differences.

The claim that addiction is not a brain disease allows us to resituate the addict in her social environment (Levy, 2007). She suffers from a disorder only insofar as her brain is dysfunctional in certain ways *and* prevailing social conditions make it likely that she will suffer from a defect of rationality or an impairment of agency as a result. This may be due to the fact that she lacks the resources to remove herself from environments in which she frequently encounters the cues that trigger cravings in her, and in which her self-control resources are depleted by constant demands, stress, and poor nutrition. It may be due to the fact that she lacks access to goods that compete with the attractions of the drug. The facts that explain her addiction, and the facts that explain her suffering (and the suffering she causes to others) are partially facts about her, and partially facts about the environment in which she is embedded. Moreover, the facts about her that explain her addiction and the associated suffering are themselves mediated by her environment (and some – and only some – of the facts about her environment are mediated by her).

Responding appropriately to addiction, as well as allocating blame between addict and other actors, requires us to be sensitive to these facts[6]. Addiction is a pathology that involves neuropsychological dysfunction, and it may be appropriate to respond to it by treating this dysfunction (pharmacologically, for instance). But addiction is a pathology only because of the addicts' social embeddedness, and it may equally be appropriate to respond to it by altering the social conditions that cause and sustain it, or which cause and sustain the impairments it gives rise to. If we are to understand addiction and respond appropriately to it, we must not focus on just the addicted individual herself, much less her brain. Our focus must be on her, in her social setting. Inevitably, that entails that *we* must ourselves come under scrutiny; perhaps we need to change as much as she does.

ACKNOWLEDGMENTS

I would like to thank Jerome Wakefield and Richard Holton for very helpful comments on an earlier version of this paper. I am also grateful to the Australian Research Council for a generous grant supporting the work leading to this article.

[6]The claim that an adequate response to addiction requires the treatment of the addict in her context, and therefore addressing the social factors that not only cause suffering but which also play a causal role in sustaining the behavior, has been sensitively developed by Hanna Pickard (see Pickard, 2012; Pickard and Pearce, forthcoming).

REFERENCES

1. Baumeister, R. F., and Vohs, K. D. (2007). Self-regulation, ego deple- tion, and motivation. *Soc. Personal. Psychol. Compass* 1, 1–14.
2. Berridge, K. C. (2007). The debate over dopamine's role in reward: the case for incentive salience. *Psychophar- macology (Berl.)* 191, 391–431.
3. Booth, M. (1996). *Opium: A history*. London: Simon and Schuster.
4. Buchanan, A., Brock, D. W., Daniels, N., and Wikler, D. (2000). *From Chance to Choice: Genetics and Justice*. Cambridge: Cambridge University Press.
5. Carter, A., and Hall, W. (2012). *Addic- tion Neuroethics: The Promises and Perils of Neuroscience Research on Addiction*. Cambridge: Cambridge University Press.
6. Cosmides, L., and Tooby, J. (1992). "Cognitive adaptations for social exchange," in *The Adapted Mind*, eds J. Barkow, L. Cosmides, and J. Tooby (New York: Oxford University Press), 163–228.
7. Cummins, R. (1975). Functional analy- sis. *J. Philos.* 72, 741.765.
8. Durrant, R., Adamson, S., Todd, F., and Sellman, D. (2009). Drug use and addiction: an evolutionary perspec- tive. *Aust. N. Z. J. Psychiatry* 43, 1049–1056.
9. Goldstein, R. Z., and Volkow, N. D. (2002). Drug addiction and its underlying neurobiological basis: neuroimaging evidence for the involvement of the frontal cortex. *Am. J. Psychiatry* 159, 1642–1652.
10. Graham, G. (2010). *The Disordered Mind*. NewYork: Routledge.
11. Koob, G. F., and Le Moal, M. (1997). Drug abuse: hedonic homeostatic dysregulation. *Science* 278, 52–58.
12. Koob, G. F., and Le Moal, M. (2008). Addiction and the brain antireward system. *Annu. Rev. Psychol.* 59, 29–53.
13. Leshner, A. I. (1997). Addiction is a brain disease, and it matters. *Science* 278, 45–44.
14. Levy, N. (2007). The social: a miss- ing term in the debate over addic- tion and voluntary control. *AJOB Neurosci.* 7, 35–36.
15. Millikan, R. G. (1984). *Language, Thought and Other Biological Cate- gories*. Cambridge, MA: MIT Press.
16. Montague, P. R., Dayan, P., and Sejnowski, T. J. (1996). A frame- work for mesencephalic dopamine systems based on predictive Heb- bian learning. *J. Neurosci.* 16, 1936–1947.
17. Murphy, D. (2006). *Psychiatry in the Sci- entific Image*. Cambridge, MA: MIT Press.
18. Murphy, D., and Stich, S. (2000). "Dar- win in the madhouse: evolution- ary psychology and the classification of mental disorders," in *Evolution and the Human Mind: Modularity, Language and Meta-Cognition*, eds P. Carruthers and A. Chamberlain (Cambridge: Cambridge University Press), 62–92.
19. Nesse, R. M., and Williams, G. C. (1995). *Why We Get Sick*. New York: Times Books.
20. Pickard, H. (2012). The purpose in chronic addiction. *AJOB Neurosci.* 3, 40–49.
21. Roe, K., and Murphy, D. (2011). "Func- tion, dysfunction, and adaptation?" in *Maladapting Minds: Philosophy, Psychiatry, and Evolutionary Theory*, ed. P. R. Adriaens and A. de Block (Oxford: Oxford University Press), 216–237.
22. Ross, D., Sharp, C., Vuchinich, R. E., and Spurrett, D. (2008). *Midbrain Mutiny: The Picoeconomics and Neu- roeconomics of Disordered Gambling*. Cambridge: MIT Press.

23. Schultz, W., Apicella, P., Scarnati, E., and Ljungberg, T. (1992). Neuronal activity in monkey ventral striatum related to the expectation of reward. *J. Neurosci.* 12, 4595–4610.
24. Schultz, W., Dayan, P., and Montague, P. R. (1997). A neural substrate of prediction and reward. *Science* 275, 1593–1159.
25. Solinas, M., Ferré, S., You, Z.-B., Karcz-Kubicha, M., Popoli, P., and Goldberg, S. R. (2002). Caffeine induces dopamine and gluta- mate release in the shell of the nucleus accumbens. *J. Neurosci.* 22, 6321–6324.
26. Sullivan, R. J., and Hagen, E. H. (2002). Psychotropic substance- seeking: evolutionary pathology or adaptation? *Addiction* 97, 389–340.
27. Sutton, R. S., and Barto, A. C. (1998). *Reinforcement learning: An introduction*. London: MIT Press.
28. Volkow, N. D., and Li, T. K. (2004). Drug addiction: the neurobiology of behaviour gone awry. *Nat. Rev. Neurosci.* 5, 963–970.
29. Wakefield, J. C. (1992). The concept of mental disorder: on the boundary between biological facts and social values. *Am. Psychol.* 47, 373–388.
30. Wilson, E. O. (1975). *Sociobiology: The New Synthesis*. Cambridge, MA: Harvard University Press.

3

The addict in us all

***Brendan Dill*[1]* *and Richard Holton*[2]**

[1] *Department of Linguistics and Philosophy, Massachusetts Institute of Technology, Cambridge, MA, USA*
[2] *Department of Philosophy, University of Cambridge, Cambridge, UK*

Edited by:
Hanna Pickard, University of Oxford, UK

Reviewed by:
Serge H. Ahmed, CNRS, France
Bennett Foddy, University of Oxford, UK

****Correspondence:***
Brendan Dill, 77 Massachusetts Avenue, 32-D808, Cambridge, MA 02139-4307, USA
e-mail: bdill@mit.edu

In this paper, we contend that the psychology of addiction is similar to the psychology of ordinary, non-addictive temptation in important respects, and explore the ways in which these parallels can illuminate both addiction and ordinary action. The incentive salience account of addiction proposed by Robinson and Berridge (1–3) entails that addictive desires are not in their nature different from many of the desires had by non-addicts; what is different is rather the way that addictive desires are acquired, which in turn affects their strength. We examine these "incentive salience" desires, both in addicts and non-addicts, contrasting them with more cognitive desires. On this account, the self-control challenge faced by addicted agents is not different in kind from that faced by non-addicted agents – though the two may, of course, differ greatly in degree of difficulty. We explore a general model of self-control for both the addict and the non-addict, stressing that self-control may be employed at three different stages, and examining the ways in which it might be strengthened. This helps elucidate a general model of intentional action.

Keywords: addiction, self-control, desire, incentive salience, ego depletion, mindfulness meditation, mental contrasting, implementation intentions

INTRODUCTION

On a common conception, addicts and non-addicts are very different. Addicts' compulsions drive them to act in ways that are quite foreign to the non-addicted. They consume drugs in the full knowledge that they are harmful, and in the face of a desire to stop, something that the normal agent does not do.

We argue here that this picture is quite misleading. Non-addicts, like addicts, have to contend with desires that are quite insensitive to their reflective judgments about what is good. And addicts, like non-addicts, have at their disposal a capacity for self-control that can enable them to resist and overcome these desires.

The situation faced by the addicted agent is thus parallel to that faced by the non-addicted agent. It is an extreme example of the same kind of thing. Both will have desires that persist even in the belief that their objects are worthless, or even actively harmful. And so both will be faced with the self-control problem of resisting these troublesome desires in the light of these beliefs. This self-control challenge, faced by both addicted and non-addicted agents, is the focus of this paper.

We begin by briefly outlining the empirical support for our first claim, that addictive desires are instances of a kind of desire common to all agents (see Desire). They result from a system – the "incentive salience" system – that has evolved to create desires, for foods and other things, that are independent from the agent's evaluations of the worth of those things. What is different in the addict is not the intrinsic nature of these desires, but their origin. Addictive drugs cause the desire-formation process to malfunction, with the result that they come to be desired with an intensity and permanence that is quite out of proportion to any pleasure they have given. However, the same problematic features of addictive desires arise even when the incentive salience system does not malfunction. We see this in more mundane desires such as the craving for chocolate. We characterize the common features of these "incentive salience" desires, and contrast them with the more reasons-sensitive desires, which we call "cognitive desires," on the basis of which agents reflectively deliberate about what to do. The competition between these two kinds of desire for control over behavior poses the problem with which we are concerned throughout the remainder of the paper: the problem of self-control.

We begin our discussion of self-control by arguing that an agent's course of action is not solely determined by the relative strengths of her desires; it also matters whether, and how, she exerts *self-control* on behalf of some desires over others. Our argument centers on two subject populations whose behaviors are, we think, best explained as resulting from selective deficits in self-control capacity: subjects with lesions in the ventromedial prefrontal cortex (vmPFC), and subjects experiencing *ego depletion* (see The Existence of Self-Control).

The picture that emerges from these first two sections portrays intentional action as the result of a competition between two systems: the incentive salience system, which automatically guides behavior on the basis of appetitive desires, and the self-control system, by means of which an agent can, with effort, bring her actions in accordance with her more reflective desires. Though the conflict between these systems is typically more dramatic in addicts, it pervades ordinary action as well.

Though we offer some new arguments in its support, this two-system picture is far from novel. The basic outlines of the approach date back to Plato [(4), *Republic* Book IV] and the more contemporary version of this picture we present here has been defended before (5–8). What we hope to add to this literature is a more detailed picture of how these two systems interact to produce behavior (see Three Stages of Self-Control). We propose that there are three distinct loci of self-control conflict – at the point of deliberation, of formation of intention, and of execution of action – which we call the *deliberative, volitional,* and *implemental* stages of self-control. Distinguishing between these stages brings into focus the nature of the self-control challenge faced by addicts and non-addicted agents alike. Drawing on a large body of empirical work, we articulate the nature of the conflict between the self-control and incentive salience systems at each stage, and suggest ways in which each kind of self-control might be improved. What emerges is a single model of human motivational psychology that captures the predicaments of addiction and ordinary temptation with equal aptitude.[1]

DESIRE

Let us start with the question of how we form desires. One might think – many have thought – that we are hedonists at heart. On such a view all of our desires stem from a fundamental intrinsic desire for pleasure. When we desire things other than pleasure we desire them *instrumentally*: that is, we desire them derivatively, because we believe that they will give us pleasure.

Many have objected that such an account makes us seem far too selfish: sometimes we want things because of the benefits that they will bring other people, independently of any benefits they may bring to us. We think that this point is probably right,[2] but it is not our primary concern here. Our argument is rather that such a picture is wrong even when we consider such simple self-regarding desires as those we have for different foods. Suppose that an agent were to sample many different foods. Some they would like, others not, and they would then go on to regulate their future desires for them accordingly. We might expect these to be instrumental desires, formed in the service of the desire for pleasure. But the empirical evidence suggests not. It suggests instead that pleasure typically causes us to have intrinsic desires for the foods themselves, which then motivate independently of any beliefs about the pleasure that such foods will bring.

The crucial evidence for this is that our desires for different foods are not always directly responsive to our explicit beliefs about how pleasurable they are to eat. The desires do not need such beliefs to bring them into existence; and they can persist in their absence. We sometimes get a sense of this in our direct experience – many of us experience a desire to eat more of a thing (chocolates? over-rich desserts? peanuts? potato chips?) even when we know that we won't enjoy it and that it may leave us feeling somewhat nauseated. However, the best evidence for this phenomenon comes from studies, not of normal foods, but of addictive drugs, and moreover, of how they work on rats. So let us start there, and then return to the case of how more normal foods work on us. Our account will follow the "incentive salience" theory developed by Robinson and Berridge (1–3).[3]

Addictive drugs artificially increase the levels of the neurotransmitter dopamine in the brain. Different drugs do this in different ways: nicotine stimulates the production of dopamine directly, opiates decrease the production of substances that inhibit the production of dopamine, cocaine reduces the activity of the system that reabsorbs dopamine after it has been released, and so on [(9), pp. 245–246]. What is remarkable is that these various substances with otherwise disparate biological and neurological effects have this single common feature: they all boost the effect of dopamine.

It is reasonable to infer that this shared neurobiological quirk must play a role in explaining these substances' more obvious common feature: that they all cause addiction. Although there remains controversy here, this idea is borne out by the evidence. By boosting dopamine levels, addictive drugs artificially stimulate the mesolimbic dopamine system, which has long been known to play an important role in motivation. That is, they stimulate it directly, and not in the normal way via an experience that also gives rise to pleasure. (Compare getting someone to see stars by banging them on the head, rather than by showing them stars.) So to understand how drug addiction works, we need to understand what role dopamine plays in motivation.

For many years dopamine was thought to be a pleasure signal. But it is not. Whilst it is typically accompanied by pleasure, that is not what it is causing or registering [for a detailed defense of this claim, see Ref. (10)]. Separate the indicators of a rat's pleasure (its facial movements) from the indicators of its desire (the effort it will expend to attain the thing), and you find that dopamine is linked to desire and not to pleasure. Artificially increase a rat's dopamine levels by giving it amphetamines, and it will work much harder to get something even if that thing gives it no pleasure, and it knows it (11). Reduce the rat's dopamine levels via genetic modification and it will fail to work for a thing even if that thing will give it great pleasure, and it knows it (12). Moreover – and this is crucial given the implications for addiction – if you increase the dopamine levels when a rat is sampling a foodstuff, what you bring about is not just an immediate desire for that foodstuff, but also a long-term dispositional desire for it (13). Show the rat the foodstuff again later, and it will still want it strongly.

What is happening here? Rats are opportunistic creatures, who need to be able to accommodate their tastes to a new environment. It makes sense for them to be able to regulate their desires in proportion to the pleasure that they get from various foodstuffs. Dopamine is clearly involved in this process. But it looks as though dopamine works directly on desires, without the need for the involvement of pleasure or beliefs about pleasure. It may be that dopamine release is typically *caused* by pleasure: in the case of most non-addictive foodstuffs, the most pleasurable ones will give the greatest dopamine release. But if dopamine is artificially increased,

[1] We do not take our account to provide an exhaustive explanation of addiction (or ordinary temptation, for that matter). It leaves out at least two important factors: affect and social context. Affect comes into the explanation of addiction in two places: first, one of the major reasons why addicts use is in order to relieve negative emotions such as stress, anxiety, and depression (135); and second, these negative emotions may significantly impair agents' ability to exert self-control (136). And as has been recognized since the earliest addiction treatment programs, social context plays a huge role in addiction: social influence often explains why the addict started taking the drug in the first place; and social support is an essential ingredient in the process of recovery from addiction. Our account has little to say about these important phenomena. Rather than attempting to survey all of the explanatory factors in addiction, we aim only to characterize two of these factors – desire and self-control – and the interactions between them. (Thanks to both Serge Ahmed and Hanna Pickard for pointing out these limitations of our account).

[2] See Batson and Shaw (137) for a classic empirical argument for this claim.

[3] The particular interpretation here follows that given in Holton and Berridge (9); readers should look there for much more detail on what is here treated far too swiftly.

as it is by addictive drugs, then this leads to the production of desire independently of pleasure.

In fact, given what we have said, we need to identify two roles that dopamine plays in the production of desire. One, the *triggering role*, involves the triggering of occurrent desire: dopamine has a role in actually getting the rat to move toward the food in the moment. The other, the *formation role*, involves the formation of dispositional desire: dopamine works to set up a long-term disposition to want the food in the future.[4] Stimulate a rat's dopamine levels at the same time that it is consuming a certain food, and it will form a dispositional desire for that food (13). This is a focused desire: it is focused on the food that was being consumed when the dopamine was released. Present the food again, or present other cues that were associated with it, and the rat will want it, even if its dopamine levels are not then being stimulated. Dopamine thus creates a dispositional desire that, when cued by the relevant food or other associated cues, triggers an occurrent desire for that food.

The formation role that dopamine plays has often been described as a learning role. But that is misleading, since, at least within the more cognitive models that now dominate psychology, learning is best taken to involve a change in belief.[5] It is not that the rat comes to believe that the food is going to bring it some advantage, and so forms an instrumental desire conditional on that belief. Rather, what is happening is that an *intrinsic* long-term desire for the substance is being created. If the desire is not reinforced, it will fade in time. But with desires put in place by addictive substances, this can take a very long time indeed – they may last for much of a rat's life.

On the basis of this evidence, Robinson and Berridge (1–3) posited a motivational system, the "incentive salience" system, which has the following features. The incentive salience system creates dispositional desires for objects on the basis of those objects' past association with reward. These dispositional desires, which we will call *incentive salience desires*, are activated – become occurrent – when the rat encounters the desired thing, or cues that have been associated with it. Once an incentive salience desire is active, it leads automatically to behavior in pursuit of the desired object. Crucially, the neural reward signal on the basis of which the incentive salience system acquires its desires is a dopamine signal. Thus addictive substances, by artificially boosting dopamine levels in the brain, produce a disproportionately large reward signal, which in turn causes the formation of a disproportionately strong incentive salience desire for the substance.

We have good reason to think this incentive salience system is present in humans as well as rats. The argument for this claim is an inference to the best explanation: the puzzling features of human addiction are best explained by the hypothesis that addictive desires are incentive salience desires. It explains the craving that is typically prompted by cues associated with the drugs: because of the artificial dopamine boost addictive drugs provide, subjects who consume these drugs acquire a long-term intrinsic desire for them, which is then triggered by the drug-associated cues. This account explains relapse, even after withdrawal: for the dispositional desire remains, ready to be triggered by the relevant cues.[6] Finally, in human subjects, the account explains why the desires for drugs are so horribly independent from beliefs about their worth. For the incentive salience system is working quite independently of belief. The addict can know perfectly well that continued consumption would destroy everything that they hold dear. That does nothing to stop the rush of desire that is triggered by the thought or sight of the drug, or, more broadly, of the people, places or paraphernalia that have surrounded its consumption.

In addiction, the process whereby incentive salience desires are acquired malfunctions. When the system is functioning normally, the dopamine signal is proportional to the reward that the subject is experiencing, and thus the desire it produces is similarly proportionate. When a subject consumes an addictive substance, however, the artificial boost in dopamine that results can sever this link between "wanting" and "liking, " leading to a desire for the substance that is way out of proportion with the pleasure it brings.[7]

But of course, much of what we have said about the incentive salience system still holds when it is not malfunctioning in this way. When it works well it still lays down long-term dispositional desires for things that have previously given pleasure; and these desires will be triggered by the relevant cues. If the things fail to give pleasure, then in time, the desire will diminish, though it will not evaporate straightaway. And if the thing continues to give pleasure, then the desire will be reinforced, even if the agent comes to believe that it is harmful.

To see this, consider the case of sugar. As far as we know, sugar has no direct effect on the dopamine system: it does not imitate dopamine, or inhibit re-uptake, or do any of the things that addictive drugs do. Nevertheless, rats that have been exposed to a sugar solution are strongly motivated to get it, just as they are motivated to get addictive drugs. In fact, if they have a choice between cocaine and sugar, around 90% of rats will take the sugar (14). It is possible that there is something special about sugar that causes the formation of long-term dispositional desires in this way. But it is equally possible that sugar is simply highly pleasurable.[8] Certainly there is no reason to think that the rats' desire-formation systems are somehow malfunctioning when they develop desires for foods that are rich in it.

[4]Holton and Berridge (9), in an attempt to avoid prejudicing the case, called these "A-signals" and "B-signals." We have replaced this terminology with something a little more memorable.

[5]Although there remains some controversy here, it looks as though the formation of beliefs can take place in the absence of dopamine (for instance, in genetically modified dopamine deficient mice) and hence in the absence of motivation. See Robinson et al. (138); and for a recent discussion of the competing hypotheses together with a proposal for compromise, see Berridge and O'Doherty (139).

[6]Indeed, withdrawal, horrible though it can be, plays a minor role in addiction; consumption is not primarily motivated by a desire to avoid it.

[7]We say "can," for it remains an open question why most people who consume addictive drugs do not become addicted to them (most people in the West drink alcohol, but most do not become alcoholics); and likewise why most animals do not consume addictive drugs if they have attractive alternatives (see below). It could be that they are less prone to form the relevant incentive salience desires; it could be that they form competing desires more strongly; or it could be that they are better at self control. For a survey of the mounting evidence for the former, see Saunders and Robinson (140).

[8]For a review of the evidence that there is more going on in the formations of desires for sugar than simply the activity of the dopamine system see DiLeone et al. (141) and Ahmed et al. (142).

Nor is there reason to think that things are any different for human beings. It has become commonplace to speak of sugar addiction; it is true that many subjects' desires for sugar have a great deal in common with addicts' desires for drugs. They too manifest in cravings that are highly cue-dependent, that are very powerful, and that persist in the face of the conviction that it would be better to eat less sugar. As with the consumption of sugar, so with many other pleasurable behaviors. Gambling, sex, surfing the web, watching daytime television – all of these have been alleged to give rise to addiction.

But we need to distinguish two things here: the "hijacking" of the desire-formation process that occurs with addictive drugs; and the nature of incentive salience desires themselves. The first of these features is unique to drugs: only substances that lead to artificial dopamine stimulation will hijack the desire-formation process in this way. We have no reason to think that sugar "addiction" results from a hijacking: there is no evidence that sugar leads to artificial boosts in dopamine. It is even more obvious that web-surfing and gambling do not stimulate dopamine in this way (since they are not ingested). So in none of these cases is there reason to think that the dopamine system has malfunctioned. Yet in every case there is reason to think that the motives to engage in these behaviors are insulated from the agent's beliefs about what would be good. Incentive salience desires have this feature regardless of how they are acquired. It is exactly this feature that leads to the talk of addiction, since it is what substance and non-substance "addictions" have in common. Agents genuinely want to stop; and yet still they feel the pull of the desire.

We are therefore faced with a terminological choice: do we reserve the term "addiction" for desires formed by means of the dopamine hijacking process, and so say that sugar and gambling addictions are not addictions proper? Or do we use the term "addiction" to refer more generally to the predicament an agent faces when she has sufficiently strong and uncontrolled incentive salience desires, whatever their origin – and thus say that sugar and gambling addictions can be genuine addictions after all? Of course in a sense nothing hinges on the choice: once we are clear on the phenomena, it should not matter how we use the words. Nevertheless, talk of addiction brings with it so many expectations that in practical terms the choice matters deeply. We are torn on this question: RH is inclined to take the first option; BD leans toward the second. In the rest of the paper, we will side with BD and take the more inclusive definition, whilst saying nothing about the difficult question of when a "normal" desire for gambling or sucrose should be seen as an addiction.

What it is important to realize is that there is a contrast between these incentive salience desires, however caused, and many of our other desires. While incentive salience desires are by nature insensitive to our judgments about what is good, not all desires share this feature. In many cases, a desire is bound up with a reason or a justification: to want something is to want it for some reason.[9] As one's confidence in the reason diminishes, so the desire diminishes. Suppose that one of your favorite companies is bringing out a new model of some device that you particularly like; moved by the advance publicity you start to develop a hankering for it. But now the reviews come out, and without fail they are dismissive. The thing is clunky, ill-conceived, badly engineered, a definite step backwards. Your desire withers. You do not need to resist or overcome it. Once your beliefs have changed so that you see no reason to continue, the desire is no longer there. We do not have to think that these reason-based desires are always instrumental, i.e., that we only have them in order to get some other thing. But they are bound up with their reasons in such a way that they do not have a life of their own: they cannot live on without them, unlike the incentive salience desires, which can. We will call such desires *cognitive desires*, since they are sensitive to our cognition in a way incentive salience desires are not.

We should also distinguish incentive salience desires from another class of motivational states, namely habits. These clearly often play a role in addiction: it is not for nothing that we speak of an addict's "habit." Like incentive salience desires they are cued by circumstance, and often result in behavior that the agent rejects. Yet in so far as we have a good behavioral grip on them – behaviors like thumb-sucking, nail-biting, hair-pulling, and muscle tics – they differ in one crucial respect. The most effective treatment for them is *habit reversal therapy*, which involves monitoring the habit, and then learning an alternative response (15).[10] And it seems that the most important part of this is simply the monitoring [(16); see also Ref. (17)]. Habits work automatically, but once they are monitored, the agent can override them. In contrast, while incentive salience desires are sometimes combined with an automatic element (reaching unawares for a cigarette), becoming aware of that element is not enough to remove their force. If they are to be resisted, they need to be overcome.

Let us summarize this section so far. We have contended that there are at least two distinct kinds of desire at play in human motivation. First, there are incentive salience desires, which are formed for objects on the basis of their previous association with either rewarding experience (when the system is functioning well) or artificial dopamine stimulation (when the system is hijacked by addictive drugs). These desires form the motivational basis of addiction, but also play an ever-present role in non-addicted agents' motivation, encompassing at least the sphere of motives we normally call "appetites" even when these are well-regulated (desires for food, drink, sex, and many other typically pleasurable stimuli). Crucially, incentive salience desires motivate independently from an agent's reflective judgments about what is valuable or even pleasurable. This distinguishes incentive salience desires from a second kind of desires, cognitive desires, which are sensitive to and based upon an agent's reflective beliefs about what is valuable; e.g., the desire to read a certain book or pursue a certain career.[11]

[9] Such an approach has been advocated, in rather different ways, by Scanlon (143) and Railton (144). We agree that some desires have this feature, but deny that this is the only kind of desire

[10] It is very effective.

[11] We do not take this distinction to be exhaustive. There could be desires that are not cognitive, in the sense that they are not sensitive to our judgments about reasons, but are not incentive salience desires either, since they are not produced by the incentive salience system. The desires involved in emotional reactions such as fear or guilt, for example, do not seem to fall neatly into either category.

How do these two kinds of desire, and our habits, interact to produce intentional action? A simple model, traditional in both psychology and philosophy, sees the efficacy of desires as simply a function of their *strength* (or of their strength together with the subject's belief in how likely they are to be realized). On such a model what an agent does is simply determined by what she most wants to do. Incentive salience desires and cognitive desires will fight it out on the basis of their strength, and the stronger desire will control behavior.

There is a great deal of empirical evidence that tells against such a model, evidence that suggests that action is not simply dictated by the strongest desire. In particular, agents are not passive spectators of the competition between their desires for domination over behavior. Rather, the agent herself plays a much more active role in determining which desire triumphs, employing self-control to resist some desires, and to act on others. What determines an agent's behavior, then, is not merely how strong her desires are, but also whether and how she exerts self-control.

Self-control is hard work. In the case of addiction, self-control is standardly employed to try to restrain incentive salience desires in the light of cognitive desires. Of course this attempt may not succeed. The addict may be aware that she (cognitively) prefers keeping her job to taking drugs, and be aware that taking drugs will cause her to lose her job, on that basis judge that she ought not to use, and yet *still* succumb to her desire for the drug. As R. Jay Wallace puts the point: "even if one succeeds, in the face of [an addictive] desire, in reasoning correctly to the conclusion that it should not be acted on, its continued presence and urgency will make it comparatively difficult to choose to comply with the deliberated verdict one has arrived at" (Ref. (18), p. 648). Moreover, even if one chooses to comply, it is hard work to convert that resolution into action.

Our contention here is that these points apply equally to *ordinary* action. For the features of addictive desire that pose self-control problems are features of incentive salience desires in general, and thus are shared by a wide range of non-addictive desires as well. Just as the motivational force of an addict's incentive salience desire for heroin persists despite her judgment that she should not take it, the motivational force of an ordinary agent's incentive salience desire for a cake will persist despite her judgment that she ought to have something more healthy instead. Whether the agent's judgment or craving prevails is a matter of self-control.

We have already elucidated the essential features of the incentive salience system, and presented empirical evidence for its existence. However, we have so far said little about the nature of self-control, and have given no empirical argument for the existence of this phenomenon. We now turn to this task (see The Existence of Self-Control). Then we will be in a position to see how the different kinds of desires are mediated by the self-control system to produce intentional action (see Three Stages of Self-Control).

THE EXISTENCE OF SELF-CONTROL

There are various reasons for believing in the existence of self-control as an independent system that is not reducible to strength of desire.[12] Here, we present just one argument. The existence of a psychological system dedicated to a particular function is frequently accepted on the basis of evidence of a selective impairment in that function. For instance, autistic persons' selective impairment in social cognition has been taken as strong evidence for the existence of a psychological system dedicated to social cognition (19), and prosopagnosic persons' selective impairment in identifying faces has been taken as strong evidence for the existence of a perceptual system dedicated to face identification (20, 21). In general, a functionally specific impairment that shows up across multiple subjects seems best explained by positing the existence of a functionally specialized psychological system that is impaired or damaged in that subject population. Furthermore, by comparing these impaired subjects to healthy controls, we can uncover the causal–functional roles of the posited system.

Here, we follow this broad strategy, contending that the behavioral abnormalities of two different populations are best explained by a selective impairment in self-control: patients with lesions in the ventromedial prefrontal cortex (vmPFC), and (healthy) subjects who have undergone *ego depletion*. However, our claim here is more limited than those that have been made about social cognition or face recognition. We are not arguing that the system involved in self-control is *exclusively* dedicated to the task: that would require showing that *only* self-control is affected in these subjects, which is far from obvious (not least because we are not yet clear on what counts as an exercise of self-control and what does not). Our point is rather that the subjects in the two groups show a systematic loss of self-control even though there is no reason to think that their desires and beliefs have been affected; and hence that we have good reason for positing some kind of system that is responsible for self-control, whether or not that system is also responsible for other, unrelated processes as well.

Our pairing of vmPFC lesions and ego depletion may seem surprising, given that the two subject groups have been studied separately and in different subdisciplines (neuropsychology and social psychology). However, these two groups have an important common feature: they both behave as we would expect people to behave who are motivated overwhelmingly by incentive salience desires. This indicates that the motivational system that counteracts incentive salience desires' effects on behavior is selectively impaired in these subject groups. As we will argue, these subjects' deficits are best explained by appeal to the impairment of a psychological system that serves the function of governing behavior on the basis of cognitive desires. That is, these subjects seem to be suffering from selective impairment of the self-control system as we have described it.

This raises the question: how *should* we expect a person to behave who is motivated solely by incentive salience desires? We can make important predictions based on a single observation about how incentive salience desires are acquired: a dispositional incentive salience desire for an end state E is formed on the basis of past associations between E and a simultaneous dopamine reward signal (usually caused by pleasure, though sometimes caused by artificial dopamine stimulation, as with addictive drugs). The strength of a dispositional incentive salience desire for any end state E is proportional to the (recency-weighted) average of the past reward signals that have been associated with E (9).

[12] See [(6), pp. 112–136].

Thus we can predict that incentive salience desires will only motivate agents to pursue ends that have been previously associated with co-occurrent reward. This means that agents will be unable to form incentive salience desires for ends that are not *immediately* rewarding, or not rewarding *to the agent*, since accomplishing these ends will not bring about a co-occurrent reward. This rules out two important kinds of ends. First, incentive salience desires will not motivate agents to pursue *long-term* goals, which produce valuable or rewarding consequences only long after their end states have been attained. Examples of such goals include the goal to pass an examination, the goal to lower one's cholesterol, and (notably) the goal to quit an addictive drug: the benefits of achieving each of these goals accrue to the agent only long after the goal has been achieved. Second, incentive salience desires will not motivate agents to pursue *other-regarding* goals that, while they produce good consequences for others, are not immediately rewarding to the agent. Many moral and altruistic goals are likely to fall under this category: e.g., the goal to be honest when there is a prudential incentive to lie, the goal to avoid socially inappropriate or offensive behavior, and the goal to help others with whom one does not empathically identify.[13] So we can predict that a person who is motivated solely by incentive salience desires will pursue predominantly *self-regarding* and *immediately rewarding* goals.[14]

Both vmPFC lesion patients and ego depleted subjects fit this prediction well. We will start with the vmPFC lesion patients, as their deficit is more dramatic.

Since Phineas Gage, the first recorded and most famous case of vmPFC lesioning, the two most salient features of vmPFC-lesioned patients have been their severe deficits in socially appropriate behavior and long-term planning (22). vmPFC lesion patients usually display "acquired sociopathy," a disorder characterized by dampened and poorly regulated emotions as well as disturbed social decision-making. This typically causes vmPFC lesion patients, post-trauma, to be unable to maintain healthy social relationships or gainful employment (23, 24).

In addition to their sociopathic behavior, vmPFC lesion patients seem unable to base their behavior on the long-term consequences of their actions. The most famous demonstration of this deficit comes from the Iowa Gambling Task [IGT; (25)]. The IGT presents subjects with four decks of cards, which give differing monetary rewards when subjects draw from them. Two high-risk decks give large immediate rewards, but result in a long-term loss by giving even larger punishments; two low-risk decks present the long-term optimal option, yielding small but consistent rewards. Healthy control subjects will start by sampling all decks, temporarily favor the high-risk decks, and then learn to choose the low-risk decks after receiving punishment. vmPFC lesion patients, on the other hand, will continue to favor the high-risk decks throughout the task. The best explanation for this pattern seems to be that the vmPFC lesion patients are motivated by the short-term rewards offered by the high-risk decks, and cannot change their behavior on the basis of the cognitive desire to maximize their long-term payoff and the judgment that those decks have a suboptimal long-term predicted payoff.[15]

As has been noted since the first studies, however, vmPFC lesion patients typically display normal intelligence, intact knowledge of social norms, and the ability to make accurate predictions about future social and non-social consequences (26, 27). This indicates that these patients' impairment is motivational rather than cognitive.

We submit that the best explanation for these results is that vmPFC lesion patients' behavior is guided overwhelmingly by the incentive salience system, which activates self-regarding and short-term goals. This is why vmPFC lesion patients show deficits in the two otherwise unrelated domains of moral behavior and long-term goal pursuit: both kinds of behavior require the capacity to set and pursue goals to achieve end states that are not immediately associated with rewarding experience.[16] However, these patients have normal explicit beliefs and evaluative judgments about what is good. So vmPFC lesion patients seem to be selectively impaired in their ability to act on their cognitive desires. This indicates that there is a psychological system, instantiated in or dependent upon the vmPFC, that (among other things) serves the function of controlling behavior on the basis of cognitive desires – i.e., the self-control system.

The self-control system can be impaired in healthy subjects as well, as is shown by studies on *ego depletion*. The ego depletion finding is that healthy (non-lesioned) subjects who exert self-control on one task will subsequently perform less well than control subjects on a second, unrelated task that also requires self-control (28). The large literature on ego depletion has demonstrated that many different kinds of task are ego depleting, from attention regulation (29) to making choices (30) to analytical thought (31). However, for our purposes, the most important ego depleting tasks are the motivational tasks, where subjects must exert self-control in order to override some desires in favor of others. On these tasks, ego depleted subjects show a similar pattern to vmPFC patients: they are selectively impaired in the pursuit of other-regarding and long-term goals.

Begin with other-regarding goals. The following results all support the claim that ego depleted subjects are less able to suppress selfish desires for the sake of other people:

- Ego depleted subjects are less likely to volunteer to help a victim of a tragedy (32).

[13]This last qualification is necessary since there is some evidence that helping those with whom one does empathize can be rewarding in itself. In general, our argument applies only to moral behavior that is not intrinsically pleasurable; and quite where the boundaries of that lie is not yet clear.

[14]It is important to emphasize that we do not take this characterization to apply generally to addicts, but only to persons driven *exclusively* by incentive salience desires; as we argue later in this section, it is implausible to think that this is true of most addicts. Thanks to Hanna Pickard for pressing us to clarify this point.

[15]For more evidence beyond the IGT supporting the idea that vmPFC lesion patients are insensitive to long-term consequences, see [Refs. (145, 146)].

[16]To return to an earlier point: we are not claiming that this is the *only* deficit that occurs in vmPFC lesion patients. Naturally occurring brain lesions are messy by nature and will rarely selectively impair a single psychological process without disrupting others. For instance, vmPFC lesion patients' reported abnormalities in moral judgment (147), social cognition (148), and affective experience (23) are not straightforwardly explained by our hypothesis that they suffer from impaired self-control. However, we think our hypothesis provides a better explanation for vmPFC lesion patients' deficits in social behavior and long-term planning than the emotion-based explanation given by Damasio (22), though we do not have the space to argue this point here.

- Ego depleted subjects are more likely to lie about their performance for monetary gain (33).
- Ego depleted subjects express more interest in sleeping with someone other than their romantic partner, are less able to suppress sexually inappropriate thoughts, and are more likely to inappropriately engage in sexual behavior with their dating partner in the laboratory when given an opportunity to do so (29).
- Ego depleted subjects are less effective at social self-presentation – for example, they are more likely to speak or disclose an inappropriate amount in conversation (34).
- Ego depleted subjects are more likely to respond destructively than constructively when their relationship partner behaves destructively (35).
- Ego depleted subjects are more likely to respond with aggression after an insult (36).

Moving on to long-term goals, the following results all support the claim that ego depleted subjects are less able to suppress short-term desires for the sake of long-term gain:

- Ego depleted subjects are less likely to choose to eat radishes rather than chocolates, or to restrain themselves from eating cookies when on a diet (28).
- Ego depleted subjects' consumption of M&M's candies is better predicted by their implicit evaluations of M&M's than by their explicitly stated desires to eat healthy, while non-depleted control subjects' consumption of M&M's is better predicted by their explicit desires to diet than by their implicit evaluations (37).
- Ego depleted subjects are less likely to restrain themselves from drinking too much beer when they expect to take a driving test afterward (38).
- Ego depleted subjects are less likely to choose to study for a test rather than procrastinate by reading magazines or playing video games (30).
- Ego depleted subjects will drink less of a healthy but bad-tasting beverage (30).
- Ego depleted subjects are more likely to spend money impulsively when given the chance (39).

All these seem to be cases where the long-term value of a future outcome (e.g., health, sobriety in a driving test, achievement, savings) needs to override a craving to pursue some immediately rewarding end (cookies, chocolate, beer, video games, and impulse spending).

Like vmPFC patients, ego depleted subjects show a selective impairment that results in the relative domination of their behavior by incentive salience desires. Non-depleted subjects are better able to pursue long-term and other-regarding goals that cannot be activated by incentive salience desires. We think this data should be explained in the same way that we have explained the motivational deficits of vmPFC-lesioned patients. Healthy, non-depleted human agents are different from vmPFC lesion patients and ego depleted subjects in that they have a fully functioning self-control system, which is impaired or absent in these other populations. The self-control system enables healthy agents to override their incentive salience desires and control their behavior in accordance with their cognitive desires. This allows their motivational repertoire to include moral considerations, altruistic concern, and the long-term consequences of their actions. The powerful explanation of these two disparate bodies of data that we attain by positing the self-control system is, we submit, sufficient reason to accept its existence.[17]

Let us pause to address a worry regarding our argument's appeal to the ego depletion findings.[18] One might be wary of drawing any conclusions from the ego depletion findings, given the controversy that surrounds them. Given how hotly debated many of Baumeister and colleagues' claims about ego depletion have been, is not it a bad idea to take those claims as premises in an argument? Though this concern is natural, closer examination reveals that the controversies surrounding ego depletion are orthogonal to our central claims.

First, there is an ongoing debate regarding the replicability of *one* of the empirical findings in the ego depletion literature. But this debate concerns not the central ego depletion finding itself, but a certain hypothesis about its physiological mechanism: Gailliot and Baumeister's (40) claim that ego depletion is mediated by depletion of glucose in the bloodstream. Despite the original findings in support of this claim, more recent experiments have called it into question [e.g., Ref. (41, 42)]. However, our argument does not rely on this questionable finding. We only appeal to the ego depletion finding itself: the finding that subjects who exert self-control on one task perform less well than controls on subsequent self-control tasks. This finding has been replicated over 100 times, according to Inzlicht and Schmeichel (43). A recent meta-analysis of 83 studies reports that the ego depletion effect is both highly statistically significant ($p < 0.001$) and of medium-to-large size [Cohen's $d = 0.62$; (44), p. 508]. Though there are still some skeptics [see Ref. (45)], the reliability and replicability of the ego depletion finding itself is widely accepted.

The other locus of controversy concerns what we call the *depletion question*: how does exerting self-control on one task impair self-control performance on subsequent tasks? Several answers to this question have been proposed. Most prominently, Roy Baumeister and colleagues have argued that self-control tasks all depend upon and use up a limited resource, which they call "willpower" (46). Their answer to the depletion question is simple: the first task uses up the willpower

[17]Levy (7) offers a similar argument for the existence of the self-control system, though he takes it to be part of System 2. However, Levy's view differs significantly from ours, in that he takes the self-control system to play an exclusively cognitive role: "ego depletion is caused by engagement in any of the much broader class of system 2 processes, which involve effortful cognitive processing" [(7), p. 147]. He argues that self-control's role in overcoming temptation is fully mediated by its role in forming accurate, unbiased beliefs about what is best to do [see also (51, 52)]. While we agree that this is *one* of the functions of self-control (see Deliberative stage), we differ from Levy in ascribing to the self-control system some directly motivational functions as well. A result of this difference is that Levy's picture omits the very role of the self-control system we have most emphasized: namely, its function of overriding an agent's incentive salience desires to control behavior in accordance with her cognitive desires. So, though Levy's argument is similar to ours, it does not suffice for the point we wish to make here.

[18]Thanks to Serge Ahmed and Bennett Foddy for both raising this worry.

resource, leaving less willpower available than is necessary for optimum performance on the second task. However, this "resource theory" has recently been challenged by alternative accounts that claim we can explain ego depleted subjects' impairment without appealing to a limited willpower resource. Several of these "anti-resource" accounts have been proposed (43, 47–49). Though the details of their accounts differ, these theorists all argue that exerting self-control decreases subjects' *motivation* to exert further self-control – either by changing their beliefs or their desires – rather than by depleting a limited self-control resource.

It may seem that we need to take a stand on this controversy, siding with the resource theorist in claiming that there is a limited willpower resource that is depleted by self-control exertion. However, our argument does not require this claim. In fact, we think our argument is consistent with both the resource and anti-resource answers to the depletion question. To see how, we need to distinguish the depletion question from an alternative question one might ask about the ego depletion finding, which we call the *covariance question.*

The covariance question is: why does ego depletion affect the particular tasks that it does, and not others? In other words, the covariance question asks why the many abilities affected by ego depletion all stand or fall *together.* What do emotion regulation, making arbitrary choices, analytic thought, resisting tempting foods, altruistic behavior, and all the other ego depleting tasks have in common, so that ability on one of these tasks covaries with ability on all of the others? Why does not ego depletion make people worse at rote memory recall, instead of impairing analytic thought? Why does ego depletion make people more selfish, rather than making them more selfless? Why does ego depletion make people more impulsive, rather than making them more cautious? All of these questions fall under the umbrella of the covariance question.

A couple hypothetical scenarios show that the covariance question is dissociable from the depletion question. First, imagine that the ego depletion effect only occurred for a single task: say, the Stroop Task. The finding would be simply that subjects who perform the Stroop Task are subsequently impaired at further trials of the Stroop Task, but equally good at all other tasks. Here, there would still be an interesting depletion question: why does doing the Stroop Task temporarily impair subjects' performance on the Stroop Task? But there would be no interesting covariance question: it is no mystery why ability on the Stroop Task covaries with ability on the Stroop Task. For the converse dissociation, imagine that instead of ego depletion, we had found an ego *augmentation* effect: that exerting self-control improved performance on subsequent self-control tasks. Clearly there is no depletion question to be had here, but rather an augmentation question, which would require a different kind of answer. If the same set of tasks were involved in ego augmentation as we have found to be involved in ego depletion, however, we would have the very same covariance question: why does performance on each of these tasks covary with performance on all of the others?

We are offering an answer to the covariance question. The best explanation for why the various abilities affected by ego depletion stand or fall together is, we propose, that they all depend upon the operation of the self-control system. To fully defend this claim, we would need to provide a theory of the causal-functional role of the self-control system, which showed how each of the tasks that is affected by ego depletion requires the self-control system, while each of the tasks that is unaffected by ego depletion does not depend upon this system. This task lies beyond the scope of this paper, though one of us (BD) hopes to undertake it in future work. Strictly speaking, our argument here defends an answer to only part of the covariance question: why does ability to act on the basis of long-term goals covary with ability to act on the basis of other-regarding goals? We have argued that the best answer to this question is that both of these abilities depend upon a system that serves the function of overriding an agent's incentive salience desires to direct action on the basis of her cognitive desires. Whether this system is also employed in the other tasks affected by ego depletion is, as far as we have argued, an open question – though we are inclined to think that it is.

Our answer to the covariance question is consistent with any of the going answers to the depletion question. Clearly, it is consistent with the resource theory: on this view, all of the tasks affected by ego depletion depend upon the operation of the self-control system, which in turn depends upon a limited resource that is depleted by its operation. It is also compatible with the anti-resource theories. These theories explain depletion by appeal to a decrease in motivation *to exert self-control.* This raises the question: what is it to "exert self-control"? The most natural answer seems to be that to exert self-control is *to utilize one's self-control system.* On the resulting anti-resource picture, depletion effects are explained by a decrease in subjects' motivation to employ their system of self-control. This picture is consistent with our view as well.

So, our view is neutral on the debate between resource and anti-resource theorists about the mechanisms of ego depletion. Our argument for the existence of the self-control system does not rely on any premise that is at issue in this controversy. So, the fact that there is controversy about the depletion question cannot provide grounds for doubting the soundness of our argument.

We have argued that intentional action is the product of a competition between two different sorts of desires that is mediated by the self-control system. This thesis holds for both addicted and non-addicted agents. Both addicts and others have incentive salience desires, as we have already argued. These desires motivate *automatically*: as soon as an incentive salience desire is triggered, it drives an agent's attention and behavior in pursuit of the desired object without conscious effort (even in spite of it). In addition, both addicts and others have cognitive desires: desires that are based in and responsive to the agent's reflective judgments about what is good. In contrast with incentive salience desires, cognitive desires may include concerns for the long-term consequences of one's actions, and the welfare of others as well as oneself. For better or worse, cognitive desires do *not* motivate behavior automatically. To guide her behavior on the basis of her cognitive desires, an agent must exert self-control. On the basis of data showing that some agents have a specific deficit in their ability to act on the basis of cognitive desires, we have argued that there is a system, the self-control system, dedicated to this task.

The self-control system serves primarily as the cognitive desires' advocate within the brain. Since cognitive desires do not motivate automatically, it is up to the self-control system to make sure they are represented in the agent's behavior. Whether an agent acts in accordance with her cognitive desires, in the face of a temptation to do otherwise, is not merely a matter of the strength of her cognitive desires, but rather a matter of her ability to exert self-control on their behalf. In other words, whether an agent's cognitive desires triumph over her incentive salience desires depends on whether the self-control system manages to override the automatic influence of the incentive salience system. We will thus more often speak of the competition between *the self-control system* and the incentive salience system than of the competition between *the cognitive desires* and the incentive salience desires. But these are just two different ways of describing the same thing.

One might be tempted to explain addiction as the result of an impairment of the self-control system, but we think this idea is a non-starter. If addicts had an impaired self-control system, we would expect them to show behavioral impairments across the board: they would not only have trouble controlling their addictive desires, but would be self-regarding and focused on the short-term across all other domains as well. But this is clearly not the case: addiction does not lead to the domain-general deficits characteristic of vmPFC lesion patients and ego depleted subjects. Unlike vmPFC lesion patients, addicts do not act like sociopaths; unlike ego depleted subjects, addicts do not seem to be impaired in *all* tasks that require self-control, such as attention regulation or analytic thought. Moreover, given the right incentives addicts do succeed in controlling even their addictive desires.[19]

Instead, we propose that the primary difference between addicted and non-addicted agents lies in the very strong incentive salience desires possessed by the former. Whether caused by artificial stimulation of the dopamine system (as in the case of cocaine or amphetamines) or by the system working in the way in which it has evolved (as in the case of sucrose) the incentive salience desires involved in addiction are likely to be stronger than any of the incentive salience desires experienced by non-addicted agents. Thus it is a far greater challenge for addicts to override their incentive salience desires, due to the abnormal motivational force of their addictive desire. Though this self-control challenge is far more difficult for addicts than it is for others, the *structure* of the challenge is the same for both, as we will now try to show.

THREE STAGES OF SELF-CONTROL

We have claimed that intentional action results from the competitive interaction amongst desires mediated by the self-control system. This is to see self-control as in the business of regulating which of the subject's desires gets to determine their behavior. But how does this work? Does self-control regulate which intentions the agent forms on the basis of their desires, or does it rather regulate whether they stick to their intentions? And might not it instead regulate which desires the agent has in the first place, or which judgments they form? We need to get clearer on what it is that self-control is controlling (or failing to control).

The philosophical literature on addiction presents several different, seemingly incompatible, answers to the question of where self-control breaks down in the case of addiction. Watson (50) and Levy (7, 51, 52) have both argued that addictive desires bias addicts' *evaluative judgments* themselves, skewing deliberation so that they come to see taking the drug as the most attractive option. "One who is defeated by appetite is more like a collaborationist than an unsuccessful freedom fighter," Watson declares colorfully [Ref. (50), p. 7]; and reiterates later: "We are not so much overpowered by brute force as seduced" (p. 10). Levy has developed this idea into a detailed account of addictive (and non-addictive) temptation, which he summarizes as follows:

> In response to temptation the subjects spontaneously generate or retrieve from memory arguments in favor of weak-willed action. Since they lack the cognitive resources to reject these arguments, they experience judgment shift. They come to judge that the benefits of succumbing to temptation are higher than they previously had thought, or the costs of giving in are lower, or both, and they act accordingly [Ref. (51), p. 101].

On this account, self-control works to control one's *judgments* in the face of the biasing influence of temptation.

In contrast, R. Jay Wallace argues that addictive desires make it difficult to *motivate* oneself to act on one's evaluative judgments once they have been formed. He emphasizes this in the passage we quoted earlier: "Even if one succeeds, in the face of such a desire, in reasoning correctly to the conclusion that it should not be acted on, its continued presence and urgency will make it comparatively difficult to choose to comply with the deliberated verdict one has arrived at" [Ref. (18), p. 648]. On this account, self-control works to turn one's judgments into a commitment to action: in other words, to form an *intention* to act.

Finally, Timothy Schroeder and Nomy Arpaly emphasize the power of *habits* in producing addictive behavior, observing that these automatic behavioral dispositions may place addicts who are trying to get sober in tempting situations, situations that tend to undercut their intentions:

> The abstinent addict will do things without thinking about them at the time, only to find a difficult situation arising. "Why did I agree to go to that party where everyone will be using?" "Why did I turn down this street that leads me close to the dealers, and not down the next street?" "Why did I end up calling my old drug buddy when I was bored?" Questions like these are often answered by an addict's unconscious behavioral tendencies [Ref. (53), p. 228].

[19] See Holton and Berridge (9) for discussion of this.

On this account, self-control works even after one has formed an intention, to *implement* that intention in the face of the obstacles posed by one's bad habits.[20]

Though each of these philosophers puts their favored locus of self-control conflict at center stage, we think there is no genuine disagreement between their claims. Instead, we favor a pluralist view: there are several distinct loci of self-control conflict. This view is advocated by Amelie Rorty in her classic article "Where Does the Akratic Break Take Place?" (54). Rorty begins by identifying several "stages on thought's way to action," and observes that "these distinctions allow us to locate the junctures where psychological akrasia can occur, in ways that explain the occurrence of behavioral akrasia" (334). These "junctures" at which self-control failure can occur are also the places where self-control might be improved: "the place where the akratic break takes place also locates the place where the self-reforming akrates can best intervene to remedy his condition" (334).

In this section, we follow Rorty's strategy: first, distinguishing different stages by which thought leads to action; second, showing how self-control conflict arises at each of these stages; and third, showing how intervention at each of these stages can help an agent win the struggle to govern her own behavior.

We propose that there are at least three distinct stages by which thought leads to action, which we will call the *deliberative* stage, the *volitional* stage, and the *implemental* stage:

(1) In the deliberative stage, the agent forms a *judgment* as to what action is best. This is the locus of self-control conflict Watson and Levy identified: the deliberative challenge of coming to a clear-eyed evaluative judgment in spite of the biasing influence of incentive salience craving.

(2) In the volitional stage, the agent chooses an *intention* to pursue. This is the locus of self-control conflict Wallace identified: the volitional challenge of willing yourself to pursue the end you have already judged to be best.

(3) In the implemental stage, the agent selects *actions* that implement her chosen intention. This is the locus of self-control conflict Schroeder and Arpaly identified: since habits are brute, unmotivated behavioral dispositions, they can cause goal-discrepant behaviors even when one is fully committed to a goal pursuit. So, it is during the implemental stage that one must grapple with and overcome one's habits.[21, 22]

We now proceed to discuss these stages in detail, with the aim of showing how self-control at each stage works similarly in addicted and non-addicted agents alike. For each stage we then briefly outline the ways in which self-control might be improved, again for both addicts and non-addicts alike.

DELIBERATIVE STAGE

Locus of deliberative self-control conflict: attention

As we have said (see The Existence of Self-Control), a central function of the self-control system is to control behavior on the basis of an agent's all-things-considered judgments of the values of potential actions and their outcomes. But in order to do this, an agent must first form the evaluative judgments on the basis of which she aims to control her behavior. This involves creating mental simulations of various potential actions and their consequences, and then comparing them against one another on the basis of relevant evaluative criteria. This task of practical deliberation requires the agent to keep several different detailed simulations of actions in working memory simultaneously, attend to the evaluatively relevant features of each, and then compare them against one another. Since the capacity of working memory is limited, an agent will only be able to focus on a subset of the potentially relevant features of her different options. Thus what judgment she ultimately forms will depend to a large extent on what evaluatively relevant considerations capture her attention.

Consider, for instance, an alcoholic deliberating about whether to have another drink at a business dinner with a client. What choice she judges best will depend on what features of her options she attends to while deliberating. If she focuses exclusively on the features she finds attractive about the drink – the refreshing, pine-tree taste of a gin and tonic, the loose euphoria of inebriation – she will judge that having another drink is the thing to do. However, if she attends to the longer-term consequences of having another drink – the resulting drunkenness rendering her unable to comport herself appropriately in front of her client, her potentially losing business as a result, and the negative consequences of this

[20]Henden (149) argues that compulsive actions (which he takes addictive actions to be) are caused by habits: "an action is compulsive, not because it is caused by an irresistible desire, but because it is part of a habit the compulsive person would find extremely difficult to discontinue even if she made a sincere effort to do so" (363). He would thus seem to be another advocate of the view that the locus of self-control conflict lies in the regulation of habits. However, Henden uses "habit" in a much wider sense than we do: he defines "habits" as "behavior patterns regularly performed in characteristic circumstances" (371). In contrast, we are using "habit" to refer to a particular psychological state, distinct from desires, goals, or intentions, that involves a strong and rigid association between a contextual cue and a behavior that causes the behavior to be automatically triggered by the cue (see Implemental stage for more detail). Thus "habits" in Henden's sense may or may not be caused by "habits" in our sense. In fact, a closer reading of Henden reveals that the "habits" he takes to underlie addiction are caused, not by the rigid stimulus-response associations we are calling "habits," but rather by incentive salience desires, which Henden calls "inclinations." Thus we do not take Henden to advocate the view that the locus of self-control is the regulation of habits, in the sense we are using the term. Thanks to Hanna Pickard for drawing our attention to this connection with Henden's work.

[21]The stages we propose are inspired by Peter Gollwitzer's highly influential *Rubicon model of action phases* (150). Though our division of stages does not correspond exactly with Gollwitzer's, we doubt this reveals a substantive disagreement, but rather reflects a difference in focus. Along similar lines, our stages are not the same as Rorty's proposed stages, but we think this is only because Rorty makes more fine-grained distinctions between stages than we do. Though we have limited ourselves to only those distinctions between stages for which we have empirical evidence, we are open to the possibility that there may be more useful distinctions between stages than we have made here.

[22]It is important to note that these stages are *goal-relative*: an agent might be in one stage relative to one goal while in a different stage relative to another. For example, an agent may have decided to take a trip to New York; having formed this intention, she is now in the implemental stage of this goal pursuit. However, in the process of implementing her intention, she will need to deliberate about further matters: should she take the train or a plane? Thus she might be in the deliberative stage regarding the question of *how to get to* New York even while she is in the implemental stage regarding her intention to *go* to New York. So the question to ask is not: what stage of self-control is this agent in *full stop*; but rather: what stage of self-control is this agent in *for this particular goal pursuit*?

for her professional reputation and career – she will likely judge that she ought to order a soda water instead. The judgment she makes about what is best to do will depend upon how she directs her attention during the process of deliberation.

The self-control and incentive salience systems will pull an agent's attention in different directions as she deliberates. An active incentive salience desire pulls an agent's attention to the attractive features of its object, thereby biasing the agent's deliberation in its favor. Only by exerting self-control can an agent attend to the reasons not to act in accordance with her incentive salience desires – i.e., the long-term consequences of her actions for things she reflectively values. It is thus over the control of attention that the deliberative stage of the competition between self-control and incentive salience is waged.

Role of the incentive salience and self-control systems in deliberation

If we are correct that the self-control system is the system that is impaired by ego depletion, then we can infer its functions from the capacities that are impaired in ego depleted subjects. It is thus instructive that ego depleted subjects show impairments in both analytic thought (31, 55, 56) and selective attention (29, 31, 40). Since practical deliberation requires both selective attention and analytic thought, we should expect ego depleted subjects to be impaired in this capacity as well. This means that the self-control system not only serves the function of controlling behavior on the basis of evaluative judgments already made, but is also deployed in the formation of evaluative judgments themselves.

However, the self-control system does not have complete sovereignty over attention. An active incentive salience desire exerts powerful influence over attention, drawing it toward the desired object and its most attractive features. This involuntary attentional pull has a significant biasing effect on practical deliberation. By automatically directing an agent's attention to the most attractive features of the desired object, an incentive salience desire can lead an agent to form evaluative judgments that give disproportionate weight to these features. This can lead agents subject to incentive salience cravings to form evaluative judgments that treat the desired object as much more valuable than they would judge it to be in the absence of craving.

This biasing effect has been demonstrated in empirical studies on both addicts and non-addicts alike. The most vivid display of this effect in non-addicts comes from a study in which the experimenters asked male subjects to answer survey questions while looking at pornography and masturbating (57). The sexually aroused subjects, when compared with non-aroused controls, reported being significantly more willing to engage in sexual behaviors they considered deviant (e.g., bisexual group sex) and to act immorally in order to have sex (e.g., slipping a woman a drug to get her to have sex). The influence of these subjects' active sexual desire went beyond their overt behavior, biasing even their *judgments* about what it would be pleasurable or morally acceptable to do. Less dramatically, some studies have shown that occurrent cravings for food make people overestimate how much they will enjoy foods in the future [(58); see also (59)]. Hence why it is dangerous to go grocery shopping while hungry.

Addictive desires have the same kind of biasing influence on evaluative judgment as sexual desire and hunger, as demonstrated by Badger et al. (60). Badger et al. studied a set of heroin addicts undertaking rehabilitation treatment who were receiving daily a heroin substitute medication Buprenorphine (BUP) to alleviate withdrawal symptoms. The experimental task asked these subjects to choose between receiving different amounts of money and receiving an extra dose of BUP, to be administered five days later.[23] The crucial manipulation was that one group of subjects was asked to make this choice while in a current state of craving, before they had received that day's dose of BUP, while a second group of subjects was asked to make the same choices while satiated, immediately after receiving their dose of BUP. The satiated subjects placed a substantially lower dollar value on the extra dose of BUP ($35) than the craving subjects, who valued the extra dose almost twice as much ($60). Notice that the difference in value here is for a dose to be received 5 days later – so subjects had no reason to think their current state of craving would have any influence on their enjoyment of the extra dose. And yet the currently craving addicts still judged receiving an extra dose 5 days later to be a more valuable outcome than the satiated addicts did. This seems best explained by the attention-biasing effect of active incentive salience desires: by drawing the craving subjects' attention to the attractive features of the extra BUP, their desire led them to judge it more valuable than they would have in the absence of craving.

How to improve deliberative self-control: mindfulness meditation

So, active incentive salience desires bias attention in both addicts and non-addicts, leading agents to disproportionately value the object of their current craving in their deliberative judgments about what is best. But agents can overcome this bias by exerting self-control, directing their own attention rather than letting it be guided by their current desire. This account yields a testable prediction: deliberative self-control can be aided by improving agents' selective attention. In other words, the better an agent's capacity to control her attention, the better she will be able to overcome the biasing influence of incentive salience-based temptation.

This prediction is confirmed by research on *mindfulness meditation*. Mindfulness is a traditional meditative practice that involves actively focusing one's attention on some aspect of one's present experience for an extended period of time. (Paradigmatically, one focuses on the experience of breathing.) Among the many psychological benefits of training in mindfulness meditation is an improvement in selective attention: both brief and long-term mindfulness training improve subjects' ability to selectively control their attention, as measured by many classic tests of attention regulation (61–63). If our picture of deliberative self-control is correct, then these improvements in selective attention should help subjects to better resist incentive salience desires. And this is exactly what the data shows.

This prediction has been robustly confirmed in studies of addicts [for a review, see Ref. (64)]. Randomized and controlled

[23] Subjects who chose the extra dose would receive two doses of BUP rather than one on the appointed day. This was a significant incentive: "Although a single dose of BUP is sufficient to eliminate addicts' acute cravings, a double dose produces a longer, more satisfying high" [(60), p. 869].

studies testing a mindfulness training intervention for addiction have shown that mindfulness training leads to a significant reduction in use of the addictive substance and a significantly lower chance of relapse, both when compared to a no-treatment baseline (65, 66) and when compared to conventional addiction treatments (67–69). One study found that smokers high on dispositional mindfulness measures are less likely to relapse after quitting than smokers lower in dispositional mindfulness (70). Finally, at least two studies have found that addicts who undergo mindfulness training not only use the addictive substance less, but also experience less intense *cravings* for the substance (68, 71).

Mindfulness-based interventions help non-addicts to overcome incentive salience temptations as well. In particular, several studies have shown mindfulness training to help obese or overweight subjects to achieve their weight-loss goals [(72–74); see also (75, 76)]. In a recent review, O'Reilly et al. (77) found that 18 out of 21 reviewed studies of mindfulness-based interventions for obesity-related behaviors reported significant decreases in the targeted behaviors.

One study directly supports our hypothesis that the mechanism behind these successful interventions is an improvement in deliberative self-control (78). This study investigated the temporal discounting of food rewards in obese and healthy-weight individuals by offering them a choice between a large, delayed food reward and a small, immediate food reward. In an initial test, obese subjects showed a much steeper discounting curve than controls – that is, they were willing to give up a larger delayed reward for a smaller immediate reward. This is what we would expect, given that the obese subjects are experiencing a stronger incentive salience craving for food, which draws their attention disproportionately to the attractive features of the immediate reward. After the initial test, some of the obese subjects undertook a 50-min training session in mindful eating, while others just watched an educational video on nutrition. These subjects then completed the temporal discounting test again. Obese subjects who underwent mindfulness training subsequently showed a significantly less steep discounting curve than they had in the initial test: they were more willing than before to give up a smaller immediate reward for the sake of a larger delayed reward. (Subjects who watched the educational video showed no such improvement.) What this suggests is that the brief mindfulness training session helped the obese subjects to overcome the biasing effect of their food cravings and form more normal judgments about the relative values of immediate and delayed rewards. In other words, mindfulness training improved these subjects' deliberative self-control.

We submit that our model of deliberative self-control provides the best explanation for the above results. An important first step in overcoming an active incentive salience desire is to form a clear-eyed evaluative judgment that indulging one's craving will lead to worse consequences than refraining from doing so. An active incentive salience desire automatically biases one's attention to the positive features of the object desired, leading agents to overestimate the value of satisfying their current desire. Mindfulness meditation training makes agents more skilled at self-controlled attention regulation, and thereby improves their ability to resist the biasing effect of active incentive salience desires on evaluative judgment. It is thus by improving agents' capacities for deliberative self-control that mindfulness meditation helps addicts and non-addicts alike resist the influence of their incentive salience desires.

VOLITIONAL STAGE

Locus of volitional self-control conflict: goals

The second stage of self-control is the volitional stage: after one judges what is best (deliberative stage), one must choose a goal to pursue (volitional stage) before one begins implementing that goal pursuit in one's behavior (implemental stage). In other words, between judgment (deliberative) and action (implemental) lies *choice* (volitional), and to exert volitional self-control is to exert self-control in choosing a course of action. This was the self-control task identified by Wallace, of "choos[ing] to comply with the deliberated verdict one has arrived at" (648).

Some readers may be skeptical that the act of making a choice is really distinct from the act of forming an evaluative judgment. Our first response would be to note that the possibility of *akrasia*, choosing against one's own best judgment, seems to require such a distinction. But, of course, people who are skeptical about the judgment/choice distinction will be skeptical about the existence of *akrasia* as well, and so this line of argument will seem to be begging the question.[24]

However, we think there is empirical evidence demonstrating that making a choice is psychologically distinct from forming an evaluative judgment. A study by Vohs et al. [(30), Study 6] shows that choosing to act on one's evaluative judgments (volition) requires more self-control than merely forming evaluative judgments (deliberation). In this study, all subjects were presented with a webpage that gave various options for customizing a desktop computer for purchase. Some subjects were asked to choose between the customizations (the choice condition), while others were asked to consider the customization options and "form an opinion of the information, thinking about what [they] would prefer" (892), but importantly, were *not* asked to implement their judgments by selecting their preferred options on the website (the deliberation condition).

The dependent measure of this study was subjects' subsequent persistence on an impossible anagram task, a task that has been shown to measure self-control capacity (28). What Vohs et al. found was that subjects in the choice condition, who had made a series of active choices, persisted significantly less on this task than subjects in the deliberation condition. This shows that the act of *choosing* involves an exertion of self-control that goes beyond the self-control required to form an evaluative judgment. These results not only dissociate choice from evaluative judgment, but also show that choice involves the exertion of self-control. In other words, this study establishes the existence of volitional self-control as a psychological task that is distinct from deliberation to a judgment.

So let us take as given the existence of volitional self-control and now ask what it involves. What is the psychological process involved in making a choice, and why might it require self-control?

---

[24]It might also be the case that evaluative judgments are formed *subsequently* to the intentions: in the light of what an agent has decided to do, cognitive dissonance motivations might lead her to form judgments that present those decisions in a good light. But we still contend that intentions and judgments have genuine independent existence [see Ref. (6), pp. 1–19].

We suggest that the exercise of choice involves the selection and activation of a kind of motivational mental state that psychologists call a "goal." A *goal*, in the technical sense used by psychologists, is a mental representation of a desired end that directs behavior in pursuit of that end.[25] We take it that such states often constitute *intentions*, as philosophers understand this term. The large research literature on goals, which we do not have the space to review here, has shown them to be a robust psychological natural kind with a distinctive suite of cognitive and behavioral signatures [for a review, see Ref. (79)]. Active goals direct attention, cognition, and behavior in a flexible and instrumentally rational way in order to bring about the end state that they represent. One primary way for a goal to be activated is simply for subjects to form a conscious, deliberate intention to pursue a certain end. We thus submit that volitional choice is best understood as the self-controlled act of activating a goal with a certain end.

Role of the incentive salience and self-control systems in volition

We have already seen how self-control plays a role in volition: Vohs et al.'s subjects had to exert self-control to go beyond forming a judgment and activate a goal to act in accordance with that judgment. Crucially for our purposes, however, self-controlled choice is not the *only* route by which goals can be activated. Goals are also activated automatically by incentive salience desires, as we shall now explain.

A series of experiments by Henk Aarts and Rudd Custers have demonstrated that a goal to pursue a certain end state can be non-consciously activated by subliminally associating positive affect with that end state (80–85). Aarts and Custers first demonstrated that subliminally associating positive affect with a goal caused subjects to report greater *wanting* to pursue the goal [(80), Study 1], and then showed in subsequent studies (cited above) that this greater wanting leads subjects to behave in the ways characteristic of goal activation. These results seem best explained by appeal to incentive salience desires. We have already seen (see Desire) that incentive salience desires are proportional in strength to the previous association of the desired object with reward, and are automatically activated by encounters with desire-associated stimuli. Thus we should expect that Aarts and Custers' intervention to associate positive affect with an end state would activate an incentive salience desire to attain that end state. And as we would predict, this association leads subjects to *want* to attain the goal. This gives us good reason to think that Aarts and Custers have activated goals in their subjects *by means of* creating and triggering incentive salience desires. Thus their findings strongly indicate that an active incentive salience desire for an object automatically and non-consciously activates a *goal* to attain that object, which then directs behavior in pursuit of its attainment.

On reflection, this is exactly what we should expect. The incentive salience cravings that addicts feel for heroin or non-addicts feel for sugar or sex do not merely influence behavior by biasing deliberative judgment. These desires seem to have *direct* motivational power, *pushing* the addict to shoot up or the non-addict to bite into the cake before either has a chance to even consider whether this is a good idea. Incentive salience desires seem to directly guide behavior in the absence of counteractive self-control, and now we can see why: cravings activate *goals*, which automatically guide action toward the attainment of the thing that is craved.

Thus, the challenge of volitional self-control in the face of an active incentive salience desire is to resist the automatic activation of the goal to attain the desired object, and instead activate an alternative goal that accords with one's deliberative judgments about what is best. Only one goal can guide behavior at a time; in fact, a dominant goal actively *suppresses* the accessibility of the most attractive alternative goals (86).[26] Thus the self-control system and the incentive salience system can be seen as competing in a "horse race" of goal activation, where the winning system is the one whose favored goal is made most active and thereby comes to dominate downstream behavior. The stronger the incentive salience desire, the more activation it will give to its favored goal, and thus the greater exertion of self-control will be required to activate an alternative goal enough to override it. This is why restraining yourself from acting on an addictive desire is far more difficult than restraining yourself from eating a chocolate cake.

How to improve volitional self-control: mental contrasting

If volitional self-control is a matter of giving sufficient activation to one's deliberatively chosen goal, then we should expect that any procedure that leads to greater activation of a consciously chosen goal will help agents to overcome temptation by incentive salience desires. The "mental contrasting" procedure, created and researched by Gabriele Oettingen, is an intervention of this kind. In this procedure, subjects who wish to attain a goal are asked to undertake two imaginative steps: first, imagine a "positive fantasy" of the goal's being attained, and all the beneficial consequences that would follow goal attainment; second, *mentally contrast* this positive fantasy with the "negative reality" of one's present distance from achieving the goal and the obstacles lying in the way of goal attainment. Several studies have shown that this mental contrasting procedure powerfully increases subjects' motivation to attain the goal, causing them to expend much more effort in pursuit of the goal (87–91). What explains this effect?

We offer the following explanation. Goal pursuit research has independently shown that the activation level of a goal

[25] We are thus using the term "goal" to refer not to the state of affairs one is pursuing (as "goal" does when used colloquially, e.g. "my goal is to lose 5 pounds"), but rather to the mental state that guides one's behavior towards bringing about that state of affairs.

[26] This claim might seem counterintuitive, if we think of goals on the model of desires. If I want to go to the opera *and* want to go to the movies, but only get to pick one, I will still desire the other: at the movies, I'll worry about what I'm missing at the opera, or vice versa. But goals are *not* like desires; they are like *intentions*. And though it is common to have conflicting desires, it is difficult to maintain conflicting intentions. Though it is possible for agents to have incompatible intentions, there is pressure, both rational and psychological, to maintain consistency among one's intentions. (Compare belief: though it is possible to have inconsistent beliefs, there is pressure, both rational and psychological, to resolve any such inconsistencies once they come to light). When I form the intention to go to the opera, my attention and behavior are directed to the pursuit of *that* end, and thereby away from the end of going to the movies. I look up the time of the opera, buy tickets, and get directions to the opera house; I *don't* look up the movie times, buy movie tickets, and get directions to the movie theatre. This tendency for goals to narrow an agent's focus, excluding incompatible courses of action, is what we have in mind when we say that "only one goal can guide behavior at a time." Thanks to Hanna Pickard for raising this concern.

is automatically modulated based on three major factors: (a) *value*, the perceived value of achieving the goal (82, 92–94); (b) *expectancy*, the perceived probability of attaining the goal (93); and (c) *discrepancy*, the perceived effort required to attain the goal (95–97). Goal activation is strongest when expectancy, value, and discrepancy are all high.

We propose that the mental contrasting procedure activates goals by means of boosting value and discrepancy: the "positive fantasy" increases the perceived value of attaining the goal, while the "negative reality" increases the perceived effort required to attain the goal. In line with this explanation is the finding that subjects who only complete the "positive fantasy" component of the procedure become *less* motivated to attain the goal (98). Though this might seem initially surprising, it is easily explained by noting that the positive fantasy on its own will sharply *decrease* the discrepancy attributed to the goal, as subjects imagine the goal to already be completed; it is this decrease in discrepancy that demotivates these subjects.[27] This is why the "negative reality" contrast, which counteracts the adverse effects of the "positive fantasy" component on discrepancy while maintaining its positive effects on value, is necessary for the mental contrasting procedure to work.

Thus the mental contrasting procedure is well-designed to increase the activation of a consciously chosen goal. So, given our characterization of volitional self-control, we should expect the mental contrasting procedure to help agents overcome temptation by incentive salience desires. And this is what we find. Oettingen et al. (89) found that the mental contrasting intervention caused smokers who wanted to quit to take more immediate action toward quitting than subjects who underwent a control intervention. And for non-addicted subjects, Johannessen et al. (99) found that dieters who performed the mental contrasting procedure were significantly more successful than control subjects at reducing their caloric intake over a 2-week period.

We have portrayed volitional self-control as involving a competition between the self-control and incentive salience systems over the activation of goals. We take this picture to be nicely confirmed by the fact that the mental contrasting procedure, which increases the activation of deliberatively chosen goals, helps agents to overcome temptation by both addictive and non-addictive incentive salience desires. Mental contrasting helps agents succeed in *motivating* themselves to act in accordance with their deliberative judgment – which, as we have seen, is not a trivial task.

IMPLEMENTAL STAGE

Locus of implemental self-control conflict: habits

As we have said, a goal, once activated, will automatically guide behavior toward its own fulfillment. Thus, one might think that choosing the right goal in the face of temptation is sufficient for controlling one's behavior. However, goal implementation – the process of executing one's chosen goal pursuit in action – itself poses non-trivial self-control challenges.

This is because goals are not the only mental states that directly influence behavior. There are also *habits*, which Neal et al. (100) define as "response dispositions that are activated automatically by the context cues that co-occurred with responses during past performance" (198). In other words, habits are associations between contexts and behaviors that lead agents to produce a certain behavior when they encounter a certain contextual cue.

For our purposes, it is important to distinguish habits both from goals and from incentive salience desires. The distinction between habits and goals is essential to understanding the difference between the volitional and implemental stages of self-control. And as we emphasized earlier (see Desire), the habits that are produced by addiction are an importantly different phenomenon from the incentive salience desires that produce addiction. Habits and incentive salience desires may each exert their influence in the absence of the other, though they often go hand in hand.

The primary feature that distinguishes habits from goals is their *motivation-independence*. As habits are associative states that produce a behavior directly when a certain context is encountered, they do not depend for their influence on any motivation to engage in the relevant behavior. This is in contrast with goals, which are almost always activated by and dependent upon a desire to achieve some end.[28] When one ceases to desire the end of a certain goal pursuit, the goal itself is deactivated (101); in contrast, when one ceases to desire the end that is served by a certain habit, the habit remains (102). One might, for instance, habitually make a turn that follows the well-worn driving route to one's workplace, when in fact one does not want to go there at all, but rather is going to a restaurant that is actually in the opposite direction. However, one will never set out to pursue the goal of going to one's workplace when in fact one has no desire whatsoever to do so.

The primary feature that distinguishes habits from incentive salience desires is their *motivational neutrality*. In addition to exerting their influence independently from (and even contrary to) one's prior motives, habits also do not *produce* any desire to perform the habitual behavior. In other words, one does not *crave* acting out one's habits. Schroeder and Arpaly (53) make this point well:

> When one does not do something one wanted to do, there is often a little disappointment or regret. But when one does not make a habitual left turn, there is no disappointment or regret that coincides with not acting out of habit ... [one] neither longingly thinks of making the left turn when at other intersections, nor is behaviorally disposed to get into a position to make the left turn. The habit only has influence upon behavior (231).

This apt observation about the different phenomenologies of habit and desire is confirmed by empirical research. As we have already mentioned (see Desire), simply learning to notice a habitual behavior seems to be sufficient for ceasing it, implying that once the subject becomes aware of the habitual behavior, it takes little additional self-control to override it (15, 16). Contrast this with incentive salience desires, which are still quite difficult to override even when one is reflectively aware of them.

---

[27] In fact, the act of imagining goal completion has been shown in one study to lead to "goal turnoff," the suppression of goal accessibility that usually occurs after the goal has *actually* been completed (151).

[28] A possible exception to this claim is the case of unconscious goal priming by exposure to words semantically associated with a goal (104).

A third feature of habits distinguishes them from both goals and incentive salience desires: their *behavioral inflexibility*. Neal and Wood (103) observe that "people rarely substitute habitual behaviors (e.g., a habit of daily jogging) for alternative behaviors that meet the same ostensible goal (e.g., switching from jogging to cycling)" [Ref. (103), p. 449]. We think this observation reflects an important fact about the structure of habits: they are associations of contexts with *a particular behavior*, not with an end that can be brought about by many different behaviors. Habits rigidly produce a certain behavior, never switching to producing a different behavior that better facilitates some goal. This is illustrated by a study on habitual popcorn eating in the cinema, in which subjects ceased to habitually eat popcorn if they were forced to do so with their non-dominant hand (102). This result shows that these subjects' habit was not really *to eat popcorn*, but rather *to scoop popcorn into their mouths using their dominant hand*. When this behavior was no longer possible, the habit did not cause the subjects to engage in the alternative behavior of eating with their non-dominant hands – because *that* is not the particular behavior they associate with the context of the cinema. In contrast, both goals and incentive salience desires are very flexible in the behaviors they produce, dynamically switching between behavioral routines when doing so is adaptive for achieving their end (104, 105).

In summary, habits are best understood as a brute, direct association between a specific context and a rigid behavior, which produces behavior in a way that is unmediated by desire. This distinguishes habits from both goals and incentive salience desires, allowing us to see the task of controlling one's habits as distinct from the task of controlling one's goals. As it arises in the implementation of one's goals, we will call this task the *implemental stage* of self-control.

Role of the incentive salience and self-control systems in creating habits

As Aristotle observed [Ref. (106), *Nicomachean Ethics* 1103a–b] and contemporary research has confirmed (107), habits are created by repetition. More precisely, a habit to perform a certain behavior in a certain context is created by an agent's performing that particular behavior in that particular context many times before. This repetition ingrains the automatic association between context and behavior that constitutes the habit.

Both the incentive salience and self-control systems can create and sustain habits by this simple method. If an incentive salience desire is served by regularly performing the same behavior in the same context (say, ordering your usual beer at your favorite bar, or reaching for the ice cream in your freezer upon arriving at home), then by repeatedly acting on that incentive salience desire, one may create a habit that serves the desire. Insofar as one disapproves of the incentive salience desire, these may be called "bad habits." Addicts, who usually spend a good while acting on their addictive desire before seeking help, will thereby acquire many habits that facilitate their addictive behavior. These "bad habits" will remain even when the addict has overcome her desire for the addictive substance, and may make it more difficult for the addict to remain in control, as Schroeder and Arpaly point out [Ref. (53), p. 228].

On the other hand, one may also inculcate "good habits" by repeatedly performing a behavior in a context that facilitates one of the cognitive desires or values on the basis of which one exerts self-control. For instance, one might create a habit of walking to the gym immediately after leaving work by simply exerting the self-control required to do so deliberately every day, until it becomes automatic and effortless. Many other examples of the self-controlled creation of habits come from athletics, music, and other skilled behaviors, where one exerts a great deal of self-control to repeat a certain behavior in a precise way during practice (whether a scale on the violin or a free-throw in basketball) and then, as one becomes skilled, is able to do the same behavior automatically and habitually. This self-controlled formation of "good habits" works just the same way as the formation of "bad habits" by the incentive salience system: produce the same behavior in the same context over and over again, and *voila!* – a habit is born.

How to improve implemental self-control: implementation intentions

Implemental self-control becomes a challenge when one has a *good goal* that may be thwarted by a *bad habit*. In other words, even once you have succeeded at *volitional* self-control, activating a goal that accords with your cognitive desires, your pursuit of this goal may be hampered by habits that lead to goal-discrepant behaviors. This problem will be especially dire if, as in the case of addicts, one's goal is to change one's behavior from a longstanding pattern produced by the pursuit of a powerful incentive salience desire. As Schroeder and Arpaly observe, bad habits may tip the balance in the addict's self-control conflict, as when an addict finds herself habitually putting herself in situations that make drugs available or tempting.

One strategy for implemental self-control is simply to directly override the habit once it has been triggered. Though this works, it is difficult, causing ego depletion in ordinary subjects (28, 32). Overriding a habit is difficult not necessarily because it is difficult to overcome a habit once it has been detected, but because it requires a great deal of attention regulation to constantly monitor for the cues that trigger the habitual behavior. Given the limitations of our resources for self-controlled attention, this strategy for overcoming bad habits is itself quite limited.

An implemental self-control strategy that may escape these limits is suggested by research on *implementation intentions*, a technique created and investigated by Peter Gollwitzer. Implementation intentions are plans of the form "*if* I encounter X cue, *then* I will perform Y response!" Subjects who form implementation intentions to aid them in a goal pursuit have been shown in a large number of studies to pursue their goals much more effectively than subjects who simply form goal intentions (of the simpler form "I will do X!"). A meta-analysis of 94 studies involving over 8,000 participants found that the improvement of goal pursuit by implementation intentions over mere goal intentions is highly statistically significant, and medium-to-large in effect size [Cohen's $d = 0.65$; (108)].

The helpful effects of implementation intentions seem to be largely due to the automatic association such intentions create between the "if" cue and the "then" response. Subjects who form implementation intentions afterward show a strong automatic association between the "if" cue and the "then" response, reacting far more quickly than controls to words associated with the "then" response after being primed with the "if" cue (109–112). This association leads subjects to quickly and automatically execute the intended "then" response when they encounter the specified "if" cue. The automaticity of this process explains why implementation intentions are just as effective (and in some cases *more* effective) when subjects suffer from impairments in executive control caused by cognitive load (113, 114), ego depletion (115), drug withdrawal (113), schizophrenia (113), ADHD (116, 117), or old age (118). The automaticity of implementation intentions is also indicated by studies showing that subjects will execute the "then" response of their implementation intentions even when the "if" cue is presented subliminally (119, 120).

The attentive reader will have already noticed that the kind of state created by implementation intentions – an automatic association between a cue and a response – is one and the same as the kind of state we have identified with *habits.* This implies that implementation intentions can enable an agent to deliberately create *new* cue-response associations that can compete with and override her old cue-response associations, i.e., her habits. If this is correct, then implementation intentions may provide a powerful tool for overriding unwanted habits and thus improving implemental self-control.

The research has borne this hypothesis out: subjects who form implementation intentions are significantly more successful at creating new habits and overriding old habits than control subjects who form mere goal intentions to do so (112, 121–125). As we would expect, reaction-time tasks indicate that implementation intentions break habits by creating a new association between the cue and the intended "then" response, which competes with the old association between the cue and the habitual response. After forming an implementation intention to break a habit, subjects react equally quickly to words associated with the intended "then" response as they do to words associated with the habitual response, indicating that the implementation intention levels the associative playing field (112). As the experimenters themselves put it: "implementation intentions eliminated the cognitive advantage of the habitual means in the 'horse race' with the alternative response" [(112), p. 503]. This gives the agent's self-control system a much better chance of winning the larger "horse race" with the incentive salience system for the control of behavior.

We should thus predict that forming implementation intentions should help agents to overcome incentive salience temptation; and the available data support this prediction. With regards to non-addicted subjects, many studies have shown implementation intentions to significantly improve success in *dieting*, an activity that requires overcoming incentive salience desires for unhealthy foods (126–128). Regarding the effectiveness of implementation intentions in overcoming addiction, there is an unfortunate dearth of research. However, one study has found that forming implementation intentions helped adolescents to quit smoking, though only for those who had a "weak or moderate" smoking habit as measured by a standard scale (125).

It is important to note that since implementation intentions aid specifically with implemental self-control, they will only facilitate self-control success among subjects who have *already* succeeded in overcoming their incentive salience desires in both the deliberative and volitional stages of self-control. If self-control fails in either of these prior stages, then the deck will be stacked too heavily in favor of the incentive salience system for a purely implemental intervention such as forming implementation intentions to make much of a difference. Perhaps this is why implementation intentions on their own did not affect the most addicted subjects' success at quitting smoking.

More generally, since success at all three stages of self-control is required for an agent to fully overcome incentive salience temptation, the most effective interventions to aid self-control will involve a combination of the stage-selective interventions we have advocated here. One existing intervention that follows this prescription is Gollwitzer and Oettingen's "Mental Contrasting with Implementation Intentions (MCII) " method, in which subjects first undergo the mental contrasting procedure – thus facilitating volitional self-control – and then form implementation intentions – thus improving implemental self-control. It should be no surprise that the MCII method is highly effective in aiding subjects to achieve their goals (117, 129–132). We can speculate that combining mindfulness training with the MCII method would augment self-control even further, comprising a "triple threat" of interventions that improve self-control in the deliberative, volitional, and implemental stages. Whether or not this "MMMCII" method (Mindfulness Meditation, Mental Contrasting, and Implementation Intentions) would in fact be effective in overcoming both addictive and non-addictive temptation is a question for further empirical work.

CONCLUSION

Intentional action is the product of a competition between at least three different motivators, incentive salience desires, cognitive desires, and habits, which is mediated by the self-control system. As we argued in "Desire," the incentive salience system is not only the source of addictive desires, but is the source of many of our ordinary, non-addictive desires as well. Due to the associative manner in which they are formed, these incentive salience desires are stubbornly independent of an agent's reflective judgments about what is valuable. This gives rise to the problem of self-control: the challenge of resisting one's incentive salience desires when they do not align with one's cognitive desires. We argued in "The Existence of Self-Control" that the capacity to exert self-control plays an independent role in determining behavior over and above the relative strengths of an agent's desires. This fact is illustrated most vividly by cases where the capacity to exert self-control is impaired (as in ego depletion) or lost altogether (as in vmPFC lesioning). The empirical evidence thus lends significant credence to the Platonic idea that there are two parts of the soul, one rational and the other appetitive, that compete for control over action.

As we argued in "Three Stages of Self-Control," this competition proceeds in stages. We distinguished three of these stages: deliberative, volitional, and implemental. In the deliberative stage, an agent forms a judgment as to what course of action would be best. Since the judgment the agent reaches depends upon the considerations she attends to when deliberating about what to do, deliberative self-control is a matter of directing *attention* in order to resist the biasing pull of craving. In the volitional stage, an agent forms an intention to act in accordance with her deliberative judgment. What this amounts to is the activation of a *goal*, a mental state that guides behavior toward the achievement of a certain end. Since incentive salience desires automatically activate goals regardless of whether the agent judges them good, an agent must exert self-control in order to make her goals accord with her evaluative judgments. Finally, in the implemental stage, an agent must guide her behavior in pursuit of her chosen goal. Whether she succeeds in doing so depends upon her habits – the automatic associations between contexts and behaviors she has formed in the past. Since habits guide behavior independently from goals, the regulation of *habits* – both by overcoming bad habits and by forming good ones – is a third task of self-control, separate from the two preceding. An agent must succeed in all three of these stages of self-control in order to conform her actions to her cognitive desires.

This single model captures the predicaments of the addict and non-addict alike. The incentive salience desires that render the addict's actions so wildly out of sync with her values are present in non-addicts as well, though in less extreme form. And thus the non-addict will also sometimes act in ways she does not endorse, driven by desires that motivate independently of her conception of the good. The non-addict can resist these desires by exerting self-control; but the addict can do this too. The task of self-control is far more difficult for the addict – which is why it is often unreasonable to blame addicts for giving in to temptation even when we might blame a non-addict for doing so. But self-control is possible for addicts, especially with strong incentives and assistance from others. Indeed, this is just what recovery from addiction is: the addictive desire does not go away, but the recovering addict learns to control her behavior in spite of it.

Thus addicts are not so different from the rest of us as we may have thought. But that may be because we underestimated our own similarity to addicts, rather than the other way around. There is a tendency to think of human agency as an entirely rational affair: we simply do whatever we think is most likely to get us what we want. The heuristics and biases literature has undermined this picture somewhat over the past few decades, but only by showing us how we are not always rational in selecting the *means* to our ends (133, 134). The model we have defended here shows that the irrationality – or arationality – of human agency goes a step deeper: our ends themselves can be set by desires that are utterly divorced from what we take to be rationally desirable. The activity of controlling our actions is thus not merely a matter of figuring out what we ought to do; it is a matter of fighting to control our minds and actions in accordance with our reasons. To borrow Plato's metaphor, being a human agent is more like struggling with stubborn horses for control over a chariot than it is like calculating a utility function. Those of us who are lucky enough not to suffer from addiction might come to understand ourselves better by acknowledging that there is an addict in us all.[29]

[29]For helpful comments and criticism, we thank Serge Ahmed, Dylan Bianchi, Bennett Foddy, Matthias Jenny, Hanna Pickard, Bernhard Salow, Ian Wells, and the participants at the Mechanisms of Self-Control Workshop at King's College London.

REFERENCES

1. Robinson TE, Berridge KC. The neural basis of drug craving: an incentive-sensitization theory of addiction. *Brain Res Rev* (1993) **18**(3):247–91. doi:10.1016/0165-0173(93)90013-P
2. Robinson TE, Berridge KC. Incentive-sensitization and addiction. *Addiction* (2001) **96**(1):103–14. doi:10.1046/j.1360-0443.2001.9611038.x
3. Robinson T, Berridge K. The incentive sensitization theory of addiction: some current issues. *Philos Trans R Soc Lond B Biol Sci* (2008) **363**(1507):3137–46. doi:10.1098/rstb.2008.0093
4. Plato. Republic. In: Cooper JM, Hutchinson DS, editors. *Plato: Complete Works.* Indianapolis, IN: Hackett Publishing Company (1997). p. 971–1224.
5. Watson G. Free agency. *J Philos* (1975) **72**(8):205–20. doi:10.2307/2024703
6. Holton R. *Willing, Wanting, Waiting.* New York, NY: Oxford University Press (2009).
7. Levy N. Resisting "weakness of the will". *Philos Phenomenol Res* (2011) **82**(1):134–55. doi:10.1111/j.1933-1592.2010.00424.x
8. Sripada CS. How is willpower possible? The puzzle of synchronic self-control and the divided mind. *Nous* (2014) **48**(1):41–74. doi:10.1111/j.1468-0068.2012.00870.x
9. Holton R, Berridge KC. Addiction between compulsion and choice. In: Levy N, editor. *Addiction and Self-Control: Perspectives from Philosophy, Psychology, and Neuroscience.* New York, NY: Oxford University Press (2013). p. 239–68.
10. Berridge K. The debate over dopamine's role in reward: the case for incentive salience. *Psychopharmacology* (2007) **191**:391–431. doi:10.1007/s00213-006-0578-x
11. Wyvell CL, Berridge KC. Intra-accumbens amphetamine increases the conditioned incentive salience of sucrose reward: enhancement of reward "wanting" without enhanced "liking" or response reinforcement. *J Neurosci* (2000) **20**(21):8122–30.
12. Robinson S, Sandstrom SM, Denenberg VH, Palmiter RD. Distinguishing whether dopamine regulates liking, wanting, and/or learning about rewards. *Behav Neurosci* (2005) **119**(1):5–15. doi:10.1037/0735-7044.119.1.5
13. Wyvell CL, Berridge KC. Incentive sensitization by previous amphetamine exposure: increased cue-triggered "wanting" for sucrose reward. *J Neurosci* (2001) **21**(19):7831–40.
14. Ahmed SH. Validation crisis in animal models of drug addiction: beyond non-disordered drug use toward drug addiction. *Neurosci Biobehav Rev* (2010) **35**(2):172–84. doi:10.1016/j.neubiorev.2010.04.005
15. Bate KS, Malouff JM, Thorsteinsson ET, Bhullar N. The efficacy of habit reversal therapy for tics, habit disorders, and stuttering: a meta-analytic review. *Clin Psychol Rev* (2011) **31**(5):865–71. doi:10.1016/j.cpr.2011.03.013
16. Ladouceur R. Habit reversal treatment: learning an incompatible response or increasing the subject's awareness? *Behav Res Ther* (1979) **17**(4):313–6. doi:10.1016/0005-7967(79)90003-2
17. Quinn JM, Pascoe A, Wood W, Neal DT. Can't control yourself? Monitor those bad habits. *Pers Soc Psychol Bull* (2010) **36**(4):499–511. doi:10.1177/0146167209360665
18. Wallace RJ. Addiction as defect of the will: some philosophical reflections. *Law Philos* (1999) **18**(6):621–54.
19. Baron-Cohen S, Leslie A, Frith U. Does the autistic child have a "theory of mind"? *Cognition* (2003) **21**(1):37–46. doi:10.1016/0010-0277(85)90022-8
20. Duchaine BC, Yovel G, Butterworth EJ, Nakayama K. Prosopagnosia as an impairment to face-specific mechanisms: elimination of the alternative hypotheses in a developmental case. *Cogn Neuropsychol* (2006) **23**(5):714–47. doi:10.1080/02643290500441296
21. Kanwisher N, Yovel G. The fusiform face area: a cortical region specialized for the perception of faces. *Philos Trans R Soc B Biol Sci* (2006) **361**(1476):2109–28. doi:10.1098/rstb.2006.1934
22. Damasio A. *Descartes' Error: Emotion, Reason, and the Human Brain.* New York, NY: Penguin Putnam (1994).
23. Damasio AR, Tranel D, Damasio H. Individuals with sociopathic behavior caused by frontal damage fail to respond autonomically to social stimuli. *Behav Brain Res* (1990) **41**(2):81–94. doi:10.1016/0166-4328(90)90144-4
24. Tranel D, Damasio H, Denburg NL, Bechara A. Does gender play a role in functional asymmetry of ventromedial prefrontal cortex? *Brain* (2005) **128**:2872–81. doi:10.1093/brain/awh643
25. Bechara A, Damasio A, Damasio H. Insensitivity to future consequences following damage to human prefrontal cortex. *Cognition* (1994) **50**:7–15. doi:10.1016/0010-0277(94)90018-3

26. Saver JL, Damasio AR. Preserved access and processing of social knowledge in a patient with acquired sociopathy due to ventromedial frontal damage. *Neuropsychologia* (1991) **29**(12):1241–9. doi:10.1016/0028-3932(91)90037-9
27. Leland J, Grafman J. Experimental tests of the somatic marker hypothesis. *Games Econ Behav* (2005) **52**(2):386–409. doi:10.1016/j.geb.2004.09.001
28. Baumeister RF, Bratslavsky E, Muraven M, Tice D. Ego depletion: is the active self a limited resource? *J Pers Soc Psychol* (1998) **74**(5):1252–65. doi:10.1037/0022-3514.74.5.1252
29. Gailliot M, Baumeister RF. Self-regulation and sexual restraint: dispositionally and temporarily poor self-regulatory abilities contribute to failures at restraining sexual behavior. *Pers Soc Psychol Bull* (2007) **33**(2):173–86. doi:10.1177/0146167206293472
30. Vohs KD, Baumeister RF, Schmeichel BJ, Twenge JM, Nelson NM, Tice DM. Making choices impairs subsequent self-control: a limited-resource account of decision making, self-regulation, and active initiative. *J Pers Soc Psychol* (2008) **94**(5):883–98. doi:10.1037/0022-3514.94.5.883
31. Schmeichel BJ, Vohs KD, Baumeister RF. Intellectual performance and ego depletion: role of the self in logical reasoning and other information processing. *J Pers Soc Psychol* (2003) **85**(1):33–46. doi:10.1037/0022-3514.85.1.33
32. DeWall C, Baumeister R, Gailliot M, Maner J. Depletion makes the heart grow less helpful: helping as a function of self-regulatory energy and genetic relatedness. *Pers Soc Psychol Bull* (2008) **34**:1653–62. doi:10.1177/0146167208323981
33. Mead NL, Baumeister RF, Gino F, Schweitzer ME, Ariely D. Too tired to tell the truth: self-control resource depletion and dishonesty. *J Exp Soc Psychol* (2009) **45**(3):594–7. doi:10.1016/j.jesp.2009.02.004
34. Vohs KD, Baumeister RF, Ciarocco NJ. Self-regulation and self-presentation: regulatory resource depletion impairs impression management and effortful self-presentation depletes regulatory resources. *J Pers Soc Psychol* (2005) **88**(4):632–57. doi:10.1037/0022-3514.88.4.632
35. Finkel EJ, Campbell WK. Self-control and accommodation in close relationship: an interdependence analysis. *J Pers Soc Psychol* (2001) **81**(2):263–77. doi:10.1037/0022-3514.81.2.263
36. DeWall C, Baumeister R, Stillman T, Gailliot MT. Violence restrained: effects of self-regulation and its depletion on aggression. *J Exp Soc Psychol* (2007) **43**(1):62–76. doi:10.1016/j.jesp.2005.12.005
37. Hofmann W, Rauch W, Gawronski B. And deplete us not into temptation: automatic attitudes, dietary restraint, and self-regulatory resources as determinants of eating behavior. *J Exp Soc Psychol* (2007) **43**(3):497–504. doi:10.1016/j.jesp.2006.05.004
38. Muraven M, Collins RL, Neinhaus K. Self-control and alcohol restraint: an initial application of the self-control strength model. *Psychol Addict Behav* (2002) **16**(2):113–20. doi:10.1037/0893-164X.16.2.113
39. Vohs KD, Faber RJ. Spent resources: self-regulatory resource availability affects impulse buying. *J Consum Res* (2007) **33**(4):537–47. doi:10.1086/510228
40. Gailliot MT, Baumeister RF. The physiology of willpower: linking blood glucose to self-control. *Pers Soc Psychol Rev* (2007) **11**(4):303–27. doi:10.1177/1088868307303030
41. Kurzban R. Does the brain consume additional glucose during self-control tasks? *Evol Psychol* (2010) **8**(2):244–59.
42. Molden DC, Hui CM, Scholer AA, Meier BP, Noreen EE, D'Agostino PR, et al. Motivational versus metabolic effects of carbohydrates on self-control. *Psychol Sci* (2012) **23**:1137–44. doi:10.1177/0956797612439069
43. Inzlicht M, Schmeichel BJ. What is ego depletion? Toward a mechanistic revision of the resource model of self-control. *Perspect Psychol Sci* (2012) **7**(5):450–63. doi:10.1177/1745691612454134
44. Hagger MS, Wood C, Stiff C, Chatzisarantis NL. Ego depletion and the strength model of self-control: a meta-analysis. *Psychol Bull* (2010) **136**(4):495–525. doi:10.1037/a0019486
45. Carter EC, McCullough ME. Is ego depletion too incredible? Evidence for the overestimation of the depletion effect. *Behav Brain Sci* (2013) **36**(6):683–4. doi:10.1017/S0140525X13000952
46. Baumeister RF, Vohs KD, Tice DM. The strength model of self-control. *Curr Dir Psychol Sci* (2007) **16**(6):351–5. doi:10.1111/j.1467-8721.2007.00534.x
47. Job V, Dweck CS, Walton GM. Ego depletion – is it all in your head? Implicit theories about willpower affect self-regulation. *Psychol Sci* (2010) **21**(11):1686–93. doi:10.1177/0956797610384745
48. Inzlicht M, Schmeichel BJ, Macrae CN. Why self-control seems (but may not be) limited. *Trends Cogn Sci* (2014) **18**(3):127–33. doi:10.1016/j.tics.2013.12.009
49. Kurzban R, Duckworth A, Kable JW, Myers J. An opportunity cost model of subjective effort and task performance. *Behav Brain Sci* (2013) **36**:661–726. doi:10.1017/S0140525X12003196
50. Watson G. Disordered appetites: addiction, compulsion, and dependence. In: Elster J, editor. *Addiction: Entries and Exits*. New York, NY: Russell Sage Foundation (1999). p. 3–28.
51. Levy N. Addiction, responsibility, and ego depletion. In: Poland J, Graham G, editors. *Addiction and Responsibility*. Cambridge, MA: The MIT Press (2011). p. 89–111.
52. Levy N. Addiction as a disorder of belief. *Biol Philos* (2014) **29**:337–55. doi:10.1007/s10539-014-9434-2
53. Schroeder T, Arpaly N. Addiction and blameworthiness. In: Levy N, editor. *Addiction and Self-Control: Perspectives from Philosophy, Psychology, and Neuroscience*. New York, NY: Oxford University Press (2013). p. 214–38.
54. Rorty AO. Where does the akratic break take place? *Australas J Philos* (1980) **58**(4):333–46. doi:10.1080/00048408012341341
55. Wheeler SC, Briñol P, Hermann AD. Resistance to persuasion as self-regulation: ego-depletion and its effects on attitude change processes. *J Exp Soc Psychol* (2007) **43**(1):150–6. doi:10.1016/j.jesp.2006.01.001
56. Masicampo EJ, Baumeister RF. Toward a physiology of dual-process reasoning and judgment: lemonade, willpower, and expensive rule-based analysis. *Psychol Sci* (2008) **19**(3):255–60. doi:10.1111/j.1467-9280.2008.02077.x
57. Ariely D, Loewenstein G. The heat of the moment: the effect of sexual arousal on sexual decision making. *J Behav Decis Mak* (2006) **19**(2):87–98. doi:10.1002/bdm.501
58. Gilbert DT, Gill MJ, Wilson TD. The future is now: temporal correction in affective forecasting. *Organ Behav Hum Decis Process* (2002) **88**(1):430–44. doi:10.1006/obhd.2001.2982
59. Van Boven L, Loewenstein G. Social projection of transient drive states. *Pers Soc Psychol Bull* (2003) **29**(9):1159–68. doi:10.1177/0146167203254597
60. Badger GJ, Bickel WK, Giordano LA, Jacobs EA, Loewenstein G, Marsch L. Altered states: the impact of immediate craving on the valuation of current and future opioids. *J Health Econ* (2007) **26**(5):865–76. doi:10.1016/j.jhealeco.2007.01.002
61. Moore A, Malinowski P. Meditation, mindfulness and cognitive flexibility. *Conscious Cogn* (2009) **18**(1):176–86. doi:10.1016/j.concog.2008.12.008
62. Jha AP, Stanley EA, Kiyonaga A, Wong L, Gelfand L. Examining the protective effects of mindfulness training on working memory capacity and affective experience. *Emotion* (2010) **10**(1):54–64. doi:10.1037/a0018438
63. Zeidan F, Johnson SK, Diamond BJ, David Z, Goolkasian P. Mindfulness meditation improves cognition: evidence of brief mental training. *Conscious Cogn* (2010) **19**(2):597–605. doi:10.1016/j.concog.2010.03.014
64. Brewer JA, Elwafi HM, Davis JH. Craving to quit: psychological models and neurobiological mechanisms of mindfulness training as treatment for addictions. *Psychol Addict Behav* (2012) **27**(2):366–79. doi:10.1037/a0028490
65. Zgierska A, Rabago D, Zuelsdorff M, Coe C, Miller M, Fleming M. Mindfulness meditation for alcohol relapse prevention: a feasibility pilot study. *J Addict Med* (2008) **2**(3):165–73. doi:10.1097/ADM.0b013e31816f8546
66. Bowen S, Marlatt A. Surfing the urge: brief mindfulness-based intervention for college student smokers. *Psychol Addict Behav* (2009) **23**(4):666–71. doi:10.1037/a0017127
67. Witkiewitz K, Marlatt GA, Walker D. Mindfulness-based relapse prevention for alcohol and substance use disorders. *J Cogn Psychother* (2005) **19**(3):211–28. doi:10.1891/jcop.2005.19.3.211
68. Bowen S, Chawla N, Collins SE, Witkiewitz K, Hsu S, Grow J, et al. Mindfulness-based relapse prevention for substance use disorders: a pilot efficacy trial. *Subst Abuse* (2009) **30**(4):295–305. doi:10.1080/08897070903250084
69. Brewer JA, Mallik S, Babuscio TA, Nich C, Johnson HE, Deleone CM, et al. Mindfulness training for smoking cessation: results from a randomized controlled trial. *Drug Alcohol Depend* (2011) **119**(1–2):72–80. doi:10.1016/j.drugalcdep.2011.05.027
70. Vidrine JI, Businelle MS, Cinciripini P, Li Y, Marcus MT, Waters AJ, et al. Associations of mindfulness with nicotine dependence, withdrawal, and agency. *Subst Abuse* (2009) **30**(4):318–27. doi:10.1080/08897070903252973
71. Westbrook C, Creswell JD, Tabibnia G, Julson E, Kober H, Tindle HA. Mindful attention reduces neural and self-reported cue-induced craving in smokers. *Soc Cogn Affect Neurosci* (2011) **8**(1):73–84. doi:10.1093/scan/nsr076
72. Forman EM, Herbert JD, Moitra E, Yeomans PD, Geller PA. A randomized controlled effectiveness trial of acceptance and commitment therapy and cognitive

therapy for anxiety and depression. *Behav Modif* (2007) **31**(6):772–99. doi:10.1177/0145445507302202

73. Lillis J, Hayes SC, Bunting K, Masuda A. Teaching acceptance and mindfulness to improve the lives of the obese: a preliminary test of a theoretical model. *Ann Behav Med* (2009) **37**(1):58–69. doi:10.1007/s12160-009-9083-x
74. Tapper K, Shaw C, Ilsley J, Hill AJ, Bond FW, Moore L. Exploratory randomised controlled trial of a mindfulness-based weight loss intervention for women. *Appetite* (2009) **52**(2):396–404. doi:10.1016/j.appet.2008.11.012
75. Alberts HJ, Mulkens S, Smeets M, Thewissen R. Coping with food cravings. Investigating the potential of a mindfulness-based intervention. *Appetite* (2010) **55**(1):160–3. doi:10.1016/j.appet.2010.05.044
76. Marchiori D, Papies EK. A brief mindfulness intervention reduces unhealthy eating when hungry, but not the portion size effect. *Appetite* (2014) **75**:40–5. doi:10.1016/j.appet.2013.12.009
77. O'Reilly GA, Cook L, Spruijt-Metz D, Black DS. Mindfulness-based interventions for obesity-related eating behaviors: a literature review. *Obes Rev* (2014) **15**(6):453–61. doi:10.1111/obr.12156
78. Hendrickson KL, Rasmussen EB. Effects of mindful eating training on delay and probability discounting for food and money in obese and healthy-weight individuals. *Behav Res Ther* (2013) **51**(7):399–409. doi:10.1016/j.brat.2013.04.002
79. Förster J, Liberman N, Friedman RS. Seven principles of goal activation: a systematic approach to distinguishing goal priming from priming of non-goal constructs. *Pers Soc Psychol Rev* (2007) **11**(3):211–33. doi:10.1177/1088868307303029
80. Custers R, Aarts H. Positive affect as implicit motivator: on the nonconscious operation of behavioral goals. *J Pers Soc Psychol* (2005) **89**(2):129–42. doi:10.1037/0022-3514.89.2.129
81. Custers R, Aarts H. Beyond priming effects: the role of positive affect and discrepancies in implicit processes of motivation and goal pursuit. *Eur Rev Soc Psychol* (2005) **16**(1):257–300. doi:10.1080/10463280500435919
82. Custers R, Aarts H. In search of the nonconscious sources of goal pursuit: accessibility and positive affective valence of the goal state. *J Exp Soc Psychol* (2007) **43**(2):312–8. doi:10.1016/j.jesp.2006.02.005
83. Aarts H, Custers R, Veltkamp M. Goal priming and the affective-motivational route to nonconscious goal pursuit. *Soc Cogn* (2008) **26**(5):555–77. doi:10.1521/soco.2008.26.5.555
84. Bijleveld E, Custers R, Aarts H. Unconscious reward cues increase invested effort, but do not change speed-accuracy tradeoffs. *Cognition* (2010) **115**(2):330–5. doi:10.1016/j.cognition.2009.12.012
85. Bijleveld E, Custers R, Aarts H. Once the money is in sight: distinctive effects of conscious and unconscious rewards on task performance. *J Exp Soc Psychol* (2011) **47**(4):865–9. doi:10.1016/j.jesp.2011.03.002
86. Shah JY, Friedman R, Kruglanski AW. Forgetting all else: on the antecedents and consequences of goal shielding. *J Pers Soc Psychol* (2002) **83**(6):1261–80. doi:10.1037/0022-3514.83.6.1261
87. Oettingen G, Pak H, Schnetter K. Self-regulation of goal setting: turning free fantasies about the future into binding goals. *J Pers Soc Psychol* (2001) **80**(5):736–53. doi:10.1037/0022-3514.80.5.736
88. Oettingen G, Mayer D, Timur Sevincer A, Stephens EJ, Pak HJ, Hagenah M. Mental contrasting and goal commitment: the mediating role of energization. *Pers Soc Psychol Bull* (2009) **35**(5):608–22. doi:10.1177/0146167208330856
89. Oettingen G, Mayer D, Thorpe J. Self-regulation of commitment to reduce cigarette consumption: mental contrasting of future with reality. *Psychol Health* (2010) **25**(8):961–77. doi:10.1080/08870440903079448
90. Oettingen G, Stephens EJ, Mayer D, Brinkmann B. Mental contrasting and the self-regulation of helping relations. *Soc Cogn* (2010) **28**(4):490–508. doi:10.1521/soco.2010.28.4.490
91. Oettingen G. Future thought and behavior change. *Eur Rev Soc Psychol* (2012) **23**(1):1–63. doi:10.1080/10463283.2011.643698
92. Aarts H, Gollwitzer PM, Hassin RR. Goal contagion: perceiving is for pursuing. *J Pers Soc Psychol* (2004) **87**(1):23–37. doi:10.1037/0022-3514.87.1.23
93. Förster J, Liberman N, Higgins ET. Accessibility from active and fulfilled goals. *J Exp Soc Psychol* (2005) **41**(3):220–39. doi:10.1016/j.jesp.2004.06.009
94. Cesario J, Plaks JE, Higgins ET. Automatic social behavior as motivated preparation to interact. *J Pers Soc Psychol* (2006) **90**:893–910. doi:10.1037/0022-3514.90.6.893
95. Rothermund K. Automatic vigilance for task-related information: perseverance after failure and inhibition after success. *Mem Cognit* (2003) **31**(3):343–52. doi:10.3758/BF03194392
96. Kawada CL, Oettingen G, Gollwitzer PM, Bargh JA. The projection of implicit and explicit goals. *J Pers Soc Psychol* (2004) **86**(4):545–59. doi:10.1037/0022-3514.86.4.545
97. Custers R, Aarts H. Goal-discrepant situations prime goal-directed actions if goals are temporarily or chronically accessible. *Pers Soc Psychol Bull* (2007) **33**(5):623–33. doi:10.1177/0146167206297404
98. Kappes HB, Oettingen G. Positive fantasies about idealized futures sap energy. *J Exp Soc Psychol* (2011) **47**(4):719–29. doi:10.1016/j.jesp.2011.02.003
99. Johannessen KB, Oettingen G, Mayer D. Mental contrasting of a dieting wish improves self-reported health behavior. *Psychol Health* (2012) **27**(sup2):43–58. doi:10.1080/08870446.2011.626038
100. Neal DT, Wood W, Quinn JM. Habits – a repeat performance. *Curr Dir Psychol Sci* (2006) **15**(4):198–202. doi:10.1111/j.1467-8721.2006.00435.x
101. Aarts H, Custers R, Holland RW. The nonconscious cessation of goal pursuit: when goals and negative affect are coactivated. *J Pers Soc Psychol* (2007) **92**(2):165. doi:10.1037/0022-3514.92.2.165
102. Neal DT, Wood W, Wu M, Kurlander D. The pull of the past: when do habits persist despite conflict with motives? *Pers Soc Psychol Bull* (2011) **37**(11):1428–37. doi:10.1177/0146167211419863
103. Neal DT, Wood W. Automaticity in situ and in the lab: the nature of habit in daily life. In: Morsella E, Bargh JA, Gollwitzer PM, editors. *Oxford Handbook of Human Action.* New York, NY: Oxford University Press (2010). p. 442–57.
104. Bargh JA, Gollwitzer PM, Lee-Chai A, Barndollar K, Trötschel R. The automated will: nonconscious activation and pursuit of behavioral goals. *J Pers Soc Psychol* (2001) **81**(6):1014. doi:10.1037/0022-3514.81.6.1014
105. Hassin RR, Bargh JA, Zimerman S. Automatic and flexible: the case of nonconscious goal pursuit. *Soc Cogn* (2009) **27**(1):20–36. doi:10.1521/soco.2009.27.1.20
106. Aristotle. Nicomachean ethics. In: Barnes J, editor. *The Complete Works of Aristotle* (Vol. 2), Princeton, NJ: Princeton University Press (1984). p. 1729–867.
107. Danner UN, Aarts H, Vries NK. Habit vs. intention in the prediction of future behavior: the role of frequency, context stability and mental accessibility of past behavior. *Br J Soc Psychol* (2010) **47**(2):245–65. doi:10.1348/014466607X230876
108. Gollwitzer PM, Sheeran P. Implementation intentions and goal achievement: a meta-analysis of effects and processes. *Adv Exp Soc Psychol* (2006) **38**:69–119. doi:10.1016/S0065-2601(06)38002-1
109. Aarts H, Dijksterhuis AP, Midden C. To plan or not to plan? Goal achievement or interrupting the performance of mundane behaviors. *Eur J Soc Psychol* (1999) **29**(8):971–9. doi:10.1002/(SICI)1099-0992(199912)29:8<971::AID-EJSP963>3.0.CO;2-A
110. Webb TL, Sheeran P. How do implementation intentions promote goal attainment? A test of component processes. *J Exp Soc Psychol* (2007) **43**(2):295–302. doi:10.1016/j.jesp.2006.02.001
111. Webb TL, Sheeran P. Mechanisms of implementation intention effects: the role of goal intentions, self-efficacy, and accessibility of plan components. *Br J Soc Psychol* (2010) **47**(3):373–95. doi:10.1348/014466607X267010
112. Adriaanse MA, Gollwitzer PM, De Ridder DT, de Wit JB, Kroese FM. Breaking habits with implementation intentions: a test of underlying processes. *Pers Soc Psychol Bull* (2011) **37**(4):502–13. doi:10.1177/0146167211399102
113. Brandstätter V, Lengfelder A, Gollwitzer PM. Implementation intentions and efficient action initiation. *J Pers Soc Psychol* (2001) **81**(5):946–60. doi:10.1037/0022-3514.81.5.946
114. Cohen A-L, Bayer UC, Jaudas A, Gollwitzer PM. Self-regulatory strategy and executive control: implementation intentions modulate task switching and Simon task performance. *Psychol Res* (2006) **72**(1):12–26. doi:10.1007/s00426-006-0074-2
115. Webb TL, Sheeran P. Can implementation intentions help to overcome ego-depletion? *J Exp Soc Psychol* (2003) **39**(3):279–86. doi:10.1016/S0022-1031(02)00527-9
116. Gawrilow C, Gollwitzer PM. Implementation intentions facilitate response inhibition in children with ADHD. *Cognit Ther Res* (2007) **32**(2):261–80. doi:10.1007/s10608-007-9150-1
117. Gawrilow C, Morgenroth K, Schultz R, Oettingen G, Gollwitzer PM. Mental contrasting with implementation intentions enhances self-regulation of goal pursuit in schoolchildren at risk for ADHD. *Motiv Emot* (2012) **37**(1):134–45. doi:10.1007/s11031-012-9288-3

118. Zimmermann TD, Meier B. The effect of implementation intentions on prospective memory performance across the lifespan. *Appl Cogn Psychol* (2009) **24**(5):645–58. doi:10.1002/acp.1576
119. Gollwitzer PM, Schaal B. Metacognition in action: the importance of implementation intentions. *Pers Soc Psychol Rev* (1998) **2**(2):124–36. doi:10.1207/s15327957pspr0202 5
120. Bayer UC, Achtziger A, Gollwitzer PM, Moskowitz GB. Responding to subliminal cues: do if-then plans facilitate action preparation and initiation without conscious intent? *Soc Cogn* (2009) **27**(2):183–201. doi:10.1521/soco.2009.27.2.183
121. Aarts H, Dijksterhuis A. Habits as knowledge structures: automaticity in goal-directed behavior. *J Pers Soc Psychol* (2000) **78**(1):53–63. doi:10.1037/0022-3514.78.1.53
122. Sheeran P, Orbell S. Using implementation intentions to increase attendance for cervical cancer screening. *Health Psychol* (2000) **19**(3):283–9. doi:10.1037/0278-6133.19.3.283
123. Holland RW, Aarts H, Langendam D. Breaking and creating habits on the working floor: a field-experiment on the power of implementation intentions. *J Exp Soc Psychol* (2006) **42**(6):776–83. doi:10.1016/j.jesp.2005.11.006
124. Orbell S, Verplanken B. The automatic component of habit in health behavior: habit as cue-contingent automaticity. *Health Psychol* (2010) **29**(4):374–83. doi:10.1037/a0019596
125. Webb TL, Sheeran P, Luszczynska A. Planning to break unwanted habits: habit strength moderates implementation intention effects on behavior change. *Br J Soc Psychol* (2010) **48**(3):507–23. doi:10.1348/014466608X370591
126. Verplanken B, Faes S. Good intentions, bad habits, and effects of forming implementation intentions on healthy eating. *Eur J Soc Psychol* (1999) **29**(56):591–604. doi:10.1002/(SICI)1099-0992(199908/09)29:5/6<591::AID-EJSP948>3.0.CO;2-H
127. Achtziger A, Gollwitzer PM, Sheeran P. Implementation intentions and shielding goal striving from unwanted thoughts and feelings. *Pers Soc Psychol Bull* (2008) **34**(3):381–93. doi:10.1177/0146167207311201
128. Adriaanse MA, Vinkers CD, De Ridder DT, Hox JJ, De Wit JB. Do implementation intentions help to eat a healthy diet? A systematic review and meta-analysis of the empirical evidence. *Appetite* (2011) **56**(1):183–93. doi:10.1016/j.appet.2010.10.012
129. Oettingen G, Hönig G, Gollwitzer PM. Effective self-regulation of goal attainment. *Int J Educ Res* (2000) **33**(7):705–32. doi:10.1016/S0883-0355(00)00046-X
130. Stadler G, Oettingen G, Gollwitzer PM. Physical activity in women: effects of a self-regulation intervention. *Am J Prev Med* (2009) **36**(1):29–34. doi:10.1016/j.amepre.2008.09.021
131. Duckworth AL, Grant H, Loew B, Oettingen G, Gollwitzer PM. Self-regulation strategies improve self-discipline in adolescents: benefits of mental contrasting and implementation intentions. *Educ Psychol* (2011) **31**(1):17–26. doi:10.1080/01443410.2010.506003
132. Houssais S, Oettingen G, Mayer D. Using mental contrasting with implementation intentions to self-regulate insecurity-based behaviors in relationships. *Motiv Emot* (2013) **37**(2):224–33. doi:10.1007/s11031-012-9307-4
133. Ariely D. *Predictably Irrational: The Hidden Forces that Shape Our Decisions.* New York, NY: HarperCollins Publishers (2008).
134. Kahneman D. *Thinking, Fast and Slow.* New York, NY: Farrar, Straus, and Giroux (2011).
135. Pickard H. The purpose in chronic addiction. *AJOB Neurosci* (2012) **3**(2):40–9. doi:10.1080/21507740.2012.663058
136. Oaten M, Cheng K. Academic examination stress impairs self-control. *J Soc Clin Psychol* (2005) **24**(2):254–79. doi:10.1521/jscp.24.2.254.62276
137. Batson CD, Shaw LL. Evidence for altruism: toward a pluralism of prosocial motives. *Psychol Inq* (1991) **2**(2):107–22. doi:10.1207/s15327965pli0202_1
138. Robinson S, Rainwater AJ, Hnasko TS, Palmiter RD. Viral restoration of dopamine signaling to the dorsal striatum restores instrumental conditioning to dopamine-deficient mice. *Psychopharmacology (Berl)* (2007) **191**(3):567–78. doi:10.1007/s00213-006-0579-9
139. Berridge K, O'Doherty J. From experienced utility to decision utility. In: Glimcher PW, Fehr E, editors. *Neuroecoconomics*, 2nd ed. Academic Press (2014). p. 335–54.
140. Saunders BT, Robinson TE. Individual variation in resisting temptation: implications for addiction. *Neurosci Biobehav Rev* (2013) **37**(9):1955–75. doi:10.1016/j.neubiorev.2013.02.008
141. DiLeone RJ, Taylor JR, Picciotto MR. The drive to eat: comparisons and distinctions between mechanisms of food reward and drug addiction. *Nat Neurosci* (2012) **15**(10):1330–5. doi:10.1038/nn.3202
142. Ahmed SH, Guillem K, Vandaele Y. Sugar addiction: pushing the drug-sugar analogy to the limit. *Curr Opin Clin Nutr Metab Care* (2013) **16**(4):434–9. doi:10.1097/MCO.0b013e328361c8b8 (2012)
143. Scanlon TM. *What We Owe to Each Other.* Cambridge: Belknap Press (1998).
144. Railton P. That obscure object, desire. *Proc Addresses Am Philos Assoc* **86**(2):22–46.
145. Schoenbaum G, Roesch M. Orbitofrontal cortex, associative learning, and expectancies. *Neuron* (2005) **47**:633–6. doi:10.1016/j.neuron.2005.07.018
146. Moretti L, Dragone D, di Pellegrino G. Reward and social valuation deficits following ventromedial prefrontal damage. *J Cogn Neurosci* (2009) **21**(1):128–40. doi:10.1162/jocn.2009.21011 *Soc*
147. Ciaramelli E, Muccioli M, Ladavas E, di Pellegrino G. Selective deficit in personal moral judgment following damage to ventromedial prefrontal cortex. *Cogn Affect Neurosci* (2007) **2**(2):84–92. doi:10.1093/scan/nsm001 (2007)
148. Shamay-Tsoory SG, Aharon-Peretz J. Dissociable prefrontal networks for cognitive and affective theory of mind: a lesion study. *Neuropsychologia* **45**:3054–67. doi:10.1016/j.neuropsychologia.2007.05.021
149. Henden E. Addictive actions. *Philos Psychol* (2013) **26**(3):362–82. doi:10.1080/09515089.2012.660688
150. Gollwitzer PM. Action phases and mind-sets. In: Higgins ET, Sorrentino RM, editors. *Handbook of Motivation and Cognition: Foundations of Social Behavior* (Vol. 2), New York, NY: The Guilford Press (1990). p. 53–92.
151. Denzler M, Förster J, Liberman N. How goal-fulfillment decreases aggression. *J Exp Soc Psychol* (2009) **45**(1):90–100. doi:10.1016/j.jesp.2008.08.021

4

The emerging role of non-coding RNAs in drug addiction

Gregory C. Sartor[1], Georges St. Laurent III[2,3] and Claes Wahlestedt[1]*

[1] Hussman Institute for Human Genomics, University of Miami Miller School of Medicine, Miami, FL, USA
[2] St. Laurent Institute, Cambridge, MA, USA
[3] Immunovirology – Biogenisis Group, University of Antioquia, Medellin, Colombia

Edited by:
Leonard Lipovich, Wayne State University, USA

Reviewed by:
Hongyan Xu, Georgia Health Sciences University, USA
Melanie Carless, Texas Biomedical Research Institute, USA

***Correspondence:**
Claes Wahlestedt, Hussman Institute for Human Genomics, University of Miami Miller School of Medicine, 1501 Northwest 10th Avenue BRB 407, Miami, FL 33136, USA.
e-mail: cwahlestedt@med.miami.edu

Prolonged drug use causes long-lasting neuroadaptations in reward-related brain areas that contribute to addiction. Despite significant amount of research dedicated to understanding the underlying mechanisms of addiction, the molecular underpinnings remain unclear. At the same time, much of the pervasive transcription that encompasses the human genome occurs in the nervous system and contributes to its heterogeneity and complexity. Recent evidence suggests that non-coding RNAs (ncRNAs) play an important and dynamic role in transcriptional regulation, epigenetic signaling, stress response, and plasticity in the nervous system. Dysregulation of ncRNAs are thought to contribute to many, and perhaps all, neurological disorders, including addiction. Here, we review recent insights in the functional relevance of ncRNAs, including both microRNAs (miRNAs), and long non-coding RNAs, and then illustrate specific examples of ncRNA regulation in the context of drug addiction. We conclude that ncRNAs are importantly involved in the persistent neuroadaptations associated with addiction-related behaviors, and that therapies that target specific ncRNAs may represent new avenues for the treatment of drug addiction.

Keywords: addiction, long non-coding RNA, microRNA, epigenetic, lncRNA, miRNA

INTRODUCTION

Evolutionary processes in the human lineage have coupled expanding genome complexity with the acquisition, processing, and distribution of ever increasing amounts of information (Sempere et al., 2006; Mattick, 2007; Berezikov, 2011). Non-coding RNAs (ncRNAs) occupy the center stage of this expanding genome complexity, with the ratio of non-coding genomic sequence to protein coding sequence growing more than 10-fold as primates evolved from simple multicellular organisms (Taft et al., 2007). ncRNAs occupy critical nodes and edges in a majority of physiological networks, frequently participating in feedback loops, stability, and fined-tuned regulatory control. The unique information processing features of ncRNAs permit them to transduce information through heterogeneous molecular machineries with relatively less energy cost than protein networks alone, making them particularly useful in the limited and thermally constrained real estate of the human central nervous system.

In light of these observations, it is not surprising that non-exonic transcripts (those mapping to regions of the genome outside annotated protein coding genes) comprise 2/3 of the total, non-ribosomal, non-mitochondrial RNA in the human brain (Kapranov et al., 2010). Highly articulated nervous system expression of miRNAs (Lagos-Quintana et al., 2002; Schratt et al., 2006; Makeyev et al., 2007) and long non-coding RNAs (lncRNAs; Mercer et al., 2008; Ponjavic et al., 2009) point to the involvement of ncRNAs in key aspects of nervous system homeostasis and plasticity. The ability of addictive stimuli to perturb and disrupt these functions suggests a broad based involvement of ncRNAs in the loss of functional coherence associated with chronic drug use (Chandrasekar and Dreyer, 2009; Hollander et al., 2010). In this review, we consider the participation of ncRNAs in the key nervous system molecular machineries affected by addiction, and the potential mechanisms of their involvement in the dimensions of this complex disorder.

INVOLVEMENT OF ncRNAs IN NEUROPLASTICITY AND LEARNING

Emerging evidence suggests that miRNAs and their processing machinery play a critical role in neuroplasticity by regulating protein dynamics in the synapse (Edbauer et al., 2010; Lippi et al., 2011; Siegel et al., 2011; Saba et al., 2012). Given that addiction is considered a maladaptive form of neuroplasticity, identifying miRNAs important in such neuroadaptations may lead to novel insights in addiction research. Demonstrating a role for miRNAs in neuroplasticity, Schratt et al. (2006) showed that miR-134 expression in the dendrites of developing hippocampal neurons is critically involved in dendritic spine formation and plasticity by inhibiting Lim domain-containing protein kinase 1, an important regulator of actin filament dynamics. Following this seminal report, other studies revealed that miR-138, miR-132, and miR-125b play an essential role in dendritic spine formation (Siegel et al., 2009; Edbauer et al., 2010). The role of miRNAs in synapse are not restricted to the those listed above, as recent reports have identified numerous dendritic- and synaptic-enriched miRNAs (Lugli et al., 2008; Eipper-Mains et al., 2011; Saba et al., 2012). Although most of the research thus far has focused on miRNAs, there is some evidence that suggests lncRNAs are also involved in synaptic plasticity. For instance, BC1 and BC200 are lncRNAs that are localized in post-synaptic dendritic compartments where they regulate local gene expression by controlling the activity of specific transcription factors (Lin et al., 2008). Other lncRNAs are also localized in the synapse and neurite extensions (French et al., 2001; Mercer et al., 2008), but their functional role in plasticity remains poorly understood.

In neurons, activity-dependent regulation of miRNAs also contributes extensively to neuroplasticity. Using the marine snail *Aplysia*, Rajasethupathy et al. (2009) demonstrated that serotonin-induced activation of sensory neurons caused a significant decrease in miR-124, leading to increased cAMP response element-binding (CREB) expression and induction of long-term facilitation. Knockdown of miR-124 also robustly increased serotonin-induced synaptic plasticity and CREB expression, revealing a functional association between miR-124 activity and CREB expression. Additional *in vivo* studies have demonstrated activity-dependent up regulation of miR-132 and miR-212 following induction of LTP in hippocampal neurons, an increase that was dependent on metabotropic glutamate receptor activation (Wibrand et al., 2010). Consistent with the role of miR-132 in neuronal activation, enhanced expression of miR-132 was observed in a number of behavioral paradigms, such as contextual fear conditioning, odorant exposure, and acute cocaine treatment (Nudelman et al., 2010). In addition, over expressing miR-132 enhances neuronal activity in cortical and hippocampal neurons (Cheng et al., 2007), possibly through miR-132-mediated inhibition of p250GAP, a protein associated with dendritic plasticity (Wayman et al., 2008).

The ability of ncRNAs to regulate transcription factors and chromatin remodeling proteins represent additional mechanisms to influence long-term neuroadaptations involved in memory formation. For example, miR-324 and miR-369, two miRNAs implicated in cocaine-induced neuroplasticity (Schaefer et al., 2010), have been shown to modulate transcription factors (MEF2 and FosB) important in reward-related learning and memory (Hiroi et al., 1997; Pulipparacharuvil et al., 2008). Additionally, miR-132 regulation of chromatin remodeling factors methyl CpG binding protein 2 (MeCP2), p300, and Jumonji and ARID domain protein 1 A (JARID1A) in the suprachiasmatic nucleus is important in neuroadaptations associated with circadian rhythm (Alvarez-Saavedra et al., 2011). Although no study to date has examined lncRNAs in learning and memory paradigms, lncRNAs could potentially be involved in long-term neuroadaptations, as they have been shown to regulate transcriptional factors, DNA methylation, and histone modifications (Rinn et al., 2007; Houseley et al., 2008; Yu et al., 2008; Khalil et al., 2009).

The studies reviewed above clearly show the importance of miRNAs (and potentially lncRNAs) in synaptic plasticity and learning and memory. However, many questions remain for future studies to better understand the role of ncRNAs in neuroplasticity. For example, the relationship between ncRNA-mediated plasticity and psychiatric disorders, such as addiction, has raised a number of intriguing questions: Are the same ncRNAs that are involved in plasticity also involved in addiction, or are other addiction-related ncRNAs involved, whose functions have yet to be determined? What are the specific targets of ncRNAs and how do these interactions contribute to the neuroadaptations associated with addiction? These are just a few questions that are currently being addressed to understand the complex relationship between ncRNA-mediated plasticity and addiction.

EMERGING ROLE FOR miRNAs IN ADDICTION

Drugs of abuse induce persistent changes in neuroplasticity by usurping gene regulatory mechanisms, in turn leading to addiction. Given the role of miRNAs in gene regulation and synaptic plasticity, recent studies have begun to examine the involvement of miRNAs in response to drugs of abuse (**Table 1**). Here, we highlight some of the recent findings that illustrate the importance of miRNAs in drug-induced synaptic plasticity, drug-seeking behaviors, and tolerance to several abused drugs.

COCAINE AND AMPHETAMINE

To investigate the role of miRNAs in cocaine addiction, Chandrasekar and Dreyer (2009) utilized *in silico* prediction models to identify miRNAs that potentially regulate cocaine-associated genes and discovered a strong prediction for miR-124, let-7d, and miR-181a. Further *in vivo* studies showed that expression of miR-181a is increased and miR-124 and let-7d are decreased in striatum of rats with a history of chronic cocaine exposure. Subsequent behavioral studies revealed that over expression of miR-124 and let-7d in the nucleus accumbens reduced cocaine conditioned place preference (CPP), whereas over expression of miR-181a enhanced cocaine preference (Chandrasekar and Dreyer, 2011). These effects on cocaine CPP were inversed when expression of the aforementioned miRNAs were inhibited. Interestingly, it was found that altering expression of these miRNAs in the nucleus accumbens modulated the expression of many addiction-related genes (Chandrasekar and Dreyer, 2009). For example, overexpression of miR-124 and let-7d increased dopamine transporter, whereas miR-181a over expression decreased it. Because the dopamine transporter is the primary target of cocaine and is importantly involved in cocaine CPP (Tilley et al., 2009), the observed behavioral changes are likely reflected, in part, by miRNA-regulation of the dopamine transporter. Notably, the expression of several other addiction-related genes, such as Brain-derived neurotrophic (BDNF), CREB, MeCP2, and ΔFosB were also regulated by these miRNAs, thus illustrating the widespread effects on addiction-related gene networks in response to changes in miRNA levels.

Using an extended access model of cocaine self-administration, Hollander et al. (2010) examined the role of miRNAs in regulating compulsive-like cocaine intake. In this study, dorsal striatal miR-212 levels were found to be significantly elevated in rats with a history of extended access to cocaine, but not in rats with short-access to cocaine or in rats receiving non-contingent cocaine exposure (yoked control). Further investigation showed that over expression or knockdown of miR-212 in the dorsal striatum decreased or enhanced cocaine self-administration under extended access conditions, respectively, suggesting that striatal miR-212 is involved in an adaptive response to inhibit escalation of cocaine intake. Reduced motivation to consume cocaine was attributed in part by miR-212-mediated upregulation of CREB, a known antagonistic regulator of cocaine reward (Carlezon et al., 1998). Subsequent studies from the same laboratory revealed that MeCP2 regulates cocaine intake via a homeostatic interaction with miR-212 to influence cocaine-mediated effects on striatal BDNF (Im et al., 2010). By revealing an important miRNA-mediated epigenetic mechanism involved in drug-seeking behaviors, this study raises a number of interesting possibilities because epigenetic

Table 1 | ncRNAs regulated by drugs of abuse (green = upregulation, red = downregulation).

Drug	ncRNAs	Mechanism(s) involved	Reference
miRNAs			
Cocaine	miR-212	Elevated following extended access to cocaine; targets CREB; interaction with MeCP2 and influences BDNF expression	Hollander et al. (2010), Im et al. (2010)
	miR-124, let-7d, miR-181a	Targets BDNF, DAT, CREB, mGluR5, FosB; involved in cocaine CPP	Chandrasekar and Dreyer (2009, 2011)
	miR-181a	Enriched in NAc synapse, regulates GluA2 expression	Saba et al. (2012)
	Ago2	Ago2 knockout in striatal D2R neurons reduces cocaine self-administration.	Schaefer et al. (2010)
	miR-8, miR-7, miR-142, and let-7 families	Upregulated in striatal PSD	Eipper-Mains et al. (2011)
	miR-200c, miR125a-5p, miR-429, miR-370, miR-183, miR-200b, miR-770-5p, miR200a	Downregulated in striatal PSD	Eipper-Mains et al. (2011)
Nicotine	miR-140	Regulates dynamin-1 expression	Huang and Li (2009b)
	miR-504	Regulates DRD1 expression	Huang and Li (2009a)
		Upregulated in hippocampus	Lippi et al. (2011)
Alcohol	miR-9	Downregulates BK channels	Pietrzykowski et al. (2008)
	miR-497, miR-302b	Involved in ethanol-induced neuronal death; targets BCL2 and cyclin D2	Yadav et al. (2011)
Opioids	miR-23b	Regulates mOR expression	Wu et al. (2009)
	let-7	Regulates mOR expression	He et al. (2010)
	miR-190	Downregulated by mOR activation via ERK signaling; targets NeuroD	Zheng et al. (2010)
	miR-133b	Morphine-induced downregulation causes enhanced Pitx3 expression	Sanchez-Simon et al. (2010)
lncRNAs			
Heroin	MIAT, MEG3, NEAT1, NEAT2	Upregulated in NAc of heroin abusers	Michelhaugh et al. (2011)
Cocaine	MIAT, MEG3, NEAT2, EMX2O	Upregulated in NAc of cocaine abusers	Michelhaugh et al. (2011)

BCL2, B-cell lymphoma 2; BDNF, brain-derived neurotrophic factor; CREB, cAMP response element-binding; CPP, conditioned place preference; DAT, dopamine transporter; DRD1, Dopamine receptor D1; D2R, dopamine receptor D2; ERK, Extracellular signal-regulated kinase; FosB, FBJ murine osteosarcoma viral oncogene homolog B; mGluR5, Metabotropic glutamate receptor 5; mOR, mu opioid receptor; NAc, nucleus accumbens; Pitx3, Pituitary homeobox 3; PSD, post-synaptic density.

factors associated with addiction have recently been the focus of intense investigation (Robison and Nestler, 2011).

Recent studies have examined synaptic expression of miRNAs in response to cocaine. By isolating striatal post-synaptic densities (PSD), Eipper-Mains et al. (2011) identified more than two dozen miRNAs that were significantly altered following chronic cocaine treatment. Interestingly, many of the PSD miRNAs affected by cocaine were found to be members of one of four families (miR-8, miR-7, miR-142, and let-7 families), suggesting that cocaine influences the expression of similar miRNAs with shared synaptic targets. In a similar study, Saba et al. (2012) utilized microarray screening to identify nine enriched and seven depleted miRNAs in the synaptodendritic compartment of the nucleus accumbens. They also revealed that miR-181a, one of the synaptically enriched miRNAs, is increased in reward-related brain regions following cocaine and amphetamine exposure, and miR-181a regulates synaptic plasticity by altering AMPA receptor subunit (GluA2) expression (Saba et al., 2012). Additional reports examining the role of miRNAs in drug-induced synaptic plasticity determined that miR-29a/b was significantly upregulated in addiction-related brain regions in mice with a history of cocaine or amphetamine exposure and plays an pivotal role in synaptic structure and function *in vitro* (Lippi et al., 2011).

Enzymes that regulate miRNA processing also appear to play a functional role in cocaine addiction. A study by Schaefer et al. (2010) revealed that knockout of argonaute 2 (Ago2, a protein important in miRNA processing) in accumbal dopamine 2 receptor expressing neurons significantly attenuated cocaine self-administration. Further investigation revealed that Ago2 regulates expression of numerous miRNAs in the striatum, and many of the Ago2-dependent miRNAs were predicted to target genes important in cocaine addiction. Consistent with the role of Ago2 in cocaine addiction, Eipper-Mains et al. (2011) showed that chronic cocaine exposure elevates Ago2 expression in the striatum. Dicer, an enzyme responsible for producing mature miRNAs, may also be necessary in cocaine addiction, as previous studies have shown that manipulation of this enzyme affects learning and memory (Konopka et al., 2010) and miRNA expression in striatum (Cuellar et al., 2008).

NICOTINE

Utilizing miRNA microarray approach, Huang and Li identified 25 miRNAs that were altered in PC12 cells following nicotine exposure. They also found that miR-140 binds and reduces expression of dynamin-1 (Huang and Li, 2009b), a GTPase that has previously been shown to be important in nicotine dependence (Hwang and Li, 2006). The same research group showed that miR-504 targets a specific dopamine receptor D1 gene containing a single nucleotide polymorphism that has been associated with nicotine dependence (Huang and Li, 2009a). Interestingly, by increasing D1 receptor expression, miR-504 may promote nicotine intake by enhancing dopamine signaling. Finally, chronic injections of nicotine increased several miRNAs in mouse hippocampus, prefrontal cortex, limbic forebrain, and midbrain (Lippi et al., 2011), indicating that nicotine has broad effects on miRNA expression in several addiction-related brain areas, though the implications are not yet clear.

ALCOHOL

In a seminal set of studies, Pietrzykowski et al. (2008) revealed that alcohol upregulates miR-9 in rat striatum and supraoptic nucleus, two regions important in alcohol tolerance. The increase in miR-9 was found to contribute to alcohol tolerance by preferentially targeting BK channel mRNA isoforms that are sensitive to alcohol. BK channels, large conductance calcium, and voltage-activated potassium channels, are important in neuronal excitability, firing frequency, and neurotransmitter release and have been one of the best described targets for alcohol tolerance (for review see Treistman and Martin, 2009). Thus, miR-9-induced destabilization of alcohol sensitive BK channels likely contributes to alcohol tolerance and addiction by promoting the expression of more tolerant BK channel isoforms. Interestingly, the role of miR-9 in alcohol dependence may not be limited to tolerance, as miR-9 was also found to target other genes that have been implicated in addiction, such as dopamine receptor D2 and histone deacetylase 5 (Pietrzykowski et al., 2008).

Other alcohol-related studies have identified miRNAs involved in ethanol dependence. Guo et al. reported differential miRNA expression patterns following chronic ethanol exposure and ethanol removal in primary cortical neuron cultures. These results may indicate that different stages of alcohol addiction (maintenance, withdrawal, etc.) have distinct miRNA expression profiles (Guo et al., 2011), information that could be important for the development of new therapeutics to treat alcohol addiction. In another study, miR-497 and miR-302b were found to be involved in ethanol-induced neuronal cell death following chronic ethanol exposure, thereby providing a possible link between miRNAs and neuronal loss associated with chronic alcohol abuse (Yadav et al., 2011). In addition, recent studies using human post-mortem tissue, revealed that 35 miRNAs were significantly upregulated in the prefrontal cortex in alcoholics (Lewohl et al., 2011), again suggesting that chronic alcohol has widespread affects on miRNA expression reward-related brain areas. The development of artificial miRNAs may be a novel approach to treating alcoholism and other forms of addiction, as one recent study showed that targeting neurokinin-1 receptor gene with an artificial miRNA significantly reduced alcohol consumption in mice (Baek et al., 2010).

OPIOIDS

Similar to alcohol, specific miRNAs have been implicated in opioid tolerance and addiction. miRNAs, let-7, and miR-23b suppress mu opioid receptor mRNA expression following long-term morphine treatment (Wu et al., 2009; He et al., 2010), demonstrating a new mechanism that might play an important role in morphine tolerance. In addition, the mu opioid receptor agonist, fentanyl, but not morphine, downregulates miR-190 expression via extracellular signal-regulated kinase (ERK) signaling (Zheng et al., 2010), indicating that specific mu opioid receptor agonists have differential influence on miRNA expression.

SUMMARY

The studies highlighted in this section illustrate a wide range of miRNA-mediated mechanisms involved in addiction. With their ability to regulate addiction-related gene networks, drug-induced plasticity, drug-seeking behaviors, and drug tolerance, miRNAs are ideal therapeutic targets for the treatment of addiction. However, much more research in this nascent field is needed to reveal miRNA targets and mechanisms that contribute importantly to the addicted state. Thus, it seems clear that future studies will reveal ever more complex and intriguing properties of these key ncRNAs in addiction.

POTENTIAL ROLE FOR LONG NON-CODING RNAs IN ADDICTION

Recent large-scale genomic studies have revealed that lncRNAs are one of the most abundant classes of ncRNAs (Jia et al., 2010; Kapranov et al., 2010). Additionally, lncRNAs have been implicated in a number of important cellular processes including gene transcription, RNA processing, and chromatin modifications (Wang and Chang, 2011). Although lncRNAs are highly expressed in the brain (Mercer et al., 2008; Belgard et al., 2011), they remain poorly characterized in this context and their role in addiction is unclear. In an attempt to determine whether lncRNAs are differently expressed in response to chronic drug use, a recent study by Michelhaugh et al. (2011) identified lncRNAs that were altered in heroin abusers by mining existing Affymetrix datasets. Of the 23 lncRNAs identified, MIAT, MEG3, NEAT1, and NEAT2 were upregulated in the nucleus accumbens of heroin abusers compared to control subjects. Preliminary reports from the same research group also found that NEAT2, MIAT, MEG3, and EMX2OS are elevated in the nucleus accumbens of cocaine abusers (Michelhaugh et al., 2011), suggesting similar aberrations in lncRNA expression in response to different drugs of abuse. The lncRNAs listed above have been implicated in a range of cellular processes including cAMP signaling (Zhao et al., 2006), GABA neuron neurogenesis (Mercer et al., 2010), and regulation of genes associated with synaptic plasticity (Bernard et al., 2010), but the functional role of these lncRNAs in addiction remains unknown. Although these initial findings are intriguing, only a small number of lncRNAs were examined, suggesting the need for more comprehensive analysis of transcriptome changes during these critical events, with emphasis on specific cell types and locus specific complexity of lncRNA expression during these changes.

Natural antisense transcripts (NATs), a subset of lncRNAs, are transcripts derived from the opposite strand of many protein coding (sense) genes. NATs bind to sense RNA and/or proteins to regulate transcription and translation. Recently, we demonstrated that BDNF, a gene known to be involved in addiction, is controlled by a conserved long non-coding antisense RNA transcript (BDNF-AS; Modarresi et al., 2012). BDNF-AS suppresses BDNF mRNA expression by altering chromatin structure at the BDNF gene locus. Inhibiting BDNF-AS by siRNA or other methods robustly increased BDNF mRNA and protein expression and enhanced neuronal outgrowth. Given the important role of BDNF in cocaine addiction (for review see Ghitza et al., 2010), it would be interesting to determine if BDNF-AS is dysregulated in response to chronic drug use and contributes to drug-seeking behaviors. Other addiction-related NATs have also been identified (Zhang et al., 2007), but their role in addiction-related neuroadaptations and behaviors merits further research.

Although initial studies have identified a potential involvement of lncRNAs in addiction, many additional questions remain – whether specific lncRNAs are necessary for drug-seeking behaviors, whether different drugs of abuse affect different lncRNAs, whether specific lncRNAs are preferentially expressed in reward-related brain areas, and whether differences across species exist (mice vs. rats vs. humans). Thus, a major research goal is to address these important unanswered questions in order to understand the underlying mechanisms of abused drugs and to identify useful targets for the treatment of addiction.

EPIGENETIC-ncRNA INTERACTIONS: POTENTIAL INVOLVEMENT IN DRUG-INDUCED NEUROADAPTATIONS

The epigenome consists of DNA methylation and several modifications (acetylation, methylation, phosphorylation, etc.) to specific amino acid residues on histone proteins. Chromatin-modifying complexes play an important role in transcriptional regulation by adding or removing covalent modifications to histone proteins. Several key chromatin-modifying proteins have recently been implicated in neuroadaptations associated with addiction. For example, specific enzymes responsible for histone acetylation, methylation, and DNA methylation in reward-related brain areas are critically involved in cocaine addiction (LaPlant et al., 2010; Maze et al., 2010; Wang et al., 2010). However, it has been largely unclear how these proteins target specific regions of the genome, given that the majority of chromatin-modifying proteins lack DNA binding capacity.

Increasing evidence now indicates that chromatin-modifying complexes are directed to their sites of action by lncRNAs. Therefore, it is possible that lncRNAs play an important role in addiction by regulating epigenetic processes. Although no study has examined lncRNA-mediated epigenetic mechanisms in the context of addiction, we speculate that such interactions are important (**Figure 1**), given that several addiction-related epigenetic factors associate with lncRNAs in tissues outside of the brain

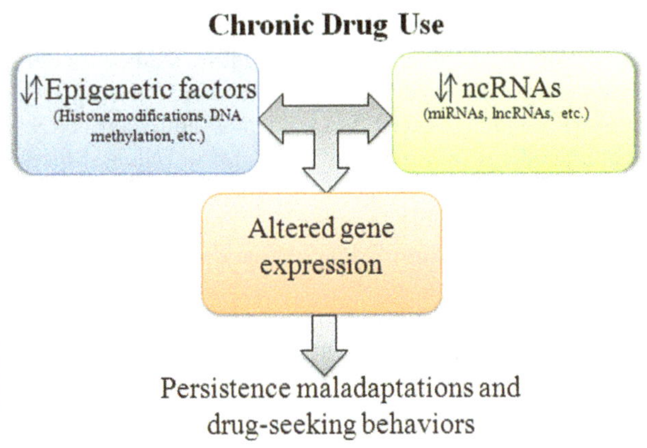

FIGURE 1 | Simplified representation of ncRNA–epigenetic interactions in response to chronic drug use. Long-term use of drugs alters expression of ncRNAs, epigenetic factors, and the interactions between these processes, causing persistent perturbations in gene expression. Chronic aberrations in gene expression are thought to evoke maladaptive neuroadaptations associated with addiction.

(Khalil et al., 2009). For example, in the placenta, lncRNAs Air, and Kcnq1ot1 regulate histone methylation by interacting with the histone methyltransferase G9a (Nagano et al., 2008; Pandey et al., 2008), an epigenetic enzyme that is downregulated in the accumbens following chronic cocaine exposure and is important in cocaine-related behaviors (Maze et al., 2010). Additionally, lncRNA-mediated regulation of histone acetylation, methylation, or DNA methylation, key modifications important in cocaine addiction (for review see, Maze and Nestler, 2011), have also been reported (Rinn et al., 2007; Houseley et al., 2008; Yu et al., 2008; Yap et al., 2010). Interestingly, not only can lncRNAs influence the activity of chromatin-modifying complexes, but evidence now indicates that alterations in epigenetic processes can alter the expression of lncRNAs (Johnson et al., 2009). Whether these specific interactions are important in the brain during drug-seeking behaviors, however, remains to be investigated.

MicroRNAs also interact with epigenetic factors important in addiction. As previously described, Im et al. (2010) found that miR-212 influences cocaine seeking by inhibiting MeCP2 in the dorsal striatum. Other epigenetic enzymes that have been implicated in addiction, such as DNA methyltransferase 3A, histone deacetylases 4, and sirtuin 1, are also regulated by specific miRNAs (Chen et al., 2006; Fabbri et al., 2007; Gao et al., 2010), but the significance of these associations in addiction-related behaviors is unknown.

Although the full spectrum of ncRNA-epigenetic associations in the CNS has yet to be seen, these interactions appear to play an essential role in fine-tuning gene expression and proper brain functioning. In drug addiction, it is possible that chronic drug use leads to long-lasting aberrations in ncRNA-mediated epigenetic mechanisms that lead to persistent drug-seeking behaviors. However, additional research is needed to determine the molecular underpinnings involved in ncRNA-epigenetic interactions in the brain and if these interactions contribute importantly to the addicted state.

FUTURE DIRECTIONS

Although a growing number of reports have implicated miRNAs in addiction-related neuroadaptations, future studies are needed to determine if lncRNAs also play a critical role in drug-seeking behaviors. Given that lncRNAs are the most abundant ncRNA in the brain and critically involved in an array of cellular processes, identifying specific lncRNAs that are regulated by drugs of abuse is likely to be a valuable approach for revealing the underlying mechanisms of addiction. With the recent development of new technologies, such as capture hybridization analysis of RNA targets (CHART) and Chromatin Isolation by RNA Purification (ChIRP; Chu et al., 2011; Simon et al., 2011), it is now possible to identify novel lncRNA-DNA or lncRNA-protein interactions involved in addiction, and future studies using these techniques will determine if these interactions are altered following prolonged drug use. In addition, as recent studies indicate that lncRNAs are differentially expressed in certain brain regions (Mercer et al., 2008; Belgard et al., 2011), identifying preferential expression of specific lncRNAs in reward-related brain areas might lead to new targets for the treatment of addiction. Finally, new therapeutic strategies and delivery approaches that target RNAs are now being explored (Bitko and Barik, 2007; Wood et al., 2007; Hung et al., 2011). Thus, using these new techniques to target ncRNAs holds great potential for treating several psychiatric disorders, including addiction.

CONCLUSION

Studies over the last several years have established a broad functional context for ncRNAs in the computational matrix of the nervous system. At the cellular level, nervous system signaling networks involve small RNAs at the synapse, where they regulate activity-dependent mRNA translation, and in turn, learning and memory-related plasticity. At the same time, in the nucleus, long RNAs function to provide temporal and spatial information to an array of epigenetic signaling systems. Chronic drug use likely perturbs these networks during the process of addiction in ways that cause a loss of plasticity and in turn establish barriers to the return to homeostasis.

Yet, the complexity of the nervous system suggests that additional layers of ncRNA-mediated events likely occur during the process of addiction. For example, recent evidence suggests that lncRNAs can serve as decoys or storage locations for small RNAs (Tay et al., 2011), in effect competing with targets for the occupancy of effector small RNAs and modulating their downstream effects (Salmena et al., 2011). In neurons this process could function together with anterograde and retrograde transport of RNA–protein vesicles, providing the potential for a link between small RNA mediated translational control at the synapse, and lncRNA-mediated chromatin signaling in the nucleus. Stresses such as repeated increases in intracellular Ca^{++} levels could reduce the performance of vesicle trafficking and lead to the progressive decoupling of such ncRNA-mediated systems relatively early in the process of addictive maladaptations.

Non-coding RNAs may also play a role in signaling between cells. Circulating exosomes and microvesicles contain many RNA species, and have the ability to traffic these RNAs from one cell type to another (Smalheiser, 2007; Dinger et al., 2008), even supporting the metastatic environment of the soma in some types of cancer. While not yet documented in the context of the nervous system, vesicle based transfer of ncRNAs could offer an additional dimension of intercellular communication in the nervous system. Such vesicles could mediate signaling between neurons and glia, for example, in response to impending cytotoxicity or other stress events. Thus, the versatility of ncRNA-based information processing provides many still unexplored avenues for function in the nervous system and involvement in the stress responses that lead to addictive maladaptations.

ACKNOWLEDGMENTS

Preparation of this review was supported by NIH grants R01 MH083733 and R01 NS063974.

REFERENCES

1. Alvarez-Saavedra, M., Antoun, G., Yanagiya, A., Oliva-Hernandez, R., Cornejo-Palma, D., Perez-Iratxeta, C., Sonenberg, N., and Cheng, H. Y. (2011). miRNA-132 orchestrates chromatin remodeling and translational control of the circadian clock. *Hum. Mol. Genet.* 20, 731–751.
2. Baek, M. N., Jung, K. H., Halder, D., Choi, M. R., Lee, B. H., Lee, B. C., Jung, M. H., Choi, I. G., Chung, M. K., Oh, D. Y., and Chai, Y. G. (2010). Artificial microRNA-based neurokinin-1 receptor gene silencing reduces alcohol consumption in mice. *Neurosci. Lett.* 475, 124–128.
3. Belgard, T. G., Marques, A. C., Oliver, P. L., Abaan, H. O., Sirey, T. M., Hoerder-Suabedissen, A., Garcia-Moreno, F., Molnar, Z., Margulies, E. H., and Ponting, C. P. (2011). A transcriptomic atlas of mouse neocortical layers. *Neuron* 71, 605–616.
4. Berezikov, E. (2011). Evolution of microRNA diversity and regulation in animals. *Nat. Rev. Genet.* 12, 846–860.
5. Bernard, D., Prasanth, K. V., Tripathi, V., Colasse, S., Nakamura, T., Xuan, Z., Zhang, M. Q., Sedel, F., Jourdren, L., Coulpier, F., Triller, A., Spector, D. L., and Bessis, A. (2010). A long nuclear-retained non-coding RNA regulates synaptogenesis by modulating gene expression. *EMBO J.* 29, 3082–3093.
6. Bitko, V., and Barik, S. (2007). Intranasal antisense therapy: preclinical models with a clinical future? *Curr. Opin. Mol. Ther.* 9, 119–125.
7. Carlezon,W. A. Jr., Thome, J., Olson, V. G., Lane-Ladd, S. B., Brodkin, E. S., Hiroi, N., Duman, R. S., Neve, R. L., and Nestler, E. J. (1998). Regulation of cocaine reward by CREB. *Science* 282, 2272–2275.
8. Chandrasekar, V., and Dreyer, J. L. (2009). microRNAs miR-124, let- 7d and miR-181a regulate cocaineinduced plasticity. *Mol. Cell. Neurosci.* 42, 350–362.
9. Chandrasekar, V., and Dreyer, J. L. (2011). Regulation of MiR-124, Let- 7d, and MiR-181a in the accumbens affects the expression, extinction, and reinstatement of cocaineinduced conditioned place preference. *Neuropsychopharmacology* 36, 1149–1164.
10. Chen, J. F., Mandel, E. M., Thomson, J. M., Wu, Q., Callis, T. E., Hammond, S. M., Conlon, F. L., and Wang, D. Z. (2006). The role of microRNA-1 and microRNA- 133 in skeletal muscle proliferation and differentiation. *Nat. Genet.* 38, 228–233.
11. Cheng, H. Y., Papp, J. W., Varlamova, O., Dziema, H., Russell, B., Curfman, J. P.,Nakazawa, T., Shimizu, K., Okamura, H., Impey, S., and Obrietan, K. (2007). microRNA modulation of circadian-clock period and entrainment. *Neuron* 54, 813–829.
12. Chu, C., Qu, K., Zhong, F. L., Artandi, S. E., and Chang, H. Y. (2011). Genomic maps of long noncoding RNA occupancy reveal principles of RNA-chromatin interactions. *Mol. Cell* 44, 667–678.
13. Cuellar, T. L., Davis, T. H., Nelson, P. T., Loeb, G. B., Harfe, B. D., Ullian, E., and McManus, M. T. (2008). Dicer loss in striatal neurons produces behavioral and neuroanatomical phenotypes in the absence of neurodegeneration. *Proc. Natl. Acad. Sci. U.S.A.* 105, 5614–5619.
14. Dinger, M. E., Mercer, T. R., and Mattick, J. S. (2008). RNAs as extracellular signaling molecules. *J. Mol. Endocrinol.* 40, 151–159.
15. Edbauer, D., Neilson, J. R., Foster, K. A., Wang, C. F., Seeburg,D. P., Batterton, M. N., Tada, T., Dolan, B. M., Sharp, P. A., and Sheng,M. (2010). Regulation of synaptic structure and function by FMRP-associated microRNAs miR-125b and miR-132. *Neuron* 65, 373–384.

16. Eipper-Mains, J. E., Kiraly, D. D., Palakodeti, D., Mains, R. E., Eipper, B. A., and Graveley, B. R. (2011). microRNA-Seq reveals cocaineregulated expression of striatal microRNAs. *RNA* 17, 1529–1543.
17. Fabbri, M., Garzon, R., Cimmino, A., Liu, Z., Zanesi, N., Callegari, E., Liu, S., Alder, H., Costinean, S., Fernandez-Cymering, C.,Volinia, S., Guler, G.,Morrison, C. D., Chan, K. K.,Marcucci, G., Calin, G. A.,Huebner, K., and Croce, C. M. (2007). MicroRNA-29 family reverts aberrant methylation in lung cancer by targeting DNA methyltransferases 3A and 3B. *Proc. Natl. Acad. Sci. U.S.A.* 104, 15805–15810.
18. French, P. J., Bliss, T. V., and O'Connor, V. (2001). Ntab, a novel noncoding RNA abundantly expressed in rat brain. *Neuroscience* 108, 207–215.
19. Gao, J., Wang, W. Y., Mao, Y. W., Graff, J., Guan, J. S., Pan, L., Mak, G., Kim, D., Su, S. C., and Tsai, L. H. (2010). A novel pathway regulates memory and plasticity via SIRT1 and miR-134. *Nature* 466, 1105–1109.
20. Ghitza,U. E., Zhai, H.,Wu,P.,Airavaara, M., Shaham, Y., and Lu, L. (2010). Role of BDNF and GDNF in drug reward and relapse: a review. *Neurosci. Biobehav. Rev.* 35, 157–171.
21. Guo, Y., Chen, Y., Carreon, S., and Qiang, M. (2011). Chronic intermittent ethanol exposure and its removal induce a different mirna expression pattern in primary cortical neuronal cultures. *Alcohol. Clin. Exp. Res.* doi: 10.1111/j.1530- 0277.2011.01689.x. [Epub ahead of print].
22. He, Y., Yang, C., Kirkmire, C. M., and Wang, Z. J. (2010). Regulation of opioid tolerance by let- 7 family microRNA targeting the mu opioid receptor. *J. Neurosci.* 30, 10251–10258.
23. Hiroi, N., Brown, J. R., Haile, C. N., Ye, H., Greenberg, M. E., and Nestler, E. J. (1997). FosB mutant mice: loss of chronic cocaine induction of Fos-related proteins and heightened sensitivity to cocaine's psychomotor and rewarding effects. *Proc. Natl. Acad. Sci. U.S.A.* 94,10397–10402.
24. Hollander, J. A., Im, H. I., Amelio, A. L., Kocerha, J., Bali, P., Lu, Q., Willoughby, D., Wahlestedt, C., Conkright, M. D., and Kenny, P. J. (2010). Striatal microRNA controls cocaine intake through CREB signalling. *Nature* 466, 197–202.
25. Houseley, J., Rubbi, L., Grunstein, M., Tollervey, D., and Vogelauer, M. (2008). A ncRNAmodulates histone modification and mRNA induction in the yeast GAL gene cluster. *Mol. Cell* 32, 685–695.
26. Huang, W., and Li, M. D. (2009a). Differential allelic expression of dopamine D1 receptor gene (DRD1) is modulated by microRNA miR- 504. *Biol. Psychiatry* 65, 702–705.
27. Huang, W., and Li, M. D. (2009b). Nicotine modulates expression of miR-140∗, which targets the 3_- untranslated region of dynamin 1 gene (Dnm1). *Int. J. Neuropsychopharmacol.* 12, 537–546.
28. Hung, G., Mazur, C., Wancewicz, E., Norris, D., and Bennet, F. (2011). *Second Generation Oligonucleotide CNS Delivery via IT Administration in-Mice,Rats andMonkey.* Society for Neuroscience,Washington, 557.06.
29. Hwang, Y. Y., and Li, M. D. (2006). Proteins differentially expressed in response to nicotine in five rat brain regions: identification using a 2- DE/MS-based proteomics approach. *Proteomics* 6, 3138–3153.
30. Im, H. I., Hollander, J. A., Bali, P., and Kenny, P. J. (2010). MeCP2 controls BDNF expression and cocaine intake through homeostatic interactions with microRNA-212. *Nat. Neurosci.* 13, 1120–1127.
31. Jia, H., Osak, M., Bogu, G. K., Stanton, L.W., Johnson, R., and Lipovich, L. (2010). Genome-wide computational identification and manual annotation of human long noncoding RNA genes. *RNA* 16, 1478–1487.
32. Johnson, R., Teh, C. H., Jia, H., Vanisri, R. R., Pandey, T., Lu, Z. H., Buckley, N. J., Stanton, L. W., and Lipovich, L. (2009). Regulation of neural macroRNAs by the transcriptional repressor REST. *RNA* 15, 85–96.
33. Kapranov, P., St Laurent, G., Raz, T., Ozsolak, F., Reynolds, C. P., Sorensen, P. H., Reaman, G., Milos, P., Arceci, R. J., Thompson, J. F., and Triche, T. J. (2010). The majority of total nuclearencoded non-ribosomal RNA in a human cell is "dark matter" unannotated RNA. *BMC Biol.* 8, 149. doi:10.1186/1741-7007-8-149
34. Khalil, A. M., Guttman, M., Huarte, M., Garber, M., Raj, A., Rivea Morales, D., Thomas, K., Presser, A., Bernstein, B. E., van Oudenaarden, A., Regev, A., Lander, E. S., and Rinn, J. L. (2009). Many human large intergenic non-coding RNAs associate with chromatin-modifying complexes and affect gene expression. *Proc. Natl. Acad. Sci. U.S.A.* 106, 11667–11672.
35. Konopka,W.,Kiryk, A.,Novak, M.,Herwerth, M., Parkitna, J. R., Wawrzyniak, M., Kowarsch, A., Michaluk, P., Dzwonek, J., Arnsperger, T., Wilczynski, G., Merkenschlager, M., Theis, F. J., Kohr, G., Kaczmarek, L., and Schutz, G. (2010). MicroRNA loss enhances learning and memory in mice. *J. Neurosci.* 30, 14835–14842.
36. Lagos-Quintana, M., Rauhut, R., Yalcin, A., Meyer, J., Lendeckel, W., and Tuschl, T. (2002). Identification of tissue-specific microRNAs from mouse. *Curr. Biol.* 12, 735–739.
37. LaPlant, Q.,Vialou,V., Covington,H. E. III, Dumitriu, D., Feng, J., Warren, B. L., Maze, I., Dietz, D. M., Watts, E. L., Iñiguez, S. D., Koo, J. W., Mouzon, E., Renthal, W., Hollis, F., Wang, H., Noonan, M. A., Ren, Y., Eisch, A. J., Bolaños, C. A., Kabbaj, M., Xiao, G., Neve, R. L.,Hurd, Y. L., Oosting, R. S., Fan, G., Morrison, J. H., and Nestler, E. J. (2010). Dnmt3a regulates emotional behavior and spine plasticity in the nucleus accumbens. *Nat. Neurosci.* 13, 1137–1143.
38. Lewohl, J. M., Nunez, Y. O., Dodd, P. R., Tiwari, G. R.,Harris, R. A., andMay_field, R. D. (2011). Up-regulation of MicroRNAs in brain of human alcohol_ics. *Alcohol. Clin. Exp. Res.* 35, 1928–1937.
39. Lin, D., Pestova, T. V., Hellen, C. U., and Tiedge, H. (2008). Translational control by a small RNA: dendritic BC1 RNA targets the eukaryotic initiation factor 4A helicase mechanism. *Mol. Cell. Biol.* 28, 3008–3019.
40. Lippi, G., Steinert, J. R., Marczylo, E. L., D'Oro, S., Fiore, R., Forsythe, I. D., Schratt, G., Zoli, M., Nicotera, P., and Young, K. W. (2011). Targeting of the Arpc3 actin nucleation factor by miR-29a/b regulates dendritic spine morphology. *J. Cell Biol.* 194, 889–904.
41. Lugli, G., Torvik, V. I., Larson, J., and Smalheiser, N. R. (2008). Expression of microRNAs and their precursors in synaptic fractions of adult mouse forebrain. *J. Neurochem.* 106, 650–661.
42. Lugli, G., Torvik, V. I., Larson, J., and Smalheiser, N. R. (2008). Expression of microRNAs and their precursors in synaptic fractions of adult mouse fore brain. *J. Neurochem.* 106, 650–661.
43. Mattick, J. S. (2007). A new paradigm for developmental biology. *J. Exp. Biol.* 210, 1526–1547.
44. Maze, I., Covington, H. E. III, Dietz, D. M., LaPlant, Q., Renthal, W., Russo, S. J., Mechanic, M., Mouzon, E., Neve, R. L., Haggarty, S. J., Ren, Y., Sampath, S. C., Hurd, Y. L., Greengard, P., Tarakhovsky, A., Schaefer, A., and Nestler, E. J. (2010). Essential role of the histonemethyltransferase G9a in cocaine-induced plasticity. *Science* 327, 213–216.
45. Maze, I., and Nestler, E. J. (2011). The epigenetic landscape of addiction. *Ann. N. Y. Acad. Sci.* 1216, 99–113.
46. Mercer, T. R., Dinger, M. E., Sunkin, S. M., Mehler, M. F., and Mattick, J. S. (2008). Specific expression of long noncoding RNAs in the mouse brain. *Proc. Natl. Acad. Sci. U.S.A.* 105, 716–721.
47. Mercer, T. R., Qureshi, I. A., Gokhan, S., Dinger, M. E., Li, G., Mattick, J. S., and Mehler, M. F. (2010). Long noncoding RNAs in neuronalglial fate specification and oligodendrocyte lineage maturation. *BMC Neurosci.* 14. doi:10.1186/1471-2202-11-14
48. Michelhaugh, S. K., Lipovich, L., Blythe, J., Jia, H., Kapatos, G., and Bannon, M.J. (2011).MiningAffymetrix microarray data for long noncoding RNAs: altered expression in the nucleus accumbens of heroin abusers. *J.Neurochem.* 116, 459–466. Modarresi, F., Faghihi, M. A., Lopez- Toledano,M. A., Fatemi, R. P.,Magistri, M.,Brothers, S. P., van der Brug, M. P., and Wahlest edt, C. (2012). Inhibition of natural antisense transcripts in vivo results in gene-specific transcriptional upregulation. *Nat. Biotechnol.* 30, 453–459.
49. Nagano, T., Mitchell, J. A., Sanz, L. A., Pauler, F. M., Ferguson-Smith, A. C., Feil, R., and Fraser, P. (2008). The Air noncoding RNA epigenetically silences transcription by targeting G9a to chromatin. *Science* 322, 1717–1720.
50. Nudelman, A. S., DiRocco, D. P., Lambert, T. J., Garelick, M. G., Le, J., Nathan son, N. M., and Storm, D. R. (2010). Neuronal activity rapidly induces transcription of the CREBregulated microRNA-132, in vivo. *Hippocampus* 20, 492–498.
51. Pandey, R. R., Mondal, T., Mohammad, F., Enroth, S., Redrup, L., Komorowski, J., Nagano, T., Mancini-Dinardo, D., and Kanduri, C. (2008). Kcnq1ot1 antisense noncoding RNA mediates lineagespecific transcrip tional silencing through chromatin-level regulation. *Mol. Cell* 32, 232–246.
52. Pietrzykowski, A. Z., Friesen, R. M., Martin, G. E., Puig, S. I., Nowak, C. L., Wynne, P. M., Siegelmann, H. T., and Treistman, S. N. (2008). Posttranscrip tional regulation of BK channel splice variant stability by miR-9 underlies neuroadaptation to alcohol. *Neuron* 59, 274–287.
53. Ponjavic, J., Oliver, P. L., Lunter, G., and Ponting, C. P. (2009). Genomic and transcriptional co-localization of protein-coding and long noncoding RNA pairs in the developing brain. *PLoS Genet.* 5, e1000617. doi:10.1371/journal.pgen.1000617
54. Pulipparacharuvil, S., Renthal,W.,Hale, C. F.,Taniguchi, M.,Xiao, G.,Kumar, A., Russo, S. J., Sikder, D., Dewey, C. M., Davis, M. M., Greengard, P., Nairn, A. C., Nestler, E. J., and Cowan, C. W. (2008). Cocaine regulates MEF2 to control synaptic and behavioral plasticity. *Neuron* 59, 621–633.
55. Rajasethupathy, P., Fiumara, F., Sheridan, R., Betel, D., Puthanveettil, S. V., Russo, J. J., Sander, C., Tuschl, T., and Kandel, E. (2009). Characterization of small RNAs in Aplysia reveals a role for miR- 124 in constraining synaptic plasticity through CREB. *Neuron* 63, 803–817.

56. Rinn, J. L., Kertesz, M., Wang, J. K., Squazzo, S. L., Xu, X., Brugmann, S. A., Goodnough, L. H., Helms, J. A., Farnham, P. J., Segal, E., and Chang, H. Y. (2007). Functional demarcation of active and silent chromatin domains in human HOX loci by noncoding RNAs. *Cell* 129, 1311–1323.
57. Robison, A. J., and Nestler, E. J. (2011). Transcriptional and epigenetic mechanisms of addiction. *Nat. Rev. Neurosci.* 12, 623–637.
58. Saba, R., Storchel,P. H.,Aksoy-Aksel, A., Kepura, F., Lippi, G., Plant,T.D., and Schratt, G. M. (2012). DopamineregulatedMicroRNAMiR- 181a controls GluA2 surface expression in hippocampal neurons. *Mol. Cell. Biol.* 32, 619–632.
59. Salmena, L., Poliseno, L., Tay, Y., Kats, L., and Pandolfi, P. P. (2011). A ceRNAhypothesis: the Rosetta Stone of a hidden RNA language? *Cell* 146, 353–358.
60. Sanchez-Simon, F. M., Zhang, X. X., Loh, H. H., Law, P. Y., and Rodriguez, R. E. (2010). Morphine regulates dopaminergic neuron differentiation via miR- 133b. *Mol. Pharmacol.* 78, 935–942.
61. Schaefer, A., Im, H. I., Veno, M. T., Fowler, C. D., Min, A., Intrator, A., Kjems, J., Kenny, P. J., O'Carroll, D., and Greengard, P. (2010).Argonaute 2 in dopamine 2 receptorexpressing neurons regulates cocaine addiction. *J. Exp. Med.* 207, 1843–1851.
62. Schratt, G. M., Tuebing, F., Nigh, E. A., Kane, C. G., Sabatini, M. E., Kiebler, M., and Greenberg, M. E. (2006). A brain-specific microRNA regulates dendritic spine development. *Nature* 439, 283–289.
63. Sempere, L. F., Cole, C. N., McPeek, M. A., and Peterson, K. J. (2006). The phylogenetic distribution of metazoan microRNAs: insights into evolutionary complexity and constraint. *J. Exp. Zool. B Mol. Dev. Evol.* 306, 575–588.
64. Siegel, G., Obernosterer, G., Fiore, R., Oehmen, M., Bicker, S., Christensen, M., Khudayberdiev, S., Leuschner, P. F., Busch, C. J., Kane, C., Hübel, K., Dekker, F., Hedberg, C., Rengarajan, B., Drepper, C., Waldmann, H., Kauppinen, S., Greenberg, M. E., Draguhn, A., Rehmsmeier, M., Martinez, J., and Schratt, G. M. (2009). A functional screen implicates microRNA-138-dependent regulation of the depalmitoylation enzyme APT1 in dendritic spine morphogenesis. *Nat. Cell Biol.* 11, 705–716.
65. Siegel, G., Saba, R., and Schratt, G. (2011). microRNAs in neurons: manifold regulatory roles at the synapse. *Curr. Opin. Genet. Dev.* 21, 491–497.
66. Simon, M. D.,Wang, C. I., Kharchenko, P. V., West, J. A., Chapman, B. A., Alekseyenko, A. A., Borowsky, M. L., Kuroda, M. I., and Kingston, R. E. (2011). The genomic binding sites of a noncoding RNA. *Proc. Natl. Acad. Sci. U.S.A.* 108, 20497–20502.
67. Smalheiser, N. R. (2007). Exosomal transfer of proteins and RNAs at synapses in the nervous system. *Biol. Direct* 2, 35.
68. Taft, R. J., Pheasant, M., and Mattick, J. S. (2007). The relationship between non-protein-coding DNA and eukaryotic complexity. *Bioessays* 29, 288–299.
69. Tay, Y., Kats, L., Salmena, L., Weiss, D., Tan, S. M., Ala, U., Karreth, F., Poliseno, L., Provero, P., Di Cunto, F., Lieberman, J., Rigoutsos, I., and Pandolfi, P. P. (2011). Coding-independent regulation of the tumor suppressorPTENby competing endogenous mRNAs. *Cell* 147, 344–357.
70. Tilley, M. R., O'Neill, B., Han, D. D., and Gu, H. H. (2009). Cocaine does not produce reward in absence of dopamine transporter inhibition. *Neuroreport* 20, 9–12.
71. Treistman, S. N., and Martin, G. E. (2009). BK Channels: mediators and models for alcohol tolerance. *Trends Neurosci.* 32, 629–637.
72. Wang, K. C., and Chang, H. Y. (2011). Molecular mechanisms of long noncoding RNAs. *Mol. Cell* 43, 904–914.
73. Wang, L., Lv, Z., Hu, Z., Sheng, J., Hui, B., Sun, J., and Ma, L. (2010). Chronic cocaine-induced H3 acetylation and transcriptional activation of CaMKIIalpha in the nucleus accumbens is critical for motivation for drug reinforcement. *Neuropsychopharmacology* 35, 913–928.
74. Wayman, G. A., Davare, M., Ando, H., Fortin, D., Varlamova, O., Cheng, H. Y., Marks, D., Obrietan, K., Soderling, T. R., Goodman, R. H., and Impey, S. (2008). An activityregulated micro RNA controls dendritic plasticity by down-regulating p250GAP. *Proc. Natl. Acad. Sci. U.S.A.* 105, 9093–9098.
75. Wibrand, K., Panja, D., Tiron, A., Ofte, M. L., Skaftnesmo, K. O., Lee, C. S., Pena, J. T., Tuschl, T., and Bramham, C. R. (2010). Differential regulation of mature and precursor micro RNA expression byNMDA and metabotropic glutamate receptor activation during LTP in the adult dentate gyrus in vivo. *Eur. J. Neurosci.* 31, 636–645.
76. Wood, M., Yin, H., and McClorey, G. (2007). Modulating the expression of disease genes with RNAbased therapy. *PLoS Genet.* 3, e109. doi:10.1371/journal.pgen.0030109
77. Wu, Q., Zhang, L., Law, P. Y., Wei, L. N., and Loh, H. H. (2009). Longterm morphine treatment decreases the association of mu-opioid receptor (MOR1) mRNA with polysomes through miRNA23b. *Mol. Pharmacol.* 75, 744–750.
78. Yadav, S., Pandey, A., Shukla, A., Talwelkar, S. S., Kumar, A., Pant, A. B., and Parmar,D. (2011). miR-497 and miR-302b regulate ethanol-induced neuronal cell death through BCL2 protein and cyclin D2. *J. Biol. Chem.* 286, 37347–37357.
79. Yap, K. L., Li, S., Munoz-Cabello, A. M., Raguz, S., Zeng, L., Mujtaba, S., Gil, J., Walsh, M. J., and Zhou, M. M. (2010). Molecular interplay of the noncoding RNA ANRIL and methylated histone H3 lysine 27 by polycomb CBX7 in transcriptional silencing of INK4a. *Mol. Cell* 38, 662–674.
80. Yu,W., Gius,D.,Onyango, P.,Muldoon- Jacobs, K., Karp, J., Feinberg, A. P., and Cui, H. (2008). Epigenetic silencing of tumour suppressor gene p15 by its antisense RNA. *Nature* 451, 202–206.
81. Zhang,Y., Li, J.,Kong, L.,Gao, G., Liu, Q. R., andWei, L. (2007).NATsDB: natural antisense transcripts DataBase. *Nucleic Acids Res.* 35, D156–D161.
82. Zhao, J., Zhang, X., Zhou, Y., Ansell, P. J., and Klibanski, A. (2006). Cyclic AMP stimulates MEG3 gene expression in cells through a cAMPresponse element (CRE) in the MEG3 proximal promoter region. *Int. J. Biochem. Cell Biol.* 38, 1808–1820.
83. Zheng, H., Zeng, Y., Zhang, X., Chu, J., Loh, H. H., and Law, P. Y. (2010). mu-Opioid receptor agonists differentially regulate the expression of miR-190 and NeuroD.*Mol. Pharmacol.* 77, 102–109.

5

The puzzling unidimensionality of DSM-5 substance use disorder diagnoses

Robert J. MacCoun*

Goldman School of Public Policy and Berkeley Law, University of California at Berkeley, Berkeley, CA, USA

Edited by:
Hanna Pickard, University of Oxford, UK

Reviewed by:
Denny Borsboom, University of Amsterdam, Netherlands
Christopher Stephen Martin, University of Pittsburgh, USA

***Correspondence:**
Robert J. MacCoun, Goldman School of Public Policy and Berkeley Law, University of California at Berkeley, 2607 Hearst Avenue, Berkeley, CA 94720-7320, USA
e-mail: maccoun@berkeley.edu

There is a perennial expert debate about the criteria to be included or excluded for the DSM diagnoses of substance use dependence. Yet analysts routinely report evidence for the unidimensionality of the resulting checklist. If in fact the checklist is unidimensional, the experts are wrong that the criteria are distinct, so either the experts are mistaken or the reported unidimensionality is spurious. I argue for the latter position, and suggest that the traditional reflexive measurement model is inappropriate for the DSM; a formative measurement model would be a more accurate characterization of the institutional process by which the checklist is created, and a network or causal model would be a more appropriate foundation for a scientifically grounded diagnostic system.

Keywords: dependence, DSM, diagnosis, psychometrics, addiction

INTRODUCTION

Since the first Diagnostic and Statistical Manual of the American Psychiatric Association (DSM) appeared in 1952, there have been six revisions – roughly one revision every decade [DSM-II in 1968, DSM-III in 1980, DSM-III-R in 1987, DSM-IV in 1994, DSM-IV-TR in 2000, and DSM-5 in 2013; see Ref. (1)]. These manuals provide an evolving checklist of possible indicators of drug abuse and/or drug dependence, some subset of which will trigger a distinct categorical diagnosis. Because these diagnoses are seen as consequential for clinicians, clients, treatment facilities, third-party payers, and for the development of addiction science, the years preceding each revision always see a lively and vigorous debate among experts about which indicators of substance abuse and dependence – e.g., withdrawal, tolerance, cravings, legal problems – do or don't belong in the checklist.

To an outside observer, the process can appear chaotic and as political as it is scientific. But somehow, the resulting checklist seems to have a noteworthy psychometric property. Using popular psychometric methods, it has been argued that the DSM diagnostic criteria for substance dependence (DSM-IV) or a substance use disorder (DSM-5) form a *unidimensional* scale – implying that they are tapping a single, coherent latent construct, either "substance abuse" (for a given substance), "substance dependence," or in the newest iteration, the combined construct "substance use disorder" [e.g., (2–6)].

But there is something odd about this. If indeed the DSM criteria form a unidimensional construct, then there should be little reason to spend years debating specific items to include in the construct. Under the measurement model that characterizes most psychometric analyses of DSM data, these indicators should be roughly interchangeable, in the same way that different items on an attitude scale, vocabulary test, or personality trait inventory tap different manifestations of the same underlying construct. And the corollary observation is that if the criteria that get debated – withdrawal, tolerance, craving, and the like – are indeed conceptually and empirically distinct (as I think they almost certainly are), then the evidence for the unidimensionality of the DSM criteria is perhaps puzzling or even troubling, rather than reassuring.

This essay does not contend the DSM diagnostic criteria are foolish or meaningless, or that adopting them was a serious mistake by some criterion of harm to patients. Rather, I argue that (a) there is confusion about the underlying structure of the DSM substance-related diagnostic criteria, and (b) greater clarity might promote the development of better science, better practice, and better inputs to management and policymaking. These are analytic issues that deserve attention in the coming decade, in anticipation of the eventual next iteration, DSM-6.

DSM-IV AND DSM-5 SUBSTANCE-USE CRITERIA

The DSM-IV (7) distinguished "substance abuse" from "substance dependence," using a checklist of seven criteria for the latter (see **Table 1**). The DSM-IV was described in terms of two dimensions (abuse and dependence), but my comments about it (and its research literature) refer to the claim that the second factor, dependence, was unidimensional. The DSM-5 (1, 8) collapses the distinction between abuse and dependence, and calls for a "substance use disorder" diagnosis, triggered by any two or more of 11 criteria, with six or more indicating a severe case. This decision was apparently based in part on evidence that the abuse items and the dependence items formed a single dimension [e.g., (6)].

ALTERNATIVE PSYCHOMETRIC MODELS FOR LATENT CONSTRUCTS

What would it mean for a list of such criteria to constitute a unidimensional latent construct? There are several alternative psychometric measurement models that can operationalize a latent construct. They quite literally imply different metaphysical

Table 1 | DSM-IV "substance dependence" and DSM-5 "substance use disorder" diagnostic criteria.

Criterion	DSM-IV substance dependence	DSM-5 substance use disorder
Tolerance	✓	✓
Withdrawal	✓	✓
Taken more/longer than intended	✓	✓
Desire/unsuccessful efforts to quit use	✓	✓
Great deal of time taken by activities involved in use	✓	✓
Use despite knowledge of problems associated with use	✓	✓
Important activities given up because of use	✓	✓
Recurrent use resulting in a failure to fulfill important role obligations		✓
Recurrent use resulting in physically hazardous behavior (e.g., driving)		✓
Continued use despite recurrent social problems associated with use		✓
Craving for the substance		✓

assumptions – ontologically, what construct exists, and epistemologically, how to do we identify it? – but also different mathematical definitions. The discussion that follows gets slightly technical, and requires a few simple equations, but to keep things simple I assume there is only one latent construct (e.g., "dependence") and that the terms in the model have unit weights (i.e., $w_i = 1$ so that $w_i X_i = X_i$).

REFLECTIVE MODELS

Traditional factor-analytic models (whether exploratory or confirmatory) are usually specified mathematically as a set of structural equations of the form $X_i = F + e_i$, where each X is one of i observed or "manifest" variables (e.g., test items or diagnostic criteria), and F is the underlying latent construct thought to cause each X to take on its observed values [e.g., (9–11)]. Importantly, the e terms reflect any idiosyncratic variance associated with the observed variables but not caused by the underlying latent construct of interest. This has an important implication; if any two observed variables share a common latent factor, it is assumed that these variables share nothing systematic in common other than that factor – they are "conditionally independent" unless the default assumption of uncorrelated error terms is explicitly overridden. Any model with these features is now commonly referred to as a "reflective model" (10). The reflective model (see **Figure 1A**) is a method of constructing unidimensional composite scales and justifying their interpretation as such.

The most common theoretical justification for this interpretation is the *domain sampling* assumption that the observed variables we retain as indicators of the latent construct are essentially interchangeable exemplars sampled arbitrarily from a much larger domain of possible expressions of the construct. "The model of domain sampling conceives of a trait as being a group of behaviors all of which have some property in common. . . .If the sample [of indicators] we draw from domain is representative, than its statistical characteristics are the same as those of the total domain" [(11), p. 211–212]. Specifically, in expectation any sufficiently large random sample of indicators from the domain should yield the same average value, and the same correlations among indicators. This notion of sampling is of course hypothetical, not literal, and that creates an important conceptual twist: "Instead of specifying a population of some set of entities and then drawing a sample randomly from it, . . . we have a sample in hand that in turn *implies* a population . . . having the same characteristics as the sample" [(11), 214 p.].

Most of the published psychometric analyses of DSM criteria that I have examined adopt the reflective model of factor analysis, without explicit justification. But this creates an unacknowledged conceptual puzzle: according to that model, any differences between two criteria – say, withdrawal symptoms vs. interference with important activities – are simply part of the error structure of the model rather than the construct itself, or its composite score. In other words, the distinctive features of each criteria that form the basis for expert debates about DSM construction are actually irrelevant to the model. Under the domain sampling assumption, there should be relatively little to argue about; we can inductively generate large sets of candidate criteria and simply cull out the ones that don't "load" on the common factor (This is basically how intelligence tests are constructed.). I very much doubt this is how most DSM experts view the diagnostic criterion list, yet this is how the analyses treat it.

FORMATIVE MODELS

There is a less familiar alternative way of specifying a latent factor model – the "formative model" [**Figure 1B**; see Ref. (9, 10)]. This model is superficially similar – it consists of the same observed indicator variables, plus one or more latent factors, and an error term. But the assumptions are quite different. In a formative model, the latent factor does not cause the observed variables; rather, they cause – or more accurately, "constitute" – the latent factor. Mathematically, the model would be represented by an equation of the form $F = \Sigma X_i + e$ but F is now the dependent variable, and there is a single error term for the factor, rather error terms for each observed variable (X). That means that anything distinctive or idiosyncratic that distinguishes two observed variables – say, withdrawal symptoms vs. interference with important activities – is part of the construct and its measurement. As a result, formative models are not assumed to be "unidimensional" and indeed, some heterogeneity among the criteria is seen as desirable.

Formative models are not inductive, at least not in the sense that a latent construct emerges from the observed variance of a reflective model. Rather, formative models are a form of "measurement by fiat." The analyst, or some other authority, decrees that certain observable criteria will collectively constitute what the latent construct actually means. An example is professional accreditation (constituted by education, degree, years of experience, a passing exam score).

A formative model seems to better capture the way many psychiatrists actually debate the DSM criteria, and it also better

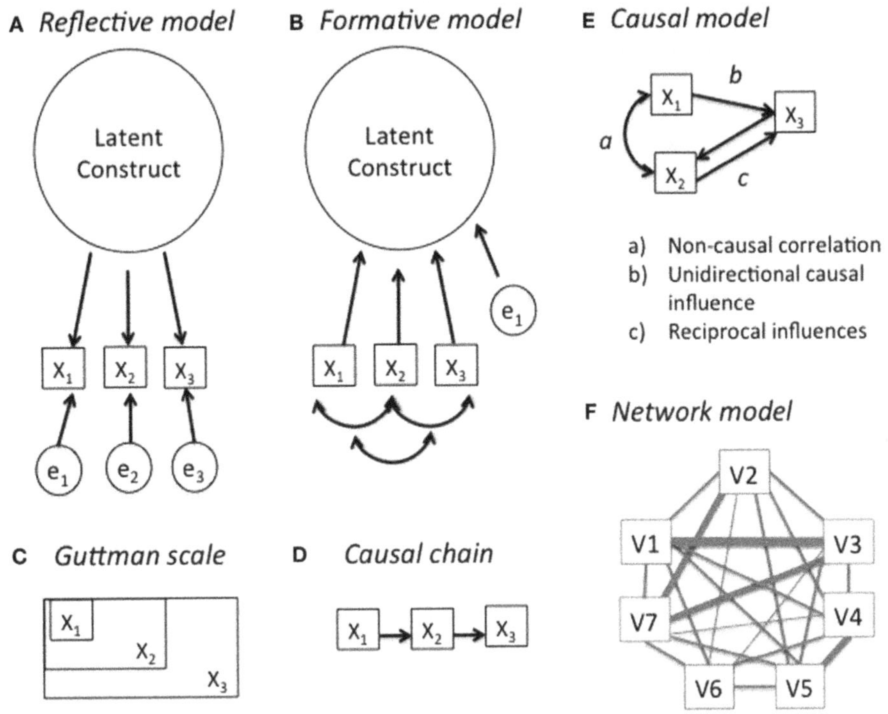

FIGURE 1 | Alternative theoretical models for interpreting a latent construct. **(A)** reflective model, **(B)** formative model, **(C)** Guttman scale, **(D)** causal chain, **(E)** causal model, and **(F)** network model.

characterizes the actual decision process – organizational fiat – that determines which criteria are included vs. excluded. But a growing number of simulation studies show that when data actually have a formative structure, fitting them using reflective models can lead to significantly biased and misleading estimates of model fit and factor scores [e.g., (13)]. Whether this helps to explain the puzzle I noted earlier – high unidimensionality despite what are surely conceptually distinct DSM criteria – would probably require focused re-analysis of major DSM data sets[1].

A GUTTMAN SCALE?

There is, however, an alternative psychometric model that might produce unidimensionality despite conceptually distinct measures – a Guttman scale [or a stochastic variant, the Mokken scale; see Ref. (16)]. As suggested by **Figure 1C**, the variables in a Guttman scale have a cumulative structure. An example might be a diagnosis of AIDS; anyone who has the disease AIDS is infected with HIV, and anyone who is infected with HIV was exposed to HIV at some earlier date when they were still HIV-negative. Thus if we determine that someone is HIV-positive, we can conclude that they were exposed to HIV, but we cannot conclude that they have AIDS or will necessarily have AIDS in the future. Like formative models, Guttman scales can emerge by fiat: with rare exceptions, we decree that those with a Ph.D. must have a Bachelors Degree, and that those with Bachelors Degree must have completed high school. Alternatively Guttman-scaled phenomena can emerge through a chain of causal processes (see **Figure 1D**) that occur in a consistent order.

If the DSM criteria formed a clear Guttman scale, this might provide a tidy resolution to the puzzle noted at the outset – the fact that psychiatrists argue over the *distinct* features of DSM criteria and yet claim that the DSM provides a *unidimensional* diagnosis of substance use disorder. But the empirical literature is not encouraging. I have only been able to locate two studies that test whether the DSM substance-use criteria form a Guttman scale. Kosten et al. (5) computed Guttman scale scores using DSM-III-R criteria for each of seven substance classes for 83 psychiatric patients. Carroll et al. (2) followed the same procedures using DSM-IV criteria for six substance classes for 521 people drawn from a variety of different clinical and general population sources. Across four substance classes, the Guttman reproducibility coefficients averaged 0.89 for the DSM-III-R study and 0.80 for the DSM-IV study. Common benchmarks for this coefficient are 0.85 or 0.90; diagnoses met the lower standard in both studies for alcohol, cocaine, and the opiates, but not for sedatives, stimulants, or marijuana. More troublingly, if we limit the focus to four criteria that are roughly the same in both version of the DSM – withdrawal, tolerance, "giving up activities," and "use despite problems" – their relative rankings within a given substance category are inconsistent across the two studies, with correlations ranging from −0.57 to 0.11 (mean $r = -0.20$). Granted, some differences are expected due to differences in year and sample, but it is difficult to see anything like a coherent

[1]An additional explanation for unidimensionality might be rater bias due to shared mental prototypes of dependence among clinicians [compare Ref. (14, 15)].

Guttman measurement model either within or across substance categories.

Another source of evidence comes from comparisons of the prevalence of each criterion, by substance, in different studies. If the criteria come close to forming a Guttman scale, then different studies should find a similar ordering, with the prevalence of some criteria (those near the low end of the scale) being consistently higher than other criteria (those near the high end of the scale). I compared prevalence estimates from three samples (2, 3, 4, 6). The average correlations of the criterion ranks across studies were only 0.54, 0.32, and 0.25 for cannabis, opiates, and cocaine, respectively.

CAUSAL MODELS AND NETWORK MODELS

One reason why items have Guttman scale properties is if they have form a simple causal chain (**Figure 1F**), but the evidence against a Guttman scale interpretation, reviewed above, also casts doubt on any simple causal model. **Figure 1E** shows a causal model that is more complex than a simple causal chain. Even a cursory examination of the DSM substance-use criteria suggests that they might have this kind of complex internal causal structure. First, many of the criteria require the clinician or the patient to make causal attributions: e.g., "Recurrent use *resulting in* a failure to fulfill important role obligations" or "continued use despite recurrent social problems *associated with* use" (italics added for emphasis).

Second, many of the criteria are likely to have causal linkages to each other. For example, tolerance implies that the user will seek larger doses, which might well increase the time taken to obtain the drug will increase. Withdrawal symptoms and craving have long been implicated in income-generating crime, needle sharing, prostitution, and other forms of physically hazardous and socially dysfunctional behavior [e.g., (17–19)].

Third, in addition to any psychopharmacological mechanisms, most of the criteria are causally influenced by the social, cultural, economic, and legal context in which substance use takes place [see Ref. (20)]. A striking illustration comes from clinical trials for heroin maintenance in Europe (21); when registered addicts are allowed easy access to high-quality heroin, their criminality drops, their health improves, and they are increasingly like to hold a job. But most clients do not quit using; on the contrary, many significantly increase their daily dose, so the intervention reduces their disorder on some criteria while possibly increasing their disorder by other criteria.

Figure 1F, reproduced from Cramer et al. (12), illustrates the kind of elaborate causal network that Borsboom, Kendler, and their colleagues have recently proposed as a more realistic model for many traits. In their framework, latent constructs neither cause observed manifestations (as in a reflective model) nor does an explicit subset of observed variables constitute the latent construct (as in a formative model). Rather, the latent construct is an emergent property of the entire network. An implication of the causal structure in **Figures 1E,F** is even when simple 1-factor models fit the data, the fit may be spurious in that the model assumed by the equations may be very different than the model that validly describes the processes that generated the data. Moreover, combining them in an "any two of the following" recipe will obscure the valuable information contained in that causal structure.

DISCUSSION

Judging from past experience, we might expect the next DSM (DSM-6) to surface in about a decade. So in the spirit of constant improvement, I respectfully urge DSM developers to consider pursuing, in parallel, at least three kinds of alternative DSM candidates: a pure reflective model, a pure formative model, and a pure causal network model. One of the three may emerge as superior. But diagnostic systems attempt to serve multiple goals, and it may be advantageous to use different systems for different purposes.

These arguments for greater theoretical and psychometric coherence might seem to have a sort of ivory-tower fastidiousness, if not outright neuroticism. After all, the perfect is surely the enemy of the good, and the DSM does a good job much of the time, at least as judged by the utility that clinicians and managed care organizations seem to find in it.

But I think there are good practical reasons for improving the coherence of the DSM substance use. One is that it might provide a better linkage to drug *policy*. A decade ago, I argued that contemporary thinking about addiction was surprisingly inconsequential for major public policy debates about drug use, or for empirical drug policy analysis (22). The DSM-5 probably helps to close that gap, as it emphasizes the harmful consequences that citizens care about. On the other hand, the gap between the DSM and drug *science* may be growing rather than shrinking. For example, a recent review of seven major scientific theories of drug addiction (23) examines whether each theory can account for various "addictive phenomena." Of the seven theories, four offer an account of withdrawal and three an account of tolerance – two explicit DSM criteria. Six offer accounts of relapse, and four an account of binging – two phenomena that aren't directly mentioned in the DSM but are closely related to other DSM criteria. But all seven offer accounts of craving, a criterion that only recently entered the DSM checklist. And four address "sensitization" – which is increasingly recognized as a signature feature of the etiology of addiction but receives no mention in the DSM.

Kosten et al. (5) attribute the unidimensional aspiration behind the DSM to a published WHO memorandum by Edwards (24). Three decades later, that memorandum is still a remarkably insightful analysis. But my reading of it is different than of Kosten et al. While Edwards et al. did argue for a *dimensional* account of dependence, they explicitly rejected the notion that it should be *unidimensional*. Edwards et al. [(24), 233 p.] argue that "what the present model would seem to propose is that a clinical or an operational definition of dependence must be multidimensional and, in terms of measurements, related to a number of phenomena within the syndrome." And the picture they offered very much seems to anticipate the kind of causal network model that Cramer et al. (9, 12) are developing:

> We believe that a system or syndrome model that seeks to take into account of the interaction between drug, person, and environment, is much to be preferred. Any interpretation that places too much emphasis on only one part of the whole system is imperfect and misleading." [(24), 232 p.].

This essay does not even begin to sketch out what a superior diagnostic system might look like; I don't even pretend to know. But I am not calling for the abandonment of the DSM-5, or even a change in the list of indicators currently in use. Rather, I am suggesting that we need a better understanding of what the patterns of covariance in DSM data actually mean. If tolerance and withdrawal and craving and psychosocial dysfunction and the other DSM criteria are distinct concepts – and I think they clearly are – why should we expect them to form a single dimension? A system that took seriously their conceptual distinctiveness would facilitate a better understanding of the causal structure that may well link them together. And a system that articulated that causal structure might improve our ability to protect high-risk clients before their problems become severe, and to more closely link treatment decisions to theory and measurement.

REFERENCES

1. American Psychiatric Association. *Diagnostic and Statistical Manual of Mental Disorders, Fifth edition.* Arlington, VA: American Psychiatric Publishing (2013).
2. Carroll KM, Rounsaville BJ, Bryant KJ. Should tolerance and withdrawal be required for substance dependence disorders? *Drug Alcohol Depend* (1994) **36**:15–22. doi:10.1016/0376-8716(94)90004-3
3. Compton WM, Saha TD, Conway KP, Grant BF. The role of cannabis use within a dimensional approach to cannabis use disorders. *Drug Alcohol Depend* (2009) **100**:221–7. doi:10.1016/j.drugalcdep.2008.10.009
4. Hasin DS, Fenton MC, Beseler C, Park JY, Wall MM. Analyses related to the development of DSM-5 criteria for substance use related disorders: 2. Proposed DSM-5 criteria for alcohol, cannabis, cocaine and heroin disorders in 663 substance abuse patients. *Drug Alcohol Depend* (2012) **122**:28–37. doi:10.1016/j.drugalcdep.2011.09.005
5. Kosten TR, Rounsaville BJ, Babor TF, Spitzer RL, Williams JBW. Substance use disorders in DSM-III-R: evidence for the dependence syndrome across different psychoactive substances. *Br J Psychiatry* (1987) **151**:834–43. doi:10.1192/bjp.151.6.834
6. Saha TD, Compton WM, Chou SP, Smith S, Ruan WJ, Huang B, et al. Analyses related to the development of DSM-5 criteria for substance use related disorders: 1. Toward amphetamine, cocaine and prescription drug use disorder continua using Item Response Theory. *Drug Alcohol Depend* (2012) **122**:38–46. doi:10.1016/j.drugalcdep.2011.09.004
7. American Psychiatric Association. *Diagnostic and Statistical Manual of Mental Disorders: DSM-IV.* Washington, DC: American Psychiatric Association (1994).
8. Compton WM, Dawson DA, Goldstein RB, Grant BF. Crosswalk between DSM-IV dependence and DSM-5 substance use disorders for opioids, cannabis, cocaine and alcohol. *Drug Alcohol Depend* (2013) **132**:387–90. doi:10.1016/j.drugalcdep.2013.02.036
9. Borsboom D, Mellenbergh GJ, van Heerden J. The theoretical status of latent variables. *Psychol Rev* (2003) **110**:203–19. doi:10.1037/0033-295X.110.2.203
10. Edwards JR, Bagozzi RP. On the nature and direction of the relationship between constructs and measures. *Psychol Methods* (2000) **5**:155–74. doi:10.1002/pon.1427
11. Ghiselli EE, Campbell JP, Zedeck S. *Measurement Theory for the Behavioral Sciences.* San Francisco: W. H. Freeman (1981).
12. Cramer AO, van der Sluis S, Noordhof A, Wichers M, Geschwind N, Aggen SH, et al. Dimensions of normal personality as networks in search of equilibrium: you can't like parties if you don't like people. *Eur J Pers* (2012) **26**:414–31. doi:10.1002/per.1866
13. Petter S, Straub D, Rai A. Specifying formative constructs in information systems research. *MIS Quart* (2007) **31**:623–56.
14. Dawes R, Faust D, Meehl PE. Clinical vs. actuarial judgment. *Science* (1989) **243**:1668–74. doi:10.1126/science.2648573
15. Westen D, Weinberger J. When clinical description becomes statistical prediction. *Am Psychol* (2004) **59**:595–613. doi:10.1037/0003-066X.59.7.595
16. Van Schuur WH. Mokken scale analysis: Between the Guttman scale and parametric item response theory. *Polit Analysis* (2003) **11**:139–63. doi:10.1093/pan/mpg002
17. Booth RE, Kwiatkowski CF, Chitwood DD. Sex-related risk behaviors: differential risk among injection drug users, crack smokers and injection drug users who smoke crack. *Drug Alcohol Depend* (2000) **58**:219–26. doi:10.1016/S0376-8716(99)00094-0
18. Gossop M, Marsden M, Stewart D, Rolfe A. Reductions in acquisitive crime and drug use after treatment of addiction problems: 1 year follow-up outcomes. *Drug Alcohol Depend* (2000) **58**:165–72. doi:10.1016/S0376-8716(99)00077-0
19. MacCoun RJ, Kilmer B, Reuter P. Research on drug-crime linkages: the next generation. *Toward a Drugs and Crime Research Agenda for the 21st Century* Washington DC: National Institute of Justice (2003). p. 65–95. Special Report (NCJ 194616).
20. MacCoun RJ, Reuter P, Schelling T. Assessing alternative drug control regimes. *J Policy Anal Manage* (1996) **15**:1–23.
21. Reuter P, MacCoun RJ. Heroin maintenance: is a U.S. experiment needed? In: Musto D, editor. *One Hundred Years of Heroin.* Westport, CT: Greenwood (2002). p. 159–80.
22. MacCoun RJ. Is the addiction concept useful for drug policy? In: Vuchinich R, Heather N, editors. *Choice, Behavioural Economics and Addiction.* Oxford: Elsevier Science (2003). p. 355–73.
23. Newlin DB, Regalia PA, Seidman TI, Bobashev G. Control theory and addictive behavior. In: Gutkin B, Ahmed SH, editors. *Computational Neuroscience of Drug Addiction.* New York: Springer Verlag (2012). p. 57–108.
24. Edwards G, Arif A, Hodgson R. Nomenclature and classification of drug- and alcohol-related problems: a WHO memorandum. *Bull World Health Organ* (1981) **51**:225–42.

6

The role of study and work in cannabis use and dependence trajectories among young adult frequent cannabis users

Nienke Liebregts[1]*, Peggy van der Pol[2], Margriet Van Laar[2], Ron de Graaf[2], Wim van den Brink[3] and Dirk J. Korf[1]

[1] *Law Faculty, Bonger Institute of Criminology, University of Amsterdam, Amsterdam, Netherlands*
[2] *Trimbos Institute, Netherlands Institute of Mental Health and Addiction, Utrecht, Netherlands*
[3] *Department of Psychiatry, Academic Medical Centre, University of Amsterdam, Amsterdam, Netherlands*

Edited by:
Richard Hammersley, University of Hull, UK

Reviewed by:
Giovanni Martinotti, Catholic University of Rome, Italy
Aviv M. Weinstein, Bristol University, UK

*Correspondence:
Nienke Liebregts, Law Faculty, Bonger Institute of Criminology, University of Amsterdam, P.O. Box 1030, 1000 BA Amsterdam, Netherlands
e-mail: n.liebregts@uva.nl

Life course theory considers events in study and work as potential turning points in deviance, including illicit drug use. This qualitative study explores the role of occupational life in cannabis use and dependence in young adults. Two and three years after the initial structured interview, 47 at baseline frequent cannabis users were interviewed in-depth about the dynamics underlying changes in their cannabis use and dependence. Overall, cannabis use and dependence declined, including interviewees who quit using cannabis completely, in particular with students, both during their study and after they got employed. Life course theory appeared to be a useful framework to explore how and why occupational life is related to cannabis use and dependence over time. Our study showed that life events in this realm are rather common in young adults and can have a strong impact on cannabis use. While sometimes changes in use are temporary, turning points can evolve from changes in educational and employment situations; an effect that seems to be related to the consequences of these changes in terms of amount of leisure time and agency (i.e., feelings of being in control).

Keywords: frequent cannabis use, cannabis dependence, young adults, qualitative research, life course approach, longitudinal study, education, employment

INTRODUCTION

Cannabis is among the most widely used illicit drugs worldwide, with between 125 and 203 million last-year users worldwide (1). In the US approximately five million persons use cannabis on a (almost) daily basis (2), and in the European Union an estimated three million individuals are (almost) daily cannabis users, most of whom are aged 15–34 years (3). Frequent (daily or nearly daily) cannabis use and particularly cannabis dependence are associated with various mental health problems and impaired functioning (4–8).

Associations between cannabis use, education, and employment have been extensively studied. Longitudinal research has shown that adolescent cannabis use is related to poor educational performance and early school dropout (9); degree attainment and university attendance (10); and reduced occupational expectations, attainment, and stability (11). A review on young adult substance use concluded that many risk and protective factors for adolescents remain for young adults, but, given the changing social contexts, factors such as college attendance and job attainment are specific for young adults (12). Regarding later life outcomes, adolescent cannabis use is related to lower income and higher unemployment in young adulthood (5). Adult past year cannabis users are more likely to quit their job to take another job, to be unemployed between jobs and to have lower levels of employment than non-past year users, including never users (13). French et al. (14) found that weekly or more frequent cannabis use was negatively related to employment, but less frequent use was not. In a longitudinal Norwegian study, cannabis users (use at least once in the past 12 months) reported lower levels of work commitment than less frequent users, regardless of individual characteristics (15). More generally, Arria et al. (11) showed that persistent drug users (at least once in every year studied) were more likely to be unemployed than non-users, and that part-time workers were more likely than full-timers to be drug dependent. Finally, Reed et al. (16) found that high job strains and low job control increased the risk on drug dependence. Together these findings suggest the presence of a reciprocal relationship between (changes in) occupational activities and (changes in) drug use and dependence, with changes in occupational activities leading to changes in drug use/dependence and changes in drug use leading to changes in occupational activities. However, little is known about the mechanisms responsible for these changes. One classical possible mechanism that could underlie this relationship is the "amotivational syndrome," as it has been proposed that heavy cannabis use would cause (temporary) cognitive impairment including diminished motivation and memory, lack of interest, and concentration problems. However, these symptoms may as well be an outcome of other factors, such as depression, and no clear evidence until now supports this association (9, 17, 18).

Life course theory considers transitions such as changes in education and work as potential turning points in explaining desistance from deviance (19). Turning points are preceded by life events, which can be abrupt or gradual. Abrupt life events make sudden, sharp distinctions between past and future. Most events, however, are more gradual, and are part of a process. Life events could (objectively) be categorized as positive or negative, but their (subjective) meaning as positive or negative depends on how they are evaluated by the person experiencing them (19). Consequently, similar events can have different meanings for different individuals. When life events lead to a lasting change over time or a redirection of an individual's course of life, including changes in deviance, they are considered turning points (20). Thus, turning points can only be identified in retrospect (21, 22). In life course theory, changes in deviance over the life course are explained within the context of age and maturation: most deviant behaviors peak in adolescence and young adulthood and then decline (19, 23). Employment has the potential to decrease deviance, because strong ties with work and informal social control could get an individual's life (back) on track; not the job *per se*, but the commitment and stability associated with work can reduce deviance (19). Also, employment limits one's time, thereby practically reducing opportunities for deviant activities (23).

Other researchers have emphasized the role of personal factors, such as "agency" in life events and desistance [cf. (24)]. In short, human agency refers to free will and (feelings of) control over one's life, and contributes to how life events are experienced and might change into a turning point (20, 24). When using the concept of agency in this study, we follow Teruya and Hser (20), who defined it as "the amount of personal choice and control over decision making individuals feel they have," and that "shapes their perceptions and the outcomes of life events and transitions and may contribute to the differential effects that the same life event may have on different people." [(20) p. 4].

Although life course theory often concerns criminal careers and desistance from crime, we assume that it also applies to cannabis use careers, since largely similar processes are involved [cf. (25)]. Life events thus can become turning points when redirecting an individual's path in substance use or dependence. In life course theory, employment, especially stable employment, is considered as one of the factors most commonly associated with desistance. The potential of employment to become a turning point is influenced by job characteristics and human agency (16, 20, 24).

Several of the earlier studies on drug use, education, and employment refer to any use in the last 12 months, which could range from only once to daily use. Consequently, it remains unclear to what extent frequent drug use, including cannabis use, is related to study and work. Probably more important is the need to better understand how and why frequent young adult cannabis users change their use, how these changes are related to transitions in and out of cannabis dependence, and how these changes and transitions are related to changes in study and occupational activities. Employment trajectories can have turning points with an impact on cannabis use and dependence, but cannabis use can also influence employment (26). To better understand the natural course of frequent cannabis use of young adults and the relation with education and work, our objectives in the current study are (1) to explore in-depth the meaning and role of education and work in using cannabis in general; (2) to analyze the relationship between events in these domains and changes in cannabis use; and (3) to analyze the role of occupational events in changes in cannabis dependence trajectories. We decided to use a qualitative approach, because the dynamics and the processes underlying the relationship of educational and work with cannabis use and dependence trajectories cannot be adequately addressed with quantitative methods and because personal narratives and in-depth interviews are deemed to improve our understanding of the processes and the context involved with these changes. This study is among the first to qualitatively capture the natural course and transitions in frequent cannabis use and dependence in young adults.

MATERIALS AND METHODS

STUDY DESIGN

The current (qualitative) study is part of a broader longitudinal study (CanDep) on cannabis use and transitions in cannabis dependence in young adult frequent cannabis users [see for details (27)]. **Figure 1** displays an overview of the different (quantitative and qualitative) interviews in the study. In brief, at baseline (T0, September 2008–April 2009) 600 frequent Dutch cannabis users (>3 days cannabis use per week in the past 12 months) aged 18–30 years were recruited in coffee shops and through respondent-driven sampling and interviewed [see for details (28)]. Participants were monitored for 3 years, with two follow-up interviews and six intermediate updates by e-mail or phone. At T0, DSM-IV diagnoses of 12-month cannabis dependence were assessed with the Composite International Diagnostic Interview (CIDI 3.0). After 18 months (T1, March–November 2010) and 36 months (T2, September 2011–March 2012) participants were interviewed again, including an assessment of their cannabis dependence status since the previous interview. At T1, four trajectories in cannabis dependence were distinguished: persistent non-dependent, persistent dependent, transition from dependent to non-dependent, and transition from non-dependent to dependent. At T2 the number of trajectories extended to eight.

In an additional qualitative sub-study, the dynamics underlying the changes in cannabis use and the transitions in cannabis dependence were investigated with special emphasis on study and occupational changes. We conducted life story interviews, in which users can express themselves through their narratives and thereby can improve our understanding of the processes and the context involved in these changes [cf. (24, 29, 30)].

From each of the four trajectories at T1, 12 participants were randomly selected, stratified for gender (8 male, 4 female), totaling 48 interviewees. At T2, these interviewees represented seven trajectories (**Table 1**). The first qualitative interview (I1) took place between December 2010 and April 2011, the second (I2) in March and April 2012. One participant could not be traced back at I2 and was excluded from the analysis, thus resulting in a final sample of 47 participants. While 47 participants is a small sample size for quantitative research methods, for qualitative methods this is not the case and a "small" sample size is considered more powerful in order to achieve depth [cf. (31, 32)].

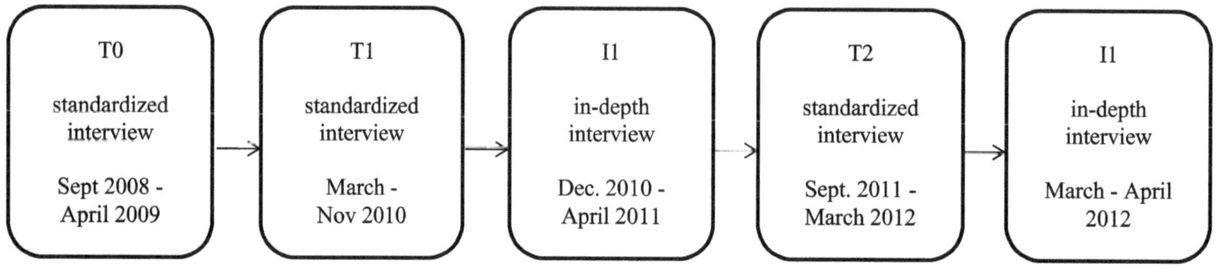

FIGURE 1 | Timeline of CanDep data collection.

Table 1 | Transitions in cannabis dependence status T0–T1–T2 and trajectory characteristics.

Cannabis dependence trajectory	*n*	T0	T1	T2	Age T0 (mean)	Age first use (mean)	Cannabis career T0 (mean years)	(Near) daily use T0	(Near) daily use T2	Female
NNN	12	Non-dependent	Non-dependent	Non-dependent	21.8	14.4	7.4	6	3	4
NDN	7	Non-dependent	Dependent	Non-dependent	20.4	14.3	6.1	4	5	2
NDD	4	Non-dependent	Dependent	Dependent	20.5	14.2	6.2	3	2	2
DNN	10	Dependent	Non-dependent	Non-dependent	21.2	13.4	7.8	7	3	3
DND	2	Dependent	Non-dependent	Dependent	22.5	14.0	8.5	1	1	1
DDN	5	Dependent	Dependent	Non-dependent	19.8	13.4	6.4	3	2	1
DDD	7	Dependent	Dependent	Dependent	22.4	15.0	7.4	5	4	3
Total	47				21.3	14.1	7.1	29	20	16

IN-DEPTH INTERVIEWS

We conducted in-depth interviews, using a topic list that included questions about participants' cannabis use career, i.e., changes in patterns of cannabis use, motives for change in cannabis use, and the occurrence of life events in various life domains. Interviewees were asked to recall changes in different life domains and in their cannabis use patterns between T0 and T1 and between T1 and T2, respectively, using detailed personal timelines [cf. (33, 34)]. One timeline referred to their cannabis use (including frequency and number of joints per occasion), the other timeline to life domains (including occupational life, i.e., education and employment). Both timelines were prepared before the interview and included data derived from the quantitative interviews and intermediate updates, which included questions about their cannabis use and occupational status (i.e., study and work). During the interviews these timelines were used as guidelines and elaborated in detail. Every interview started with an open question ["Thinking about your life between …. (T0 or T1) and … (T1 or T2), what has happened and what experiences have been important to you?"], and ended with a similar, but slightly different question ["Looking back at the period between … (T0 or T1) and … (T1 or T2), what experiences or processes do you consider to have had a (positive or negative) impact on your life and cannabis use?"]. While in the first in-depth interview (I1) participants' entire cannabis career and life history until baseline (T0) were discussed, the focus in both in-depth interviews (I1 and I2) was on the period between the standardized interviews (T0–T1 and T1–T2 respectively). The study was approved by a Medical Ethics Committee. All participants provided written informed consent at the start of the study, acknowledging that their participation was voluntary. They all were assured that the interviews were confident and data was kept safe, separated from any personal information and that anonymity was guaranteed. Interviews took place at a quiet location; mostly at participants' home and sometimes at the research institute. The interviews lasted between 1.5 and 3.5 h. After completion, participants received a financial compensation of €25.

ANALYSIS

All interviews were digitally recorded (with participant's consent), transcribed verbatim, and imported into QSR Nvivo. Transcripts were analyzed combining deductive and inductive strategies. Codes and categories were partly developed beforehand, based on the literature [*a priori* coding: (35)]. In addition, new codes and categories evolved from the data, and new patterns emerged. Interview transcripts were read and reread to identify and link evolving codes, categories, and themes [pattern coding: (35)]. To guarantee anonymity, interviewees were identified with fictitious names and sometimes quotations were slightly adapted.

RESULTS

PARTICIPANTS

Age of participants at baseline ranged from 18 to 30 years (**Table 1**). One third was female (by selection). Age at first use varied from 11 to 18 years (mean = 14 years).

At baseline, the length of cannabis use careers ranged from 1 to 15 years (mean = 7 years), for some with intervals of no use.

At baseline (T0), 29 participants were (near) daily users (5–7 days per week) and the remaining 18 participants used on 3–4 days per week. During the study there was an overall decline in cannabis use frequency. At T2, 20 participants were (near)daily users, 19 participants used at least three times a week but not (near)daily, 3 participants had not used cannabis for 1 year or more and said they had quit permanently, and in the 5 remaining participants cannabis use varied from 1 day per week to less than monthly, including 3 participants who basically considered themselves as quitters, and had been using cannabis only a few times in the past year. Also quantity of cannabis used decreased, from on average 2.9 joints per using day at T0 to 2.4 at T2 (excluding three non-past year users). At T0, 24 participants were last-year cannabis dependent and 23 participants were non-dependent. At T2 this had changed to 13 dependent and 34 non-dependent participants. At baseline dependent and non-dependent interviewees were rather similar concerning mean age at initiation, mean age at baseline, gender and (near)daily use. At T2 cannabis dependent interviewees were more frequently (near)daily users than non-dependent participants, but also in NDN many participants were using (near)daily. Besides, relatively more females than males were dependent at T2.

EDUCATION, EMPLOYMENT, AND COMMITMENT

Regarding occupational status, three categories were distinguished: students, employed and neither student nor employed. At baseline, almost two-thirds of the participants (31/47) were fulltime students. At the time of the last in-depth interview some had stopped studying without a qualification, some had graduated, but most (24) were still studying. Type of study varied from a vocational training to academic studies. Most students had a job on the side; some regularly 3 days a week, others every now and then when they felt in need of money. The most popular job among these students was working in cafes or restaurants. At baseline, about a quarter of the interviewees (11/47) were in paid fulltime employment (32 or more hours weekly). At T2 more than one third was employed (18/47), all but one fulltime. By then, some interviewees still worked at the same company, and sometimes had been promoted, while others had switched work several times during these 3 years. The growing number of employed participants is partly explained by participants graduating and then starting their job career, and partly by participants quitting their study unfinished and getting employed. The employment sectors were diverse, for example some worked in bars, others in academic professions. In the course of the study, one participant became unemployed at T2. At T0, the remaining five interviewees were neither student nor employed: three defined themselves as a fulltime parent, one was on social benefits, and one was in a reintegration program (with probation). Of these participants, the one on probation had become a student at T2 and the occupational status of the other four remained unchanged. To summarize, in the course of the study the number of students dropped from 31 to 24, the number of employed (almost exclusively fulltime) increased from 11 to 18, and the number of participants without study or work remained stable at 5.

Although the importance that student and employed interviewees attached to their study or work varied, only a few of them felt that it was not very important and that life was more about social activities and "having fun."

> *My study is somewhere on the background in my life. Of course it's important for me to keep thinking about the future, and it plays a large role in that I have to go there a couple of times every week, and have to study for it, but if I fail a test, I fail a test, that doesn't really bother me. (. . .) I'm not much of a scholar, for me the fun things in life are more important.* (Julius, I1, DNN)

however, most students attached goals to their study, for instance attaining their undergraduate diploma in due time, or getting high grades. some had intermediate study delays, but sooner or later commitment often grew and study became a priority.

> *Now, my school is very important, I don't want to do retakes, because I can't choose another study again. My student grant ends at some time and anyhow I have to pay the next three years myself. I want to do it well and timely, not being 30 when I graduate. Imagine I'm 30 and by then I have to start my career, find a husband and possibly have kids. And that has to happen before a certain age. That's also why I want to pass my exams in one time.* (Kim, I1, DDD)

In their narratives, interviewees often expressed commitment to study and work, and to strive for a steady job career. Evidently, the more important participants considered their study or job, the more effort they put into it and the more committed they felt.

> *When I'm at work, I'm ambitious. In my last job I got promoted to supervisor within one year, and that is something I want to achieve. I have higher aspirations, and I cannot simply work somewhere for 8 hours and watch the clock. I envy people who are able to do that: have a job, do their work and that's it. I am not like that; my work always follows me home. Yeah, I'm pretty ambitious.* (Kevin, I2, NNN)

CANNABIS USE IN RELATION TO STUDY AND WORK

Most interviewees believed that heavy cannabis use would negatively impact their daily occupational functioning and most of them had experienced adverse effects themselves, such as difficulties getting out of bed the next day, functioning more slowly and sloppy, trouble memorizing, and postponing tasks. However, almost one in five participants (8/47) reported better functioning in some tasks when being high or stoned, mainly because they believed it improved their concentration. With cannabis, they felt like being "in a bubble" and less distracted by other people, actions or thoughts. Interestingly, all these interviewees stated to have ADHD and/or ADD (all except one clinically diagnosed), and some said that cannabis was like "natural Ritalin" or a kind of "self-medication."

> *"Recently I finished that training, and started my own company. It goes really well. I'm much more concentrated in my work after using cannabis. And when I'm programming when I'm stoned, I'm like in the codes straight away, type everything effortlessly. Sober I start thinking about how it's working, the syntaxes, commando's, but stoned all of that happens fully automatic. I get into a kind of vibe to program completely uninterrupted. It makes a big difference."* (Ben, I1, DNN)

Almost all student and employed interviewees took it for granted not to use cannabis before or at school or work or when studying mainly to avoid adverse effects and/or out of responsibility.

> *Interviewer: Why don't you smoke cannabis at work? Interviewee: Well, it's kind of... On the one hand I think that they wouldn't be cool with that. I think they want to hire the sober Jacob. On the other hand: sometimes, when you have smoked a couple of joints you lose a little attention to details. And that is something that's really important in my job, the details. So, not using cannabis at work out of feelings of responsibility, but perhaps also to distinguish work from leisure. Like: you're not here to chill but to work.* (Jacob, I2, NNN)

Other reasons for not using cannabis at work or at school were fear that colleagues would notice it and fear of possible consequences, such as being taken less seriously or being fired. Most interviewees said colleagues or fellow students did not know about their cannabis use. They believed that cannabis use was a private matter, and preferred to keep it to themselves. The dominant patterns in the narratives was to be rather firm in stating that it was inappropriate to be intoxicated while at work, at school or when studying. Using cannabis belonged to the leisure domain, and they reported that they only used cannabis after finishing study or work. As a result, most employed participants barely used cannabis at daytime, and more on weekends than on weekdays. With students, there was more variation, as their daily life was less structured around fixed hours throughout the week. They sometimes used cannabis at daytime, and more often during holidays. Among the participants without study and work, the three that were full time parents sometimes used cannabis at daytime when the children were at school, but more often at night when the children were asleep; they used less or not at all during school holidays.

Despite interviewees generally holding strong views on not using cannabis before and during study or work, some did admit it had happened occasionally. While employed participants seemed to be most strict in not using when at work, students sometimes believed that study differs from work, as there is less social control at college (e.g., when not showing up or not paying attention in classes).

> *I am very strict: when I have to work or go to school I don't smoke. Well, school . . . occasionally, when my class begins late, at 2 PM, a friend drops by and then we'll have a cup of coffee and smoke a joint, but not heavy. The first class is also very boring, I go stare out the window or distract others.* (Tess, I1, NDN)

> *It's perhaps more practical not to be too stoned during lectures, but hey, occasionally it doesn't do any harm. Sometimes, when the lecture begins at 5 PM, well, I sometimes smoke a joint at 3 PM and I think: I shouldn't have to. I'm trying to take the study really serious, but sometimes it doesn't work out and I think: oh well, I'll do it tomorrow. No one is bothered by it; it doesn't affect anyone.* (Eduard, I2, DDD)

RELATION BETWEEN STUDY AND WORK EVENTS AND CHANGES IN CANNABIS USE

Not surprisingly given their stage of life, most interviewees reported life events related to study or work that had taken place in the course of our study. In total, participants reported 97 events, averaging 2.1 events per interviewee (**Table 2**). Four participants reported no events.

Most changes and events concerned starting a new study or job, graduating, finishing a study, quitting work or a study prematurely, and stress related to study or work. Slightly more events were evaluated as positive than as negative. Getting high grades, graduation, and starting a new job always had positive meanings to the interviewees, and starting a new study very often as well. Being fired from a job, getting low grades, and stress were always experienced as negative. Only a few events, although reported as important to interviewees, were perceived as neutral (neither positive nor

Table 2 | Events related to study or work.

Trajectory (*n*) > life event experienced (*n*)	Cannabis use	NNN (12)	NDN (7)	NDD (4)	DNN (10)	DND (2)	DDN (5)	DDD (7)	Total (47)
T0–T2 (TOTAL)									
Negatively (van der Pol et al., forthcoming)	More	2	–	3	3	2	3	3	16
	Stable	6	5	–	5	–	–	2	18
	Less	2	1	–	2	–	3	–	8
	Total	10	6	3	10	2	6	5	42
Neutral (5)	More	–	–	–	1	–	–	–	1
	Stable	–	1	1	2	–	–	–	4
	Total	–	1	1	3	–	–	–	5
Positively (50)	More	–	1	1	1	1	1	–	5
	Stable	14	6	1	7	3	3	2	36
	Less	1	1	1	1	–	3	2	9
	Total	15	8	3	9	4	7	4	50
AVERAGE NUMBER EVENTS PER PARTICIPANT									
Negatively		0.8	0.9	0.8	1.0	1.0	1.2	0.7	0.9
Neutral		–	0.1	0.3	0.2	–	–	–	0.1
Positively		1.3	1.1	0.8	0.9	2.0	1.4	0.6	1.1
Total		2.1	2.1	1.8	2.1	3.0	2.6	1.3	2.1

negative, or both positive and negative), all being study-related (e.g., study delay or starting graduate courses). Quitting a study was experienced the most ambiguously, mainly depending on whether or not this happened voluntary. In line with Rönkä et al. (36), we found that interviewees associated positively experienced events more often with personal choice than negatively experienced events. Nevertheless, interviewees reported almost as many negatively experienced events with little or no personal choice as negatively experienced events where personal choice was present. Over one third of the interviewees reported more than one event, mostly both a negatively and a positively experienced event, such as being fired from work (negative) and getting a new job (positive).

Interviewees talked about changes in their cannabis use in terms of more use (i.e., more frequently, more joints per occasion, or larger amounts of cannabis), or less use (i.e., less frequently, less joints per occasion, or smaller amounts), or said their cannabis use had not changed (stable use). Negatively experienced events were most frequently associated with stable use (43%), somewhat less frequently with more use (38%), and least frequently with less use (19%). In contrast, positively experienced events were most frequently associated with stable use (72%) and much less frequently with less use (18%) or more use (10%). In more than half of the events, interviewees said that they had not impacted their cannabis use. This mainly concerned events that interviewees perceived as positive, but also as planned and not really changing their daily life, or as neutral. As Wheaton and Gotlib (22) stated, "contrast" is important for events to become turning points. In our study, many participants who became graduate students after having attained their bachelor's degree, although they were surely happy with their certificate, did not change their life drastically. Likewise, employed participants who had switched from a job to a similar one, often considered their new job, although they were pleased with it, as little influential on their daily life. Therefore, these changes in study or work did not really influence their cannabis use.

Generally, increases or decreases in cannabis use were transient, and according to the interviewees these changes in cannabis use largely depended on changes in the amount of leisure time that went along with events or temporary changes. For instance, becoming unemployed or having a quiet study period led to more leisure time and thereby more cannabis use, whereas a new job or a busy study period led to less leisure time, and consequently to less cannabis use.

> *[about the timeline] The more demanding my study, the lesser I smoke. When I'm free, there is a peak in my use. Let's see. In June and July I've used less, because I worked at a bank for 2 months, nine-to-five job, little leisure time. Then in August, an increase in use, like "long live freedom! Now I can smoke again". After that, a normal level for a while. December slowly a decrease, because then the exams come closer. January a drop, heavy times and tough exams, 4-5 exams in one week, so then it's 0-1 joint per day. And then February suddenly again 'freedom!', so daily use, 2 joints anyhow.* (Zoë, I1, NNN)

> *When I have a lot of leisure time, I smoke more and sooner. When I'm busier and more serious, then I smoke less. And that is certainly a correlation, when there is an ascending line with responsibilities and working hard, there is simultaneously a descending line with cannabis use.* (Robert, I2, DDN)

In addition, agency came to the forefront as an important factor, most clearly in the narratives of students. Several students reported considerable delay in their study, which they all experienced as negative and some were facing a demanding last year of studies. Some expressed a low level of agency regarding their study, did not feel in control, gave up, and subsequently started to use more cannabis.

> *I felt really bad that period. I did go out with friends, but I didn't do much for my study and I only worked now and then. I didn't give it my all. I smoked a lot and I started to use that, as an excuse. I had no priorities, things just happened. Life happened to me, and I sort of endorsed it...* (Julian, I2, DDD)

In contrast, other students chose and managed to restructure their daily life and to study hard, and, although they did not necessarily blame their study delay on cannabis, they actively reduced their cannabis use. They all stated that they were highly motivated to change their cannabis use and were convinced that they could succeed. In the course of our study, three participants reported to have quit using cannabis, giving their occupational life as the main reason, as they thought cannabis was not conducive to their functioning. They said that quitting did not occur overnight, but was a gradual process: they went from daily use to only in weekends, and step-by-step cut back. At the last interview they had not used cannabis for over a year and neither had the intention to start again.

> *My medical study was suffering from my cannabis use. Whenever I have an exam I have to study very hard, a full week every day, spending the whole day in the library, otherwise I won't make it. When I was using cannabis, being there at 8:30 AM was a problem anyhow, because I couldn't wake up early. Also, after 3 PM I didn't feel like studying anymore, no concentration, I wasn't able to memorize things. Factual knowledge doesn't go together with cannabis use. I always stopped using a week before the exams, but you need three days to get active and to get adjusted, and in fact you're too late. Also, smoking cannabis at night does not go well with lectures early in the morning. I often overslept and didn't go. All in all my study delay was one year. Last year, I decided: I don't want to use cannabis, I want to catch up on my study. And I did! Now I do great, I pass the exams, so I shouldn't smoke anymore. The difference between when I was smoking cannabis and now is huge.(...) I feel in control of my life now more than ever.* (Sofie, I1, DDN)

Of the six participants who lost their job during our study, no one reported this was related to their cannabis use. While one could argue that cannabis may have affected their functioning and thus indirectly caused job loss, this did not seem the case as mostly their dismissal was due to cut-backs related to the crisis.

RELATION BETWEEN STRESS AND CHANGES IN CANNABIS USE

A recurring topic in many narratives was stress related to study or work, though not *per se* in conjunction with events. For students such stress mainly involved study delays and exam periods, especially their final project or master thesis. For employed interviewees it was largely connected with deadlines, having to work too many hours and reorganizations or job loss. Participants without study or work perceived stress mainly related to financial problems and sometimes parenting. Stress came with ups and downs, and could have a strong impact on participants' mood and everyday life functioning, including cannabis use. Some interviewees explained how cannabis use could be functional in dealing with stress, because it helped them to distract their mind, making it easier to relax and taking a moment for oneself. For some, smoking a joint at the end of the day was also a reward for their hard work. Consequently, it was not uncommon for interviewees to explain increases in their cannabis use by stressful and busy times.

> *When I'm stressed, or more stressed, then I'm gonna smoke more. Just to forget a bit. It won't solve anything, but for the moment it does, you can simply let things go.* (Samantha, I2, NNN)

> *When I'm stressed, the urge to smoke increases. I don't know if that's positive or negative, probably not positive, but hey, it gives me some peace. By then I think: ok, now I have a break, it's ok now. If I don't have that break I'm a bit stuck with that frustration. Additionally, it relaxes me. Except that the next day at work I'm a little less alert and probably it's not beneficial, but at least it relieves the evening itself.* (Jonas, I2, DDD)

Conversely, other participants explained a decrease in their cannabis use by stressful times. Some thought that with stress cannabis use was not helpful, since it might intensify emotions and lead to more stress or worries. For some others, like Kevin, using less cannabis in times of stress was not so much because of possible unpleasant effects, but primarily a matter of time and personal choice.

> *Interviewee: At that time I used less. See, when you've had a really busy day and you come home at 8 PM and you want to go to the gym and cook a meal and also have to smoke a joint and get up at 7h the next morning, no, that won't work. Interviewer: To what extent is it about priorities? Interviewee: Yeah, it depends on your priorities, but for me it's not cannabis, I prioritize my job. No, when I'm stressed I'm not going to smoke more, but less instead.* (Kevin, I2, NNN)

In five participants, chronic stress ended in a situation of "burnout." They all experienced this as very negative and it took them at least a couple of months to recover. Two of these interviewees thought their cannabis use was worsening their mental health and stopped using (one permanently and one temporarily with the intention to quit permanently). One of these interviewees remained stable in her cannabis use and two others used more cannabis during their burnout and said that this was because they had more leisure time.

RELATION BETWEEN STUDY AND WORK EVENTS AND CANNABIS DEPENDENCE TRAJECTORIES

Regarding cannabis dependence, seven different trajectories evolved, with persistent non-dependent (NNN; $n = 12$) and transitions from dependent at baseline to non-dependent at T1 and T2 (DNN; $n = 10$) being the most common trajectories (**Table 1**). On average 2.1 events were reported, but this was only 1.3 in the group of persistent dependent participants (DDD; $n = 7$; **Table 2**).

Although numbers of participants in most trajectories are small ($n = 2$–12), some patterns seem to become manifest. In response to occupational events, interviewees who were non-dependent at T2 (NNN, NDN, DNN, DDN) mostly had not changed their use (49/75 events) or rather equally often used less (14/75) or more cannabis (12/75). Interviewees who were dependent at T2 (DDD, DND, and NDD), though they also quite often said that their cannabis use had not changed because of events (9/22 events), were somewhat more likely to use more (10/22) than less (3/22).

Concerning occupational status (study, work, or neither) and trajectories some interesting patterns emerged. Firstly, many participants remained student during our study (23/47) and, although they can be found in six different trajectories, the overall tendency over time is away from cannabis dependence (**Table 3**). Four of these students were persistent non-dependent (NNN). While 14/23 participants who remained student were dependent at T0, only five were at T2. In general, the students who became non-dependent (7 DNN, 4 DDN, 3 NDN) stated that their study became more demanding as it progressed, which they found difficult to combine with frequent cannabis use. From their narratives it became clear that they decided for more control over their cannabis use, through being more selective in when to use and when not and/or through less frequent use.

> *I concluded for myself that if I really want to succeed in life, I have to fully go for this study now. And that has changed my cannabis use as well. I still use, every week I do, but not daily anymore. Because when I do, the next day I don't feel alert, I notice I can't really concentrate. That interferes with what I want to do, my study. So now I only smoke in the weekends, or when I don't have any obligations the next days. I plan my use, take it into account. More seriously. My study is the first priority now, definitely. From February till June 2011 it wasn't, and I*

Table 3 | Occupational status and cannabis dependence trajectories T0–T1–T2 ($n = 47$).

T0	T1	T2	NNN (12)	NDN (7)	NDD (4)	DNN (10)	DND (2)	DDN (5)	DDD (7)	Total (47)
Study	Study	Study	4	3	2	7	–	4	3	23
Study	Study	Work	1	1	–	–	–	–	–	2
Study	Work	Work	3	–	–	2	–	–	–	5
Work	Study	Work	–	–	–	1	–	–	–	1
Work	Work	Work	2	2	2	–	1	1	2	10
Neither	Study	Study	1	–	–	–	–	–	–	1
Neither	Neither	Neither	1	1	–	–	–	–	2	4
Study	Work	Neither	–	–	–	–	1	–	–	1

used cannabis very often. That was less serious, I wasn't devoted to my study and I attended the university mainly to socialize. (Max, I2, DDN)

In contrast, four of the five participants who remained student and who were dependent at T2 (3 DDD, 2 NDD) expressed in their narratives a lower level of agency regarding their study, e.g., reported that they did not take their study very seriously, or did not spend enough time on it.

I can't convince myself of the need to quit using cannabis. I don't encounter adverse effects. There are things, such as my study delay, that cannabis contributed to. But the real decisive factor is if I really had the willpower and would go for it, then I would succeed in my study. Even when using that much cannabis. It's just my own laxity I think. I have had that my whole life. (Eduard, I2, DDD)

Secondly, all seven students who became employed, either after quitting their study (by choice or involuntary due to poor performance) or after graduation, were non-dependent at T2. Four (with stable or reduced cannabis use) showed a persistent non-dependent trajectory (NNN) and three shifted from dependent to non-dependent (1 NDN, 2 DNN) in the same period as their occupational status changed from student to employed. Although this shift co-occurred with change in occupational status, it was not necessarily induced by events related to study or work. Mike (DNN), for example, said that between T0 and T1 he felt that the use of cannabis sometimes made him a bit paranoid. Therefore he decided to decrease his cannabis use, and finally he quit. In the meantime he discontinued his study and started working fulltime. Similarly, Isabel (DNN) expressed that the way she used cannabis evolved as part of a general change in lifestyle rather than specifically because of a shift in occupational status from study to work.

Like with other things, you need to find a certain balance in cannabis use. For cannabis I have found that balance, I guess. I have that for a year now. Also because I live on my own now, I really got to know myself. You're alone, there is nobody else around. It has changed me, made me more independent. (Isabel, I1, DNN)

Regarding the group that remained employed (10/47), no clear patterns in trajectories could be observed. These participants were represented in six different trajectories (2 NNN, 2 NDN, 2 NDD, 1 DND, 1 DDN, 2 DDD). At T0 this group included four dependent participants versus five at T2. The extent to which employed participants said that they were committed to their job varied, and also their type of job, but this did not appear to be related to their cannabis dependence status. However, sometimes change in cannabis use did not result in a dynamic trajectory, as was the case with Jonas, who stated that over time he had taken more control over his cannabis use, but was diagnosed as persistent dependent (DDD).

The regularity got out of my cannabis use. I used to smoke every day, a joint before bedtime, perhaps one in the early evening and when I had a day off I could sometimes start in the afternoon. Well, that's not really something to be proud of, and I always thought: if I want, I can stop using. It was time to prove that. It was a rude awaking [laughs]. Before, I didn't try to control my use, I never saw the need to. But I began to feel the effects: the relatively easy college life was over, employed life was more demanding, and I had to better take care of myself. Perhaps I still don't fully regulate my use, I sometimes have relapses. It's difficult, because after I haven't been smoking for a while, I think: why not smoke? I don't have any problems with my use, I'm functioning fine, also when I smoke. I can do my job well, or quite well and my social life as well. (Jonas, I2, DDD)

Also in the case of the other participants (7/47) no consistent patterns could be observed in the relationship between cannabis dependence trajectories and (events in) the occupational domain. Alternatively, agency, more specifically their ability to regulate their cannabis use appears to be related to (transitions in) their dependence status. This became most clear for three participants with young children in the neither group (NNN, NDN, DDD). During our study these three mothers experienced the event of one or two children going to school for the first time, which created a considerable change in their daily time schedule. Although they all underlined not to use cannabis in presence of their children, the way they organized their cannabis use was quite different. Samantha (NNN) believed to be in control over her cannabis use. She used cannabis mainly at night, before going to sleep, and only after she had taken care of her daily responsibilities. Contrariwise, Charlotte (DDD) said that her kids often arrived too late at school, because she had difficulties getting up in the morning, and that she smoked a joint right after she had brought her children to school, even though she knew that by doing so she often postponed her daily tasks. She felt addicted, not in control over her use and in both in-depth interviews she said she would want to quit. Nathalie (NDN), on the other hand, often used cannabis after having finished her daily tasks, but between T0 and T1, when her son started to attend school, she experienced a period that she used more frequently and also in the morning. In retrospect, she believed during that time she was addicted to cannabis, and she had decided to change her use and to (successfully) retake control over it.

DISCUSSION

In this qualitative study we explored the role of study and work in cannabis use among a group of young adult initially frequent cannabis users. We were particularly interested in analyzing how study and work, and more specifically events related to these domains, contributed to transitions in cannabis use and dependence. We interviewed 47 young adults in-depth twice retrospectively covering a period of 3 years. All interviewees were frequent cannabis users at the start of the study (T0). During the follow-up period, there were wide variations and strong dynamics in their patterns of cannabis use, the presence of cannabis dependence, and their occupational situation. Overall, there was a declining tendency in frequency and quantity of cannabis use, including a few interviewees who had quit using cannabis altogether at the second in-depth interview. Various trajectories concerning cannabis dependence appeared. One quarter of the sample remained persistent non-dependent during the study. Some participants were persistent dependent, and others switched from a dependent to non-dependent status and vice versa, yet, at the end of the study more participants were non-dependent than at baseline (34 versus 23 of all 47 interviewees).

Almost two-thirds of the interviewees were students (often with a job on the side) at baseline and remained student during the total study period. Most other participants were in paid employment, and in the course of our study some students became employed as well, indicating that long-term frequent cannabis use does not necessarily restrain individuals in their professional life [cf. (37, 38)]. Most interviewees considered cannabis use as inappropriate before or during hours of study or work [cf. (39)].

As expected in this age group (mean age 21 years), life events related to study or work were quite common, nearly all participants experienced at least one such an event. Overall, participants evaluated slightly more events as positive than negative. Similar events could be valued differently, and it was evident that agency did matter. In line with Rönkä et al. (36), events were likely to be experienced positively when personal choice was felt to be present, e.g., when students decided themselves to discontinue a study rather than being forced to stop, or when individuals choose to start a new job rather than being fired. Our study shows that events in the context of study or work have the potential to, but not necessarily do, influence cannabis use. It should be noted that events that did have an impact on cannabis use often were gradual rather than abrupt, and often cannabis use changed gradually. The feeling of being in control, i.e., agency, in the case of occupational events also appeared relevant for cannabis use. Many events did not lead to changes in cannabis use, but negatively experienced events were mainly associated with stable (43%) or more (38%) cannabis use, whereas positively experienced events were mainly associated stable (72%) or less (18%) cannabis use. Our findings further suggested that increases or decreases in cannabis use related to occupational events are at least partly explained by changes in the amount of leisure time. For example, participants tended to report more use after becoming unemployed, while those who started a new job reported less cannabis use. Changes in cannabis use were also explained by job and study-related stress and how interviewees managed stress. Some reported less use, because using while stressed would enhance negative emotions, or simply because of too little time left to use. Conversely, others reported more use in stressful periods, because cannabis helped them to relax, or was a reward at the end of a day of study or work.

We also found indications for reverse causation, i.e., changes in cannabis use can lead to changes in study or work. Several interviewees, because of events such as study delays, or (expected) stressful times, gradually managed to rigorously cut back or even quit their cannabis use, which eventually was conducive to their occupational performance. Overall, interviewees, who considered their study or work as being rather important, were more committed and motivated and were more willing to rule out any possible influence of their cannabis use on their occupational functioning.

Inspections on occupational events in relation to cannabis dependence (trajectories) revealed that in response to events, participants who were non-dependent at T2 mostly had not changed their use, or equally often used less or more cannabis. In contrast, interviewees who were dependent at T2 were more likely to use more rather than less in response to (negative) occupational events. Besides, interesting patterns emerged concerning occupational status (study, work, or neither). Among participants who remained student during our study, the overall tendency over time was away from cannabis dependence. The students who switched to non-dependence found their study, as it progressed and became more demanding, hard to combine with frequent cannabis use and decided for more control, through being more selective in timing and frequency of use. All students who became employed during our study were non-dependent at T2. Besides, none of the students who entered the workforce were dependent at T2, although the transition was not necessarily induced by study or work events.

For other participants, including those who remained employed, no clear patterns in trajectories could be observed. Alternatively, agency, more specifically their ability to regulate their cannabis use, appeared to be related to (transitions in) their dependence status.

Taken together, our study supports a reciprocal relationship between occupational life (events) and frequent cannabis use and dependence. On the one hand cannabis use and dependence impact occupational life either negatively, in terms of worsened occupational functioning, or positively, e.g., when users deliberately cut back on or stop using cannabis to improve their professional performance. On the other hand our findings support Laub and Sampson's (23) line of reasoning that employment and education impact cannabis use and (indirectly) dependence by limiting leisure time and facilitating structure resulting in attenuated cannabis use. However, it could be argued, and as indicated by our findings, that the available leisure time is influenced by several factors, such as the way participants give meaning to their life and study or job, including motivation, priorities, and agency. For example, some interviewees prioritized study over cannabis use and thereby had less leisure time, while others prioritized cannabis use over study, thus had more leisure time. This might require a certain level of agency, i.e., feelings of being in control or believing in one's own capabilities. In this perspective, the restricting impact of leisure time on cannabis use might be ascribed to the amount of leisure time one *has* as well as to the amount of leisure time one *creates* to use cannabis. As our findings show the relationship works both ways, this provides a nuance for the debate on the "amotivational syndrome." Our study also supports previous research stating that occupational stress can bring about an increase in drug use (16), yet, might depend on the person (characteristics) experiencing it. For some participants cannabis use was a way of managing everyday demands [see also (37, 38)] or coping with psychiatric symptoms. Especially for AD(H)D participants, cannabis use may reduce symptoms, attenuate sleep problems, and improve social functioning (self-medication) (40). Regarding the relationship between stress, depression, and cannabis use, this self-medication hypothesis – and its potential contra productive effect – is somewhat supported by our quantitative findings that coping motives (although not specifically for depression) were one of the few cannabis related differences between dependent and non-dependent frequent users (8), a predictor of cannabis dependence onset (41), and a predictor of dependence persistence (van der Pol et al., forthcoming).

LIMITATIONS

Our findings add to the growing insight into the relationship between occupational life and cannabis use of young adult cannabis users. Nonetheless several factors might limit the results of this study.

An enriched sample was selected, and therefore we cannot guarantee representativeness. However, this does not necessarily mean that the sample is highly biased. Our sample includes many students, but being a student is rather common for young adults in the Netherlands. Cannabis use and occupational status in our study were quite dynamic, but to some extent this was affected by the study design. We deliberately included dynamic dependence trajectories between T0 and T1 for in-depth interviews. More generally, our sample of young adults is likely to be dynamic or even volatile in different aspects, including education and employment. From the life course theory perspective, a decline in cannabis use during young adulthood was to be expected with aging.

Moreover, we investigated the process of cannabis use in the periods between interviews (T0–T1–T2), whereas cannabis dependence was dichotomously captured in diagnoses of dependence versus non-dependence, based on the presence of symptoms within a certain period. Not only could much variation underlie these diagnoses, since they refer to the time between two interviews, also the "effect" of an event related to study or work on cannabis dependence might not have been revealed, and only become apparent afterward, in a next interview. Likewise, participants who had stopped using were categorized as non-dependent, while they were actually non-users.

Furthermore, it should be noted that some results presented here may not be universally replicable because they are related to the country where the study is conducted. Dutch policy officially tolerates possession and sale of small amounts of cannabis, and this may limit extrapolation of our results to countries with formal penalties. Yet, we intended to explore in-depth the role of study and work in cannabis use and dependence rather than to portray a representation of all cannabis users. Although research suggests cannabis laws have little impact on cannabis use patterns of regular users [e.g., Ref. (42–44)], their experiences of certain life events, feelings of personal choice and control, and therefore the outcomes of life events might be indirectly affected by cannabis policy. Hence, a comparable study in another country might therefore find different results.

Finally, as mentioned before, our analyses are based on the narratives of the interviewees, and they largely create their own reconstructions of their cannabis careers and lives. Consequently, their self-perception and self-reflection formed the foundation of our analyses and interpretations. It should be noted that when interpreting the results, all data were based on self-report. We mainly looked into the subjective, not objectified, meanings of (occupational) events. Although subjective, participants' evaluation of events often corresponded with how one would categorize them objectively (from an outsider's perspective). Also the use of context-based timelines, including data participants (quantitatively) reported intermediately, positively contributed to the recall of their lives and cannabis use. More importantly, our approach gave novel insights in the perceptions, experiences, and attributed meanings of participants, which is reflected in the emerging importance of agency in the narratives. For example, although many interviewees stated that they had to learn by their own experience how cannabis use can impact job or study performance, most prioritized their obligations, out of personal motivations or an overall strong work ethic.

How can we explain that occupational events left cannabis use largely unchanged? An explanation could be that for young adults, events such as a new study or a job switch are quite normal and part of a normal career. In fact, sometimes these events were not changing participants' daily lives. Besides, cannabis use appeared to be primarily a leisure activity. These findings relate to the normalization thesis, which suggests that in the past decades, for many users cannabis use has become a normal part of their life, which includes clear choices about whether, where and when (not) to use (45, 46). Cannabis use assimilates quite well with studying and/or being employed, but rules and norms are applied: users do not use cannabis just anytime and anywhere. Cannabis is preferably not used with colleagues and is reserved for leisure time. In this study we focused on the professional life domain, thereby somewhat artificially taking this domain out of its wider context. Life events in other domains, for example social relationships with relatives, partners, and friends, might be equally or even more important.

Life course theory appeared a useful framework to explore how and why education and employment are related to cannabis use and dependence over time. Our study showed that life events in the realm of education and employment were rather common in young adults' lives and can have a strong impact on their cannabis use. Changes in cannabis use are sometimes temporary, but turning points in cannabis use careers can evolve from events in education and employment, as became most clear for the interviewees who fully quit using cannabis. To conclude, and similar to desistance from crime, cessation of cannabis use often is a gradual process, in which agency plays a major role. Besides, regarding the occupational life of young adult cannabis users, leisure time is a (important) factor underlying changes in frequent cannabis use.

ACKNOWLEDGMENTS

This research was funded by a grant from the Netherlands Organization for Health Research and Development (Grant number 31160009).

REFERENCES

1. UNODC. World Drug Report 2011. United Nations Publication (2011) [cited 2013 Jun 18]. Available from: http://www.unodc.org/documents/ data-and-analysis/WDR2011/ World_Drug_Report_2011_ebook. pdf
2. Substance Abuse and Mental Health Services Administration. *Results from the 2011 National Survey on Drug Use and Health: Sum- mary of National Findings.* (No. NSDUH Series H-44, HHS Publica- tion No. (SMA) 12-4713). Rockville, MD: Substance Abuse and Men- tal Health Services Administration (2012).
3. European Monitoring Centre for Drugs and Drug Addiction. *Annual Report 2012: The State of the Drugs Problem in Europe.* Luxembourg: Publications Office of the European Union (2013).
4. Degenhardt L, Coffey C, Romaniuk H, Swift W, Carlin JB, Hall WD, et al. The persistence of the association between adolescent cannabis use and common mental disorders into young adulthood. *Addiction* (2013) 108(1):124–33. doi:10.1111/j.1360-0443.2012. 04015.x
5. Fergusson DM, Boden JM. Cannabis use and later life outcomes. *Addiction* (2008) 103(6):969–76. doi:10.1111/j.1360- 0443.2008.02221.x
6. Hall WD. The adverse health effects of cannabis use: what are they, and what are their implica- tions for policy? *Int J Drug Pol- icy* (2009) 20:458–66. doi:10.1016/ j.drugpo.2009.02.013
7. Martinotti G, Di Iorio G, Sepede G, De Berardis D, De Risio L, Di Giannantonio M. Cannabis use and psychosis: theme introduction. *Curr Pharm Des* (2012) 18(32):4991–8. doi:10.2174/138161212802884627

8. van der Pol P, Liebregts N, de Graaf R, ten Have M, Korf DJ, van den Brink W, et al. Mental health dif- ferences between frequent cannabis users with and without dependence and the general population. *Addic- tion* (2013) 108:1459–69. doi:10. 1111/add.12196
9. Lynskey M, Hall W. The effects of adolescent cannabis use on educational attainment: a review. *Addiction* (2000) 95(11):1621–30. doi:10.1046/j.1360-0443.2000. 951116213.x
10. Horwood LJ, Fergusson DM, Hay- atbakhsh MR, Najman JM, Cof- fey C, Patton GC, et al. Cannabis use and educational achievement: findings from three Australasian cohort studies. *Drug Alcohol Depend* (2010) 110(3):247–53. doi:10.1016/ j.drugalcdep.2010.03.008
11. Arria AM, Garnier-Dykstra LM, Cook ET, Caldeira KM, Vincent KB, Baron RA, et al. Drug use pat- terns in young adulthood and post- college employment. *Drug Alco- hol Depend* (2013) 127(1–3):23– 30. doi:10.1016/j. drugalcdep.2012. 06.001
12. Stone AL, Becker LG, Huber AM, Catalano RF. Review of risk and protective factors of sub- stance use and problem use in emerging adulthood. *Addict Behav* (2012) 37(7):747–75. doi:10.1016/j. addbeh.2012.02.014
13. Hoffmann JP, Dufur M, Huang L. Drug use and job quits: a lon- gitudinal analysis. *J Drug Issues* (2007) 37(3):569–96. doi:10.1177/ 002204260703700305
14. French MT, Roebuck MC, Alexan- dre PK. Illicit drug use, employment, and labor force participation. *South Econ J* (2001) 68(2):349–68. doi:10.2307/1061598
15. Hyggen C. Does smoking cannabis affect work commitment? *Addic- tion* (2012) 107(7):1309–15. doi:10. 1111/j.1360-0443.2012.03796.x
16. Reed PL, Storr CL, Anthony JC. Drug dependence enviromics: job strain in the work environment and risk of becoming drug-dependent. *Am J Epidemiol* (2006) 163(5):404– 11. doi:10.1093/aje/kwj064
17. Fernández-Artamendi S, Fernández-Hermida JR, Secades- Villa R, García-Portilla P. Cannabis and mental health. *Actas Esp Psiquiatr* (2011) 39(3):180–90.
18. Hall W, Solowij N, Lemon J. *The Health and Social Consequences of Cannabis Use. Monograph Series No. 25.* Canberra: Australian Govern- ment Publishing Service (1994).
19. Laub JH, Sampson RJ. Turning points in the life course: why change matters to the study of crime. *Criminology* (1993) 31(3):301–25. doi:10.1111/j.1745-9125.1993.tb01132.x
20. Teruya C, Hser Y. Turning points in the life course: current findings and future directions in drug use research. *Curr Drug Abuse Rev* (2010) 3(3):189–95. doi:10.2174/ 1874473711003030189
21. Hutchison ED. The life course per- spective: a promising approach for bridging the micro and macro worlds for social workers. *Fam Soc* (2005) 86:143–52. doi:10.1606/ 1044-3894.1886
22. Wheaton B, Gotlib IH. Trajecto- ries and turning points over the life course: concepts and themes. In: Gotlib IH, Wheaton B editors. *Stress and Adversity over the Life Course: Trajectories and Turning Points.* New York: Cambridge University Press (1997). p. 1–25.
23. Laub JH, Sampson RJ. *Shared Begin- nings, Divergent Lives: Delinquent Boys to Age 70.* Cambridge: Harvard University Press (2003).
24. Maruna S. *Making Good: How Ex- Convicts Reform and Rebuild their Lives.* Washington, DC: American Psychological Association (2001).
25. Laub JH, Sampson RJ. Understand- ing desistance from crime. *Crime Justice* (2001) 28:1–69.
26. Huang DYC, Evans E, Hara M, Weiss RE, Hser Y. Employment trajecto- ries: exploring gender differences and impacts of drug use. *J Vocat Behav* (2011) 79(1):277–89. doi:10. 1016/j.jvb.2010.12.001
27. van der Pol P, Liebregts N, de Graaf R, Korf DJ, van den Brink W, van Laar M. The Dutch cannabis dependence (CanDep) study on the course of frequent cannabis use and dependence: objectives, meth- ods and sample characteristics. *Int J Methods Psychiatr Res* (2011) 20(3):169–81. doi:10.1002/mpr.345
28. Liebregts N, Benschop A, van der Pol P, van Laar M, de Graaf R, van den Brink W, et al. Cannabis depen- dence and peer selection in social networks of frequent users. *Con- temp Drug Probl* (2011) 38(1):93– 120.
29. Carlsson C. Using 'Turning points' to understand processes of change in offending. *Br J Criminol* (2012) 52(1).1–16. doi.10.1093/bjc/azr062
30. Sampson RJ, Laub JH. A life- course view of the development of crime. *Ann Am Acad Polit Soc Sci* (2005) 602:12–45. doi:10.1177/ 0002716205280075
31. Crouch M, McKenzie H. The logic of small samples in interview-based qualitative research. *Soc Sci Info* (2006) 45(4):483–99. doi:10.1177/ 0539018406069584
32. Bourgois P. Theory, method, and power in drug and HIV- prevention research: a participant- observer's critique. *Subst Use Misuse* (1999) 34(14):2155–72. doi:10.3109/10826089909039443
33. Bedi G, Redman J. Self-reported ecstasy use: the impact of assess- ment method on dosage estimates in recreational users. *J Psychophar- macol* (2006) 20(3):432–6. doi:10. 1177/0269881106063272
34. Vervaeke HKE, Korf DJ. Long- term ecstasy use and the man- agement of work and relation- ships. *Int J Drug Policy* (2006) 17(6):484–93. doi:10.1016/j. drugpo.2006.09.002
35. Miles MB, Huberman AM. *Quali- tative Data Analysis: An Expanded Sourcebook.* London: Sage Ltd (1994).
36. Rönkä A, Oravala S, Pulkkinen L. Turning points in adults' lives: the effects of gender and the amount of choice. *J Adult Dev* (2003) 10(3):203–15. doi:10.1023/ A:1023418414709
37. Osborne GB, Fogel C. Under- standing the motivations for recreational marijuana use among adult Canadians. *Subst Use Misuse* (2008) 43(3-4):539–72. doi:10.1080/10826080701884911
38. Hathaway AD. Marijuana and lifestyle: exploring tolerable deviance. *Deviant Behav* (1997) 18(3):213–32. doi:10.1080/ 01639625.1997.9968056
39. Frank VA, Christensen AS, Dahl HV. Cannabis use during a life course–integrating cannabis use into everyday life. *Drugs Alcohol Today* (2013) 13(1):44–50. doi:10. 1108/17459261311310844
40. Gudjonsson GH, Sigurdsson JF, Sig- fusdottir ID, Young S. An epidemiological study of ADHD symp- toms among young persons and the relationship with cigarette smok- ing, alcohol consumption and illicit drug use. *J Child Psychol Psychia- try* (2012) 53:304–12. doi:10.1111/ j.1469-7610.2011.02489.x
41. van der Pol P, Liebregts N, de Graaf R, Korf DJ, van den Brink W, van Laar M. Predicting the tran- sition from frequent cannabis use to cannabis dependence: a three- year prospective study. *Drug Alco- hol Depend* (2013). doi:10.1016/j. drugalcdep.2013.06.009
42. Fergusson DM, Swain-Campbell NR, Horwood LJ. Arrests and convictions for cannabis related offences in a New Zealand birth cohort. *Drug Alcohol Depend* (2003) 70(1):53–63. doi:10.1016/S0376- 8716(02)00336-8
43. Korf DJ. Dutch coffee shops and trends in cannabis use. *Addict Behav* (2002) 27(6):851–66. doi:10.1016/ S0306-4603(02)00291-5
44. Reinarman C. The limited relevance of drug policy: cannabis in Amsterdam and in San Francisco. *Am J Public Health* (2004) 94:836–42. doi:10.2105/AJPH.94.5.836
45. Measham F, Shiner M. The legacy of 'normalisation': the role of classi- cal and contemporary criminologi- cal theory in understanding young people's drug use. *Int J Drug Policy* (2009) 20(6):502–8. doi:10.1016/j. drugpo.2009.02.001
46. Parker H. Normalization as a barometer: recreational drug use and the consumption of leisure by younger Britons. *Addict Res Theory* (2005) 13(3):205–15. doi:10.1080/ 16066350500053703

7

Intertemporal bargaining in addiction

George Ainslie[1,2] *

[1] School of Economics, University of Cape Town, Cape Town, South Africa
[2] Department of Veterans Affairs, Coatesville, PA, USA

Edited by:
Hanna Pickard, University of Oxford, UK

Reviewed by:
Serge H. Ahmed, CNRS, France
Bennett Foddy, University of Oxford, UK

***Correspondence:**
George Ainslie, 151 Veterans Affairs Medical Center, Coatesville, PA 19320 USA
e-mail: george.ainslie@va.gov

The debate between disease models of addiction and moral or voluntarist models has been endless, and often echoes the equally endless debate between determinism and free will. I suggest here that part of the problem comes from how we picture the function of motivation in self-control. Quantitative experiments in both humans and non-humans have shown that delayed reward loses its effectiveness in proportion to its delay. The resulting instability of preference is best controlled by a recursive self-prediction process, intertemporal bargaining, which is the likely mechanism of both the strength and the experienced freedom of will. In this model determinism is consistent with more elements of free will than compatibilist philosophers have heretofore proposed, and personal responsibility is an inseparable, functional component of will. Judgments of social responsibility can be described as projections of personal responsibility, but normative responsibility in addiction is elusive. The cited publications that are under the author's control can be downloaded from www.picoeconomics.org.

Keywords: addiction, hyperbolic discounting of reward, intertemporal choice, self-control, brain imaging of motivation

Many factors promote the impulse for an addictive activity. In addition to social and informational differences between individuals, the differential attractiveness of such activity is associated with heritable differences in the highs people get from a given activity, differences in their inborn tendency to discount delayed rewards, and adaptation of their brain reward structures to repeated addictive activity (1). Prior factors that have increased the differential reward for addictive activities – even the self-inflicted adaptation factor – could be said to have created a disease, in that the person's current level of temptation is not subject to voluntary control. Eczema is called a disease, after all, even though the involuntary process is the itching, whereas voluntary scratching is what does the damage. However, discovery of the physical roots of temptation should not obscure the process of motivated choice that is never bypassed in addiction.

Addiction is sometimes identified with physiological patterns such as intoxication, tolerance, and withdrawal, regardless of how the person values them. However, the kind of addiction that a person complains of has two essential elements: temporary preference for inferior rewards, and failure to forestall the recurrent surrender to this preference. The first element arises from the universal over-valuation of imminent rewards, which will produce temporary preferences for them to the extent that the person does not compensate for it. It has been suggested that this over-valuation represents just the arousal of appetites or emotions (2), but a more fundamental pattern is now well documented (3–5). People have inherited a hyperbolic delay discount function from our non-human ancestors:

$$\text{Present value} = \text{Value}_0 / \left[1 + (k \times \text{Delay})\right]$$

where Value_0 = value if immediate and k is degree of impatience.

This function makes the value of an event inversely proportional to its expected delay, which means that many objectively smaller sooner (SS) rewards will tend to be temporarily preferred to larger later (LL) alternatives when the SS rewards are imminent (**Figure 1**). The hyperbolic shape of the value/delay function probably survived natural selection because it is a basic psychophysical relation, the same as that for sensory perceptions such as brightness and heaviness (6). In species where instinct generates present reward for future-oriented tasks (hoarding, dam-building, migrating...) this shape is probably not maladaptive, but it gives humans a temptation problem.

Modern people are set up for addictions at birth. Since Isaac Marks' seminal article (7) many activities have been identified as addictive without the involvement of substances, or even external rewards. Analysis of hyperbolic discounting suggests how the great human ability to coin reward by imagination can be channeled into addictive temptations, by patterns of outcomes that serve as occasions for reward but that make no prediction at all of external rewarding events, as in video games (8). What differentiates the addict from her neighbor is not the strong temptation, when close up, to seek options that she would avoid from a distance. Rather it is the collapse of her resistance to this temptation. This is the other essential element of addiction. We normally reach compromises with our urges, and set boundaries to our bad habits. Understanding this failure – indeed understanding why "compromise" is the right word – will be key to understanding responsibility in addiction.

RECURSIVE SELF-PREDICTION

Motivation for impulse control comes from the value described by the hyperbolic discount function at long delays, which is proportional to objective value when both alternatives are distant – and

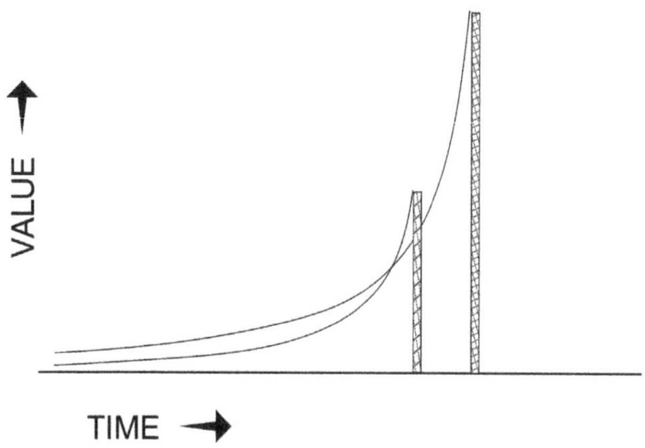

FIGURE 1 | Hyperbolic curves describing the values of a smaller, sooner (SS) reward and a larger, later (LL) reward as the delay before they will be available decreases. An early choice (near the left edge) would favor the LL reward, but a choice when the pair is close would favor the SS reward.

much higher for each than is described by either conventional exponential or "quasi-hyperbolic" (cue-driven) functions (9). The need to adopt protections for long term plans is unique to humans, and the number of these that the new human species has been able to learn has been limited: to some extent a person can avoid paths that take her close to SS alternatives, or she can avoid revaluation of them when close, but these strategies will necessarily be hard to maintain for long periods. Alternatively she can set up incentives, especially social ones, that will add deterrence at crucial moments. However, I have argued that a great part of impulse control in an individualistic society is accomplished by the person's perception that large future benefits depend on regular choices of a particular kind – such as not to drink, spend, or play too much – and that each current choice is a test case for the choices she can expect future selves to make (4, 9). Such self-prediction creates a potentially strong but somewhat rigid mechanism of impulse control, willpower, without the need for a separate organ or faculty. The person can then afford to live closer to temptations, although her self-control will be at risk from her thinking of reasons that a future self should not count a present indulgence as a lapse – that is, from rationalizations.

The person will see a current abstinence as worth the effort if and only if this is necessary to maintain a credible pattern of abstinence, a perception that organizes her relevant choices into a repeated prisoner's dilemma – or self-enforcing contract – where a current defection jeopardizes future cooperation. The devil is in the word "relevant." If the person can see how a current consumption should not change her future expectation – "today is special" – then she may get to enjoy it without damaging her long term prospects. Auditioning rationales for their credibility and modifying them accordingly is a recursive, often rapid process. If successful, it maintains the compromise between urges and long term expectations. Rationalizations may not be especially risky when the stakes are low ("I resolve to clean my room today"), but the risk becomes demonstrable when large amounts of incentive hinge on the test, as when a recovering alcoholic decides to try drinking just once. This plan is apt to follow the same logic as the decision of a party to a self-enforcing contract to cheat her partner; defection by a current self often leads to the notorious abstinence violation effect (10; for dieters, see 11). Such a sudden loss of control after a single lapse has sometimes been blamed on a physical stimulation of appetite; however, when alcoholic volunteers are given either alcohol punch or an indistinguishable placebo, the belief that they have had alcohol leads to craving whereas the alcohol itself does not (12).

EVIDENCE OF RECURSIVE SELF-PREDICTION IN WILL

Recursive (fed-back) processes are notoriously hard to experiment on, even in physical systems (e.g., 13, pp. 191–211), let alone motivational ones, a difficulty which may have concealed their prevalence. Recursive self-prediction is most evident in common intuitions about the motivational consequence of a single lapse in a diet or sobriety, as above, which are sharpened in thought problems such as Kavka's, Monterosso's, and Newcomb's (14). There have been some suggestive experiments: pointing out to subjects that their current choice in a series of SS/LL reward choices may be predictive of their future preferences raises their frequency of LL choices, although not as much as does obligatory commitment for the whole series with their first choice (15, 16). The intertemporal bargaining model fits the properties of will specified by the early psychologists who analyzed will (4, pp. 79–80, 117–120), and predicts the behavior of subjects in 2- and *N*-person prisoner's dilemma analogs (4, pp. 90–94; 17). However, given that intertemporal bargaining depends on intrapsychic contingencies, we might hope for better evidence from brain imaging.

Unfortunately, imaging experience is rudimentary. Using functional magnetic resonance imaging (fMRI), Luo et al., found that equal preference between a LL reward and a SS alternative cannot be predicted from the activity in brain reward centers when those alternatives are offered singly, outside of the choice situation (18). After establishing a behavioral indifference point, subjects were given chances to respond for each outcome separately. They showed less activity in their reward centers for what had been the LL rewards than for the erstwhile SS rewards, even though they had been indifferent when choosing between these rewards, and were still indifferent when the choice contingency was offered again. That is, the mere establishment of a choice contingency changes the relative value of SS and LL outcomes, in favor of the LL one. The implication is that when impulse control is relevant, motivation beyond what arises from the current rewards themselves must be active. In other studies the lateral frontal cortex has been found to be more active when a subject makes LL choices (e.g., 19), but a recent experiment raises a question of whether this activity is tracking motivation for those LL choices. Luo et al. observed individual subjects' stochasticity (variability) of SS/LL choice over time (20). By finding the ratio of SS to LL amount that produced equal preference, and then offering differing amounts in the same ratio at the same alternative delays, it was possible in effect to offer a subject the same choice repeatedly in a way that the subject would not recognize, and thus to observe small, spontaneous variations over trials of SS vs. LL preference. Lateral frontal cortical activity was indeed often greater with LL choice, but mostly in subjects who showed relatively great stochasticity – the ones who wavered most. This somewhat counterintuitive finding suggests that activity in lateral frontal cortical "executive centers" may not reflect preference for LL alternatives *per se*, but perhaps represents a response by which subjects compensate for a perceived unreliability of such preference. These studies are far from definitive, but they suggest that self-control in SS/LL choices may be determined by processes on at least two levels above the spontaneous valuation of rewards that is seen in non-choice designs: mental effort, possibly reflected in lateral frontal cortical activity; and a non-effortful evaluative process in which the most stable long term preferences are established – possibly by intertemporal bargaining – which so far lacks fMRI correlates. It may be significant that subjects with relatively great ventromedial prefrontal cortical activity when imagining future selves also prefer LL rewards relatively more than do other subjects (21), but the role of such "prospection" centers in self-control has not been explored.

FREEDOM OF WILL

Assuming that recursive self-prediction is the basis of will, what are the implications for addicts' responsibility? Intertemporal bargaining increases the power of self-control but also its potential volatility. A recovering alcoholic may notice that she is procrastinating about an unrelated issue and interpret that as evidence of her will being weaker than she thought, which may in turn reduce her expectation of staying sober. That reduction may motivate increased rigidity to prove she is strong, or it may snowball into expectations that are too greatly lowered for their peril to deter a drinking episode. The potential for small or merely symbolic choices to shift much larger motives gives the will an element of chaos, in the technical sense (13). Whatever awareness of this process a person has acquired is apt to weigh on every choice that she notices to be evidence of her predilections. This extra motivation provides a rationale for strength of will – and also, arguably, for a mechanism that meets common definitions of freedom of will.

As characterized by Richard Holton, people's insistence on the freedom of will largely stems from two kinds of experience: the unpredictability of one's own behavior ("For all I know, I might have done otherwise") and the initiation of one's behavior ("Action is experienced as something that the agent instigates, rather than something that just happens to the agent as the result of the state that they were antecedently in" – 22). We do not feel as if we are passively responding to the incentives we detect. Chaotic systems such as weather have been proposed as models for the unpredictability of our choices (23), but critics have pointed out that being buffeted by the weather would not feel like being free, more like having seizures (24, p. 231). However, the feeding back of tentative choices to the process of choice itself makes the agent a participant in her motivational weather. In a simple linear choice I might decide how much food to take at a buffet lunch on the basis of how hungry I am or how long I expect to go without food in the afternoon. But if I am a restricted eater those considerations may be overshadowed by estimating whether the food I take looks like I am lapsing, and knowing that the prospect of lapsing may increase my hunger. [Recursive self-prediction as a cause of "conditioned" (cue-driven) appetite is discussed in 5, pp. 222–229]. The latter, recursive estimation is of the same cognitive kind as the linear, but the sensation that my making estimates is changing those estimates as I make them has an added quality. Choosing under the influence of the choice itself pulls attention back from the ostensible alternatives to an inward dialog, one that should produce a feeling of agency at the same time that it makes choice unpredictable from its original incentives. The outcome is still strictly determined, of course, but recursively rather than linearly, a distinction that keeps the self from being that old bugbear of determinism, a throughput – a mere conveyor of incentives (fuller discussion in 25).

RESPONSIBILITY FOR ADDICTIVE CHOICES

Much of the effort that has gone into finding rationales for free will stems from its supposed necessity for holding people responsible for their choices (26). A theory that derives the functional properties of free will from recursive self-prediction is still deterministic, and thus does not seem at first to be a solution. However, the way that this theory relates strength to freedom of will suggests a functional framework for responsibility without indeterminacy – and thus a space in which the voluntarist model of addiction can be valid. Rather than testing this possibility by the truth or falsehood of determinism, it makes more sense for us to look at the practical roots of responsibility. Psychology has generally assumed that a personal sense of responsibility comes from internalization of pressure that is brought to bear by parents and other socializers, but with the logic of intertemporal bargaining their precepts cease to be needed to provide incentive, only to suggest compromises between internal interests. A serious lapse threatens such compromises, not because the person makes a decision to punish herself but because of the realistic fall in her expectation of future self-control. (This model is not contradicted by social psychology experiments in which subjects who read statements espousing determinism subsequently indulge in minor antisocial behaviors – see 22.)

Personal responsibility is thus an operational component of will. Its inseparability from volition raises the possibility that when people judge someone else to be guilty, they are projecting their own experience with lapses – feeling personal guilt empathically: "If I were in her shoes, I would feel guilty." That is, our understanding of other people's responsibility comes from our intuition of our own. Such a process would supply the element of deservingness that is missing from determinist models that explain social responsibility as a manipulation to create deterrence, which are intuitively unsatisfying (27). Thus for both personal and social responsibility, the truth of determinism is not relevant (discussed in 25). However, the question remains of how responsibility is affected by addiction.

An addict undeniably faces disease factors, but my argument is that they operate *through* motivation, not instead of it. Addiction becomes "hopeless" when the addict has no rationale by which abstention at crucial choice points would sufficiently increase the believability of her future sobriety. As described above, such belief is sensitively dependent on many self-generated signs and symbols, but at some point the addict has tried and spoiled all the ones she can think of. She is not sick in the sense of being beyond motivation, but her inability to propose any credible intertemporal deal constitutes a kind of bankruptcy, and she could be argued thus not to be responsible – except that, unlike a financial bankrupt, she sometimes has a sudden epiphany that re-orders her accounts (28). The advice of the Anonymous organizations that the addict is helpless against her addiction does not imply the irrelevance of intertemporal bargaining, but rather the danger of trying rationalizations where the bargaining is full of mistrust. Their injunction to resolve sobriety for only 1 day at a time aims at restarting the bargaining process with a low level of trust. To acknowledge helplessness against a temptation without attempting to renounce it forever sounds illogical, but it is often the only successful compromise after long histories of grand resolution and total collapse. These organizations have intuited most of the tactics that an intertemporal bargaining model would prescribe (which is not to argue for or against their clinical effectiveness).

CONCLUSION

As is the case with so many ancient debates, both the disease theory and the moral theory of addiction have part of the truth on their side. The physical roots of addictive temptation are increasingly known, as is their unequal distribution among individuals and within the same individual at different points in her addictive history. In her current moment forces gathered by heredity, exposure, and even her own past behavior are givens, and could fairly be judged to constitute a disease. However, their force is still one of temptation, even when giving in promises only a joyless oblivion instead of the pain of short-lived self-control. The error of policy-makers who rely on negative incentives is not their belief that addictive behavior is motivated, but their miscalculation of how much punishment can make up for the bankruptcy of a person's intertemporal bargaining process. Unless they have experienced such bankruptcy themselves, trying to put themselves in the addict's shoes leads them to conclude that she just needs an extra push, whereas in fact she needs to re-establish a relationship with her prospective future selves. Certainly cures for temptation itself can be a factor – for instance, buprenorphine for opiate craving – as can simply structuring modest incentives with a view toward immediacy and reliability (e.g., 29). And certainly, blanket forgiveness of bad deeds that have sprung from an addiction would create perverse incentives, "moral hazard." But beyond these straightforward contingencies, the difference between sobriety and ruin often lies with the turnings of intertemporal bargaining, which defy simplification.

ACKNOWLEDGMENTS

This material is the result of work supported with resources and the use of facilities at the Department of Veterans Affairs Medical Center, Coatesville, PA, USA. The opinions expressed are not those of the Department of Veterans Affairs or of the US Government.

REFERENCES

1. Redish AD, Jensen S, John- son A. A unified framework for addiction: vulnerabilities in the decision process. *Behav Brain Sci* (2008) 31:415–87. doi:10.1017/S0140525X0800472X
2. Berns GS, Laibson D, Loewenstein G. Intertemporal choice – toward an integrative framework. *Trends Cogn Sci* (2007) 11:482–8. doi:10.1016/j.tics.2007.08.011
3. Green L, Myerson J. A discount- ing framework for choice with delayed and probabilistic rewards. *Psychol Bull* (2004) 130:769–92. doi: 10.1037/0033-2909.130.5.769
4. Ainslie G. *Breakdown of Will*. Cam- bridge: Cambridge University Press (2001).
5. Ainslie G. The core process in addic- tions and other impulses: hyper- bolic discounting versus condition- ing and cognitive framing. In: Ross D, Kincaid H, Spurrett D, Collins P, editors. *What is Addiction?* Cam- bridge: MIT (2010). p. 211–45.
6. Gibbon J. Scalar expectancy the- ory and Weber's law in animal timing. *Psychol Rev* (1977) 84: 279–325. doi:10.1037/0033-295X. 84.3.279
7. Marks I. Behavioural (non- chemical) addictions. *Br J Addict* (1990) 85:1389–94. doi:10.1111/j. 1360-0443.1990.tb01625.x
8. Ainslie G. Grasping the impalpa- ble: the role of endogenous reward in choices, including process addic- tions. *Inquiry* (2013). doi:10.1080/0020174x.2013.806129
9. Ainslie G. Pure hyperbolic discount curves predict "eyes open" self- control. *Theory Decis* (2012) 73: 3–34. doi:10.1007/s11238-011- 9272-5
10. Marlatt GA, Gordon JR. Deter- minants of relapse: implications for the maintenance of behavior change. In: Davidson PO, David- son SM, editors. *Behavioral Med- icine: Changing Health Lifestyles*. Pergamon: Brunner/Mazel (1980). p. 410–52.
11. Polivy J, Herman CP. Dieting and binging: a causal analysis. *Am Psy- chol* (1985) 40:193–201. doi:10. 1037/0003-066X.40.2.193
12. Maisto S, Lauerman R, Adesso V. A comparison of two experimen- tal studies of the role of cogni- tive factors in alcoholics drink- ing. *J Stud Alcohol* (1977) 38: 145–9.
13. Gleick J. *Chaos: Making a New Sci- ence*. New York: Viking Penguin (1987).
14. Ainslie G. Can thought experi- ments prove anything about the will? In: Spurrett D, Ross D, Kincaid H, Stephens L, editors. *Distributed Cognition and the Will: Individual Volition and Social Context*. Cam- bridge: MIT (2007). p. 169–96.
15. Kirby KN, Guastello B. Making choices in anticipation of similar future choices can increase self- control. *J Exp Psychol Appl* (2001) 7:154–64. doi:10.1037/1076-898X. 7.2.154
16. Hofmeyr A, Ainslie G, Charlton R, Ross D. The relationship between addiction and reward bundling: an experiment comparing smok- ers and non-smokers. *Addiction* (2010) 106:402–9. doi:10.1111/j. 1360-0443.2010.03166.x
17. Monterosso JR, Ainslie G, Toppi- Mullen P, Gault B. The fragility of cooperation: a false feedback study of a sequential iterated prisoner's dilemma. *J Econ Psy- chol* (2002) 23:437–48. doi:10.1016/ S0167-4870(02)00095-8
18. Luo S, Giragosian L, Ainslie G, Mon- terosso J. Behavioral and neural evidence of incentive bias for imme- diate rewards relative to preference-matched delayed rewards. *J Neurosci* (2009) 29:14820–7. doi:10.1523/JNEUROSCI.4261-09. 2009
19. Hare TA, Camerer CF, Rangel Self-control in decision- making involves modulation of the vmPFC valuation sys- tem. *Science* (2009) 324:646–8. doi:10.1126/science.1168450
20. Luo S, Ainslie G, Pollini D, Giragosian L, Monterosso JR. Moderators of the association between brain activation and farsighted choice. *Neuroimage* (2012) 59:1469–77. doi:10.1016/j. neuroimage.2011.08.004
21. Mitchell JP, Schirmer J, Ames DL, Gilbert DT. Medial prefrontal cor- tex predicts intertemporal choice. *J Cogn Neurosci* (2010) 23:857–66. doi:10.1162/jocn.2010.21479
22. Holton R. Determinism, self- efficacy, and the phenome- nology of free will. *Inquiry* (2009) 52:412–28. doi:10.1080/ 00201740903087383
23. Garson JW. Chaos and free will. *Phi- los Psychol* (1995) 8:365–74. doi:10.1080/09515089508573165
24. Kane R. Two kinds of incompat- ibilism. *Philos Phenomenol Res* (1989) 50:220–54. doi:10.2307/ 2107958
25. Ainslie G. Free will as recursive self-prediction: does a determinis- tic mechanism reduce responsibil- ity? In: Poland J, Graham G, editors. *Addiction and Responsibility*. Cam- bridge: MIT (2011). p. 55–87.
26. Haji I. Compatibilist views of freedom and responsibility. In: Kane R, editor. *The Oxford Handbook of Free Will*. Oxford: Oxford University Press (2002). p. 202–28.
27. Greene J, Haidt J. How (and where) does moral judgment work? *Trends Cogn Sci* (2002) 6:517–23. doi:10. 1016/S1364-6613(02)02011-9
28. Heyman GM. *Addiction: A Disorder of Choice*. Cambridge: Harvard University Press (2009).
29. Olmstead TA, Sindelar JL, Petry NM. Cost-effectiveness of prize- based incentives for stimulant abusers in outpatient psychosocial treatment programs. *Drug Alco- hol Depend* (2007) 16:175–82. doi:10.1016/j.drugalcdep.2006.08. 012

8

Disentangling the correlates of drug use in a clinic and community sample: a regression analysis of the associations between drug use, years-of-school, impulsivity, IQ, working memory, and psychiatric symptoms

Gene M. Heyman[1]*, Brian J. Dunn[2] and Jason Mignone[3]

[1] *Department of Psychology, Boston College, Chestnut Hill, MA, USA*
[2] *Department of Psychology, Center for Studies in Behavioral Neurobiology, Concordia University, Montreal, QC, Canada*
[3] *Prime, Buchholz & Associates, Inc., Portsmouth, NH, USA*

Edited by:
Hanna Pickard, University of Oxford, UK

Reviewed by:
Nick Heather, Northumbria University, UK
Don Ross, The University of Cape Town, South Africa

****Correspondence:***
Gene M. Heyman, Department of Psychology, Boston College, Chestnut Hill, MA 02467, USA
e-mail: heymang@bc.edu, gheyman@fas.harvard.edu

Years-of-school is negatively correlated with illicit drug use. However, educational attainment is positively correlated with IQ and negatively correlated with impulsivity, two traits that are also correlated with drug use. Thus, the negative correlation between education and drug use may reflect the correlates of schooling, not schooling itself. To help disentangle these relations we obtained measures of working memory, simple memory, IQ, disposition (impulsivity and psychiatric status), years-of-school and frequency of illicit and licit drug use in methadone clinic and community drug users. We found strong zero-order correlations between all measures, including IQ, impulsivity, years-of-school, psychiatric symptoms, and drug use. However, multiple regression analyses revealed a different picture. The significant predictors of illicit drug use were gender, involvement in a methadone clinic, and years-of-school. That is, psychiatric symptoms, impulsivity, cognition, and IQ no longer predicted illicit drug use in the multiple regression analyses. Moreover, high risk subjects (low IQ and/or high impulsivity) who spent 14 or more years in school used stimulants and opiates less than did low risk subjects who had spent <14 years in school. Smoking and drinking had a different correlational structure. IQ and years-of-school predicted whether someone ever became a smoker, whereas impulsivity predicted the frequency of drinking bouts, but years-of-school did not. Many subjects reported no use of one or more drugs, resulting in a large number of "zeroes" in the data sets. Cragg's Double-Hurdle regression method proved the best approach for dealing with this problem. To our knowledge, this is the first report to show that years-of-school predicts lower levels of illicit drug use after controlling for IQ and impulsivity. This paper also highlights the advantages of Double-Hurdle regression methods for analyzing the correlates of drug use in community samples.

Keywords: drug use, educational attainment, impulsivity, IQ, working memory, non-treatment drug users, methadone clinic, Cragg's Double-Hurdle regression

INTRODUCTION

According to journalists, public officials, and even popular song writers, kids who drop out of school early are inviting disaster. Not only are they undermining their future earnings, but life on the streets paves the way to delinquency, drugs, and worse. In his 1966 hit, "Don't be a drop out," rhythm and blues star James Brown warns that "without an education you might as well be dead," and in an interview in the *New Yorker*, the current American Secretary of Education, Arne Duncan, comments that his friends who did not go to college are now casualties of drugs and crime (1). Yet, despite the widely assumed benefits of staying in school, the relationship between education and future prospects is not well understood. This is particularly true of drug use, the focus of the study described in this report. First, there is the question of the causal relations. There is evidence that early drug use causes students to drop out of school [e.g., Ref. (2, 3)], and, conversely, there is evidence that early success in school protects against later drug use (4, 5). Of course these are not mutually exclusive connections, and it is also possible that educational attainment and drug use are symptomatic of one or more common factors such as IQ and/or conscientiousness, so that school functions as a proxy for its correlates and is not itself a causal factor. For instance, educational attainment is correlated with IQ, psychiatric symptoms, and impulsivity (6–8), and each of these factors is also correlated with drug use in just the way predicted by the hypothesis that they are linked to drug use by way of years spent in school.

Our goal was to better understand the relations between drug use, cognition, impulsivity, and years-of-school. Our approach differed from previous studies in several ways. We recruited non-clinic drug users as well as clinic drug users. This increased the chances that our measures varied over a wide range, and it increased the likelihood that the sample reflected most drug users, since most drug users, including those who meet the criteria for dependence, do not make use of treatment facilities [e.g., Ref. (9)]. Second, we obtained cognitive, dispositional, and demographic correlates of drug use so that we could use multiple regression methods to test whether significant zero-order correlates remained significant when they were entered as one of several simultaneous predictors of drug use. For example, would impulsivity continue to predict drug use if differences in years-of-school, IQ, and psychiatric symptoms were controlled for? Third, we used a "two-tier" multiple regression method, an approach that is much more common in economics than in drug research. This method allowed us to distinguish between the predictors of ever using a particular drug and the predictors of how often the drug was used. This distinction is helpful when the subjects of a study do not all use the same drugs.

One of the convenient aspects of studying drug use in clinic populations is that all of the subjects use drugs and likely use many of the same ones. However, clinic populations may provide a distorted picture of drug use since most drug users do not take advantage of clinic services [e.g., Ref. (9–11)]. In principle, community samples provide the opportunity for more representative accounts of the determinants of drug use, but they come with their own challenges. For instance, most of our subjects did not use every drug that we were interested in evaluating. This resulted in data sets that included many zero frequencies, which is incompatible with the assumptions of ordinary least squares regression. Researchers interested in the determinants of consumer behavior face an analogous problem when one or more commodities of interest are purchased by some but not all consumers. Following their experience, we adopted Cragg's Double-Hurdle regression method (1971). This is a two-tier approach, which allowed us to model the decision to use a drug and the frequency of drug use conditional on use as two separate stochastic processes. Probit regression analysis determined the predictors of ever using a drug, and Truncated Ordinary Least Squares regression determined the predictors of frequency of drug use.

The sort of complexity that applies to cognition and drug use applies to the relationship between impulsivity and drug use. The basic finding is that higher scores on measures of impulsivity are positively correlated with differences in drug use. This holds for studies in which impulsivity was measured by questionnaires [e.g., Ref. (12)], by choice procedures which used hypothetical rewards [e.g., Ref. (13)], and by choice procedures which pitted actual sooner smaller rewards against later larger rewards [e.g., Ref. (14, 15)]. However, impulsivity is correlated with IQ [e.g., Ref. (16)], working memory [e.g., Ref. (17)], and years-of-school [e.g., Ref. (18, 19)]. Possibly, then, just as years-of-school may be a proxy for differences in cognition, impulsivity may be a proxy for differences in cognition and/or years-of-school. Consequently, we proceeded in a two-step manner. First, we asked whether there was a correlation between impulsivity and drug use, as others have found, and then we asked whether the correlation held up when common correlates of drug use and impulsivity were included in the analysis. Thus, our study used multiple regression analyses to better understand the correlates of drug use, with emphasis on the distinction between years-of-school and cognition and, similarly, the possible distinctions between impulsivity, cognition, and years-of-school.

MATERIALS AND METHODS

PARTICIPANTS

One hundred and eighty-four subjects participated in the study. Seventy-seven were recruited from Boston methadone clinics and the others were from Boston area communities. At the clinics, we distributed flyers that described the study and asked for paid volunteers. To recruit community subjects, we placed ads in neighborhood newspapers and online (boston.craigslist.org). The ads stated that paid volunteers were sought for a study on drug use. We excluded volunteers who reported a history of head injury or were younger than 21 or older than 65 years of age. To ensure that the subjects could read and understand the questionnaires, we asked for evidence of reading skill in English. We accepted anyone who was fluent in English and said they had graduated high school or passed a General Equivalency Test for high school. (How this criterion may have influenced the results is reviewed in the Section "Discussion.") The clinic subjects were tested at their clinics; the community subjects were tested at the Behavioral Pharmacology Research Laboratory of McLean Hospital. All subjects signed an approved consent form and were informed that the study was designed so as to insure the subjects' anonymity. The McLean Hospital Institutional Review Board for Human Subject Research evaluated and approved all procedures and the consent form.

MATERIALS AND PROCEDURE

The study session consisted of a series of questionnaires and cognitive tests. The questionnaires obtained information on demographic characteristics, years-of-school (including technical training, nursing classes, hair styling classes, and so on), drug use history, impulsivity [Barratt Impulsiveness Scale (20)], and psychiatric symptoms [Symptom Check List-90-Revised (21)]. The cognitive procedures included short-term and working memory span tests (22) and the vocabulary and matrix reasoning subtests of the Wechsler Abbreviated Scale of Intelligence, WASI (23).

Short-term and working memory span tests

The verbal span tests asked subjects to recall a list of letters. The instructions and stimuli were displayed on a laptop computer. Each letter (78 point Lucinda Sands Unicode font) appeared for 1.5 s, one-after-the-other, with the series varying in length in pseudo-random fashion from three to eight letters. The end of the series was marked by a prompt showing three question marks. The subject was then asked to identify the just-displayed series of letters in the order that they had appeared on a prepared form. In the working memory version of this test, there was an additional "interference" task. Prior to each letter, the monitor displayed an array of colored circles and squares. The subject's task was to count out loud the blue–green circles. At the completion of the count, the experimenter advanced the screen to the next letter in the span.

Thus, in the working memory task, subjects were asked to keep in mind a series of letters while completing a counting task.

In the spatial cognition task, the screen displayed a side or diagonal of a rectangle, with an arrow head at one end to indicate directionality. Each line segment appeared for 1.5 s, and, as in the letter version of this task, the subject was asked to recall each display in the order that it appeared, writing down their responses on a prepared form. With one exception, the procedure was the same as the letter spans. Pilot tests indicated that this task was more difficult than the letter spans so that the longest spatial span was six rather than eight items.

Each of the four span tests was preceded by instructions and three practice spans to insure that the subject understood the task. The experimental events and stimuli were controlled by E-Prime software programs (Psychology Software Tools, Inc.).

Vocabulary and matrix reasoning subtests, Wechsler Abbreviated Scale of Intelligence

The vocabulary subtest consists of a list of 42 words that the subject is asked to define. Like its predecessors (the vocabulary subtests of the WISC-III and WAIS-III) the WASI verbal test is said to measure crystallized or acquired intelligence. The matrix reasoning subtest consists of a series of 35 different geometric and colored patterns that the subject completed by identifying the correct stimulus from a set of five choices. It is similar to the matrix reasoning subtest in the WAIS-III, and, like this test, is said to measure "non-verbal fluid reasoning and general intellectual ability." On the basis of national norms, these two tests provide an estimate of full scale IQ. For instance, the correlation between the WASI and the WAIS-III IQ was 0.87 in a large national sample (23). Neither test was timed.

Measuring drug consumption

The subjects answered detailed questionnaires regarding their history of illicit drug use, alcohol consumption, and smoking. The questions were fashioned after those found in other drug research programs [e.g., *Addiction Severity Index* (24) and *Personal Drinking History Questionnaire* (25)]. The illicit drug questionnaire identified six drug categories: marijuana/hashish, hallucinogens, amphetamine, cocaine, opiates, and "other drugs." For each drug the subjects were asked to describe their: (1) level of use, as measured in days per week, (2) mode of self-administration, and (3) periods of use at a given overall frequency, as measured in two different ways: calendar year and age. On the basis of these data, we estimated: (1) total occasions that a drug was used, (2) duration of "regular use," where regular use was defined as three or more times a week for a year or more, and (3) the current pattern of use. The questionnaires for smoking and drinking followed a similar format, yielding similar measures.

Urine sampling for current drug use

Methadone clinic subjects provided urine samples so that we could test for current drug use. The assay (Instant-View Multi-Drug Screen Urine Test) checked for the presence of 12 drugs, including morphine, methadone, various stimulants, benzodiazepines, marijuana/hashish, MDMA, and PCP.

Impulsiveness and current psychiatric symptoms

The Barratt Impulsiveness Scale (20) is a widely used, 30-item self-report questionnaire. Subjects rate themselves on a four point scale on questions regarding planning, spontaneity, patience, and susceptibility to boredom.

The Symptom Check List-90-R (SCL) is a self-report, psychiatric symptom inventory. It asks subjects to rate the degree to which they experienced 90 different symptoms as stressful over the previous 7 days. On the basis of research and clinical experience, the 90 verbal descriptions are grouped into nine symptom categories, plus a residual category. The categories are generally accepted symptom clusters, such as depression and anxiety. The SCL rating scale has five levels, ranging from "not at all" stressful to "extremely" stressful.

Demographic questionnaire

We also administered a questionnaire that gathered demographic information, including age, marital status, ethnicity, and years spent in school. School was broadly defined as any type of training, including hair dressing, nursing, and other forms of preparation for occupational roles.

Statistical analyses

We used multiple regression methods to identify the variables that predicted differences in drug use. This approach entailed two challenges. First, the drug frequency distributions were positively skewed, and, second, many subjects did not use a particular drug so that there were many "zero" scores in the frequency distributions. To correct for positive skew we transformed the frequencies so that they would better approximate a normal distribution. Guided by Stata's Box-Cox test, we evaluated various "power" transformations of the frequencies, ranging from logarithmic to 0.5 (square root) and chose the two that most closely produced a normal distribution in drug use frequencies according to the Shapiro–Wilk test and visual inspection of the probability graphs (see Results).

The list of methods for analyzing data sets with a large number of zeroes includes logistic models, zero-inflated Poisson regression, and "two-tier" Tobit and Double-Hurdle regression analyses. Econometric researchers developed the two two-tier methods as a way of quantifying the likelihood of purchasing a good (participation) and then conditional on the purchase, the frequency of purchases (26, 27). Although both methods are widely used in economics, the Double-Hurdle has the advantage of allowing the researcher to evaluate whether the predictors of participation and predictors of frequency of participation differ. For instance, when the two sets are the same, the Double-Hurdle reduces to the Tobit analysis. Thus, Cragg's Double-Hurdle approach is more flexible and inclusive, so we used it [see Ref. (28) for a helpful introduction to the method]. The first tier uses a probit regression equation to model whether an individual ever used a particular drug or not. The second tier uses a truncated regression equation to model the frequency of drug use, conditional on having used the drug at least once. Thus, each tier yields a set of regression coefficients and their significance levels. We entered the same set of predictors for both tiers, but this was not necessary. The analyses were conducted with SYSTAT 13 and Stata 12 statistical software.

RESULTS

DEMOGRAPHICS

The average age of the subjects was 40.7 (10.04) years, 57% were female, 73% were White, and the average number of years-of-school was 14.3 (2.6) – parentheses enclose the standard deviations. With one exception, the community and clinic demographic characteristics were quite similar. The average ages differed by <2 years (40.0 and 41.7), the proportions of males and females were nearly the same (58 and 56%), and the proportions of whites and non-whites were also similar (31 and 25%), respectively. However, community subjects typically spent more time in school than did clinic subjects. Almost all community subjects graduated high school and the majority had some post high school training (73%). In contrast, 34% of the clinic subjects earned a GED degree rather than graduating high school, and 60% went no further than the 12th grade. Overall, the average difference in years-of-school for the two groups was 3.5, which was statistically significant [12.3 and 15.8 years; $F(1,182) = 135.4$, $p < 0.0005$].

NUMBER OF DRUG USE OCCASIONS

Table 1 summarizes the reported levels of illicit and licit drug use for all subjects and for clinic and community subjects taken separately. For a given drug, consumption levels varied widely, and for every drug the average consumption level was considerably greater than the median consumption level, implying that the frequency distributions were positively skewed (as pointed out in the Section "Materials and Methods"). The community and clinic drug frequency distributions were also positively skewed, with the exception of cigarette smoking in clinic subjects. Also note that with the exception of stimulants, the maximum consumption level for a given drug was about the same for community and clinic subjects. Indeed, the maximum consumption level for a given drug was as likely to come from the community sample as the clinic sample. However, there were also differences in drug use. On average, drug consumption was much higher in the clinic sample, particularly for illicit drugs, and, in line with this finding, more community subjects reported little or no use of a particular drug. Consequently, the median consumption levels for community subjects were often zero. Put somewhat differently, the range of drug use frequencies was wider in the community sample, with many community subjects reporting no drug use and others reporting levels that matched the clinic subjects.

Figure 1 shows normal probability plots for our five measures of drug use. We combined the frequencies of opiate and stimulant use into a single category because they were highly correlated with each other ($r = 0.77$) and doing so resulted in a more orderly distribution of drug use frequencies, while maintaining a faithful reflection of each drug. (The correlation between the frequency of opiate use and the combined score was $r = 0.92$, and the correlation between the frequency of stimulant use and the combined score was $r = 0.91$.) On the x-axes are the obtained frequencies of drug use, and on the y-axes are the expected frequencies assuming that they were normally distributed. Thus, deviations from a straight line fit indicate deviations from normality. The left panels indicate that the untransformed frequencies were not normally distributed. The right panels show the same data transformed as indicated in the graph. We used Stata's Box-Cox test to guide the search for the transformation that provided the best fit to a normal distribution, and on the basis of these results and visual inspection of the graphs, we settled on the square root transformation for stimulants and opiates, years of use and cigarettes, and power transformations of 0.18 for alcohol binges and marijuana use. According to the Shapiro–Francia test, the transformed drug use

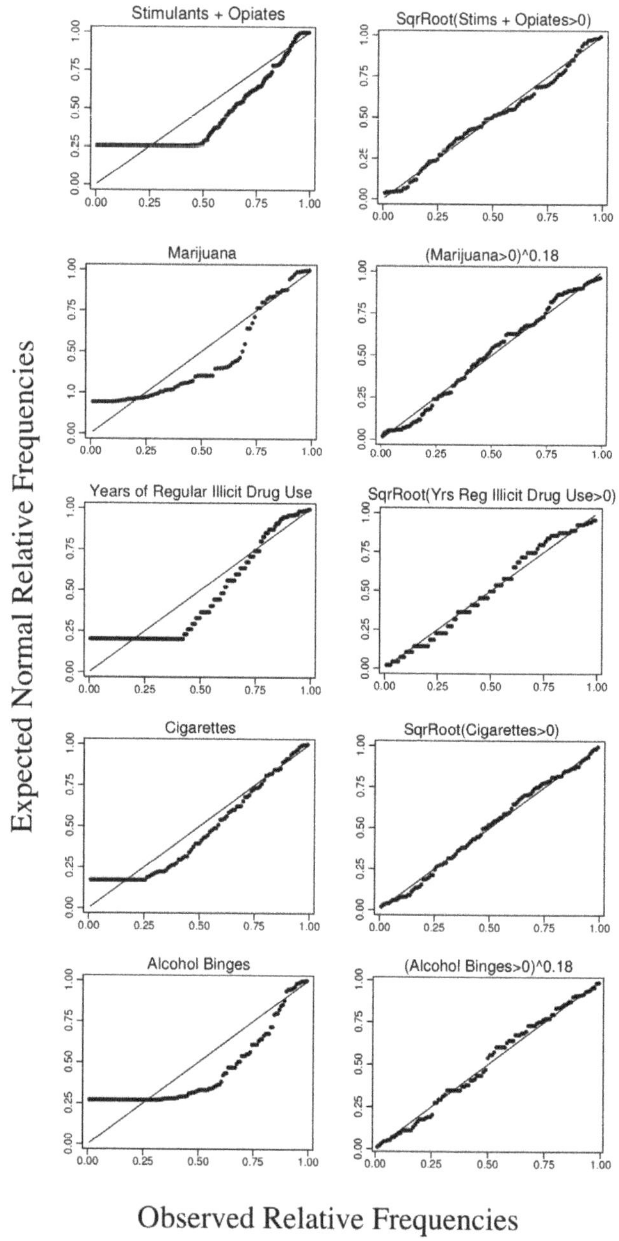

FIGURE 1 | Normal probability graphs of frequency of drug use and years of regular illicit drug use (>2/week for a year or more). The diagonal line plots a perfect correlation between the observed relative frequencies of use and the predicted relative frequencies assuming a normal distribution. The left panels show the untransformed frequencies including subjects who reported no use. The right panels show the transformed frequencies (square root or power with an exponent of 0.18) for subjects who used one or more times.

frequencies did not deviate significantly from normality, with the exception of marijuana ($p < 0.05$). However, as indicated by the graph, the distribution of marijuana use frequencies was not that different from the frequency distributions for other drugs. Thus, the transformed drug use frequencies approximated the regression model ideal of normally distributed variables. (Normality tests of the residuals are presented with the regression results.)

COGNITIVE, PSYCHIATRIC, AND DRUG USE CORRELATIONS

Table 2 lists the correlations between the number of times a drug was used, the six cognitive measures, impulsiveness, the total scores on the psychiatric symptoms check list, and years-of-school. The asterisks indicate significance at the 0.05 level, taking into account the number of comparisons (Bonferroni corrected).

Most of the correlations were statistically significant, and the pattern of correlations revealed an underlying order across drugs and psychological measures. The correlations were highest for opiates and stimulants and lowest for alcohol. Second, although the absolute magnitudes of the correlations varied as a function of drug, the relative strengths of the correlations did not. For every drug, the correlations between frequency of use and working memory were stronger than the correlation between frequency of use and simple memory. For every drug, the correlations between frequency of use and verbal (letter) working memory span tests were stronger than the correlation between frequency of use and spatial (line) working memory span tests. And, similarly, for every drug the correlations with frequency of use were higher for the vocabulary component of the IQ test than for the matrix reasoning component of the IQ test. That is, for every drug, verbal cognition was a stronger correlate of frequency of use than was spatial cognition. There was an analogous orderliness to the dispositional measures (psychiatric symptoms and impulsivity). In six of the eight tests, impulsivity was more strongly correlated with drug use than were psychiatric symptoms. However, these differences were quite small.

The last column of **Table 2** reveals that the strongest correlate of drug use was years-of-school. This was true for every drug, with the correlations varying from −0.36 (alcohol) to −0.66 (stimulants/opiates and years of illicit drug use). Also notice that years-of-school was significantly correlated with the cognitive measures and with impulsiveness and psychiatric symptoms. These correlations mirror the drug correlations in that they were stronger for the verbal tests, stronger for the working memory tests, and stronger for impulsiveness than for psychiatric symptoms. Thus, years-of-school was most strongly correlated with those variables that were most strongly correlated with drug use, and the rank order of the correlations was nearly identical for every drug, with scores on verbal tests outpacing scores on spatial tests.

CURRENT DRUG USE

We also evaluated the relations between current drug use and cognition. Twenty-nine of 77 clinic subjects tested positive for one or more illicit drugs. However, their scores on the cognitive tests were similar to those of the clinic subjects who did not test positive for an illicit drug. For instance, the average IQ scores for the two groups were nearly identical: 94.6 and 94.0, none of the differences were statistically significant, and on two of the six tests, those who tested positive for drug use scored slightly higher. On the basis of verbal reports, 34 clinic subjects reported that they had used one or more illicit drugs in the 30 days prior to the interview. That is, verbal reports provided somewhat higher rate of recent drug use than did metabolic tests, a result reported by others as well [e.g., Ref. (29)]. The cognitive scores for those who reported past month drug use were similar to the scores of those who reported no drug use in the last 30 days, and none of the differences were statistically significant. We also asked community subjects about current drug use. Twenty-nine met the criteria for lifetime regular drug use, and of this subset, six reported that they had used an illicit drug at least once in the last 30 days. This is a very small sample. Nevertheless, we should report that their cognitive scores were about the same as those of subjects reporting no recent drug use (e.g., average IQ scores of 109.3 and 106.6, respectively).Thus, there was no evidence that current drug use influenced performance on the cognitive tests.

MULTIPLE REGRESSION ANALYSES OF THE CORRELATES OF DRUG USE

Years-of-school, scores on the cognitive tests, and scores on the dispositional questionnaires were correlated with one another as well as with drug use. To better understand the structure of the correlations we recalculated them using multiple regression methods. First, we applied principal component analyses to reduce the number of predictors and to establish predictors that were not correlated with each other (with varimax rotation of the factors). Three factors accounted for 81% of the variance in the six cognitive tests. These will be referred to as "IQ," "verbal cognition," and "spatial cognition," with the labels identifying the cognitive test or tests that the factor was most strongly correlated with. Two factors accounted for 80% of the variance in Barratt scale results and the 10 Symptom Check-List symptoms. These will be referred to as "impulsiveness" and "psychiatric symptoms," in accordance with their correlates. Thus, we reduced 17 cognitive and dispositional predictors of drug use to 5, and in each set the predictors were statistically independent of one another. To these five predictors we added three demographic predictors of drug use: age, gender, and "clinic status." The latter was a binary measure that distinguished clinic and community subjects. Our goal was to dissociate being in treatment and years-of-school. For instance, if years-of-school was largely a proxy for clinic status then including clinic status in the analysis would reduce the correlation between years-of-school and drug use, perhaps to the extent that it was no longer a significant correlate of drug use. However, since a prerequisite for treatment was a diagnosis of opiate dependence, clinic status was necessarily a significant predictor of illicit drug use, and **Table 1** suggests it may also predict drinking bouts and cigarette smoking. Thus, it was not obvious that the correlates of drug use listed in **Table 2** would remain significant when clinic status was included in the regression equations.

REGRESSION (CRAGG'S DOUBLE-HURDLE) ANALYSES OF THE CORRELATES OF DRUG USE

Tables 3 and **4** summarize the regression analyses for licit and illicit drugs. For each drug – identified in the top row – the first two columns list the coefficients for the predictors of any use and their significance levels, as determined by probit regression. The third

Table 1 | Frequency of drug use.

	All subjects				Community				Clinic			
	Min.	Med.	Avg.	Max.	Min.	Med.	Avg.	Max.	Min.	Med.	Avg.	Max.
Opiates[a]	0	0	1468	13,416	0	0	204	13,416	130	2548	3225	11,284
Stimulants[b]	0	12	876	12,064	0	12	225	5102	0	1300	1780	12,064
Marijuana[c]	0	221	1464	11,284	0	221	750	9282	0	1456	2456	11,284
Years regular[d]	0	4.5	8.5	34	0	4.5	2.6	34	3	15	16.7	34
Total occasions[e]	0	1508	4375	25,351	0	1508	1281	25,351	874	7332	8702	24,128
Alcohol binges[f]	0	48	728	9072	0	48	452	8640	0	432	1112	9072
Cigarettes/100[g]	0	538	1066	6388	0	538	561	6388	0	1752	1768	5183

[a]F(1,182) = 1034, p < 0.001; [b]F(1,182) = 177, p < 0.001; [c]F(1,182) = 57, p < 0.001; [d]F(1,182) = 164, p < 0.001; [e]F(1,182) = 195, p < 0.001; [f]F(1,182) = 21, p < 0.001; [g]F(1,182) = 66, p < 0.001.

Table 2 | Drug use, cognition, psychological disposition, and years-of-school correlations*.

	Letter STM+	Letter WM+	Spatial STM	Spatial WM	IQ vocab test	IQ Matrix teas test	Impulsiveness+	Psych sympt total+	Years school
Opiate	−0.26*	−0.39*	−0.24*	−0.31*	−0.53*	−0.24*	0.37*	0.35*	−0.61*
Stimulant	−0.32*	−0.37*	−0.17*	−0.25*	−0.48*	−0.28*	0.31*	0.28*	−0.56*
Stimulant and opiate	−0.31*	−0.42*	−0.24*	−0.31*	−0.57*	−0.27*	0.39*	0.37*	−0.66*
Marijuana	−0.11	−0.14	−0.08	−0.22*	−0.35*	−0.21*	0.30*	0.33*	−0.46*
Years regular	−0.26*	−0.39*	−0.20*	−0.32*	−0.58*	−0.34*	0.38*	0.39*	−0.66*
Alcohol	−0.02	−0.04	−0.05	−0.15*	−0.26*	−0.21*	0.32*	0.25*	−0.36*
Cigs	−0.24*	−0.31*	−0.17*	−0.30*	−0.41*	−0.32*	0.25*	0.24*	−0.53*
Years school	0.31*	0.39*	0.21*	0.37*	0.63*	0.39*	−0.41*	−0.39*	

**p* < 0.05, Bonferroni corrected.

+*STM refers to short-term memory; WM refers to working memory; Impulsiveness refers to the participant's score on the Barratt questionnaire; Psych sympt total refers to the participant's total score on the Symptom Check List-90 questionnaire. Correlations are based on the transformed drug frequencies.*

and fourth columns list the coefficients of the predictors and their statistical significance for the frequency of use among users (truncated regression), that is, conditional on use. The significance levels were set according to Stata's "robust" command, which corrects for heteroskedastic residuals and observations that might have endue influence ("leverage"). We eliminated spatial cognition and verbal cognition from the regression analyses because preliminary tests revealed that their fitted coefficients were not significantly different from zero for any drug. Stata's multicollinearity test among the predictors resulted in a median Variance Inflated Factor of 1.37 (or, alternatively, median tolerance of 0.75), which is well below the recommended maximum of 4.0 or 5.0. According to the Shapiro–Wilk test, the residuals were normally distributed, with the exception of those for smoking. For both licit and illicit drugs the Double-Hurdle regression models were significant [with an average Wald χ^2 (7) = 459.9, $p > 0.0000$].

ILLICIT DRUGS

Table 3 shows that the statistically significant predictors of any use and frequency of use conditional on any use differed. Clinic status was, of course, a significant predictor of any illicit drug use. Impulsivity was a significant predictor of any stimulant and opiate use, and years-of-school was also a significant predictor of any opiate and stimulant use and had a null-hypothesis p value of 0.052 for one or more years of illicit drug use. The correlations for school were negative, meaning the more years that an individual spent in school, the less likely he or she was to use an illicit drug. The significant predictors of frequency of illicit drug use, conditional on any use, were age, gender, and years-of-school. For instance, the frequency of stimulant and opiate use and number of years of regular illicit drug use (three or more times a week) varied as a function of age, gender, and years-of-school (as well as clinic status). Marijuana had a somewhat different profile in that age and gender were the only significant predictors of frequency of use. Thus, of the significant zero-order correlations in **Table 2**, years-of-school remained a robust predictor of drug use when other predictors were included in the analyses, whereas IQ, impulsivity, and psychiatric symptoms did not.

LICIT DRUGS

Table 4 shows that the regression results for licit drugs differed from those of the illicit drugs, particularly in the case of drinking bouts. The significant predictors of ever smoking (> 100 cigarettes) were age, clinic stats, and years-of-school. The significant predictors of one or more drinking bouts (five or more drinks/occasion) were gender and impulsivity. The only significant predictor of number of cigarettes smoked among regular smokers was age. The significant predictors of the frequency of drinking bouts were

Table 3 | Double-Hurdle (Cragg's) regression analysis: coefficients, robust standard errors, and significance.

Predictors	Stimulants/opiates				Marijuana				Years regular use			
	Use/probit	p	Freq|Use TruncReg	p	Use/probit	p	Freq|Use TruncReg	p	Use/probit	p	Freq|Use TruncReg	p
Age	0.020 (0.014)	0.164	1.05*** (0.247)	0.000	−0.004 (0.010)	0.705	0.021*** (0.009)	0.017	0.001 (0.014)	0.960	0.057*** (0.009)	0.000
Gender	0.344 (0.307)	0.264	10.61*** (5.26)	0.001	0.177 (0.216)	0.414	0.562*** (0.171)	0.001	0.556 (0.293)	0.058	0.787*** (0.170)	0.000
Clinic	5.99*** (0.247)	0.000	39.19*** (9.36)	0.000	0.639* (0.275)	0.020	0.485 (0.248)	0.051	5.97*** (0.251)	0.000	0.934*** (0.251)	0.000
IQ	−0.012 (0.015)	0.409	0.264 (0.227)	0.246	0.007 (0.010)	0.506	−0.004 (0.009)	0.616	−0.122 (0.015)	0.401	−0.003 (0.007)	0.683
Impulsivity	0.576** (0.194)	0.003	0.771 (3.112)	0.805	0.168 (0.113)	0.138	0.113 (0.104)	0.278	0.333 (0.176)	0.063	−0.0370.100	0.711
Psych symptoms	0.248 (0.205)	0.226	−0.234 (2.547)	0.927	0.168 (0.113)	0.529	0.179 (0.093)	0.055	0.236 (0.189)	0.212	0.054 (0.093)	0.561
Years school	−0.145* (0.071)	0.038	−5.53*** (1.73)	0.001	−0.097 (0.054)	0.076	−0.055 (0.060)	0.364	−0.139 (0.072)	0.052	−0.139*** (0.059)	0.019

gender and impulsivity. For the legal drugs, clinic status was not a predictor of frequency of use, and as with the illicit drugs IQ and psychiatric symptoms were no longer significant predictors of ever using a licit drug or the frequency of licit drug use, conditional on any use. However, impulsivity continued to predict drinking bouts in the multiple regression analyses.

AGE

Age was positively correlated with frequency of drug use for drug users. This could simply mean that older individuals had more time to use drugs. To test this inference, we repeated the analyses with rate of drug use as the dependent variable rather than frequency of drug use. If the relationship with age reflected nothing more than opportunity to use more, the correlation between age and rate of drug use would not be significant. The denominator for calculating rate of drug use was years of use (current age minus onset age). Age was not a significant predictor of rate of drug use.

YEARS-OF-SCHOOL, IMPULSIVENESS, AND IQ

Figure 2 plots the relationship between years-of-school and stimulant and opiate use for the most and least impulsive subjects as measured by Barratt scores and for the least and most academically able subjects as measured by IQ scores (e.g., individuals who were "most impulsive" had a Barratt score above the 59th percentile, whereas individuals who were "least impulsive" had a Barratt score below the 41st percentile). Consider impulsiveness first (the left half of the graphs).

There was an inverse relationship between years-of-school and drug use for both the most and least impulsive subjects. Moreover, the relationship with school was strong enough to reverse the typical association between impulsiveness and drug use. For instance, a comparison of the top and middle panels shows that subjects who scored in the top two quintiles on the impulsivity questionnaire but who spent 14 years or more in school typically used stimulants and opiates less than did subjects who scored in the bottom two quintiles of the impulsivity scale but had spent <14 years in school (on average 848 and 3495 occasions, respectively). These two panels also show that for the more impulsive subjects there was about a fivefold increase in opiate and stimulant use for those with <14 years-of-school (4346 and 848 occasions), and the slopes of the fitted lines reveal that years-of-school had a slightly stronger association with differences in drug use for the more impulsive subjects.

To insure that years-of-school was not a proxy for clinic status, we tested the associations between school, impulsiveness, and drug use in a sample composed exclusively of community subjects. The bottom left panel shows the results. For subjects with <14 years-of-school, drug use differed markedly as a function of impulsiveness: 233 and 2048 occasions for low and high impulsiveness, respectively. However, community subjects who scored high on impulsivity but had 14 or more years-of-school used stimulants and opiates less frequently (233 occasions) than did community subjects who scored low on impulsivity but who went to school for fewer than 14 years (408 occasions). That is, for the community subjects, the typical link between impulsivity and drug use did not hold when years-of-school was included in the analyses.

Table 4 | Double-Hurdle (Cragg's) regression analysis: coefficients, robust standard errors, and significance.

	Cigarettes				Alcohol bouts			
Predictors	**Use/probit**	***p***	**Freq|Use TruncReg**	***p***	**Use/probit**	***p***	**Freq|Use TruncReg**	***p***
Age	0.035** (0.011)	0.002	8.71*** (1.13)	0.000	−0.029** (0.010)	0.005	0.019 (0.010)	0.058
Gender	−0.100 (0.230)	0.662	12.76 (27.86)	0.647	0.913*** (0.224)	0.000	0.451** (0.168)	0.007
Clinic	0.819** (0.297)	0.006	61.22 (37.59)	0.103	0.422 (0.300)	0.154	0.095 (0.234)	0.685
IQ	−0.017 (0.011)	0.122	−1.04 (1.06)	0.324	0.0.003 (0.010)	0.726	−0.008 (0.006)	0.210
Impulsivity	0.056 (0.142)	0.691	6.91 (14.00)	0.622	0.254* (0.113)	0.025	0.282** (0.092)	0.002
Psych symptoms	−0.151 (0.134)	0.259	12.68 (10.14)	0.211	0.089 (0.111)	0.425	0.052 (0.083)	0.531
Years school	−0.154* (0.061)	0.012	−8.84 (7.83)	0.259	−0.052 (0.057)	0.369	−0.031 (0.046)	0.511

The three panels on the right side of **Figure 2** plot the relationship between years-of-school and drug use for high and low scorers on the IQ test. There was an inverse relationship between years-of-school and drug use for both groups, and as with impulsiveness, the relationship with school was strong enough to reverse the overall correlation between IQ and drug use. For instance, low IQ subjects with 14 or more years-of-school tended to use opiates and stimulants somewhat less than did high IQ subjects with <14 years-of-school (1593 and 2269 occasions on average, respectively). Also note that the slopes of the fitted lines imply that years-of-school had a slightly stronger relationship with drug use for the low IQ subjects, which parallels the results for differences in impulsiveness.

The bottom panel shows stimulant and opiate use as a function of IQ and school for community subjects only. The results parallel the impulsivity results. Community subjects who scored in the two lowest quintiles for IQ but attended school for 14 or more years used stimulants and opiates less frequently than did community subjects who scored in the top two IQ quintiles but who failed to go to school for 14 or more years (48 and 741 occasions, respectively).

DISCUSSION

The subjects in our study varied widely in terms of drug histories, educational history, and psychological characteristics, yet, the results were orderly. (1) In all but one case, the transformed frequencies of drug use approximated a normal distribution – and the probability plot for the one exception (marijuana) was quite similar to the others. (2) As in previous studies, the frequency of drug use was positively correlated with impulsivity and negatively correlated with cognition and years-of-school. (3) The magnitudes of the correlations varied as a function of type of drug, but the rank order of the correlations was the same for each drug. The correlations were stronger for verbal tests than for spatial tests and were stronger for working memory than for simple memory. (4) However, in the multivariate analyses, the relationship between cognition and frequency of drug use (conditional upon any use) was no longer significant. Similarly, the relationship between impulsivity and drug use did not remain significant, with the exception of drinking bouts. In contrast, the relationship between years-of-school and frequency of drug use remained significant for any stimulant and opiate use, any smoking, frequency of stimulant and opiate use, and years of regular illicit drug use. (5) In line with the multivariate dissociation of educational attainment and cognition, **Figure 2** showed that high risk individuals who had been in school for 14 or more years used opiates and stimulants at lower levels than did low risk individuals with less schooling (where risk was defined by low IQ or high impulsivity). Similarly, among community subjects with 14 years or more of school, **Figure 2** revealed that stimulant and opiate use was not associated with differences in impulsiveness or IQ. This is significant in that it suggests that with the exception of alcohol, time spent in school helps reduce drug use. However, before discussing these findings in more detail, there are several methodological issues to attend to. Are the results reliable, and are there reasons to expect that they apply beyond the individuals who served as the subjects in this report?

RELIABILITY OF SELF-REPORTED DRUG HISTORIES

Researchers have tested the reliability of self-reported drug use by comparing their informants' words with physiological assays of drug use. The basic finding is that when the subjects appeared not to fear possible negative consequences for a candid account, self-reported levels of use approximated the metabolic estimates of levels of use. In contrast, when censure or worse was possible, participants under reported drug use (29–32). The present study approximated the conditions of the research projects that fostered reliable self-reported drug use. We guaranteed our informants anonymity, and we had no actual or apparent connection with the judicial system. In support of this point, and in line with previous findings, our verbal accounts of recent drug use indicated higher levels of recent use than did the metabolic tests. However, there is a second way to test the reliability of our self-report.

Experimental and self-report correlations

To determine the reliability of the subjects' accounts of their drug histories, we can examine the correlations between the experimental session test results (e.g., working memory scores) and estimated frequencies of drug use based on self-report. If the reports are reliable then it is possible, although not necessary, that drug use frequency will correlate with the variables that the experimenter selected to study. However, if the self-reports are unreliable then such correlations could only appear by chance, and, accordingly, would be highly unlikely. For every drug years-of-school was the strongest correlate of frequency of use, for every drug verbal IQ was a stronger correlate of frequency of use than was spatial IQ,

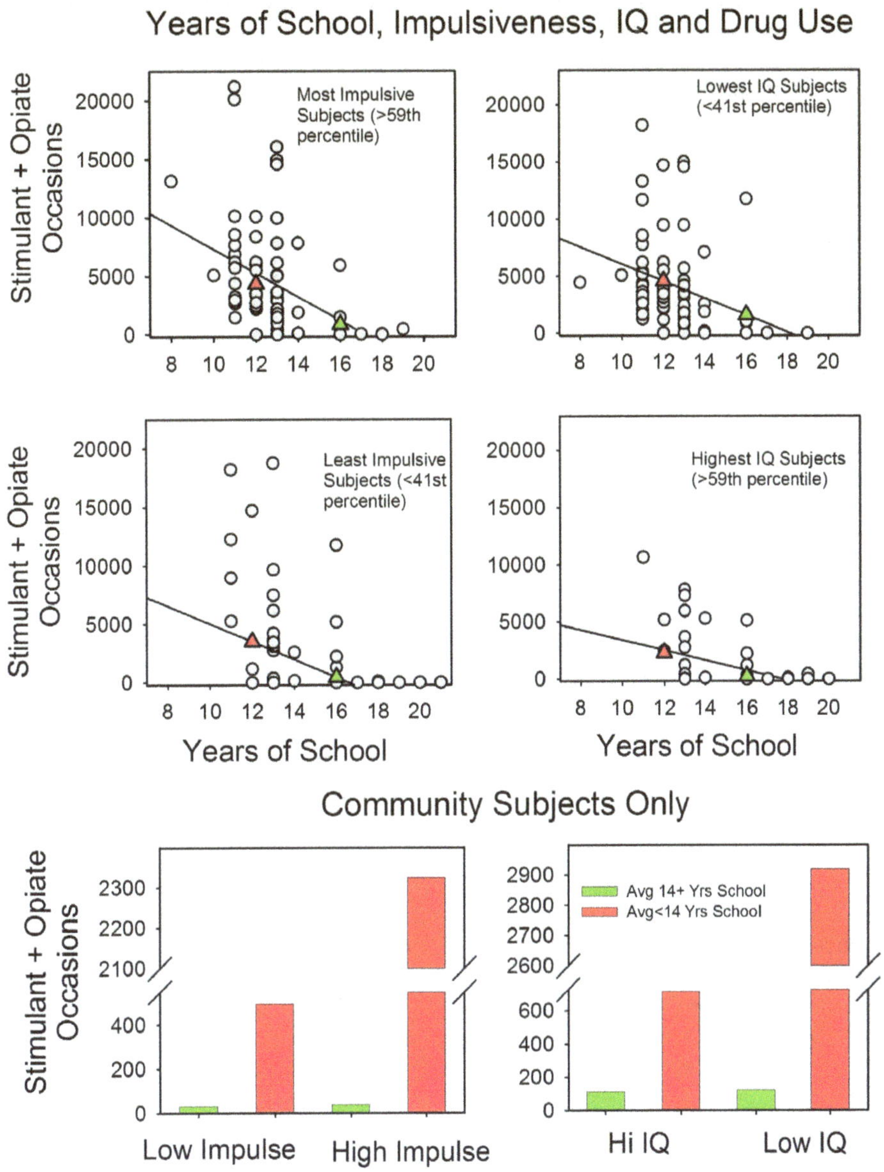

FIGURE 2 | The relationship between years-of-school and the frequency of stimulant and opiate use in the most and least at risk subjects (as measured by the Barratt Impulsiveness Scale and IQ). The top four panels show the findings from both clinic and community subjects. See text for details. The filled triangles indicate the averages for subjects with <14 years-of-school (red) and 14 or more years-of-school (green). The bottom two panels show these relations for just the community subject sample.

and for every drug working memory was a stronger correlate of frequency of use than was short-term memory. It is implausible that the subjects concocted drug histories that were so systematically related to their performance in the cognitive procedures. Put another way, the results are highly orderly, and it is much more plausible that this order reflects valid self-reports (and orderly correlations with cognition and psychological disposition) than accident or artifice.

GENERALITY OF THE RESULTS

We can compare our results with previous studies to evaluate the generality of the present findings. First, the zero-order correlations are consistent with scores of previous studies on the relations between educational attainment, impulsivity, and drug use, including large, national surveys that selected participants so as to match national demographic trends [e.g., Ref. (33)]. Similarly, the multiple regression analyses produced results that match previous findings. For instance, in a large prospective study of IQ and adult outcomes, Fergusson et al. (34), found that childhood IQ was correlated with educational attainment and a long list of dysfunctional adult behaviors. But then in the multivariate analyses with social covariates, IQ's association with criminal activity, illicit drug use, and other dysfunctional activities shrank significantly. This is analogous to our results. We found strong zero-order correlations between IQ, years-of-school, and drug use, but IQ no longer predicted frequency of drug use when years-of-school was a covariate in the Double-Hurdle regression analyses. Thus, even though the present research recruited volunteers, the results match those of similar studies that used selection criteria that would necessarily reduce the biases that can accompany self-selected subjects.

ALCOHOL

The pattern of correlations for bouts of heavy drinking differed from those of illicit drug use and smoking. Most notably, years-of-school did not predict heavy drinking, although impulsivity did. The most obvious explanation is that being in school limits access to illicit drugs but not to alcohol. This is consistent with recent research showing that dependence persists much longer for licit drugs than illicit drugs (35, 36). For instance, if years-of-school is negatively correlated with illicit drug use but not bouts of heavy drinking, then bouts of heavy drinking should persist longer, all else being equal.

INTERPRETATIONS OF THE FINDINGS

The multiple regression analyses show that years-of-school, clinical status, and gender remained significant predictors of the frequency of illicit drug use. Although each predictor is important to the understanding of drug use and addiction, we will focus largely on years-of-school. It was the strongest zero-order correlate of drug use, and it was typically the strongest zero-order correlate of the cognitive and dispositional correlates that were themselves significantly correlated with drug use.

The logical possibilities

There are three possible relationships between drug use and years-of-school: (1) drug use curtailed educational attainment, (2) educational attainment and drug use are not causally related but reflect one or more common factors, and (3) educational attainment and/or its correlates curtailed drug use. Each hypothesis has empirical support, and they are not mutually exclusive relations.

Did early drug use cut short time spent in school?

In a study with over a thousand subjects, Engberg and Morral (37) found that reducing drug use in young people increased school attendance. Their subjects were adolescents who had been admitted to drug treatment centers. This suggests that the correlations that we observed reflect in part or whole the negative influence of early drug use on staying in school. We examined this idea by evaluating the correlations between age of onset of drug use and years-of-school. If drugs curtailed school there should be a positive correlation between these two measures, i.e., younger age of onset and fewer years-of-school. For all subjects that had used an illicit drug one or more times, the correlation was in the expected direction, but small and not statistically significant ($r = 0.09, p = 0.30$). But perhaps the correlation would be stronger if the analysis was restricted to just those individuals who became regular illicit drug users (three times a week or more for at least a year)? The results were about the same ($r = 0.07$, $p = 0.44$). In similar analyses for drinking and smoking, those who started smoking at an earlier age tended to leave school earlier, but the correlation was weak ($r = 0.17$) and not statistically significant ($p = 0.21$). In contrast, the correlation between age of onset for binge drinking and years-of-school was negative, meaning there was a tendency for those who stayed in school longer to report more binge drinking episodes. However, as was the case for illicit drugs and smoking, the association was not statistically significant ($r = -0.18, p = 0.07$). Thus, for both licit and illicit drugs the relationship between age of onset of drug use and years-of-school was weak.

As a second check on the relationship between school and drug use, we compared the correlations between IQ and years-of-school for regular illicit drug users and not-regular illicit drug users. If drug use cut short school then it is reasonable to suppose that it also weakened the correlation between IQ and years-of-school (see, e.g., **Table 2**). The IQ and years-of-school correlation for regular drug users was $r = 0.49$ and for not-regular drug users it was $r = 0.36$. That is, IQ was a slightly better predictor of years-of-school in those who used illicit drugs more. Thus, for the subjects in this study, we did not find evidence that the onset of drug use cut short schooling.

That our results did not replicate those of Engberg and Morral (37) may reflect differences in the participants. Engberg and Morral's subjects had already been admitted to drug treatment programs although they were still in their teen years. In contrast, the subjects in our study were not necessarily at risk for drug use as teenagers. Most – including the clinic subjects – had completed high school. Thus, it seems reasonable to suppose that drug use is much more likely to undermine education in youngsters who are already at risk for not finishing high school.

Is there a common underlying factor?

It is plausible that the factors that influence years-of-school also strongly influence years of drug use so that the two outcomes are different aspects of a single syndrome. In the limit, the "single syndrome" thesis predicts that there is no causal relationship between school and drug use. Cognition, impulsiveness, and psychiatric symptoms are reasonable common factors. However, years-of-school remained a unique predictor of drug use when these factors were included in the regression analyses. Thus, the limiting case that educational attainment has no causal tie to drug use (despite zero-order correlations) was not supported. It is easy, though, to imagine other common factors. For example, "conscientiousness" predicts performance in school [e.g., Ref. (38)] and drug use (39). Thus, in future studies on the role of education in drug use it would be of interest to measure the influence of conscientiousness and other personality traits.

Did years-of-school help limit drug use?

According to the regression analyses, years-of-school was a significant predictor of whether someone became a stimulant and opiate user or a smoker and of the frequency of stimulant and opiate use and years of regular use of any illicit drug. Although this is a cross-sectional study, the pattern of correlations is most simply understood in terms of the influence of years-of-school on drug use.

First, as has been emphasized, verbal cognition was a stronger predictor of drug use than was spatial cognition and this held for cigarettes and alcohol as well as for illegal drugs. There is no known pharmacological explanation for this result, and given the very disparate pharmacological properties of the drugs, it seems highly unlikely that one exists. However, the rank order of the correlations makes sense if years-of-school played a key role in limiting drug use. First, **Table 2** shows that cognition, impulsivity, and psychiatric symptoms showed the same pattern of correlations with drug use as they did with years-of-school. Verbal cognition was more strongly correlated with both frequency of drug use and years-of-school than was spatial cognition. Similarly working memory scores were more strongly correlated with both frequency of drug use and years-of-school than was simple memory. The simplest interpretation is that the cognitive differences resulted in differences in educational attainment, which, in turn, led to differences in drug use. In support of the first point, researchers routinely find that verbal cognition is a better predictor of academic performance than spatial cognition [e.g., Ref. (40, 41)]. In support of the second point, longitudinal studies of at risk children repeatedly find that those children who do better in school, even in the elementary grades, have better adolescent and adult outcomes [e.g., Ref. (5, 42)]. That is, there are empirical precedents for the interpretation that school provides social and health benefits, such as less illicit drug use. (What is new is this report is that the correlation between educational attainment and drug use remained after controlling for IQ and impulsivity.)

LIMITATIONS

We see several limitations: (1) the study relies on self-report, (2) the subjects were not selected randomly, (3) the analysis was correlational, and (4) we restricted the subjects to those who graduated high school or obtained a GED. We have discussed the first three, as it seemed essential to do so before considering the implications of the findings. The problem with the GED or high school graduation requirement is that it may have limited the range of values for years-of-school. Nevertheless, years-of-school was the best predictor of drug use, cognition, and psychiatric symptoms. Moreover, according to **Figure 2** the critical number of years-of-school is 14 or more. This is close to the median value for the subjects in this study, so that the range of variation in years-of-school was appropriate for detecting the critical 14-year mark. These findings suggest that the most likely consequence of widening the educational criteria would be stronger evidence for the importance of education in drug use.

RELEVANCE TO THE UNDERSTANDING OF ADDICTION

Methodological relevance

Years-of-school was the strongest zero-order correlate of drug use and the most consistent predictor of illicit drug use in the multiple regression analyses. However, we would not have discovered this had we followed the more typical research methodology of studying just those drug users who were in treatment, as this would have restricted the range of variation in educational attainment. This raises the possibility that there may be other little studied variables that are also powerful predictors of drug use and/or variables, which predict both years-of-school and drug use. However, in order to investigate these questions researchers must include subjects who vary widely demographically, which will likely result in data sets with a large number of zeroes. We found that Cragg's Double-Hurdle regression method offered a handy solution to this problem, and it should do the same for other researchers who recruit subjects from the community as well as from the clinic.

Conceptual relevance

Addiction is often referred to as a "chronic relapsing disease" [for discussion and history of this viewpoint, see Ref. (43)]. In line with this definition, the directors and spokespersons of the American federal addiction research institutes promote molecular, pharmacological accounts of excessive drug use [e.g., Ref. (44)]. They claim that drug use transforms voluntary drug experimenters into involuntary "addicts" who have lost the capacity to say "no" [e.g., Ref. (45)]. However, the results presented here support the idea that social processes, such as time spent in school, play an important role in drug use. In support of these findings, national surveys reveal that educational attainment is a potent predictor of who quits smoking cigarettes (46, 47) and who quits heavy drug use [e.g., Ref. (33)]. Moreover, according to the regression analyses what mattered for the subjects in this study was time in school, not its cognitive or dispositional correlates. Put more generally, although addiction researchers have emphasized individual differences in the likelihood that drug use leads to excessive use, it may turn out that historical and other social factors are at least if not more important. For example, cohort differences in prevalence are substantially larger for addiction than for other psychiatric disorders [Ref. (43), Figure 2.3].

Relevance for interventions

Figure 2 points to the potential practical significance of the results. For those subjects who were most at risk for stimulant and opiate use (as measured by IQ and impulsivity), years-of-school was associated with lower than expected levels of drug use. Indeed the high risk subjects with 14 years or more of school used opiates and stimulants less than did the low risk subjects who had <14 years-of-school. This is important. To our knowledge, there are no reliable programs for boosting IQ or curbing impulsivity. In contrast, efforts to increase schooling have been successful. For instance, in the United States over the last 10 years there has been about a 25% increase in the number of individuals aged 25 and older who completed college (48). This suggests that a plausible approach to excessive drug use is indirect: promote programs that increase post high school training. Also note that there is nothing in our results or those that we reviewed that say that such schooling has to be college oriented. In the present study, years-of-school included a wide range of programs, not just academic ones. In support of this point are the results from an interesting report on the relationships between time in the classroom, academic skills, and safe-sex. The researchers (49) measured years-of-school, reading ability, evidence of learning disabilities, and prudent sexual behavior among female prison inmates. Years-of-school predicted the likelihood of taking precautions against contracting HIV; language skills and learning disabilities did not. That is, how long the women went to school, not what they had learned in school, predicted healthy behaviors.

How might years in school influence drug use?

This last observation raises the issue of how might time spent in school have constrained drug use? Much has been written about this question [e.g., Ref. (50)]. Lleras-Muney (51), an economist, found that years-of-school was correlated with increased life span in the United States even after controlling for region of the country, occupation, access to medical care, and gender. She and a colleague, David Cutler and Lleras-Muney (52), speculate that "increasing levels of education lead to different thinking and decision-making patterns" that promote more prudent behavior. In a longitudinal study, Henry et al. (42) found that years-of-school markedly weakened the correlation between early childhood measures of impulsiveness and antisocial behavior as measured at age 21. Importantly, these effects were greatest for those who scored highest on the "Lack of Control" behavioral scale. The authors speculate that attending school strengthens ties to social institutions and values, and that this inhibits antisocial behavior, particularly in those who are most likely to be antisocial.

In addition to the possible cognitive and social benefits of time spent in school, **Figure 2** suggests that school may function something like a physical barrier against frequent illicit drug use. The graphs show that school had a more pronounced effect on drug use for those who spent 14 or more years in the classroom. Put in terms of age, those with 14 years or more of school tended to be in a classroom at least part of the day during their late teens and early twenties. This is just the age at which heavy, illicit drug use typically starts [e.g., Ref. (53)]. Thus, participation in post high school education and professional programs may keep young adults "off the streets" at just the age when they are most likely to become frequent drug users. This not to say that school is a panacea. Individuals with secure careers become heavily involved with drugs (54), and most individuals who have <14 years-of-school do not become drug addicts. These two points do not undermine the role that school plays in promoting healthy behavior. Rather they simply show that school is not the only predictor of drug use.

CONCLUSION

To our knowledge, this is the first study to simultaneously evaluate the correlations between impulsiveness, cognition, years-of-school, and drug use. The simplest interpretation of the results is that to a significant degree the cognitive and dispositional correlates of drug use (listed in **Table 2**) were in place prior to drug use, and that the negative correlations between years-of-school and illicit drug use and between years-of-school and smoking were due in some part to school itself, not its correlates. The practical significance of these findings is that programs that promote education and training, particularly in young adults, will pay dividends as measured by decreases in drug use. Moreover, the results suggest that such programs may be most useful for those most at risk. These are testable ideas and according to the results presented here, promising ideas.

ACKNOWLEDGMENTS

We would like to thank Caitlin Ravichandran of McLean Hospital and Hiram Brownell of Boston College for their comments on earlier versions of this manuscript. Special thanks go to Federico Mantovanelli of the Boston College Research Services and Don Ross of University of Cape Town for their useful suggestions regarding the regression analyses. The research was supported by a grant from the National Institute of Drug Abuse (R01 DA14387) to Gene M. Heyman.

REFERENCES

1. Rotella C. *Class Warrior: Arne Duncan's Bid to Shake Up Schools*. New Yorker (2010). p. 24–9.
2. Mensch BS, Kandel DB. Dropping out of high school and drug involvement. *Sociol Educ* (1988) **61**:95–113. doi:10.2307/2112267
3. Lynskey MT, Coffey C, Degenhardt L, Carlin JB, Patton G. A longitudinal study of the effects of adolescent cannabis use on high school completion. *Addiction* (2003) **98**:685–92. doi:10.1046/j.1360-0443.2003.00356.x
4. Brunswick AF, Titus SP. Heroin patterns and trajectories in an African American cohort (1969-1990). In: Inciardi JA, Harrison LD, editors. *Heroin in the Age of Crack-Cocaine*. (Vol. 6), Thousand Oaks, CA: Sage Publications (1998). p. 77–108.
5. Fothergill KE, Ensminger ME, Green KM, Crum RM, Robertson J, Juon HS. The impact of early school behavior and educational achievement on adult drug use disorders: a prospective study. *Drug Alcohol Depend* (2008) **92**:191–9. doi:10.1016/j.drugalcdep.2007.08.001
6. Kessler RC, Foster CL, Saunders WB, Stang PE. Social consequences of psychiatric disorders, I: educational attainment. *Am J Psychiatry* (1995) **152**: 1026–32.
7. Lozano JH, Gordillo F, Pérez MA. Impulsivity, intelligence, and academic performance: testing the interaction hypothesis. *Pers Individ Dif* (2014) **61**:63–8. doi:10.1016/j.paid.2014.01.013
8. Tambs K, Sundet JM, Magnus P, Berg K. Genetic and environmental contributions to the covariance between occupational status, educational attainment, and IQ: a study of twins. *Behav Genet* (1989) **19**:209–22. doi:10.1007/BF01065905
9. Stinson FS, Grant BF, Dawson D, Ruan WJ, Huang B, Saha T. Comorbidity between DSM-IV alcohol and specific drug use disorders in the United States: results from the national epidemiological survey on alcohol and related conditions. *Drug Alcohol Depend* (2005) **80**:105–16. doi:10.1016/j.drugalcdep.2005.03.009
10. Regier DA, Farmer ME, Rae DS, Locke BZ, Keith SJ, Judd LL, et al. Comorbidity of mental disorders with alcohol and other drug abuse. Results from the epidemiologic catchment area (ECA) study. *JAMA* (1990) **264**:2511–8. doi:10.1001/jama.1990.03450190043026
11. Robins LN. Vietnam veterans' rapid recovery from heroin addiction: a fluke or normal expectation? *Addiction* (1993) **88**:1041–54. doi:10.1111/j.1360-0443.1993.tb02123.x
12. Nielsen DA, Ho A, Bahl A, Varma P, Kellogg S, Borg L, et al. Former heroin addicts with or without a history of cocaine dependence are more impulsive than controls. *Drug Alcohol Depend* (2012) **124**:113–20. doi:10.1016/j.drugalcdep.2011.12.022
13. Madden GJ, Bickel WK, Jacobs EA. Discounting of delayed rewards in opioid-dependent outpatients: exponential or hyperbolic discounting functions? *Exp Clin Psychopharmacol* (1999) **7**:284–93. doi:10.1037/1064-1297.7.3.284
14. Heyman GM, Gibb SP. Delay discounting in college cigarette chippers. *Behav Pharmacol* (2006) **17**:669–79. doi:10.1097/FBP.0b013e3280116cfe
15. Mitchell SH. Measures of impulsivity in cigarette smokers and non-smokers. *Psychopharmacology* (1999) **146**:455–64. doi:10.1007/PL00005491
16. de Wit H, Flory JD, Acheson A, McCloskey M, Manuck SB. IQ and non-planning impulsivity are independently associated with delay discounting in middle-aged adults. *Pers Individ Dif* (2007) **42**:111–21. doi:10.1016/j.paid.2006.06.026
17. Hinson JM, Jameson TL, Whitney P. Impulsive decision making and working memory. *J Exp Psychol Learn Mem Cogn* (2003) **29**:298–306. doi:10.1037/0278-7393.29.2.298
18. Freeney Y, O'Connell M. Wait for it: delay-discounting and academic performance among an Irish adolescent sample. *Learn Individ Differ* (2010) **20**:231–6. doi:10.1016/j.lindif.2009.12.009
19. Jaroni JL, Wright SM, Lerman C, Epstein LH. Relationship between education and delay discounting in smokers. *Addict Behav* (2004) **29**:1171–5. doi:10.1016/j.addbeh.2004.03.014
20. Patton JH, Stanford MS, Barratt ES. Factor structure of the Barratt Impulsiveness Scale. *J Clin Psychol* (1995) **51**:768–74. doi:10.1002/1097

21. Derogatis LR. *Symptom Checklist-90-Revised: Administration, Scoring and Procedures Manual.* 3rd ed. Minneapolis, MN: NCS Pearson, Inc (1994).
22. Kane MJ, Engle RW. The role of prefrontal cortex in working-memory capacity, executive attention, and general fluid intelligence: an individual-differences perspective. *Psychon Bull Rev* (2002) **9**:637–671. doi:10.3758/BF03196323
23. Psychological Corporation. *Wechsler Abbreviated Scale of Intelligence Manual.* San Antonio, TX: Psychological Corporation (1999).
24. McLellan AT, Kushner H, Metzger D, Peters R, Smith I, Grissom G, et al. The fifth edition of the addiction severity index. *J Subst Abuse Treat* (1992) **9**:199–213. doi:10.1016/0740-5472(92)90062-S
25. Vogel-Sprott M. *Alcohol Tolerance and Social Drinking: Learning the Consequences.* New York, NY: Guilford Press (1992).
26. Cragg JG. Some statistical models for limited dependent variables with application to the demand for durable goods. *Econometrica* (1971) **39**(5):829–44. doi:10.2307/1909582
27. Tobin J. Estimation of relationships for limited dependent variables. *Econometrica* (1958) **26**:24–36.
28. Burke WJ. Fitting and interpreting Cragg's tobit alternative using Stata. *Stata J* (2009) **9**:584–92.
29. Darke S. Self-report among injecting drug users: a review. *Drug Alcohol Depend* (1998) **51**:253–63. doi:10.1016/S0376-8716(98)00028-3
30. Land DB, Kushner R. Drug abuse during pregnancy in an inner-city hospital: prevalence and patterns. *J Am Osteopath Assoc* (1990) **90**:421–426.
31. Nair P, Rothblum S, Hebel R. Neonatal outcome in evidence of fetal exposure to opiates, cocaine, and cannabinoids. *Clin Pediatr* (1994) **33**:280–8. doi:10.1177/000992289403300505
32. Weatherby NL, Needle R, Cesari H, Booth R, McCoy CB, Watters JK, et al. Validity of self-reported drug use among injection drug users and crack cocaine users recruited through street outreach. *Eval Program Plann* (1994) **17**:347–55. doi:10.1016/0149-7189(94)90035-3
33. Warner LA, Kessler RC, Hughes M, Anthony JC, Nelson CB. Prevalence and correlates of drug use and dependence in the United States: results from the national comorbidity survey. *Arch Gen Psychiatry* (1995) **52**:219–29. doi:10.1001/archpsyc.1995.03950150051010
34. Fergusson DM, Horwood LJ, Ridder EM. Show me the child at seven II: childhood intelligence and later outcomes in adolescence and young adulthood. *J Child Psychol Psychiatry* (2005) **46**:850–8. doi:10.1111/j.1469-7610.2005.01472.x
35. Heyman GM. Quitting drugs: quantitative and qualitative features. *Annu Rev Clin Psychol* (2013) **9**:29–59. doi:10.1146/annurev-clinpsy-032511-143041
36. Lopez-Quintero C, Hasin DS, de los Cobos JP, Pines A, Wang S, Grant BF, et al. Probability and predictors of remission from life-time nicotine, alcohol, cannabis or cocaine dependence: results from the national epidemiologic survey on alcohol and related conditions. *Addiction* (2011) **106**:657–69. doi:10.1111/j.1360-0443.2010.03194.x
37. Engberg J, Morral AR. Reducing substance use improves adolescents' school attendance. *Addiction* (2006) **101**:1741–51. doi:10.1111/j.1360-0443.2006.01544.x
38. Cheng W, Ickes W. Conscientiousness and self-motivation as mutually compensatory predictors of university-level GPA. *Pers Individ Dif* (2009) **47**:817–22. doi:10.1016/j.paid.2009.06.029
39. Terracciano A, Löckenhoff CE, Zonderman AB, Ferrucci L, Costa PT. Personality predictors of longevity: activity, emotional stability, and conscientiousness. *Psychosom Med* (2008) **70**:621–7. doi:10.1097/PSY.0b013e31817b9371
40. de Koning BB, Loyens SM, Rikers RP, Smeets G, van der Molen HT. Generation Psy: student characteristics and academic achievement in a three-year problem-based learning bachelor program. *Learn Individ Differ* (2012) **22**:313–23. doi:10.1016/j.lindif.2012.01.003
41. Ormiston M. The bearing of general and special abilities upon scholastic success at the beginning and end of a secondary school career. *Br J Educ Psychol* (1939) **9**:213–23. doi:10.1111/j.2044-8279.1939.tb03209.x
42. Henry B, Caspi A, Moffitt TE, Harrington H, Silva PA. Staying in school protects boys with poor self-regulation in childhood from later crime: a longitudinal study. *Int J Behav Dev* (1999) **23**:1049–73. doi:10.1080/016502599383667
43. Heyman GM. *Addiction: A Disorder of Choice.* Cambridge, MA: Harvard University Press (2009).
44. Volkow ND, Li TK. Drug addiction: the neurobiology of behaviour gone awry. *Nat Rev Neurosci* (2004) **5**:963–70. doi:10.1038/nrn1539
45. Leshner AI. Addiction is a brain disease, and it matters. *Science* (1997) **278**:45. doi:10.1126/science.278.5335.45
46. U.S. Department of Health & Human Services. *The Health Benefits of Smoking Cessation: A Report of the Surgeon General.* Rockville, MD: U.S. Department of Health and Human Services, Public Health Service, Centers for Disease Control, Center for Chronic Disease Prevention and Health Promotion, Office of Smoking and Health. DHHS Publication No. (CDC) 90-8416 (1990).
47. U.S. Department of Health & Human Services. Cigarette smoking among adults – United States, 1993. *Morb Mortal Wkly Rev* (1994) 43:925–30.
48. United States Census Bureau. (n.d.). Available from: http://www.census.gov/hhes/socdemo/education/data/cps/historical/Fig3.pg
49. Paasche-Orlow MK, Clarke JG, Hebert MR, Ray MK, Stein MD. Educational attainment but not literacy is associated with HIV risk behavior among incarcerated women. *J Womens Health* (2005) **14**:852–9. doi:10.1089/jwh.2005.14.852
50. Bachman JG, editor. *The Education-Drug Use Connection: How Successes and Failures in School Relate to Adolescent Smoking, Drinking, Drug Use, and Delinquency.* New York, NY: Lawrence Erlbaum Associates (2008).
51. Lleras-Muney A. The relationship between education and adult mortality in the United States. *Rev Econ Stud* (2005) **72**:189–221. doi:10.1111/0034-6527.00329
52. Cutler DM, Lleras-Muney A. *Education and Health: Evaluating Theories and Evidence* (No. w12352). Cambridge, MA: National Bureau of Economic Research (2006).
53. Kessler RC, Berglund P, Demler O, Jin R, Merikangas KR, Walters EE. Lifetime prevalence and age-of-onset distributions of DSM-IV disorders in the national comorbidity survey replication. *Arch Gen Psychiatry* (2005) **62**:593–602. doi:10.1001/archpsyc.62.6.617
54. Coombs RH. *Drug-Impaired Professionals.* Cambridge, MA: Harvard University Press (1997).

Food cravings, appetite, and snack-food consumption in response to a psychomotor stimulant drug: the moderating effect of "food-addiction"

Caroline Davis[1]*, Robert D. Levitan[2], Allan S. Kaplan[2], James L. Kennedy[2] and Jacqueline C. Carter[3]

[1] *Kinesiology and Health Science, York University, Toronto, ON, Canada*
[2] *Centre for Addiction and Mental Health, Toronto, ON, Canada*
[3] *Department of Psychology, Memorial University of Newfoundland, St. John's, NL, Canada*

Edited by:
Adrian Meule, University of Wuerzburg, Germany

Reviewed by:
Kristin Miller Von Ranson, University of Calgary, Canada
Gene-Jack Wang, National Institutes of Health, USA

***Correspondence:**
Caroline Davis, Kinesiology and Health Science, York University, 343 Bethune College, 4700 Keele Street, Toronto, ON M3J1P3, Canada
e-mail: cdavis@yorku.ca

There is mounting evidence that many highly processed foods have addictive properties, and that some cases of compulsive overeating resemble an addiction disorder. While support for the *Yale Food Addiction Scale* (YFAS) as a valid diagnostic tool has been impressive and continues to increase, to date, no research has examined the food-addiction construct in response to an actual food stimulus, and in relation to direct measures of appetite and food consumption. As part of a larger community-based study of overeating in healthy adults who were predominately overweight and obese (aged 25–50 years), 136 participants completed the YFAS, of whom 23 met the diagnostic criteria for food-addiction. They took part in a 2-day, double-blind, cross-over, single-dose drug challenge using a psychomotor stimulant (methylphenidate) and placebo. Participants were first assessed on ratings of appetite and food cravings after holding and tasting their favorite snack food, after which they were able to eat all or part of the snack, as they wished. Three separate repeated-measures analysis-of-variance procedures were carried out, each with two between-subjects factors (Diagnosis: food-addiction vs. non-food addiction) and (Sex: male vs. female) and 1 within-subjects factor (Days: drug vs. placebo). As anticipated, for all three dependent variables, there was a significant main effect for Days with a response decrease from placebo to the drug condition. With respect to *food cravings* and *appetite ratings*, results indicated that the food addiction group had significantly higher scores on both variables. For *food consumption*, there was a significant Days × Diagnosis interaction whereby the food-addiction group showed no food-intake suppression across days compared to the non-food-addiction group who demonstrated a significant decrease in snack-food consumption with methylphenidate. The finding that the food-addiction group was resistant to the food-intake suppression typically induced by a dopamine agonist supports evidence of dopamine signaling-strength differences in individuals with compulsive overeating compared to those without this disorder. This represents the first demonstration that individuals defined by their food-addiction status have a unique pattern of food-intake following a pharmacologic challenge with such agents.

Keywords: food cravings, appetite, food consumption, psychomotor stimulant, food-addiction

INTRODUCTION

In its recently released 5th edition, the *Diagnostic and Statistical Manual of Mental Disorders* (DSM-5) has acknowledged the existence of behavioral addictions for the first time (American Psychiatric Association, 2013). Currently, however, pathological gambling is the only one listed in the newly labeled "non-substance-related disorders" category. Although other excessive behaviors related to sex, exercise, eating, and shopping had been considered for inclusion, none was deemed to have sufficient peer-reviewed evidence for identification as a mental health problem at the time of publication (Potenza, 2014). Of these conditions, the one receiving the most discussion and research investigation in recent years is *food addiction* – the rather unsuitably named[1] syndrome describing compulsive overeating accompanied by strong cravings and extreme difficulty in abstaining from highly palatable fare. To illustrate, a keywords search in *Web of Science* (an online scientific citation indexing service) for the year 2013 –

[1]There has been justified criticism of the contiguousness of the words "food" and "addiction" in this putative diagnostic label because the word "food" connotes substances essential for survival and fundamental to human existence, while "addiction" implies psychopathology and even antisocial behavior. More appropriate perhaps would be terms like "hyper-palatable processed food" or "high fat, sweet, and salty food" because those that are intensely craved and over-consumed, and that comprise most binge episodes are not grown or raised in nature. Instead they are highly processed foods, calorically dense in fat, sugar, and salt, and are almost universally perceived as very appetizing (Curtis and Davis, 2014).

using the terms "food addiction," "sex addiction," and "shopping addiction," consecutively – rendered 48, 8, and 0 citations, in that order.

The growing legitimacy of the food-addiction concept has been heavily influenced by the premise that hyper-palatable foods, rich in sugar, fat, and salt, have the potential to foster excessive consumption and a state of dependence (Gearhardt et al., 2011a; Davis and Carter, 2014), and that some cases of compulsive overeating have striking clinical and neurophysiologic similarities to drugaddiction (Davis and Carter, 2009; Davis, 2013). Compelling preclinical research laid the groundwork and a solid foundation of evidence for biobehavioral parallels between the excessive consumption of sugar and fat and that of addictive drugs like cocaine and heroin. Readers are referred to several excellent reviews of this body of research (Avena et al., 2008, 2012; Corwin et al., 2011). The systematic study of clinical cases of food addiction came somewhat later, but has increased rapidly. This work began to flourish with the development of the *Yale Food Addiction Scale* (YFAS; Gearhardt et al., 2009) – a diagnostic tool based on the seven DSM-IV (American Psychiatric Association, 1994) symptom criteria for substance dependence, with the word "food" substituting for drugs in the questionnaire items. To date, studies have found substantial co-morbidity between binge eating disorder (BED) and YFAS food addiction, in addition to many shared psychological and biological risk factors (Davis et al., 2011; Gearhardt et al., 2011b, 2012). An even greater overlap was found in an earlier study of women diagnosed with BED where 92% of the sample met the DSM-IV criteria for dependence during a structured telephone interview – again when food replaced the drug/substance nomenclature in the assessment questions (Cassin and von Ranson, 2007). A recent qualitative study also confirmed that a high proportion of obese women with and without BED endorsed DSM symptoms of substance dependence when food was the "substance" in question (Curtis and Davis, 2014). These women felt that "loss-of-control" overeating, the inability to stop this behavior despite strong wishes to do so, and extreme cravings were the characteristics of their disorder which most resembled an addiction.

The first case-control study of food addiction in obese men and women found that those who met the YFAS diagnostic criteria had a significantly greater prevalence of BED than their age- and weight-matched counterparts (Davis et al., 2011). They also reported more intense trait-related food cravings and greater emotional and hedonic overeating than the control participants. Other research has found similar results using the YFAS symptom score (Meule et al., 2012). In addition, preliminary genetic evidence demonstrated that a composite polymorphic index of elevated dopamine signaling strength was greater in those who met the YFAS criteria for food addiction, and this profile score correlated positively with binge eating severity, food cravings, and emotional eating (Davis et al., 2013). Together these results support the view that risk for food addiction is greater in those with a hyper-sensitivity to reward and a greater appetitive motivation for reinforcing stimuli. In a study of weight-loss treatment-seeking adults, YFAS-symptom scores were also associated with lower weight loss after several weeks of treatment, suggesting that food addiction, with related signs of tolerance and withdrawal, may undermine efforts to lose weight in those trying to adopt better eating habits (Burmeister et al., 2013). A later study, however, failed to replicate these results (Lent et al., 2014).

In a recent general-population study, adults who met the YFAS criteria for food addiction had significantly higher body mass index (BMIs) and a greater percentage of adipose tissue compared to their non-food-addicted counterparts (Pedram et al., 2013). They also self-reported eating more calories from fat and protein. In addition, it was found that overweight and obese women had a significantly higher prevalence of food addiction than weight-matched men. Interestingly, this sex bias reflects the pattern of findings from drug-addiction research. For example, while drug abuse has traditionally been more widespread in men than in women (Wittchen et al., 2011), the gap seems to be narrowing, suggesting that earlier differences may simply reflect variation in opportunity and gender-biased expectations rather than in vulnerability (Becker, 2009; Colell et al., 2013). Indeed, it appears that many addiction risk factors are greater in women than in men. Women tend to increase their rate of drug consumption more quickly than men, are more likely to relapse, and to have longer periods of drug use before their next attempt at abstinence (Elman et al., 2001; Evans and Foltin, 2010) – a phenomenon known as *telescoping*, which describes an accelerated progression from the commencement of drug use to the development of dependence and admission to treatment (Greenfield et al., 2010). Women who abuse drugs also report more severe cravings and subjective drug effects than their male counterparts (Back et al., 2011), and this pattern seems to be similar for most addictive substances (Becker and Ming, 2008).

There is now compelling evidence that the cravings for addictive drugs and for hyper-palatable foods are fostered by similar biological mechanisms whereby excessive consumption of either provokes neuro-adaptations resulting in a *blunted* dopamine signal in brain reward circuitry – in particular, the nucleus accumbens and the ventral tegmental area (VTA; Volkow et al., 2013). Excessive consumption also contributes to a heightened motivational salience for the reward, which, together with dopamine down-regulation, increases the "wanting," or an intense craving, for the substance in question (Robinson and Berridge, 2013). *Cravings* are therefore an important component of the addiction process, especially because they appear to increase the risk for relapse following abstinence (Sinha et al., 2006). In this context, it is noteworthy that conventional weight-loss programs, including dietary restriction and increased physical activity, are typically ineffective in the long term for patients with problematic overeating and obesity (Begin et al., 2006; Mann et al., 2007). Indeed, numerous obesity studies have linked cravings to overeating and weight gain, to the lack of success in attempts to restrict calories, and to early drop-out from bariatric treatment programs (Batra et al., 2013).

Not surprisingly, given the down-regulatory neurophysiologic processes in addiction, treatments that serve to increase dopamine signaling have shown some success in reducing episodes of overeating. For example, in a randomized-control trial, pharmacotherapy with an amphetamine-based stimulant medication was effective in lowering the frequency of binge episodes in those with compulsive overeating (Shaffer, 2012; Gasior et al., 2013). Similar medications have also been successful in producing weight loss in those with intractable obesity and co-morbid symptoms of attention deficit/hyperactivity disorder (ADHD; Levy et al., 2009). Likewise, laboratory studies of single-dose administrations of methylphenidate [a dopamine transporter (DAT) blocker] have also shown decreased food cravings and food consumption in obese adults and those with BED (Leddy et al., 2004; Goldfield et al., 2007; Davis et al., 2012). And finally, non-invasive dorsolateral prefrontal cortical (DLPFC) neurostimulation – a procedure which is believed to increase dopamine excretion via interconnections between the DLPFC and the VTA and nucleus accumbens – has also produced reductions in drug and food cravings (Jansen et al., 2013).

THE PRESENT STUDY

Although various studies have used food-related cues in their experimental paradigms (Gearhardt et al., 2011b; Meule et al., 2012), to the best of our knowledge, there are no *objective* food consumption studies in human food-addiction research. Since self-report measures of food intake may be subject to biased recall, it is also important to have objective food-intake data for a more complete understanding of the phenomenology of disordered (and other) eating behaviors. The purpose of the current study was therefore to compare appetite, cravings, and consumption between adults diagnosed with and without YFAS food addiction, in response to a snack-food challenge following a single-dose administration of methylphenidate versus placebo. Given the generally experienced, appetite-suppression, effects of stimulant drugs, and their suggested therapeutic use in reducing binge episodes (Levy et al., 2009; Shaffer, 2012; Gasior et al., 2013), the primary purpose for including the drug challenge in the study protocol was to identify possible factors moderating response magnitude to methylphenidate, given the considerable response variability among patients taking such medications[2].

Sex differences were also assessed in this 3-way mixed model, double-blind, cross-over design. It was anticipated that the food-addiction group would report greater appetite and food cravings and consume more of their favorite snack during the placebo condition than the non-food-addiction group. Another goal of this study was to investigate whether food addiction moderated the appetite-suppression effects typically found following administration of methylphenidate. It was speculated that the stronger appetitive responses to food associated with food-addiction (Davis et al., 2013) might buffer the normally experienced suppression effect from methylphenidate. Finally, and based on other sex differences in clinical and pre-clinical drug-response research, it was predicted that females would be more responsive to the appetite and food consumption suppression effects of methylphenidate than males.

[2]These potential moderators included genetic factors, results for which will be published elsewhere for the larger study.

MATERIALS AND METHODS

PARTICIPANTS

As part of a larger community-based study of overeating in healthy adults who were predominately overweight and obese and between the ages of 25 and 50 years, 136 participants (women = 92; male = 44) completed the YFAS, of whom 23 met the diagnostic criteria for food addiction. The food-addiction group had a mean BMI of 34.6 ± 7.0 and a mean age of 33.9 ± 5.9 years compared to the non-food-addiction group with a mean BMI of 33.8 ± 8.4 and a mean age of 32.4 ± 6.6 years. These values were not significantly different. Participants were recruited from posters, newspaper advertisements, and online sites like Craigslist and Kijiji. Inclusion criteria were residence in North America for at least 5 years and fluency in written and spoken English. Women were also required to be pre-menopausal as indicated by the reporting of regular menstrual-cycles. Exclusion criteria were a current diagnosis (or history) of any psychotic disorder, panic disorder, or substance abuse as diagnosed by the Structured Clinical Interview for DSM-IV (SCID), any serious medical condition like cancer, or heart disease, and any medications contraindicated for methylphenidate (e.g., certain antidepressants like Wellbutrin). Twenty-six percent of the food-addiction group, and 20 percent of the control group were regular smokers. Women who were pregnant or breast-feeding, or who had given birth within the past 6 months were also excluded. This study was approved by the institutional Research Ethics Boards and was carried out in accordance with the Declaration of Helsinki.

MEASURES

Food addiction

Food addiction was diagnosed by the 25-item YFAS (Gearhardt et al., 2009) – a self-report questionnaire measure – using the dichotomous scoring procedure proposed by its authors. Based on the DSM-IV (American Psychiatric Association, 1994) criteria for substance dependence, a diagnosis is given if the respondent endorses three or more of the symptom subscales "over the past year" and if s/he also confirms the "clinically significant impairment" criterion.

Food cravings

Food cravings were assessed by the 15-item *State* version of the *General Food Cravings Questionnaire* (Cepeda-Benito et al., 2000). This well-validated scale (Nijs et al., 2007) was personalized for each participant by replacing the general words "tasty food" with the specific snack-food each participant had identified. For example, where appropriate, item one was changed from "I'm craving tasty food" to "I'm craving potato chips," and so on. The alpha coefficients for Day 1 and Day 2 were 0.93 and 0.92, respectively.

Appetite ratings

Appetite ratings were assessed, after participants had been given their snack, by the sum of 3 Likert-scale questions, each scored from 1 ("not at all") to 10 ("a great deal"): (1) How hungry does it make you feel to see your favorite snack? (2) How much would you like to eat some of your favorite snack – even just a small portion? (3) Now that you've had a taste of your favorite snack, how strong is your desire to have some more? After the second question, participants were asked to take a few bites of their snack, before the third question was asked.

Snack-food consumption

Snack-food consumption was quantified as the weight of the snack (to the nearest gram) at the end of the session subtracted from the initial weight of the snack. The amount consumed was then converted to a percentage of the initial snack weight. For example, a score of zero indicated that none of the snack was eaten and a score of 100 indicated the entire snack was eaten.

PROCEDURES

The data reported in this study are part of a larger and more extensive protocol involving three separate assessment sessions. They comprise a sub-set of participants who were assessed on the YFAS. Using a randomized, double-blind, cross-over design, participants were administered either a dose of oral methylphenidate equivalent to 0.5 mg/kg body weight (to a maximum dose of 55 mg), or placebo, at the same time of day and the same day of the week, separated by 1 week. This dose was selected because it has been used successfully in other drug challenges with healthy adults (Volkow et al., 2001). Methylphenidate was titrated for BMI because of evidence-based recommendations that this compound should be prescribed on a weight-adjusted basis (Shader et al., 1999). Methylphenidate and placebo were packaged in identical colored capsules to prevent detection of the drug by taste or color.

Day 1

Demographic information was obtained, a psychiatric assessment was administered, and questionnaire measures were distributed to be completed at home and returned at the second assessment. Participants had height and weight measured, blood pressure was taken, and an electrocardiogram was carried out to confirm eligibility for the subsequent drug challenge sessions. Participants were also asked to indicate their "favorite snack food" in preparation for the food challenge taking place at the 2nd and 3rd session. The most commonly chosen snacks were potato chips, chocolate bars, and cookies. For a more detailed explanation of the protocol see Davis et al. (2012).

Days 2 and 3

Both 2.5-h sessions were scheduled at the same time of day and the same day of the week, separated by 1 week. Prior to each session, participants were told to eat a normal meal 2 h before their appointment and to abstain from drinking any caffeinated beverage or smoking nicotine on the day of, and prior to, their appointments. These dietary restrictions were confirmed on each testing day. Upon arrival at the laboratory, a 10-item, visual-analog, mood adjective scale was given at baseline and every 15 min after the ingestion of the capsule. The peak uptake for methylphenidate is approximately 1 h. During that time, participants were seated in a quiet area and encouraged to occupy themselves with reading materials. About an hour and 15 min after the ingestion of the capsule, participants were given their favorite snack-food to hold, and the appetite rating questions were asked, after which they were given the craving questionnaire to complete. Participants were then told that the study tasks were finished and they could eat as much of their snack as they wished. At this point more than 3 h had elapsed since their last meal.

RESULTS

In order to assess whether there were group differences in the initial weight of the snack food – since each participant chose his/her own – a 2 (Sex) × 2 (Diagnostic Group) analysis of variance (ANOVA) was carried out. Results confirmed there were no differences between men and women ($p = 0.828$) or between the food-addiction and the non-food-addiction groups ($p = 0.413$), and there was no significant interaction between these two variables ($p = 0.974$).

REPEATED MEASURES ANOVA

Three separate 2 × 2 × 2 mixed model, repeated measures ANOVAs were computed – one for each of the dependent variables: food cravings, appetite ratings, and percentage of food consumed. There was one within-subjects factor (Days: placebo vs. drug) and two between-subjects factors: (Sex: male vs. female) and (Diagnostic Group: food-addiction vs. non-food-addiction)[3].

With *food cravings* and *appetite ratings* as the dependent variables, there was a significant main effect for Diagnostic Group ($p < 0.0001$ for both: $\eta_p^2 = 0.157$ and 0.128, respectively) with the food-addiction group reporting higher scores than the non-food-addiction group. In both cases, there was also a significant main effect for Days, indicating a diminution in scores in the drug condition compared to the placebo condition ($p = 0.006$ and 0.031, and $\eta_p^2 = 0.056$ and 0.035, respectively), but these decreases on the drug day were not significantly different between those with and without food addiction. These results are presented graphically in **Figures 1** and **2**.

[3]Each of the three repeated measures ANOVAs was re-run with BMI included as a co-variate. In each case, BMI did not correlate with the dependent variable nor were the Days × BMI interaction terms statistically significant, indicating that BMI did not contribute to the variance in the appetite, cravings, and food-consumptions variables. Therefore it was removed from the models. The values reported in the Table and the Figures are the results without BMI.

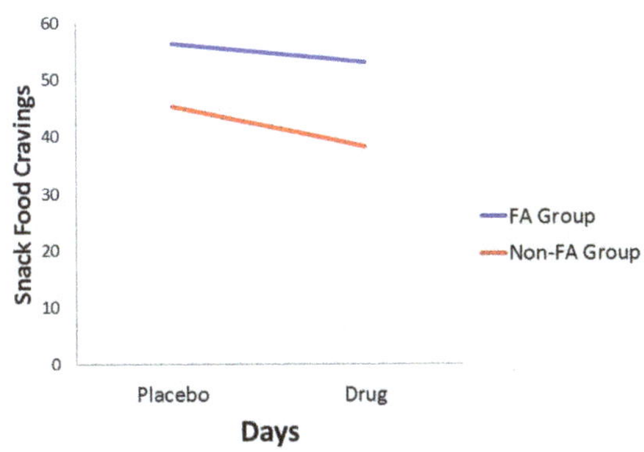

FIGURE 1 | Plot for the Diagnostic Group × Days interaction with food cravings as the dependent variable.

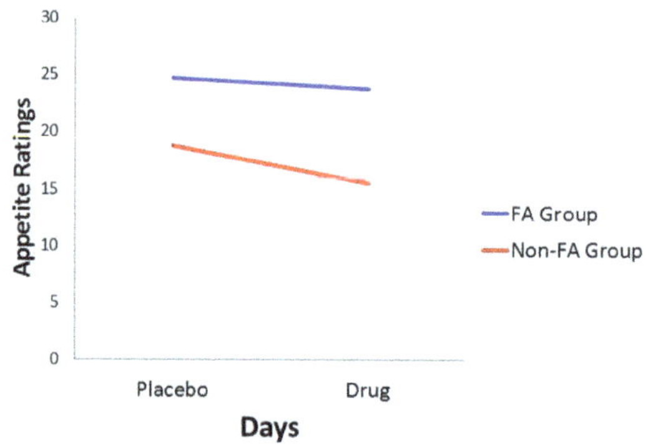

FIGURE 2 | Plot for the Diagnostic Group × Days interaction with appetite ratings as the dependent variable.

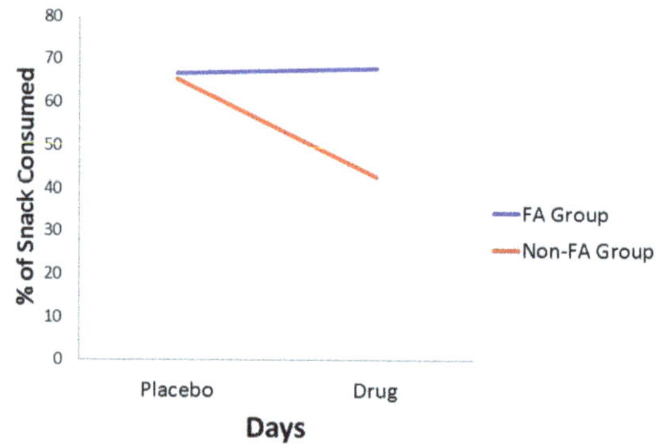

FIGURE 3 | Plot for the Diagnostic Group × Days interaction with percentage of snack-food consumption as the dependent variable.

In conformance with statistical convention, the absence of a significant interaction between the food-addiction and non-food-addiction variable and the placebo vs. drug variable precludes the legitimate testing of *post hoc* individual-Group comparisons across Days. It is important to note, however, that this interaction is testing the significance of the *difference in slopes* between the two groups. It is not testing whether either slope is different from zero. In this case, a slope not different from zero indicates no drug-suppression effect. Since the primary question of interest in the current study was whether one or both of the food-addiction groups displayed a suppression effect – not simply whether they differed from each other – a test of simple slopes was carried out for each group, strictly acknowledging that the results are investigational and preliminary. In the non-food-addiction group, the decrease from the placebo to the methylphenidate condition for appetite ratings and food cravings was statistically significant in both instances ($p < 0.0001$: $\eta_p^2 = 0.260$ and 0.1.86, respectively). In the food-addiction group, neither comparison was statistically significant ($p = 0.257$ and 0.198, respectively).

There were no significant differences between men and women, nor did they differ on their food cravings and appetite ratings when they were taking the placebo or the drug.

For the *percentage of consumed snack-food*, there was a statistically significant interaction between Diagnostic Group and Days (see **Table 1**). As indicated in **Figure 3**, and according to *post hoc* comparisons, the food-addiction group showed no reduction in food-intake in the drug condition from the placebo condition, while there was a significant decrease in the non-food-addiction group ($p < 0.0001$: $\eta_p^2 = 0.276$). There was also a significant main effect for Sex ($p = 0.022$: $\eta_p^2 = 0.039$) with men consuming a greater percentage of their snack than women (see **Figure 4**)[4].

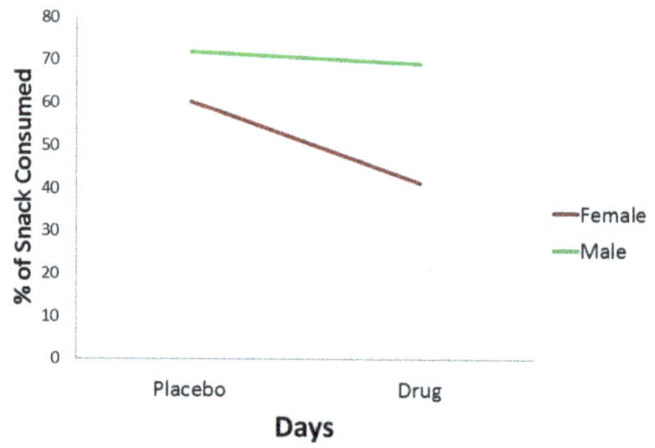

FIGURE 4 | Plot for the Sex main effect with percentage of snack-food consumption as the dependent variable.

Table 1 | Summary statistics for the within subject contrasts for the 2 [Days] × 2 [Sex] × 2 [Diagnostic Group] ANOVA with Food Consumption as the dependent variable.

Source	Type III SS	df	*f*	*p* =
Days	1464.50	1	5.25	0.023
Days × Sex	833.22	1	2.99	0.086
Days × Diagnosis	1611.53	1	5.78	0.018
Days × Sex × Diagnosis	704.36	1	2.53	0.114
Error (Days)	36512.17	131	–	–

MOOD RATINGS

In light of the food consumption group differences in response to methylphenidate, it was decided to assess whether this finding reflected variation in subjective mood response to the drug, possibly as a result of differences in uptake or metabolism. The first item on the visual-analog scale, which was given every 15 min after ingestion of the capsule, asked participants whether they felt any mood or emotional changes that could be attributed to taking a stimulant medication. Participants indicated their response by making a pencil mark on a line 147 mm long, where the left

[4]As a *post hoc* analysis, we investigated whether the methylphenidate effect on food-intake was associated with its effect on food cravings and appetite ratings. We calculated a difference score (placebo – drug) for each of the three food-related variables and examined their bivariate inter-correlations. The food consumption difference score was moderately correlated with the cravings and appetite difference scores ($r = 0.39$ $p < 0.0001$, and $r = 0.35$ $p < 0.0001$, respectively), which were themselves highly correlated ($r = 0.76$, $p < 0.0001$).

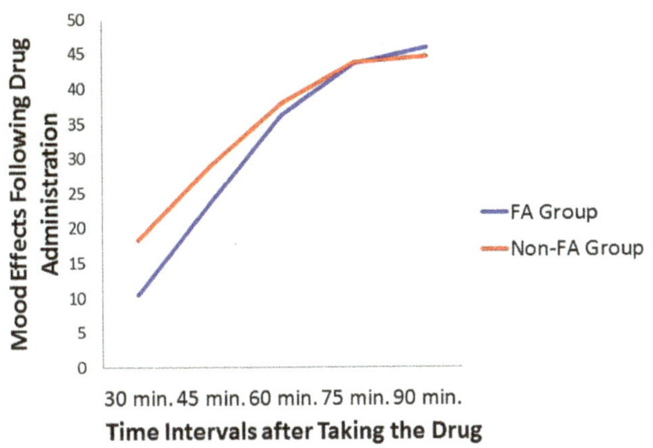

FIGURE 5 | Plot for the Diagnostic Group × Time Interval relationship with mood ratings on the drug day as the dependent variable.

end of the line indicated "no effect" and the right end of the line meant a "very strong" effect. Scores therefore varied between 0 and 147.

Repeated measure ANOVA was employed to assess the rating at time periods: 30, 45, 60, 75, and 90 min after ingestion of the capsule on the drug day. Similar to the previous analyses, between-subjects factors were Sex and Diagnostic Group. Results indicated a significant effect across time periods ($p < 0.0001$: $\eta_p^2 = 0.254$) with a linear increase which stabilized at 75 min post ingestion. There were, however, no differences between the food-addiction and the control groups, nor a difference between men and women. There was also no interaction between these two variables. **Figure 5** depicts the Time effect with separate lines for the food-addiction and the non-food-addiction groups. It is noteworthy that the peak subjective effect of the drug occurred at approximately 75 min after the capsule was taken – the time the snack-food challenge took place – after which the effect appeared to plateau in both groups.

DISCUSSION

This study represents the first empirical support for the food-addiction theory, based on *actual* food intake. Results demonstrated significant eating-related differences in response to a snack-food challenge between those diagnosed with YFAS food addiction and the non-diagnosed control group. The former reported stronger food cravings and greater appetite ratings following a taste of their favorite snack, and these differences remained stable in both the placebo and the methylphenidate conditions. While there was an overall diminution in these self-reports from placebo to drug, as was expected, this effect was driven primarily by a decrease in the non-food-addiction group, since there was no diminution among those with food addiction. With respect to food consumption, there was a significant interaction between Diagnostic Group and Days, again showing a substantial decrease in snack-food consumption in the non-food-addiction group, while there was no change in the food-addiction group.

Interestingly, and contrary to prediction, there was no difference between the food-addiction and the non-food-addiction groups in the percentage of food consumed in the placebo condition. Since appetite ratings and food cravings were both higher in the food-addiction group after the snack food was presented, it is difficult to explain why their food intake was also not greater on the drug-free testing day. One possibility is that a ceiling effect accounted for the null finding. Specifically, each participant was given a *single* snack item such as a chocolate bar, a cookie, or a small bag of chips. When analyzing the data, it was noted that a large proportion of the sample consumed the entire snack in the placebo condition – viz. 55% of the food-addiction group and 44% of the controls, compared to 45 and 25% respectively in the drug condition. If the size of the snack had been larger, thereby providing an opportunity for greater variability at the high-consumption end of the distribution, it is possible that placebo group differences may have emerged.

To summarize, in response to the methylphenidate challenge, the food-addiction group appeared resistant to the typical appetite-suppression effects of this drug. One can only speculate on the mechanisms underlying these results. Methylphenidate is lipophilic and therefore some of the drug may be sequestered in fat tissue. However, since the mean BMI values were equivalent in the two groups, differences in fat mass are unlikely to account for the observed group effects. In addition, the absence of any difference between the groups in the reporting of subjective drug effects, or on the timing of the peak subjective effects (see **Figure 5**), suggests that metabolic variation is unlikely to account for the appetite/eating group differences. Because methylphenidate's mechanism of action is very similar to that of cocaine – both block the DAT – some biological insights may be gleaned from preclinical research using a strain of cocaine-insensitive mice. The DAT-CI is a knock-in mouse line containing three point mutations in the DAT gene. This genetic alteration reduces DAT function and thereby leads to a hyper-dopaminergic state as reflected by heightened spontaneous locomotion in these animals compared to wild-type strains (O'Neill and Gu, 2013). Since inhibition of the DAT is necessary for a response to cocaine, as expected these genetically modified animals also do not display an increase in locomotion following cocaine administration, nor a conditioned place preference (O'Neill et al., 2013).

It is relevant that in previous human research we found evidence of an increased striatal dopamine signal – as indexed by a multi-locus genetic profile – in a group of adults diagnosed with YFAS food addiction compared to their age- and weight-matched counterparts (Davis et al., 2013). These findings are consistent with behavioral evidence that hyper-responsive brain reward mechanisms may serve as a risk factor for the tendency to over-consume highly palatable foods. Like the DAT-CI mice, individuals with a predisposition to elevated dopamine activity may also be relatively inured to the typical effects of stimulant drugs like cocaine and methylphenidate. Our results may therefore have potential clinical implications because methylphenidate is the first-line drug treatment for adults with ADHD, and similar stimulant drugs have recently shown some efficacy in reducing binge episodes in adults with BED (Shaffer, 2012; Gasior et al., 2013). Moreover, in light of the evidence that food addiction may reflect a more severe form of BED (Davis, 2013), the results of this study could assist in the development of personalized treatment management for patients with compulsive overeating. Indeed, many patients who use stimulant drugs therapeutically are non-responsive or discontinue treatment because of negative side effects – findings which suggest that pharmacogenetic research is needed to better understand the factors that influence drug effectiveness and toxicity. Regrettably, few adult studies have been conducted in this field, although some positive findings have identified influential markers on the DAT1 gene in relation to drug responsiveness (Contini et al., 2013).

With respect to sex differences, we found little support for our prediction that females would be more responsive to methylphenidate than males. Considering there were no Sex × Days interactions, our results do not mesh well with pre-clinical research demonstrating a stronger response to methylphenidate in females compared to males. For example, adolescent female rats showed a more robust sensitization to a dose of methylphenidate compared to their male counterparts (Brown et al., 2012), although later research found no sex differences in conditioned-place preference using the same drug (Cummins et al., 2013). It is also noteworthy that these drug effects were moderated by the strain of rats and by the drug dose (Chelaru et al., 2012).

Overall, the present study has added to the growing body of research supporting the validity of the food-addiction construct. To the best of our knowledge, this is the first study to use a well-controlled, laboratory-based, food challenge to make eating-related comparisons between adults with and without YFAS-diagnosed food addiction. In accord with our previous evidence of strong links between food addiction and trait-like food cravings (Davis et al., 2011), the current study also found elevated state-related food cravings in response to the physical presence of a highly palatable snack, which participants were asked to taste and invited to eat. Nevertheless, it is important to emphasize that replication is needed with larger samples of individuals meeting YFAS criteria for food addiction in order to improve confidence in the outcomes of this research. In the present study, the sample lacked adequate power to test the Sex × Diagnostic Group interaction due to small frequencies in some of the cells. Future researchers are also encouraged to provide a greater quantity in the snack-food challenge in order to increase the range of food-consumption scores. In addition, larger samples will allow researchers to take account of menstrual-cycle status in female participants since estrogen and progesterone levels are known to influence response to stimulant drugs (Evans and Foltin, 2010). And finally, we encourage studies going forward to search for mechanisms to explain the apparent food-related insensitivity to methylphenidate in those with YFAS food addiction by using sophisticated brain imaging techniques.

REFERENCES

American Psychiatric Association. (1994). *Diagnostic and Statistical Manual of Mental Disorders,* 4th Edn, Washington, DC.

American Psychiatric Association. (2013). *Diagnostic and Statistical Manual of Mental Disorders,* 5th Edn, Arlington, VA: American Psychiatric Publishing.

Avena, N. M., Bocarsly, M. E., and Hoebel, B. G. (2012). Animal models of sugar and fat bingeing: relationship to food addiction and increased body weight. *Methods Mol. Biol.* 829, 351–365. doi: 10.1007/978-1-61779-458-2_23

Avena, N. M., Rada, P., and Hoebel, B. G. (2008). Evidence of sugar addiction: behavioral and neurochemical effects of intermittent, excessive sugar intake. *Neurosci. Biobehav. Rev.* 32, 20–39. doi: 10.1016/j.neubiorev.2007.04.019

Back, S. E., Payne, R. L., Wahlquist, A. H., Carter, R. E., Stroud, Z., Haynes, L., et al. (2011). Comparative profiles of men and women with opioid dependence: results from a national multisite effectiveness trial. *Am. J. Drug Alcohol Abuse* 37, 313–323. doi: 10.3109/00952990.2011.596982

Batra, P., Das, S. K., Salinardi, T., Robinson, L., Saltzman, E., Scott, T., et al. (2013). Relationship of cravings with weight loss and hunger. Results from a 6 month worksite weight loss intervention. *Appetite* 69, 1–7. doi: 10.1016/j.appet.2013.05.002

Becker, J. B. (2009). Sexual differentiation of motivation: a novel mechanism? *Horm. Behav.* 55, 646–654. doi: 10.1016/j.yhbeh.2009.03.014

Becker, J. B., and Ming, H. (2008). Sex differences in drug use. *Front. Neuroendocrinol.* 29:36–47. doi: 10.1016/j.yfrne.2007.07.003

Begin, C., Gagnon-Girouard, M. P., Provencher, V., and Lemieux, S. (2006). Obesity treatment supporting individual in appropriation of his steps. *Can. Psychol.* 47, 316–332.

Brown, R. W., Hughes, B. A., Hughes, A. B., Sheppard, A. B., Perna, M. K., Ragsdale, W. L., et al. (2012). Sex and dose-related differences in methylphenidate adolescent locomotor sensitization and effects on brain-derived neurotropic factor. *J. Psychopharmacol.* 26, 1480–1488. doi: 10.1177/0269881112454227

Burmeister, J. M., Hinman, N., Koball, A., Hoffman, D. A., and Carels, R. A. (2013). Food addiction in adults seeking weight loss treatment. Implications for psychosocial health. *Appetite* 60, 103–110. doi: 10.1016/j.appet.2012.09.013

Cassin, S. E., and von Ranson, K. M. (2007). Is binge eating experienced as an addiction? *Appetite* 49, 687–690. doi: 10.1016/j.appet.2007.06.012

Cepeda-Benito, A., Gleaves, D. H., Williams, T. L., and Erath, S. A. (2000). The development and validation of the state and trait food-cravings questionnaires. *Behav. Ther.* 31, 151–173. doi: 10.1016/S0005-7894(00)80009-X

Chelaru, M. I., Yang, P. B., and Dafny, N. (2012). Sex differences in the behavioral response to methylphenidate in three adolescent rat strains (WKY, SHR, SD). *Behav. Brain Res.* 226, 8–17. doi: 10.1016/j.bbr.2011.08.027

Colell, D., Sanchez-Niubo, A., and Domingo-Salvany, A. (2013). Sex differences in the cumulative incidence of substance use by birth cohort. *Int. J. Drug Policy* 24, 319–325. doi: 10.1016/j.drugpo.2012.09.006

Contini, V., Rovaris, D. L., Victor, M. M., Grevet, E. H., Rohde, L. A., and Bau, C. H. D. (2013). Pharmacogenetics of response to methylphenidate in adults patients with Attention-Deficit/Hyperactivity Disorder (ADHD): a systematic review. *Eur. Neuropsychopharmacol.* 23, 555–560. doi: 10.1016/j.euroneuro.2012.05.006

Corwin, R. I., Avena, N. M., and Boggiano, M. M. (2011). Feeding and reward: perspectives from three rat models of binge eating. *Physiol. Behav.* 104, 87–97. doi: 10.1016/j.physbeh.2011.04.041

Cummins, E. D., Griffin, S. B., Burgess, K. C., Peterson, D. J., Watson, B. D., and Buendia, M. A. (2013). Methylphenidate place conditioning in adolescent rats: an analysis of sex differences and the dopamine transporter. *Behav. Brain Res.* 257, 215–223. doi: 10.1016/j.bbr.2013.09.036

Curtis, C., and Davis, C. (2014). A qualitative study of binge eating disorder and obesity from an addiction perspective. *Eat. Disord.* 22, 19–32. doi: 10.1080/10640266.2014.857515

Davis, C. (2013). From passive overeating to "food addiction": a spectrum of compulsion and severity. *ISRN Obes.* 2013:435027. doi: 10.1155/2013/435027

Davis, C., and Carter, J. C. (2009). Compulsive overeating as an addiction disorder: a review of theory and evidence. *Appetite* 53, 1–8. doi: 10.1016/j.appet.2009.05.018

Davis, C., and Carter, J. C. (2014). If certain foods are addictive, how might this change the treatment of compulsive overeating and obesity? *Curr. Addict. Rep.* doi: 10.1007/s40429-014-0013-z

Davis, C., Curtis, C., Levitan, R. D., Carter, J. C., Kaplan, A. S., and Kennedy, J. L. (2011). Evidence that 'food addiction' is a valid phenotype of obesity. *Appetite* 57, 711–717. doi: 10.1016/j.appet.2011.08.017

Davis, C., Fattore, L., Kaplan, A. S., Carter, J. C., Levitan, R. D., and Kennedy, J. L. (2012). The suppression of appetite and food consumption by methylphenidate: the moderating effects of gender and weight in healthy adults. *Int. J. Neuropsychopharmacol.* 15, 181–187. doi: 10.1017/S1461145711001039

Davis, C., Loxton, N. J., Levitan, R. D., Kaplan, A. S., Carter, J. C., and Kennedy, J. L. (2013). 'Food addiction' and its associations with a dopaminergic multilocus genetic profile. *Physiol. Behav.* 118, 63–69. doi: 10.1016/j.physbeh.2013.05.014

Elman, I., Karlsgodt, K. H., and Gastfriend, D. R. (2001). Gender differences in cocaine craving among non-treatment-seeking individuals with cocaine dependence. *Am. J. Drug Alcohol Abuse* 27, 193–202. doi: 10.1081/ADA-100103705

Evans, S. M., and Foltin, R. W. (2010). Does the response to cocaine differ as a function of sex or hormonal status in human and non-human primates? *Horm. Behav.* 58, 13–21. doi: 10.1016/j.yhbeh.2009.08.010

Gasior, M., McElroy, S. L., Mitchell, J., Wilfley, D., Ferreira-Cornwell, C., Gao, J., et al. (2013). "Efficacy and safety of lisdexamfetamine dimesylate in treatment of adults with moderate to severe binge eating disorder: a randomized, double-blind, placebo-controlled trial," in *Poster Presented at the Annual Meeting of the Eating Disorder Research Society*, Baltimore.

Gearhardt, A. N., Corbin, W. R., and Brownell, K. D. (2009). Preliminary validation of the Yale Food Addiction Scale. *Appetite* 52, 430–436. doi: 10.1016/j.appet.2008.12.003

Gearhardt, A. N., White, M. A., Masheb, R. M., Morgan, P. T., Crosby, R. D., and Grilo, C. M. (2012). An examination of the food addiction construct in obese patients with binge eating disorder. *Int. J. Eat. Disord.* 45, 657–663. doi: 10.1002/eat.20957

Gearhardt, A., Davis, C., Kushner, R., and Brownell, K. (2011a). The addiction potential of hyperpalatable foods. *Curr. Drug Abuse Rev.* 4, 140–145. doi: 10.2174/1874473711104030140

Gearhardt, A. N., Yokum, S., Orr, P. T., Stice, E., Corbin, W. R., and Brownell, K. D. (2011b). Neural correlates of food addiction. *Arch. Gen. Psychiatry* 32, E1–E9.

Goldfield, G. S., Lorello, C., and Doucet, E. (2007). Methylphenidate reduces energy intake and dietary fat intake in adults: a mechanism of reduced reinforcing value of food? *Am. J. Clin. Nutr.* 86, 308–315.

Greenfield, S. F., Back, S. E., Lawson, K., and Brady, K. T. (2010). Substance use in women. *Psychiatr. Clin. North Am.* 33, 339–355. doi: 10.1016/j.psc.2010.01.004

Jansen, J. M., Daams, J. G., Koeter, M. W. J., Veltman, D. J., van den Brink, W., and Goudriaan, A. E. (2013). Effects of non-invasive neurostimulation on craving: a meta-analysis. *Neurosci. Biobehav. Rev.* 37, 2472–2480. doi: 10.1016/j.neubiorev.2013.07.009

Leddy, J. J., Epstein, L. H., Jaroni, J. L., Roemmich, J. N., Paluch, R. A., Goldfield, G. S., et al. (2004). Influence of methylphenidate on eating in obese men. *Obes. Res.* 12, 224–232. doi: 10.1038/oby.2004.29

Lent, M. R., Eichen, D. M., Goldbacher, E., Wadden, T. A., and Foster, G. D. (2014). Relationship of food addiction to weight loss and attrition during obesity treatment. *Obesity (Silver Spring)* 22, 52–55. doi: 10.1002/oby.20512

Levy, L. D., Fleming, J. P., and Klar, D. (2009). Treatment of refractory obesity in severely obese adults following management of newly diagnosed attention deficit hyperactivity disorder. *Int. J. Obes. (Lond.)* 33, 326–334. doi: 10.1038/ijo.2009.5

Mann, T., Tomiyama, A. J., Westling, E., Lew, A. M., Samuels, B., and Chatman, J. (2007). Medicare's search for effective obesity treatments: diets are not the answer. *Am. Psychol.* 62, 220–233. doi: 10.1037/0003-066X.62.3.220

Meule, A., Lutz, A., Voegele, C., and Kubler, A. (2012). Women with elevated food addiction symptoms show accelerated reactions, but no impaired inhibitory control, in response to pictures of high-calorie food-cues. *Eat. Behav.* 13, 423–428. doi: 10.1016/j.eatbeh.2012.08.001

Nijs, I. M., Franken, I. H., and Muris, P. (2007). The modified Trait and State Food-Craving Questionnaire: development and validation of a general index of food craving. *Appetite* 49, 38–46. doi: 10.1016/j.appet.2006.11.001

O'Neill, B., and Gu, H. H. (2013). Amphetamine-induced locomotion in a hyperdopaminergic ADHD mouse model depends on genetic background. *Pharmacol. Biochem. Behav.* 103, 455–459. doi: 10.1016/j.pbb.2012.09.020

O'Neill, B., Tilley, M. R., and Gu, H. H. (2013). Cocaine produces conditioned place aversion in mice with a cocaine-insensitive dopamine transporter. *Genes Brain Behav.* 12, 34–38. doi: 10.1111/j.1601-183X.2012.00872.x

Pedram, P., Wadden, D., Amini, P., Gulliver, W., Randell, E., Cahill, F., et al. (2013). Food addiction: its prevalence and significant association with obesity in the general population. *PLoS ONE* 8:e74832. doi: 10.1371/journal.pone.0074832

Potenza, M. N. (2014). Non-substance addictive behaviors in the context of DSM-5. *Addict. Behav.* 39, 1–2. doi: 10.1016/j.addbeh.2013.09.004

Robinson, M. J. F., and Berridge, K. C. (2013). Instant transformation of learned repulsion into motivational 'wanting.' *Curr. Biol.* 23, 282–289. doi: 10.1016/j.cub.2013.01.016

Shader, R. I., Harmatz, J. S., Oesterheld, J. R., Parmlee, D. X., Sallee, F. R., and Greenblatt, D. J. (1999). Population pharmacokinetics of methylphenidate in children with attention-deficit hyperactivity disorder. *J. Clin. Pharmacol.* 39, 775–785. doi: 10.1177/00912709922008425

Shaffer, C. (2012). Pharma: clinic roundup. *BioWorld Today.* 23, 9.

Sinha, R., Garcia, M., Paliwal, P., Kreek, M. J., and Rounsaville, B. J. (2006). Stress-induced cocaine craving and hypothalamic-pituitary-adrenal responses are predictive of cocaine relapse outcomes. *Arch. Gen. Psychiatry* 63, 324–331. doi: 10.1001/archpsyc.63.3.324

Volkow, N. D., Wang, G. J., Tomasi, D., and Baler, R. D. (2013). The addictive dimensionality of obesity. *Biol. Psychiatry* 73, 811–818. doi: 10.1016/j.biopsych.2012.12.020

Volkow, N. D., Wang, G.-J., Fowler, J. S., Logan, J., Gerasimov, M., Maynard, L., et al. (2001). Therapeutic doses of oral methylphenidate significantly increase extracellular dopamine in the human brain. *J. Neurosci.* 21, 1–5.

Wittchen, H. U., Jacobi, F., Rehm, J., Gustavsson, A., Svensson, M., Jonsson, B., et al. (2011). The size and burden of mental disorders and other disorders of the brain in Europe 2010. *Eur. Neuropsychopharmacol.* 21, 655–679. doi: 10.1016/j.euroneuro.2011.07.018

10

Explaining human recreational use of 'pesticides': the neurotoxin regulation model of substance use vs. the hijack model and implications for age and sex differences in drug consumption

Edward H. Hagen[1]*, Casey J. Roulette[1] and Roger J. Sullivan[2]

[1] Department of Anthropology, Washington State University, Vancouver, WA, USA
[2] Department of Anthropology, California State University, Sacramento, CA, USA

Edited by:
Hanna Pickard, University of Oxford, UK

Reviewed by:
Serge H. Ahmed, Centre national de la recherche scientifique, France
Bennett Foddy, University of Oxford, UK

***Correspondence:**
Edward H. Hagen, Department of Anthropology, Washington State University, 14204 NE Salmon Creek Avenue, Vancouver, WA 98686-9600, USA
e-mail: ehagen@gmail.com

Most globally popular drugs are plant neurotoxins or their close chemical analogs. These compounds evolved to deter, not reward or reinforce, consumption. Moreover, they reliably activate virtually all toxin defense mechanisms, and are thus correctly identified by human neurophysiology as toxins. Acute drug toxicity must therefore play a more central role in drug use theory. We accordingly challenge the popular idea that the rewarding and reinforcing properties of drugs "hijack" the brain, and propose instead that the brain evolved to carefully regulate neurotoxin consumption to minimize fitness costs and maximize fitness benefits. This perspective provides a compelling explanation for the dramatic changes in substance use that occur during the transition from childhood to adulthood, and for pervasive sex differences in substance use: because nicotine and many other plant neurotoxins are teratogenic, children, and to a lesser extent women of childbearing age, evolved to avoid ingesting them. However, during the course of human evolution many adolescents and adults reaped net benefits from regulated intake of plant neurotoxins.

Keywords: pharmacophagy, zoopharmacognosy, drug reward, evolution, self-medication, evolutionary medicine

The mesolimbic dopamine system (MDS)[1] plays a key, though still not fully understood, role in the ability of laboratory animals to learn an association between a stimulus, such as a tone, and a natural reward, such as sugar water, and to approach and consume the reward (1–6). Drugs of abuse have neurobiological and behavioral effects that closely resemble the effects of sugar and other natural rewards, activating the MDS and producing approach and consummatory behavior, positive feelings, and the learning of cues that predict drug availability. Drugs *are* rewards (7). Moreover, drugs and sugar are chemically similar: both are small organic molecules that act as ligands for various receptors. In fact, fermentation converts 1 glucose molecule into 2 ethanol molecules (and 2 CO_2 molecules), and ethanol contains more calories per gram than glucose (7 vs. 4), underscoring the comparability of a natural reward and a drug. On what basis, then, do neurobiologists classify drug reward as abnormal and food reward as normal?

1. THE HIJACK HYPOTHESIS

Numerous, highly cited articles that review the neurobiology of drug use employ similar metaphors to distinguish natural rewards from drugs: natural rewards "activate" the MDS, whereas drugs "hijack," "usurp," "co-opt," or artificially stimulate it [e.g., Ref. (7–15)]. Kelley and Berridge [(9), p. 3306], for instance, open their review with:

> Addictive drugs act on brain reward systems, although the brain evolved to respond not to drugs but to natural rewards, such as food and sex. Appropriate responses to natural rewards were evolutionarily important for survival, reproduction, and fitness. In a quirk of evolutionary fate, humans discovered how to stimulate this system artificially with drugs.

In another review, Hyman [(11), p. 1414] leads into a section titled "A Hijacking of Neural Systems Related to the Pursuit of Rewards" with:

> [A]ddiction represents a pathological usurpation of the neural mechanisms of learning and memory that under normal circumstances serve to shape survival behaviors related to the pursuit of rewards and the cues that predict them.

On the evolutionary novelty of drug dependence, Wise [(8), p. 27] is perhaps most explicit:

> Addiction is quite a recent phenomenon, largely dependent upon the controlled use of fire (smoking), hypodermic syringes (intravenous injection), and the cork and bottle (storage and transportation of alcohol). Thus, while brain dopamine is activated by most drugs of abuse, the drugs have undergone mostly human selection for their ability to activate the system; the system has not undergone natural selection because of its sensitivity to the drugs.

[1]The MDS comprises dopamine (DA) neurons located in the midbrain structures of the ventral tegmental area (VTA) and substantia nigra pars compacta (SNc) that project to the nucleus accumbens (NAc) and dorsal striatum.

We refer to these arguments as the "hijack hypothesis." We recognize, on the one hand, that this is a metaphor invoked by drug researchers to help explain the effects of drugs of abuse on the brain. On the other hand, its frequent appearance in prominent review articles suggests that drug abuse researchers consider it to provide a fundamental distinction between addictive substances and food. This distinction is based on the following Darwinian propositions: the MDS evolved to enhance access to some substances, like sugar, that increased fitness[2]; these are termed "natural rewards." It did not evolve to respond to known drugs of abuse because these did not increase fitness and because repeated consumption of such substances is an evolutionary novelty[3].

Unfortunately, most drug researchers do not seem to regard the hijack hypothesis as a hypothesis. Instead, it is treated as an axiom or truism that requires little supporting evidence. The most important point of our commentary is that the evolutionary premises of the hijack hypothesis are *empirically testable.*

Previous work has criticized the hijack hypothesis on a number of grounds (see, for instance, articles in this special issue). In particular, although laboratory studies demonstrate that animals will self-administrate most drugs of abuse, these studies rarely provide the animals with alternative rewarding choices. In studies that do provide a rewarding alternative, such as sweetened water or social interactions (as in the famous Rat Park experiment), most animals choose the alternative, not the drug, undermining the claim that drugs hijack decision-making machinery (19).

Here we briefly summarize our previous critique of the hijack hypothesis' evolutionary premises (20–22). It is important to emphasize that we only critique these premises, *not* the evidence on the neurobiological mechanisms involved in drug use nor the various interpretations of dopamine function. We then sketch an evolutionary alternative to the hijack hypothesis: the *neurotoxin regulation* hypothesis. We conclude by considering age and sex differences in substance use in light of both hypotheses.

A caveat: neurobiological theory of drug use usually contrasts initial seeking and use with longer-term phenomena such as drug tolerance and addiction. We focus on initial drug seeking and use for several reasons: there are a small number of simple information-processing models of initial drug seeking and use, often dubbed "reward models." Current research on drug tolerance and addiction, in contrast, lacks a similarly concise, well-accepted conceptual framework [for a review of various theories of addiction, see Ref. (23)]. Moreover, tolerance and addiction are generally attributed, in part, to complex changes in neurobiology induced by long-term drug exposure. It is difficult to evaluate which changes are due to the effects of drugs and which to the nervous system's attempt to adapt to drug exposure, complicating an evolutionary analysis.

[2] By "fitness" we mean biological fitness – the average contribution to the gene pool of the next generation. For a review of fitness concepts, see Ref. (16).

[3] Some have recently argued that sugar is itself a potential substance of abuse [e.g., Ref. (17)], which again requires an appeal to evolutionary novelty, in this case the novelty of access to relatively unconstrained quantities of sugar [e.g., Ref. (18)].

2. MOST DRUGS ARE PLANT DEFENSIVE CHEMICALS OR CLOSE CHEMICAL ANALOGS

Terrestrial plants and animals appeared ~400 million years ago. Animals evolved to exploit plant tissues and energy stores, and in response, plants evolved numerous defenses, including toxins. These toxins appear in high concentrations in some organs, like leaves, that are critical for plant growth, survival, and reproduction, and in low concentration in other organs, like ripe fruits, that evolved to be consumed by herbivores to aid seed dispersal, which is beneficial for the plant.

Plant drugs, such as caffeine, nicotine, cocaine, and THC, belong to a subcategory of toxins that evolved to interfere with neuronal signaling in herbivores. Depending on the toxin, this includes interference with: (1) neurotransmitter synthesis, storage, release, binding, and re-uptake, (2) receptor activation and function, and (3) key enzymes involved in signal transduction (24). Plant drugs therefore did evolve to "hijack" herbivore nervous systems, but for an effect that is precisely the opposite of the hijack hypothesis: to deter, not reward, or reinforce, plant consumption. (We prefer describing these effects as "interference" rather than "hijacking.")

Plant toxins have had a profound influence on the evolution of herbivore neurophysiology, resulting in: (1) numerous chemosensors including bitter taste receptors, (2) detoxification mechanisms including cytochrome P450 and other enzymes, (3) cellular membrane carrier proteins for toxin transport, including ATP-binding cassette proteins, and (4) aversive learning mechanisms that permit selective feeding on less toxic tissues (25, 26). Many herbivore defensive proteins are expressed in the blood-brain barrier and the brain itself, including in humans (27–30), indicating the fitness advantages of protecting the CNS specifically from plant neurotoxins and other xenobiotics.

From an herbivore's perspective, then, the value of a plant substance usually comprises the benefits of useable macronutrients (carbohydrates, fats, and proteins) minus the costs of toxin exposure.

2.1. BENEFITS OF TOXIN CONSUMPTION IN NON-HUMAN ANIMALS

Although exposure to plant toxins is ordinarily costly for herbivores, herbivores have also evolved to exploit plant toxins for herbivore benefit, which often involves prophylactic or therapeutic effects against pathogens, i.e., self-medication (also known as pharmacophagy or zoopharmacognosy) (31–43). Originally proposed as a primate behavior, evidence for self-medication is now available from diverse non-human species, including fruit flies (40, 41), ants (44), moths (39), butterflies (45, 46), honeybees (47, 48), birds (42), sheep (49), goats (50), and Neanderthals (51). In many of these studies (but not all), animals increase toxin intake in response to infection. More generally, there is growing recognition that animal defenses against pathogens include not only immune system responses, but also behavioral responses, termed *behavioral immunity* or *non-immunological defense*, of which self-medication is one example (52, 53).

In summary, animals have been exposed to plant toxins, likely including those affecting the CNS, for hundreds of millions of years. Animals can also extract benefits from such exposure. Thus, the evolutionary premises of the hijack hypothesis – that, for humans, drug exposure is evolutionarily novel and has no fitness benefits – are questionable and cannot be accepted without considerable further evidence.

2.2. NICOTINE AS A MODEL DRUG

In what follows we will often rely on studies of tobacco and nicotine for the following reasons: first, nicotine is globally popular and highly addictive. Second, it is a plant drug, and therefore belongs to the category of substances that most animals were regularly exposed to during their evolution. Third, it is not out of the question that humans have chewed or smoked various psychoactive plants for hundreds of thousands of years, just as tobacco is consumed today. Fourth, the role of nicotine as a plant defensive chemical is well-documented (54, 55). And fifth, there is extensive research on nicotine.

We will also draw on the extensive research on pharmaceuticals and pesticides because often these are derived from plant toxins (e.g., nicotine, which has therapeutic applications and is also widely used as a pesticide), chemically resemble plant toxins, or have neurophysiological effects analogous to plant toxins. Data on them will therefore help us illuminate neurophysiological responses to plant toxins.

2.3. NICOTINE TOXICITY

Although neurobiology emphasizes the rewarding properties of nicotine, nicotine is an extremely potent neurotoxin. In humans, the lethal dose of nicotine is ~10 mg in children and 30–60 mg in adults, a toxicity comparable to hydrogen cyanide (56). Death can occur within 5 min after consumption of concentrated nicotine insecticides (57). A single cigarette typically contains 10–20 mg of nicotine, but much of it is burned; smokers thus absorb 0.5–2 mg per cigarette, and users of smokeless tobacco about twice this much (58).

Despite the evolutionary novelty of human exposure to nicotine[4], nicotine activates most known human toxin defense mechanisms, such as bitter taste receptors in the mouth and gut (62), bitter taste pathways in the peripheral nervous system (63), xenobiotic-sensing nuclear receptors (64), xenobiotic-metabolizing enzymes (58), aversion circuitry in the CNS (65), and conditioned taste avoidance (66).

In individuals not habituated to nicotine, 0.6 mg (one "light" cigarette) can induce sweating, nausea, dizziness, coldness of hands, palpitations, headache, and upset stomach (67); 4–8 mg often produces serious symptoms, including burning sensations in the mouth and throat, profuse salivation, vomiting, abdominal pain, and diarrhea (57).

Human neurophysiology thus correctly identifies nicotine as a dangerous toxin and generates appropriate avoidance and expulsion responses. Because nicotine is not thought to be directly responsible for the chronic diseases caused by smoking (68) [cf. Ref. (69)], its toxicity plays little role in research on tobacco use. More generally, although drug researchers have long recognized that drugs are toxins and have aversive effects, and that drug toxicity and aversiveness is at odds with drug reward [for reviews, see Ref. (70–72)], this insight has had little influence on drug use theory (72). In the framework we develop here, however, drug toxicity plays a central role.

3. THE NEUROTOXIN REGULATION HYPOTHESIS

Herbivores and omnivores, including humans, obtain substantial macronutrients from plants. Plant choice in non-human animals is heavily influenced by toxin concentration, which appears to be assessed by chemosensors in, e.g., the mouth and gut, followed by conditioned learning and social learning (e.g., observing mother's plant choices) (73, 74). Complete avoidance of plant toxins is not an option, however. Mammalian herbivores cap the daily amount of ingested plant toxins by modulating intake to accommodate changes in the dietary concentration of toxins. They are able to do this even for toxins that are, for them, evolutionarily novel (75). It appears that herbivores regulate the dose of plant toxins to keep blood concentrations below a critical level [Ref. (76), and references therein]. At the same time, because plant toxins can provide fitness benefits, regulatory mechanisms should not, and could not, completely eliminate exposure to plant toxins but instead balance dose-dependent costs vs. benefits, and adjust intake accordingly [Ref. (74, 77, 78), and references therein].

In our view, drug toxicity poses two major challenges to any theory of drug use. First, why do humans ignore cues of toxicity, like bitter taste and nausea, to regularly and deliberately consume non-trivial doses of potentially lethal substances that provide essentially no macronutrients? Second, given that humans do consume such substances, how and why does human neurophysiology successfully meter their intake? The hijack hypothesis seems to imply that drug consumption is regulated, at least in part, by the same mechanism that regulates consumption of sugar and other foods. Humans consume tens-to-hundreds of grams of sugar and other carbohydrates per meal. Typical doses of recreational drugs, on the other hand, are tiny – on the order of milligrams or tens of milligrams – and are not far below a lethal dose (79); yet overdoses and death are relatively rare[5]. We find it surprising that the inadvertent triggering of a mechanism that evolved to reward and reinforce intake of large quantities of macronutrients results in the precisely metered intake of minute quantities of neurotoxins.

We therefore propose that the brain might not accidentally reward or reinforce consumption of nicotine and other addictive drugs, as the hijack model proposes, nor generate purely aversive reactions, as drug toxicity would suggest, but instead has evolved specialized mechanisms to precisely *regulate* drug consumption to minimize costs and maximize benefits [Ref. (22) cf. Ref. (81)].

[4]Whereas humans evolved in the Old World, all but one of the 60–70 tobacco species (genus *Nicotiana*) are native to the Americas or Oceania (one species is native to Africa). *N. tabacum*, the species of primary commercial importance, was domesticated by Native Americans within the last several thousand years, and spread to the Old World in the last few hundred years (59–61). Although nicotine is present in a number of plants native to the Old World, it is currently difficult to make the case that human ancestors were regularly exposed to nicotine.

[5]Drugs that are injected, and thus bypass peripheral chemosensors, are a partial exception. In the US in 2008, for example, there were about 1.9 million cocaine users and 5100 cocaine-related lethal poisonings, for an annual rate of 0.27%, which includes users who injected cocaine (CDC, NIH). A study of lethal cocaine-related deaths in Australia found that 86% involved cocaine injection and 81% also involved other drugs, mostly opioids, alcohol, and benzodiazepines (80). Thus, death from non-injected cocaine is rare.

A neurotoxin regulation mechanism would only evolve if, in fact, there were fitness benefits to neurotoxin consumption. We have proposed numerous potential benefits of psychoactive drug use, including enhancement of attention, memory and other aspects of cognition and physiology, and redressing nutrient deficiencies and neurotransmitter dysregulation (20–22). Later, we sketch another possible benefit involving attraction of mates and other social partners.

Our principal hypothesis, however, has been that human consumption of plant neurotoxins helps prevent or treat infection by parasites with nervous systems, i.e., macroparasites such as helminths [see also Ref. (82)], similar to the self-medication observed in many other animals species. Helminth parasites have been an important selection pressure in vertebrate and mammalian evolution, and in human evolution specifically (83, 84). Over one third of the global population remains infected by them (85). Helminths are often able to evade the immune system (86, 87), so chemotherapeutic intervention is frequently necessary to clear infections. There is increasing evidence that some non-human animals consume plant toxins specifically to prevent or treat helminth infections (49, 50) [but see Ref. (88)].

Intriguingly, three of the world's most popular psychoactive drugs – nicotine, arecoline (from betel-nut) and THC – are effective against helminths and other macroparasites; to this day some farmers and veterinarians deworm animals with nicotine or arecoline (89–98). Some helminth species have a larval stage that migrates through the lung (84), which perhaps was a selection pressure specifically to smoke neurotoxic plants[6].

An evolved mechanism to self-medicate with psychoactive substances should up-regulate consumption and down-regulate elimination of such substances in response to infection and/or infection risk. There are intriguing hints that infection risk and immune system signals do just that[7]. The "proinflammatory hypothesis of drug abuse" has emerged from growing evidence of immune involvement in drug reinforcement (102–104). Opioids, for instance, perhaps acting as xenobiotic-associated molecular patterns, activate toll-like receptor 4 (TLR4) signaling (important for pathogen recognition and immune activation), which surprisingly reinforces opium consumption via the mesolimbic dopamine reward pathway (105). Especially intriguing is direct evidence that the immune system modulates intake of the psychoactive drug ethanol (106, 107). One genome-wide association study found that smoking behavior might be regulated by IL-15, which is involved in immune signaling (108). Such results indicate an intimate relationship between psychoactive drug use and immunity, and, importantly, that central immune signals can modulate drug consumption.

Down-regulation of drug metabolism during infections would increase blood concentrations of potentially therapeutic agents. Infection and inflammation are indeed associated with a broad down-regulation of xenobiotic-metabolizing enzymes and transporters in humans and laboratory animals (albeit with complications for CYP2A6, which metabolizes nicotine), which often results in a pronounced increase in plasma concentrations of various drugs. This well-documented but poorly understood phenomenon (109) could also be evidence for a self-medication mechanism.

Although it might not be intuitive to reconceptualize recreational drug use as a means to prevent or treat macroparasite infections (chemoprophylaxis and chemotherapy, respectively), we point out that prior to the discovery of sodium's role in body fluid homeostasis, our evolved appetite for salt was utterly mysterious.

There is considerable evidence that nicotine intake is tightly controlled. If nicotine were purely rewarding or reinforcing, then lethal nicotine overdoses among adult tobacco users should be common. Instead, they are extremely rare (79). Behaviorally, cigarette smokers appear to titrate nicotine, altering their smoking behavior in response to changes in nicotine content so as to maintain a relatively constant blood concentration of nicotine (110). Both facts support the existence of a regulatory mechanism.

The putative regulatory mechanism might involve the MDS, which seems to play a central role in weighing the costs of behaviors, not just benefits. A subpopulation of dopamine neurons in the MDS is excited by aversive stimuli and cues that predict aversive stimuli (111–113). There is even one report that bitter taste receptors are expressed in the rat MDS (30). Given the anatomical proximity of the targets of aversion- and reward-related dopamine, their interaction could be the neurophysiological basis for weighing costs against benefits (2, 114). Interestingly, the MDS appears to be involved in the neurophysiological system that evolved to regulate intake of small quantities of sodium (115, 116). We envision the hypothesized neurotoxin regulation mechanism to be somewhat analogous to the salt appetite regulation mechanism in that it would employ numerous peripheral and central chemosensors and feedback circuits to precisely meter intake of milligrams of environmental chemicals.

Unlike the sodium regulation mechanism, the putative neurotoxin regulation mechanism must titrate a diverse range of compounds, many of which would be evolutionary novel for the organism: plants are constantly evolving new chemical defenses, and both plants and animals migrate. Currently, it is not possible to fully explain how a limited number of toxin defense proteins, which would be the foundation of a regulatory mechanism, selectively bind to a large range of chemically diverse toxins. Understanding the relationship between the physiochemical properties of a toxin molecule and its biological activity – its structure-activity relationship – is a dynamic and challenging area of research [e.g., Ref. (117)]. Part of the answer is that most toxins belong to one of a smaller group of chemical families, such as fatty acids, peptides, amino acids, amines, amides, azacycloalkanes, N-heterocyclic compounds, ureas, thioureas, carbamides, esters, lactones, carbonyl compounds, phenols, crown ethers, terpenoids, secoiridoids, alkaloids, glycosides, flavonoids, and steroids (118). Molecules belonging to the same family tend to share chemical properties[8]. Thus, binding regions of defensive proteins might be specific for classes of compounds.

[6]Contrary to Wise (8), there is archeological evidence for controlled use of fire c. 790 KYA – 1 MYA (99, 100), long before the evolution of *Homo sapiens*.

[7]The prevailing view is that the causal arrow usually points in the opposite direction, i.e., that drug abuse increases infection risk by impairing immunity (101).

[8]But it is not uncommon for small chemical changes to result in large changes in bioactivity.

In addition, chemically diverse toxins can interfere with the same signaling pathway (e.g., nicotine, a small organic molecule, and botulinum toxin, a protein, both interfere with cholinergic signaling). We speculate that a neurotoxin regulation mechanism might be able to detect interference with neural signaling pathways, and modulate intake accordingly. We also speculate that individual learning plays an important role in the neurotoxin regulation mechanism. Given exposure to a novel neurotoxin with unknown costs and benefits, a user should first ingest minute quantities, gradually increasing intake to optimize benefits vs. costs, which resembles patterns exhibited by laboratory animals and humans with extended access to drugs (119).

4. AGE DIFFERENCES IN DRUG USE: A DEVELOPMENTAL SWITCH?

There are dramatic changes in substance use across the lifespan, which provide an opportunity to empirically test the hijack hypothesis against the neurotoxin regulation hypotheses. Do these changes reflect changes in vulnerability to hijacking? Or do they reflect age-related changes in the costs and benefits of exposure to plant toxins that should up- or down-regulate ingestion?

Users of popular psychoactive substances report virtually no use prior to the age of 10 (with the partial exception of alcohol). Starting about the age of 12 there is a rapid increase in substance use, so that almost everyone who will ever use a substance has done so by age 20 (**Figure 1**). The pattern suggests the existence of a developmental "switch."

The complete lack of child substance use seen in the self-report data in **Figure 1** are corroborated by serum cotinine values from a nationally representative US sample (**Figure 2**). Cotinine, the primary metabolite of nicotine, is a reliable and widely used biomarker of exposure to tobacco, via either tobacco consumption or environmental tobacco smoke (ETS) (121). The cotinine concentration of a smoker is usually ~100 ng/ml, whereas that of a non-smoking child living with smokers is usually <10 ng/ml (121, 122)[9].

Figure 2 depicts 12 years of data (1999–2010) that include 5932 children ages 3–10 (123), 1111 of whom (19%) lived with a smoker, and thus presumably had easier access to tobacco. Among all children, 94.5% of the cotinine concentrations are ≤3 ng/ml and 99.4% are ≤10 ng/ml. These values are within the range of values seen in non-smokers exposed to ETS, e.g., from a smoking parent or other caregiver[10]. Only 33 children (0.6%) had cotinine values >10 ng/ml, and 6 (0.1%) had values >20 ng/ml, with the maximum value (32.4 ng/ml) occurring in a 4-year old. These values overlap with the values of smokers who haven't smoked recently, but are still within the range of values that could result from heavy ETS, such as traveling in a car with a heavy smoker (121)[11].

What explains the dramatic lack of child substance use, and the equally dramatic transition to substance use during adolescence?

4.1. THE HIJACK MODEL OF CHILDREN'S LOW-TO-NON-EXISTENT SUBSTANCE USE

The hijack hypothesis predicts that anyone with a functional MDS, that is, anyone for whom sugar is rewarding or reinforcing, will be susceptible to tobacco and other drugs. The everyday experience that children enjoy sweets, and thus have a functional reward system, is confirmed by studies of: (1) diet across the lifespan that show that a substantial fraction of the daily energy intake for US children and adolescents comes from sugar added to beverages and foods (125, 126), and (2) reinforcement learning that find that although children and older adults do show "deficits" in some aspects of reward processing relative to younger adults, reward-based learning mechanisms are quite functional in children (127). The hijack hypothesis therefore predicts that, all else equal, children would consume drugs of abuse at rates similar to adolescents and adults, contrary to the evidence in **Figure 1**. On its own, the hijack hypothesis cannot explain the dramatic changes in substance use across the lifespan. Drug use researchers therefore typically invoke additional explanations.

An influential hypothesis attributes the onset of drug use to a transient "imbalance" between the MDS and the prefrontal cortex (PFC) that emerges in adolescence. The PFC is believed to be responsible for executive control functions such as self-regulation, abstract reasoning, deliberation, response inhibition, and planning ahead (128–130). According to the hypothesis, these functions manage or curb the rewarding and reinforcing signals from the MDS, including those generated by drug use. The key insight of this hypothesis is that the MDS and PFC have different developmental trajectories: the MDS is largely mature by adolescence but the PFC is still developing into early adulthood. It is thought that the still-maturing PFC cannot adequately control the heightened reward responsiveness stemming from the mature MDS, thus explaining why adolescents engage in risky behaviors, such as unprotected sex and drug use [e.g., Ref. (129–131), and references therein].

How does the imbalance model explain the lack of child drug use? To our knowledge, the proponents of this model have not explicitly discussed child drug use. However, the clear implication would seem to be that in children, prefrontal cortex circuits, and the MDS, though still developing, are "balanced," so the PFC is able to successfully manage the MDS, explaining why children typically do not engage in risky behavior. Specifically, child enjoyment of drugs would be successfully overridden by the executive control circuits of the PFC. This requires that children know that drug use is risky. We guess that proponents of this model would argue that parents and others teach children about the dangers of drugs. In addition, parents and society impose restrictions on child access to drugs.

[9] Distinguishing smokers from non-smokers exposed to ETS based on cotinine values alone is complicated by the many sources of variability, such as amount of nicotine exposure, time between last exposure and sample collection, and differences in nicotine and cotinine metabolism due to, e.g., common polymorphisms in the enzymes that metabolize them (primarily CYP2A6). A smoker who hadn't smoked recently and a non-smoker exposed to heavy ETS might both have a cotinine concentration of 10 ng/ml, for instance. Estimates of the optimal serum cotinine concentration for distinguishing tobacco users from non-users exposed to ETS range from 3 to 15 ng/ml (121).

[10] In children living with smokers, the highest cotinine values in occurred in the younger children, suggesting physical proximity to a primary caregiver who is a smoker, or greater absorption and/or slower clearance of nicotine in younger children.

[11] A study of 42 non-smoking bar staff, for example, found a mean cotinine value of 9.28 ng/ml, with 3 individuals having values >20 ng/ml, and a maximum value of 31.3 ng/ml (124).

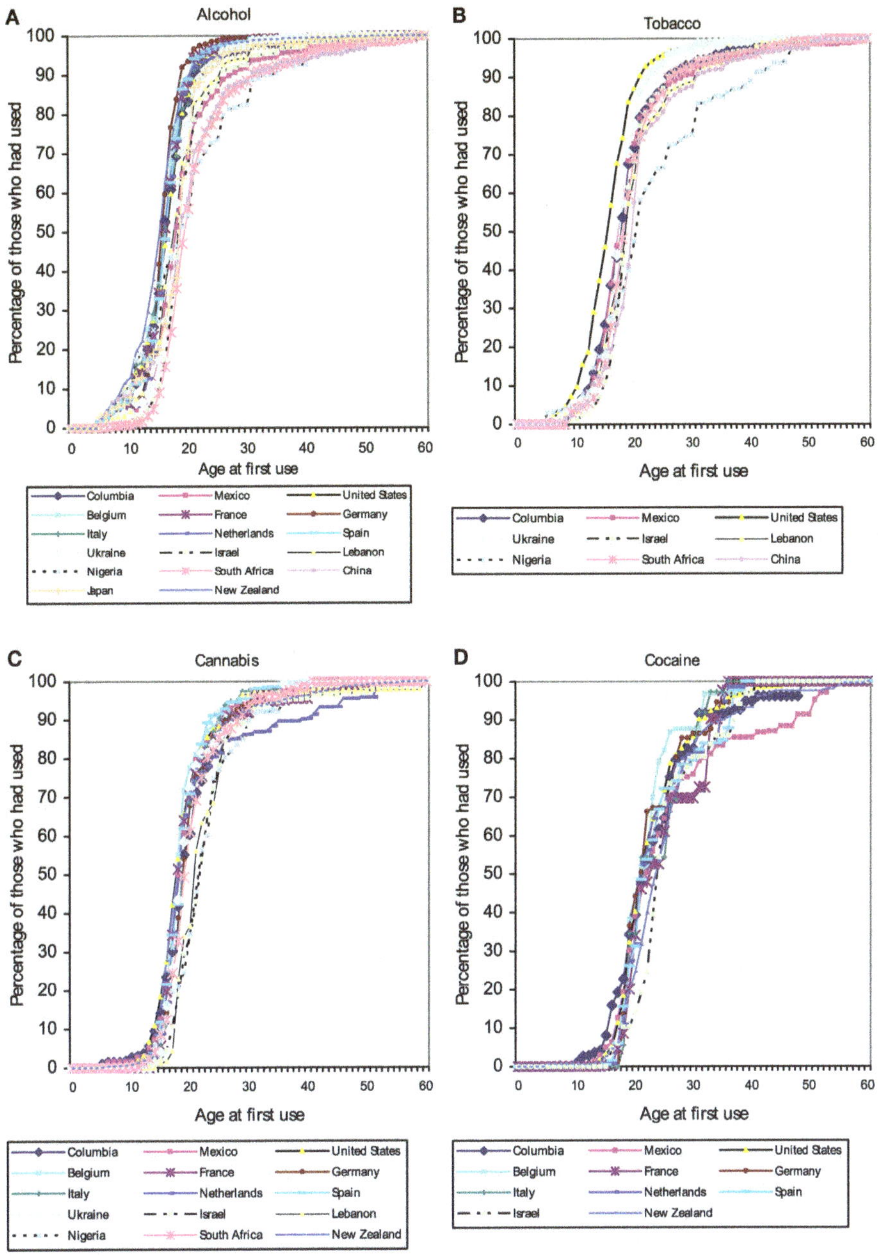

FIGURE 1 | Cumulative distribution of self-reported age of first use of **(A)** alcohol, **(B)** tobacco, **(C)** cannabis, and **(D)** cocaine in a large ($N = 85{,}052$) cross-national sample of users of these substances from the World Mental Health Survey Initiative. These patterns suggest the existence of a developmental "switch" that flips during adolescence. Figures from Ref. (120).

Restricted access to tobacco could explain low-to-non-existent child use. In the US, the sale of tobacco to minors is illegal in all 50 states. Moreover, the US spends over $500 million annually on tobacco control measures (132), which include mass media anti-tobacco campaigns; disseminating health warnings via, e.g., cigarette packages and advertising; enforcing bans on tobacco marketing; monitoring tobacco use; enforcing some smoke-free legislation; and providing some tobacco cessation health care programs. Tobacco taxes also deter use.

If such warnings and social restrictions account for low child substance use, then, according the hijack model, children should readily consume plant drugs when they are absent. Caffeine, a bitter-tasting plant toxin[12], is a psychostimulant that strongly

[12]There are two hypotheses for the evolution of caffeine, which is found in several plant species: herbivore defense, and allelopathy – inhibiting the germination of competing plants (133). Caffeine in nectar might have evolved to enhance pollinator memory (134).

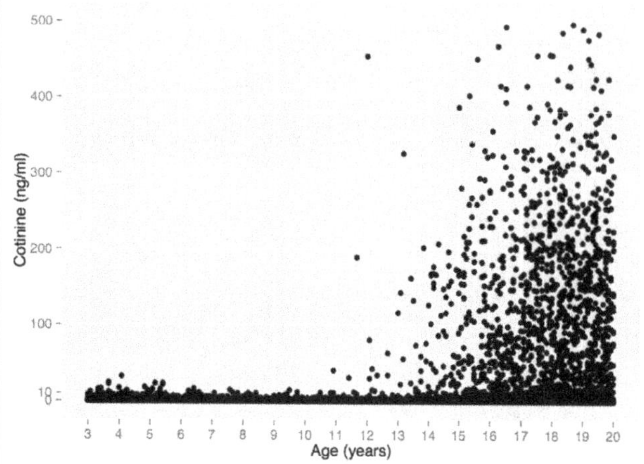

FIGURE 2 | Serum cotinine concentration vs. age in a sample of 18,382 children, adolescents, and young adults from the US National Health and Nutrition Examination Survey 1999–2010. There is no unequivocal evidence of tobacco consumption prior to age 11. (6 Cotinine values >500 ng/ml were omitted for clarity, all from individuals >17 years old.) Data from Ref. (123).

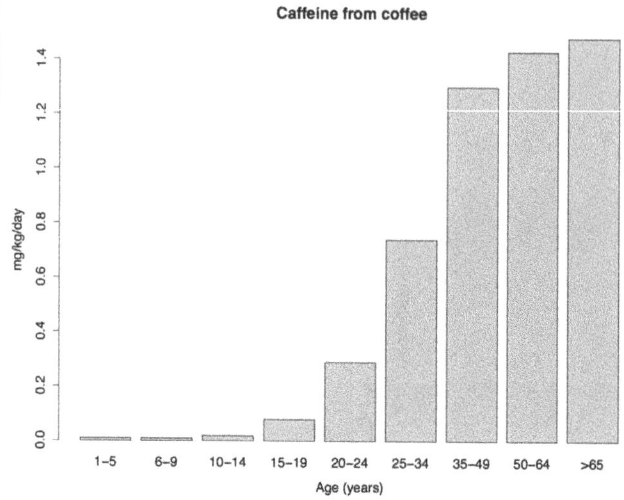

FIGURE 3 | Daily caffeine intake from coffee per kilogram of body weight in a sample of US caffeine consumers. Data from Ref. (136).

interacts with the central dopaminergic systems via antagonism of endogenous adenosine (135). Caffeine is added to numerous beverages marketed to children, which suggests that parents and society are not overly concerned about child caffeine consumption. In fact, the daily amount of caffeine consumed from soft drinks is similar in US children, adolescents, and adults (136). It is far from clear, however, that the rewarding properties of caffeine motivate child consumption of soft drinks. Soft drinks contain high levels of sugar and other sweeteners, and, compared to coffee, about 1/3 the concentration of caffeine. The rewarding properties of sugar and artificial sweeteners obviously play a major role in child consumption of soft drinks; the role of caffeine is unclear.

Coffee consumption patterns should be informative because coffee contains a rewarding psychoactive substance (caffeine), does not necessarily contain sugar, and, unlike tobacco, is not subject to national or global efforts to control its consumption. Under the imbalance model, consumption of coffee should therefore be similar in children and adults. Yet coffee consumption is extremely low in US children, with a transition to adult levels occurring in adolescence and early adulthood (**Figure 3**), resembling the age pattern of tobacco use. The similar age patterns of tobacco and coffee consumption despite the profound difference in social restrictions on child access to tobacco vs. coffee, shows, at a minimum, that such restrictions play a smaller role in child drug consumption patterns than is commonly thought (we do not dispute their importance for adolescent and adult drug use prevalence). As we argue next, low drug use by children is probably better explained by child aversion to drugs.

4.2. THE NEUROTOXIN REGULATION MODEL OF CHILDREN'S LOW-TO-NON-EXISTENT SUBSTANCE USE

Because we take an evolutionary perspective, we consider the biological fitness consequences of plant toxin exposure to ancestral human children, who subsisted on wild foods. Virtually all wild plant foods, including fruits, contain toxins (137). A wild fruit contains substantial macronutrients, however, whose benefits can offset the cost of its toxins. A dried leaf of a neurotoxic plant, on the other hand, has virtually no macronutrients to offset the costs of its toxins. Thus, under the neurotoxin regulation hypothesis, consumption of the dried leaf would only occur when the benefits of toxin exposure outweigh the costs. Our basic premise, which we explain in detail next, is that during childhood the costs of toxin exposure outweigh the benefits, so that drug use is very low, but during adolescence the balance shifts, so that increased benefits outweigh diminishing costs, leading to substantial drug use.

4.2.1. Age differences in the costs of neurotoxin exposure

We focus first on the fitness costs of exposure, and how these change during development. Due to differences in body mass alone, the cost of ingesting, e.g., 10 mg of nicotine, is much more dangerous to a 5-year old than a 15-year old. In addition, children have a considerably higher daily caloric requirement per kilogram of body mass: 2 year olds (a typical age of weaning in natural fertility populations) require about 80 kcal/kg/day, which decreases by young adulthood to about 40–50 kcal/kg/day (138, 139). This means that young children are eating almost twice as much food per kilogram of body mass as adults. Because ancestral humans relied on wild foods, higher caloric intake per unit mass implies potentially greater exposure to plant toxins per unit mass (depending on the "quality" of the diet, e.g., the mix of plant and animal foods).

This higher potential exposure has a number of implications. First, toxin defense pathways have limited capacities and can become saturated (140). Hence, consumption of a plant drug in addition to toxin-rich plant foods could cause toxin levels to reach dangerous levels. Second, toxin metabolism and elimination is energetically expensive (141), reducing energy available for, e.g., growth and immunity.

Disruption of development is perhaps the greatest cost of plant toxin exposure for children, though, because it can permanently impair functionality. Indeed, there is an entire discipline – teratology – devoted to investigating the role of environmental compounds in developmental disruption. Developmental toxicity is often distinct from systemic toxicity. For instance, low doses of some pesticides that cause little systemic toxicity nevertheless disrupt neural development, whereas near lethal doses of other pesticides have no discernible effect on neural development (142). The thalidomide tragedy provides another example: thalidomide was a sedative that was also effective against pregnancy sickness. Due to its low acute toxicity and the absence of teratogenic effects in rodents, it became quite popular in the 1960s until its severe teratogenic effects in humans – deformed limbs and organ defects in 20–30% of exposed infants – were recognized (143). The lack of teratogenicity in rodents might be due, in part, to their ability to rapidly metabolize and eliminate thalidomide, compared to much slower elimination in humans (144). These examples demonstrate that, for children, exposure to plant toxins can have costs above and beyond systemic toxicity, and that toxin metabolism is a key defense[13].

Some popular plant drugs are indeed potent teratogens. Nicotine, for example, interferes with acetylcholine signaling, which has a unique trophic role in brain development, modulating the patterns of brain cell replication and differentiation, synaptic outgrowth, and architectural modeling. All phases of brain assembly, from the early embryonic stage through adolescence, are profoundly vulnerable to disruption by nicotine exposure (145, 146). Even child exposure to environmental tobacco smoke (cotinine concentrations of ~1 vs. >100 ng/ml in tobacco users) is associated with deficits in neurodevelopment, intelligence, attention, and academic achievement (147, 148). Cholinergic signaling also plays an important role in non-neuronal cells, including those of the immune system, lungs, gut, and testes (149, 150), so nicotine and other cholinergic toxins could disrupt their development and function as well.

Consistent with these facts, there is considerable evidence for heightened toxin defenses during childhood. The best defense is to avoid ingesting toxic substances, and children reject many more foods than adults. Not surprisingly, vegetables and fruits are the most frequently rejected foods. There are two distinct, but closely related, psychological factors related to rejection of foods prior to ingestion: neophobia (rejection of novel foods), and "picky/fussy" eating (rejection of many foods, regardless of their novelty).

Neophobic food rejection occurs primarily due to visual cues. Foods that do not "look right" – green vegetables for example, or foods that resemble known bitter foods – are rejected without being placed in the mouth. Food neophobia is low at weaning, increases sharply as a child becomes more mobile (so parents would have less control over food choice), peaks between 2 and 6, and then decreases with age, becoming relatively stable in adulthood. Some studies show an inflection point at the onset of adolescence. The developmental trajectory of neophobia is widely interpreted to reflect an evolved defense against plant teratogens (151, 152). We see an important role for parental warnings in child ingestive behavior. Children should be averse to substances described by others as bitter or "bad." Unlike the imbalance model, however, parental warnings about drugs are taken as cues of toxicity rather than an attempt to restrict access to desired substances.

Foods that are placed in the mouth are rejected primarily based on taste, especially bitter taste (though sometimes on texture) (152). Taste is responsible for evaluating the nutritious content of food and preventing the ingestion of toxic substances (see **Box 1** for discussion of bitter taste physiology and genetics). Detection thresholds for bitter compounds are extremely low, in some cases as low as nano- or micro-molar concentrations (153), whereas those for sucrose are about 1000× higher (154).

Children 7–8 years old have a higher density of taste buds on the tip of the tongue than adults, and density is positively related to taste sensitivity. This density decreases to the adult level by about 9–10, with developmental changes complete by about age 11–12 (160). Children are indeed more sensitive to the bitter taste of PROP than adults, and are up to twice as likely to be supertasters (161), with the transition to adult sensitivity seeming to occur in adolescence [Ref. (162, 163), and references therein]. This age dependence might be greatest in T2R38 heterozygotes (163). (See **Box 1**). High bitter taste sensitivity leads to reduced consumption of bitter vegetables (e.g., cabbage, broccoli, asparagus, and spinach), especially in children (161).

All common recreational plant drugs, including nicotine, taste bitter. Ethanol has both bitter and sweet taste components (164). Thus, taste receptors properly recognize most popular psychoactive drugs as toxic. Given children's heightened neophobia, bitter sensitivity, and pickiness, they probably find most psychoactive drugs to be especially unpalatable[14].

The second major toxin defense is neutralization and elimination of ingested toxic substances, often via metabolism in the liver. As a percentage of body mass, liver volume is about 60% bigger in young children than in adults (165). Child drug clearance rates are very low at birth but reach adult levels by about 1 year, and then surpass adult levels, perhaps due to the increased relative size of the liver and/or higher expression of xenobiotic-metabolizing enzymes (166)[15].

Based on non-fatal poisoning data from the US, child toxin avoidance and metabolism mechanisms seem to work well: poisoning rates are highest in 1–2 year olds and then drop rapidly from 2 to 6, remaining low until adolescence (**Figure 4**), a pattern that mirrors the ontogeny of neophobia. Of course, this pattern might reflect other factors, such as increasingly tight restrictions on access

[13]Metabolism can also convert non toxic compounds into toxins (e.g., thalidomide metabolites are biologically active), which probably illustrates the truism that no defense mechanism is perfect.

[14]Chocolate, a concoction of sugar and fermented cacao beans, sometimes with milk and other flavors, is an exception as it contains several psychoactive plant xanthine alkaloids, including theobromine and caffeine. However, the version popular with children is mostly sugar, fat, and protein.

[15]Pediatric drug clearance is the subject of continuing theoretical and empirical investigation, and it is possible that the increased drug clearance in children relative to adults is an artifact of linear scaling by weight instead of allometric scaling by 3/4 power or body surface area (167). Regardless, children achieve near-adult levels of drug clearance at an early age.

Box 1 | Bitter taste physiology and genetics.

To understand the strengths and limitations of the evidence for age and sex differences in taste, especially in bitter taste (toxin detection), it is helpful to know a bit about taste physiology and genetics, and the history of taste research. Taste receptor cells are each tuned to one of the five basic taste modalities: sweet and umami, which identify sugars and amino acids, respectively, two key nutrients; salty, which helps ensure proper electrolyte balance; and sour and bitter, which detect toxins. Taste buds, which are distributed across the tongue and palate epithelium, comprise 50–150 taste receptor cells. Circumvallate papillae are located at the back of the tongue and contain thousands of taste buds; foliate papillae are located along the back edge of the tongue and contain a dozen to hundreds of taste buds; fungiform papillae are located in the front two-thirds of the tongue and contain one or a few taste buds (155).

In the early 1930s it was discovered that the ability to taste the bitter compound phenylthiocarbamide (PTC) was inherited in a nearly Mendelian fashion (156, 157), with PTC taste blindness due to a recessive "non-taster" allele at a single locus having a population frequency of about 50% (158). Thus, about 25% of the population are homozygous for the non-taster allele and are non-tasters, and about 75% possesses at least one copy of the dominant taster allele and are "tasters." The high frequency of the non-tasting allele implies balancing selection (e.g., heterozygote advantage), but the selective factor remains unknown.

An enormous body of research has explored variation in ability to taste PTC and a related substance, propylthiouracil (PROP), that has methodological advantages over PTC. One important finding is that PROP is intensely bitter for a subset of tasters, termed "supertasters," and only mildly bitter for other tasters. Although it is tempting to conclude that supertasters are those who are homozygous for the taster allele, genotype, number of fungiform papillae (FP), and perhaps other factors make separate contributions to perceived PROP bitterness (159).

In the early 2000s, the genes for bitter, sweet, and umami taste receptors were identified. Whereas only 3 genes are involved in sweet and umami taste (T1R1, T1R2, and T1R3), about 25 functional genes code for human bitter taste receptors (the T2R family). This makes sense because the chemical diversity of toxins vastly exceeds that of macronutrients. Some bitter taste receptors respond to as many as 1/3 of known bitter compounds, whereas others respond to only a few; many bitter compounds active multiple receptors (118).

The gene responsible for the bimodal taste distribution of PTC/PROP was finally identified as one of the bitter taste receptors, T2R38, with tasters being homozygous or heterozygous for the PAV allele, and non-tasters being homozygous for the AVI allele (158). Thus, although human bitter taste is mediated by 25 taste receptors – all with allelic variation, all whose phenotypic expression is undoubtedly modified by other genes and environmental factors, and which, as a group, respond to thousands of compounds – most research on human bitter taste is based on the taste response to PTC or PROP, which is largely (but not entirely) mediated by two alleles of a single bitter taste receptor with a distinctive pattern of balancing selection. [Quinine, which activates 9 T2R receptors (118), is another bitter taste stimulant used in many studies.]

A further complication is that both T2R38 genotype and PROP phenotype predict intensity of non-bitter tastants, such as NaCl (salty), sucrose (sweet), and citric acid (sour). And even after controlling for T2R38 genotype, number of fungiform papillae, and nonoral sensory standards, PROP bitterness predicts intensity of other tastants (159). This means, among other things, that inter-individual differences in the intensity of toxicity signals inferred from T2R genotype or PROP phenotype might also predict differences in the intensity of nutrient signals, with potentially complex effects on ingestion.

to toxic substances and/or improved training of children with age. Poisoning rates increase sharply at the onset of adolescence, paralleling reduced neophobia and the onset of substance use.

The apparent existence of heightened toxin defenses in children strongly suggests that, for much of human evolution, the costs of exposure to plant toxins during childhood have been high, but diminished as brain and other organ development neared completion, i.e., in adolescence. Although ancestral human children could not completely avoid plant toxins, we propose that during childhood the costs of consuming plant substances with high levels of neurotoxins but low levels of macronutrients almost always outweighed the benefits. The result is that children's heightened toxin defense mechanisms usually prevent drug ingestion, which explains children's virtually non-existent drug use.

4.2.2. Increases in fitness benefits across development

The hypothesized neurotoxin regulation mechanism functions to minimize the costs of exposure, and maximize the benefits. In addition to the evidence that the costs of neurotoxin exposure were diminishing in adolescence, there is also evidence that the putative anti-parasite benefits were increasing. In populations with endemic helminth infections (which presumably include ancestral human populations), individuals are born without infections but acquire them as they age. At the same time, they gradually acquire protective immunity. As a likely result of these two processes, infection levels peak in middle childhood or adolescence in many populations, with the age of the peak dependent on the parasite transmission rate and the rate at which individuals become immune (a higher transmission rate leads to an earlier, more intense peak) (169–171). See **Figure 5A**. This peak could have selected for a predisposition to initiate drug use at this time to maximize prophylactic or therapeutic benefits. Intriguingly, in populations with endemic *Schistosoma haematobium* infection the immune system itself appears to undergo an age-related antibody switch. Theoretical and empirical results suggest this reflects a transition from an early non-protective response based on exposure to eggs to a later protective response stimulated by the death of adult worms (172) (**Figure 5B**). If the immune system response to a helminth infection exhibits a switch-like transition in adolescence, then so, too, might behavioral defenses, such as self-medication.

Attracting mates is another possible benefit for adolescents but not children. Sexually selected signals, such as peacock tails and bird songs, are widespread in nature and usually emerge at the end of the juvenile period to advertise sexual maturity and mate quality to the opposite sex (173, 174). Similarly, conspicuous psychoactive substance use, which under the hypothesis cannot begin until the risk of teratogenesis has abated, would be a reliable cue or signal that a developmental milestone had been achieved, such as maturation of the nervous system and perhaps gonads or other organs[16]. Such a signal might attract mates (175) and other social partners because a developmentally mature individual would be able to provide them greater benefits. A reliable cue or signal of developmental maturity would be especially important in populations, such as most hunter-gatherers, that do not keep track of chronological age yet choose mates and social partners based on qualities that vary with age but are otherwise difficult to discern.

[16]It would also signal well-functioning detoxification mechanisms, of course.

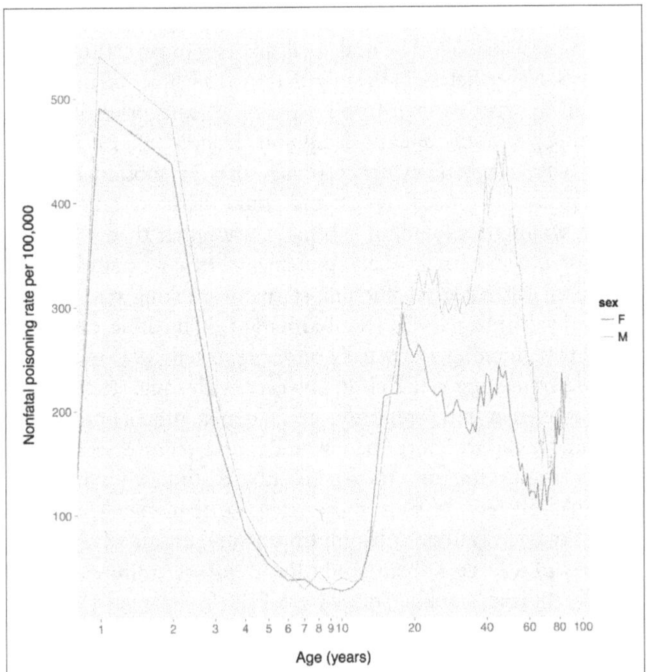

FIGURE 4 | US unintentional non-fatal poisoning rate vs. age, 2001–2011. There is a dramatic decline in rates during childhood, a dramatic increase during adolescence, and the female (but not male) rate declines steadily during women's reproductive years (about age 18–38). The x-axis is on a log scale to improve display of the lower age range. Data from Centers for Disease Control and Prevention (168).

In support of this hypothesis, the age of onset of sexual behavior closely parallels that of drug use (compare **Figures 1** and **6**). Smoking initiation is significantly influenced by perceived benefits like looking grown up (176); and in adolescents, perceived maturity, substance use, sexual behavioral, and prestige are all correlated (177, 178). Young smokers are also more risk taking and impulsive, traits that characterize males engaged in intrasexual competition (179–181), and engage in earlier sexual behavior (182), all of which suggest a link between substance use and mating. Indeed, higher mating effort is related to more smoking and more lenient attitudes toward drug use (183, 184). But, smoking has well-documented negative effects on female reproductive function [reviewed in Ref. (185)], and there is also evidence that it negatively impacts male reproduction, including erectile function (186, 187), so the signaling benefits to either sex would need to outweigh these costs[17].

The neurotoxin regulation hypothesis, like the imbalance hypothesis, involves a cost-benefit analysis by children, but it differs from the imbalance hypothesis in a number of ways. First, we hypothesize that neurotoxin regulation involves specialized circuits and is not based solely on domain-general learning. Second, although these mechanisms take into account warnings from others, they rely heavily on bitter taste receptors and other chemosensors. Third, because the cost of ingesting too much neurotoxin vastly outweighs the cost of not ingesting enough, the mechanisms are biased against consumption. Fourth, the circuitry is well-developed in early childhood, although its functioning changes across development to reflect changes in the costs and benefits of neurotoxin exposure.

5. SEX DIFFERENCES IN SUBSTANCE USE

There is a global male bias in substance use among adults, albeit one that is less dramatic than the age bias, and that varies by nation, substance, age, birth cohort, and other factors. Male prevalence of smoking is almost always greater than female prevalence, for instance (**Figure 7**). The two exceptions in these data are Nauru (a small island in the south Pacific) and Sweden. The Swedish data

[17]It is possible that such costs could increase the credibility of the signal, sensu (188, 189).

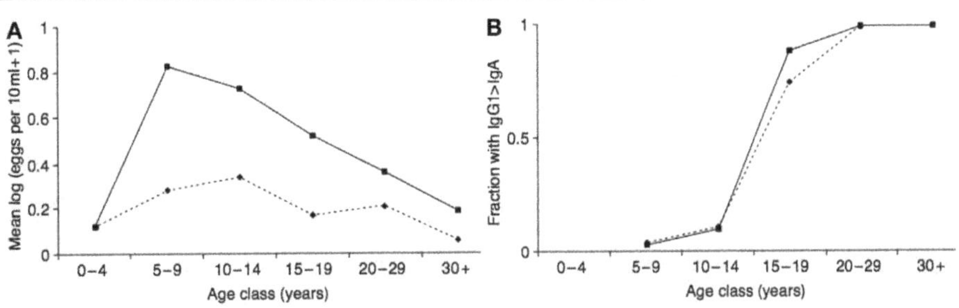

FIGURE 5 | (A) Intensity of *Schistosoma haematobium* infection in two Zimbabwean populations with high transmission rate (solid line) and low transmission rate (dashed line). **(B)** The resulting antibody switch. The y-axis represents fractions of the two populations with high levels of anti-soluble egg antigen specific IgG1 relative to IgA (as absorbance at 492 nm). Reproduced from Ref. (170).

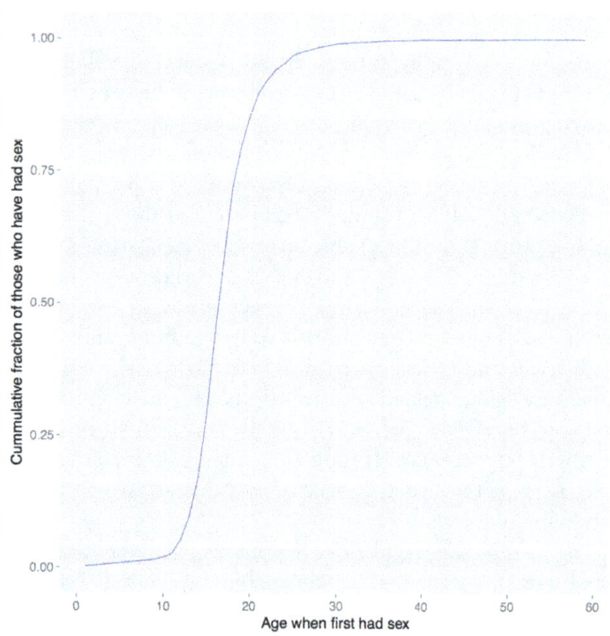

FIGURE 6 | Age of first sexual intercourse in NHANES data. This cumulative distribution closely resembles that of age of first substance use seen in **Figure 1**. Data from Ref. (123).

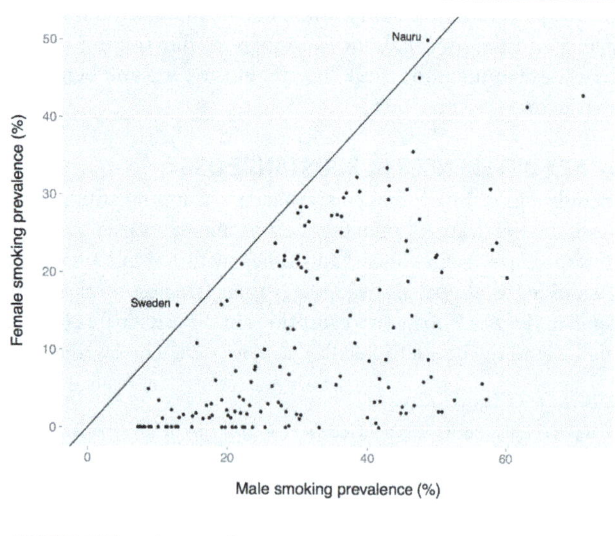

FIGURE 7 | Female vs. male smoking prevalence across nations. The solid diagonal line represents equal prevalence. Values coded as "<1%" set to 0. Data from the Tobacco Atlas (http://www.tobaccoatlas.org).

are misleading, however, because the use of oral tobacco products is high among Swedish men but low among Swedish women. Thus, far more Swedish men use tobacco (40%) than do Swedish women (23%) (190).

The large cross-national WMHSI study (120) found that the odds ratio of women initiating use of alcohol, tobacco, cannabis, and cocaine use in any year of life, vs. men, ranged from 0 for tobacco use in Nigeria and 0.1 for cocaine use in Mexico and Columbia (large male biases) to a non-significant 0.8 for cannabis use in France (no sex bias). Although most of these ratios indicated a statistically significant male bias, when sex differences were examined by age there was clear evidence that, for some substances in some populations, they were narrowing in younger cohorts, especially for the legal drugs alcohol and tobacco, and in several cases there were no significant sex differences. In no case, though, were women significantly *more* likely to initiate use of these substances than men.

In contrast to the foregoing substances that either show a clear male bias, or no bias, there are some drugs that are more likely to be used by females of certain ages in some populations. For example, there is historical evidence for a female bias in the use of opioids in the late 19th and early 20th century US (191). In the US in recent years, adolescent girls (12–17) were more likely than adolescent boys to use alcohol and be non-medical users of psychotherapeutic drugs. Nevertheless, in the population as a whole, US men were more likely than women to be users of all categories of drugs, including psychotherapeutic drugs and alcohol (192, 193).

As with age bias, evidence of sex bias in substance use is based primarily on self-report, and could therefore reflect a sex bias in willingness to admit substance use rather than a sex bias in substance use itself. A comprehensive review of studies that compared self-reported smoking status to smoking status determined by cotinine levels (the biomarker of nicotine exposure) found that smoking was usually under-reported (194). A sex bias in under-reporting is less clear, however, with some studies finding that women under-report more than men, others finding that men under-report more than women, and culture seeming to play an important role. In two recent US studies, for instance, women's self-reports were more accurate than men's, or even overestimated cigarette consumption relative to men (195, 196), whereas in a large Korean study the ratios of cotinine-verified to self-reported smoking rates were 2.36 for women (substantial under-reporting) and 1.12 for men. Even so, cotinine-verified smoking rates were much higher in Korean men (50.0%) than women (13.9%) (197).

In short, unlike the nearly uniform global absence of child drug use (**Figure 1**), there is considerable heterogeneity in the prevalence of adult drug use by sex (e.g., **Figure 7**). This heterogeneity suggests that multiple factors differentially affect women's and men's drug use, perhaps including sex differences in access to drugs and sex differences in formal and informal social penalties and rewards for using drugs. At the same time, a greater prevalence among women appears to be the exception rather than the rule (e.g., **Figure 7**), which suggests that biological sex itself might play an important role in the decision to use, or not use, drugs.

5.1. THE HIJACK MODEL OF SEX DIFFERENCES IN SUBSTANCE USE

Women enjoy sugar, needless to say, and, in the US at least, eat as much of it as men (as a fraction of total calories) (198). This implies that there are no gross differences in food reward that would explain sex differences in substance use. On the other hand, there are numerous sex differences in motivation, reinforcement, and reward, and their underlying neural mechanisms that might. We will focus on the work of Becker and colleagues, who have written extensively on sex differences in the neurobiology of motivation and reward, and the implications for sex differences in drug use (199–202).

Becker and colleagues base their model on a plausible evolutionary account of sex differences in motivation rooted in parental investment theory. Parental investment is any investment, such as food or protection, by the parent in an individual offspring that increases the offspring's survival (and hence reproduction) at the cost of the parent's ability to invest in other offspring (203). Females in most animal species, including those that serve as models in drug research (e.g., rats, monkeys), invest more in offspring than males via, e.g., larger gamete size, internal gestation, and various forms of postnatal care, such as lactation. Male investment in offspring is minimal. As a consequence, female and male reproductive strategies diverge. Female fitness is largely constrained by access to the resources necessary to support high levels of parental investment, whereas male fitness is largely constrained by access to mates. Males therefore compete with other males for females, and females are choosey about mates (e.g., mating with males that exhibit higher genetic quality).

Becker et al. argue that, in rats, sex differences in parental investment have resulted in the evolution of sex differences in sexual and parenting motivation, and that some of these differences are shared with humans (200). In rats, male sexual motivation is constant, in line with a male strategy to maximize fitness by maximizing the number of mates. Male sexual motivation (but not mounting) is mediated by the MDS. Female sexual motivation, in contrast, depends on context and timing. Female rats are sexually receptive (estrus) for about 1 day of their 4–5 day estrous cycle. At this time, females "pace" copulations, and pregnancy is more likely to result when coital stimulation occurs at a particular rate. This appears to be a mechanism of female choice because dominant male rats contribute more intromissions and tend to give each female more ejaculations than subordinates (204). Female pacing is mediated by the MDS, and dopamine increases only when females anticipate receiving copulatory stimulation at their preferred rate of intromission.

There are also pronounced sex differences in parental motivation. Female rats exhibit a strong motivation to gain access to pups but males do not. There is some evidence that the MDS is involved in maternal motivation.

According to Becker et al., these sex differences in rat neurobiology emerge, in part, from the effects of gonadal hormones on the developing brain, particularly during the perinatal and peripubertal periods[18]. In addition, sex differences in gonadal hormones can result in sex differences in adult brain function.

Becker and Taylor [(200), p. 185] postulate that "Once sex differences in motivational circuits had evolved ... there were unforeseen consequences that resulted in many other motivations systems being sexually dimorphic as well. Nowhere is this so striking as in drug addiction. Sex differences emerge in all phases of the addiction process including initiation and prevalence of use, patterns and levels of use, the progression to addiction, withdrawal, and relapse." To more specifically link sex differences in drug use to sex differences in motivation, Becker and Taylor [(200), p. 178] argue that "motivation in females is modulated by gonadal hormones, and the female brain is more vulnerable to be co-opted by exogenous agents that induce constant activation (e.g., drugs of abuse) than are males." And, "Sex differences in neural circuitry of attachment may spill over into other motivational systems too, including non-reproductive motivations for drugs. The development of strong attachments, and addictions or compulsive behaviors may occur through activation of the neural system that mediates maternal motivation; thus, females can become addicted to drugs more rapidly than males."

Becker and colleagues cite a wealth of evidence from laboratory rats and humans that gonadal steroid hormones modulate drug-related behaviors, and that, by a number of measures, females in both species are more vulnerable to the effects of drugs (particularly cocaine). These sex-specific effects include more rapid progression from initial drug use to dependence in women, and more rapid acquisition of cocaine self-administration in female rats; greater stress-induced drug craving in women and female rats; and greater stress-induced reinstatement of drug use in women and female rats. Becker et al. (202) argue, further, that whereas men tend to use drugs for sensation seeking (positive reinforcement), women tend to use drugs to reduce stress or self-medicate psychological distress (negative reinforcement). Stressed or psychologically distressed individuals "enter into the downward spiral [toward addiction] already burdened with neurological changes that may promote their transition to addiction more rapidly."

In summary, in rats the neurobiology of sexual and parental motivation and reward differs among the sexes and involves sex differences in the response of the MDS, and Becker et al. argue that these sex differences underlie sex differences in the animals' responses to drugs of abuse. Many sex differences in human drug use are rooted in sex differences in human neurobiology that resemble those seen in rats. The upshot of most sex differences is that females are more vulnerable to the co-opting effects of drugs than males.

Becker and colleagues' conclusion would seem to predict that the prevalence of drug use would be higher in women. Instead, for most drugs in most populations, the prevalence is higher, often much higher, in men (e.g., **Figure 7**). Becker et al. acknowledge higher male prevalence, and contend that it is a consequence of historical, cultural, and social factors. But the Becker et al. model is almost exclusively one of neurobiological sex differences and only briefly sketches what those historical and sociocultural factors might be: "Overall, availability of drugs coupled with dissatisfying social conditions, stress, anxiety, and depression tends to exacerbate drug abuse and addiction in women. While such conditions can also increase drug use in men, it is our hypothesis that on the average this happens more often in women" [Ref. (202), p. 5]. Maybe so, but of these factors, only "availability of drugs" has a plausible male bias that might explain the pervasive male bias in the prevalence of drug use. Like the imbalance model of drug

[18] Becker et al. aim to explain sex differences in drug use, not age differences. But their theory could explain the dramatic age differences discussed earlier. If drugs specifically hijacked the mechanisms underlying sexual behavior, parenting, or pair-bonding, then drug use would only occur when these systems became active, i.e., during adolescence. This would seem to imply, however, that drug use would then be more closely associated with sexual, parenting, or pair-bonding emotions, which is debatable.

use in children, then, the Becker et al. model puts the onus for lower prevalence in women on their socially restricted access to drugs.

5.2. THE NEUROTOXIN REGULATION MODEL OF SEX DIFFERENCES IN DRUG USE

The neurotoxin regulation model of sex differences, like the Becker et al. model, is grounded in evolved sex differences in parental investment (and thus applies to adults, not children). According to the neurotoxin regulation model, the decision to ingest plant neurotoxins reflects an evolved calculus that weighs fitness benefits against costs. Because we take an evolutionary perspective, we consider the fitness benefits and costs of neurotoxin intake to ancestral men and women. Most of the fitness benefits and costs of regulated neurotoxin intake would probably have been similar for men and women, but women of childbearing age faced an additional cost: potential disruption of fetal and infant development.

Ancestral women had no access to highly reliable modern contraceptive technologies. Across contemporary hunter-gatherer societies that also lack such technologies, the median age at first birth is 19.25, the median weaning age is 2.5 years, the median interbirth interval is 3.2 years, and the median total fertility rate is 5.5 (205). Thus, for much of her late teens to her late thirties the median hunter-gatherer woman is pregnant or lactating.

Ancestral women's plant ingestion therefore had a profound impact on the exposure of their fetuses and infants to plant toxins. Throughout gestation, for instance, maternal serum or urine cotinine levels correlate strongly with concentrations in fetal tissues and fluids such as cord blood, umbilical cord tissue, meconium, amniotic fluid, and placenta [Ref. (206), and references therein]. In infants breastfed by smoking mothers, cotinine concentrations in the urine are in the range of adult smokers (207). Fetal exposure to nicotine and other tobacco teratogens is associated with reduced academic achievement and intellectual abilities later in life (208).

Among contemporary hunter-gatherers, a median 21% of children die within the first year of life, and 45% within the first 15 years of life, rates similar to those seen in chimpanzees (205), which implies intense selection to protect offspring from harm. We therefore propose that, to maximize the fitness benefits from their high investment in offspring, women evolved to be more averse to toxins in their reproductive years, and to metabolize and eliminate them more rapidly. The tradeoffs of increased toxin defense included dietary restrictions and thus either reduced nutrient intake or increased search and processing times, and energy allocation to toxin metabolism at the expense of, e.g., activity levels and immunity.

Contemporary hunter-gatherer societies are characterized by a sexual division of labor, with men typically hunting or fishing, women typically gathering plant foods, and food widely shared among all group members (there is considerable variability, however, and women often hunt and men often gather) (205). If ancestral human societies were also characterized by a similar sexual division of labor involving foraging of plant vs. animal foods, then this could have been an additional factor for the evolution of sex differences in chemosensing and toxin defense.

Drugs of abuse activate most toxin defense mechanisms, including those governing intake such as bitter taste receptors and conditioned taste avoidance, and higher bitter sensitivity seems to reduce drug intake. For instance, T2R38 genotype predicts drug use in adults, with tasters consuming less than non-tasters. Ethanol tastes bitter, and beer and wine both contain additional bitter compounds (209–211). Alcohol intake is lowest in PAV homozygotes PAV/AVI heterozygotes (tasters); in one study (212) it was almost half that reported by AVI homozygotes (non-tasters) [reviewed in Ref. (213)]. A number of studies suggest that high bitter taste sensitivity in adults is also protective against nicotine dependence (214–219), albeit with some inconsistencies [e.g., Ref. (216)].

We therefore propose that heightened toxin defense in women (evidence for which we discuss next) results in their lower prevalence of drug use. We also propose that learning plays a key role: the effects of plant toxins on fetal and infant development are not completely predictable from their immediate physiological effects (e.g., bitter taste, nausea), so women should be attentive to information from others regarding the negative effects on offspring (or lack thereof) of ingesting particular plants, and adjust intake accordingly.

There is considerable evidence for sex differences in toxin disposition. Less clear is whether these differences are a consequences of greater toxin defense in women, particularly pregnant or lactating women, or instead are byproducts of, e.g., sex differences in physiology, such as body size and composition. Women have a higher percentage of body fat than men, for example, and lipophilic drugs, such as THC, are sequestered in fat tissue, which might account for some sex differences in response to THC (220). Sex differences in toxin disposition could even be due to sex differences in exogenous factors like diet. To give one example, grapefruit juice inhibits CYP3A4, an important drug metabolizing enzyme (221). If there were a sex difference in consumption of grapefruit juice, this could result in sex differences in the disposition of many drugs and toxins.

We will briefly review evidence that seems to suggest enhanced toxin defenses in women, while acknowledging considerable uncertainty in the interpretation of this evidence, that much evidence suggests no sex differences, and that some evidence points in the opposite direction. The challenge in resolving the nature of sex differences in toxin defense mechanisms is exacerbated by a lack of data on drug disposition in women, as pharmaceutical research often excluded women, particularly pregnant women, from clinical trials over concerns of possible drug teratogenicity.

We divide women's lives into 3 distinct reproductive phases: a sexually active but pre-reproductive phase that starts in early-to-mid adolescence and ends at the age of first pregnancy; a reproductive phase involving alternating periods of pregnancy and lactation; and a post-reproductive phase that begins with menopause. We propose maximum sex differences in toxin defense during the reproductive phase, especially during pregnancy and lactation, and consequently maximum sex differences in the prevalence of substance use, but reduced sex differences in toxin defense in the pre- and post-reproductive phases, and consequently reduced sex differences in the prevalence of substance use.

Modern birth control technologies complicate interpretation of sex differences in drug use patterns and toxin defense mechanisms because for the first time in our evolutionary history women can indefinitely extend their sexually active pre-reproductive phase;

reliably alternate psychoactive drug use with pregnancy and lactation; minimize breastfeeding by rapidly transitioning to infant formula; and sharply limit total fertility. In other words, during their reproductive years most modern women can, if they choose, use psychoactive drugs much of the time with little risk of fetal or infant exposure. Hormonal birth control introduces a further complication in that steroid hormones modulate xenobiotic metabolism (see below), and might also alter psychobehavioral toxin defense mechanisms.

5.2.1. Heightened toxin detection in women

Women have more fungiform papillae and more taste buds than men and, according to most studies, are able to detect lower concentrations of PROP and are more likely to be supertasters (222). High bitter sensitivity, in turn, generally predicts reduced vegetable intake in both women and men [e.g., Ref. (223); for review, see Ref. (224)]. The major caveat is that research on bitter taste has been dominated by investigation of two compounds, PTC and PROP, which primarily activate a single bitter taste receptor, T2R38 (see **Box 1**); it is unknown whether sex differences in bitter taste sensitivity extend to a broad range of ecologically important substances and all bitter taste receptors.

5.2.2. Heightened drug metabolism in women

Nicotine metabolism is accelerated in women (225). Nicotine and most other drugs are metabolized by liver cytochrome P450 enzymes. About a dozen of the 57 human P450 enzymes are primarily responsible for xenobiotic metabolism. Of the many factors influencing sex differences in drug disposition, there is widespread agreement that sex differences in hepatic enzyme activity play a major role.

The CYP3A family is the most abundant P450 in the liver, and is responsible for the metabolism of >50% of all commercial drugs. Most studies have found that women have about 20–30% higher CYP3A-mediated clearance, albeit with considerable variation across drugs and individuals (226, 227). Nuclear receptors (NR) are transcription factors that are activated by small lipophilic molecules, including plant toxins; NR, in turn, regulate the expression of many genes, including P450 enzymes. In rodents, sex differences in NR-regulated liver metabolism raise the possibility that the female liver is more efficient in neutralizing substances (228). In a study of 374 drug metabolizing and transporter genes in human liver tissue, sex differences in expression were found in 77 (21%). Of these, 58 (75%) had higher expression in women (229).

Other evidence suggests few sex differences in metabolism, or, for some substances, even a male bias. For instance, other than CYP3A, sex differences in the activities of most xenobiotic-metabolizing P450s are unresolved (227, 230). Some substrates of CYP1A2 and CYP2E1, which metabolize 4 and 2% of known commercial drugs, respectively (231), are more rapidly metabolized in men (232), and men appear to have greater hepatic expression of p-glycoprotein, an important drug transporter (230).

Based on FDA data, women suffer more prescription drug-related adverse events, and these events are of a more serious nature. This might indicate that women are *more* vulnerable to toxins, not less. It could also reflect the fact that most drug trials have involved men, and thus dosages are inappropriate for women due to smaller body size, differences in body composition, sex differences in pharmacokinetics, sex differences in pharmacodynamics (the effects of the drug), biased reporting, or perhaps that women more often use multiple drugs, increasing the risk of an adverse event (230). Because xenobiotics can both induce and inhibit P450 expression, sex differences in diet could also contribute to sex differences in adverse events.

In contrast to the FDA data on adverse events for prescription drugs, US non-fatal poisoning rates indicate that although there is no sex difference in adolescence, women have a markedly lower rate than men from age 20–75 (**Figure 4**). It is not clear whether this reflects heightened toxin defenses in women (including avoidance), or one or more of the many other factors influencing toxin ingestion, metabolism, physiological effects, and elimination.

5.2.3. Pregnancy

During pregnancy, women have to meet increasing demands for macro and micronutrients while at the same time protecting their fetuses from plant teratogens, which exist in higher concentrations in the wild foods consumed by ancestral women than in the domesticated grains, vegetables, and fruits consumed by most women today. In addition, to accommodate a fetus expressing paternal genes, as well as changes in vulnerabilities to infection, there are substantial changes in maternal immunity.

Studies based on PTC/PROP find that bitter taste reaches a maximum in the first trimester of pregnancy, which would make women particular good "poison detectors" to protect the fetus from teratogens (233). A study using caffeine, however, which activates different T2Rs, found reduced bitter taste sensitivity in pregnant women vs. non-pregnant controls, an effect the authors interpret as functioning to increase variation in diet in order to increase weight during pregnancy (234).

Approximately 50–90% of pregnancies involve heightened food aversions, and up to 80% involve nausea and vomiting. This is puzzling given the increased micro- and macro-nutrient requirements of pregnancy. Yet nausea and vomiting in pregnancy (NVP), which tends to occur in the first trimester, is associated with positive pregnancy outcomes. Two complimentary adaptationist accounts of NVP have garnered widespread attention. One highlights aversions to meat, because meat is likely to harbor pathogens, and women are immunosuppressed in their first trimester (235, 236). The other, supporting the view we advance here, highlights aversions to toxic plants because these pose a risk to the developing fetus, especially during organogenesis (237, 238); for review, see (239). The two hypotheses broadly overlap, however, because microbial food-borne pathogens produce some of the most toxic substances known to science. Botulinum toxin, for instance (a cholinergic toxin like nicotine) has a lethal dose on the order of nanograms per kilogram of body mass (240).

Pregnancy-related aversions include drugs like alcohol, coffee, and tobacco (239, 241), and these aversions appear to reduce drug intake. Women smokers, for example, often reduce or cease smoking during pregnancy, and one important reason seems to be sensory aversions to tobacco smoke (242).

There are also pregnancy-related increases in drug metabolism. Nicotine metabolism, for instance, is accelerated in pregnancy (243). Activities of CYP3A4, CYP2C9, and CYP2D6, which together are responsible for the metabolism of >80% of commercial drugs, are increased several-fold during pregnancy. There is also evidence for increased activity of the phase II enzyme UGT1A4, as well as the drug transporters p-glycoprotein, OATP1B1, and OCT2. However, CYP1A2, which is responsible for the metabolism of about 4% of commercial drugs, is down-regulated. Pregnancy-related changes in activities of other P450 enzymes are equivocal, with some evidence for increased activity of CYP2B6.

Pregnancy hormones are obvious potential modulators of P450 enzymes. An *in vitro* study found that pregnancy-levels of estradiol enhanced CYP2A6, CYP2B6, and CYP3A4 expression, whereas progesterone induced CYP2A6 (minor), CYP2B6, CYP2C8, CYP3A4, and CYP3A5 expression (244). For reviews of drug disposition in pregnancy, see (231, 245–247).

5.2.4. Menopause

If female toxin defenses are heightened to protect their fetuses and nursing infants, and if heightened defenses involve tradeoffs against other important functions and behaviors, then defenses should decrease to male levels post menopause. Consistent with this view, perceived bitterness of PROP remains relatively constant for women in their childbearing years, and then declines after menopause, whereas for men it shows a more gradual and steady decline from their 30s onward (233). Nicotine metabolism is accelerated in younger women compared to men, but is no different in menopausal and postmenopausal women than men (225). Data on the relationship between menopause and clearance of other drugs is conflicting, however. For example, some substrates of CYP3A4 are cleared less rapidly in menopausal and postmenopausal women, consistent with the hypothesis, but others show no difference (230).

5.2.5. Summary of sex differences

In summary, there is enough evidence to propose (but not to conclude) that toxin defenses are heightened in women during their childbearing years; that the enhancement serves, at least in part, to protect the fetus and infant; that it reduces intake of drugs; and that it is partially responsible for the lower prevalence of drug use of women in their 20s and 30s. We speculate that the diminishing sex differences in use of some substances in younger cohorts might partially reflect the global fertility transition over the last several decades that involves increased use of birth control, later age at marriage, delay of first birth, and lower total fertility (248), all of which would allow women, especially younger women, to increase drug intake while limiting fetal and infant exposure. If the fertility transition is partly a consequence of reduced child mortality rates combined with women's increasing economic importance in society and their need for increased education, and thus a reduced emphasis on their reproductive roles, this might also have reduced social disapproval of drug use in women relative to men, further increasing women's access to, and willingness to use, drugs.

Finally, we suggest that, for the human data at least, the Becker et al. and neurotoxin regulation models are complimentary rather than contradictory. Whereas the neurotoxin regulation model of sex differences emphasizes female avoidance and elimination of plant toxins, the Becker et al. model primarily applies to women who have already chosen to use drugs, and who therefore differ from the general female population; given lower female prevalence of drug use, they might differ more than male drug users differ from the general male population. In addition, as Becker et al. emphasize, men and women often use drugs for different reasons, with women more often using drugs to alleviate stress or depression and men more often as a type of risk taking. It is not so surprising that people who use drugs for very different reasons would also exhibit important differences in many other facets of drug use.

6. CONCLUDING REMARKS

We have taken the idea that drugs hijack the brain and reframed it as a testable hypothesis. We then developed a testable alternative, the neurotoxin regulation hypothesis. In our view, the dramatic age and sex differences in drug use are better explained by age and sex differences in the costs vs. benefits of toxin exposure than by age and sex differences in reward, supporting the neurotoxin regulation hypothesis. The case is far from closed, however, and there is little reason to accept either hypothesis without considerable further research. The hijack hypothesis would be supported by finding that the child MDS generates a pro-drug motivation that is overridden by deliberations in the prefrontal cortex, perhaps in response to adult warnings, and/or is thwarted by socially restricted access to drugs. It would also be supported by finding that the sex differences in substance use are largely due to sex differences in social restrictions on drug use that are independent of childbearing, and not due to sex differences in a preference to consume drugs.

The neurotoxin regulation hypothesis would be supported by finding, instead, that child drug use is rare regardless of adult warnings or restrictions, there is no pro-drug use signal from the MDS to override, children are strongly averse to drugs, and, at least in ancestral populations, there were fitness benefits to drug use, which first exceeded the costs in adolescence. It would also be supported by finding that sex differences in drug use are partly a consequence of maternal toxin defense mechanisms that function to protect the fetus and infant. Increased drug use by pre- and post-reproductive women is not surprising, and recent diminishing of sex differences for some drugs in some populations might be linked to the fertility transition. Product engineering aimed at increasing women's drug use, which includes adding sugar and flavorings to alcoholic beverages and cigarettes (249, 250), probably also plays a role in reducing sex differences.

Tobacco use and abuse of alcohol and other drugs are major contributors to global disease burden (251, 252). Many pharmacological treatments for drug abuse aim to reduce reward (253). Research on the treatment of substance abuse might benefit by also investigating pharmacological manipulation and enhancement of toxin defense mechanisms[19].

---

[19] Disulfiram is a partial example. It inhibits acetaldehyde dehydrogenase, which, in individuals who drink, leads to high levels of acetaldehyde, a toxic alcohol metabolite. The resulting unpleasant reaction deters drinking.

REFERENCES

1. Glimcher PW. Colloquium paper: understanding dopamine and reinforcement learning: the dopamine reward prediction error hypothesis. *Proc Natl Acad Sci U S A* (2011) 108(Suppl 3):15647–54. doi:10.1073/pnas.1014269108
2. Morris G, Schmidt R, Bergman H. Striatal action-learning based on dopamine concentration. *Exp Brain Res* (2009) 200:307–17. doi: 10.1007/s00221-009-2060-6
3. Redgrave P, Gurney K, Reynolds J. What is reinforced by phasic dopamine signals? *Brain Res Rev* (2008) 58(2):322–39. doi:10.1016/ j.brainresrev.2007.10.007
4. Schultz W. Behavioral dopamine signals. *Trends Neurosci* (2007) 30(5):203–10. doi:10.1016/j.tins. 2007.03.007
5. Berridge KC. The debate over dopamine's role in reward: the case for incentive salience. *Psychopharmacology (Berl)* (2007) 191(3):391–431. doi:10.1007/s00213-006-0578-x
6. Salamone JD, Correa M, Far- rar A, Mingote SM. Effort-related functions of nucleus accumbens dopamine and associated fore- brain circuits. *Psychopharmacol- ogy* (2007) 191(3):461–82. doi:10. 1007/s00213-006-0668-9
7. Schultz W. Potential vulner- abilities of neuronal reward, risk, and decision mecha- nisms to addictive drugs. *Neuron* (2011) 69(4):603–17. doi:10.1016/j.neuron.2011.02.014
8. Wise RA. Addiction becomes a brain disease. *Neuron* (2000) 26(1):27–33. doi:10.1016/S0896- 6273(00)81134-4
9. Kelley AE, Berridge KC. The neu- roscience of natural rewards: rele- vance to addictive drugs. *J Neurosci* (2002) 22(9):3306–11.
10. Gardner E. Endocannabinoid sig- naling system and brain reward: emphasis on dopamine. *Phar- macol Biochem Behav* (2005) 81(2):263–84. doi:10.1016/j.pbb. 2005.01.032
11. Hyman SE. Addiction: a disease of learning and memory. *Am J Psychi- atry* (2005) 162:1414–22. doi:10. 1176/appi.ajp.162.8.1414
12. Kauer JA, Malenka RC. Synaptic plasticity and addiction. *Nat Rev Neurosci* (2007) 8(11):844–58. doi: 10.1038/nrn2234
13. Sulzer D. How addictive drugs disrupt presynaptic dopamine neurotransmission. *Neuron* (2011) 69(4):628–49. doi:10.1016/j.neuron.2011.02.010
14. Volkow ND, Baler RD, Goldstein RZ. Addiction: pulling at the neural threads of social behaviors. *Neuron* (2011) 69(4):599–602. doi: 10.1016/j.neuron.2011.01.027
15. Goldstein RZ, Volkow ND. Dys- function of the prefrontal cortex in addiction: neuroimaging findings and clinical implications. *Nat Rev Neurosci* (2011) 12(11):652–69. doi:10.1038/nrn3119
16. Orr HA. Fitness and its role in evo- lutionary genetics. *Nat Rev Genet* (2009) 10(8):531–9. doi:10.1038/ nrg2603
17. Avena NM, Rada P, Hoebel BG. Evidence for sugar addic- tion: behavioral and neurochem- ical effects of intermittent, exces- sive sugar intake. *Neurosci Biobe- hav Rev* (2008) 32(1):20–39. doi: 10.1016/j.neubiorev.2007.04.019
18. Ahmed SH, Avena DNM, Berridge DKC, Gearhardt DAN, Guillem DK. Food addiction. In: Pfaff DW, editor. *Neuroscience in the 21st Century*. New York: Springer (2013). p. 2833–57.
19. Ahmed SH, Lenoir M, Guillem K. Neurobiology of addiction ver- sus drug use driven by lack of choice. *Curr Opin Neurobiol* (2013) 23(4):581–7. doi:10.1016/j. conb.2013.01.028
20. Sullivan RJ, Hagen EH. Psy- chotropic substance-seeking: evolutionary pathology or adaptation? *Addiction* (2002) 97:389–400. doi:10.1046/j.1360-0443.2002.00024.x
21. Sullivan RJ, Hagen EH, Hammer- stein P. Revealing the paradox of drug reward in human evolution. *Proc Biol Sci* (2008) 275:1231–41. doi:10.1098/ rspb.2007.1673
22. Hagen EH, Sullivan RJ, Schmidt R, Morris G, Kempter R, Ham- merstein P. Ecology and neurobi- ology of toxin avoidance and the paradox of drug reward. *Neuro- science* (2009) 160:69–84. doi:10. 1016/j.neuroscience.2009.01.077
23. West R. Theories of addiction. *Addiction* (2001) 96(1):3–13. doi:10.1046/j.1360-0443.2001. 96131.x
24. Wink M. Interference of alkaloids with neuroreceptors and ion chan- nels. In: ur Rahman A, editor. *Bioactive Natural Products (Part B)* (Vol. 21). Amsterdam: Elsevier (2000). p. 3–122.
25. Karban R, Agrawal AA. Herbi- vore offense. *Annu Rev Ecol Syst* (2002) 33:641–64. doi:10.1146/ annurev.ecolsys.33.010802.150443
26. Petzinger E, Geyer J. Drug trans- porters in pharmacokinetics. *Naunyn Schmiedebergs Arch Pharmacol* (2006) 372(6):465–75. doi:10.1007/s00210-006-0042-9
27. Dauchy S, Dutheil F, Weaver RJ, Chassoux F, Daumas-Duport C, Couraud P-O, et al. ABC transporters, cytochromes P450 and their main transcription fac- tors: expression at the human blood-brain barrier. *J Neurochem* (2008) 107(6):1518–28. doi:10. 1111/j.1471-4159.2008.05720.x
28. Dehkordi O, Rose JE, Fatemi M, Allard JS, Balan KV, Young JK, et al. Neuronal expression of bitter taste receptors and downstream signal- ing molecules in the rat brainstem. *Brain Res* (2012) 1475:1–10. doi: 10.1016/j.brainres.2012.07.038
29. Dutheil F, Beaune P, Loriot M-A. Xenobiotic metabolizing enzymes in the central nervous system: contribution of cytochrome P450 enzymes in normal and patho- logical human brain. *Biochimie* (2008) 90(3):426–36. doi:10.1016/ j.biochi.2007.10.007
30. Singh N, Vrontakis M, Parkinson F, Chelikani P. Functional bitter taste receptors are expressed in brain cells. *Biochem Biophys Res Com- mun* (2011) 406(1):146–51. doi: 10.1016/j.bbrc.2011.02.016
31. Janzen DH. Complications in interpreting the chemical defenses of trees against tropical arboreal plant-eating vertebrates. In: Mont- gomerie GC, editor. *The Ecology of Arboreal Folivores*. Washington, DC: Smithsonian Institution Press (1978). p. 73–84.
32. Wrangham RW, Nishida T. *Aspilia* spp. leaves: a puzzle in the feed- ing behavior of wild chimpanzees. *Primates* (1983) 24(2):276–82. doi: 10.1007/BF02381090
33. Johns T. *With Bitter Herbs They Shall Eat It: Chemical Ecology and the Origins of Human Diet and Medicine*. Tucson: University of Arizona Press (1990).
34. Glander KE. Nonhuman primate self-medication with wild plant foods. In: Etkin NL, editor. *Eating on the Wild Side: The Pharmaco- logical, Ecologic, and Social Impli- cations of Using Noncultigens*. Tuc- son: University of Arizona Press (1994). p. 227–39.
35. Huffman MA. Current evidence for self-medication in primates: a multidisciplinary perspective. *Am J Phys Anthropol* (1997) 104(S25):171–200. doi:10.1002/ (SICI)1096-8644(1997)25+<171: :AID-AJPA7>3.3.CO;2-K
36. Ode PJ. Plant chemistry and nat- ural enemy fitness: effects on herbivore and natural enemy interactions. *Annu Rev Entomol* (2006) 51:163–85. doi:10.1146/ annurev.ento.51.110104.151110
37. Villalba JJ, Provenza FD. Self- medication and homeosta- tic behaviour in herbivores: learning about the benefits of nature's pharmacy. *Ani- mal* (2007) 1(09):1360–70. doi:10.1017/S1751731107000134
38. Huffman MA. Primate self- medication. In: Campbell C, Fuentes A, MacKinnon K, Panger M, Bearder S, editors. *Primates in Perspective*. Oxford: University of Oxford Press (2007). p. 677–90.
39. Singer MS, Mace KC, Bernays EA. Self-medication as adaptive plas- ticity: increased ingestion of plant toxins by parasitized caterpillars. *PLoS One* (2009) 4(3):e4796. doi: 10.1371/journal.pone.0004796
40. Milan NF, Kacsoh BZ, Schlenke TA. Alcohol consumption as self- medication against blood-borne parasites in the fruit fly. *Curr Biol* (2012) 22(6):488–93. doi:10.1016/ j.cub.2012.01.045
41. Kacsoh BZ, Lynch ZR, Mor- timer NT, Schlenke TA. Fruit flies medicate offspring after seeing parasites. *Sci- ence* (2013) 339(6122):947–50. doi:10.1126/science.1229625
42. Suárez-Rodríguez M, López-Rull I, Garcia CM. Incorporation of ciga- rette butts into nests reduces nest ectoparasite load in urban birds: new ingredients for an old recipe? *Biol Lett* (2013) 9(1):20120931. doi:10.1098/rsbl.2012.0931
43. de Roode JC, Lefevre T, Hunter MD. Self-medication in animals. *Science* (2013) 340(6129):150–1. doi:10.1126/science.1235824
44. Castella G, Chapuisat M, Christe P. Prophylaxis with resin in wood ants. *Anim Behav* (2008) 75(4):1591–6. doi:10.1016/j. anbehav.2007.10.014
45. Lefèvre T, Chiang A, Kelavkar M, Li H, Li J, de Castillejo CLF, et al. Behavioural resistance against a protozoan parasite in the monarch butterfly. *J Anim Ecol* (2012) 81(1):70–9. doi:10.1111/j. 1365-2656.2011.01901.x
46. Lefevre T, Oliver L, Hunter MD, de Roode JC. Evidence for trans- generational medication in nature. *Ecol Lett* (2010) 13(12):1485–93. doi:10.1111/j.1461-0248.2010. 01537.x
47. Köhler A, Pirk CW, Nicolson SW. Honeybees and nectar nico- tine: deterrence and reduced survival versus potential health benefits. *J Insect Physiol* (2012) 58(2):286–92. doi:10.1016/j. jinsphys.2011.12.002
48. Simone-Finstrom MD, Spivak M. Increased resin collection after parasite challenge: a case of self- medication in honey bees? *PLoS One* (2012) 7(3):e34601. doi:10. 1371/journal.pone.0034601
49. Villalba JJ, Provenza FD, Hall JO, Lisonbee LD. Selection of tannins by sheep in response to gastrointestinal nematode infection. *J Anim Sci* (2010) 88(6): 2189–98. doi:10.2527/jas.2009- 2272
50. Villalba JJ, Landau SY. Host behav- ior, environment and ability to self-medicate. *Small Rumin Res* (2012) 103(1):50–9. doi:10.1016/j. smallrumres.2011.10.018

51. Hardy K, Buckley S, Collins MJ, Estalrrich A, Brothwell D, Copeland L, et al. Nean- derthal medics? Evidence for food, cooking, and medi- cinal plants entrapped in dental calculus. *Naturwis- senschaften* (2012) 99(8):617–26. doi:10.1007/s00114-012-0942-0
52. Parker BJ, Barribeau SM, Laughton AM, de Roode JC, Gerardo NM. Non-immunological defense in an evolutionary framework. *Trends Ecol Evol* (2011) 26:242–8. doi:10. 1016/j.tree.2011.02.005
53. Schaller M, Duncan LA. Schaller M, Duncan LA. The behavioral immune system: its evolution and social psychological implications. In: Forgas JP, Haselton MG, von Hippel W, editors. *Evolution and the Social Mind: Evolutionary Psy- chology and Social Cognition*. New York, NY: Psychology Press (2007). p. 293–307.
54. Baldwin IT. An ecologically motivated analysis of plant- herbivore interactions in native tobacco. *Plant Phys- iol* (2001) 127(4):1449–58. doi:10.1104/ pp.010762
55. Steppuhn A, Gase K, Krock B, Halitschke R, Baldwin IT. Nico- tine's defensive function in nature. *PLoS Biol* (2004) 2(8):E217. doi: 10.1371/journal. pbio.0020217
56. Gosselin RE, Smith RP, Hodge HC. *Clinical Toxicology of Commercial Products*. 5th ed. (Vol. II). Balti- more, MD: Williams and Wilkin (1984).
57. de Landoni JH. Nicotine. Poisons Information Monographs, Inter- national Programme on Chemical Safety (1991). Available from: http: //www. inchem.org/documents/ pims/chemical/nicotine.htm
58. Hukkanen J, Jacob P, Benowitz NL. Metabolism and disposition kinetics of nicotine. *Pharmacol Rev* (2005) 57(1):79–115. doi:10.1124/ pr.57.1.3
59. Wilbert J. *Tobacco and Shamanism in South America*. New Haven, CT: Yale University Press (1987).
60. Winter JC. *Tobacco Use by Native North Americans: Sacred Smoke and Silent Killer*. Norman: Univer- sity of Oklahoma Press (2000).
61. Lewis RS, Nicholson JS. Aspects of the evolution of *Nicotiana tabacum L.* and the status of the United States *Nicotiana* germplasm col- lection. *Genet Resour Crop Evol* (2006) 54(4):727–40. doi:10.1007/s10722-006-0024-2
62. Wu SV, Rozengurt N, Yang M, Young SH, Sinnett-Smith J, Rozen- gurt E. Expression of bitter taste receptors of the T2R fam- ily in the gastrointestinal tract and enteroendocrine STC-1 cells. *Proc Natl Acad Sci U S A* (2002) 99(4):2392–7. doi:10.1073/ pnas.042617699
63. Oliveira-Maia AJ, Stapleton- Kotloski JR, Lyall V, Phan TT, Mummalaneni S, Melone P, et al. Nicotine activates TRPM5- dependent and independent taste pathways. *Proc Natl Acad Sci U S A* (2009) 106(5):1596–601. doi:10.1073/pnas.0810184106
64. Lamba V. PXR (NR1I2): splice variants in human tissues, includ- ing brain, and identification of neurosteroids and nicotine as PXR activators. *Toxicol Appl Pharma- col* (2004) 199(3):251–65. doi:10. 1016/j.taap.2003.12.027
65. Laviolette SR, van der Kooy D. The neurobiology of nicotine addic- tion: bridging the gap from mol- ecules to behaviour. *Nat Rev Neu- rosci* (2004) 5(1):55–65. doi:10. 1038/nrn1298
66. Kumar R, Pratt JA, Stolerman IP. Characteristics of conditioned taste aversion produced by nico- tine in rats. *Br J Pharmacol* (1983) 79(1):245–53. doi:10.1111/j.1476- 5381.1983.tb10518.x
67. Foulds J, Stapleton JA, Bell N, Swettenham J, Jarvis MJ, Rus- sell MAH. Mood and physio- logical effects of subcutaneous nicotine in smokers and never- smokers. *Drug Alcohol Depend* (1997) 44(2–3):105–15. doi:10. 1016/ S0376-8716(96)01327-0
68. Hecht SS. Tobacco carcinogens, their biomarkers and tobacco- induced cancer. *Nat Rev Cancer* (2003) 3(10):733–44. doi:10.1038/ nrc1190
69. Ambrose JA, Barua RS. The patho- physiology of cigarette smoking and cardiovascular disease: an update. *J Am Coll Cardiol* (2004) 43(10):1731–7. doi:10.1016/j.jacc. 2003.12.047
70. Verendeev A, Riley AL. Condi- tioned taste aversion and drugs of abuse: history and interpre- tation. *Neurosci Biobehav Rev* (2012) 36(10):2193–205. doi:10. 1016/j.neubiorev.2012.08.004
71. Davis CM, Riley AL. Condi- tioned taste aversion learning: implications for animal models of drug abuse. *Ann N Y Acad Sci* (2010) 1187(1):247–75. doi:10. 1111/j.1749-6632.2009.05147.x
72. Hunt T, Amit Z. Conditioned taste aversion induced by self- administered drugs: paradox revis- ited. *Neurosci Biobehav Rev* (1987) 11(1):107–30. doi:10.1016/S0149- 7634(87)80005-2
73. Provenza FD, Balph DF. Diet learn- ing by domestic ruminants: the- ory, evidence and practical impli- cations. *Appl Anim Behav Sci* (1987) 18(3):211–32. doi:10.1016/ 0168-1591(87)90218-8
74. Forbey JS, Dearing MD, Gross EM, Orians CM, Sotka EE, Foley WJ. A pharm-ecological perspec- tive of terrestrial and aquatic plant- herbivore interactions. *J Chem Ecol* (2013) 39(4):465–80. doi:10.1007/ s10886-013-0267-2
75. Torregrossa A-M, Azzara AV, Dear- ing MD. Testing the diet-breadth trade-off hypothesis: differential regulation of novel plant sec- ondary compounds by a specialist and a generalist herbivore. *Oecolo- gia* (2012) 168(3):711–8. doi:10. 1007/s00442-011-2121-y
76. Torregrossa A-M, Dearing MD. Nutritional toxicology of mam- mals: regulated intake of plant secondary compounds. *Funct Ecol* (2009) 23(1):48–56. doi:10.1111/j. 1365-2435.2008.01523.x
77. Forbey JS, Harvey AL, Huff- man MA, Provenza FD, Sulli- van R, Tasdemir D. Exploitation of secondary metabolites by ani- mals: a response to homeostatic challenges. *Integr Comp Biol* (2009) 49(3):314–28. doi:10.1093/ icb/icp046
78. Raubenheimer D, Simpson SJ. Nutritional PharmEcol- ogy: doses, nutrients, toxins, and medicines. *Integr Comp Biol* (2009) 49(3):329–37. doi:10.1093/ icb/icp050
79. Gable RS. Comparison of acute lethal toxicity of commonly abused psychoactive substances. *Addiction* (2004) 99(6):686–96. doi:10.1111/ j.1360-0443.2004.00744.x
80. Darke S, Kaye S, Duflou J. Cocaine-related fatalities in New South Wales, Australia 1993–2002. *Drug Alcohol Depend* (2005) 77(2):107–14. doi:10.1016/j. drugalcdep.2004.07.004
81. Tsibulsky VL, Norman AB. Sati- ety threshold: a quantitative model of maintained cocaine self-administration. *Brain Res* (1999) 839(1):85–93. doi:10.1016/ S0006-8993(99)01717-5
82. Rodriguez E, Cavin JC, West JE. The possible role of Ama- zonian psychoactive plants in the chemotherapy of parasitic worms – a hypothesis. *J Ethnophar- macol* (1982) 6(3):303–9. doi:10. 1016/0378-8741(82)90053-8
83. Mascie-Taylor CGN. The bur- den of chronic disease. *Science* (2003) 302:1921–2. doi:10.1126/ science.1092488
84. Jackson J, Friberg I, Little S, Bradley J. Review series on helminths, immune modulation and the hygiene hypothesis: immunity against helminths and immunological phenomena in modern human populations: coevolutionary legacies? *Immunol- ogy* (2009) 126(1):18–27. doi:10. 1111/j.1365-2567.2008.03010.x
85. Hotez PJ, Brindley PJ, Bethony JM, King CH, Pearce EJ, Jacobson J. Helminth infections: the great neglected tropical diseases. *J Clin Invest* (2008) 118(4):1311–21. doi: 10.1172/JCI34261
86. Maizels RM, Yazdanbakhsh M. Immune regulation by helminth parasites: cellular and molecular mechanisms. *Nat Rev Immunol* (2003) 3(9):733–44. doi:10.1038/ nri1183
87. Yazdanbakhsh M, Sacks DL. Why does immunity to parasites take so long to develop? *Nat Rev Immunol* (2010) 10(2):80–1. doi:10.1038/ nri2673
88. Debban CL, Dyer KA. No evi- dence for behavioural adapta- tions to nematode parasitism by the fly *Drosophila putrida*. *J Evol Biol* (2013) 26(8):1646–54. doi:10. 1111/jeb.12158
89. Hammond JA, Fielding D, Bishop SC. Prospects for plant anthelmintics in tropical vet- erinary medicine. *Vet Res Commun* (1997) 21:213–28. doi:10.1023/A:1005884429253
90. World Health Organization. Guidelines for surveillance, pre- vention and control of echinococ- cosis/hydatidosis. In: Eckert J, Gemmell MA, Soulsby EJL, edi- tors. *Echinococcosis-Hydatidosis Surveillance, Prevention and Control*. FAO/UNEP/WHO (1981). Available from: http://apps.who. int/iris/ handle/10665/66490
91. Iqbal Z, Lateef M, Jabbar A, Ghayur MN, Gilani AH. In vitro and in vivo anthelmintic activity of *Nicotiana tabacum* L. leaves against gastrointestinal nema- todes of sheep. *Phytother Res* (2006) 20(1):46–8. doi:10.1002/ ptr.1800
92. Msolla P, Mmbuji WE, Kasuku AA. Field control of bovine para- sitic otitis. *Trop Anim Health Prod* (1987) 19(3):179–83. doi:10.1007/ BF02239717
93. Kabelik J, Krejei Z, Santavy F. Cannabis as a medicament. *Bull Narc* (1960) 12:5–23.
94. Kohler P. The biochemical basis of anthelmintic action and resis- tance. *Int J Parasitol* (2001) 31(4):336–45. doi:10.1016/S0020- 7519(01)00131-X
95. Tomizawa M, Casida JE. Neon- icotinoid insecticide toxicol- ogy: mechanisms of selective action. *Annu Rev Pharma- col Toxicol* (2005) 45:247–68. doi:10.1146/annurev.pharmtox. 45.120403.095930
96. Grewal PS. Nematicidal effects of some plant-extracts to *Aphe- lenchoides composticola* (nema- toda) infesting mushroom, *Agari- cus bisporus*. *Rev Nematol* (1989) 12(3):317–22.
97. McPartland JM. Cannabis as repel- lent and pesticide. *J Int Hemp Assoc* (1997) 4(2):89–94.
98. McPartland JM, Glass M. Nemati- cidal effects of hemp (*Cannabis sativa*) may not be mediated by cannabinoid receptors. *N Z J Crop Hortic Sci* (2001) 29:301–7. doi:10. 1080/01140671.2001.9514191

99. Berna F, Goldberg P, Horwitz LK, Brink J, Holt S, Bamford M, et al. Microstratigraphic evi- dence of in situ fire in the Acheulean strata of Wonderwerk Cave, Northern Cape province, South Africa. *Proc Natl Acad Sci U S A* (2012) 109(20):E1215–20. doi:10.1073/pnas.1117620109
100. Goren-Inbar N, Alperson N, Kislev ME, Simchoni O, Melamed Y, Ben-Nun A, et al. Evidence of hominin control of fire at Gesher Benot Yaaqov, Israel. *Science* (2004) 304(5671):725–7.
101. Friedman H, Newton C, Klein TW. Microbial infections, immunomodulation, and drugs of abuse. *Clin Microbiol Rev* (2003) 16(2):209–19. doi:10.1128/CMR. 16.2.209-219.2003
102. Hutchinson MR, Watkins LR. Why is neuroimmunopharmacol- ogy crucial for the future of addic- tion research? *Neuropharmacology* (2013) 76(Pt B):218–27. doi:10. 1016/j.neuropharm.2013.05.039
103. Coller JK, Hutchinson MR. Implications of central immune signaling caused by drugs of abuse: mechanisms, mediators and new therapeutic approaches for prediction and treatment of drug dependence. *Pharmacol Ther* (2012) 134(2):219–45. doi:10. 1016/j.pharmthera.2012.01.008
104. Mayfield J, Ferguson L, Har- ris RA. Neuroimmune signal- ing: a key component of alcohol abuse. *Curr Opin Neurobiol* (2013) 23(4):513–20. doi:10.1016/j.conb. 2013.01.024
105. Hutchinson MR, Northcutt AL, Hiranita T, Wang X, Lewis SS, Thomas J, et al. Opioid activation of toll-like receptor 4 contributes to drug reinforcement. *J Neurosci* (2012) 32(33):11187–200. doi:10. 1523/JNEUROSCI.0684-12.2012
106. Blednov YA, Ponomarev I, Geil C, Bergeson S, Koob GF, Har- ris RA. Neuroimmune regulation of alcohol consumption: behav- ioral validation of genes obtained from genomic studies. *Addict Biol* (2012) 17(1):108–20. doi:10.1111/ j.1369-1600.2010.00284.x
107. Blednov YA, Benavidez JM, Geil C, Perra S, Morikawa H, Har- ris RA. Activation of inflam- matory signaling by lipopolysac- charide produces a prolonged increase of voluntary alcohol intake in mice. *Brain Behav Immun* (2011) 25:S92–105. doi:10.1016/j. bbi.2011.01.008
108. Liu YZ, Pei YF, Guo YF, Wang L, Liu XG, Yan H, et al. Genome-wide association analyses suggested a novel mechanism for smoking behavior regulated by IL15. *Mol Psychiatry* (2009) 14(7):668–80. doi:10.1038/mp.2009.3
109. Morgan ET, Goralski KB, Piquette- Miller M, Renton KW, Robert- son GR, Chaluvadi MR, et al. Regulation of drug-metabolizing enzymes and transporters in infec- tion, inflammation, and can- cer. *Drug Metab Dispos* (2008) 36(2):205–216. doi:10.1124/dmd. 107.018747
110. Scherer G. Smoking behaviour and compensation: a review of the literature. *Psychopharmacology* (1999) 145(1):1–20. doi:10.1007/ s002130051027
111. Joshua M, Adler A, Mitelman R, Vaadia E, Bergman H. Mid- brain dopaminergic neurons and striatal cholinergic interneurons encode the difference between reward and aversive events at dif- ferent epochs of probabilistic clas- sical conditioning trials. *J Neurosci* (2008) 28(45):11673–84. doi:10. 1523/JNEUROSCI.3839-08.2008
112. Brischoux F, Chakraborty S, Brier- ley DI, Ungless MA. Phasic exci- tation of dopamine neurons in ventral VTA by noxious stim- uli. *Proc Natl Acad Sci U S A* (2009) 106(12):4894–9. doi:10. 1073/pnas.0811507106
113. Matsumoto M, Hikosaka O. Two types of dopamine neuron dis- tinctly convey positive and neg- ative motivational signals. *Nature* (2009) 459(7248):837–41. doi:10. 1038/nature08028
114. Schmidt R, Morris G, Hagen EH, Sullivan RJ, Hammerstein P, Kempter R. The dopamine puz- zle. *Proc Natl Acad Sci U S A* (2009) 106(27):E75. doi:10.1073/ pnas.0905153106
115. McCarron DA. Physiology, not policy, drives sodium intake. *Am J Hypertens* (2013) 26(10):1191–3. doi:10.1093/ajh/hpt151
116. Geerling JC, Loewy AD. Central regulation of sodium appetite. *Exp Physiol* (2008) 93(2):177–209. doi: 10.1113/expphysiol.2007.039891
117. Muster W, Breidenbach A, Fis- cher H, Kirchner S, Müller L, Päh- ler A. Computational toxicology in drug development. *Drug Dis- cov Today* (2008) 13(7–8):303–10. doi:10.1016/j.drudis.2007.12.007
118. Meyerhof W, Batram C, Kuhn C, Brockhoff A, Chudoba E, Bufe B, et al. The molecular recep- tive ranges of human TAS2R bit- ter taste receptors. *Chem Senses* (2010) 35:157–70. doi:10.1093/ chemse/bjp092
119. Ahmed SH, Koob GF. Transi- tion from moderate to exces- sive drug intake: change in hedo- nic set point. *Science* (1998) 282(5387):298–300. doi:10.1126/ science.282.5387.298
120. Degenhardt L, Chiu WT, Samp- son N, Kessler RC, Anthony JC, Angermeyer M, et al. Toward a global view of alcohol, tobacco, cannabis, and cocaine use: find- ings from the WHO World Mental Health Surveys. *PLoS Med* (2008) 5(7):e141. doi:10. 1371/journal.pmed.0050141
121. Benowitz NL. Cotinine as a bio- marker of environmental tobacco smoke exposure. *Epidemiol Rev* (1996) 18(2):188–204.doi:10.1093/oxfordjournals. epirev.a017925
122. Marano C, Schober SE, Brody DJ, Zhang C. Secondhand tobacco smoke exposure among children and adolescents: United states, 2003–2006. *Pediatrics* (2009) 124(5):1299–305. doi:10.1542/peds.2009-0880
123. Centers for Disease Control and Prevention (CDC). *National Center for Health Statistics (NCHS). National Health and Nutrition Examination Survey Data.* Hyattsville, MD: U.S. Department of Health and Human Services, Centers for Disease Control and Prevention (1999-2010). Available from: http://www.cdc.gov/nchs/nhanes/ nhanes_questionnaires.htm
124. Jarvis MJ, Foulds J, Feyerabend Exposure to passive smok- ing among bar staff. *Br J Addict* (1992) 87(1):111–3. doi:10.1111/j. 1360-0443.1992. tb01906.x
125. Ervin RB, Kit BK, Carroll MD. *Consumption of Added Sugar Among Us Children and Adoles- cents, 2005–2008.* Hyattsville, MD: National Center for Health Statis- tics (2012). NCHS Data Brief No. 87.
126. Wang YC, Bleich SN, Gortmaker SL. Increasing caloric contri- bution from sugar-sweetened beverages and 100% fruit juices among US children and adolescents, 1988–2004. *Pedi- atrics* (2008) 121(6):e1604–14. doi:10.1542/ peds.2007-2834
127. Hämmerer D, Eppinger B. Dopaminergic and prefrontal con- tributions to reward-based learn- ing and outcome monitoring dur- ing child development and aging. *Dev Psychol* (2012) 48(3):862–74. doi:10.1037/a0027342
128. Miller EK, Cohen JD. An inte- grative theory of prefrontal cor- tex function. *Annu Rev Neu- rosci* (2001) 24(1):167–202. doi:10. 1146/annurev. neuro.24.1.167
129. Casey BJ, Jones RM, Hare TA. The adolescent brain. *Ann N Y Acad Sci* (2008) 1124:111–26. doi:10.1196/ annals.1440.010
130. Steinberg L. A social neu- roscience perspective on adolescent risk-taking. *Dev Rev* (2008) 28(1):78–106. doi:10.1016/j.dr.2007.08.002
131. Chambers RA, Taylor JR, Potenza MN. Developmental neurocircuitry of motivation in adolescence: a critical period of addiction vulnerability. *Am J Psychiatry* (2003) 160(6):1041–52. doi:10.1176/appi.ajp.160.6.1041
132. World Health Organization. *WHO Report on the Global Tobacco Epidemic* (2013). Available from: http://www.who.int/tobacco/ global_report/2013/en/
133. Ashihara H, Sano H, Crozier A. Caffeine and related purine alka- loids: biosynthesis, catabolism, function and genetic engi- neering. *Phytochemistry* (2008) 69(4):841–56. doi:10.1016/j. phytochem.2007.10.029
134. Wright GA, Baker DD, Palmer MJ, Stabler D, Mustard JA, Power EF, et al. Caffeine in floral nectar enhances a pol- linator's memory of reward. *Science* (2013) 339(6124):1202–4. doi:10.1126/science.1228806
135. Ferré S. An update on the mech- anisms of the psychostimulant effects of caffeine. *J Neurochem* (2008) 105(4):1067–79. doi:10. 1111/j.1471-4159.2007.05196.x
136. Knight CA, Knight I, Mitchell DC, Zepp JE. Beverage caffeine intake in US consumers and subpopu- lations of interest: estimates from the share of intake panel sur- vey. *Food Cosmet Toxicol* (2004) 42(12):1923–30. doi:10.1016/j.fct. 2004.05.002
137. Cipollini ML, Levey DJ. Sec- ondary metabolites of fleshy vertebrate-dispersed fruits: adaptive hypotheses and impli- cations for seed dispersal. *Am Nat* (1997) 150(3):346–72. doi:10.1086/286069
138. Butte NF, Wong WW, Hopkinson JM, Heinz CJ, Mehta NR, Smith EO. Energy requirements derived from total energy expenditure and energy deposition during the first 2 y of life. *Am J Clin Nutr* (2000) 72(6):1558–69.
139. World Health Organization and Others. *Human Energy Require- ments.* Technical Report, Report of a Joint FAO/WHO/UNU Expert Consultation, Rome (2001). Avail- able from: ftp://ftp.fao.org/docrep/ fao/007/y5686e/ y5686e00.pdf
140. Roberts DM, Buckley NA. Pharmacokinetic considera- tions in clinical toxicology. *Clin Pharmacokinet* (2007) 46(11):897–939. doi:10.2165/ 00003088-200746110-00001
141. Sorensen JS, McLister JD, Dear- ing MD. Plant secondary metabo- lites compromise the energy bud- gets of specialist and general- ist mammalian herbivores. *Ecology* (2005) 86(1):125–39. doi:10.1890/ 03-0627
142. Slotkin TA, Levin ED, Seidler FJ. Comparative developmental neurotoxicity of organophosphate insecticides: effects on brain devel- opment are separable from sys- temic toxicity. *Environ Health Per- spect* (2006) 114(5):746–51. doi: 10.1289/ehp.8828
143. von Moos R, Stolz R, Cerny T, Gillessen S. Thalidomide: from tragedy to promise. *Swiss Med Wkly* (2003) 133(5/6):77–87.
144. Chung F, Lu J, Palmer BD, Kestell P, Browett P, Baguley BC, et al. Thalidomide pharmacoki- netics and metabolite formation in mice, rabbits, and multiple myeloma patients. *Clin Cancer Res* (2004) 10(17):5949–56. doi:10. 1158/1078-0432.CCR-04-0421

145. Slotkin TA. Cholinergic systems in brain development and disrup- tion by neurotoxicants: nicotine, environmental tobacco smoke, organophosphates. *Toxicol Appl Pharmacol* (2004) 198(2):132–51. doi:10.1016/j.taap.2003.06.001
146. Dwyer JB, Broide RS, Leslie FM. Nicotine and brain development. *Birth Defects Res C Embryo Today* (2008) 84(1):30–44. doi:10.1002/ bdrc.20118
147. DiFranza JR, Aligne CA, Weitz- man M. Prenatal and postna- tal environmental tobacco smoke exposure and children's health. *Pediatrics* (2004) 113(Suppl 3): 1007–15.
148. Chen R, Clifford A, Lang L, Anstey KJ. Is exposure to sec- ondhand smoke associated with cognitive parameters of chil- dren and adolescents? A system- atic literature review. *Ann Epi- demiol* (2013) 23(10):652–61. doi: 10.1016/j.annepidem.2013.07.001
149. Albuquerque EX, Pereira EFR, Alkondon M, Rogers SW. Mammalian nicotinic acetylcholine receptors: from structure to function. *Phys- iol Rev* (2009) 89(1):73–120. doi:10.1152/physrev.00015.2008
150. Schirmer SU, Eckhardt I, Lau H, Klein J, DeGraaf YC, Lips KS, et al. The cholinergic system in rat testis is of non-neuronal origin. *Repro- duction* (2011) 142(1):157–66. doi: 10.1530/REP-10-0302
151. Cashdan E. Adaptiveness of food learning and food aver- sions in children. *Soc Sci Inform* (1998) 37(4):613–32. doi:10.1177/053901898037004003
152. Dovey TM, Staples PA, Gib- son EL, Halford JC. Food neo- phobia and "picky/fussy" eating in children: a review. *Appetite* (2008) 50(2–3):181–93. doi:10. 1016/j.appet.2007.09.009
153. Behrens M, Meyerhof W. Bitter taste receptor research comes of age: from characterization to mod- ulation of TAS2Rs. *Semin Cell Dev Biol* (2013) 24(3):215–21. doi:10. 1016/j.semcdb.2012.08.006
154. Drewnowski A, Gomez-Carneros Bitter taste, phytonutrients, and the consumer: a review. *Am J Clin Nutr* (2000) 72(6):1424–35.
155. Chandrashekar J, Hoon MA, Ryba NJP, Zuker CS. The receptors and cells for mammalian taste. *Nature* (2006) 444(7117):288–94. doi:10. 1038/nature05401
156. Fox AL. The relationship between chemical constitution and taste. *Proc Natl Acad Sci U S A* (1932) 18(1):115–20. doi:10.1073/ pnas.18.1.115
157. Blakeslee AF. Genetics of sensory thresholds: taste for phenylthiocar- bamide. *Proc Natl Acad Sci U S A* (1932) 18:120–30. doi:10.1073/ pnas.18.1.120
158. Wooding S. Phenylthiocarbamide: a 75-year adventure in genetics and natural selection. *Genetics* (2006) 172(4):2015–23.
159. Hayes JE, Bartoshuk LM, Kidd JR, Duffy VB. Supertasting and PROP bitterness depends on more than the TAS2R38 gene. *Chem Senses* (2008) 33(3):255–65. doi:10.1093/ chemse/bjm084
160. Correa M, Hutchinson I, Laing DG, Jinks AL. Changes in fungi- form papillae density during devel- opment in humans. *Chem Senses* (2013) 38(6):519–27. doi:10.1093/ chemse/bjt022
161. Negri R, Di Feola M, Di Domenico S, Scala MG, Artesi G, Valente S, et al. Taste perception and food choices. *J Pediatr Gastroen- terol Nutr* (2012) 54(5):624–9. doi: 10.1097/MPG.0b013e3182473308
162. Mennella JA, Pepino MY, Reed DR. Genetic and environmen- tal determinants of bitter percep- tion and sweet preferences. *Pedi- atrics* (2005) 115(2):e216–22. doi: 10.1542/peds.2004-1582
163. Mennella JA, Pepino MY, Duke FF, Reed DR. Age modifies the genotype-phenotype relationship for the bitter receptor TAS2R38. *BMC Genet* (2010) 11(1):60. doi: 10.1186/1471-2156-11-60
164. Scinska A, Koros E, Habrat B, Kukwa A, Kostowski W, Bienkowski P. Bitter and sweet components of ethanol taste in humans. *Drug Alcohol Depend* (2000) 60(2):199–206. doi:10. 1016/S0376-8716(99)00149-0
165. Johnson TN, Tucker GT, Tan- ner MS, Rostami-Hodjegan A. Changes in liver vol- ume from birth to adult- hood: a meta-analysis. *Liver Transpl* (2005) 11(12):1481–93. doi:10.1002/lt.20519
166. Ginsberg G, Hattis D, Son- awane B. Incorporating phar- macokinetic differences between children and adults in assess- ing children's risks to environ- mental toxicants. *Toxicol Appl Pharmacol* (2004) 198(2):164–83. doi:10.1016/j.taap.2003.10.010
167. Anderson BJ, Holford NHG. Mechanism-based concepts of size and maturity in pharma- cokinetics. *Annu Rev Pharmacol Toxicol* (2008) 48(1):303–32. doi:10.1146/annurev.pharmtox. 48.113006.094708
168. Centers for Disease Control and Prevention. *Web-based Injury Sta- tistics Query and Reporting Sys- tem (WISQARS)*. National Center for Injury Prevention and Control, Centers for Disease Control and Prevention (2003).
169. Anderson RM, May RM. Herd immunity to helminth infection and implications for parasite control. *Nature* (1985) 315(6019):493–6. doi:10.1038/315493a0
170. Woolhouse M. Patterns in parasite epidemiology: the peak shift. *Para- sitol Today* (1998) 14(10):428–34. doi:10.1016/S0169-4758(98) 01318-0
171. Blackwell AD, Gurven MD, Sugiyama LS, Madimenos FC, Liebert MA, Martin MA, et al. Evidence for a peak shift in a humoral response to helminths: age profiles of IgE in the Shuar of Ecuador, the Tsimane of Bolivia, and the U.S. NHANES. *PLoS Negl Trop Dis* (2011) 5(6):e1218. doi:10.1371/ journal.pntd.0001218
172. Mitchell KM, Mutapi F, Savill NJ, Woolhouse MEJ. Protective immunity to *Schistosoma haema- tobium* infection is primarily an anti-fecundity response stimulated by the death of adult worms. *Proc Natl Acad Sci U S A* (2012) 109(33):13347–52. doi:10. 1073/pnas.1121051109
173. Darwin C. *The Descent of Man, and Selection in Relation to Sex*. Lon- don: John Murray (1871).
174. Andersson MB. *Sexual Selection*. Princeton, NJ: Princeton Univer- sity Press (1994).
175. Diamond JM. *The Third Chim- panzee*. New York: HarperCollins (1992).
176. Song AV, Morrell HER, Cornell JL, Ramos ME, Biehl M, Kropp RY, et al. Perceptions of smoking- related risks and benefits as pre- dictors of adolescent smoking ini- tiation. *Am J Public Health* (2009) 99(3):487–92. doi:10.2105/AJPH. 2008.137679
177. Arbeau KJ, Galambos NL, Mikael Jansson S. Dating, sex, and sub- stance use as correlates of adoles- cents' subjective experience of age. *J Adolesc* (2007) 30(3):435–47. doi: 10.1016/j.adolescence.2006.04.006
178. Galambos NL, Kolaric GC, Sears HA, Maggs JL. Adolescents' sub- jective age: an indicator of per- ceived maturity. *J Res Adolesc* (1999) 9(3):309–37. doi:10.1207/ s15327795jra0903_4
179. Hill EM, Chow K. Life-history the- ory and risky drinking. *Addiction* (2002) 97(4):401–13. doi:10.1046/ j.1360-0443.2002.00020.x
180. Lende DH, Smith EO. Evolution meets biopsychosociality: an analysis of addictive behavior. *Addiction* (2002) 97(4):447–58. doi:10.1046/j.1360-0443.2002. 00022.x
181. Wilson M, Daly M. Competitive- ness, risk taking, and violence: the young male syndrome. *Ethol Sociobiol* (1985) 6(1):59–73. doi: 10.1016/0162-3095(85)90041-X
182. Sussman S. The relations of cig- arette smoking with risky sex- ual behavior among teens. *Sex Addict Comp* (2005) 12(2–3): 181–99.
183 Jones DN, Figueredo AJ. Mating effort as a predictor of smoking in a college sample. *Curr Res Soc Psy- chol* (2007) 12:186–95.
184. Kurzban R, Dukes A, Weeden J. Sex, drugs and moral goals: repro- ductive strategies and views about recreational drugs. *Proc Biol Sci* (2010) 277(1699):3501–8. doi:10. 1098/rspb.2010.0608
185. Dechanet C, Anahory T, Math- ieu Daude JC, Quantin X, Reyft- mann L, Hamamah S, et al. Effects of cigarette smoking on reproduction. *Hum Reprod Update* (2010) 17(1):76–95. doi:10.1093/ humupd/dmq033
186. Cao S, Yin X, Wang Y, Zhou H, Song F, Lu Z. Smoking and risk of erectile dysfunction: system- atic review of observational stud- ies with meta-analysis. *PLoS One* (2013) 8(4):e60443. doi:10.1371/ journal.pone.0060443
187. Vine MF. Smoking and male repro- duction: a review. *Int J Androl* (1996) 19(6):323–37. doi:10.1111/ j.1365-2605.1996.tb00523.x
188. Spence M. Job market signaling. *Q J Econ* (1973) 87(3):355–74. doi: 10.2307/1882010
189. Zahavi A. Mate selection-a selec- tion for a handicap. *J Theor Biol* (1975) 53:205–14. doi:10. 1016/0022-5193(75)90111-3
190. Patja K, Hakala SM, Bostrom G, Nordgren P, Haglund M. Trends of tobacco use in Swe- den and Finland: do differ- ences in tobacco policy relate to tobacco use? *Scand J Public Health* (2009) 37(2):153–60. doi:10.1177/ 1403494808100277
191. Kandall SR. *Substance and Shadow: Women and Addiction in the United States*. Cambridge, MA: Harvard University Press (1999).
192. Cotto JH, Davis E, Dowling GJ, Elcano JC, Staton AB, Weiss SRB. Gender effects on drug use, abuse, and dependence: a special analysis of results from the National Sur- vey on Drug Use and Health. *Gend Med* (2010) 7(5):402–13. doi:10. 1016/j.genm.2010.09.004
193. Substance Abuse and Mental Health Services Administration. *Results from the 2011 National Survey on Drug Use and Health: Summary of National Findings*. Rockville, MD: Substance Abuse and Mental Health Services Administration (2012). NSDUH Series H-44 HHS Publication No. (SMA) 12-4713.
194. Gorber SC, Schofield-Hurwitz S, Hardt J, Levasseur G, Tremblay M. The accuracy of self-reported smoking: a systematic review of the relationship between self- reported and cotinine-assessed smoking status. *Nicotine Tob Res* (2009) 11(1):12–24. doi:10.1093/ ntr/ntn010

195. Assaf AR, Parker D, Lapane KL, McKenney JL, Carleton RA. Are there gender differences in self- reported smoking practices? Cor- relation with thiocyanate and coti- nine levels in smokers and non- smokers from the Pawtucket Heart Health Program. *J Womens Health (Larchmt)* (2002) 11(10):899–906. doi:10.1089/154099902762203731
196. Gan WQ, Cohen SB-Z, Man SFP, Sin DD. Sex-related differences in serum cotinine concentrations in daily cigarette smokers. *Nicotine Tob Res* (2008) 10(8):1293–300. doi:10.1080/14622200802239132
197. Jung-Choi K-H, Khang Y-H, Cho H-J. Hidden female smokers in Asia: a comparison of self-reported with cotinine-verified smoking prevalence rates in represen- tative national data from an Asian population. *Tob Control* (2012) 21(6):536–42. doi:10.1136/tobaccocontrol-2011-050012
198. Ervin RB, Ogden CL. *Consump- tion of Added Sugars Among US Adults, 2005-2010*. Hyattsville, MD: National Center for Health Statistics (2013). NCHS Data Brief No. 122.
199. Becker JB, Hu M. Sex differences in drug abuse. *Front Neuroendocrinol* (2008) 29(1):36–47. doi:10.1016/j. yfrne.2007.07.003
200. Becker JB, Taylor JR. Sex differ- ences in motivation. In: Becker JB, Berkley KJ, Geary N, Hamp- son E, Herman JP, Young EA, edi- tors. *Sex Differences in the Brain: From Genes to Behavior*. New York: Oxford University Press (2008). p. 177–99.
201. Becker JB. Sexual differentiation of motivation: a novel mechanism? *Horm Behav* (2009) 55(5):646–54. doi:10.1016/j.yhbeh.2009.03.014
202. Becker JB, Perry AN, Westenbroek C. Sex differences in the neural mechanisms mediating addiction: a new synthesis and hypothesis. *Biol Sex Differ* (2012) 3(1):1–35. doi:10.1186/2042-6410-3-14
203. Trivers RL. Parental investment and sexual selection. In: Camp- bell B, Campbell B, editors. *Sexual Selection and the Descent of Man 1871-1971*. Chicago, IL: Aldine (1972). p. 139–79.
204. McClintock MK, Anisko JJ, Adler NT. Group mating among Nor- way rats. II. The social dynamics of copulation: competition, coopera- tion, and mate choice. *Anim Behav* (1982) 30(2):410–25. doi:10.1016/ S0003-3472(82)80052-3
205. Marlowe FW. Hunter- gatherers and human evo- lution. *Evol Anthropol Issues News Rev* (2005) 14(2):54–67. doi:10.1002/evan.20046
206. Vyhlidal CA, Riffel AK, Haley KJ, Sharma S, Dai H, Tantisira KG, et al. Cotinine in human placenta predicts induction of gene expres- sion in fetal tissues. *Drug Metab Dispos* (2013) 41(2):305–11. doi: 10.1124/ dmd.112.049999
207. Schulte-Hobein B, Schwartz- Bickenbach D, Abt S, Plum C, Nau H. Cigarette smoke exposure and development of infants through- out the first year of life: influence of passive smoking and nursing on cotinine levels in breast milk and infant's urine. *Acta Paediatr* (1992) 81(6–7):550–7. doi:10. 1111/j.1651-2227.1992.tb12293.x
208. Clifford A, Lang L, Chen R. Effects of maternal cigarette smoking during pregnancy on cognitive parameters of children and young adults: a literature review. *Neurotoxicol Teratol* (2012) 34(6):560–70. doi:10.1016/j. ntt.2012.09.004
209. Intelmann D, Batram C, Kuhn C, Haseleu G, Meyerhof W, Hofmann T. Three TAS2R bitter taste recep- tors mediate the psychophysical responses to bitter compounds of hops (*Humulus lupulus L.*) and beer. *Chemosens Percept* (2009) 2(3):118–32. doi:10.1007/s12078- 009-9049-1
210. Hufnagel JC, Hofmann T. Quan- titative reconstruction of the nonvolatile sensometabolome of a red wine. *J Agric Food Chem* (2008) 56(19):9190–9. doi:10.1021/jf801742w
211. Hufnagel JC, Hofmann T. Orosensory-directed identifi- cation of astringent mouthfeel and bitter-tasting compounds in red wine. *J Agric Food Chem* (2008) 56(4):1376–86. doi:10.1021/jf073031n
212.0Hayes JE, Wallace MR, Knopik VS, Herbstman DM, Bartoshuk LM, Duffy VB. Allelic variation in TAS2R bitter receptor genes associates with variation in sen- sations from and ingestive behav- iors toward common bitter bever- ages in adults. *Chem Senses* (2011) 36(3):311–9. doi:10.1093/ chemse/ bjq132
213. Hayes JE, Feeney EL, Allen AL. Do polymorphisms in chemosen- sory genes matter for human inges- tive behavior? *Food Qual Prefer* (2013) 30(2):202–16. doi:10.1016/ j.foodqual.2013.05.013
214. Kaplan AR, Glanville EV, Fischer R. Taste thresholds for bitter- ness and cigarette smoking. *Nature* (1964) 202(4939):1366. doi:10. 1038/2021366a0
215. Enoch MA, Harris CR, Goldman D. Does a reduced sensitivity to bitter taste increase the risk of becom- ing nicotine addicted? *Addict Behav* (2001) 26(3):399–404. doi: 10.1016/S0306-4603(00)00117-9
216. Cannon DS, Baker TB, Piper ME, Scholand MB, Lawrence DL, Drayna DT, et al. Asso- ciations between phenylthiocar- bamide gene polymorphisms and cigarette smoking. *Nicotine Tob Res* (2005) 7(6):853–8.
217. Snedecor S, Pomerleau C, Mehringer A, Ninowski R, Pomerleau O. Differences in smoking-related variables based on phenylthiocar- bamide "taster" status. *Addict Behav* (2006) 31(12):2309–12. doi:10.1016/j.addbeh.2006.02.016
218. Mangold JE, Payne TJ, Ma JZ, Chen G, Li MD. Bitter taste recep- tor gene polymorphisms are an important factor in the develop- ment of nicotine dependence in African Americans. *J Med Genet* (2008) 45(9):578–82. doi:10.1136/ jmg.2008.057844
219. Weber AM. Determining the prevalence of bitter tasters in a sample of college smokers. *J Undergrad Res Ohio State* (2011) 2(1).
220. Fattore L, Fratta W. How impor- tant are sex differences in cannabinoid action? *Br J Pharmacol* (2010) 160(3):544–8. doi:10.1111/j.1476-5381.2010.00776.x
221. Seden K, Dickinson L, Khoo S, Back D. Grapefruit-drug interactions. *Drugs* (2010) 70(18):2373–407. doi:10.2165/ 11585250-000000000-00000
222. Bartoshuk LM, Duffy VB, Miller IJ. PTC/PROP tasting: anatomy, psy- chophysics, and sex effects. *Physiol Behav* (1994) 56(6):1165–71.
223. Duffy VB, Hayes JE, Davidson AC, Kidd JR, Kidd KK, Bar- toshuk LM. Vegetable intake in college-aged adults is explained by oral sensory phenotypes and TAS2R38 genotype. *Chemosens Percept* (2010) 3(3–4):137–48. doi: 10.1007/s12078-010-9079-8
224. Feeney E. The impact of bitter per- ception and genotypic variation of TAS2R38 on food choice. *Nutr Bull* (2011) 36(1):20–33. doi:10.1111/j. 1467-3010.2010.01870.x
225. Benowitz NL, Lessov-Schlaggar CN, Swan GE, Jacob P III. Female sex and oral contracep- tive use accelerate nicotine metab- olism. *Clin Pharmacol Ther* (2006) 79(5):480–8.
226. Greenblatt DJ, von Moltke LL. Gender has a small but statisti- cally significant effect on clearance of CYP3A substrate drugs. *J Clin Pharmacol* (2008) 48(11):1350–5. doi:10.1177/0091270008323754
227. Nicolson TJ, Mellor HR, Roberts RR. Gender differences in drug toxicity. *Trends Pharmacol Sci* (2010) 31(3):108–14. doi:10.1016/ j.tips.2009.12.001
228. Rando G, Wahli W. Sex differences in nuclear receptor-regulated liver metabolic pathways. *Biochim Bio- phys Acta* (2011) 1812(8):964–73. doi:10.1016/j.bbadis.2010.12.023
229. Yang L, Li Y, Hong H, Chang CW, Guo LW, Lyn-Cook B, et al. Sex differences in the expression of drug-metabolizing and trans- porter genes in human liver. *J Drug Metab Toxicol* (2012) 3:119.
230.Soldin OP, Chung SH, Matti- son DR. Sex differences in drug disposition. *J Biomed Biotechnol* (2011) 2011:1–14. doi:10.1155/ 2011/187103
231. Anzenbacher P, Anzenbacherova E. Cytochromes P450 and metabo- lism of xenobiotics. *Cell Mol Life Sci* (2001) 58(5–6):737–47. doi:10. 1007/ PL00000897
232. Waxman DJ, Holloway MG. Sex differences in the expres- sion of hepatic drug metab- olizing enzymes. *Mol Phar- macol* (2009) 76(2):215–28. doi:10.1124/mol.109.056705
233. Prutkin J, Duffy VB, Etter L, Fast K, Gardner E, Lucchina LA, et al. Genetic variation and infer- ences about perceived taste inten- sity in mice and men. *Physiol Behav* (2000) 69(1):161–73.
234. Kölble N, Hummel T, von Mer- ing R, Huch A, Huch R. Gusta- tory and olfactory function in the first trimester of pregnancy. *Eur J Obstet Gynecol Reprod Biol* (2001) 99(2):179–83. doi:10.1016/S0301- 2115(01)00408-0
235. Flaxman SM, Sherman PW. Morn- ing sickness: a mechanism for protecting mother and embryo. *Q Rev Biol* (2000) 75(2):113–48. doi:10. 1086/393377
236. Fessler DMT. Reproductive immunosuppression and diet: an evolutionary perspective on pregnancy sickness and meat con- sumption. *Curr Anthropol* (2002) 43(1):19–61. doi:10.1086/324128
237. Hook EB. Dietary cravings and aversions during pregnancy. *Am J Clin Nutr* (1978) 31(8):1355–62.
238. Profet M. Pregnancy sickness as adaptation: a deterrent to maternal ingestion of teratogens. In: Barkow JH, Cosmides L, Tooby J, editors. *Adapted Mind: Evolutionary Psy- chology and the Generation of Cul- ture*. New York: Oxford University Press (1995). p. 327–66.
239. Patil CL, Abrams ET, Steinmetz AR, Young SL. Appetite sensa- tions and nausea and vomit- ing in pregnancy: an overview of the explanations. *Ecol Food Nutr* (2012) 51(5):394–417. doi: 10.1080/03670244.2012.696010
240. Gill DM. Bacterial toxins: a table of lethal amounts. *Microbiol Rev* (1982) 46(1):86–94.
241. Pepper GV, Roberts SC. Rates of nausea and vomiting in preg- nancy and dietary characteristics across populations. *Proc Biol Sci* (2006) 273(1601):2675–9. doi:10. 1098/rspb.2006.3633

242. Pletsch PK, Pollak KI, Peterson BL, Park J, Oncken CA, Swamy GK, et al. Olfactory and gustatory sen- sory changes to tobacco smoke in pregnant smokers. *Res Nurs Health* (2008) 31(1):31–41.
243. Dempsey D, Jacob P III, Benowitz NL. Accelerated metabolism of nicotine and cotinine in pregnant smokers. *J Pharmacol Exp Ther* (2002) 301(2):594–8. doi:10.1124/ jpet.301.2.594
244. Choi S-Y, Koh KH, Jeong H. Isoform-specific regulation of cytochromes P450 expression by estradiol and progesterone. *Drug Metab Dispos* (2012) 41(2):263–9. doi:10.1124/dmd. 112.046276
245. Tracy TS, Venkataramanan R, Glover DD, Caritis SN. Tem- poral changes in drug metab- olism (CYP1A2, CYP2D6 and CYP3A activity) during preg- nancy. *Am J Obstet Gynecol* (2005) 192(2):633–9. doi:10.1016/j.ajog. 2004.08.030
246. Anderson GD. Pregnancy-induced changes in pharmacokinetics: a mechanistic-based approach. *Clin Pharmacokinet* (2005) 44(10):989–1008. doi:10.2165/ 00003088-200544100-00001
247. Isoherranen N, Thummel KE. Drug metabolism and trans- port during pregnancy: how does drug disposition change during pregnancy and what are the mechanisms that cause such changes? *Drug Metab Dispos* (2013) 41(2):256–62. doi:10.1124/dmd.112.050245
248. United Nations. *World Fertility Report 2009*. New York: Depart- ment of Economic and Social Affairs, Population Division (2011).
249. Cubbin C, Soobader M-J, LeClere FB. The intersection of gender and race/ethnicity in smok- ing behaviors among menthol and non-menthol smokers in the United States: smoking behaviors among menthol and non-menthol smokers. *Addiction* (2010) 105:32–8. doi:10.1111/j. 1360-0443.2010.03191.x
250. Simonson R. *Flavored Whiskeys Expand the Market*. The New York Times (2013). Available from: http://www.nytimes.com/2013/06/ 26/dining/flavored-whiskeys- expand-the-market.html
251. Degenhardt L, Hall W. Extent of illicit drug use and dependence, and their contribution to the global burden of disease. *Lancet* (2012) 379(9810):55–70. doi:10. 1016/S0140-6736(11)61138-0
252. Mathers CD, Loncar D. Projec- tions of global mortality and bur- den of disease from 2002 to 2030. *PLoS Med* (2006) 3(11): e442. doi:10.1371/journal.pmed. 0030442
253. The National Center on Addic- tion and Substance Abuse at Columbia University. *Addic- tion Medicine: Closing the Gap Between Science and Practice* (2012). Available from: http: //www.casacolumbia.org/upload/ 2012/20120626addictionmed.pdf

11

Addiction and will

Brian Johnson*

Department of Psychiatry, State University of New York Upstate Medical University, Syracuse, NY, USA

Edited by:
Henrik Kessler, University of Bonn, Germany

Reviewed by:
Claudio Colace, AUSL Viterbo, Italy
Andrea Clarici, University of Trieste, Italy

***Correspondence:**
Brian Johnson, Department of Psychiatry, State University of New York Upstate Medical University, 750 East Adams Street, Syracuse, NY 13210, USA
e-mail: johnsonb@upstate.edu

A hypothesis about the neurobiological bases of drive, drive reduction and will in addictive illness is presented. Drive reduction seems to require both SEEKING and gratification. Will is the everyday term for our experience of drives functioning within us. Addictive drugs take over the will by altering neurotransmission in the SEEKING system. As a result of this biological change, psychological defenses are arrayed that allow partial gratification and reduce anxiety about the consequences of drug use. Repeated partial gratification of the addictive drive creates a cathexis to the drug and the drug seller. It also keeps the addicted person in a permanent state of SEEKING. The cathexis to the drug and drug seller creates a difficult situation for psychoanalytic therapists. The actively addicted patient will have one set of feelings for the analyst, and a split off set of feelings for the drug dealer. Addictive neuroses, which feature a split transference, are contrasted with Freud's concept of transference and narcissistic neuroses. For treatment of an actively addicted patient, the treater must negotiate the split transference. By analyzing the denial system the relationship with the drug dealer ends and the hostility involved in addictive behavior enters the transference where it can be interpreted. Selling drugs that take over the will is a lucrative enterprise. The addictive drug industry, about the size of the oil and gas industry worldwide, produces many patients in need of treatment. The marketers of addictive drugs understand the psychology of inducing initial ingestion of the drugs, and of managing their addicted populations. The neuropsychoanalytic understanding of addiction might be used to create more effective public health interventions to combat this morbid and mortal illness.

Keywords: neuropsychoanalysis, SEEKING, drive, psychoanalysis, addiction, toxoplasmosis, cathexis, will

INTRODUCTION

Toxoplasma gondii, a single-celled protozoan parasite, manipulates the brain of the rat to shift their response to cat odor from defensive to sexual attraction (House et al., 2011). *Toxoplasma* in the environment gain entry into the rat by skin contact. They multiply in brain and muscle tissue. The immune response of the rat results in cyst formation.

The pathways for the defensive and reproductive pathways run in parallel from the olfactory bulb to the medial amygdala and hypothalamus in close anatomical proximity (House et al., 2011). *Toxoplasma* cysts elaborate tyrosine beta hydroxylase, the rate-limiting enzyme in the pathway from the tyrosine in food to dopamine. Prandovszky et al. (2011) found that infected brain cell cultures had a threefold increase in dopamine compared to uninfected cells. Alteration in brain dopamine results in a subtle shift in behavior. Rats infected with *T. gondii* shift their behavior from fearing/avoiding cats to approaching them as if they were desirable mates. The rats get eaten by the cats.

The organism makes its way into its preferred host, the cat, by taking over the brain of the rat (House et al., 2011). The rat behaves normally in all ways except that instead of avoiding cats, it seeks them out. This behavioral change is not for the survival of the rat, but for the survival of the *T. gondii* parasite.

The goal of this communication is to ask the question about whether a homologous process in the human has to do with the sale of addictive drugs. Like the process involving *T. gondii*, the mechanism would involve the dopaminergic system. The conclusion would be that, like the rat serving the *Toxoplasma* organism, the behavior of a human taking addictive drugs into their brain has to do with the benefit of the drug seller; even at the cost of the life of the addicted human.

There is almost no clinical material in this paper. Psychoanalytic and neuropsychoanalytic treatment of addiction has been extensively presented by the author in numerous clinical papers covering alcohol (Johnson, 1992, 1993, 2003a, 2011), marijuana (Jones et al., 2005), cocaine (Johnson, 2009a), heroin (Johnson, 1999, 2001, 2010), nicotine (Johnson, 2003a), and drug dreams (Johnson, 2001, 2003b, 2006, 2012) including papers describing whole psychoanalyses with 9-year follow ups after treatment for alcohol addiction (Johnson, 2011) and heroin addiction (Johnson, 2010). After 10 mostly clinical papers, this discussion focuses on the general implications of concepts derived from the confluence of neuroscience and clinical psychoanalytic work.

DRIVE AND CATHEXIS: KEY CONCEPTS FOR ADDICTION NEUROPSYCHOANALYSIS

Drive and cathexis are concepts that originated during Freud's pre-psychoanalytic period of neuroscience research (Compton, 1983a). Since then, the field has struggled with the problem of how to combine clinical observational data with theoretical constructs that involve a completely unconscious aspect of motivation. Freud originally identified drive as the engine of relatedness, the primary conceptual device in psychoanalysis for explaining mind, body, and environment relationships (Compton, 1983b). For some psychoanalysts, the concept of drive has taken on the extreme opposite quality. For example, Aron (1999, p. 259) stated, "...The classical drive/structure metapsychology ... narrows our view of people, deprives them of subjectivity, and reduces them to objects. This limitation is true of any asocial, 'one-person' psychology."

On the other hand, drive or motivation has become a focus of the neuroscience approaches to addiction. For example, Kalivas and Volkow (2005, p. 1403) stated, "As the pursuit for the neural basis of addiction advances, it is clear that the search intimately involves understanding the neurobiological basis of motivation and choice for biological reward, such as food and sex, as well as more cognitively and experientially based reward, such as friendship, family and social status." Neuroscientists working in the field of motivation and volition have varying opinions as to the origin of motivation. Some reviews (Zhu, 2003; Haggard, 2008) look to cortical pathways as the initiators of actions. Others (Berridge, 2004; Kalivas and Volkow, 2005) focus on the dopaminergic pathway that leads from the ventral tegmental area (VTA) of the midbrain through the lateral hypothalamus to the nucleus accumbens as the central structural pathway involved in motivation. This is the SEEKING system (Panksepp, 1998).

In neuropsychoanalyst Jaak Panksepp's model, derived from his extensive experimentation with animals, the SEEKING system has the capacity to shift activity from one to another motivational system, depending on internal and environmental inputs. This supraordinate flexibility is exactly what Berridge (2004, p.201) cited against the drive model. "The most dramatic evidence against dedicated drive neurons came from studies of motivation by electrical brain stimulation... For example, if one stimulated the lateral hypothalamus of different rats, many rats might show eating behavior. But a few rats might show drinking behavior, a few show sexual behavior, or others show predatory aggressive behavior, depending on the availability of stimuli and on the disposition of the individual rat being stimulated." This phenomenon, that various motivated behaviors are prompted by one system, is exactly the concept of drive; a constant pressure from inside the organism to do work (Freud, 1915; Shevrin, 1997; 2003).

In an earlier contribution (Johnson, 2008) I considered addiction researchers Robinson and Berridge (1993), Berridge and Robinson (2003) distinction between "wanting" and "liking." In that paper I posited that Panksepp's SEEKING system is the same system that Freud (1915) hypothesized to exist deep in the brain, libidinal drive. My assumption was not based on a historical study. I was and am using Freud's thinking only because, in many cases, it is still the most perspicacious description integrating nomothetic neuroscience with ideographic psychoanalytic observation. I suggested that Freud's concept of the pleasure principle was connected to Panksepp's many observations of endorphin/opioid function in the brain (Panksepp, 1981, 1990, 1998, 1999; Panksepp and Watt, 2011, etc.). Importantly, the pleasure system is tied to the drive system via opioid receptors in the VTA and nucleus accumbens shell (NAS), where they potentiate glutamatergic and dopaminergic processes that intensify drive.

Using the SEEKING system to stand in for Freud's drive system obviates the objection that it excludes a focus on relatedness, since SEEKING and other instinctual systems, CARE, PLAY, LUST, and PANIC (Panksepp, 1998), offer a biologically based and much more articulated set of instinctual drivers toward forming relationships. It gives us a model for clinical work that preserves Freud's concept of libidinal drive while responding to Aron's concern that drive produces an "asocial, one person psychology." We SEEK relationships. Panksepp's neuropsychoanalytic formulation of instinct, which is based in animal research, solves problems which could not be understood by an approach that is purely based on clinical experiences with patients.

Freud described "cathexis" as an initially mobile instinctual energy that could be bound to persons, body parts, ideas, or dream elements (Freud, 1920, p.34). In the 21st century we have information that allows us to describe the neuroscience of libidinal investment (Johnson, 2008). Dopamine is released in the nucleus accumbens of mother rats following pup exposure. VTA or nucleus accumbens (drive/SEEKING system) lesions disrupt maternal behavior (Insel, 2003). Dopamine (D1) receptors are necessary for rats to develop place conditioning for opioids. Opioid receptor antagonists block the development of partner preference in rats after mating. Both drive and pleasure need to be functioning to produce attachment. Without the drive of the dopaminergic system, there can be no libidinal investment. In order to form a sexual bond, rats have to remember that mating was a pleasant, not just a driven, experience.

Other neural systems are involved when animals come to prefer specific mates. Medial orbital frontal, amygdalar, and hippocampal memory inputs are involved. Hormonal systems interact with drive and pleasure systems. Oxytocin potentiates endorphin release during mating. Oxytocin is essential for partner preference, as has been demonstrated repeatedly in experiments comparing the prairie vole, which has an oxytocin system, with the montane vole, which does not (Insel, 2003; Johnson, 2008). Prairie voles form sexual partnerships, montane voles do not. In summary, cathexis has to do with an ensemble of drive, pleasure, memory, hormones – but there is no cathexis without drive.

One conclusion of the 2008 paper was that versions of the 1993 Robinson and Berridge distinction between wanting and liking had already been discovered by previous investigators. Freud had described it in 1920 in his essay, "Beyond the Pleasure Principle." Panksepp had shown the distinction between wanting and liking in his papers on the SEEKING and endorphin systems (Panksepp, 1981, 1990, 1998; Panksepp and Watt, 2011, etc.). But the main conclusion of the paper was that in biological or "physical" (Johnson, 1999, 2003b) addiction, addictive drugs had changed the drive system so that they were urgently wanted; whether intoxication was pleasant or not. This conclusion is an elaboration of the concept that is generally accepted in the neuroscience community that addiction begins with an alteration in the mesolimbic dopamine system (Hyman et al., 2006; Koob and Volkow, 2010). Addiction represents the usurpation of neural processes that underlie pursuit of food, water, sex, and relationships. Implicit was an idea about cathexis that will be developed below; cathexis for drugs or drug sellers can complete with cathexis for people who are loved.

DRIVE REDUCTION AND DRIVE

Why is the concept of drive reduction dead? I believe it is because Freud's thinking about this topic has been ignored by current neuroscientists. For example, when Berridge (2004) discussed why drive reduction had been disproved by animal experiments, he explained that animals who only SEEK will do it forever, and animals who are only gratified, for example by having caloric requirements satisfied by gastric feeding, were still motivated to pursue food. An important source of his confusion is the behaviorist term "reward," which conflates the concepts of SEEKING/drive and gratification. It is only by separating these two components of drive reduction that we can understand how they operate.

Freud gave the fullest description of drive reduction in his 1923 paper, "The Ego and the Id" (Freud, 1923, pp. 21–23).

"Internal perceptions yield sensations of processes arising in the most diverse and certainly also the deepest strata of the mental apparatus. . .they are more primordial, more elementary than sensations arising externally. . .

Sensations of a pleasurable nature do not have anything inherently impelling about them, whereas unpleasurable ones have it in the highest degree. The latter impel toward change, toward discharge, and that is why we interpret unpleasure as implying a heightening and pleasure a lowering of energetic cathexis. . .

This something behaves like a repressed impulse. It can exert driving force without the ego noticing the compulsion. . . Not until there is a resistance to the compulsion, a hold-up in the discharge reaction, does the 'something' at once become conscious as unpleasure. . .

The part played by word-presentations now becomes perfectly clear. By their interposition internal thought-processes are made into perceptions. . . We are all 'lived' by unknown and uncontrollable forces."

The ego's relationship with the id, "Is like a man on horseback, who has to hold in check the superior strength of the horse. . . Often a rider, if he is not to be parted from the horse, is obliged to guide it where it wants to go."

Drive reduction involves a combination of the rapacious, insistent drive building to a state where it demands satisfaction, and the pleasure of complete gratification. Both must operate sequentially for the drive to be reduced. Drive alone, in the case of addiction the constant drive for addictive drugs, is only increased by exposure to drugs. Once addicted, exposure to alcohol, cocaine, nicotine, or opioids causes a brief diminution of desire, followed by an increase of the urgent wish for the drug.

In the case of self-stimulation of the drive center (lateral hypothalamus), animals wired to be able to activate this area will push the "on" button constantly until they die. The unpleasure of briefly relieved drive apparently causes endless fruitless attempts to achieve drive reduction. In contrast, pure gratification without activation of SEEKING is in the end unsatisfying. Pornography addiction may be an example of gratification that is endlessly unsatisfying. Masturbation may be unsatisfying because it gratifies sexually without engaging the SEEKING system. Apparently, animals or humans who can't reduce drive by combining SEEKING and satisfaction sometimes endlessly engage in activities that activate only one or the other half of drive reduction.

We have taken as a hypothesis that drive involves activation of the ventral tegmental dopaminergic SEEKING system running from the midbrain through the lateral hypothalamus to the nucleus accumbens. A second hypothesis is that drive reduction requires both activation of the SEEKING system and gratification; food, sex, a relationship, something that requires work (Freud, 1915; Shevrin, 1997), and involves the complete relaxation of gratification. Addictive behaviors cause a brief and incomplete reduction of drive that result in endless drug seeking. The Freudian concept of will is necessary to understand how drive and drive reduction operate in the individual to change behavior.

THE CONCEPT OF WILL

In the Project for a Scientific Psychology (aka "Psychology for Neurologists") Freud explained, ". . .in the interior. . .there arises the impulsion which sustains all psychical activity. We know this power as the *will* – the derivative of the drives" (quoted/translated by Schmidt-Hellerau, 2001, p. 61). The experience of drives operating inside us can impel us to do things that we do not consciously "want" to do. This often leads to an interpretation by the analyst that certain behaviors are, "intentional but not conscious." The reasons that we do things are often not apparent to us.

In fact, the lay term "will power" sometimes seems to exist as a denial of true intention. People will say things like, "I wanted to eat the whole pint of ice cream, but I exercised will power and only had half." Or even less consciously, "I really wanted to stay on my diet and I struggled not to eat all that ice cream, but I did it anyway; I ate that ice cream against my will." Much of the work of psychoanalysis has to do with patients becoming conscious of their real motives, what the true goals of their will is (Wheelis, 1956; The philosophical and psychoanalytic intersection of will and drive was reviewed in Young and Brook, 1994).

As Freud said so presciently, it is the repeated stimulation of neuronal pathways that leads to cathexis (Schmidt-Hellerau, 2001, pp. 54–58). The process of facilitation of neuronal pathways, leading to structural changes in the brain, would nowadays be referred to as long-term potentiation (Kandel, 2006). The combination of experience and brain changes under the influence of neurotransmitters, neuropeptides, and hormones leads to the development of interests that are different for every person (Johnson, 2008). In other words, inborn givens take shape and definition through the interaction with the social environment and establish patterns of maintaining contact and relatedness with others. This phenomenon of modulation of cathexis by a combination of innate biology, development, and experience means that every person is a little different in their tastes. The urgent needs generated by the drive system, once specific tastes in object and patterns of relatedness become fixed, are matched up against external reality. The degree of pleasure and fulfillment resulting from actualization of one's drives and cathexes lead to either gratification or neurotic frustration (Johnson, 2008). In the case where expression of will leads to frustration, individuals feel that their life is not going well and yet are often not be able to articulate where the problem lies.

Interpretation of conflicts between conscious and unconscious goals, often described as "neurotic conflict," is the constant occupation of any psychoanalyst. Meissner (2005, p. 28) discussed "intrasystemic id conflicts" involving motivational systems. One might love one's mother consciously, and yet also wish to destroy her unconsciously. Both urges could be described as id-driven. This conflict generates anxiety – a signal that there is trouble in a relationship (Freud, 1926; Watt and Panksepp, 2009). There is a conflict between the wish for additive drugs and the wish for relationships. Both could be characterized as id-driven.

In a typically parallel neuropsychoanalytic way, the intrasystemic id conflict of addiction can be seen psychologically and also neurobiologically. Psychologically, one might love one's mother consciously, and also unconsciously want to destroy her by destroying oneself with heroin. The use of addictive drugs can be understood as an unconscious expression of rage (Dodes, 1990). Neurobiologically, the conflict has to do with a conflict between urgently wanting a drug, and still wanting other goals of the drive system including a relationship with one's mother. The experience that the mothers of heroin users are wildly upset while the heroin user sees themselves is single-mindedly pursuing drug use, is an everyday experience on an addiction treatment service.

HOW THE WILL IS TAKEN OVER BY ADDICTIVE CHEMICALS

There are only about 20 chemicals known to humans that alter the drive system so as to create a new drive (Johnson, 2008). These substances: alcohol, nicotine, benzodiazepines, opioids, stimulants, marijuana, phencyclidine, etc., all work by diverse mechanisms (Nestler, 2005), but with the same uniform end result. They cause sensitization of the ventral tegmental dopaminergic SEEKING system to the chemical (Robinson and Berridge, 1993). After sufficient exposure to the chemical, the person begins to want the drug; irrationally and insistently.

There is a triangle on the lower right half of **Figure 1** which shows the hypothesized mechanism of physical addiction for stimulant drugs. The corners of the triangle are the VTA, the NAS, and the prefrontal cortex. Cocaine and methamphetamine increase

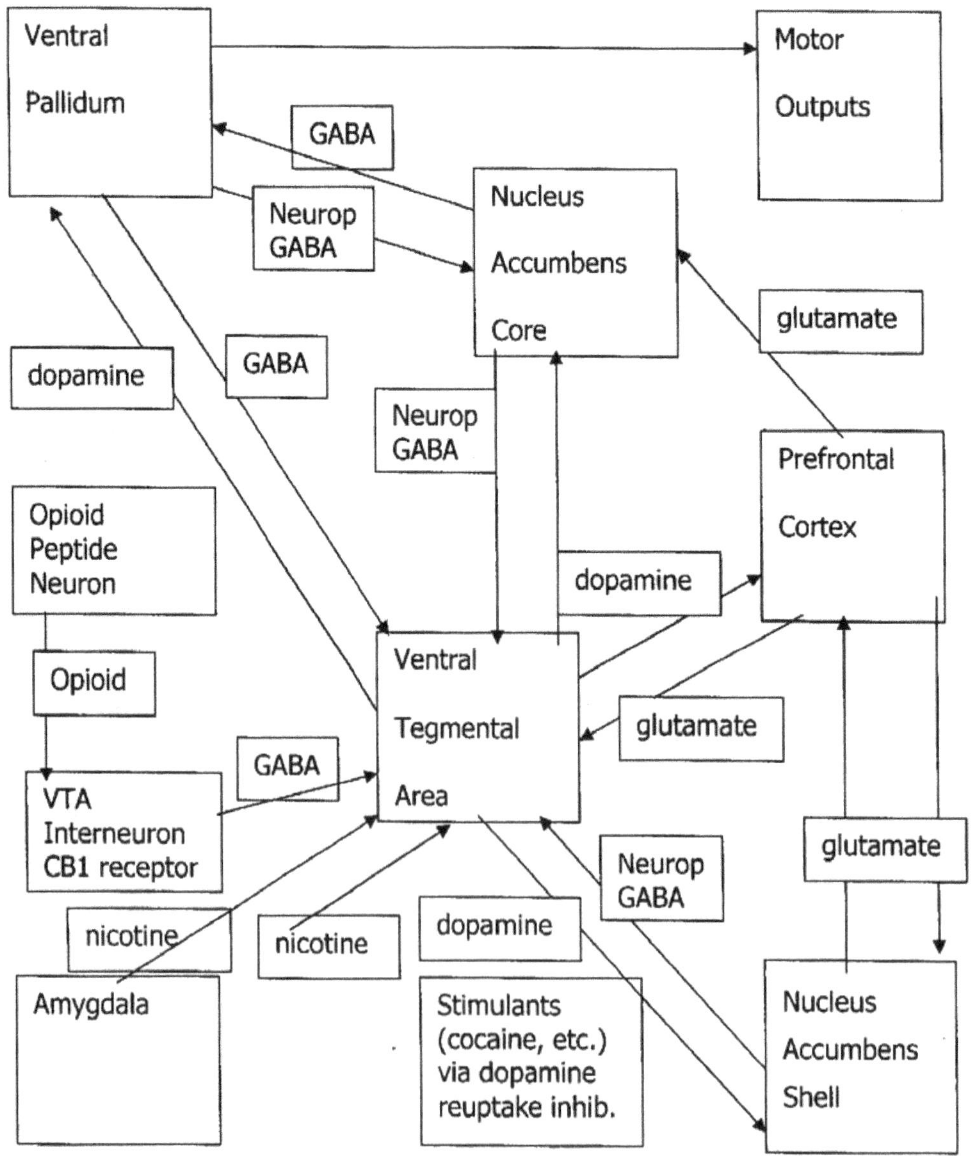

FIGURE 1 | Craving/dreaming pathways: Neurop, neuropeptides; GABA, gamma amino butyric acid, CB, cannabinoid.

dopaminergic neural activation from the VTA directly to the NAS (Niehaus et al., 2009) by blocking the dopamine reuptake transporter protein. Nicotine has receptors on the VTA, and stimulates activating signaling from the amygdala (Nestler, 2005).

There is a tonic brake on the VTA created by GABAergic inhibition by a set of interneurons. This set of interneurons is represented by a box directly to the left of the VTA box that occupies the center of **Figure 1**. Opioids act as a brake on an inhibitory system involving GABAergic interneurons that slow dopamine neurotransmission from the VTA to the NAS (Nestler, 2005). Removing this inhibition from the VTA results in increased dopamine activation of the NAS. Marijuana's tetrahydrocannabinol lodges in endocannabinoid receptors in inhibitory GABAergic VTA interneurons, inhibiting this brake so that there is increased dopaminergic stimulation of the NAS (Fattore et al., 2008). The mechanism for alcohol and benzodiazepines may be that in withdrawal from these GABAergic drugs, there is a lessening of GABAergic inhibition of the VTA, and dopamine neurotransmission is increased (Enoch, 2008).

The mechanism of physical addiction for every addictive drug is that dopamine neurotransmission from the VTA to the NAS is altered. Craving, the psychological manifestation of dopaminergic drive activity in this pathway (Shevrin, 1997), is induced by drug exposure. After repeated exposure to the addictive chemicals that produce dopaminergic activation of the SEEKING system, the chemicals become wanted, desired, craved; just like so called, "natural reinforcers," food, water, sex, and relationships.

The pathway does not end with the NAS. As seen in **Figure 1**, there are limbic and frontal centers connected with this subcortical pathway. As the effects of stimulation in the subcortical pathway cause long-term potentiation of higher centers, and drugs are wanted, drug cues recognized at pathways involving amygdalar, hippocampal, and frontal activation provoke neural firing, and downgoing glutamatergic pathways increase craving by stimulating more dopamine release. The higher centers notice possible availability of drugs, and turn up craving.

The pathways in **Figure 1** allow for the concept that there are two mechanisms of induction of craving; the "upper" and the "downer" pathways. The terms "upper" and "downer" are street language for whether the user experiences a drug as activating or relaxing. These terms may also reflect a difference in neurobiological action. The upper pathway, activated by cocaine, methamphetamine, and nicotine, directly increases firing from the VTA to the NA. The downer pathway is less direct. The interneuron braking system is deactivated, leading to increased activation of VTA to NAS dopamine. This would account for the fact that the upper drugs cause drug craving so commonly and are harder to become abstinent from, while downer drugs such as marijuana, alcohol, opioids, or benzodiazepines provoke addiction with lower frequency. When drugs in the downer group are used for recreational or medical reasons, most users do not become addicted.

Persons whose brains have been changed by addictive drugs must obtain the chemical or they are punished by ferocious unpleasure if there is, "A resistance to the compulsion, a hold-up in the discharge reaction." These chemicals are used to take over the will of the victim. For example, one might say that the person who is smoking a cigarette while having fantasies of dying of cancer, heart disease, or emphysema is not following their own will, but actually enacting the desire of the cigarette manufacturer, who is selling the cigarettes.

We might say that human children, who begin using nicotine on average in the United States at age 13, are controlled by a process homologous to rats infected by toxoplasmosis. Their behavior has been subtly altered by a change in dopamine/SEEKING. They behave in almost every way as if they are themselves. But inhaling nicotine, along with particles that can produce cancer or ruin the lung's ability to obtain oxygen, is in the service of the cigarette sellers.

DRUG-INDUCED RELATIONSHIPS

By using these drugs, individuals begin to "want" them for no reason other than brain changes. By associative learning, the purveyors of the drugs are also wanted. The state of drug craving is intensely emotional, urgent, energetic, searching for a means of gratification. By providing the drug, the seller becomes wanted, cathected.

Relationships with drug providers can have a yearning, romantic cast. As one patient told me, despite being in treatment for addiction, and sober, "I love my dealer!" A patient with attention deficit hyperactivity disorder (ADHD), cocaine and nicotine addiction suspected I would profit from having him buy a prescription for the antidepressant bupropion, used to treat ADHD and nicotine dependence. This suggests a transference from his drug sellers to me, with their/my drug as the intermediary causing a cathexis. A third patient, early in his treatment for opioid addiction, called the drug dealer to whom he had paid $200,000, his "best friend." When in emotional distress, my patient refused to call my cell phone, but rather, kept relapsing because he would call his drug dealer's cell phone.

There are secondary changes in the brain as addiction progresses. Later brain changes involve routinization of drug SEEKING by reorganization of pathways (Koob and Volkow, 2010) involving the nucleus accumbens core (Everitt and Robbins, 2005; Kalivas and Volkow, 2005) and diminished prefrontal inhibition (Bechara, 2005), especially if there are losses of brain tissue due to the various degrading effects of these drugs (reviewed in Johnson, 2009b). The longer addiction goes on, the harder it is to recover. Initiating brain changes with one drug results in faster adaptation with craving for a second addictive drug (Robinson and Berridge, 2000). For example, individuals who start smoking cigarettes before the age of 15 are 80 times more likely to use illicit drugs (Lai et al., 2000).

Exposure to addictive drugs can cause brain changes that result in permanent craving. This makes perfect sense if you think of the reason that drives are built into animals. We need to have a steady pressure to obtain items in the environment that are related to survival. If we learn where these items are, or how to recognize their possible availability, we need to have our craving turned on at that moment when we recognize availability cues so that we intensify our search for the proximal, life-supporting item, no matter how long ago we learned about the linkage between cue and drive goal. After learning about the constant availability of reward in the environment, SEEKING them can become a more automatic, unconscious behavior – modulated in the nucleus accumbens core.

However, this survival mechanism has its drawbacks. One Freudian discovery was that this constant pressure to act can come into conflict with other considerations that have to do with living in a social environment. The original paradigm of the Oedipus Complex was the conflict between the sexual drive and the presence of a larger, older, same-gender parent who was in the way of the child's closeness with the parent of the opposite gender (Freud, 1909).

Conflict is also generated regarding drug-seeking. Once addictive drugs get entrained into the drive pathway, there is a constant pressure to act to procure the drug experience again, no matter how unpleasant and dysfunctional the consequences. This is no different conceptually than yearning for a parent of the opposite gender when one is too young to effectively or safely compete. Lust can be dangerous; whether for love or drugs. Life provokes internal conflict.

Drives are so deeply unconscious that it is hard to experience them directly. Describing "craving" is a difficult task (reviewed in Johnson, 2012). Craving seems absent 1 min, overwhelming the next. An unconscious basal state may be altered by the provocation of dopamine neurotransmission in the VTA/nucleus accumbens pathway when drug cues activate frontal or limbic centers. With a drug cue or intense emotion, the previously unconscious drive enters awareness.

Finally, just as food, water, sex, and relational needs provoke dreams, so does the hunger for drugs (Johnson, 2001). Drug dreams are a unique aspect of physical addiction (Johnson, 2003b). Craving for drugs that is not conscious can be made conscious by the interpretation of dreams (Johnson, 2001).

PSYCHOLOGICAL SEQUELAE OF PHYSICAL ADDICTION

As soon as the drug has had sufficient impact on the neural pathways shown in **Figure 1**, there is a reorganization of thinking. We are in a position to actually see the impact of physical factors in the brain on psychology by talking to persons who have undergone this change. The victim of this process begins to have the experience described above that they become uncomfortable as the drug washes out of their brain. The addicted person has that inner sensation that they absolutely must have more of the drug to ward off the unpleasure of craving. They suffer from endless drug SEEKING. Persons with alcohol dependence show up at the bar at 8 am. Persons with heroin dependence knock on their dealer's door early in the morning. Cigarette smokers get off planes and have a cigarette before they do anything else. The unpleasure of craving is so intense that addicted individuals do everything they can to get rid of it. But it always comes right back.

Defenses are arrayed by the ego to modulate the new drive state. Consistent with Freud's metaphor of horse and rider (quoted in the drive reduction and drive section), the newly addicted person urgently wants to procure and use their drug. Their ego is aware of the potential liabilities in using it again. The ego deploys a series of explanations about why using the drug again is, "OK."

Psychological defenses reduce anxiety at the expense of obscuring reality. It is customary in the field of addiction to talk about "denial." However, there is no reason that a single defense, denial, would be arrayed against a drive. There are as many defenses arrayed against the drive for addictive chemicals as there are against any other drive. For example, an addicted person might use projection of responsibility, "I'm using because she/he treated me badly." The defense could be minimization, "Going to work late because I was hung over from drinking isn't such a big deal."

Each person's denial system is their own unique set of explanations about why they should keep using their addictive drug(s). To the outside observer, their denial system, the particular set of psychological defenses set up to protect continued dangerous drug use, makes no sense. This is because the defenses are arrayed against internal stimuli. The observer cannot feel the drive to use the drug. In fact, one of the problems of identifying with addicted individuals is that the observer or psychoanalyst usually has not had the patient's experience of pursuing drugs. The best way to make an empathic identification is to imagine one of the basic drive goals, such as food. One can think about how hard it is to lose weight by tolerating the urge to eat things that are off the weight-loss diet. One will notice that defenses are arrayed to protect eating foods that are not consistent with the diet, just as addicted persons have defenses about using when they also wish to be abstinent.

The denial system of the physically addicted person is based on their craving for the drug, and on their allegiance to the seller of their drug. This may sound like an odd claim; isn't the drug the object? The answer to this question puts us back where Freud started. Human relationships are grounded in the gratification of drives. In adult sexual relationships, attraction leads to increasing involvement, sexual gratification, cathexis, and loyalty.

We can understand how drive precedes cathexis in relationships if we observe the SEEKING system functioning with the drive for addictive drugs. Persons who become addicted develop an allegiance to the seller of the drug. Cigarette manufacturers are keenly aware of cathexis. Their goal is to make the user of cigarettes fall in love with the brand that contains their nicotine.

In the United States, about 20 million persons buy illegal drugs, and it is almost unheard of for an addicted person to turn in their drug dealer. In part this is because the drug users fear that they will be killed if they alert police that their dealer is selling drugs. But mostly it comes from cathexis. Addicted persons have warm feelings toward their dealers; even as they may also fear being killed by them. Warm feelings that cover a fear of being killed is the defense, "idealization."

Craving provokes idealization. Idealization of the drug is a constant and indispensable part of denial. This defense, as described by Klein (1957), involves fear of the object (drug/drug seller). Addicted people are terrified by their behaviors. Yet this information is unavailable to them consciously. Their conscious experience is that, whatever the drug, its use is wonderful. People who smoke cigarettes are staying slim, being free to defy authority, expressing their emotions, and their sexuality – just like cigarette smoking actors do in the movies. Some persons addicted to alcohol pride themselves on how much they can drink. Some users of heroin feel that it is a cooler drug than any other. For addictive drugs that are legal, advertising has the theme of ideal behavior; that the drug or alcohol is connected with social dominance or pleasure in sports or relationships. I summarize various aspects of this idealization in **Table 1** (explained at length in Johnson, 1993, 1998).

Idealization, like laughter, is catching. This may be an underlying dynamic of the social nature of the spread of cigarette smoking (Christakis and Fowler, 2008). When a 12-year-old child sees a 16-year-old child smoking a cigarette, the 16-year-old is using idealization internally to defend against their panic about seeing how out of control their behavior is and to defend against their perception of physical changes such as cough and shortness of breath. This idealization is represented to the 12-year-old interpersonally. The 16-year-old idealizes their ability to smoke a cigarette without having to cough when the irritating smoke enters their lungs, an aspect of tolerance. They communicate to the 12-year-old that smoking is appealing, "cool." As a result, the 12-year-old victim will tolerate the aversive aspects of smoking until tolerance, craving, and denial set in. This victim is then in a position to pass the addiction on to another young victim. Other drugs work by the same mechanism. It doesn't matter what the chemical is, the defense of idealization is uniform for addictive drugs.

TREATMENT IMPLICATIONS OF THE NEUROPSYCHOANALYTIC CONCEPTS OF DRIVE, DRIVE REDUCTION, AND WILL

Freud had a set of conditions that he felt had to do with the distribution of libido by the ego. In the "transference neuroses" libido was available to be cathected to the analyst. This was ideal for psychoanalytic treatment. In the "narcissistic neuroses" (Freud, 1917, pp. 420–423) libido was withdrawn from objects, therefore from the analyst, and psychoanalytic treatment was impossible. As a hypothesis, we could add to this list "addictive neuroses." Some libido is cathected to the drug/drug seller, some to other people – including the analyst. There is a splitting of the transference, just as there is a splitting of the patient's experience (**Table 1**). What the analyst observes is that the patient has many ordinary dynamic interactions in the hour, but keeps the addictive urges outside the hour.

The patient does with the analyst (of course) what they do with all relationships. The patient very much wants to be engaged with the analyst, but has another cathexis for her/his libido that has nothing to do with the analyst. The patient's conscious experience is that behaviors having to do with obtaining and using drugs have little to do with other relationships. Their libidinal investment is dissociated into the part that cares deeply about the analyst and the part that cares deeply about obtaining and using drugs.

One result of this situation is the familiar complaint of some addicted individuals who claim that their psychoanalysis did nothing to change their addiction. This is because the patient felt that their addiction had nothing to do with their analyst (their true experience) and their analyst was not in a position to hear about the effects of the addictive drug. In these psychoanalyses, the patient and analyst worked on their relationship, while the relationship with the drug/drug dealer remained unexamined. The unintended result of this approach can be that the patient who has completed such a psychoanalysis is even more adept at having relationships with people while using their drug addictively. Lying midway between the transference neuroses and the narcissistic neuroses, the addictive neuroses require some alterations of technique in order for the patient to benefit from treatment.

What can an analyst do when faced with an addictive neurosis that has a split cathexis/transference? The answer has something to do with developing conscious conflict about drug use within the relationship with the analyst. The patient knows that they are in trouble because of their relationship with the drug and with the drug dealer, but not consciously. The patient knows that they cannot both fully engage in the relationship with the analyst, and stay involved with the drug/drug dealer, but not consciously. The relationship with the drug/drug dealer is based on a system of beliefs which make perfect sense to the patient because they exist to diminish the anxiety about using a drug that is creating damage and may result in death. For example, many persons who are addicted to nicotine will say things like, "Sure cigarettes may kill me. We all have to die some time!"

Therefore, in many cases the analyst will have to divide the treatment into two phases. In the first, the transference is not explored because it is split. The analyst appreciates that attacking the relationship with the drug/drug dealer is not going to work. A strong cathexis has been established after many experiences of great unpleasure relieved by drugs and/or alcohol. The analyst limits their interventions to clarifications and confrontations that intensify conscious conflict between the wish to use and the symptoms of addiction that ensue from use. By using these non-transference interpretations, the analyst works on the denial system. It is only after the patient has moved through the "stages of change" by virtue of increasing dismay about the consequences of drug and/or alcohol use, and stopped using, that the treatment enters the second phase.

Addicted persons are like children in a divorce who don't want to tell one parent what is going on with the other. They feel an alliance with both, but understand that the allegiance to one is

Table 1 | Addictive idealization/splitting.

The addiction	
Experiencing ego/psychic reality	**Observing ego/external reality**
Facilitates relationships	Makes close relationships difficult (wards off fear of control/merger)
Creates pleasure	Creates pain
Gives a sense of omnipotence	Makes one impaired
Is a rebellion that creates a feeling of separateness	Is a compliance with the attacking introject that undercuts the use of aggression needed to be separate

essentially disloyal to the other. Just as one divorced parent often does not hear what the child is doing with the other, the analyst often does not hear what is going on with the drug dealer. Not being open and honest is the result. This formulation allows the treating clinician to shift from, "My patient lied to me," to, "I encountered a split transference." The first reaction might produce anger, the second interest, and a feeling of a technical challenge.

For any psychotherapy treatment, a key ingredient of healing has to do with the therapeutic alliance (Nissen-Lie et al., 2010). If addiction therapists use non-specific or intuitive interventions that are warmly related, outcomes might be the same despite different theoretical orientations. Therapists who intuit the underlying neuropsychodynamics more accurately might have better outcomes, but be unable to explain why. For the therapist who was able to explain what they were doing with neuroscience and metapsychology, there might be better outcomes – but this hypothesis has not been empirically tested.

An innovative psychoanalytic treatment of alcohol use disorders in borderline personality disorder, Dynamic Deconstructive Psychotherapy, subjects showed a significant decrease in heavy drinking accompanied by complete cessation of other drug use. In contrast, subjects in optimal community care received more treatment but showed increased drinking and increased drug use over the 30 month post-treatment follow up study (Gregory et al., 2010). This kind of naturalistic comparison of outcomes for patients who are initially randomized into neuropsychoanalytic or conventional treatment groups would be a way to empirically test the concepts described here.

Talking with patients during active addiction, one becomes aware that use is procedural, automatic, unconsidered. The technique of the first phase of neuropsychoanalytic treatment of addiction is to sharpen the conscious conflict between the drive derivative that is in evidence during use, but not conscious, and the ego's alarm at the reality of the consequences. Caring is communicated. Denial is undercut. We must remember the earlier quote from Freud regarding the function of word-representation as the mechanism by which internal unconscious thought processes are made into perceptions. In order for the addicted person to continue to be actively addicted, they can't think about what they are doing. Talking about one's urge to use drugs and alcohol takes place within a relationship. As Freud said about word presentation, "It is like the theorem that all knowledge has its origin in external perception.... A hypercathexis of the process of thinking takes place, thoughts are *actually* perceived – as if they came from without – and are consequently held to be true" (Freud, 1923, p. 23). Talking about craving and addictive behaviors changes them from precontemplative unformulated experience to more conscious problems that require work in psychotherapy.

If the goal of the ego is to serve the id, like the rider guiding the horse where it wants to go, then the patient will resist talking about their addiction because it disrupts the ability to go get drugs. In this way, the powerful urges created by exposure to addictive chemicals debilitate ego functioning. This impairment is often experienced by the analyst as having a patient who says, "Nothing comes to mind," or who does not arrive for treatment. Recognition of this injury to ego functioning by an altered drive state can be ameliorated by interpreting the lack of association or the missing of appointments as manifestations of craving. For example, the analyst may respond to a patient who says, "Nothing comes to mind," with, "Perhaps you are thinking about using drugs, and you are trying NOT to talk to me about that."

The psychoanalyst should not take idealization at face value. A patient who romances their addictive behavior can be listened to until the negative/frightened side of the thinking emerges. The alternative to addictive idealization is conscious ambivalence.

What happens when the denial system is interpreted sufficiently so that the patient stops using? My observation is that the split transference collapses, and the issues that had been diverted into addictive drug use enter the transference. I reported, "The psychoanalysis of a man with active alcoholism," where the end of alcoholic drinking during days per week psychoanalysis resulted in intense hostility entering the transference (Johnson, 1992). In the second phase of treatment, aggressive derivatives (Dodes, 1990) that had been expressed through the use of alcohol entered the transference relationship, where they were explored and ameliorated (Johnson, 1992). For some patients, when addictive behavior stops, the analyst has to be prepared for a siege of hostility that had never been in evidence during the first phase of treatment. The addictive behaviors had expressed the hostility and displaced it away from the transference.

I reported the 4 days per week psychoanalysis of a man with heroin addiction where cessation of heroin use resulted in an intense anaclitic depression entering the transference (Johnson, 2010). The patient went from a cool, unrelated person to an intensely needy and frightened person. The amelioration of the anaclitic depression within the transference resulted in a 9-year absence of addictive symptoms at the time of the report.

PUBLIC HEALTH APPLICATIONS OF THE NEUROPSYCHOANLYTIC MODEL

Psychoanalysis has been since its early days a theory of culture as well as of the individual mind (Paul, 2011). The discussion so far has described an illness that is based in a brain system that is deeply unconscious. Items that impinge on the drive pathway are "needed." Addictive drugs are a commodity. The property of these drugs, that they take over the will by creating dysphoria/craving/unpleasure during abstinence, means that addicted persons will do just about anything to obtain their drug.

How widespread is addiction, and how much money is involved in addiction? Let's think about the number of brains involved. 26% (World Health Organization [WHO], 2010) of the world's population of almost seven billion smokes cigarettes. This amounts to about 600 billion cigarettes/year sold (World Health Organization [WHO], 2008). 13% of the world's population drinks at least 40 g of alcohol (three drinks) per day (World Health Organization [WHO], 2010). There are nearly two billion people using nicotine and one billion people drinking substantial amounts of alcohol.

The amount of money involved in selling legal drugs seems not to be carefully tracked worldwide. We know facts such as Philip Morris International was the 14th most profitable company in the United States in 2008, making $6.89 billion in profits (CNN-Money.com 2010). The United Nations Office on Drugs and Crime (United Nations Development Programme, 1999; Reuter et al., 2009, p. 3) estimates that the illicit drug industry accounts for 8% of world trade, about the same size as the oil and gas industry or world tourism. Drugs that impinge on the SEEKING system have many customers.

How lethal and morbid are drugs and alcohol? Worldwide tobacco accounts for 9% of all deaths, 18% in high income (>$10,000 US) countries (World Health Organization [WHO], 2010). Alcohol causes 4% of deaths worldwide, 2% in high income countries (World Health Organization [WHO], 2010). Alcohol is the #3 leading global risk for burden of disease behind starvation and unsafe sex, and tobacco is #5 (World Health Organization [WHO], 2010). Cigarettes kill about half of the persons who use them (World Health Organization [WHO], 2008), which adds up to 443,000/year in the United States (Centers for Disease Control [CDC], 2009) and about four million/year in the world (World Health Organization [WHO], 2008).

How would we account for this apparently "irrational" economic activity? The SEEKING system of cigarette smokers has been captured by nicotine. If a seller can induce a potential victim to expose their brain to an addictive drug a few times, the alteration in the drive pathway will make the person want the addictive drug despite the danger. For this reason, purveyors of addictive drugs use a sophisticated psychological understanding of idealization and splitting to attract and manage their customers. For example, the nephew of Sigmund Freud, Edward Bernays, and one of the founders of American psychoanalysis, A. A. Brill, went to work for American tobacco companies in the 1920s to help with campaigns to attract new populations to the smoking of cigarettes (Brandt, 2007).

Many smokers say that they don't want to smoke, even though they show that they do want to smoke. Whose will are they following? The addicted person is following the will of the seller. While the smoker knows they cannot possibly benefit from their addictive behavior, the entire industry of production, marketing, and sales benefits enormously. This is true of any industry that produces a chemical that becomes urgently wanted by altering the drive pathway; whether a government deems that chemical legal or illegal.

We may be attracted to many people, but we make relationships based on cathexis. We fall in love with people who can meet our needs; conscious or otherwise. Love is irrational. The addictive drug industry is successful by capturing the will and the cathexis of its victims.

This information is of value in combating addiction. Public health initiatives informed by concepts such as the capture of will and cathexis, idealization of drug use, and the financial consequences of having a commodity with these properties, would lead to much different behavior by governments. For example, the addictive drug industry might be nationalized to divert money away from those who profit by deceptive advertising to teenagers, and to properly inform the public about how addictive drugs work in the brain to produce bizarre behaviors. It is more desirable from a harm reduction standpoint to have heroin sold in state stores by drug counselors than by gangs on the street with guns. It is more desirable from a harm reduction standpoint to have methamphetamine profits go to government revenues than drug cartels.

Finally, returning to the idea of the homology of the way that *T. gondii* controls the brain of the rat, and the way that protagonists of the addictive drug industry control the brain of the addicted customer, we notice that in both cases there are examples of random collateral damage. Toxoplasmosis is an important human disease, affecting about 1/3 humans in the world (House et al., 2011). There is no particular advantage for the *Toxoplasma* to inhabit the human brain since the organism dies there when the human dies.

There is speculation that the parasite expresses dopamine in the human brain, producing in some hosts schizophrenia or obsessive compulsive disorder (House et al., 2011). The dopamine blocker haloperidol moves the behavior of both humans and rats back toward normal. It completely abolishes the rat's interest in cats and restores their normal fear (Prandovszky et al., 2011).

It may be that while there are many individuals in the addictive drug industry who consciously manipulate the brains of their customers, there are other individuals such as physicians who are mystified by the way their attempts to help patients with pain or anxiety using medications in the opioid and benzodiazepine classes results in addictive behaviors. Patients who were initially grateful for the help of the physician later begin to manifest manipulative and hostile drug-seeking behaviors that cause consternation in the physician. It may be that without thinking about this process, physicians are seeding their patient population with medications that may become urgently wanted by some who undergo the brain change described here. This formulation about how drugs alter the will may facilitate more careful prescribing.

SUMMARY

Combining developing concepts about the brain effects of addictive drugs with psychoanalytic observations, new hypotheses about the disease of addiction have been generated. Addictive drugs take over the will by transiently increasing dopamine firing in the SEEKING pathway. A new drive to obtain the drug results in the formation of a series of psychological defenses that both promote gratification and shield the person from the anxiety produced by addictive behaviors, the denial system. Idealization of the drug is a ubiquitous defense. Addicted persons cathect the seller of the drug as a result of repeated gratification of the drive. They fall in love with the drug and the seller/dealer.

The first task in treating actively addicted patients involves negotiating the split cathexis. The treater rides the line between ignoring the addiction, and directly opposing the cathexis with the drug/drug dealer. Clarification and confrontation are the two main types of interpretation that are used until alcohol or drug use ceases.

After cessation of use, the treater has to explore underlying hostile/aggressive urges and dependency needs that had been encapsulated by the addictive behavior. It is rare to see a purely physical addiction. In most cases, the very reason that the addiction was adopted has to do with an inability to use aggression effectively to negotiate relationships and inability to depend on people. Without a thorough exploration of these dynamics, the patient is prone to relapse to use of the addictive drug.

Selling addictive drugs is a huge industry in the world. Sellers use their understanding of the psychodynamics of addiction to capture brains. A public health approach can use the formulations above to help potential victims understand that the drugs work by taking over the will and causing warm feelings toward individuals who don't mind having their customers die.

The author has suggested a homology between the way the *T. gondii* parasite takes over the will of the rat, and the way addictive drugs take over the will of a person. In both instances "the will" involves dopaminergic function. One aspect of the behavior of the victim involves being willing to sacrifice their life to propitiate the welfare of the parasite or the welfare of the drug dealer.

ACKNOWLEDGMENTS

Thanks to Robert Gregory M.D., David Brand Ph.D., Brandon Yeager M.D., and Akos Mersich M.D, Ph.D, who made trenchant suggestions about earlier versions of this manuscript.

REFERENCES

1. Aron, L. (1999). "The patient's experi- ence of the analyst's subjectivity," in *Relational Psychoanalysis, the Emer- gence of a Tradition*, eds S. A. Mitchell and L. Aron (Hillsdale: Analytic Press).
2. Bechara, A. (2005). Decision making, impulse control and loss of willpower to resist changes: a neurocognitive perspective. *Nat. Neurosci.* 8, 1458- 1463. doi: 10.1038/nn1584
3. Berridge, K. C. (2004). Motiva- tion concepts in behavioral neuro- science. *Physiol. Behav.* 81, 179- 209. doi: 10.1016/j.physbeh.2004. 02.004
4. Berridge, K. C., and Robinson, T. E. (2003). Parsing reward. *Trends Neurosci.* 26, 507–513. doi: 10.1016/S0166-2236(03)00233-9
5. Brandt, A. M. (2007). *The Cigarette Century*. New York: Basic Books.
6. Centers for Disease Control (CDC). (2009). Available at: cdc.gov
7. Christakis, N. A., and Fowler, J. H. (2008). The collective dynamics of smoking in a large social network. *N. Engl. J. Med.* 358, 2249–2258. doi: 10.1056/NEJMsa0706154
8. Compton, A. (1983a). The cur- rent status of the psychoanalytic theory of instinctual drives, I: drive concept, classification and development. *Psychoanal. Q.* 52, 364–401.
9. Compton, A. (1983b). The current sta- tus of the psychoanalytic theory of instinctual drives, II: the relation of the drive concept to structures, regulatory principles, and objects. *Psychoanal. Q.* 52, 402–426.
10. Dodes, L. M. (1990). Addiction, help- lessness, and narcissistic rage. *Psychoanal. Q.* 59, 398–419.
11. Enoch, M. (2008). The role of GABAA receptors in the development of alcoholism. *Biochem. Behav.* 90, 95–104. doi: 10.1016/j.pbb.2008. 03.007
12. Everitt, B. J., and Robbins, T. W. (2005). Neural systems of reinforcement for drug addiction: from actions to habits to compulsion. *Nat. Neu- rosci.* 8, 1481–1489. doi: 10.1038/ nn1579
13. Fattore, L., Fadda, P., Spano, M. S., Pistis, M., and Fratta, W. (2008). Neurobiological mechanisms of cannabinoid addiction. *Mol. Cell. Endocrinol.* 286(Suppl. 1), S97–S107. doi: 10.1016/j.mce.2008. 02.006
14. Freud, S. (1909). "Analysis of a phobia in a five year old boy," in *Standard Edi- tion*, Vol. 10 (Basingstoke: Palgrave Macmillan), 5–149.
15. Freud, S. (1915). "Instincts and their vicissitudes," in *Standard Edition*, Vol. 14 (London: Hogarth Press), 117- 140.
16. Freud, S. (1917). "Introductory lec- tures on psychoanalysis" in *Standard Edition*, Vol. 17, (New York: W.W. Norton), 420–423.
17. Freud, S. (1920). "Beyond the pleasure principle," in *Standard Edition*, Vol. 18, (Basingstoke: Palgrave Macmil- lan), 1–64.
18. Freud, S. (1923). "The ego and the id," in *Standard Edition*, Vol. 19, (London: Hogarth Press), 21–23.
19. Freud, S. (1926). "Inhibitions, symp- toms and anxiety," in *Standard Edition*, Vol. 20, (Basingstoke: Palgrave Macmillan), 77–175.
20. Gregory, R. J., Delucia-Deranja, E., and Mogle, J. A. (2010). Dynamic deconstructive psychotherapy ver- sus optimized community care for borderline personality disor- der co-occurring with alcohol use disorders, a 30 month follow- up. *J. Nerv. Ment. Dis.* 198, 292–298. doi: 10.1097/NMD.0b013e3181d6172d
21. Haggard, P. (2008). Human volition: towards a neuroscience of will. *Nat. Rev. Neurosci.* 9, 934–946. doi: 10.1038/nrn2497
22. House, P. K., Vyas, A., and Sapolsky, R. (2011). Predator cat odors activate sexual arousal pathways in brains of *Toxoplasma gondii* infected rats. *PLoS ONE* 6:e23277. doi: 10.1371/jour- nal.pone.0023277
23. Hyman, S. E., Malenka, R. C., and Nestler, E. J. (2006). Neu- ral mechanisms of addicton: the role of reward-related learn- ing and memory. *Annu. Rev. Neurosci.* 29, 565–598. doi: 10.1146/annurev.neuro.29.051605. 113009
24. Insel, T. R. (2003). Is social attachment an addictive disorder? *Physiol. Behav.* 79, 351–357. doi: 10.1016/S0031- 9384(03)00148-3
25. Johnson, B. (1992). The psychoanaly- sis of a man with active alcoholism. *J. Subst. Abuse Treat.* 9, 111–123. doi: 10.1016/0740-5472(92)90077-2
26. Johnson, B. (1993). A developmental model of addiction, and its relationship to the twelve step program of alcoholics anonymous. *J. Subst. Abuse Treat.* 10, 23–32. doi: 10.1016/0740- 5472(93)90095-J
27. Johnson, B. (1998). The mechanism of codependence in the prescription of benzodiazepines to patients with addiction. *Psychiatr. Ann.* 28, 166- 171.
28. Johnson, B. (1999). Three perspec- tives on addiction. *J. Am. Psy- choanal. Assoc.* 47, 791–815. doi: 10.1177/00030651990470031301
29. Johnson, B. (2001). Drug dreams: a neu- ropsychoanalytic hypothesis. *J. Am. Psychoanal. Assoc.* 49, 75–96. doi: 10.1177/00030651010490011101
30. Johnson, B. (2003a). A Neuropsycho- analytic approach to addiction. *Neuropsychoanalysis* 5, 29–34.
31. Johnson, B. (2003b). Psychological addiction, physical addiction, addictive character, addictive personal- ity disorder: a new nosology of addiction. *Can. J. Psychoanal.* 11, 135–160.
32. Johnson, B. (2006). Commentary on Simon Boag's Freudian dream theory, dream bizarreness and the disguise- censor controversy. *Neuropsycho- analysis* 8, 33–40.
33. Johnson, B. (2008). Just what lies beyond the pleasure principle? *Neu- ropsychoanalysis* 10, 201–212.
34. Johnson, B. (2009a). A 'neuropsycho- analytic' treatment of a patient with cocaine dependence. *Neuropsycho- analysis* 11, 151–167.
35. Johnson, B. (2009b). "Depression and addiction," in *Depression: Treatment Strategies and Management*, Second Edition, eds T. L. Schwartz and T. J. Petersen (New York: Taylor & Fran- cis).
36. Johnson, B. (2010). The psychoanal- ysis of a man with heroin depen- dence; implications for neurobiolog- ical theories of attachment and drug craving. *Neuropsychoanalysis* 12, 207–215.
37. Johnson, B. (2011). Psychoana- lytic treatment of psychological addiction to alcohol (alcohol abuse). *Front. Psychol.* 2:362. doi: 10.3389/fpsyg.2011.00362
38. Johnson, B. (2012). "Drug abuse, dreams and nightmares," in *Drug Abuse and Addiction in Medical Ill- ness*, eds J. C. Verster, K. M. Brady, and M. Galanter (Totowa: Humana Press), 385–392. doi: 10.1007/978-1- 4614-3375-0_31
39. Jones, D. S., Krotick, S., Johnson, B., and Morrison, A. P. (2005). Clinical challenge: waiting for res- cue, an attorney who will not advo- cate for himself. *Harv. Rev. Psy- chiatry* 13, 344–356. doi: 10.1080/ 10673220500250989
40. Kalivas, P. W., and Volkow, N. D. (2005). The neural basis of addiction: a pathology of motiva- tion and choice. *J. Am. Psychi- atr. Assoc.* 162, 1403–1413. doi: 10.1176/appi.ajp.162.8.1403
41. Kandel, E. R. (2006). *In Search of Mem- ory: The Emergence of a New Science of the Mind*. New York: W.W. Norton.
42. Klein, M. (1957). "Envy and Gratitude," in *Envy and Gratitude and Other Works 1946- 1963*. London: The Hogarth Press.
43. Koob, G. F., and Volkow, N. D. (2010). Neurocircuitry of addiction. *Neuropsychopharmacology* 35, 217- 238. doi: 10.1038/npp.2009.110
44. Lai, S., Lai, H., Page, J. B., and McKoy, C. B. (2000). The associa- tions between cigarette smoking and drug abuse in the United States. *J. Addict. Dis.* 19, 11–24. doi: 10.1300/ J069v19n04_02
45. Meissner, W. W. (2005). "The dynamic unconscious," in Textbook of Psychoanalysis Arlington, eds E. S. Person, A. M. Cooper, and G. O. Gab- bard. (Arlington: American Psychi- atric Publishing), 21–37.

46. Nestler, E. J. (2005). Is there a common molecular pathway for addiction? *Nat. Neurosci.* 8, 1445–1449. doi: 10.1038/nn1578
47. Niehaus, J. L., Cruz-Bermudez, N. D., and Kauer, J. A. (2009). Plas- ticity of addiction: a mesolim- bic dopamine short-circuit? *Am. J. Addict.* 18, 259–271. doi: 10.1080/10550490902925946
48. Nissen-Lie, H. A., Monsen, J. T., and Ronnestad, M. H. (2010). Ther- apist predictors of early patient- rated working alliance: a multilevel approach. *Psychother. Res.* 20, 627– 646. doi: 10.1080/10503307.2010. 497633
49. Panksepp, J. (1981). "Brain opioids: a neurochemical substrate for narcotic and social dependence," in *Progress in Theory in Psychopharmacology*, ed. S. Cooper (London: Academic Press) 149–175.
50. Panksepp, J. (1990). "A role for "affec- tive neuroscience" in understanding stress: the case of separation distress circuitry," in *Psychobiology of Stress*, ed. S. Puglisi-Allegra and A. Oliv- erio (Dordrecht: Kluwer Academic Publish- ers), 41–58.
51. Panksepp, J. (1998). *Affective Neuroscience.* New York: Oxford University Press.
52. Panksepp, J. (1999). Emotions as viewed by psychoanalysis and neuroscience: an exercise in consilience. *Neuropsy- choanalysis* 1, 15–37.
53. Panksepp, J., and Watt, D. (2011). Why does depression hurt? Ancestral primary-process separation- distress (PANIC/GRIEF) and diminished brain reward (SEEK- ING) processes in the genesis of depressive affect. *Psychiatry* 74, 5–21. doi: 10.1521/psyc.2011. 74.1.5
54. Paul, R. A. (2011). Cultural narratives and the succession scenario: Slumdog Millionaire and other popular films and fictions. *Int. J. Psychoanal.* 92, 451–470. doi: 10.1111/j.1745- 8315.2011.00405.x
55. Prandovszky, E., Gaskell, E., Mar- tin, H., Duby, J. P., Web- ster, J. P., and McConkey, G. A. (2011). The neurotropic parasite *Tox- oplasma gondii* increases dopamine metabolism. *PLoS ONE* 6:e23866. doi: 10.1371/journal. pone.0023866
56. Reuter, P. H., Trautmann, F., Pacula, R. L., Kilmer, B., Gageldonk, A., and van derGouwe, D. (2009). *Technical Series #6, Assessing changes in global drug problems, 1998-2007.* Rand Europe, Available at: www.rand.org
57. Robinson, T. E., and Berridge, K. C. (1993). The neural basis of drug craving, an incentive-sensitization the- ory of addiction. *Brain Res. Rev.* 18, 247–291. doi: 10.1016/0165- 0173(93)90013-P
58. Robinson, T. E., and Berridge,K. C. (2000). The psychology and neurobiology of addiction: an incentive-sensitization view. *Addiction* 95 (Suppl. 2), S91– S117. doi: 10.1046/j.1360-0443.95. 8s2.19.x
59. Schmidt-Hellerau, C. (2001). *Life Drive & Death Drive, Libido & Lethe.* New York: Other Press.
60. Shevrin, H. (1997). Psychoanalysis as the patient – high in feeling, low in energy. *J. Am. Psychoanal. Assoc.* 45, 841–864. doi: 10.1177/00030651970450031101
61. Shevrin, H. (2003). The psycho- analytic theory of drive in the light of recent neuroscience find- ings and theories. *First Annual C. Philip Wilson Memorial Lec- ture, Lenox Hill Hospital* 9/15/2003, New York.
62. United Nations Development Pro- gramme. (UNDP). (1999). *Human Development Report 1999.* Oxford: Oxford University Press, 103.
63. Watt, D. F., and Panksepp, J. (2009). Depression: an evolutionar- ily conserved mechanism to termi- nate separation distress? A review of aminergic, peptidergic, and neural network perspectives. *Neuropsycho- analysis* 11, 7–51.
64. Wheelis, A. (1956). Will and psy- choanalysis. *J. Am. Psychoanal. Assoc.* 40, 285–303. doi: 10.1177/ 000306515600400205
65. World Health Organization (WHO). (2008). Report on Global Tobacco Epidemic 2008.
66. World Health Organization (WHO). (2010). *Global Health Risks.* (2010). Geneva: World Health Organization. Young, C., and Brook, A. (1994). Schopenhauer and Freud. *Int. J. Psy- choanal.* 75, 101–118.
67. Zhu, J. (2003). Locating volition. *Con- scious. Cogn.* 13, 302–322. doi: 10.1016/j.concog.2003.09.003

12

Modulation of the endocannabinoid system: vulnerability factor and new treatment target for stimulant addiction

Stéphanie Olière[1], Antoine Jolette-Riopel[1], Stéphane Potvin[2,3] and Didier Jutras-Aswad[1,2]*

[1] Addiction Psychiatry Research Unit, Research Center, Centre Hospitalier de l'Université de Montréal (CRCHUM), Montreal, QC, Canada
[2] Department of Psychiatry, University of Montreal, Montreal, QC, Canada
[3] Research Center, Institut Universitaire en Santé Mentale de Montréal, Montreal, QC, Canada

Edited by:
Elizabeth Clare Temple, University of Ballarat, Australia

Reviewed by:
Elizabeth Clare Temple, University of Ballarat, Australia
Luigi Janiri, Università Cattolica del S. Cuore, Italy

***Correspondence:**
Didier Jutras-Aswad, CRCHUM, St-Luc Hospital, Édouard-Asselin Pavilion, 264 René-Lévesque Blvd. East, Montreal, QC H2X 1P1, Canada
e-mail: didier.jutras-aswad@umontreal.ca

Cannabis is one of the most widely used illicit substance among users of stimulants such as cocaine and amphetamines. Interestingly, increasing recent evidence points toward the involvement of the endocannabinoid system (ECBS) in the neurobiological processes related to stimulant addiction. This article presents an up-to-date review with deep insights into the pivotal role of the ECBS in the neurobiology of stimulant addiction and the effects of its modulation on addictive behaviors. This article aims to: (1) review the role of cannabis use and ECBS modulation in the neurobiological substrates of psychostimulant addiction and (2) evaluate the potential of cannabinoid-based pharmacological strategies to treat stimulant addiction. A growing number of studies support a critical role of the ECBS and its modulation by synthetic or natural cannabinoids in various neurobiological and behavioral aspects of stimulants addiction. Thus, cannabinoids modulate brain reward systems closely involved in stimulants addiction, and provide further evidence that the cannabinoid system could be explored as a potential drug discovery target for treating addiction across different classes of stimulants.

Keywords: addiction, stimulants, psychostimulants, cocaine, cannabis, cannabinoids or endocannabinoids

INTRODUCTION

Addiction to psychostimulants such as cocaine, amphetamine, and its derivatives [i.e., methamphetamine, *N*-methyl-3,4-methylenedioxymethamphetamine (MDMA)] is a significant global public health problem which affects many aspects of social and economic life. Worldwide, between 16 and 51 million people are users of these types of substances (1). Amphetamines have been identified as the second world's most widely used illicit drug after cannabis, with an annual prevalence ranging from 0.3 to 1.2% in the adult population. Methamphetamine consumption has increased dramatically the last years, especially in the western and mid-western parts of the United States, although there also appears to be an eastward trend in use (2). Over 15 million people worldwide are cocaine users and 5.9 million of them live in North America (3, 4). Although the prevalence of cocaine consumption has declined in the past decade, cocaine use increased in 2011; dependence to this drug remains a significant issue in North America, Western and Central Europe, particularly in metropolitan areas where crime and violence have increased (4). Given its association with high rates of mental and physical problems as well as premature mortality, cocaine abuse is still an unresolved medical and socio-economic concern which carries a heavy burden for abusers and their families alike (3, 5–7).

In recent decades, development of new treatments for psychostimulant addiction has been a major focus of multidisciplinary research efforts and have included molecular approaches, preclinical behavioral studies, and clinical trials. However, in spite of these research endeavors, no specific pharmacological therapy has been found to be truly effective in alleviating psychostimulant cessation symptoms like craving and anxiety, or to prevent relapse (8–11). Neuropharmacological agents such as antidepressants, anticonvulsants, and antipsychotics have been tested as treatments for cocaine dependence but these medications have yielded negative clinical outcomes (12–14). Subsequent attempts at targeting other neurotransmitters such as the dopaminergic and γ-aminobutyric acid (GABA) systems (10, 15, 16), and developing a cocaine vaccine (17) to promote abstinence in cocaine-dependent individuals, have shown promising results but still require further investigation. Importantly, many clinical studies have focused on cocaine addiction rather than other psychostimulants such as amphetamines and methylphenidate. Whether the outcomes related to cocaine addiction can be applied to other psychostimulants remains unclear (18).

Given the need to better understand neurobiological mechanisms that underly psychostimulants addiction and to develop innovative treatment strategies, researchers have explored the involvement of specific neurotransmitter systems and brain structures in the motivational and addictive properties of this class of drugs. Increasing evidence indicates that the endocannabinoid system (ECBS) - a group of neuromodulatory lipids and receptors – plays a central role in various cognitive and physiological processes associated with addiction such as reward, stress responsiveness, and drug-related synaptic plasticity (19–21). The potential of ECBS modulation in treating stimulant addiction has recently been highlighted in human and animal studies investigating its effects on acquisition, maintenance, and relapse of drug-taking behavior. Moreover, endogenous and exogenous cannabinoids such as plant-derived cannabinoid ligands (i.e., Δ^9-THC, cannabidiol, CBD) modulate specific neurotransmitter systems which are also pharmacological targets for cocaine. Interestingly, cannabis is widely used by psychostimulant-dependent individuals (22); while it is recognized that components of the ECBS are implicated in psychostimulants, more specifically in cocaine-seeking behaviors, very few studies have focused on an understanding of the neural and behavioral effects of cannabis on psychostimulants use in humans.

The current review will focus on the neurobiological basis of the addictive process from psychostimulant initiation to drug abuse and addiction. The involvement of critical neurotransmitters and neural circuits underlying the pathological modifications at each of these stages will be highlighted with a specific attention given to the ECBS. In turn, this overview will serve as foundations to look at the ECBS as a specific target of pharmacotherapeutic interventions to reduce the addictive effects of psychostimulants.

NEUROBIOLOGY OF PSYCHOSTIMULANTS

Occasional use of psychostimulants like cocaine, at low doses, provokes a so-called "rush" (i.e., euphoria) in humans, giving them a sensation of vigilance and increased energy. Higher doses of cocaine induces symptoms described as "cocaine high," which include enhancement of a euphoric sensation, an increase in motor activity, amplification of sensory perception, talkativeness, and suppression of appetite and thirst (23). Unfortunately, these positive subjective effects (i.e., euphorigenic state) are often followed by repetitive and frequent cocaine abuse which develops into addiction. Drug addiction is a chronically relapsing disorder characterized by loss of control over drug-seeking and the compulsive desire (referred as craving) to use drugs in spite of negative consequences (24). Drug cravings increase with exposure to drug and drug-related-cues, and in the context of emotional stress or negative moods (25, 26). Because addiction is a highly complex disorder, numerous studies have attempted to determine the molecular and cellular factors implicated in the pleasurable effects induced by drug consumption, and their role in the development of addictive behaviors (27–31).

NEUROTRANSMITTERS INVOLVED IN PROCESSES LEADING TO PSYCHOSTIMULANTS ADDICTION

Psychostimulants affect the central nervous system by modulating the mesocorticolimbic dopamine (DA) system which is involved in several physiological processes such as cognition, memory, and reward-driven learning (32). The mesocorticolimbic system, which has been found to play a role in drug reward and addiction, includes DA projections from cell bodies in the ventral tegmental area (VTA) to limbic structures such as the nucleus accumbens (NAc) (33), amygdala in the forebrain (34, 35), hippocampus (36), and to cortical areas such as the prefontal cortex (PFC), including the orbitofrontal cortex (OFC) and anterior cingulate (AC) (37). Psychostimulants exert their effects on the CNS via a number of mechanisms; cocaine, amphetamines, methamphetamines, and methylphenidate alter normal DA receptor functions by binding the dopamine transporter (DAT) and forming a complex that blocks the transporter's function. The psychostimulant/DAT complex inhibits DA reuptake into the presynaptic nerve terminal, leading to an excess of DA in the synaptic cleft within the NAc – recognized as the center of the rewarding process (38–40). This phenomenon results in an increased and prolonged post-synaptic effect of dopaminergic signaling at DA receptors on the receiving neuron (30, 31). However, unlike cocaine, which interferes mainly with plasma membrane transporters, other psychostimulants modulate the CNS through a host of mechanisms. First, methamphetamines and amphetamines act as substrate-type releasers (41, 42) to enhance DA efflux. These substrate-type releasers have two modes of action: (i) they reverse the process of transporter-mediated exchange by interacting with specific transporter proteins which are subsequently brought into the cytoplasm of the nerve terminal; (ii) they also increase cytoplasmic levels of DA by interfering with vesicular storage (43, 44). Moreover, these drugs increase cytosolic DA levels by shutting-down the activity of the monoamine oxidase (MAO) – an important enzyme for the catabolism of monoaminergic neurotransmitters. Finally, psychostimulants also enhance the activity and expression of the tyrosine hydroxylase (TH), the DA-synthesizing enzyme [reviewed in Ref. (45)]. However, exactly how these high levels of DA in the NAc mediates drug reward remains partially understood.

Even though DA has been identified as one of the primary mechanisms involved in drug reinforcement initiation, studies reveal that mice lacking the gene expressing the DAT continue to self-administer cocaine (46, 47). Interestingly, several reports have suggested the indirect implication of other neurotransmitter systems [i.e., serotonin (5-HT), norepinephrine (NE), glutamate (GLU), GABA, opioid peptides, and endocannabinoids (48–50)] in the incentive sensitization and reinforcing effects of psychostimulants (29, 51). Indeed, psychostimulants also reduce 5-HT and norepinephrine NE reuptake, which in turn leads to an increase in extracellular monoamines concentrations and contributes to the rewarding subjective feelings mediated by these drugs (42, 52–54). Surprisingly, knock-down of NET, or SERT, or NET/SERT genes does not abolish but rather potentiates the rewarding or aversive effects of cocaine (55, 56). Recently, further lines of evidence have suggested that NE plays a role in the reinstatement of drug seeking, although it does not influence the maintenance phase of cocaine self-administration (SA) (57–59). Blockage of NE cognate receptors – α1-adrenergic receptors (α1ARs) and β-adrenergic receptors (βARs) – in a mice model of addiction diminishes cocaine-primed and foot shock-induced reinstatement respectively, whereas inhibition of both receptors reduces cue-induced reinstatement (60, 61).

Long-term use of psychostimulants leads to homeostatic dysregulation of normal (i.e., without cocaine) dopaminergic signaling. This hypo-dopaminergic state contributes to the appearance of some withdrawal symptoms (i.e., depressive mood disorders), often observed in abstinent psychostimulant addicts, and, also the maintenance of drug-use behaviors. Similarly, withdrawal symptoms from chronic cocaine use have been also associated with cocaine-induced alterations in 5-HT neurotransmission. Interestingly, rodent studies show that enhancement of serotonergic transmission in the NAc through administration of exogenous 5-HT served to offset the DA deficit caused by cocaine withdrawal (62); indeed, accumulating studies suggest that increasing brain 5-HT activity could reduce the behavioral-stimulant and reinforcing properties of psychostimulants (reviewed in Ref. (44)]. Thus, modulation of 5-HT and DA levels might sensitize an important brain reward circuit to the reinforcing effects of psychostimulants contributing to the intractable nature of addiction and relapse.

The glutamatergic system is another important neuronal substrate of behaviors induced by drugs of abuse (63, 64). Indeed, GLU is an excitatory neurotransmitter essential to numerous processes including neuroplasticity, linked to long-term potentiation (LTP), long-term depression (LTD), extinction, and reward-related learning (65–68). Like DA, GLU levels in the NAc core decrease during the early phase of cocaine abstinence (69, 70), whereas both stress and drug-induced reinstatement of cocaine-seeking are associated with an increase of extracellular GLU levels in the NAc in rodents (63, 64, 70–73). Thus, the data suggests that both a decrease in basal GLU transmission and an enhanced GLU response may constitute a neurobiological substrate of cocaine-, cocaine-associated cue-triggered relapse.

While discovery of numerous neurotransmitter systems have yielded significant advances in defining psychostimulants' effects on the brain neurochemistry, the precise mechanisms underlying their role in addictive behaviors are not as straightforward. While DA and GLU appear to be critical in the development and persistence of stimulant addictive behaviors, a growing body of evidence points toward the impact of other neurotransmission systems, including the ECBS, in various physiological and behavioral processes associated with psychostimulant addiction, through both DA/GLU related and unrelated mechanisms. An overview of this evidence will be presented in Section "The Endocannabinoid System," with a particular focus on the potential exogenous and endogenous cannabinoids influence on psychostimulant reinforcement, drug-related synaptic plasticity, and drug-seeking behavior.

NEURAL REGIONS INVOLVED IN ADDICTION PROCESS TO PSYCHOSTIMULANTS

A central challenge in addiction research is understanding the neurobiological substrates involved in drug-taking behavior. Over the last two decades, neuroimaging has provided substantial insight into that question by: (i) allowing researchers to investigate the roles of different neural regions in drug-induced euphoria and subsequent craving; (ii) enabling the gathering of tremendous information regarding the neurochemical and physiological adaptations of the brain during the addiction process.

Brain imaging studies of subjects addicted to psychostimulants indicate that the NAc – known to play a fundamental role in goal-directed behaviors (74) – is organized into two functionally distinct sub-compartments termed the shell and core (33). The shell and the VTA are critical in inducing motivational salience and responding to novel rewarding stimuli (75). The core mediates the expression of learned behaviors, and receives glutamatergic afferents from the PFC (33, 75). DA release into the core occurs in response to cues predicting a motivating event (76, 77). The NAc receives information regarding motivationally relevant events from the VTA, amygdala, hippocampus, and PFC, and responds by providing output to brain circuits which modulate the expression of the behavioral response (e.g., to seek the drug or not) (78). Chronic exposure to psychostimulants leads to the dysregulation of the mesolimbic circuitry, which in turn enhances the motivation to take drugs and decreases the ability to regulate the behavioral response to drug cues (33, 74).

The numerous neuroimaging methods used to study the chronic effects of psychostimulants on the brains of drug-addicted individuals have consistently found abnormalities in both cortical and subcortical neural areas (37, 79). More specifically, chronic exposure to psychostimulants causes functional alterations within frontal brain areas, including the dorsolateral prefrontal cortex (DLPFC), the OFC, and the anterior cingulate cortex (ACC) involved in goal identification; selection (80); decision making; impulsivity; behavioral inhibition (81), and assessment of consequences (82), respectively. It has been proposed that abnormalities within these three PFC-striatothalamic circuits play a central role in emotional response to drug cues, craving, compulsive drug-seeking, and relapse (26, 35, 83–85). Moreover, structural magnetic resonance imaging (structural MRI) studies associate chronic use of psychostimulants with alterations in white-matter integrity and gray-matter volume, which are strongly correlated with lower abstinence-based outcomes (86) and drug-induced compulsivity, decision making, and attention impairments in cocaine-dependent subjects, respectively (85). Furthermore, exposure to emotional distress and aversive stimuli also activates the cortico-limbic circuits, including prefrontal, AC, middle frontal, and orbitofrontal regions, limbic and paralimbic structures such as the amygdala, hippocampus, parahippocampal gyrus, fusiform gyrus, and other midbrain areas, but not the ventral striatum (87, 88). Overall, the data shows that chronic use of psychostimulants modulates a set of neural regions implicated in stress, emotions, impulsivity, and reward processing control which precipitate relapse in drug-abstinent individuals.

THE ENDOCANNABINOID SYSTEM

Though the significant role played by various neurotransmitters, genetic factors and specific brain structures in reinforcing the properties of psychostimulants has been established, the common mechanisms underlying the development of addictive behaviors have yet to be fully elucidated. A growing body of evidence points to the involvement of the ECBS in the acquisition and maintenance of drug-taking behaviors and in various physiological, as well as behavioral processes associated with addiction. Interestingly, a characteristic of psychostimulants abuse is the concurrent consumption of other substances including delta-9-tetrahydrocannabinol (Δ^9-THC) – the main cannabinoid found in cannabis [reviewed in Ref. (89)]. This poly-substance pattern of use has prompted researchers to investigate the potential interaction with, and effect of, these drug on neuropsycho-biological processes related to addiction. For example, some studies reveal that cannabis consumption enhances the incentive to use cocaine in individuals dependent on both, while others suggested that cannabis reduced withdrawal symptoms in abstinent cocaine-addicted subjects (22, 90, 91). Although it is recognized that components of the ECBS are involved in cocaine-seeking behaviors, very few studies have focused on understanding the neural and behavioral effects of endogenous and exogenous cannabinoids on psychostimulant use. In this section, we will first provide an overview of the ECBS, and then focus on recent findings pointing toward a role of the ECBS in the circuitry underlying psychostimulant addiction.

OVERVIEW

The ECBS consists of a family of lipid signaling molecules referred to as endocannabinoids, their cognate receptors and specific metabolic enzymes which are responsible for degradation of the endocannabinoids – anandamide (AEA) and 2-arachidonoylglycerol (2-AG). The neurobiological properties of endocannabinoids are complex, but it is now well established that they modulate a wide diversity of physiological processes including pain and inflammation, immune responses, food intake, synaptic transmission, cognition, reward, and motor activity (92). Endocannabinoids also influence mechanisms involved in addiction and relapse.

RECEPTORS

There are currently two well described subtypes of cannabinoid receptors, termed CB1 and CB2, which differ in their signaling mechanisms and tissue distribution. Even though CB1 receptors are considered the most abundant and widely distributed G-protein-coupled receptors found in the CNS, they are also present in peripheral organs and tissues (i.e., endocrine glands, leukocytes, spleen, heart, and gastrointestinal tracts, etc.) (93–97). CB1 receptors are localized in TH-expressing neurons, probably dopaminergic neurons of the NAc, VTA, striatum, and pyriform cortex, suggesting that the ECBS may directly influence dopaminergic reward mechanisms. In addition, CB1 receptors are expressed in other neural regions related to reward, motivation and memory processing (i.e., basolateral amygdala, hippocampus, and cerebral cortex), movement (i.e., basal ganglia, cerebellum), pain modulation (i.e., certain parts of the spinal cord, periaqueductal gray). Endocannabinoids induce LTD of the inhibitory synapses in the hippocampus, contributing to the synaptic plasticity involved in the learning processes related to addictive behaviors. CB1 receptors are confined at the terminals of central and peripheral nerves, where they inhibit the release of excitatory and inhibitory neurotransmitters (release on command, retrograde signaling) (98–100). Thus, the activation of CB1 receptors protects the nervous system from over-activation or over-inhibition by neurotransmitters and thereby promotes the latter's prominent role in anxiety, depression, cognition, addiction, motor function, feeding behavior, and pain (101). CB2 receptors are mainly found in immune cells (i.e., spleen, tonsils, and thymus gland) (102–104), although recent experimental data indicate CB2 receptors expression in the cerebellum, brainstem, and cortex (105–107) as well as activated microglial within the CNS (108–110). Simulation of CB2 receptors on microglia modulates the neuro-inflammatory response by regulating cytokines release in the brain (111–113).

Increasing evidence points toward the existence of additional cannabinoid receptors subtypes in the CNS. Indeed, recent preclinical studies suggest the persistence of cannabinoid-like properties after cannabinoid agonists have been administered to mice lacking CB1 and CB2 receptors ($CB1^{-/-}$ and $CB2^{-/-}$) in neuronal subpopulations. This indicates that these agonists recognize non-CB1/CB2 cannabinoid receptors (114–117). Among these receptors, the orphan G-protein-coupled receptors modulate the ECBS. GPR55 specifically is found in the striatum and to a lesser extent in the hippocampus, the thalamus and the cerebellum (118). GPR55 is phylogenetically different from CB1 and CB2 receptors, in that it is activated by the CB1 antagonists – rimonabant and AM251 – but blocked by the cannabinoid agonist CP55, 940 (119–121). Thus, GPR55 is considered as a non-CB receptor with a binding site for cannabinoid ligands [reviewed in Ref. (122)]. Though a recent study from Rusakov's group suggests that GPR55 enhances neurotransmitters release at central synapses (123), further studies are required to confirm its neurophysiological function.

The actions of endocannabinoids are not only restricted to the CB1, CB2, and GPR receptors. Transient receptor potential (TRP) receptors have also been identified as sites of endocannabinoid interaction. Exogenous and endogenous cannabinoids interact with at least five TRP receptors (124); AEA binds to the transient receptor vanilloid potential 1 (TRVP1) with low affinity. TRVP1 is found on sensory neurons, where they are partly coexpressed with CB1 receptor, but also in several central nuclei including the hypothalamus and basal ganglia, the hippocampus and cerebellum (125). The efficacy and potency of AEA at TRVP1 is increased when the AEA degrading enzyme FAAH (fatty acid amide hydrolase) is suppressed (126–128). Surprisingly, pharmacological or genetic inhibition of FAAH enhances AEA, but decreases 2-AG levels via TRVP1 receptors (129). Interestingly, both endocannabinoids AEA and 2-AG decrease the excitatory GLU and the inhibitory GABAergic inputs to striatal neurons (130, 131). Therefore, it is likely that the potential of AEA to reduce 2-AG levels by activating TRVP1 receptors might represent a mechanism to integrate excitatory and inhibitory inputs in the basal ganglia.

ENDOCANNABINOIDS AND THEIR METABOLIZING ENZYMES

In the CNS, endocannabinoids mediate forms of short-term synaptic plasticity known as depolarization-induced suppression of inhibition (DSI) (132, 133) and depolarization-induced suppression of excitation (DSE) (134). Thus, endocannabinoids are considered as retrograde messengers that neuromodulate diverse physiological processes. AEA and 2-AG are the two most characterized endocannabinoids (135, 136), although other studies have identified of additional endocannabinoids such as 2-arachidonylglyceryl ether (noladin ether) (137), *N*-arachidonoyl-dopamine (NADA) (128), and *O*-arachidonoyl-ethanolamine (virodhamine) (138). However, the physiological functions of these endocannabinoids are still being investigated. While 2-AG acts as a full agonist at CB1 and CB2 receptors, AEA behaves as a partial agonist at both receptors subtypes and can also interact with GPR55 and TRVP1 receptors.

Unlike other neurotransmitters, AEA and 2-AG are not synthesized and stored in the nerve cells. Rather, they are produced on an "as needed" basis by their membrane lipid precursors in a Ca^{2+} dependent fashion (133, 139). Although additional studies are needed to ascertain the exact role of the *N*-acylphosphatidylethanolamine phospho-lipase D in the ECBS, it has been proposed that this enzyme might play a significant role in the synthesis of AEA (140). The enzyme responsible for 2-AG synthesis is the diacylglycerol lipase alpha (141). Upon depolarization of post-synaptic neurons, the endocannabinoids released into the synaptic cleft bind to and activate the presynaptic CB1 receptors, which in turn suppress the release of both excitatory and inhibitory different neurotransmitters [see for review (142)]. Then, AEA and 2-AG are rapidly deactivated by cellular reuptake into both neurons and glial cells and metabolized by specific enzymes (143). AEA can be metabolized by either the FAAH (144), or monoacylglycerol lipase (MAGL), which degrades specifically 2-AG (145). In addition to MAGL, recent studies have suggested that the enzymes ABHD6 and ABHD12 could also be involved in 2-AG metabolism (146, 147). FAAH is over-expressed in the CNS and FAAH-positive neurons are localized in proximity to CB1 receptor-containing terminals, underlining the role for this enzyme in endocannabinoids inhibition (148). Thus, selective inhibition of FAAH (149) and MAGL (150) can prolong the effects of endocannabinoids. Pre-clinical studies have demonstrated that pharmacological inhibition of FAHH with URB597 (149) or PF-3845 compounds (151) induced-anxiolytic-like effects (152, 153) and anti-nociceptive properties in mice (152, 154). Inhibition of MAGL with JZL184 inhibitor causes analgesia, hypothermia, and hypomotility (155). However, chronic exposure to JZL184 impairs endocannabinoid-mediated synaptic plasticity in mouse hippocampus and cerebellum via 2-AG upregulation. It also induces tolerance to the analgesic effects, physical dependence, and persistent activation as well as desensitization of brain CB1 receptors (156). Surprisingly, MAGL knockout mice show enhanced learning behavior and have normal locomotor activity, suggesting the possible role of MAGL in cognitive function (157, 158).

EXOGENOUS CANNABINOIDS: Δ^9-THC VS. CBD

Cannabis is the world's most commonly used illicit drug (159, 160). Between 119 and 224 million people are cannabis users worldwide (4). Cannabis contains over 85 different chemical substances unique to the plant and termed phytocannabinoids. Among them, Δ^9-tetrahydrocannabinol (Δ^9-THC) and CBD are the two main components of cannabis, which has been used for thousands of years for both recreational and medicinal purposes. Most studies regarding cannabis properties have focused on Δ^9-THC, which is the main psychoactive constituent in cannabis extracts (161). Although Δ^9-THC possesses a number of therapeutic effects (e.g., on pain, spasms, inflammation), its negative impact on the CNS has been highlighted in several clinical studies on subjects smoking cannabis, documenting impulsive behavior, cognitive impairment, consumption of addictive substances, and psychiatric disorders (e.g., schizophrenia, depression, and anxiety) (162–165). For example, Δ^9-THC has been shown to induce psychotic-like and anxiogenic effects when administered intravenously to healthy subjects (166, 167). Other experimental studies revealed that Δ^9-THC injection in animal models causes hypolocomotion, catalepsy, antinociception, and hypothermia (168).

Pharmacological studies in animal models suggest that not all therapeutic effects related to cannabis administration can be ascribed to Δ^9-THC [reviewed in Ref. (169)]. Indeed, CBD – the second most abundant cannabinoid found in cannabis – acts as an antidepressant and possesses anticonvulsant, antiemetic, anxiolytic, and sleep-promoting as well as neuroprotective properties in humans (160, 170–176). CBD mediates its neuropharmacological properties by acting as an inverse agonist on CB1 and CB2 receptors (177, 178); it also stimulates the TRVP1 and TRVP2 (179) which serve as so-called ionotropic cannabinoid receptors. In addition, CBD inhibits FAAH, the main catabolic enzyme that alters the hydrolysis of the endogenous cannabinoid neurotransmitter AEA (180) (see above section), and is also an antagonist at the putative GPR55 receptor. The clinical association of the modulation of the ECBS by CBD remains to be fully investigated; this effect could arguably be related to DA uptake inhibition (181). Interestingly, ECBS interacts closely with other neurobiological structures which are implicated in the neural adaptations observed during chronic use of drugs and vulnerability to addiction. For example, CBD plays a role in the modulation of extracellular levels of DA (182) as well as μ and δ opioid receptors (183); it increases adenosine signaling through inhibition of uptake (184). Moreover, μ opioid and CB1 receptors colocalized within neural regions are known to modulate reward, goal-directed behavior, and habit formation relevant to addiction including striatal output projection neurons of the NAc and dorsal striatum (185, 186). While further studies are required to better understand the impact of CBD on GLU neurotransmission, its protective effects on GLU toxicity (187) and its psychopharmacologic interaction with ketamine (188), a *N*-methyl-D-aspartic (NMDA) receptor antagonist, are well documented. CBD activates also the serotoninergic receptors 5-HT1A (5-hydroxytryptamine) (171, 176, 189–193), which in turn diminishes vulnerability to stress and has anxiolytic-like effects in animal models (170, 172, 189, 190, 192–195). Similar results were observed in humans, where CBD administration decreases autonomic arousal and subjective anxiety (196). Interestingly, these anxiolytic effects have been linked to the modulation of core regions involved in the "emotional brain," including limbic system structures such as the AMG and the ACC (197, 198). CBD's anxiolytic effects were further confirmed by a study indicating that the effective connectivity between ACC and AMG is attenuated during the emotional processing of fearful faces, while resting activity of the left parahippocampus gyrus is increased. (196, 199). Remarkably, these neural structures are activated during drug craving in cocaine addiction (197, 200). It also decreases compulsive behaviors in rodents, which is hypothesized to be related to CB1-related mechanisms (201, 202).

While CBD has neuroprotective properties (187, 203, 204) and Δ^9-THC administration have been shown to cause neurotoxic effects (205), these opposing properties have been highlighted in brain imaging studies where Δ^9-THC and CBD activate different brain regions during tasks engaging verbal memory (206, 207), response inhibition (208), and emotional processing (196, 209–211). When given at appropriate doses, CBD counteracts Δ^9-THC properties. Thus, CBD can modulate the functional effects of Δ^9-THC (177, 178). Pre-clinical studies demonstrate that CBD decreases Δ^9-THC-induced conditioned place aversion and social interaction of on operant behavior model (212, 213). In addition, CBD diminishes Δ^9-THC-induced anxiety and psychotic-like symptoms in humans (214, 215). Together, this data clearly suggests that CBD limits Δ^9-THC adverse effects. Thus, administered together, CBD might increase Δ^9-THC clinical efficacy (216, 217). It has been established that unlike, Δ^9-THC, CBD possesses therapeutic properties that could reduce withdrawal symptoms often present in individuals with addictive disorders (e.g., anxiety, psychotic, mood symptoms, insomnia, and pain). For example, a recent pre-clinical study from Hurd's group aimed at assessing the effects of cannabinoids on opioid-seeking behaviors in rats indicates that while Δ^9-THC potentiates heroin SA, CBD inhibits cue-induced heroin-seeking behaviors for up to 2 weeks following the last administration (218). In addition, CBD is well tolerated and has no gross effects on motor function (such as locomotor activity). CBD is also protects against damages caused by various substances; it reverses binge ethanol-induced neurotoxicity (219) and mitigates the cardiac effects of Δ^9-THC (220, 221). Together this data illustrates the different, and sometimes opposite, neurobiological properties of the two main constituents of cannabis – CBD and Δ^9-THC – that are linked to neural circuits which might play significant roles in addiction disorders. However, while numerous studies have highlighted the participation of the ECBS in the rewarding and addictive properties of drugs of abuse such as opioids, nicotine, and alcohol over the last decades, relatively few studies have focus on the impact of this system on addiction to psychostimulants.

INTERACTION OF THE eCBS WITH BIOLOGICAL AND BEHAVIORAL CORRELATES OF PSYCHOSTIMULANTS ADDICTION

HUMAN STUDIES

Human studies aimed at understanding the interaction of the ECBS with biological and behavioral correlates of addiction to psychostimulants have mostly focused on ECBS-related risk factors leading to drug dependence. Interestingly, cannabis use is strongly associated with the abuse and/or dependence of several class of drugs including psychostimulants such as cocaine (222). Moreover, exogenous cannabinoids have been shown to modulate the acute rewarding effects of cocaine. These lines of evidence may suggest an association between ECBS and liability to psychostimulant by pointing toward a possible involvement of the ECBS in the motivational effects mediated by psychostimulants (223) [reviewed in Ref. (224)]. Based on these observations, scientific efforts have been devoted to investigate the influence of various genetic (e.g., ECBS-related genes) and environmental characteristics (e.g., previous or current exposure to cannabinoid agonists) in individual progression from occasional use to psychostimulant addiction.

"The gateway theory" and addiction to psychostimulants

Association of prior or concomitant cannabis consumption with other illicit drugs including psychostimulants such as methamphetamine and cocaine, forms the basis of a well-known hypothesis – " the gateway theory," which suggests a causal role for cannabis in the development of subsequent drug use and addiction (225). While data indicate that smoking cannabis is positively associated with cocaine consumption, it would be inappropriate to assume that cannabis *per se* leads to cocaine use. A study from Lynskey et al. in human twins reveals that early cannabis use in life increases the odds of subsequent cocaine use, supporting the causative model of the "gateway theory." However, results of this study have been refuted by Kandel et al. (226) which argues that several additional genetic, social, and environmental factors, such as life experiences, might link cannabis use with subsequent cocaine consumption (227, 228). Actual neurobiological causal mechanisms underlying this "gateway theory" remain mostly unidentified. Interestingly, Tomasiewicz and colleagues show that Δ^9-THC exposure induces epigenetic dysregulation of the endogenous opioid proenkephalin in adolescents; these findings indicate that cannabis exposure, in and of itself, can be considered as a risk factor that acts "above the genome" and can "write" on the existing epigenetic background of adolescent neurodevelopment. Thus, in adolescents, Δ^9-THC exposure-mediated epigenetic effects may act in concert with other environmental or social factors to augment future behavioral responses to drugs of abuse via stable and long-term regulation of genes at the transcriptional level. However, while these data establish a direct link between Δ^9-THC-induced changes in proenkephalin expression and susceptibility to opiate drugs, no studies have confirmed that this mechanism can be applied to psychostimulants (229).

Genetic determinants of the ECBS and psychostimulant addiction

It is worth mentioning that not every subject who experiences the pleasurable effects of psychostimulants will become a chronic user. Indeed it is more likely that additional factors such as: (1) genetic variabilities (e.g., polymorphisms in the catechol *O*-methyltransferase gene (Val158met) and in the serotonin transporter gene (5-HTTLPR) (230, 231); (2) monoamine receptors deficiency – either genetically or as a result of their drug excesses – also contribute to the psychostimulants addiction process (232–235) (see **Table 1**). In the ECBS, different genetic variants of the CB1 receptors – *CNR1* – and *FAAH* genes have been associated with increased susceptibility to drug addiction. Indeed, genetic analyses demonstrate that the *CNR1* gene exhibits elevated numbers of (AAT)n triplet repetition in a sample of 192 non-Hispanic Caucasian subjects. Interestingly, this *CNR1* polymorphism increases the risk of intravenous drug use in this population, with strongest correlation observed in cocaine, amphetamine, and marijuana dependence (236). Similarly, a study from Ballon and colleagues shows that detection of this *CNR1* polymorphism in a sample of 142 African-Caribbean individuals predisposed them to cocaine addiction (237). Unfortunately, while single sequence repetitions can alter transcriptional rates and thereby induced gene overexpression or silencing (238), the functional nature of the microsatellite polymorphism triplet repetition (AAT)n in modulating *CNR1* gene expression remains blurred (239). It has been hypothesized that the presence of long alleles with high numbers of AAT triplets alter *CNR1* transcriptional gene expression, ultimately leading to low levels of CNR1 protein synthesis (240). A recent meta-analysis of 11 studies aimed at investigating the contribution of three *CNR1* polymorphisms (rs1049353, rs806379, and the AAT triplet repetitions) to drug dependence vulnerability confirmed the presence of (AAT)n repeats, but only in the Caucasian population [reviewed in Ref. (239)]. Unfortunately, the effect of the three *CNR1* polymorphisms appeared to be insignificant and showed high heterogeneity. Important caveats have to be considered when looking at these studies. First, the ethnicity of the different subjects may prove important, as some studies included several ethnic groups in their samples, and in some cases, these groups were not even mentioned (241, 242). Some reports also examined *CNR1* gene polymorphisms in connection with a different phenotype or stage of drug addiction such as craving, drug consumption, dependence, or drug withdrawal

Table 1 | ECBS and factors contributing to vulnerability to psychostimulants in humans.

Aspect	Conclusion	Reference
Genetic risks factors	CNR1 (AAT)n repeat polymorphism associated with IV drug use, including amphetamine and cocaine, in a non-Hispanic Caucasian population and with cocaine dependence in an African-Caribbean population	Comings et al. (236), Ballon et al. (237)
	CNR1 gene single nucleotide polymorphisms associated with cocaine addiction in an African-American population	Clarke et al. (244)
	FAAH gene mis-sense mutation associated with drug dependence	Sipe et al. (245), Flanagan et al. (246)
Cannabis effect in addiction to psychostimulants	Self-reported of cannabis smoking by crack-cocaine abusers alleviates withdrawal symptoms and drug-craving	Labigalini et al. (90)
	Post-discharge use of cannabis by American cocaine addicts increases risk of relapse	Aharonovich et al. (91)
	Cannabis use correlates with syringe sharing in injection drug users	Jutras-Aswad et al. (22)
	Recent cannabis use decreases activation of frontal cortices area during emotional stress stimulation in cocaine-dependent individuals	Li et al. (247)

(243). Furthermore, a detailed description of the repercussions of *CNR1* polymorphisms on CB1 function from a neurobiological standpoint is lacking from the reviewed studies.

Polymorphisms in the gene coding for the endocannabinoid-inactivating enzyme *FAAH* may constitute another risk factor for problematic drug use, as described by initial reports identifying C385A, a mis-sense single nucleotide polymorphism (SNP) causing reduced FAAH enzymatic activity (245, 246). Indeed, a study from Sipe et al. reveals significant association between C385A SNP and street drug abuse in a sample of 1737 Caucasian subjects with addictive disorders. Neuroimaging studies combined with genetic analysis reveal that low FAAH activity enhances AEA protein expression levels which, in turn, modulate brain regions implicated in drug addiction and reward circuitry such as the OFC, AC gyrus, and NAc (242). Additional neuroimaging studies show that C385A carriers exhibit increased ventral striatal reactivity – a correlate for heightened impulsivity and reward sensitivity. C385A carriers display low threat-related amygdala reactivity – a pattern observed in individuals with high familial risk of alcoholism. Moreover, C385A polymorphism-reduced FAAH functional activity increases risk-taking behavior associated with addiction through abnormal impulsivity and threat perception [reviewed in Ref. (224, 243)]. Contribution of SNPs that modulate FAAH functions to stimulant addiction remain to be explored as the aforementioned data were not obtained in individuals specifically addicted to stimulants.

Effect of exogenous cannabinoids on psychostimulant reward

As mentioned previously (see The Endocannabinoid System), an intriguing characteristic of psychostimulants abuse is the concurrent consumption of cannabis. Parallel to studies on the long-term effects of cannabis exposure on subsequent psychostimulant use, researchers also examined the acute rewarding effects of cannabis use on concurrent psychostimulant addiction (91, 222). However, studies aimed at investigating such interactions are sparse. Conflicting results from Foltin et al. and Lukas et al. provide evidence that cannabinoids modulate cocaine-mediated euphoric actions. First, data from Foltin and colleagues show that human volunteers who smoked cannabis prior to intravenous cocaine experience a prolongation of the "high" sensation (248). Second, a study from Lukas and colleagues reveals that smoking Δ^9-THC, 30 min prior to intranasal cocaine decreases the latency to onset of cocaine-induced euphoria significantly, from 1.87 to 0.53 min, as well as the duration of cocaine-induced dysphoria, from 2.1 to 0.5 min (249). Interestingly, when both drugs are administered concomitantly, no changes are observed in cocaine- and Δ^9-THC-induced positive subjective properties. Furthermore, Δ^9-THC increases the peak plasma levels and bioavailability of cocaine considerably. This increase might be the result of Δ^9-THC-induced vasodilation of the nasal mucosa which, in turn, reduces cocaine-induced vasoconstriction, thereby increasing cocaine's absorption. In addition, the discrepancies between these two studies might be also due to pharmacodynamic mechanisms including differences in cocaine absorption or in the ratio of CBD/Δ^9-THC levels found in the type of cannabis used for each study.

Using fMRI technology combined with script-guided imagery paradigm in which subjects imagined being in a real-life stressful situation, Rajita Sinha's group found that cannabis abuse contributed to stress-induced blood-oxygen-level-dependent (BOLD) contrast in a group of cocaine-dependent individuals. More specifically, cannabis consumption decreases emotional stress cue-induced frontal and cingulate activation in cocaine-dependent individuals (247). These findings suggest an abnormal cognitive control mechanism during affective processing in association with heavy cannabis use. An important caveat to consider in the latter study is that cocaine-dependent individuals were abstinent for several weeks prior to the neuroimagery session and were not current users of cannabis. Thus the study did not allow to examine the acute effect of cannabis on neural and behavioral responses. However, the fact that this cannabis-induced alteration in stress-response can be translated to cocaine craving and relapse vulnerability has definitely piqued further interest, and initial data on this matter already exists. Indeed, the effects of cannabis consumption on abstinence and relapse to cocaine use have been provided in a study from Labigalini and colleagues, in which 25 cocaine-crack dependent individuals reported to smoke cannabis in order to get relief from abstinence mediated-cocaine-withdrawal symptoms. From this sample, 68% of addicts achieved crack-cocaine cessation while using cannabis during the 9 months duration of the study (90). However, the self-reported nature of this study and its limited duration suggest cautiousness in interpreting its outcome. In a more recent study, Aharonovich et al. drew opposite conclusions on the consequences of smoking cannabis on cocaine relapse. In this study, researchers investigated whether cannabis use after the discharge of 144 drug-addicts from inpatient treatment program could help them to maintain abstinence and thereby preventing relapse to cocaine use. Results from this study suggest that smoking cannabis reduced the achievement of sustained remission and increased relapse to cocaine use (91) (see **Table 1**). Surprisingly, a study from Jutras-Aswad et al. supports the assumption that irregular cannabis use increases risky behaviors (syringe sharing) of cocaine and opioid users, as opposed to regular cannabis use, suggesting a complex dose-effect relationship between cannabis and addictive behaviors (22). The possibility that cannabis use by recently abstinent cocaine-dependent individuals influences relapse to drug and other related behaviors remains poorly documented.

ANIMAL STUDIES

Over the last decades, development of animal models have allowed a better understanding of psychostimulant effects and addiction-related behaviors. These studies would not be available through clinical studies for ethical and practical reasons. Notably, invasive measures such as catheter installation for drug administration and surgical brain procedures for assessment of drug-induced neurobiological changes, as well as strictly controlled conditioning protocols involving restrictive environments, have extended the knowledge of psychostimulants effect on neurotransmission. These methods have also allowed observations of specific behavioral aspects of psychostimulant addiction. Thus, studies on animal models of psychostimulants abuse have provided tremendous insights on the role of ECBS in various aspects of psychostimulant addiction, spanning from drug reward, acquisition, and relapse.

Influence of ECBS on psychostimulants-induced behavioral and reinforcing effects

As mentioned above (see Neurobiology of Psychostimulants), substantial evidence indicates that behavioral and addictive properties of psychostimulants come from the interactions of psychostimulants with brain monoamines. Specifically, increase of extracellular levels of DA through promotion of DA release by amphetamine and MDMA, as well as inhibition of DA reuptake by cocaine, represent the primary mechanisms involved in rewarding effects mediated by psychostimulants (224). In animal models of intracranial self-stimulation (ICSS), the rewarding properties of drugs of abuse typically translate into lowering of the so-called reward threshold established after operant training [see Ref. (250) for description]. Initial experiments showed no effect of CB1 antagonist SR141716A on cocaine's ability to lower ICSS threshold in rats (251), although careful data analysis suggests a tendency toward attenuation. However, different results were obtained when using a more potent antagonist – AM251. This antagonist proves CB1 blockade's effectiveness in inhibiting cocaine's action on brain stimulation reward (250). Paradoxically, the non-selective cannabinoid agonist – WIN55, 212-2 – and the endocannabinoid transmission enhancer – AM404 – are also able to abolish cocaine's reinforcing effects as assessed by ICSS (252). Whether these apparently contradictory findings may indicate an inverse U-shape effect of CB1 stimulation function on rewarding properties of stimulants is not entirely clear. However, these results clearly indicate that cannabinoids might interfere with brain systems responsible for psychostimulants rewarding effects, and the mechanism underlying this phenomenon should be further explored.

Li and colleagues recently found significant reductions in DA levels in striatum of mice lacking the *CNR1* gene, when compared to their wildtype counterparts following acute cocaine administration and during the basal state (253). This observation shows consistency with above-cited ICSS studies and with a previous report on the inhibition of cocaine-induced DA release in rats by CB1 antagonist SR141716A (254). In contrast, initial findings suggested that neither basal levels nor cocaine-induced increases in extracellular NAc DA of CB1 knockout mice differed from that of normal mice (255), and that CB1 inactivation by antagonists AM251 and SR141716A failed to alter the increase in extracellular NAc DA responsible for cocaine-mediated rewarding effects in rats (256, 257). Differences in experimental methods used to measure DA levels (voltammetry vs. *in vivo* microdialysis) and in the genetic background of the knockout animals (C57BL/6J vs. CD1) could account for such discrepancies. Notably, compensatory neurobiological changes due to lack of CB1 receptors could explain the subnormal basal DA levels observed in Li et al. study. This subnormal basal DA levels could also have contributed to apparent attenuation of DA levels enhancement produced by cocaine. Overall, the extent to which ECBS interaction with psychostimulants-mediated reward effects depends on DA transmission seems limited, especially when CB1 is targeted. It remains a controversial issue, with subsequent reports of attenuation of cocaine-enhanced extracellular NAc DA activity by CB2 agonists JWH133 and GW405833 in mice (258), but not by the pharmacological FAAH inhibitor URB597 in rats (259) adding to the complexity of the matter (see **Table 2**).

The increase of DA neurotransmission in the NAc and other striatal regions responsible for psychostimulant-induced rewarding parallels the stimulation of locomotor activity following acute drug administration. Sensitization to hyperlocomotor responses produced by psychostimulants occurs after chronic treatment, reflecting adaptive changes in DA transmission and potentially correlating with drug-seeking and reinstatement behavior (254, 262). In various studies, neither genetic deletion (262–264) nor pharmacological inhibition of CB1 receptors by SR141716A (265, 266) altered cocaine's ability to induce acute motor effects or behavioral sensitization in rats and mice. However, a comparable number of reports described contradictory results, showing attenuation of both of these outcomes in CB1 knockout mice (253, 267) (see **Table 3**) as well as impairment of sensitization

Table 2 | Pharmacological inhibition of FAAH inhibition and properties of psychostimulants.

FAAH inhibitors	Drug	Animal	Outcome	Effects	Reference
AM404	Cocaine	Rat	Drug-induced lowering of brain reward/self-stimulation threshold	Impaired	Vlachou et al. (252)
			Drug-induced acute hyperlocomotion	Attenuated	Vlachou et al. (252)
URB597	Cocaine	Monkey	SA – effect of agonist after drug-taking extinction	No effect	Justinova et al. (260)
			SA – drug-taking behavior	No change	Justinova et al. (260)
		Rat	Cocaine-induced increase in VTA DA activity	Preserved	Luchicchi et al. (259)
			Cocaine-induced alterations in firing of NAc shell spiny neurons	Attenuated	Luchicchi et al. (259)
URB597, PMSF	Cocaine	Rat	SA – drug-seeking responses/intake	No change	Adamczyk et al. (261)
			SA – drug-induced reinstatement	Attenuated	Adamczyk et al. (261)
			SA – cue-induced reinstatement	Attenuated	Adamczyk et al. (261)

in animals pretreated with SR141716A (254, 268) or AM251 (267). Interestingly, although chronic cocaine use still induced sensitization in mice with invalidated CB1 receptors, sensitized response appeared somewhat changed when compared to control animals. Corbille et al. also found that AM251, unlike SR141716A (269), only impaired sensitization to cocaine after a single exposure, but not upon repeated administration. Similar experiments with cannabinoid agonists showed mixed results, as non-selective WIN 55,212-2 reduced cocaine's motor effects, probably in a non-CB1 mediated fashion (252, 270). Likewise, CB2 agonists JWH133 and GW405833 decreased both acute hyperlocomotion and sensitization in rats (258), which parallels findings observed in mice genetically overexpressing CB2 (271). Δ^9-THC failed to alter cocaine's motor effects in rats (268, 272). Similarly, cannabinoid-amphetamine interactions studies demonstrate that acute cannabinoid exposure antagonizes amphetamine's locomotion effects in a dose-dependent manner in rats. On the other hand, chronic exposure to Δ^9-THC induces sensitization to the psychomotor effects mediated by amphetamine in rats (273). Taken together, these experiments suggest that the acute motor stimulant effects of psychostimulant and the induction of cocaine sensitization may not depend on endocannabinoid tone, even though CB1 receptors could play a minor modulating role in this regard [reviewed in Ref. (274)].

Overall, while some evidence of ECBS involvement in the neurobiological and behavioral correlates of psychostimulant reinforcing properties exists, influence of ECBS on acute psychostimulant reward is modest and probably involves a combination of mechanisms which may not directly involve DA activity in the NAc or CB1 receptors.

Influence of ECBS on acquisition and maintenance of psychostimulant-induced seeking behaviors

Models of conditioning such as the SA paradigm and the conditioned place-preference (CPP) procedure illustrate the reinforcing properties of drugs of abuse and demonstrate their ability to induce and maintain drug-seeking behaviors. Consistent with findings showing the limited involvement of the ECBS in the reinforcing properties of psychostimulants (see Influence of ECBS on Psychostimulants-Induced Behavioral and Reinforcing Effects), modulation of the ECBS appears to have a modest influence on acquisition and maintenance of psychostimulant-taking behavior in animals. In CPP experiments, while CB1 receptor deletion did not affect psychostimulant-induced place conditioning in mice, SR141716A impaired cocaine-, methamphetamine-, and MDMA-induced place conditioning in both rats and mice (262–265, 281, 286, 287). Difference in species, compensatory changes in the knockout animals due to the lack of CB1 receptors, as well as use of more intense conditioning and higher doses of drugs in the genetic deletion studies may have contributed to this discrepancy. This suggests that intensity of conditioning could overcome the effects of blocking ECBS signaling [reviewed in Ref. (274)]. It is important to note that the weaker cannabinoid antagonist CBD did not affect establishment of amphetamine-induced CPP in rats (290) and that the genetic overexpression of cannabinoid receptor CB2 impaired acquisition of both cocaine-induced CPP and SA (271). Thus the CPP model indicates that, although not directly interfering with the rewarding properties of psychostimulant drugs, ECBS could play a role in the perception and memory of psychostimulant reward, depending on environment-related factors.

In general, CB1 receptor invalidation does not seem to affect SA of psychostimulants. Experiments with genetic deletion of CB1 show conflicting results, as both knockout and SR141716A-treated mice still acquired amphetamine- and cocaine-taking behavior in restrained mobility conditions (266, 275), whereas knockout mice showed impaired SA behavior in other protocols (255, 258). Overall, results suggest that learning SA behavior might not require extensive ECBS involvement. Maintenance of such behavior may not depend on CB1 either, as drug-taking responses under a fixed-ratio schedule in animals that had already acquired cocaine SA remained unaffected after CB1 blockade by SR141716A in mice (266, 283), monkeys (280), and rats (250, 256, 269, 283) and by AM251 in rats (250, 277). Only one contradicting report exists in which AM251 decreased methamphetamine SA in conditioned rats (278). Cannabinoid signaling enhancement by the pharmacological FAAH inhibitors – URB597 and PMSF – also failed to affect maintenance of fixed-ratio drug-taking behavior in rats (261) and monkeys (260). On the other hand, cannabinoid stimulation by CB1 agonists had significant effects in several studies.

Table 3 | Effects of CB1 cannabinoid receptor deletion and properties of psychostimulants; CB1 receptor antagonists and properties of psychostimulants.

Genotype	Drug	Animal	Outcome	Effects	Reference
CB1 KO	Cocaine	Mouse	Drug-induced acute hyperlocomotion	Preserved	Martin et al. (262), Houchi et al. (263), Miller et al. (264)
			Drug-induced acute hyperlocomotion	Attenuated	Corbille et al. (267), Li et al. (253)
			Drug-induced motor sensitization	Preserved	Martin et al. (262)
			Drug-induced motor sensitization	Attenuated	Corbille et al. (267)
			Drug-induced increase in NAc DA levels	Preserved	Soria et al. (255)
			Drug-induced increase in NAc DA levels	Attenuated	Li et al. (253)
			CPP – behavior acquisition under chronic unpredictable stress exposure	Preserved	Martin et al. (262), Houchi et al. (263), Miller et al. (264)
				Enhanced	Miller et al. (264)
			SA – behavior acquisition in restrained mobility protocol	Impaired	Soria et al. (255), Xi et al. (258)
				Preserved	Cossu et al. (275)
			SA – breaking point under PR schedule	Decreased	Soria et al. (255)
	Amphet.		Drug-induced acute hyperlocomotion	Preserved	Houchi et al. (263)
			Drug-induced acute hyperlocomotion	Attenuated	Corbille et al. (267)
			Drug-induced motor sensitization	Attenuated	Corbille et al. (267)
			SA – behavior acquisition in restrained mobility protocol	Preserved	Cossu et al. (275)
Antagonist	**Drug**	**Animal**	**Outcome**	**Effects**	**Reference**
AM251	Cocaine	Mouse	Drug-induced acute hyperlocomotion	Attenuated	Corbille et al. (267)
			Drug-induced motor sensitization (induction)	Attenuated	Corbille et al. (267)
			Drug-induced motor sensitization (expression)	Preserved	Corbille et al. (267)
			CPP – drug-induced reinstatement	Preserved	Vaughn et al. (276)
			CPP – stress-induced reinstatement	Impaired	Vaughn et al. (276)
		Rat	Drug-induced lowering of brain reward/self-stimulation threshold	Attenuated	Xi et al. (250)
			Drug-induced increase in NAc DA levels	Preserved	Xi et al. (257)
			Drug-induced increase in NAc glutamate	Attenuated	Xi et al. (257)
			SA – drug-induced reinstatement	Attenuated	Xi et al. (257), Adamczyk et al. (277)
			SA – cue-induced reinstatement	Attenuated	Adamczyk et al. (277)
			SA – drug-seeking responses/intake	No change	Xi et al. (250), Adamczyk et al. (277)
			SA – breaking point under PR schedule	Decreased	Xi et al. (250)
	METH	Rat	SA – drug-seeking responses/intake	Decreased	Vinklerova et al. (278)
SR141716A	Amphet., cocaine	Gerbils	Drug-induced acute hyperlocomotion	Decreased	Poncelet et al. (279)
			Reinstatement of drug-seeking	Decreased	Poncelet et al. (279)
	Cocaine	Monkey	SA – drug-seeking responses/intake	No change	Tanda et al. (280)
		Mouse	Drug-induced acute hyperlocomotion	Attenuated	Gerdeman et al. (268)
				Preserved	Lesscher et al. (266)
			Drug-induced motor sensitization (induction)	Attenuated	Gerdeman et al. (268)
				Preserved	Lesscher et al. (266)

(Continued)

Table 3 | Continued

Antagonist	Drug	Animal	Outcome	Effects	Reference
			Drug-induced motor sensitization (expression)	Preserved	Gerdeman et al. (268)
			Drug-induced motor sensitization (maintenance – specific to a drug-paired environment)	Reversed	Gerdeman et al. (268)
			CPP – behavior acquisition	Impaired	Yu et al. (281)
			CPP – drug-induced reinstatement	Impaired	Yu et al. (281)
			SA – behavior acquisition	Preserved	Lesscher et al. (266)
			SA – "extinction burst responding"	Attenuated	Ward et al. (282)
			SA – time for behavior extinction	Decreased	Ward et al. (282)
			SA – cue-induced reinstatement	Attenuated	Ward et al. (282)
			SA – drug-seeking responses/intake	No change	De Vries et al. (283), Lesscher et al. (266)
			SA – breaking point under PR schedule	Decreased	Soria et al. (255)
		Rat	Drug-induced acute hyperlocomotion	Preserved	Chaperon et al. (265)
				Attenuated	Cheer et al. (254)
			Drug-induced motor sensitization (expression)	Attenuated	Filip et al. (269)
			Drug-induced lowering of brain reward/self-stimulation threshold	Preserved	Vlachou et al. (251), Xi et al. (250)
			Drug-induced decrease in VP GABA efflux	Preserved	Caille and Parsons (256)
			Drug-induced increase in NAc DA levels	Preserved	Caille and Parsons (256)
				Suppressed	Cheer et al. (254)
			Drug discrimination	Preserved	Filip et al. (269)
			SA – drug-seeking responses/intake	No change	De Vries et al. (283), Caille and Parsons (256), Filip et al. (269), Xi et al. (250)
			SA – breaking point under PR schedule	No change	Xi et al. (250)
				Decreased	Orio et al. (284)
			SA – drug-induced reinstatement	Attenuated	De Vries et al. (283), Filip et al. (269)
			SA – HU210-induced reinstatement	Attenuated	De Vries et al. (283)
			SA – cue-induced reinstatement	Attenuated	De Vries et al. (283), Filip et al. (269)
			SA – stress-induced reinstatement	Preserved	De Vries et al. (283)
			CPP – behavior acquisition	Impaired	Chaperon et al. (265)
			CPP – behavior expression	Preserved	Chaperon et al. (265)
	MDMA	Mouse	CPP – drug-induced reinstatement	Increased	Daza-Losada et al. (285)
			CPP – behavior acquisition	Impaired	Rodriguez-Arias et al. (286)
		Rat	CPP – behavior acquisition	Impaired	Braida et al. (287)
			SA – drug-seeking responses/intake	Increased	Braida and Sala (288)
	METH	Mouse	CPP – behavior acquisition	Impaired	Yu et al. (281)
			CPP – drug-induced reinstatement	Impaired	Yu et al. (281)
		Rat	Drug-induced reinstatement of drug-seeking behavior	Attenuated	Anggadiredja et al. (289)
			Cue-induced reinstatement of drug-seeking behavior	Attenuated	Anggadiredja et al. (289)

Indeed, WIN 55,212-2 increased acquisition of MDMA SA in mice (286) and exposure to CP55,940 enhances development of cocaine SA in female rats (291). THC failed to alter acquisition of cocaine SA and amphetamine SA in monkeys (272) and rats (290), respectively. In regard to maintenance of drug intake in animals with SA behavior, cannabinoid agonists decreased drug-taking responses in rats – CP55,940 diminished MDMA intake (288) and WIN55,212-2 decreased cocaine administration (292) – and in monkeys – Δ^9-THC also decreased cocaine intake (272). Fattore et al. first interpreted the shift in psychostimulant intake produced by CB1 agonists as indicative of a synergistic action of CB1 stimulation on reinforcing properties of the drugs, which, incidentally, could account for the frequent use of cannabis among human psychostimulants users (292). Complementary experiments using progressive-ratio schedules also reveal interaction of CB1 receptors with psychostimulant-induced reinforcing properties. In PR schedules, both genetic deletion and antagonist treatment of CB1 receptors produce a decrease in the maximal effort mice provided to self-administer cocaine, as made apparent by decreases in breaking point measures induced by SR141716A (255, 277, 284) and by AM251 (250) (SR141716A producing no effect in this specific report). This adds to the evidence that the CB1 receptors, while not indispensable for acquisition or maintenance of cocaine-seeking behavior, may exert a specific modulation on motivation and reward salience in psychostimulant addiction.

Role of ECBS in extinction and reinstatement of drug-taking behaviors

Although the mechanism used by endocannabinoid signaling to modulate psychostimulant reward and acquisition or maintenance is still the subject of debate, some form of consensus exists in the literature about the pivotal role of the ECBS in extinction and reinstatement in animal behavioral models of psychostimulant addiction [reviewed in Refs. (89) and (274)]. In conditioning procedures, extinction refers to the learning phase that follows the removal of the reinforcer (i.e., psychostimulant drugs), during which rates of conditioned responses (i.e., SA or CPP) progressively decline back to pre-conditioning levels. After drug-seeking behavior becomes extinct, several behavioral phenomena can reinstate drug-seeking behavior. These include not only re-exposure to the abused drug itself, but also exposure to contextual cues associated with previous drug administration and to environmental stressors (274, 293).

In a recent study from Ward et al. mice treated with SR141716 after removal of cocaine in a SA paradigm altered the burst in cocaine-seeking observed in the initial phase of extinction learning, while decreasing the time required to achieve complete extinction of cocaine-seeking behavior when compared to vehicle-treated mice (282). CB1 blockade by SR141716A also significantly decreases cue-induced reinstatement of cocaine SA behavior following extinction, supporting similar reports of attenuation of cue-induced reinstatement of cocaine-seeking by CB1 antagonism in rats (269, 277, 283). Evaluation of reinstatement of SA behavior induced by drug-priming produced similar results: SR141716A blocks cocaine-induced reinstatement (269, 283), and both AM251 (257, 277) and SR141716A inhibit methamphetamine-induced reinstatement (289). It is worth noting that CB2 antagonism also has an anti-reinstatement effect in cocaine-primed, but not in cue-exposed rats (277). In CPP models, CB1 blockade by SR141716A, but not by AM251 (276), impaired drug-induced reinstatement in cocaine-conditioned mice (281). SR141716A also impaired methamphetamine-induced reinstatement of CPP (281). Few studies focused on stress-induced reinstatement of psychostimulant-seeking. Vaughn et al. recently found that AM251 reverses stress-induced CPP (276). De Vries et al. could not find an impact of SR141716A on stress-induced SA reinstatement (283).

Stimulation of CB1 receptors produced opposite results to those obtained in pharmacological blockade experiments (see **Table 4**). WIN55,212-2 increases time for extinction of CPP and enhances drug-induced reinstatement in MDMA-conditioned mice (285, 286). Similarly, Δ^9-THC increases cue-induced reinstatement of methamphetamine SA in rats (289). However, studies from Parker et al. and Adamczyk et al. complexify the interpretation of these results (290). Indeed, Adamczyk's group showed that FAAH inhibition impairs cue- and drug-induced reinstatement of cocaine SA. Using the place-preference conditioning paradigm, Parker et al. have assessed the potential of both exogenous cannabinoids – Δ^9-THC and CBD – to potentiate the extinction of cocaine- and amphetamine-induced CPP (290). After the establishment of cocaine-induced and amphetamine-induced place preference, rats were given an extinction trial, 30 min prior to which they were injected with a low dose of Δ^9-THC, CBD, or vehicle. During conditioning trials, researchers also injected rats with cannabinoids, or vehicle, prior to an amphetamine injection, to determine the effects of Δ^9-THC or CBD on the establishment and expression of a place preference. Results indicate that Δ^9-THC and CBD potentiate the extinction of stimulant-CPP learning, which is not mediated by an alteration of learning or retrieval. CBD does not have a reinforcing or hedonic property on its own, suggesting that it does not have the addictive potential of Δ^9-THC, a significant advantage in terms of therapeutic use. The non-reinforcing aspect of CBD has been replicated in studies looking at the co-administration of CBD and Δ^9-THC (212, 294). These discrepancies probably result from the lack of receptor selectivity in the methods used to enhanced cannabinoid signaling. Nonetheless, these experiments support a significant involvement of ECBS in the extinction and reinstatement of behaviors related to psychostimulant addiction. Overall, the positive results of CB1 antagonists on extinction and prevention of reinstatement of psychostimulant SA, combined with their lack of reinforcing properties, suggest a therapeutic potential for CB1 modulation in treatment of psychostimulant addiction.

CONCLUSION

A growing number of studies have investigated the neurobiological and behavioral mechanisms leading to psychostimulants dependence. A key feature of drug dependence is the relapse to drug use even after long period of abstinence. While greatly improved in recent years, treatment strategies for psychostimulants have

Table 4 | CB1 receptor agonists and properties of psychostimulants.

Agonists	Drugs	Models	Outcome	Effects	Reference
CP55,940	Cocaine	Mouse	SA – effect of agonist after drug-taking extinction	No effect	Vaughn et al. (276)
		Rat	SA – behavior acquisition following exposure during adolescence in female specimen	Enhanced	Higuera-Matas et al. (291)
	MDMA	Rat	SA – drug-seeking responses/intake	Decreased	Braida and Sala (288)
HU210	Cocaine	Rat	SA – effect of agonist after drug-taking extinction	Reinstatement	De Vries et al. (283)
Δ^9-THC	Amphet.	Rat	CPP – behavior acquisition	Preserved	Parker et al. (290)
			CPP – behavior extinction	Potentiated	Parker et al. (290)
	Cocaine	Monkey	SA – effect of agonist after drug-taking extinction	Reinstatement	Justinova et al. (260)
		Mouse	Drug-induced motor sensitization	Preserved	Gerdeman et al. (268)
		Rat	Drug-induced acute hyperlocomotion	Preserved	Panlilio et al. (272)
			Drug-induced motor sensitization	Preserved	Panlilio et al. (272)
			Drug-induced anxiety	Increased	Panlilio et al. (272)
			SA – behavior acquisition	Preserved	Panlilio et al. (272)
			SA – drug-seeking responses under PR schedule	Decreased	Panlilio et al. (272)
			CPP – behavior extinction	Potentiated	Parker et al. (290)
	METH	Rat	SA – cue-induced reinstatement	Increased	Anggadiredja et al. (289)
			SA – drug-induced reinstatement	Attenuated	Anggadiredja et al. (289)
WIN-55	Cocaine	Rat	Drug-induced acute hyperlocomotion	Attenuated	Przegalinski et al. (270), Vlachou et al. (252)
			Drug-induced lowering of brain reward/self-stimulation threshold	Impaired	Vlachou et al. (251)
			SA – drug-seeking responses/intake	Decreased	De Vries et al. (283)
	MDMA	Mouse	CPP – behavior acquisition	Increased	Rodriguez-Arias et al. (286)
			CPP – time for behavior extinction	Increased	Rodriguez-Arias et al. (286)
			CPP – drug-induced reinstatement	Increased	Rodriguez-Arias et al. (286), Daza-Losada et al. (285)

yet to address effectively drug-seeking behaviors linked to high rates of relapse, persistent drug use as well as subsequent health, mental, and social problems. There is consequently an urgent need for researchers to identify compounds that might help patients (1) initiate abstinence and (2) avoid relapse. The ECBS appears to play a critical role in dependence to psychostimulants and experimental studies are now providing evidence that while it does not participate in the primary reinforcing properties of psychostimulants, it reliably modulates relapse to drugs. Interestingly, emerging human data supports a role for ECBS modulation in vulnerability to psychostimulant addiction, and more significantly in addictive behaviors among dependent individuals. Accumulating evidence thus points to the ECBS as a critical target for the development of pharmacotherapies for the treatment of addiction to psychostimulants. Given the various neuropharmacological actions of exogenous cannabinoids, and their ability to modulate the acute reinforcing effects of drugs, data on Δ^9-THC and CBD is particularly promising as to the potential use of cannabinoids in relapse prevention strategies for psychostimulant-dependent individuals. The effects of these compounds on stimulant use outcomes in humans remains to be clearly established and could be assessed with well-designed controlled trials. The neurobiological correlates of cannabinoids' impact on stimulant-seeking behaviors could also be examined with neuroimaging studies in stimulants dependent individuals. Among potential barriers, social and scientific acceptability of cannabinoid-based therapy, side effects profiles, as well as addictive potential of certain cannabinoid such as Δ^9-THC, have to be taken into consideration.

ACKNOWLEDGMENTS

Stéphane Potvin is holder of a Junior 1 research award from the *Fonds de Recherche du Québec en Santé* (FRSQ). This work was supported by the CHUM Department of Psychiatry; Université de Montréal Department of Psychiatry; and the CHUM Research Center (Didier Jutras-Aswad).

REFERENCES

1. UNODC.*World Drug Report 2009*. Vienna: United Nations Office on Drugs and Crime (2009).
2. Substance Abuse and Mental Health Services Administration, Office of Applied Studies. *The DASIS Report: Geographic Differences in Substance Abuse Treatment Admissions for Methamphetamine/ Amphetamine and Marijuana: 2005*. Rockville,MD (2008).
3. Degenhardt L, Hall W. Extent of illicit drug use and dependence, and their contribution to the global burden of disease. *Lancet* (2012) 379:55–70. doi:10.1016/ S0140-6736(11)61138-0
4. UNODC. *World Drug Report*. Vienna: United Nations Publication (2012).
5. BenDiane MK,Feroni I, Poncet M, Obadia Y. Chief health risks associatedwith intravenous heroin and cocaine abuse. *Presse Med* (2000) 29:453–7.
6. Arendt M,Munk-Jorgensen P, Sher L, Jensen SO. Mortality among individuals with cannabis, cocaine, amphetamine,MDMA,and opioid use disorders: a nationwide followup study of Danish substance users in treatment. *Drug Alcohol Depend* (2011) 114(2–3):134– 9. doi:10.1016/j.drugalcdep.2010.09.013
7. Pavarin R, Lugoboni F, Mathewson S, Ferrari AM, Guizzardi G, Quaglio G. Cocainerelated medical and trauma problems: a consecutive series of 743 patients from a multicentre study in Italy. *Eur J Emerg Med* (2011) 18(4):208–14. doi:10.1097/ MEJ.0b013e3283440f25
8. Gorelick DA, Gardner EL, Xi ZX. Agents in development for the management of cocaine abuse. *Drugs* (2004) 64:1547–73. doi:10. 2165/00003495-200464140-00004
9. Vocci FJ, Elkashef A. Pharmacotherapy and other treatments for cocaine abuse and dependence. *Curr Opin Psychiatry* (2005) 18:265–70. doi:10.1097/01.yco. 0000165596.98552.02
10. Karila L, Gorelick D, Weinstein A, Noble F, Benyamina A, Coscas S, et al. New treatments for cocaine dependence: a focused review. *Int J Neuropsychopharmacol* (2008) 11:425–38. doi:10.1017/ S1461145707008097
11. Christopher Pierce R, O'Brien CP, Kenny PJ, Vanderschuren LJ. Rational development of addiction pharmacotherapies: successes, failures, and prospects. *Cold Spring Harb Perspect Med* (2012) 2:a012880. doi:10.1101/cshperspect.a012880
12. Lima MS, Reisser AA, Soares BG, Farrell M. Antidepressants for cocaine dependence. *Cochrane Database Syst Rev* (2003):CD002950.
13. Amato L, Minozzi S, Pani PP, Davoli M. Antipsychotic medications for cocaine dependence. *Cochrane Database Syst Rev* (2007):CD006306.
14. Minozzi S,Amato L,Davoli M,Farrell M, Lima Reisser AA, Pani PP, et al. Anticonvulsants for cocaine dependence. *Cochrane Database Syst Rev* (2008):CD006754. doi:10. 1002/14651858.CD006754.pub2
15. Xi ZX, Gardner EL. Hypothesisdriven medication discovery for the treatment of psychostimulant addiction. *Curr Drug Abuse Rev* (2008) 1:303–27. doi:10.2174/ 1874473710801030303
16. Perez-Mana C, Castells X, Vidal X, Casas M, Capella D. Efficacy of indirect dopamine agonists for psychostimulant dependence: a systematic review and meta-analysis of randomized controlled trials. *J Subst Abuse Treat* (2011) 40:109–22. doi:10.1016/j. jsat.2010.08.012
17. Martell BA, Orson FM, Poling J, Mitchell E, Rossen RD, Gardner T, et al. Cocaine vaccine for the treatment of cocaine dependence in methadone-maintained patients: a randomized, doubleblind, placebo-controlled efficacy trial. *Arch Gen Psychiatry* (2009) 66:1116–23. doi:10.1001/ archgenpsychiatry.2009.128
18. Ries RK, Fiellin DA, Miller SC, Saitz R. *Principles of Addiction Medecine*. 4th ed. Philadelphia: Lippincott Williams & Wilkins (2009). p. 707–22.
19. Gardner EL. Endocannabinoid signaling system and brain reward: emphasis on dopamine. *Pharmacol Biochem Behav* (2005) 81:263–84. doi:10.1016/j.pbb.2005.01.032
20. Heifets BD, Castillo PE. Endocannabinoid signaling and longterm synaptic plasticity. *Annu Rev Physiol* (2009) 71:283–306. doi:10.1146/annurev.physiol. 010908.163149
21. Lutz B. Endocannabinoid signals in the control of emotion. *Curr Opin Pharmacol* (2009) 9:46–52. doi:10.1016/j.coph.2008.12.001
22. Jutras-Aswad D, Zang G, Bruneau J. Cannabis use correlates of syringe sharing among injection drug users. *Am J Addict* (2010) 19:231–7. doi:10.1111/j.1521-0391.2010.00031.x
23. WHO. *Neuroscience of psychoactive substance use and dependence*. Geneva: World Health Organization (2004).
24. Hyman SM, Fox H,Hong KI,Doebrick C, Sinha R. Stress and drugcue- induced craving in opioiddependent individuals in naltrexone treatment. *Exp Clin Psychopharmacol* (2007) 15:134–43. doi:10.1037/1064-1297.15.2.134
25. O'Brien CP, Childress AR, Ehrman R, Robbins SJ. Conditioning factors in drug abuse: can they explain compulsion? *J Psychopharmacol* (1998) 12:15–22. doi:10. 1177/026988119801200103
26. Sinha R, Lacadie C, Skudlarski P, Fulbright RK, Rounsaville BJ, Kosten TR, et al. Neural activity associated with stress-induced cocaine craving: a functional magnetic resonance imaging study. *Psychopharmacology (Berl)* (2005) 183:171–80. doi:10.1007/s00213- 005-0147-8
27. Lingford-Hughes AR, Davies SJ, McIver S, Williams TM, Daglish MR, Nutt DJ. Addiction. *Br Med Bull* (2003) 65:209–22. doi:10. 1093/bmb/65.1.209
28. Robinson TE, Berridge KC. Addiction. *Annu Rev Psychol* (2003) 54:25–53. doi:10.1146/annurev. psych.54.101601.145237
29. Kalivas PW, Volkow ND. The neural basis of addiction: a pathology of motivation and choice. *Am J Psychiatry* (2005) 162:1403–13. doi:10.1176/appi.ajp.162.8.1403
30. Everitt BJ, Belin D, Economidou D, Pelloux Y, Dalley JW, Robbins TW. Review. Neural mechanisms underlying the vulnerability to develop compulsive drugseeking habits and addiction. *Philos Trans R Soc Lond B Biol Sci* (2008) 363:3125–35. doi:10.1098/ rstb.2008.0089
31. Feltenstein MW, See RE. The neurocircuitry of addiction: an overview. *Br J Pharmacol* (2008) 154:261–74. doi:10.1038/bjp.2008. 51
32. Chen PC, Lao CL, Chen JC. The D(3) dopamine receptor inhibits dopamine release in PC-12/hD3 cells by autoreceptor signaling via PP-2B, CK1, and Cdk-5. *J Neurochem* (2009) 110:1180–90. doi:10.1111/j.1471-4159.2009.06209.x
33. Di Chiara G. Nucleus accumbens shell and core dopamine: differential role in behavior and addiction. *Behav Brain Res* (2002) 137:75–114. doi:10.1016/S0166- 4328(02)00286-3
34. Meil WM, See RE. Lesions of the basolateral amygdala abolish the ability of drug associated cues to reinstate responding during withdrawal from selfadministered cocaine. *Behav Brain Res* (1997) 87:139–48. doi:10. 1016/S0166-4328(96)02270-X
35. Childress AR,Mozley PD,McElgin W, Fitzgerald J, Reivich M,O'Brien CP. Limbic activation during cueinduced cocaine craving. *AmJ Psychiatry* (1999) 156:11–8.
36. Robbins TW, Everitt BJ, Nutt DJ. Introduction. The neurobiology of drug addiction: new vistas. *Philos Trans R Soc Lond B Biol Sci* (2008) 363:3109–11. doi:10.1098/ rstb.2008.0108
37. Goldstein RZ, Volkow ND. Drug addiction and its underlying neurobiological basis: neuroimaging evidence for the involvement of the frontal cortex. *Am J Psychiatry* (2002) 159:1642–52. doi:10.1176/ appi.ajp.159.10.1642
38. Koob GF, Swerdlow NR. The functional output of the mesolimbic dopamine system. *Ann N Y Acad Sci* (1988) 537:216–27. doi:10. 1111/j.1749-6632.1988.tb42108.x
39. Volkow ND, Wang GJ, Fischman MW, Foltin RW, Fowler JS, Abumrad NN, et al. Relationship between subjective effects of cocaine and dopamine transporter occupancy. *Nature* (1997) 386:827–30. doi:10.1038/386827a0
40. Fowler JS, Volkow ND, Wang GJ, Gatley SJ, Logan J. [(11)]Cocaine: PET studies of cocaine pharmacokinetics, dopamine transporter availability and dopamine transporter occupancy. *Nucl Med Biol* (2001) 28:561–72. doi:10.1016/ S0969-8051(01)00211-6
41. Fleckenstein AE, Gibb JW,Hanson GR. Differential effects of stimulants on monoaminergic transporters: pharmacological consequences and implications for neurotoxicity. *Eur J Pharmacol* (2000) 406:1–13. doi:10.1016/S0014-2999(00)00639-7
42. Rothman RB, Baumann MH. Monoamine transporters and psychostimulant drugs. *Eur J Pharmacol* (2003) 479:23–40. doi:10.1016/ j.ejphar.2003.08.054
43. Rudnick G, Clark J. From synapse to vesicle: the reuptake and storage of biogenic amine neurotransmitters. *Biochim Biophys Acta* (1993) 1144:249–63. doi:10.1016/ 0005-2728(93)90109-S
44. Howell LL, Kimmel HL. Monoamine transporters and psychostimulant addiction. *Biochem Pharmacol* (2008) 75:196–217. doi:10.1016/j.bcp.2007.08.003
45. Barr AM, Panenka WJ, Macewan GW,Thornton AE, Lang DJ,Honer WG, et al. The need for speed: an update on methamphetamine addiction. *J Psychiatry Neurosci* (2006) 31:301–13.
46. Rocha BA, Fumagalli F, Gainetdinov RR, Jones SR, Ator R, Giros B, et al. Cocaine self-administration in dopamine-transporter knockout mice. *Nat Neurosci* (1998) 1:132–7. doi:10.1038/381

47. Sora I, Wichems C, Takahashi N, Li XF, Zeng Z, Revay R, et al. Cocaine reward models: conditioned place preference can be established in dopamine- and in serotonin-transporter knockout mice. *Proc Natl Acad Sci U S A* (1998) 95:7699–704. doi:10.1073/ pnas.95.13.7699
48. Lee B, Tiefenbacher S, Platt DM, Spealman RD. Role of the hypothalamic-pituitary-adrenal axis in reinstatement of cocaineseeking behavior in squirrel monkeys. *Psychopharmacology (Berl)* (2003) 168:177 83. doi:10.1007/ s00213-003-1391-4
49. Arnold JC. The role of endocannabinoid transmission in cocaine addiction. *Pharmacol BiochemBehav* (2005) 81:396–406. doi:10.1016/j.pbb.2005.02.015
50. Backstrom P, Hyytia P. Ionotropic and metabotropic glutamate receptor antagonism attenuates cue-induced cocaine seeking. *Neuropsychopharmacology* (2006) 31:778–86. doi:10.1038/sj.npp.1300845
51. Lingford-Hughes A, Nutt D. Neurobiology of addiction and implications for treatment. *Br J Psychiatry* (2003) 182:97–100. doi:10. 1192/bjp.182.2.97
52. Broderick PA, Olabisi OA, Rahni DN, Zhou Y. Cocaine acts on accumbens-monoamines and locomotor behavior via a 5-HT2A/2C receptor mechanism as shown by ketanserin: 24-h follow-up studies. *Prog Neuropsychopharmacol Biol Psychiatry* (2004) 28:547–57. doi: 10.1016/j.pnpbp.2004.01.007
53. Filip M. Role of serotonin (5- HT)2 receptors in cocaine selfadministration and seeking behavior in rats. *Pharmacol Rep* (2005) 57:35–46.
54. Wee S, Wang Z, He R, Zhou J, Kozikowski AP, Woolverton WL. Role of the increased noradrenergic neurotransmission in drug self-administration. *Drug Alcohol Depend* (2006) 82:151–7. doi:10.1016/j.drugalcdep.2005.09.002
55. Sora I, Hall FS, Andrews AM, Itokawa M, Li XF, Wei HB, et al. Molecular mechanisms of cocaine reward: combined dopamine and serotonin transporter knockouts eliminate cocaine place preference. *Proc Natl Acad Sci U S A* (2001) 98:5300–5. doi:10.1073/ pnas.091039298
56. Hall FS, Li XF, Sora I, Xu F, Caron M, Lesch KP, et al. Cocaine mechanisms: enhanced cocaine, fluoxetine and nisoxetine place preferences following monoamine transporter deletions.*Neuroscience* (2002) 115:153–61. doi:10.1016/ S0306-4522(02)00379-2
57. Shaham Y, Erb S, Stewart J. Stress-induced relapse to heroin and cocaine seeking in rats: a review. *Brain Res Brain Res Rev* (2000) 33:13–33. doi:10.1016/ S0165-0173(00)00024-2
58. Weinshenker D, Schroeder JP. There and back again: a tale of norepinephrine and drug addiction. *Neuropsychopharmacology* (2007) 32:1433–51. doi:10.1038/sj.npp. 1301263
59. Gaval-Cruz M, Weinshenker D. Mechanisms of disulfiraminduced cocaine abstinence: antabuse and cocaine relapse. *Mol Interv* (2009) 9:175–87. doi:10.1124/mi.9.4.6
60. Leri F, Flores J, Rodaros D, Stewart J. Blockade of stress-induced but not cocaine-induced reinstatement by infusion of noradrenergic antagonists into the bed nucleus of the stria terminalis or the central nucleus of the amygdala. *JNeurosci* (2002) 22:5713–8.
61. Smith RJ, Aston-Jones G. alpha(2) Adrenergic and imidazoline receptor agonists prevent cue-induced cocaine seeking. *Biol Psychiatry* (2011) 70:712–9. doi:10.1016/j. biopsych.2011.06.010
62. Parsons LH, Weiss F, Koob GF. Serotonin1b receptor stimulation enhances dopamine-mediated reinforcement. *Psychopharmacology (Berl)* (1996) 128:150–60. doi:10.1007/s002130050120
63. Tzschentke TM, Schmidt WJ. Glutamatergic mechanisms in addiction. *Mol Psychiatry* (2003) 8:373–82. doi:10.1038/sj.mp.4001269
64. Kalivas PW, Lalumiere RT, Knackstedt L, Shen H. Glutamate transmission in addiction. *Neuropharmacology* (2009) 56(Suppl 1):169–73. doi:10.1016/ j.neuropharm.2008.07.011
65. Sarti F, Borgland SL, Kharazia VN, Bonci A. Acute cocaine exposure alters spine density and longterm potentiation in the ventral tegmental area. *Eur J Neurosci* (2007) 26:749–56. doi:10.1111/j. 1460-9568.2007.05689.x
66. Chen Q, Xiong X, Lee TH, Liu Y, Wetsel WC, Zhang X. Neural plasticity and addiction: integrinlinked kinase and cocaine behavioral sensitization. *J Neurochem* (2008) 107:679–89. doi:10.1111/j. 1471-4159.2008.05619.x
67. Knackstedt LA, Kalivas PW. Glutamate and reinstatement.*CurrOpin Pharmacol* (2009) 9:59–64. doi:10. 1016/j.coph.2008.12.003
68. Novak M, Halbout B, O'Connor EC, Rodriguez Parkitna J, Su T, Chai M, et al. Incentive learning underlying cocaine-seeking requires mGluR5 receptors located on dopamine D1 receptorexpressing neurons. *J Neurosci* (2010) 30:11973–82. doi:10.1523/ JNEUROSCI.2550-10.2010
69. Baker DA, McFarland K, Lake RW, Shen H, Tang XC, Toda S, et al. Neuroadaptation in cystineglutamate exchange underlie cocaine relapse. *Nat Neurosci* (2003) 6:743–9. doi:10.1038/ nn1069
70. McFarland K, Lapish CC, Kalivas PW. Prefrontal glutamate release into the core of the nucleus accumbens mediates cocaine-induced reinstatement of drug-seeking behavior. *J Neurosci* (2003) 23:3531–7.
71. Cornish JL, Kalivas PW. Glutamate transmission in the nucleus accumbens mediates relapse in cocaine addiction. *J Neurosci* (2000) 20:RC89.
72. McFarland K, Davidge SB, Lapish CC, Kalivas PW. Limbic and motor circuitry underlying footshock-induced reinstatement of cocaine-seeking behavior. *J Neurosci* (2004) 24:1551 60. doi:10.1523/JNEUROSCI.4177- 03.2004
73. Backstrom P, Hyytia P. Involvement of AMPA/kainate, NMDA, and mGlu5 receptors in the nucleus accumbens core in cueinduced reinstatement of cocaine seeking in rats. *Psychopharmacology (Berl)* (2007) 192:571–80. doi: 10.1007/s00213-007-0753-8
74. DiChiara G,BassareoV,Fenu S,De Luca MA, Spina L, Cadoni C, et al. Dopamine and drug addiction: the nucleus accumbens shell connection. *Neuropharmacology* (2004) 47(Suppl 1):227–41. doi:10.1016/j. neuropharm.2004.06.032
75. Ito I, Kimura T, Watanabe S, Kirino Y, Ito E. Modulation of two oscillatory networks in the peripheral olfactory system by gamma-aminobutyric acid, glutamate, and acetylcholine in the terrestrial slug *Limax marginatus*. *J Neurobiol* (2004) 59:304–18. doi: 10.1002/neu.10328
76. Di Ciano P, Cardinal RN, Cowell RA, Little SJ, Everitt BJ. Differential involvement of NMDA, AMPA/kainate, and dopamine receptors in the nucleus accumbens core in the acquisition and performance of pavlovian approach behavior. *J Neurosci* (2001) 21:9471–7.
77. Kalivas PW, McFarland K. Brain circuitry and the reinstatement of cocaine-seeking behavior. *Psychopharmacology (Berl)* (2003) 168:44–56. doi:10.1007/s00213-003-1393-2
78. Robbins TW, Everitt BJ. Neurobehavioural mechanisms of reward and motivation. *Curr Opin Neurobiol* (1996) 6:228–36. doi:10.1016/ S0959-4388(96)80077-8
79. Jentsch JD, Taylor JR. Impulsivity resulting from frontostriatal dysfunction in drug abuse: implications for the control of behavior by reward-related stimuli. *Psychopharmacology (Berl)* (1999) 146:373–90. doi:10.1007/PL00005483
80. Rogers RD, Ramnani N, Mackay C, Wilson JL, Jezzard P, Carter CS, et al. Distinct portions of anterior cingulate cortex and medial prefrontal cortex are activated by reward processing in separable phases of decision-making cognition. *Biol Psychiatry* (2004) 55:594–602. doi:10.1016/j. biopsych.2003.11.012
81. Dom G, Hulstijn W, Sabbe B. Differences in impulsivity and sensation seeking between early- and late-onsetalcoholics. *Addict Behav* (2006) 31:298–308. doi:10.1016/j. addbeh.2005.05.009
82. Yucel M, Lubman DI. Neurocognitive and neuroimaging evidence of behavioural dysregulation in human drug addiction: implications for diagnosis, treatment and prevention.*DrugAlcohol Rev* (2007) 26:33–9. doi:10.1080/ 09595230601036978
83. KiltsCD, Schweitzer JB, Quinn CK, Gross RE, Faber TL,Muhammad F, et al.Neural activity related to drug craving in cocaine addiction. *Arch Gen Psychiatry* (2001) 58:334–41. doi:10.1001/archpsyc.58.4.334
84. Sinha R, Lacadie C, Skudlarski P, Wexler BE. Neural circuits underlying emotional distress in humans. *Ann N Y Acad Sci* (2004) 1032:254–7. doi:10.1196/ annals.1314.032
85. Ersche KD, Barnes A, Jones PS, Morein-Zamir S, Robbins TW, Bullmore ET. Abnormal structure of frontostriatal brain systems is associated with aspects of impulsivity and compulsivity in cocaine dependence. *Brain* (2011) 134:2013–24. doi:10.1093/ brain/awr138
86. Xu J, Devito EE, Worhunsky PD, Carroll KM, Rounsaville BJ, Potenza MN. White matter integrity is associated with treatment outcomemeasures in cocaine dependence. *Neuropsychopharmacology* (2010) 35:1541–9. doi:10. 1038/npp.2010.25
87. Phan KL, Wager T, Taylor SF, Liberzon I. Functional neuroanatomy of emotion: a metaanalysis of emotion activation studies in PET and fMRI. *Neuroimage* (2002) 16:331–48. doi:10.1006/nimg.2002.1087
88. Sinha R, Rounsaville BJ. Sex differences in depressed substance abusers. *J Clin Psychiatry* (2002) 63:616–27. doi:10.4088/ JCP.v63n0715
89. Tanda G. Modulation of the endocannabinoid system: therapeutic potential against cocaine dependence. *Pharmacol Res* (2007) 56:406–17. doi:10.1016/j. phrs.2007.09.001
90. Labigalini E Jr, Rodrigues LR, Da Silveira DX. Therapeutic use of cannabis by crack addicts in Brazil. *J Psychoactive Drugs* (1999) 31:451–5. doi:10.1080/02791072. 1999.10471776
91. Aharonovich E, Liu X, Samet S, Nunes E, Waxman R, Hasin D. Postdischarge cannabis use and its relationship to cocaine, alcohol, and heroin use: a prospective study. *Am J Psychiatry* (2005) 162: 1507–14. doi:10.1176/appi. ajp. 162.8.1507

92. Pacher P, Batkai S, Kunos G. The endocannabinoid system as an emerging target of pharmacotherapy. *Pharmacol Rev* (2006) 58:389–462. doi:10.1124/pr.58.3.2
93. Herkenham M, Lynn A, Little M, Johnson M, Melvin L, De Costa B, et al. Cannabinoid receptor localization in brain. *Proc Natl Acad Sci USA* (1990) 87:1932. doi:10.1073/ pnas.87.5.1932
94. Howlett AC, Bidaut-Russell M, Devane WA, Melvin LS, Johnson MR, Herkenham M. The cannabinoid receptor: biochemical, anatomical and behavioral characterization. *Trends Neurosci* (1990) 13:420–3. doi:10.1016/ 0166-2236(90)90124-S
95. Herkenham M, Lynn AB,De Costa BR, Richfield EK. Neuronal localization of cannabinoid receptors in the basal ganglia of the rat. *Brain Res* (1991) 547:267–74. doi: 10.1016/0006-8993(91)90970-7
96. Herkenham M, Lynn AB, Johnson MR,Melvin LS, De Costa BR, Rice KC. Characterization and localization of cannabinoid receptors in rat brain: a quantitative in vitro autoradiographic study. *J Neurosci* (1991) 11:563–83.
97. Batkai S, Jarai Z, Wagner JA, Goparaju SK, Varga K, Liu J, et al. Endocannabinoids acting at vascular CB1 receptors mediate the vasodilated state in advanced liver cirrhosis. *Nat Med* (2001) 7:827–32. doi:10.1038/89953
98. Alger BE. Retrograde signaling in the regulation of synaptic transmission: focus on endocannabinoids. *Prog Neurobiol* (2002) 68:247–86. doi:10.1016/S0301-0082(02)00080-1
99. Szabo B, Schlicker E. Effects of cannabinoids on neurotransmission. *Handb Exp Pharmacol* (2005) 168:327–65. doi:10.1007/3- 540-26573-2_11
100. Vaughan CW, Christie MJ. Retrograde signalling by endocannabinoids. *Handb Exp Pharmacol* (2005) 168:367–83. doi:10.1007/3- 540-26573-2_12
101. Kano H, Niranjan A, Novotny J Jr, Bhatnagar J, Flickinger JC, Lunsford LD. Radiosurgery for desmoplastic melanoma of the head and neck using the Leksell Gamma Knife Perfexion technology: a case report. *Stereotact Funct Neurosurg* (2009) 87:61–5. doi:10. 1159/000195721
102. Munro S, Thomas KL, Abu-Shaar M. Molecular characterization of a peripheral receptor for cannabinoids. *Nature* (1993) 365:61–5. doi:10.1038/365061a0
103. Galiegue S, Mary S, Marchand J, Dussossoy D, Carriere D, Carayon P, et al. Expression of central and peripheral cannabinoid receptors in human immune tissues and leukocyte subpopulations. *Eur J Biochem* (1995) 232:54–61. doi:10. 1111/j.1432-1033.1995.tb20780.x
104. Fride E, Foox A, Rosenberg E, Faigenboim M, Cohen V, Barda L, et al. Milk intake and survival in newborn cannabinoid CB1 receptor knockout mice: evidence for a "CB3" receptor. *Eur J Pharmacol* (2003) 461:27–34. doi:10.1016/ S0014-2999(03)01295-0
105. Onaivi ES, Ishiguro H, Gong JP, Patel S, Perchuk A, Meozzi PA, et al. Discovery of the presence and functional expression of cannabinoid CB2 receptors in brain. *Ann N Y Acad Sci* (2006) 1074:514–36. doi:10.1196/annals.1369.052
106. Ashton JC, Glass M. The cannabinoid CB2 receptor as a target for inflammation-dependent neurodegeneration. *Curr Neuropharmacol* (2007) 5:73–80. doi:10. 2174/157015907780866884
107. Onaivi ES, Ishiguro H, Gong JP, Patel S, Meozzi PA, Myers L, et al. Brain neuronal CB2 cannabinoid receptors in drug abuse and depression: from mice to human subjects. *PLoS ONE* (2008) 3:e1640. doi:10.1371/ journal.pone.0001640
108. Witting A, Walter L, Wacker J, Moller T, Stella N. P2X7 receptors control 2-arachidonoylglycerol production by microglial cells. *Proc Natl Acad Sci U S A* (2004) 101:3214–9. doi:10.1073/pnas.0306707101
109. Maresz K, Pryce G, Ponomarev ED, Marsicano G, Croxford JL, Shriver LP, et al.Direct suppression of CNS autoimmune inflammation via the cannabinoid receptor CB1 on neurons and CB2 on autoreactive T cells. *Nat Med* (2007) 13:492–7. doi:10.1038/nm1561
110. Cabral GA, Raborn ES, Griffin L, Dennis J, Marciano-Cabral F. CB2 receptors in the brain: role in central immune function. *Br J Pharmacol* (2008) 153:240–51. doi:10. 1038/sj.bjp.0707584
111. Racz I, Bilkei-Gorzo A, Markert A, Stamer F, Gothert M, Zimmer A.Anandamide effects on 5-HT(3) receptors in vivo. *Eur J Pharmacol* (2008) 596:98–101. doi:10.1016/j. ejphar.2008.08.012
112. Atwood BK, Mackie K. CB2: a cannabinoid receptor with an identity crisis. *Br J Pharmacol* (2010) 160:467–79. doi:10.1111/j. 1476-5381.2010.00729.x
113. Stella N. Cannabinoid and cannabinoid-like receptors in microglia, astrocytes, and astrocytomas. *Glia* (2010) 58:1017–30. doi:10.1002/glia.20983
114. Marsicano G, Moosmann B, Hermann H, Lutz B, Behl C. Neuroprotective properties of cannabinoids against oxidative stress: role of the cannabinoid receptor CB1. *J Neurochem* (2002) 80:448–56. doi:10.1046/j.0022-3042.2001.00716.x
115. Begg M, Pacher P, Batkai S, Osei- Hyiaman D, Offertaler L, Mo FM, et al. Evidence for novel cannabinoid receptors. *Pharmacol Ther* (2005) 106:133–45. doi:10.1016/j. pharmthera.2004.11.005
116. Cristino L, De Petrocellis L, Pryce G, Baker D, Guglielmotti V, Di Marzo V. Immunohistochemical localization of cannabinoid type 1 and vanilloid transient receptor potential vanilloid type 1 receptors in the mouse brain. *Neuroscience* (2006) 139:1405–15. doi:10.1016/ j.neuroscience.2006.02.074
117. Brown AJ. Low-carb diets, fasting and euphoria: is there a link between ketosis and gammahydroxybutyrate (GHB)? *Med Hypotheses* (2007) 68:268–71. doi:10.1016/j.mehy.2006.07.043
118. Godlewski G, Offertaler L, Osei- Hyiaman D, Mo FM, Harvey- White J, Liu J, et al. The endogenous brain constituent Narachidonoyl L-serine is an activator of large conductance Ca2+- activatedK+channels. *J Pharmacol Exp Ther* (2009) 328:351–61. doi: 10.1124/jpet.108.144717
119. JohnsDG, Behm DJ,Walker DJ,Ao Z, Shapland EM, Daniels DA, et al. The novel endocannabinoid receptor GPR55 is activated by atypical cannabinoids but does notmediate their vasodilator effects. *Br J Pharmacol* (2007) 152:825–31. doi:10. 1038/sj.bjp.0707419
120. Kapur A, Hurst DP, Fleischer D, Whitnell R,Thakur GA,Makriyannis A, et al. Mutation studies of Ser7.39 and Ser2.60 in the human CB1 cannabinoid receptor: evidence for a serine-induced bend in CB1 transmembrane helix 7. *Mol Pharmacol* (2007) 71:1512–24. doi:10.1124/mol.107. 034645
121. Ryberg E, Larsson N, Sjogren S, Hjorth S, Hermansson NO, Leonova J, et al. The orphan receptor GPR55 is a novel cannabinoid receptor. *Br J Pharmacol* (2007) 152:1092–101. doi:10.1038/sj.bjp. 0707460
122. Giuffrida A, Seillier A. New insights on endocannabinoid transmission in psychomotor disorders. *Prog Neuropsychopharmacol Biol Psychiatry* (2012) 38:51–8. doi:10.1016/j.pnpbp.2012.04.002
123. Sylantyev S, Jensen TP, Ross RA, Rusakov DA. Cannabinoidand lysophosphatidylinositolsensitive receptor GPR55 boosts neurotransmitter release at central synapses. *Proc Natl Acad Sci U S A* (2013) 110:5193–8. doi:10.1073/pnas.1211204110
124. Patapoutian A, Tate S, Woolf CJ. Transient receptor potential channels: targeting pain at the source. *Nat Rev Drug Discov* (2009) 8:55–68. doi:10.1038/nrd2757
125. Mezey E, Toth ZE, Cortright DN, Arzubi MK,Krause JE, Elde R, et al. Distribution of mRNA for vanilloid receptor subtype 1 (VR1), and VR1-like immunoreactivity, in the central nervous system of the rat and human. *Proc Natl Acad Sci U S A* (2000) 97:3655–60. doi:10.1073/ pnas.97.7.3655
126. Szolcsanyi J. Anandamide and the question of its functional role for activation of capsaicin receptors. *Trends Pharmacol Sci* (2000) 21:203–4. doi:10.1016/ S0165-6147(00)01484-X
127. De Petrocellis L, Harrison S, Bisogno T, Tognetto M, Brandi I, Smith GD, et al. The vanilloid receptor (VR1)-mediated effects of anandamide are potently enhanced by the cAMP-dependent protein kinase. *J Neurochem* (2001) 77:1660–3. doi:10.1046/j. 1471-4159.2001.00406.x
128. Huang SM, Bisogno T, Trevisani M, Al-Hayani A, De Petrocellis L, Fezza F, et al. An endogenous capsaicin-like substance with high potency at recombinant and native vanilloid VR1 receptors. *Proc Natl Acad Sci U S A* (2002) 99:8400–5. doi:10.1073/pnas.122196999
129. Maccarrone M, Rossi S, Bari M, De Chiara V, Fezza F, Musella A, et al. Anandamide inhibits metabolism and physiological actions of 2-arachidonoylglycerol in the striatum. *Nat Neurosci* (2008) 11:152–9. doi:10.1038/nn2042
130. Gerdeman GL, Ronesi J, Lovinger DM. Postsynaptic endocannabinoid release is critical to long-term depression in the striatum. *Nat Neurosci* (2002) 5:446–51.
131. Gubellini P, Picconi B, Bari M, Battista N, Calabresi P, Centonze D, et al. Experimental parkinsonism alters endocannabinoid degradation: implications for striatal glutamatergic transmission. *J Neurosci* (2002) 22:6900–7.
132. Ohno-Shosaku T, Maejima T, Kano M. Endogenous cannabinoids mediate retrograde signals fromdepolarized postsynaptic neurons to presynaptic terminals. *Neuron* (2001) 29:729–38. doi:10. 1016/S0896-6273(01)00247-1
133. Wilson RI, Nicoll RA. Endogenous cannabinoids mediate retrograde signalling at hippocampal synapses. *Nature* (2001) 410:588–92. doi:10.1038/35069076
134. Kreitzer AC, Regehr WG. Cerebellar depolarization-induced suppression of inhibition is mediated by endogenous cannabinoids. *J Neurosci* (2001) 21:RC174.
135. Devane WA, Hanus L, Breuer A, Pertwee RG, Stevenson LA, Griffin G, et al. Isolation and structure of a brain constituent that binds to the cannabinoid receptor. *Science* (1992) 258:1946–9. doi:10. 1126/science.1470919

136. Sugiura T, Kondo S, Sukagawa A, Nakane S, Shinoda A, Itoh K, et al. 2-Arachidonoylglycerol: a possible endogenous cannabinoid receptor ligand in brain. *Biochem Biophys Res Commun* (1995) 215:89–97. doi:10.1006/bbrc.1995.2437
137. Hanus L, Abu-Lafi S, Fride E, Breuer A, Vogel Z, Shalev DE, et al. 2-Arachidonyl glyceryl ether, an endogenous agonist of the cannabinoid CB1 receptor. *Proc Natl Acad Sci U S A* (2001) 98:3662–5. doi:10.1073/pnas.061029898
138. Porter AC, Sauer JM, Knierman MD, Becker GW, Berna MJ, Bao J, et al. Characterization of a novel endocannabinoid, virodhamine, with antagonist activity at the CB1 receptor. *J Pharmacol Exp Ther* (2002) 301:1020–4. doi:10.1124/jpet.301.3.1020
139. Wilson RI, Kunos G, Nicoll RA. Presynaptic specificity of endocannabinoid signaling in the hippocampus. *Neuron* (2001) 31:453–62. doi:10.1016/S0896- 6273(01)00372-5
140. Okamoto Y, Wang J, Morishita J, Ueda N. Biosynthetic pathways of the endocannabinoid anandamide. *Chem Biodivers* (2007) 4:1842–57. doi:10.1002/cbdv.200790155
141. Tanimura A, Yamazaki M, Hashimotodani Y, Uchigashima M, Kawata S, Abe M, et al. The endocannabinoid 2- arachidonoylglycerol produced by diacylglycerol lipase alpha mediates retrograde suppression of synaptic transmission. *Neuron* (2010) 65:320–7. doi:10.1016/j.neuron.2010.01.021
142. Fride E. Endocannabinoids in the central nervous system: from neuronal networks to behavior. *Curr Drug Targets CNS Neurol Disord* (2005) 4:633–42. doi:10.2174/ 156800705774933069
143. Hillard CJ. Biochemistry and pharmacology of the endocannabinoids arachidonylethanolamide and 2-arachidonylglycerol. *Prostaglandins Other Lipid Mediat* (2000) 61:3–18. doi:10.1016/ S0090-6980(00)00051-4
144. Cravatt BF, Giang DK, Mayfield SP, Boger DL, Lerner RA, Gilula NB. Molecular characterization of an enzyme that degrades neuromodulatory fatty-acid amides. *Nature* (1996) 384:83–7. doi:10. 1038/384083a0
145. Nomura DK, Blankman JL, Simon GM, Fujioka K, Issa RS, Ward AM, et al. Activation of the endocannabinoid system by organophosphorus nerve agents. *Nat Chem Biol* (2008) 4:373–8. doi:10.1038/nchembio.86
146. Blankman JL, Simon GM, Cravatt BF. A comprehensive profile of brain enzymes that hydrolyze the endocannabinoid 2-arachidonoylglycerol. *Chem Biol* (2007) 14:1347–56. doi:10.1016/j. chembiol.2007.11.006
147. Marrs WR, Blankman JL, Horne EA, Thomazeau A, Lin YH, Coy J, et al. The serine hydrolase ABHD6 controls the accumulation and efficacy of 2-AG at cannabinoid receptors. *Nat Neurosci* (2010) 13:951–7. doi:10.1038/nn.2601
148. McKinney MK, Cravatt BF. Structure and function of fatty acid amide hydrolase. *Annu Rev Biochem* (2005) 74:411–32. doi:10.1146/annurev.biochem.74. 082803.133450
149. Fegley D, Gaetani S, Duranti A, Tontini A, Mor M, Tarzia G, et al. Characterization of the fatty acid amide hydrolase inhibitor cyclohexyl carbamic acid 3-carbamoyl-biphenyl-3-yl ester (URB597): effects on anandamide and oleoylethanolamide deactivation. *J Pharmacol Exp Ther* (2005) 313:352–8. doi:10.1124/jpet.104.078980
150. Straiker A,Hu SS, Long JZ, Arnold A, Wager-Miller J, Cravatt BF, et al. Monoacylglycerol lipase limits the duration of endocannabinoidmediated depolarization-induced suppression of excitation in autaptic hippocampal neurons. *Mol Pharmacol* (2009) 76:1220–7. doi: 10.1124/mol.109.059030
151. Ahn K, Johnson DS, Mileni M, Beidler D, Long JZ, McKinney MK, et al. Discovery and characterization of a highly selective FAAH inhibitor that reduces inflammatory pain. *Chem Biol* (2009) 16:411–20. doi:10.1016/j.chembiol.2009.02.013
152. Piomelli D, Tarzia G, Duranti A, Tontini A, Mor M, Compton TR, et al. Pharmacological profile of the selective FAAH inhibitor KDS-4103 (URB597). *CNS Drug Rev* (2006) 12:21–38. doi:10.1111/ j.1527-3458.2006.00021.x
153. Kinsey SG, O'Neal ST, Long JZ, Cravatt BF, Lichtman AH. Inhibition of endocannabinoid catabolic enzymes elicits anxiolyticlike effects in the marble burying assay. *Pharmacol Biochem Behav* (2011) 98:21–7. doi:10.1016/j.pbb. 2010.12.002
154. Naidu PS,Kinsey SG,Guo TL,Cravatt BF, Lichtman AH. Regulation of inflammatory pain by inhibition of fatty acid amide hydrolase. *J Pharmacol Exp Ther* (2010) 334:182–90. doi:10.1124/jpet.109. 164806
155. Long JZ, Nomura DK, Vann RE, Walentiny DM, Booker L, Jin X, et al. Dual blockade of FAAHandMAGLidentifies behavioral processes regulated by endocannabinoid crosstalk in vivo. *Proc Natl Acad Sci U S A* (2009) 106:20270–5. doi:10.1073/ pnas.0909411106
156. Schlosburg JE, Blankman JL, Long JZ,Nomura DK, Pan B, Kinsey SG, et al. Chronic monoacylglycerol lipase blockade causes functional antagonism of the endocannabinoid system. *Nat Neurosci* (2010) 13:1113–9. doi:10.1038/nn.2616
157. Chanda PK, Gao Y, Mark L, Btesh J, Strassle BW, Lu P, et al. Monoacylglycerol lipase activity is a critical modulator of the tone and integrity of the endocannabinoid system. *Mol Pharmacol* (2010) 78:996–1003. doi:10.1124/mol.110.068304
158. Pan B, Wang W, Zhong P, Blankman JL, Cravatt BF, Liu QS. Alterations of endocannabinoid signaling, synaptic plasticity, learning, andmemory inmonoacylglycerol lipase knock-out mice. *J Neurosci* (2011) 31:13420–30. doi:10. 1523/JNEUROSCI.2075-11.2011
159. Watson SJ, Benson JA Jr, Joy JE. Marijuana and medicine: assessing the science base: a summary of the 1999 Institute of Medicine report. *Arch Gen Psychiatry* (2000) 57:547–52. doi:10.1001/archpsyc. 57.6.547
160. Zuardi AW, Crippa JA, Hallak JE, Moreira FA, Guimaraes FS. Cannabidiol, a Cannabis sativa constituent, as an antipsychotic drug. *Braz J Med Biol Res* (2006) 39:421–9. doi:10.1590/S0100- 879X2006000400001
161. Curran HV, Brignell C, Fletcher S, Middleton P, Henry J. Cognitive and subjective dose-response effects of acute oral Delta 9- tetrahydrocannabinol (THC) in infrequent cannabis users. *Psychopharmacology (Berl)* (2002) 164:61–70. doi:10.1007/s00213- 002-1169-0
162. Fried PA, Smith AM. A literature review of the consequences of prenatal marihuana exposure. An emerging theme of a deficiency in aspects of executive function. *Neurotoxicol Teratol* (2001) 23:1–11. doi:10.1016/ S0892-0362(00)00119-7
163. Arseneault L, Cannon M, Poulton R, Murray R, Caspi A, Moffitt TE. Cannabis use in adolescence and risk for adult psychosis: longitudinal prospective study. *BMJ* (2002) 325:1212–3. doi:10.1136/bmj.325. 7374.1212
164. Kandel DB. Does marijuana use cause the use of other drugs? *JAMA* (2003) 289:482–3. doi:10. 1001/jama.289.4.482
165. Huizink AC, Mulder EJ. Maternal smoking, drinking or cannabis use during pregnancy and neurobehavioral and cognitive functioning in human offspring. *Neurosci Biobehav Rev* (2006) 30: 24–41. doi:10.1016/j.neubiorev. 2005.04.005
166. D'Souza DC, Perry E, Macdougall L, Ammerman Y, Cooper T, Wu YT, et al. The psychotomimetic effects of intravenous delta-9- tetrahydrocannabinol in healthy individuals: implications for psychosis. *Neuropsychopharmacology* (2004) 29:1558–72. doi:10.1038/sj. npp.1300496
167. D'Souza DC, Ranganathan M, Braley G, Gueorguieva R, Zimolo Z, Cooper T, et al. Blunted psychotomimetic and amnestic effects of delta-9-tetrahydrocannabinol in frequent users of cannabis. *Neuropsychopharmacology* (2008) 33:2505–16. doi:10.1038/sj.npp. 1301643
168. Compton DR, Johnson MR, Melvin LS, Martin BR. Pharmacological profile of a series of bicyclic cannabinoid analogs: classification as cannabimimetic agents. *J Pharmacol Exp Ther* (1992) 260:201–9.
169. Williamson EM, Evans FJ. Cannabinoids in clinical practice. *Drugs* (2000) 60:1303–14. doi:10. 2165/00003495-200060060-00005
170. Guimaraes FS, De Aguiar JC, Mechoulam R, Breuer A. Anxiolytic effect of cannabidiol derivatives in the elevated plus-maze. *Gen Pharmacol* (1994) 25:161–4. doi:10.1016/0306-3623(94) 90027-2
171. Russo EB, Burnett A, Hall B, Parker KK. Agonistic properties of cannabidiol at 5-HT1a receptors. *NeurochemRes* (2005) 30:1037–43. doi:10.1007/s11064-005-6978-1
172. Moreira FA, Aguiar DC, Guimaraes FS. Anxiolytic-like effect of cannabidiol in the rat Vogel conflict test. *Prog Neuropsychopharmacol Biol Psychiatry* (2006) 30:1466–71. doi:10.1016/j.pnpbp.2006.06.004
173. Hermann D, Sartorius A, Welzel H, Walter S, Skopp G, Ende G, et al. Dorsolateral prefrontal cortex N-acetylaspartate/total creatine (NAA/tCr) loss in male recreational cannabis users. *Biol Psychiatry* (2007) 61:1281–9. doi:10. 1016/j.biopsych.2006.08.027
174. El-Alfy AT, Ivey K, Robinson K, Ahmed S, Radwan M, Slade D, et al. Antidepressant-like effect of delta9-tetrahydrocannabinol and other cannabinoids isolated from Cannabis sativa L. *Pharmacol Biochem Behav* (2010) 95:434–42. doi:10.1016/j.pbb.2010.03.004
175. Long LE, Chesworth R, Huang XF, McGregor IS, Arnold JC, Karl T. A behavioural comparison of acute and chronic Delta9-tetrahydrocannabinol and cannabidiol in C57BL/6JArc mice. *Int J Neuropsychopharmacol* (2010) 13:861–76. doi:10.1017/S1461145709990605
176. Zanelati TV, Biojone C, Moreira FA, Guimaraes FS, Joca SR. Antidepressant-like effects of cannabidiol in mice: possible involvement of 5-HT1A receptors. *Br J Pharmacol* (2010) 159:122–8. doi:10.1111/j.1476-5381.2009. 00521.x

177. Thomas A, Baillie GL, Phillips AM, Razdan RK, Ross RA, Pertwee RG. Cannabidiol displays unexpectedly high potency as an antagonist of CB1 and CB2 receptor agonists in vitro. *Br J Pharmacol* (2007) 150:613–23. doi:10.1038/sj. bjp.0707133
178. Pertwee RG. The diverse CB1 and CB2 receptor pharmacology of three plant cannabinoids: delta9-tetrahydrocannabinol, cannabidiol and delta9-tetrahydrocannabivarin. *Br J Pharmacol* (2008) 153:199–215. doi:10.1038/sj.bjp.0707442
179. Qin N, Neeper MP, Liu Y, Hutchinson TL, Lubin ML, Flores CM. TRPV2 is activated by cannabidiol and mediates CGRP release in cultured rat dorsal root ganglion neurons. *J Neurosci* (2008) 28:6231–8. doi:10. 1523/JNEUROSCI.0504-08.2008
180. Bisogno T, Hanus L, De Petrocellis L, Tchilibon S, Ponde DE, Brandi I, et al. Molecular targets for cannabidiol and its synthetic analogues: effect on vanilloid VR1 receptors and on the cellular uptake and enzymatic hydrolysis of anandamide. *Br J Pharmacol* (2001) 134:845–52. doi:10.1038/sj. bjp.0704327
181. Pandolfo P, Silveirinha V, Dos Santos-Rodrigues A, Venance L, Ledent C, Takahashi RN, et al. Cannabinoids inhibit the synaptic uptake of adenosine and dopamine in the rat and mouse striatum. *Eur J Pharmacol* (2011) 655:38–45. doi:10.1016/j.ejphar.2011.01.013
182. Murillo-Rodriguez E, Palomero- Rivero M, Millan-Aldaco D, Mechoulam R, Drucker-Colin R. Effects on sleep and dopamine levels of microdialysis perfusion of cannabidiol into the lateral hypothalamus of rats. *Life Sci* (2011) 88:504–11. doi:10.1016/j.lfs.2011.01.013
183. Kathmann M, Flau K, Redmer A, Trankle C, Schlicker E. Cannabidiol is an allosteric modulator at mu- and delta-opioid receptors. *Naunyn Schmiedebergs Arch Pharmacol* (2006) 372:354–61. doi:10. 1007/s00210-006-0033-x
184. Carrier EJ, Auchampach JA, Hillard CJ. Inhibition of an equilibrative nucleoside transporter by cannabidiol: a mechanism of cannabinoid immunosuppression. *Proc Natl Acad Sci U S A* (2006) 103:7895–900. doi:10.1073/pnas.0511232103
185. Rodriguez JJ,Mackie K, PickelVM. Ultrastructural localization of the CB1 cannabinoid receptor in muopioid receptor patches of the rat Caudate putamen nucleus. *J Neurosci* (2001) 21:823–33.
186. Schoffelmeer AN, Hogenboom F, Wardeh G, De Vries TJ. Interactions between CB1 cannabinoid and mu opioid receptors mediating inhibition of neurotransmitter release in rat nucleus accumbens core. *Neuropharmacology* (2006) 51:773–81. doi:10.1016/j.neuropharm.2006. 05.019
187. Hampson AJ,Grimaldi M,Axelrod J, Wink D. Cannabidiol and (-)Delta 9-tetrahydrocannabinol are neuroprotective antioxidants. *Proc Natl Acad Sci U S A* (1998) 95:8268–73. doi:10.1073/pnas.95.14.8268
188. Hallak JE,Dursun SM,BosiDC,De Macedo LR, Machado-De-Sousa JP, Abrao J, et al. The interplay of cannabinoid and NMDA glutamate receptor systems in humans: preliminary evidence of interactive effects of cannabidiol and ketamine in healthy human subjects. *Prog Neuropsychopharmacol Biol Psychiatry* (2011) 35:198–202. doi:10.1016/j.pnpbp.2010.11.002
189. Campos AC, Guimaraes FS. Involvement of 5HT1A receptors in the anxiolytic-like effects of cannabidiol injected into the dorsolateral periaqueductal gray of rats. *Psychopharmacology (Berl)* (2008) 199:223–30. doi:10.1007/s00213-008-1168-x
190. Alves FH, Crestani CC, Gomes FV, Guimaraes FS, Correa FM, Resstel LB. Cannabidiol injected into the bed nucleus of the stria terminalis modulates baroreflex activity through 5-HT1A receptors. *Pharmacol Res* (2010) 62:228–36. doi: 10.1016/j.phrs.2010.05.003
191. Magen I, Avraham Y, Ackerman Z, Vorobiev L, Mechoulam R, Berry EM. Cannabidiol ameliorates cognitive and motor impairments in bile-duct ligated mice via 5-HT1A receptor activation. *Br J Pharmacol* (2010) 159:950–7. doi:10.1111/ j.1476-5381.2009.00589.x
192. Soares Vde P, Campos AC, Bortoli VC, Zangrossi H Jr, Guimaraes FS, Zuardi AW. Intra-dorsal periaqueductal gray administration of cannabidiol blocks panic-like response by activating 5-HT1A receptors. *Behav Brain Res* (2010) 213:225–9. doi:10.1016/j.bbr.2010. 05.004
193. Gomes FV, Reis DG, Alves FH, Correa FM, Guimaraes FS, Resstel LB. Cannabidiol injected into the bed nucleus of the stria terminalis reduces the expression of contextual fear conditioning via 5- HT1A receptors. *J Psychopharmacol* (2012) 26:104–13. doi:10.1177/ 0269881110389095
194. Guimaraes FS, Chiaretti TM, Graeff FG, Zuardi AW. Antianxiety effect of cannabidiol in the elevated plus-maze. *Psychopharmacology (Berl)* (1990) 100:558–9. doi:10.1007/BF02244012
195. Granjeiro EM, Gomes FV, Guimaraes FS, Correa FM, Resstel LB. Effects of intracisternal administration of cannabidiol on the cardiovascular and behavioral responses to acute restraint stress. *Pharmacol Biochem Behav* (2011) 99:743–8. doi:10.1016/j.pbb.2011.06.027
196. Fusar-Poli P, Crippa JA, Bhattacharyya S, Borgwardt SJ, Allen P, Martin-Santos R, et al. Distinct effects of {delta}9-tetrahydrocannabinol and cannabidiol on neural activation during emotional processing. *Arch Gen Psychiatry* (2009) 66:95–105. doi:10. 1001/archgenpsychiatry.2008.519
197. Crippa JA,ZuardiAW, Garrido GE, Wichert-Ana L, Guarnieri R, Ferrari L, et al. Effects of cannabidiol (CBD) on regional cerebral blood flow. *Neuropsychopharmacology* (2004) 29:417–26. doi:10. 1038/sj.npp.1300340
198. Crippa JA, Derenusson GN, Ferrari TB, Wichert-Ana L, Duran FL, Martin-Santos R, et al. Neural basis of anxiolytic effects of cannabidiol (CBD) in generalized social anxiety disorder: a preliminary report. *J Psychopharmacol* (2011) 25:121–30. doi:10.1177/ 0269881110379283
199. Fusar-Poli P, Allen P, Bhattacharyya S, Crippa JA, Mechelli A, Borgwardt S, et al. Modulation of effective connectivity during emotional processing by Delta 9-tetrahydrocannabinol and cannabidiol. *Int J Neuropsychopharmacol* (2010) 13(4): 421–32. doi:10.1017/S1461145709990617
200. Pessoa L. On the relationship between emotion and cognition. *Nat Rev Neurosci* (2008) 9:148–58. doi:10.1038/nrn2317
201. Casarotto PC, Gomes FV, Resstel LB, Guimaraes FS. Cannabidiol inhibitory effect on marbleburying behaviour: involvement of CB1 receptors. *Behav Pharmacol* (2010) 21:353–8. doi:10.1097/FBP. 0b013e32833b33c5
202. Deiana S,Watanabe A, Yamasaki Y, Amada N, Arthur M, Fleming S, et al. Plasma and brain pharmacokinetic profile of cannabidiol (CBD), cannabidivarine (CBDV), Delta(9)-tetrahydrocannabivarin (THCV) and cannabigerol (CBG) in rats and mice following oral and intraperitoneal administration and CBD action on obsessive-compulsive behaviour. *Psychopharmacology (Berl)* (2012) 219(3):859–73.
203. Mechoulam R, Parker LA, Gallily R. Cannabidiol: an overview of some pharmacological aspects. *J Clin Pharmacol* (2002) 42:11S–9S.
204. Lastres-Becker I, Molina-Holgado F, Ramos JA, Mechoulam R, Fernandez-Ruiz J. Cannabinoids provide neuroprotection against 6-hydroxydopamine toxicity in vivo and in vitro: relevance to Parkinson's disease. *Neurobiol Dis* (2005) 19:96–107. doi:10.1016/j.nbd.2004.11.009
205. Sarne Y, Mechoulam R. Cannabinoids: between neuroprotection and neurotoxicity. *Curr Drug Targets CNS Neurol Disord* (2005) 4:677–84. doi:10.2174/156800705774933005
206. Bhattacharyya S, Fusar-Poli P, Borgwardt S, Martin-Santos R, Nosarti C,O'Carroll C, et al.Modulation of mediotemporal and ventrostriatal function in humans by Delta9-tetrahydrocannabinol: a neural basis for the effects of Cannabis sativa on learning and psychosis. *Arch Gen Psychiatry* (2009) 66:442–51. doi:10.1001/ archgenpsychiatry.2009.17
207. Bhattacharyya S, Morrison PD, Fusar-Poli P, Martin-Santos R, Borgwardt S, Winton-Brown T, et al. Opposite effects of delta-9-tetrahydrocannabinol and cannabidiol on human brain function and psychopathology. *Neuropsychopharmacology* (2010) 35:764–74. doi:10.1038/npp.2009.184
208. Borgwardt SJ, Allen P, Bhattacharyya S, Fusar-Poli P, Crippa JA, Seal ML, et al. Neural basis of delta-9-tetrahydrocannabinol and cannabidiol: effects during response inhibition. *Biol Psychiatry* (2008) 64:966–73. doi:10. 1016/j.biopsych.2008.05.011
209. Fox HC, Hong KI, Siedlarz K, Sinha R. Enhanced sensitivity to stress and drug/alcohol craving in abstinent cocaine-dependent individuals compared to social drinkers. *Neuropsychopharmacology* (2008) 33:796–805. doi:10. 1038/sj.npp.1301470
210. Katona I, Freund TF. Endocannabinoid signaling as a synaptic circuit breaker in neurological disease. *Nat Med* (2008) 14:923–30. doi:10.1038/nm.f.1869
211. Lalumiere RT, Kalivas PW. Glutamate release in the nucleus accumbens core is necessary for heroin seeking. *J Neurosci* (2008) 28:3170–7. doi:10.1523/ JNEUROSCI.5129-07.2008
212. Vann RE, Gamage TF, Warner JA, Marshall EM, Taylor NL, Martin BR, et al. Divergent effects of cannabidiol on the discriminative stimulus and place conditioning effects of Delta(9)- tetrahydrocannabinol. *Drug Alcohol Depend* (2008) 94:191–8. doi: 10.1016/j.drugalcdep.2007.11.017
213. Malone DT, Jongejan D, Taylor DA. Cannabidiol reverses the reduction in social interaction produced by low dose Delta(9)-tetrahydrocannabinol in rats. *Pharmacol Biochem Behav* (2009) 93:91–6. doi:10.1016/j.pbb.2009.04.010
214. Karniol IG, Takahashi RN, Musty RE. Effects of delta9- tetrahydrocannabinol and cannabinol on operant performance in rats. *Arch Int Pharmacodyn Ther* (1974) 212:230–7.
215. ZuardiAW, Shirakawa I, Finkelfarb E, Karniol IG. Action of cannabidiol on the anxiety and other effects produced by delta 9-THC in normal subjects. *Psychopharmacology (Berl)* (1982) 76:245–50. doi:10. 1007/BF00432554

216. Pertwee RG. Inverse agonism and neutral antagonism at cannabinoid CB1 receptors. *Life Sci* (2005) 76:1307–24. doi:10.1016/j. lfs.2004.10.025
217. Russo E, Guy GW. A tale of two cannabinoids: the therapeutic rationale for combining tetrahydrocannabinol and cannabidiol. *Med Hypotheses* (2006) 66:234–46. doi:10.1016/j.mehy.2005.08.026
218. Ren Y, Whittard J, Higuera-Matas A,Morris CV,Hurd YL. Cannabidiol, a nonpsychotropic component of cannabis, inhibits cueinduced heroin seeking and normalizes discrete mesolimbic neuronal disturbances. *J Neurosci* (2009) 29:14764–9. doi:10.1523/ JNEUROSCI.4291-09.2009
219. Hamelink C, Hampson A, Wink DA, Eiden LE, Eskay RL. Comparison of cannabidiol, antioxidants, and diuretics in reversing binge ethanol-induced neurotoxicity. *J Pharmacol Exp Ther* (2005) 314:780–8. doi:10.1124/ jpet.105.085779
220. Trouve R, Nahas G, Stuker O, Latour C. Antagonistic effects of two natural cannabinoids on the isolated heart. *C R Seances Acad Sci III* (1983) 297:191–4.
221. Nahas G, Trouve R. Effects and interactions of natural cannabinoids on the isolated heart. *Proc Soc Exp Biol Med* (1985) 180:312–6. doi:10.3181/00379727-180-42181
222. Agrawal A, Neale MC, Prescott CA, Kendler KS. Cannabis and other illicit drugs: comorbid use and abuse/dependence in males and females. *Behav Genet* (2004) 34:217–28. doi:10.1023/B:BEGE. 0000017868.07829.45
223. Miller NS, Klahr AL, Gold MS, Sweeney K,Cocores JA. The prevalence of marijuana (cannabis) use and dependence in cocaine dependence. *N Y State J Med* (1990) 90:491–2.
224. Serrano A, Parsons LH. Endocannabinoid influence in drug reinforcement, dependence and addiction-related behaviors. *Pharmacol Ther* (2011) 132:215–41. doi:10.1016/j.pharmthera.2011. 06.005
225. Fergusson DM, Boden JM, Horwood LJ. Cannabis use and other illicit drug use: testing the cannabis gateway hypothesis. *Addiction* (2006) 101:556–69. doi:10.1111/j.1360-0443.2005. 01322.x
226. Kandel DB, Yamaguchi K, Klein LC. Testing the gateway hypothesis. *Addiction* (2006) 101:470–2. doi:10.1111/j.1360-0443.2006. 01426.x discussion 474-476.
227. Lynskey MT, Vink JM, Boomsma DI. Early onset cannabis use and progression to other drug use in a sample of Dutch twins. *Behav Genet* (2006) 36:195–200. doi:10. 1007/s10519-005-9023-x
228. Agrawal A, Lynskey MT, Bucholz KK, Martin NG, Madden PA, Heath AC. Contrasting models of genetic co-morbidity for cannabis and other illicit drugs in adult Australian twins. *Psychol Med* (2007) 37:49–60. doi:10. 1017/ S0033291706009287
229. Tomasiewicz HC, Jacobs MM, Wilkinson MB, Wilson SP, Nestler EJ, Hurd YL. Proenkephalin mediates the enduring effects of adolescent *Cannabis* exposure associated with adult opiate vulnerability. *Biol Psychiatry* (2012) 72(10):803–10. doi:10.1016/j. biopsych.2012.04.026
230. Mattay VS, Goldberg TE, Fera F, Hariri AR, Tessitore A, Egan MF, et al. Catechol O-methyltransferase val158-met genotype and individual variation in the brain response to amphetamine. *Proc Natl Acad Sci U S A* (2003) 100: 6186–91. doi:10.1073/pnas. 0931309100
231. Hariri AR, Tessitore A, Mattay VS, Fera F,Weinberger DR. The amygdala response to emotional stimuli: a comparison of faces and scenes. *Neuroimage* (2002) 17:317–23. doi:10.1006/nimg.2002.1179
232. Volkow ND, Fowler JS, Wolf AP, Schlyer D, Shiue CY, Alpert R, et al. Effects of chronic cocaine abuse on postsynaptic dopamine receptors. *Am J Psychiatry* (1990) 147:719–24.
233. Volkow ND, Fowler JS, Wang GJ, Hitzemann R, Logan J, Schlyer DJ, et al. Decreased dopamine D2 receptor availability is associated with reduced frontal metabolism in cocaine abusers. *Synapse* (1993) 14:169–77. doi:10.1002/ syn.890140210
234. Volkow ND, Chang L, Wang GJ, Fowler JS, Ding YS, Sedler M, et al. Low level of brain dopamine D2 receptors in methamphetamine abusers: association with metabolism in the orbitofrontal cortex. *Am J Psychiatry* (2001) 158:2015–21. doi:10.1176/appi.ajp.158.12.2015
235. Andersen SL, Napierata L, Brenhouse HC, Sonntag KC. Juvenile methylphenidate modulates reward-related behaviors and cerebral blood flow by decreasing cortical D3 receptors. *Eur J Neurosci* (2008) 27:2962–72. doi:10.1111/j. 1460-9568.2008.06254.x
236. Comings DE, Muhleman D, Gade R, Johnson P, Verde R, Saucier G, et al. Cannabinoid receptor gene (CNR1): association with i.v. drug use. *Mol Psychiatry* (1997) 2:161–8. doi:10.1038/sj.mp. 4000247
237. Ballon N, Leroy S, Roy C, Bourdel MC, Charles-Nicolas A, Krebs MO, et al. (AAT)n repeat in the cannabinoid receptor gene (CNR1): association with cocaine addiction in an African-Caribbean population. *Pharmacogenomics J* (2006) 6:126–30. doi:10.1038/sj. tpj.6500352
238. LiYC,Korol AB, Fahima T,Nevo E. Microsatellites within genes: structure, function, and evolution. *Mol Biol Evol* (2004) 21:991–1007. doi: 10.1093/ molbev/msh073
239. Benyamina A, Kebir O, Blecha L, Reynaud M, Krebs MO. CNR1 gene polymorphisms in addictive disorders: a systematic review and a meta-analysis. *Addict Biol* (2011) 16:1–6. doi:10.1111/j.1369- 1600.2009.00198.x
240. Barrero FJ, Ampuero I, Morales B, Vives F, De Dios Luna Del Castillo J, Hoenicka J, et al. Depression in Parkinson's disease is related to a genetic polymorphism of the cannabinoid receptor gene (CNR1). *Pharmacogenomics J* (2005) 5:135–41. doi:10.1038/sj. tpj.6500301
241. Haughey HM,Marshall E, Schacht JP, Louis A, Hutchison KE. Marijuana withdrawal and craving: influence of the cannabinoid receptor 1 (CNR1) and fatty acid amide hydrolase (FAAH) genes. *Addiction* (2008) 103:1678–86. doi:10.1111/j.1360-0443.2008. 02292.x
242. Filbey FM, Schacht JP, Myers US, Chavez RS, Hutchison KE. Individual and additive effects of the CNR1 and FAAH genes on brain response to marijuana cues. *Neuropsychopharmacology* (2010) 35:967–75. doi:10.1038/npp.2009. 200
243. Lopez-Moreno JA, Echeverry- Alzate V, Buhler KM. The genetic basis of the endocannabinoid system and drug addiction in humans. *J Psychopharmacol* (2012) 26:133–43. doi:10.1177/0269881111416689
244. Clarke TK, Bloch PJ, Ambrose- Lanci LM, Ferraro TN, Berrettini WH, Kampman KM, et al. Further evidence for association of polymorphisms in the CNR1 gene with cocaine addiction: confirmation in an independent sample and meta-analysis. *Addict Biol* (2013) 18(4):702–8. doi:10.1111/j. 1369-1600.2011.00346.x
245. Sipe JC, Chiang K, Gerber AL, Beutler E, Cravatt BF. A missensemutation in human fatty acid amide hydrolase associated with problem drug use. *Proc Natl Acad SciUSA* (2002) 99:8394–9. doi:10. 1073/pnas.082235799
246. Flanagan JM, Gerber AL, Cadet JL, Beutler E, Sipe JC. The fatty acid amide hydrolase 385 A/A (P129T) variant: haplotype analysis of an ancient missense mutation and validation of risk for drug addiction. *Hum Genet* (2006) 120:581–8. doi:10.1007/ s00439-006-0250-x
247. Li CS,Milivojevic V, Constable RT, Sinha R. Recent cannabis abuse decreased stress-induced BOLD signals in the frontal and cingulate cortices of cocaine dependent individuals. *Psychiatry Res* (2005) 140:271–80. doi:10.1016/j. pscychresns.2005.09.002
248. Foltin RW, Fischman MW, Pippen PA, Kelly TH. Behavioral effects of cocaine alone and in combination with ethanol or marijuana in humans. *Drug Alcohol Depend* (1993) 32:93–106. doi:10. 1016/0376-8716(93)80001-U
249. Lukas SE, Sholar M, Kouri E, Fukuzako H, Mendelson JH. Marihuana smoking increases plasma cocaine levels and subjective reports of euphoria in male volunteers. *Pharmacol Biochem Behav* (1994) 48:715–21. doi:10. 1016/0091-3057(94)90338-7
250. Xi ZX, Spiller K, Pak AC, Gilbert J, Dillon C, Li X, et al. Cannabinoid CB1 receptor antagonists attenuate cocaine's rewarding effects: experiments with self-administration and brain-stimulation reward in rats. *Neuropsychopharmacology* (2008) 33:1735–45. doi:10.1038/sj.npp.1301552
251. Vlachou S, Nomikos GG, Panagis G. WIN 55,212-2 decreases the reinforcing actions of cocaine through CB1 cannabinoid receptor stimulation. *Behav Brain Res* (2003) 141:215–22. doi:10.1016/ S0166-4328(02)00370-4
252. Vlachou S, Stamatopoulou F, Nomikos GG, Panagis G. Enhancement of endocannabinoid neurotransmission through CB1 cannabinoid receptors counteracts the reinforcing and psychostimulant effects of cocaine. *Int J Neuropsychopharmacol* (2008) 11:905–23. doi:10.1017/S1461145708008717
253. Li X, Hoffman AF, Peng XQ, Lupica CR, Gardner EL, Xi ZX. Attenuation of basal and cocaineenhanced locomotion and nucleus accumbens dopamine in cannabinoid CB1-receptor-knockout mice. *Psychopharmacology (Berl)* (2009) 204:1–11. doi:10.1007/s00213-008-1432-0
254. Cheer JF, Wassum KM, Sombers LA, Heien ML, Ariansen JL, Aragona BJ, et al. Phasic dopamine release evoked by abused substances requires cannabinoid receptor activation. *J Neurosci* (2007) 27:791–5. doi:10.1523/ JNEUROSCI.4152-06.2007
255. Soria G,Mendizabal V, Tourino C, Robledo P, Ledent C, Parmentier M, et al. Lack of CB1 cannabinoid receptor impairs cocaine selfadministration. *Neuropsychopharmacology* (2005) 30:1670–80. doi: 10.1038/sj.npp.1300707
256. Caille S, Parsons LH. Cannabinoid modulation of opiate reinforcement through the ventral striatopallidal pathway. *Neuropsychopharmacology* (2006) 31:804–13. doi:10.1038/sj.npp.1300848
257. Xi ZX, Gilbert JG, Peng XQ, Pak AC, Li X, Gardner EL. Cannabinoid CB1 receptor antagonist AM251 inhibits cocaine-primed relapse in rats: role of glutamate in the nucleus accumbens. *J Neurosci* (2006) 26:8531–6. doi:10. 1523/JNEUROSCI.0726-06.2006

258. Xi ZX, Peng XQ, Li X, Song R, Zhang HY, Liu QR, et al. Brain cannabinoid CB(2) receptors modulate cocaine's actions in mice. *Nat Neurosci* (2011) 14:1160–6. doi:10.1038/nn.2874
259. Luchicchi A, Lecca S, Carta S, Pillolla G, Muntoni AL, Yasar S, et al. Effects of fatty acid amide hydrolase inhibition on neuronal responses to nicotine, cocaine and morphine in the nucleus accumbens shell and ventral tegmental area: involvement of PPARalpha nuclear receptors.*Addict Biol* (2010) 15:277–88. doi:10.1111/j. 1369-1600.2010.00222.x
260. Justinova Z, Mangieri RA, Bortolato M, Chefer SI, Mukhin AG, Clapper JR, et al. Fatty acid amide hydrolase inhibition heightens anandamide signaling without producing reinforcing effects in primates. *Biol Psychiatry* (2008) 64:930–7. doi:10.1016/j.biopsych. 2008.08.008
261. Adamczyk P, McCreary AC, Przegalinski E, Mierzejewski P, Bienkowski P, Filip M. The effects of fatty acid amide hydrolase inhibitors on maintenance of cocaine and food self-administration and on reinstatement of cocaine-seeking and food-taking behavior in rats. *J Physiol Pharmacol* (2009) 60:119–25.
262. Martin M, Ledent C, Parmentier M, Maldonado R, Valverde O. Cocaine, but not morphine, induces conditioned place preference and sensitization to locomotor responses in CB1 knockout mice. *Eur J Neurosci* (2000) 12:4038–46. doi:10.1046/j. 1460-9568.2000.00287.x
263. Houchi H, Babovic D, Pierrefiche O, Ledent C, Daoust M, Naassila M. CB1 receptor knockout mice display reduced ethanol-induced conditioned place preference and increased striatal dopamine D2 receptors. *Neuropsychopharmacology* (2005) 30:339–49. doi:10. 1038/sj.npp.1300568
264. Miller LL, Ward SJ, Dykstra LA. Chronic unpredictable stress enhances cocaine-conditioned place preference in type 1 cannabinoid receptor knockout mice. *Behav Pharmacol* (2008) 19:575–81. doi:10.1097/FBP. 0b013e-32830ded11
265. Chaperon F, Soubrie P, Puech AJ, Thiebot MH. Involvement of central cannabinoid (CB1) receptors in the establishment of place conditioning in rats. *Psychopharmacology (Berl)* (1998) 135: 324–32. doi:10.1007/s002130050518
266. Lesscher HM, Hoogveld E, Burbach JP, Van Ree JM, Gerrits MA. Endogenous cannabinoids are not involved in cocaine reinforcement and development of cocaineinduced behavioural sensitization. *Eur Neuropsychopharmacol* (2005) 15:31–7. doi:10.1016/j.euroneuro. 2004.04.003
267. Corbille AG, Valjent E, Marsicano G, Ledent C, Lutz B, Herve D, et al. Role of cannabinoid type 1 receptors in locomotor activity and striatal signaling in response to psychostimulants. *J Neurosci* (2007) 27:6937–47. doi:10.1523/ JNEUROSCI.3936-06.2007
268. Gerdeman GL, Schechter JB, French ED. Context-specific reversal of cocaine sensitization by the CB1 cannabinoid receptor antagonist rimonabant. *Neuropsychopharmacology* (2008) 33:2747–59. doi:10.1038/sj.npp.1301648
269. Filip M, Golda A, Zaniewska M, McCreary AC, Nowak E, Kolasiewicz W, et al. Involvement of cannabinoid CB1 receptors in drug addiction: effects of rimonabant on behavioral responses induced by cocaine. *Pharmacol Rep* (2006) 58:806–19.
270. Przegalinski E, Gothert M, Frankowska M, Filip M. WIN 55,212-2-induced reduction of cocaine hyperlocomotion: possible inhibition of 5-HT(3) receptor function. *Eur J Pharmacol* (2005) 517:68–73. doi:10.1016/j.ejphar.2005.05.014
271. Aracil-Fernandez A, Trigo JM, Garcia-Gutierrez MS, Ortega- Alvaro A, Ternianov A, Navarro D, et al. Decreased cocaine motor sensitization and selfadministration in mice overexpressing cannabinoid CB(2) receptors. *Neuropsychopharmacology* (2012) 37:1749–63. doi:10.1038/npp.2012.22
272. Panlilio LV, Solinas M, Matthews SA, Goldberg SR. Previous exposure to THC alters the reinforcing efficacy and anxietyrelated effects of cocaine in rats. *Neuropsychopharmacology* (2007) 32:646–57. doi:10.1038/sj.npp.1301109
273. Gorriti MA,RodriguezDe Fonseca F, Navarro M, Palomo T. Chronic (-)-delta9-tetrahydrocannabinol treatment induces sensitization to the psychomotor effects of amphetamine in rats. *Eur J Pharmacol* (1999) 365:133–42. doi:10. 1016/S0014-2999(98)00851-6
274. Wiskerke J, Pattij T, Schoffelmeer AN, De Vries TJ. The role of CB1 receptors in psychostimulant addiction. *Addict Biol* (2008) 13:225–38. doi:10.1111/j. 1369-1600.2008.00109.x
275. Cossu G, Ledent C, Fattore L, Imperato A, Bohme GA, Parmentier M, et al. Cannabinoid CB1 receptor knockout mice fail to self-administer morphine but not other drugs of abuse. *Behav Brain Res* (2001) 118:61–5. doi:10.1016/ S0166-4328(00)00311-9
276. Vaughn LK, Mantsch JR, Vranjkovic O, Stroh G, Lacourt M, Kreutter M, et al. Cannabinoid receptor involvement in stressinduced cocaine reinstatement: potential interaction with noradrenergic pathways. *Neuroscience* (2012) 204:117–24. doi:10.1016/j. neuroscience.2011.08.021
277. Adamczyk P, Miszkiel J, McCreary AC, Filip M, Papp M, Przegalinski E. The effects of cannabinoid CB1, CB2 and vanilloid TRPV1 receptor antagonists on cocaine addictive behavior in rats. *Brain Res* (2012) 1444:45–54. doi:10.1016/j. brainres.2012.01.030
278. Vinklerova J, Novakova J, Sulcova A. Inhibition of methamphetamine self-administration in rats by cannabinoid receptor antagonist AM 251. *J Psychopharmacol* (2002) 16:139–43. doi:10.1177/ 026988110201600204
279. Poncelet M, Barnouin MC, Breliere JC, Le Fur G, Soubrie P. Blockade of cannabinoid (CB1) receptors by 141716 selectively antagonizes drug-induced reinstatement of exploratory behaviour in gerbils. *Psychopharmacology (Berl)* (1999) 144:144–50. doi: 10.1007/s002130050987
280. Tanda G, Munzar P, Goldberg SR. Self-administration behavior is maintained by the psychoactive ingredient of marijuana in squirrel monkeys. *Nat Neurosci* (2000) 3:1073–4. doi:10.1038/80577
281. Yu LL, Zhou SJ, Wang XY, Liu JF, Xue YX, Jiang W, et al. Effects of cannabinoid CB(1) receptor antagonist rimonabant on acquisition and reinstatement of psychostimulant reward memory in mice. *Behav Brain Res* (2011) 217: 111–6. doi:10.1016/j.bbr.2010.10. 008
282. Ward SJ, Rosenberg M, Dykstra LA, Walker EA. The CB1 antagonist rimonabant (SR141716) blocks cue-induced reinstatement of cocaine seeking and other context and extinction phenomena predictive of relapse. *Drug Alcohol Depend* (2009) 105:248–55. doi: 10.1016/j.drugalcdep.2009.07.002
283. De Vries TJ, Shaham Y, Homberg JR, Crombag H, Schuurman K, Dieben J, et al. A cannabinoid mechanism in relapse to cocaine seeking.*NatMed* (2001) 7:1151–4. doi:10.1038/nm1001-1151
284. Orio L, Edwards S, George O, Parsons LH, Koob GF. A role for the endocannabinoid systemin the increased motivation for cocaine in extended-access conditions. *J Neurosci* (2009) 29:4846–57. doi:10.1523/JNEUROSCI.0563- 09.2009
285. Daza-Losada M,Minarro J,Aguilar MA, Valverde O, Rodriguez-Arias M.Acute blockade of CB1 receptor leads to reinstatement of MDMAinduced conditioned place preference. *Pharmacol Biochem Behav* (2011) 100:33–9. doi:10.1016/j. pbb.2011.07.011
286. Rodriguez-Arias M, Manzanedo C, Roger-Sanchez C, Do Couto BR, Aguilar MA, Minarro J. Effect of adolescent exposure to WIN 55212-2 on the acquisition and reinstatement of MDMA-induced conditioned place preference. *Prog Neuropsychopharmacol Biol Psychiatry* (2010) 34:166–71. doi:10. 1016/j.pnpbp.2009.10.019
287. Braida D, Iosue S, Pegorini S, Sala M. 3,4 Methylenedioxymethamphetamineinduced conditioned place preference (CPP) is mediated by endocannabinoid system. *Pharmacol Res* (2005) 51:177–82. doi:10.1016/j.phrs.2004.07.009
288. Braida D, Sala M. Role of the endocannabinoid system in MDMA intracerebral selfadministration in rats. *Br J Pharmacol* (2002) 136:1089–92. doi:10.1038/sj.bjp.0704825
289. Anggadiredja K, Nakamichi M, Hiranita T, Tanaka H, Shoyama Y, Watanabe S, et al. Endocannabinoid system modulates relapse to methamphetamine seeking: possible mediation by the arachidonic acid cascade. *Neuropsychopharmacology* (2004) 29:1470–8. doi:10. 1038/sj.npp.1300454
290. Parker LA, Burton P, Sorge RE, Yakiwchuk C, Mechoulam R. Effect of low doses of delta9- tetrahydrocannabinol and cannabidiol on the extinction of cocaine-induced and amphetamine-induced conditioned place preference learning in rats. *Psychopharmacology (Berl)* (2004) 175:360–6. doi:10.1007/s00213-004-1825-7
291. Higuera-Matas A, Soto- Montenegro ML, Del Olmo N, Miguens M, Torres I, Vaquero JJ, et al. Augmented acquisition of cocaine self-administration and altered brain glucose metabolism in adult female but not male rats exposed to a cannabinoid agonist during adolescence. *Neuropsychopharmacology* (2008) 33:806–13. doi:10.1038/sj.npp.1301467
292. Fattore L, Martellotta MC, Cossu G, Mascia MS, Fratta W. CB1 cannabinoid receptor agonistWIN 55,212-2 decreases intravenous cocaine self-administration in rats. *Behav Brain Res* (1999) 104:141–6. doi:10.1016/S0166-4328(99)00059-5
293. Sinha R, Fuse T, Aubin LR, O'Malley SS. Psychological stress, drug-related cues and cocaine craving. *Psychopharmacology (Berl)* (2000) 152:140–8. doi:10.1007/s002130000499
294. Jarbe TU, Henriksson BG, Ohlin GC. Delta9-THC as a discriminative cue in pigeons: effects of delta8-THC, CBD, and CBN. *Arch Int Pharmacodyn Ther* (1977) 228:68–72.

13

Addiction and choice: theory and new data

Gene M. Heyman*

Department of Psychology, Boston College, Boston, MA, USA

Edited by:
Hanna Pickard, University of Oxford, UK

Reviewed by:
Serge H. Ahmed, CNRS, France
Bennett Foddy, University of Oxford, UK

****Correspondence:***
Gene M. Heyman, Department of Psychology, McGuinn Hall, Boston College, Boston, MA 02467, USA.
e-mail: heymang@bc.edu; gheyman@harvard.fas.edu

Addiction's biological basis has been the focus of much research. The findings have persuaded experts and the public that drug use in addicts is compulsive. But the word "compulsive" identifies patterns of behavior, and all behavior has a biological basis, including voluntary actions. Thus, the question is not whether addiction has a biology, which it must, but whether it is sensible to say that addicts use drugs compulsively. The relevant research shows most of those who meet the American Psychiatric Association's criteria for addiction quit using illegal drugs by about age 30, that they usually quit without professional help, and that the correlates of quitting include legal concerns, economic pressures, and the desire for respect, particularly from family members. That is, the correlates of quitting are the correlates of choice not compulsion. However, addiction is, by definition, a disorder, and thereby not beneficial in the long run. This is precisely the pattern of choices predicted by quantitative choice principles, such as the matching law, melioration, and hyperbolic discounting. Although the brain disease model of addiction is perceived by many as received knowledge it is not supported by research or logic. In contrast, well established, quantitative choice principles predict both the possibility and the details of addiction.

Keywords: addiction, choice theory, remission, correlates of recovery, brain disease model

INTRODUCTION

Addictive drugs change the brain, genetic studies show that alcoholism has a substantial heritability, and addiction is a persistent, destructive pattern of drug use (e.g., Cloninger, 1987; American Psychiatric Association, 1994; Robinson et al., 2001). In scientific journals and popular media outlets, these observations are cited as proof that "addiction is a chronic, relapsing brain disease, involving compulsive drug use" (e.g., Miller and Chappel, 1991; Leshner, 1999; Lubman et al., 2004; Quenqua, 2011). Yet, research shows that addiction has the highest remission rate of any psychiatric disorder, that most addicts quit drugs without professional help, and that the correlates of quitting are those that attend most decisions, such as financial and familial concerns (e.g., Biernacki, 1986; Robins, 1993; Stinson et al., 2005; Klingemann et al., 2010). However, addiction is "disease-like" in the sense that it persists even though on balance its costs outweigh the benefits (e.g., most addicts eventually quit). Thus, in order to explain addiction, we need an account of voluntary behavior that predicts the persistence of activities that from a global bookkeeping perspective (e.g., long-term) are irrational. That is, addiction is not compulsive drug use, but it also is not rational drug use. Several empirical choice principles predict the possibility of relatively stable yet suboptimal behavior. They include the matching law, melioration, and hyperbolic discounting (e.g., Herrnstein, 1990; Ainslie, 1992). These principles were discovered in the course of experiments conducted in laboratories and natural settings, and in experiments these same principles also distinguish addicted from non-addicted drug users (e.g., Kirby et al., 1999). For example, ex and current heavy drug users were more likely to suboptimally "meliorate" than were non-addicts in a choice procedure that invited both long-term maximizing and melioration (Heyman and Dunn, 2002). Thus, we have on hand a research based, non-disease account of the defining features of addiction, which is to say its destructive and irrational aspects. As this essay is based on how those we call addicts behave, it would be most efficient to begin with a brief summary of key aspects of the natural history of addiction.

LIKELIHOOD OF REMISSION AND TIME COURSE OF ADDICTION

Figure 1 shows the cumulative frequency of remission as a function of the onset of dependence in a nation-wide representative sample of addicts (United States, Lopez-Quintero et al., 2011). The researchers first recruited a sample of more than 42,000 individuals whose demographic characteristics approximated those of the US population for individuals between the ages of 18 and 64 (Grant and Dawson, 2006). The participants were interviewed according to a questionnaire designed to produce an APA diagnosis when warranted. For those who currently or in the past met the criteria for "substance dependence" (the APA's term for addiction), there were additional questions aimed at documenting the time course of clinically significant levels of drug use. **Figure 1** summarizes the findings regarding remission and the duration of dependence.

On the *x*-axis is the amount of time since the onset of dependence. On the *y*-axis is the cumulative frequency of remission, which is the proportion of individuals who met the criteria for lifetime dependence but for the past year or more had been in remission. The fitted curves are negative exponentials, based on the assumption that each year the likelihood of remitting remained constant, independent of the onset of dependence (Heyman, 2013).

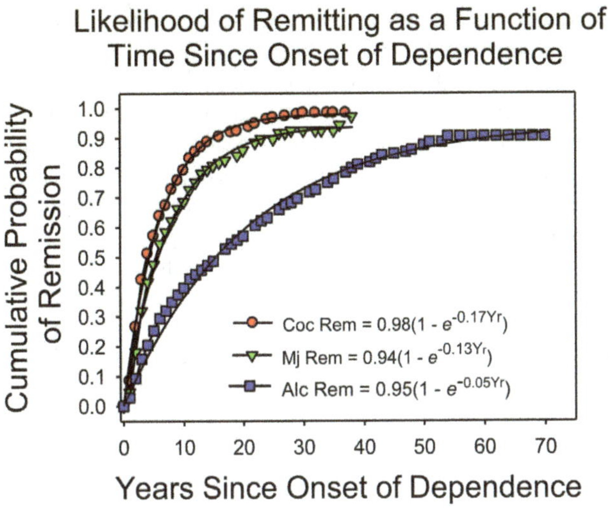

FIGURE 1 | The cumulative frequency of remission as a function of time since the onset of dependence, based on Lopez-Quintero et al.'s (2011) report. The proportion of addicts who quit each year was approximately constant. The smooth curves are based on the negative exponential equations listed in the figure.

The cumulative frequency of remission increased each year for each drug. Indeed, the theoretical lines so closely approximated the observations that the simplest account is that each year a constant proportion of those who had not yet remitted did so regardless of how long they had been addicted. By year 4 (since the onset of dependence) half of those who were ever addicted to cocaine had stopped using cocaine at clinically significant levels; for marijuana the half-life of dependence was 6 years; and for alcohol, the half-life of dependence was considerably longer, 16 years. As the typical onset age for dependence on an illicit drug is about 20 (Kessler et al., 2005a), the results say that most people who become addicted to an illicit drug are "ex-addicts" by age 30. Of course, addicts may switch drugs rather than quit drugs, but other considerations indicate that this does not explain the trends displayed in **Figure 1**. For example, dependence on any illicit drug decreases markedly as a function of age, which would not be possible if addicts were switching from one drug to another (Heyman, 2013).

The graph also shows that there is much individual variation. Among cocaine users, about 5% continued to meet the criteria for addiction well into their 40s; among marijuana users, about 8% remained heavy users well into their 50s, and for alcoholics, more than 15% remained heavy drinkers well into their 60s. Thus, for both legal and illegal drugs some addicts conform to the expectations of the "chronic disease" label. However, as noted below, the correlates of quitting drugs are the correlates of decision making, not the correlates of the diseases addiction is said to be similar to.

CAN WE TRUST THE DATA?

The results in **Figure 1** replicate the findings of previous nationwide surveys and targeted studies that selected participants so as to obtain representative samples (e.g., Robins and Murphy, 1967; Anthony and Helzer, 1991; Robins, 1993; Warner et al., 1995; Kessler et al., 2005a,b). For instance, in every national scientific survey of mental health in the United States, most of those who met the criteria for dependence on an illicit drug no longer did so by age 30, and addiction had the highest remission rate of any other psychiatric disorder. However, research on remission faces well-known methodological pitfalls. Those in remission may relapse at some post-interview date, and the subject rosters of the large epidemiological studies may be biased in favor of those addicts who do quit. For instance, addicts who remain heavy drug users may not cooperate with researchers or may be hard to contact because of their life style, illnesses, or have higher mortality rates. These issues have been discussed in some detail elsewhere (Heyman, 2013). The key results were that remission after age 30 was reasonably stable, and that it was unlikely that there were enough missing or dead addicts to alter significantly the trends displayed in **Figure 1**.

THE CORRELATES OF QUITTING AND THE ROLE OF TREATMENT

The correlates of quitting include the absence of additional psychiatric and medical problems, marital status (singles stay addicted longer), economic pressures, fear of judicial sanctions, concern about respect from children and other family members, worries about the many problems that attend regular involvement in illegal activities, more years spent in school, and higher income (e.g., Waldorf, 1983; Biernacki, 1986; Waldorf et al., 1991; Warner et al., 1995). Put in more personal terms, addicts often say that they quit drugs because they wanted to be a better parent, make their own parents proud of them, and not further embarrass their families (e.g., Premack, 1970; Jorquez, 1983). In short, the correlates of quitting are the practical and moral concerns that affect all major decisions. They are not the correlates of recovery from the diseases addiction is said to be like, such as Alzheimer's, schizophrenia, diabetes, heart disease, cancer, and so on (e.g., Leshner, 1999; McLellan et al., 2000; Volkow and Li, 2004).

Much of what we know about quitting drugs has been provided by researchers who study addicts who are not in treatment (e.g., Klingemann et al., 2010). This is because most addicts do not seek treatment. For instance, in the survey that provided the data for **Figure 1**, only 16% of those who currently met the criteria for dependence were in treatment, and treatment was broadly defined so as to include self-help organizations as well as services by trained clinicians (Stinson et al., 2005). Since most addicts quit, the implication is that most addicts quit without professional help. Research supports this logic (e.g., Fiore et al., 1993).

A NON-DISEASE ETIOLOGY FOR PERSISTENT SELF-DESTRUCTIVE DRUG USE

Although self-destructive, irrational behavior can be a sign of pathology, it need not be. The self-help industry is booming, which reflects the tendency of so many of us to procrastinate, overeat, skip exercising, and opt for whatever is most convenient. Why buy a book or go to a lecture on how to improve your life if you did not realize that (1) you were behaving imprudently, (2) knew you probably could change, but (3) so far have not taken the requisite steps. Similarly, human irrationality drives the story-line of most novels, memoirs, movies, and plays. Agamemnon sacrifices his own daughter to advance his political and personal goals but then publicly embarrasses Achilles his most powerful and skillful warrior. Both actions are selfish, and the second undermines the goals of the first, which anyone could have foretold. However, Homer is portraying human nature not writing a psychiatric text. Thus, it seems fair to say that who cite selfishness and myopic choices as evidence of pathology (e.g., "she has to be sick because she bought drugs rather than groceries") naively misread human nature.

In support of the poet's as opposed to the brain disease account of human nature, behavioral psychologists and economists have discovered principles that predict self-defeating, selfish patterns of behavior. They include "hyperbolic discounting," "melioration," and the "matching law" (Herrnstein, 1970, 1990; Rachlin and Green, 1972; Ainslie, 1992; Rachlin, 2007). These are quantitative, empirical laws of choice that predict how different species, including humans, choose between different commodities and activities, such as food, water, and exercise. Their relevance to addiction and other self-defeating behaviors is that under some conditions they predict relatively stable yet suboptimal patterns of behavior. For example, Heyman and Herrnstein (1986) arranged an experiment in which the matching predicted the lowest possible rate of reinforcement. As predicted the subjects shifted to matching, lowering their overall reinforcement rate as they did so. This finding has been replicated numerous times (e.g., Herrnstein et al., 1997), and it is analogous as to what happens as drug use turns into addiction.

Or, put another way, general principles that apply to everyday choices, also predict compulsive-like consumption patterns that are consistent with the behavior of addicts.

These choice laws reflect a basic, but often overlooked property, of most choice situations. There is more than one "optimal" strategy (Heyman, 2009). One is optimal from the perspective of the most immediate circumstances, such as the current values of the options, taking into account just the most pressing needs and goals. The others are optimal in terms of wider time horizons and the perspectives of others. For example, in settings in which current choices affect the values of future options, it is possible for the current best choice to be the worst long-term choice (e.g., Herrnstein et al., 1993; Heyman and Dunn, 2002). This is relevant because a common feature of addictive drugs is that they provide immediate benefits but delayed costs. Thus, it is possible that the drug is the best choice when the frame of reference is restricted to the current values of the immediately available options but the worst choice when the frame of reference expands to include future costs and other people's needs. According to this account, persistent drug use reflects the workings of a local optimum, whereas controlled drug use or abstinence reflects the workings of a global optimum. Put somewhat differently, whether or not drug use persists depends on the factors that influence decision making, particularly values that emphasize global as opposed to a local frame of reference (e.g., values related to family, the future, one's reputation, and so on). Scores of studies support this analysis (e.g., Waldorf, 1983; Biernacki, 1986; Mariezcurrena, 1994; Klingemann et al., 2010).

OLD CLINICAL FOLLOW-UP STUDIES: EMPIRICAL SUPPORT FOR THE DISEASE ACCOUNT

Imagine that what we knew about addiction was restricted to those individuals who make up the right-hand tails of the cumulative distribution curves in **Figure 1**. We would have good reason to believe that addiction is a chronic relapsing disease. This is precisely the situation for much of the history of addiction research. Until the mid 1970s virtually all empirical studies of addicts were based on individuals who had been in treatment, which was most often detoxification in American prison/hospitals or similar institutions (e.g., Brecher, 1972; Vaillant, 1973; Maddux and Desmond, 1980; Hser et al., 1993). In some studies virtually all of the participants were males with extensive arrest records, poor work histories, lower than average marriage rates, and lower than average educational achievement (e.g., Vaillant, 1973). That is, the understanding of addiction as a chronic disorder was based on a population of drug users whose demographic characteristics – we now know – match those that predict not quitting (e.g., Klingemann et al., 2010). In the 1960s illicit drug use spread to college campuses and upscale neighborhoods. This new generation of addicts included individuals who were employed, married, and well-educated (e.g., Waldorf et al., 1991). With these demographic changes, the natural history of addiction changed. More often than not, the pressures of family, employment, and the hassles of an illegal life style eventually trumped getting high. **Figure 1**, which is representative of every major epidemiological study conducted over the past 30 years, reflects this reality; received opinion does not.

BUT DRUGS CHANGE THE BRAIN

With the exception of alcohol, addictive drugs produce their biological and psychological changes by binding to specific receptor sites throughout the body. As self-administered drug doses greatly exceed the circulating levels of their natural analogs, persistent heavy drug use leads to structural and functional changes in the nervous system. It is widely – if not universally – assumed that these neural adaptations play a causal role in addiction. In support of this interpretation brain imaging studies often reveal differences between the brains of addicts and comparison groups (e.g., Volkow et al., 1997; Martin-Soelch et al., 2001) However, these studies are cross-sectional and the results are correlations. There are no published studies that establish a causal link between drug-induced neural adaptations and compulsive drug use or even a correlation between drug-induced neural changes and an increase in preference for an addictive drug. For example, in a frequently referred to animal study, Robinson et al. (2001) found dendritic changes in the striatum and the prefrontal cortex of rats who had self-administered cocaine. They concluded that this was a "recipe for addiction." However, they did not evaluate whether their findings with rodents applied to humans, nor did they even test if the dendritic modifications had anything to do with changes in preference for cocaine in their rats. In principle then it is possible that the drug-induced neural changes play little or no role in the persistence of drug use. This is a testable hypothesis.

First, most addicts quit. Thus, drug-induced neural plasticity does not prevent quitting. Second, in follow-up studies, which tested Robinson et al.'s claims, there were no increases in preference for cocaine. For instance in a preference test that provided both cocaine and saccharin, rats preferred saccharin (Lenoir et al., 2007) even after they had consumed about three to four times more cocaine than the rats in the Robinson et al study, and even though the cocaine had induced motoric changes which have been interpreted as signs of the neural underpinnings of addiction (e.g., Robinson and Berridge, 2003). Third, **Figure 1** shows that the likelihood of remission was constant over time since the onset of dependence. Although this is a surprising result, it is not without precedent. In a longitudinal study of heroin addicts, Vaillant (1973) reports that the likelihood of going off drugs neither increased nor decreased over time (1973), and in a study with rats, Serge Ahmed and his colleagues (Cantin et al., 2010) report that the probability of switching from cocaine to saccharin (which was about 0.85) was independent of past cocaine consumption. Since drugs change the brain, these results suggest that the changes do not prevent quitting, and the slope of **Figure 1** implies that drug-induced neural changes do not even decrease the likelihood of quitting drugs once dependence is in place.

BUT THERE IS A GENETIC PREDISPOSITION FOR ADDICTION

Twin and adoption studies have repeatedly demonstrated a genetic predisposition for alcoholism (e.g., Cloninger, 1987), and the limited amount of research on the genetics of illicit drug use suggests the same for drugs such as heroin, cocaine, and marijuana (Tsuang et al., 2001). However, all behavior has a genetic basis, including voluntary acts. The brain is the organ of voluntary action, and brain structure and development follow the blueprint set by DNA. Thus, there is no necessary connection between heritability and compulsion. In support of this point, monozygotic twins are much more likely to share similar religious and political beliefs than are dizygotic twins, even when they are separated before the age of 1 year old (e.g., Waller et al., 1990; McCourt et al., 1999). That is, learned, voluntary religious and political beliefs have substantial heritabilities just as do many involuntary human characteristics. The relevance to addiction is that a genetic predisposition is not a recipe for compulsion, just as brain adaptations are not a recipe for compulsion.

SUMMING UP

Addiction involves an initial "honey moon" period, followed by alternating periods of remission and relapse, and then an eventual return to a more sober life. Most addicts quit using drugs at clinically significant levels, they typically quit without professional help, and in the case of illicit drugs, they typically quit before the age of 30. The correlates of quitting include many of the factors that influence voluntary acts, but not, according to **Figure 1**, drug exposure once drug use meets the criteria for dependence. Thus, we can say that addiction is ambivalent drug use, which eventually involves more costs than benefits (otherwise why quit?). Behavioral choice principles predict ambivalent preferences, semi-stable suboptimal behavior patterns, and the capacity to shift from one option to another. In contrast, the brain disease account of addiction fails to predict the high quit rates; it fails to predict the correlates of quitting; it fails to predict the temporal pattern of quitting; and it is tied to unsupportable assumptions, such as the claims that neural adaptations, heritability, and irrationality are *prima facie* evidence of disease. To be sure "compulsion" and "choice" can be seen as points on a continuum, but **Figure 1** and research on quitting make it clear that addiction is not a borderline case.

It is time to think about addiction in terms of what the research shows, particularly the more recent epidemiological studies, and it is time to abandon the medical model of addiction. It does not fit the facts. The matching law, melioration, and hyperbolic discounting predict that drugs and similar commodities will become the focus of destructive, suboptimal patterns of behavior. These same choice models also predict that individuals caught in a destructive pattern of behavior retain the capacity to improve their lot and that they will do so as a function of changes in their options and/or how they frame their choices. This viewpoint fits the facts of addiction and provides a practical guide to measures that will actually help addicts change for the better.

REFERENCES

1. Ainslie, G. (1992). *Picoeconomics: The Strategic Interaction of Successive Motivational States Within the Per- son*. Cambridge: Cambridge Univer- sity Press.
2. American Psychiatric Association. (1994). *Diagnostic and Statisti- cal Manual of Mental Disorders: DSM-IV*, 4th Edn. Washington, DC: American Psychiatric Association.
3. Anthony, J. C., and Helzer, J. E. (1991). "Syndromes of drug abuse and dependence," in *Psychiatric Disorders in America*, eds L. N. Robins and D. A. Regier (New York: The Free Press), 116–154.
4. Biernacki, P. (1986). *Pathways from Heroin Addiction: Recovery Without Treatment*. Philadelphia, PA: Temple University Press.
5. Brecher, E. M. (1972). *Licit and Illicit Drugs; The Consumers Union Report on Narcotics, Stim- ulants, Depressants, Inhalants, Hallucinogens, and Marijuana–Including Caffeine, Nicotine, and Alcohol*, 1st Edn. Boston, MA: Little, Brown.
6. Cantin, L., Lenoir, M., Augier, E., Vanhille, N., Dubreucq, S., Serre, F., et al. (2010). Cocaine is low on the value ladder of rats: possible evidence for resilience to addiction. *PLoS ONE* 5:e11592. doi:10.1371/journal.pone.0011592
7. Cloninger, C. R. (1987). Neurogenetic adaptive mechanisms in alcoholism. *Science* 236, 410–416.
8. Fiore, M. C., Newcomb, P., and McBride, P. (1993). "Natural his- tory of tobacco use and addic- tion," in *Nicotine Addiction: Prin- ciples and Management*, eds. C. T. Orleans and J. Slade (New York: Oxford University Press), 89–104.
9. Grant, B. F., and Dawson, D. A. (2006). Introduction to the National epidemiologic survey on alcohol and related conditions. *Alcohol Res. Health* 29, 74–78.
10. Herrnstein, R. J. (1970). On the law of effect. *J. Exp. Anal. Behav.* 13, 243–266.
11. Herrnstein, R. J. (1990). Behavior, rein- forcement, and utility. *Psychol. Sci.* 1, 217–224.
12. Herrnstein, R. J., Rachlin, H., and Laib- son, D. I. (1997). *The Matching Law: Papers in Psychology and Economics*. New York: Russell Sage Foundation.
13. Herrnstein, R. J., Loewenstein, G. F., Prelec, D., and Vaughan, W. (1993). Utility maximization and melio- ration: internalities in individual choice. *J. Behav. Decis. Mak.* 6, 149–185.
14. Heyman, G. M. (2009). *Addiction: A Disorder of Choice*. Cambridge, MA: Harvard University Press.
15. Heyman, G. M. (2013). Quitting drugs: quantitative and qualitative features. *Annu. Rev. Clin. Psychol.* 9, 29–59.
16. Heyman, G. M., and Dunn, B. (2002). Decision biases and persistent illicit drug use: an experimental study of distributed choice in drug clinic patients. *Drug Alcohol Depend.* 67, 192–203.
17. Heyman, G. M., and Herrnstein, R. J. (1986). More on concurrent interval ratio schedules. *J. Exp. Anal. Behav.* 46, 331–351.
18. Hser, Y. I., Anglin, D., and Powers, K. (1993). A 24-year follow-up of California narcotics addicts. *Arch. Gen. Psychiatry* 50, 577–584.
19. Jorquez, J. S. (1983). The retirement phase of heroin using careers. *J. Drug Issues* 13, 343–365.
20. Kessler, R. C., Berglund, P., Dem- ler, O., Jin, R., Merikangas, K. R., and Walters, E. E. (2005a). Lifetime prevalence and age-of-onset distrib- utions of DSM-IV disorders in the National comorbidity survey repli- cation. *Arch. Gen. Psychiatry* 62, 593–602.

21. Kessler, R. C., Chiu, W. T., Demler, O., Merikangas, K. R., and Walters, E. E. (2005b). Prevalence, severity, and comorbidity of 12-month DSM-IV disorders in the National comor- bidity survey replication. *Arch. Gen. Psychiatry* 62, 617–627.
22. Kirby, K., Petry, N., and Bickel, W. (1999). Heroin addicts discount delayed rewards at higher rates than non-drug-using controls. *J. Exp. Psy- chol. Gen.* 128, 78–87.
23. Klingemann, H. K., Sobell, M. B., and Sobell, L. C. (2010). Continuities and changes in self-change research. *Addiction* 105, 1510–1518.
24. Lenoir, M., Serre, F., Cantin, L., and Ahmed, S. H. (2007). Intense sweetness surpasses cocaine reward. *PLoS ONE* 2:e698. doi:10.1371/journal.pone.0000698
25. Leshner, A. I. (1999). Science-based views of drug addiction and its treatment. *J. Am. Med. Assoc.* 282, 1314–1316.
26. Lopez-Quintero, C., Hasin, D. S., de los Cobos, J. P., Pines, A., Wang, S., Grant, B. F., et al. (2011). Probabil- ity and predictors of remission from life-time nicotine, alcohol, cannabis or cocaine dependence: results from the National epidemiologic survey on alcohol and related conditions. *Addiction* 106, 657–669.
27. Lubman, D. I., Yucel, M., and Pan-telis, C. (2004). Addiction, a condi- tion of compulsive behaviour? Neu- roimaging and neuropsychological evidence of inhibitory dysregula- tion. *Addiction* 99, 1491–1502.
28. Maddux, J. F., and Desmond, D. P. (1980). New light on the matur- ing out hypothesis in opioid depen- dence. *Bull. Narc.* 32, 15–25.
29. Mariezcurrena, R. (1994). Recovery from addictions without treatment: literature review. *Scand. J. Behav. Ther.* 23, 131–154.
30. Martin-Soelch, C., Chevalley, A.-F., Kunig, G., Missimer, J., Magyar, S., Mino, A., et al. (2001). Changes in reward-induced brain activation in opiate addicts. *Eur. J. Neurosci.* 14, 1360–1368.
31. McCourt, K. B., Thomas, J. Jr., Lykken, D. T., Tellegen, A., and Keyes, M. (1999). Authoritarianism revisited: genetic and environmental influ- ences examined in twins reared apart and together. *Pers. Individ. Differ.* 27, 985–1014.
32. McLellan, A. T., Lewis, D. C., O'Brien, C. P., and Kleber, H. D. (2000). Drug dependence, a chronic medical illness: implications for treatment, insurance, and outcomes evaluation. *J. Am. Med. Assoc.* 284, 1689–1695.
33. Miller, N. S., and Chappel, J. N. (1991). History of the disease concept. *Psychiatr. Ann.* 21, 196–205.
34. Premack, D. (1970). "Mechanisms of self-control," in *Learning Mecha- nisms in Smoking*, ed. W. A. Hunt (Chicago: Aldine), 107–123.
35. Quenqua, D. (2011). *July 10. Rethinking Addiction's Roots, and Its Treatment.* New York Times. Available at: http://www.nytimes.com/2011/07/ 11/ health/11addictions.html
36. Rachlin, H. (2007). In what sense are addicts irrational? *Drug Alcohol Depend.* 90(Suppl.), S92–S99.
37. Rachlin, H., and Green, L. (1972). Com- mitment, choice, and self-control. *J. Exp. Anal. Behav.* 17, 15–22.
38. Robins, L. N. (1993). Vietnam veterans' rapid recovery from heroin addiction: a fluke or normal expectation? *Addiction* 188, 1041–1054.
39. Robins, L. N., and Murphy, G. (1967). Drug use in a normal popula- tion of young Negro men. *Am. J. Public Health Nations Health* 57, 1580–1596.
40. Robinson, T. E., and Berridge, K. E. (2003). Addiction. *Ann. Rev. Psychol.* 54, 25–53.
41. Robinson, T. E., Gorny, G., Mitton, E., and Kolb, B. (2001). Cocaine self-administration alters the mor- phology of dendrites and den- dritic spines in the nucleus accum- bens and neocortex. *Synapse* 39, 257–266.
42. Stinson, F. S., Grant, B. F., Dawson, D., Ruan, W. J., Huang, B., and Saha, T. (2005). Comorbidity between DSM- IV alcohol and specific drug use disorders in the United States: results from the National epidemiological survey on alcohol and related con- ditions. *Drug Alcohol Depend.* 80, 105–116.
43. Tsuang, M. T., Bar, J. L., Harley, R. M., and Lyons, M. J. (2001). The Har- vard twin study of substance abuse: what we have learned. *Harv. Rev. Psychiatry* 9, 267–279.
44. Vaillant, G. E. (1973). A 20-year follow-up of New York narcotic addicts. *Arch. Gen. Psychiatry* 29, 237–241.
45. Volkow, N. D., and Li, T. K. (2004). Drug addiction: the neurobiology of behaviour gone awry. *Nat. Rev. Neurosci.* 5, 963–970.
46. Volkow, N. D., Wang, G. J., and Fowler, J. S. (1997). Decreased stri- atal dopaminergic responsiveness in detoxified cocaine-dependent sub- jects. *Nature* 386, 830–833.
47. Waldorf, D. (1983). Natural recov- ery from opiate addiction: some social-psychological processes of untreated recovery. *J. Drug Issues* 13, 237–279.
48. Waldorf, D., Reinarman, C., and Mur- phy, S. (1991). *Cocaine Changes: The Experience of Using and Quitting.* Philadelphia, PA: Temple University Press.
49. Waller, N. G., Kojetin, B. A., and Bouchard, T. (1990). Genetic and environmental influences on reli- gious interests, attitudes, and val- ues: a study of twins reared apart and together. *Psychol. Sci.* 1, 138–142.
50. Warner, L. A., Kessler, R. C., Hughes, M., Anthony, J. C., and Nelson, C. B. (1995). Prevalence and cor- relates of drug use and depen- dence in the United States. results from the National comorbidity survey. *Arch. Gen. Psychiatry* 52, 219–229.

14

Pleasure and addiction

***Jeanette Kennett*[1*†], *Steve Matthews*[2†] *and Anke Snoek*[1†]**

[1] *Department of Philosophy, Macquarie University, Sydney, NSW, Australia*
[2] *Australian Catholic University, Sydney, NSW, Australia*

Edited by:
Hanna Pickard, University of Oxford, UK

Reviewed by:
Bennett Foddy, University of Oxford, UK
Owen Flanagan, Duke University, USA

****Correspondence:***
Jeanette Kennett, Department of Philosophy, Macquarie University, Building W6A Room 736, Sydney, NSW 2109, Australia
e-mail: jeanette.kennett@mq.edu.au

†Jeanette Kennett, Steve Matthews and Anke Snoek have contributed equally to this work.

What is the role and value of pleasure in addiction? Foddy and Savulescu (1) have claimed that substance use is just pleasure-oriented behavior. They describe addiction as "strong appetites toward pleasure" and argue that addicts suffer in significant part because of strong social and moral disapproval of lives dominated by pleasure seeking. But such lives, they claim, can be autonomous and rational. The view they offer is largely in line with the choice model and opposed to a disease model of addiction. Foddy and Savulescu are sceptical of self-reports that emphasize the ill effects of addiction such as loss of family and possessions, or that claim an absence of pleasure after tolerance sets in. Such reports they think are shaped by social stigma which makes available a limited set of socially approved addiction narratives. We will not question the claim that a life devoted to pleasure can be autonomously chosen. Nor do we question the claim that the social stigma attached to the use of certain drugs increases the harm suffered by the user. However our interviews with addicts (as philosophers rather than health professionals or peers) reveal a genuinely ambivalent and complex relationship between addiction, value, and pleasure. Our subjects did not shy away from discussing pleasure and its role in use. But though they usually valued the pleasurable properties of substances, and this played that did not mean that they valued an addictive life. Our interviews distinguished changing attitudes towards drug related pleasures across the course of substance use, including diminishing pleasure from use over time and increasing resentment at the effects of substance use on other valued activities. In this paper we consider the implications of what drug users say about pleasure and value over the course of addiction for models of addiction.

Keywords: addiction, pleasure, autonomy, choice theory, reward and motivation

> Well don't get me wrong, I love using mate. If I could use successfully I would. I'd still be using. I love using. I just don't like the shit that comes with it. (R50)

INTRODUCTION

According to the so-called Moral Model (or Lay View), held by many, perhaps the majority of ordinary people, drug use by people who satisfy standard definitions of addiction is not the product of a disease or disorder that undermines the autonomy of the user. Drug use is voluntary behavior motivated by pleasure. The Lay or Moral Model of addiction takes a stern normative stance on the seeking of pleasure in this way – it regards it as parasitic, irresponsible, hedonism.

The minimal Liberal view of addiction expounded by Foddy and Savulescu (1) rejects the moralism of the Lay view but agrees with it that drug use in addicts is voluntary, pleasure-seeking behavior, and that we can draw no adverse conclusions about the autonomy of addicts from their repetitive drug-seeking behavior. In arguing against neurobiological versions of the Disease Model of addiction they say this:

> In plain English, if we repeatedly obtain some pleasurable experience we start to want it more. It moves up the rankings of experiences we would like to repeat. If we regularly engage in an extremely pleasurable experience, it is only natural that we will come to place a higher importance on that experience. The Liberal View is not so minimal that it cannot say what addictions are. They are strong appetites toward pleasure. (2010: p. 15)[1]

On their view, although an addicted person may well periodically regret his addictive behavior, he nevertheless at the moment of consumption acts in order to satisfy an appetite for pleasure and this choice is not obviously either irrational or lacking autonomy.

The Lay and Liberal positions provoke an inquiry into the relation between pleasure and addiction; in particular, they provoke us to consider what role pleasure plays in the moral psychology of the addicted agent. Are addicted persons motivated by pleasure alone? And is pleasure the object of their actions throughout the course of their addiction?

We will address these questions in two ways: first, we will examine the Choice account of motivation that we take to underlie the Liberal View to test the status of the claim that addictive motivation can be explained in terms of pleasure-seeking. What is meant by this claim and what would count as evidence against it? Second, we will probe the role that pleasure plays in addictive actions via evidence sourced from addicted persons themselves. In a recent study

[1] All 2010 in-text references to Foddy and Savulescu will be to this work.

($n = 69$), semi-structured interviews were undertaken to explore the effects of substance use on what addicted persons value, specifically in relation to the ways addiction has impacted on the course of their lives. During these interviews many of our subjects offered accounts of the phenomenology of addiction and addictive motivation. Our research indicates that there are important nuances to the role that pleasure plays in addiction; that changes in motivations for substance use occur over the course of addiction; and that there is variation in how pleasure itself is evaluated by the individuals concerned. We hope in these two ways to supply a richer and more informative account of motivation in addiction than is currently accepted by holders of either the Lay or Liberal view. Our results, together with other evidence, suggest that addictive motivation is complex, and make it doubtful that severely addicted persons' consumption can be subsumed under the category of ordinary weakness of will.

CHOICE MODELS OF ADDICTION

Recently, models of addiction which arise from behavioral economics and the psychology of choice have taken center stage in the ongoing debate over how best to characterize what goes wrong in addiction. Choice theorists see this model as breaking the impasse between Medical models (including the brain disease model), which remove or diminish, perhaps unacceptably, the agency of those who are addicted, and Moral or Lay models which condemn them. Disease models claim that the behavior of addicts is substantially involuntary – that it is caused by processes which bypass deliberation and choice or that are impervious to them. Moral models deny this and claim that the goals and values of the addicted person are bad or their choices and actions are weak in ways which reflect poorly on them.

By contrast, prominent choice theorists such as George Ainslie (24) and Gene Heyman (25) argue that the universal principles of choice that underlie ordinary behavior also explain the drug-seeking behavior of addicts. If we want to explain what people choose and do we must understand it in terms (broadly speaking) of satisfactions sought or pains avoided. George Ainslie claims that an economic theory of action must assume that the "individual is constrained to choose the option with the greatest expected reward of all those she considers." [(2), p. 116] It is impossible for the agent to be more motivated to pursue a lesser perceived reward over a greater reward when both are available to her. The addicted person follows this pattern: her choices, like all other choices, aim at reward and are responsive to incentives. She uses drugs because they offer her more in the way of pleasure or reward than the available alternatives. Seen like this we may think that her choices are, in themselves, no more to be condemned than those of people who are preoccupied with exercising, work, stamp-collecting, or gourmet food – though like these other choices they may be criticized if they impose unacceptable costs on others or are pursued by unlawful means. Drug users, including those who are called addicts, choose to use drugs, and upon examination the explanation for what they do is of a piece with explanations of the voluntary behavior by non-addicts. This, we take it, is central to the Liberal View.

Models of addiction which propose that the user aims at the highest reward on offer face an obvious problem that choices in other domains usually do not: that of the not infrequent cases in which continued drug use incurs heavy costs, such as loss of employment, damaged relationships, legal penalties, and poor health. Additionally the initial intense pleasure that drug use delivers tends to fade over time and so it is hard to see the pleasure gained as outweighing the obvious costs. Ainslie and Heyman explain the addicted person's chronic drug-seeking in the face of diminishing rewards and higher costs in the following way. Activities that are initially extremely highly rewarding set up inflated expectations of future reward. The promise of drug rewards in the immediate future combined with overly steep discounting of the value of other more distant rewards is further exacerbated by the toxic effects of addictive rewards on other natural rewards which drain them of the pleasure which could normally be expected from them. Drug use thus continues to promise, and they claim to deliver, more reward than the *immediately* available alternatives, even though the amount of pleasure on offer is substantially reduced and even though, were the drug user to delay gratification for long enough they would reap greater long-term rewards. This model is argued to provide a more useful and more optimistic framework than the disease model in providing directions for treatment based on positive incentives that can out-compete drug rewards.

One of us has argued elsewhere (3, 4) that the choice model and the reward account of motivation on which it rests fails to provide an adequate explanation of the actions of a small but significant subset of those who are called addicts and so fails to set aside the possibility that the disease model applies to this group. We will not rehearse all of those arguments here but we flag our concern that disease theorists and choice theorists may not be applying the term "addict" to the same group and thus that conclusions that may be warranted for the larger group of substance abusers who mature out of harmful drug use upon acquisition of new interests and responsibilities do not transfer to those hard core users with whom clinicians are concerned.

Another concern with the Choice account centers on the meaning of the term "reward" in the theory. According to this account, even where it is difficult or impossible for us or for the person concerned to identify the reward that drug-taking offers – as for example in some cases of chronic alcoholism where the physical ill effects of use are immediate and severe – ex hypothesis there must be such a reward or the person would not keep choosing to use drugs. In our view this claim is either trivial or false. We address the triviality claim here; we will provide reason to think that any substantive claim is false in a later section.

If we stipulate that *all* action aims at some reward (or relief), then the conclusion that drug users are motivated by the rewarding properties of their substance of choice follows from the fact that their behavior is intentional. Choice reveals preference. Of course, we can make this stipulation if we want. Our claims about the role of reward in addiction will then be unfalsifiable, and so of no interest, since the notion of reward is detached from its ordinary meaning and loses any explanatory value. On this technical reading of the notion of reward to say that some episode of drug use aimed at reward means *no more* than to say that it was motivated. This we do not dispute. The interesting question is whether reward in the everyday sense is what motivates drug use in addiction.

THE LIBERAL ACCOUNT OF ADDICTION

We see the Liberal View of addiction as arising from the picture of human motivation promulgated by the choice theorists and as gaining some warrant from it. Like the Choice theory the Liberal view says we must start from the assumption that addicts act to satisfy their strongest preferences and the driver for preferences that Foddy and Savulescu nominate is an appetite for the pleasure that drug use offers. They say "we should accept that many addicts may be choosing to use drugs because they desire drug use more than any other thing" (2010: p. 14).

Like choice theorists, Foddy and Savulescu reject the disease model and its claims that addictive action is non-autonomous. They claim that there is nothing special about the choices of those who are addicted – their ordering of values may be different to the non-addict, however, we cannot infer from this that their will is diseased or their choice-making disordered (2010: p. 14). But while choice theorists acknowledge the apparent irrationality of addicted choices and seek to explain why addicts choose what appears to be objectively worse for them over the long run, the Liberal View holds that there is no principled reason to think that addictive actions are irrational at all. Although, *some* actions performed in the course of addiction may turn out to be non-autonomous, so too may the apparently autonomous actions of non-addicts (2010: p. 15). We are not entitled to make the judgment that the bad or weak-willed choices of the addicted person are worse or different in kind to bad or weak-willed choices made by the non-addict.

Foddy and Savulescu's target is the normative framework and assumptions that surround drug use and inform both the Disease and Moral Models. Absent the normative assumption that a life devoted to the pleasures offered by drug use is lacking in value we have no reason to suppose that the addict is lacking autonomy. Foddy and Savulescu think that if we adopt a neutral Liberal position on the values at stake we must remain agnostic on the question of the rationality and autonomy of addicts. The main contours of their argument are as follows:

A. Neurobiological accounts of addiction that support the Disease model do not sufficiently distinguish the behavior of addicted persons from habitual behaviors for other non-drug-like substances, such as sugar, or activities like gambling (2010: p. 4–6)
B. Addictive behaviors are not irrational, nor can we say that they are non-autonomous (2010: p. 7–8)
C. It is important not to confuse any negative consequences resulting from the consumption of addictive drugs arising from cultural norms and legal sanctions against those practices, with the consequences of consumption of those same drugs absent those norms and sanctions (2010: p. 9) (A related point is a normative bias in the Disease View: the DSM, for instance, nominates as one diagnostic criterion continued use despite knowledge that it is causing "a persistent or recurrent physical or psychological problem.").
D. Once we eliminate the errors of the opposing views all we can safely say is that substance addiction involves the seeking and taking of drugs in response to strong, regular, appetitive desires (2010: p. 14).

Let us now unpack the points above in more detail. Habitual actions that aim at satisfying desires for pleasure, considered as a general category, lead to changes in neural architecture and adaptations which cement new patterns of the same behavior. The noteworthy thing about illicit drugs, say Foddy and Savulescu, is *only* that the causal pathway to neural modification is special: certain pleasure-involving receptors are targeted directly, and the intensity of the effect is typically relatively high. But many foods and non-drug-like substances also modify brain biology, they say, as well as practices such as sex or gambling.

This observation leads to an argument: if these other substances, such as sugar, cause the same kinds of brain changes, and addiction to illicit drugs is a brain disease, then regular consumption of sugar is also a brain disease; but of course it is not. Why single out illicit drugs then? Foddy and Savulescu suggest that the reason illicit drugs are thought addictive and deserving of the disease tag, is that the category emerges from "unjustifiable factual claims" based on cultural prejudices. For example, the attribution of compulsion in addiction is generated by a normative bias that is built into philosophical, political, and popular conceptions of what a life ought to contain. In particular it should not contain the selfish and destructive pleasure-seeking that addiction brings about. But, say Foddy and Savulescu, this is indeed a bias, and it has no place in deciding the criteria for addiction, *qua* a condition that allegedly compromises rational autonomy. Their view is that we do not know whether autonomy is compromised in addiction. So, they claim, we should be skeptical of claims that addicted persons are *compelled* in their behavior around the securing and taking of drugs.

Why, according to Foddy and Savulescu, should we be skeptical about the claims that the nature of addiction compromises the capacity of persons to be effective in decision-making? Again, their argument is complex, but two points they make stand out.

First, the cultural ideology around the evils of taking illicit drugs provides powerful motivating reasons to internalize a narrative that paints the addicted person as helpless and powerless to control their urges to take mind-altering substances. Indeed, addicted persons themselves utilize this conception of their situation to deflect the stigma and opprobrium attaching to this behavior. They may even be self-deceived. This would not be surprising, say Foddy and Savulescu, for this reason: "[g]iven that the average person subscribes to some version of the Lay View, the worst thing an addict could say is that she used drugs because she wanted to or because she enjoyed it." (2010: p. 9)

Second, Foddy and Savulescu nominate a heterogeneous set of reasons, particularly from medicine and epidemiology, for doubting the claims of compulsion. Again, they say, there is a stereotypical view of drugs as causing withdrawal, but this is overstated and cannot be generalized from the key case, heroin addiction. In addition they note, with the choice theorists that most people ultimately give up their drug habit by the age of 35. And many base their drug-taking behavior or abstention around rational considerations, e.g., life choices such as pregnancy (2010: pp. 12–14). If their behavior was compelled it would not be responsive to rational considerations and ordinary life incentives.

In the light of all this, Foddy and Savulescu sum up their own view this way:

> The Liberal View contains only three claims about addiction. First, we do not know whether an addict values anything more than the satisfaction of his addictive desires. Second, we do not know whether an addict behaves autonomously when they use drugs. Third, addictive desires are just strong, regular appetitive desires. (2010: p. 14)

The conclusion is that we should err on taking at face value the behavior of drug addicts – that they are rational choosers who value drugs for their rewarding properties more than they value the alternatives. Avoiding "normative bias" they say, we should accept that on face value addicts are autonomous. The Liberal account says that non-autonomy is not a *defining* condition of addiction, even though some cases of addictive behavior might turn out not to be autonomous. Addiction on the Liberal View is a matter of acting on one's strong appetitive desires for pleasure, and that is all.

The Liberal view developed by Foddy and Savulescu can escape the charge of triviality directed at the choice account, insofar as it assumes that what motivates drug use in addiction is pleasure and it characterizes pleasure as "[a] conscious sensation produced by the brain that has the quality of being pleasant, satisfying, or enjoyable" (2010: p. 19). Central to the Liberal View, is the claim that addicted persons respond to incentives – that is what justifies the *prima facie* assumption of autonomy – and the driving incentive much of the time is pleasure (Foddy and Savulescu do agree that drug use may fail to deliver on its aim of fulfilling pleasure.). We will return to the question of responsiveness to incentives in addiction later in this paper. Our main interest here is the role of pleasure in addiction. Let us be clear: we do not question the claim that a life devoted to pleasure-seeking may be autonomously chosen. Nor do we deny that some of those who are called addicts are autonomously choosing a life centered on drug pleasures or that many of the harms suffered by drug users are the result of illiberal social and legal policies which stigmatize such pleasures (though we note this does not apply to the very significant harms caused by legal and socially approved drugs like alcohol). What we do deny is that pleasure or reward plays the central motivating role assigned to it by Choice theorists and by Liberal accounts in an important set of cases and these are precisely the cases where we have most reason to question the autonomy of the addict.

Our self-report data suggest strongly that we should construe the role of pleasure somewhat differently to how the choice accounts would have it, especially when it is conceived as part of a narrative dynamic. The role of pleasure in addiction must be understood as changing over time. While a strong desire for pleasure plays a crucial role for many, perhaps most, people in establishing addiction, it is not so clear that pleasure or the expectation of pleasure plays this role in maintaining addiction. If it does not and we cannot easily construe the behavior of the addict as aiming at reward then there will be reason to question each of the three claims made by the Liberal View.

In Section "The Diachronic Value of Pleasure in Addiction" we present our self-report data to support our claims around the more nuanced understanding of pleasure in addiction. Before that, however, we respond to the claim made by Foddy and Savulescu that the self-report data from those with addiction problems is unreliable.

CAN WE RELY ON SELF-REPORT DATA TO UNDERSTAND THE ROLE OF PLEASURE IN ADDICTION?

Foddy and Savulescu claim that because of the taboo nature of addiction, it becomes, according to those who reject self-report data, "...*impossible* to obtain *honest* accounts from addicted persons themselves..." (2010: p. 3, our italics). They say, "[t]here is enormous social pressure for addicts to provide an alternative explanation for their drug use" [(1): p. 9]. This echoes a similar observation by Dalrymple (5) who has said that when working as a psychiatrist, he was always struck by how differently users described their addiction to him (in terms of suffering and involuntariness) compared with what they would say to their peers in the hallway (in terms of pleasure). The claim is that addicted persons will be reluctant to express to professionals and others the pleasure-incentive that is really driving their addictive actions. This claim presupposes that addicted persons are being honest and truthful with their peers and not with professionals.

While it is plausible to suppose that socially available narratives of addiction influence what users say to clinicians, courts and other concerned parties about their drug use, we think that the claim that it is impossible to obtain from them honest accounts of their motivations for use is overstated, unfair to those who seek help for their drug use or who participate in research projects, and lacking a solid evidential basis.

We suggest that: (i) Addicted persons may be ambivalent about their using and this will be reflected in differing accounts given to different groups. (ii) What they say to peers is not obviously more reliable than what they say to professionals from whom they have sought help, but even if it is, the data that we have collected is not subject to these biases. (iii) There is also social pressure on many people struggling with addiction to *remain* users when they would prefer to quit, or to use more than they want to, and this social pressure plausibly influences what they say to peers. (iv) We should distinguish between the heat of the moment and the cool reflective moment in determining what it is that people really prefer.

First, we think that insofar as users express different attitudes to different groups this may reflect genuine ambivalence about their drug use, as different considerations are brought to the fore. When with family the damage done to family relationships and the hurt suffered by those near to them will be more salient than it is with peers. With professionals damage to health and to long-term prospects comes to the fore. With peers, the pleasures induced by the drug and its social aspects will be most prominent. The question, then, is not whether the individual is lying to one of these groups. The question is, of the accounts they give, which, if any, should be privileged in providing reliable testimony concerning what motivates their drug use. Given the expression of different attitudes to different groups, attitudes underpinned by a rationale responsive to that context, there is no *a priori* reason for thinking one of these groups is privileged as the group to receive the truthful account. In particular we do not know whether an addicted person's statement to a fellow user misrepresents their understanding of what motivates them.

Second, the responses to our own study provide reasons to doubt that addicted persons are honest with their peers (a context where the taboo of taking drugs for pleasure does not operate) and not with those professionals with whom they are engaged. Our questionnaire reflected none of the normative biases Foddy and Savulescu identify, and we made clear to the participants that our role as philosophers (not treatment professionals), oriented us to an interest in their story, and their experiences. Our open style of questioning was designed to avert any sense of being judgmental and the semi-structured nature of the interviews meant that we maximized the possibility of eliciting clear and reflective accounts of respondents' understandings of the role pleasure played in their addictive experiences. Respondents repeatedly stated that they wanted to be honest with us, that they enjoyed the conversation and felt listened to. Sometimes they asked us directly if we wanted the socially accepted explanation or if we wanted to hear what they really thought. It became clear that respondents were not reluctant to express to us the nature of their using, its extent, and the kinds of incentives that drove this behavior, including pleasure. We will explore their reflections on pleasure in the next section.

Third, some of the responses we collected suggest that we should be cautious about privileging what they say to their peers over professionals and others, in seeking to explain their behavior. Social pressure cuts both ways and many long-term addicts live in a social milieu in which using is expected and abstinence is seen as a threat, an implied criticism, or socially unacceptable.

> The other addicts aren't really . . .they don't want to see someone get on with their life "cause then... oh this is what I think, then... it's saying to them, may be you can do this but they don't want to... they're comfortable. I don't know, it's kind of like misery loves company... you can have so many friends when you're miserable and everybody wants to hear all your problems and they're all so consoling you know but sometimes I wonder if they're not being patronizing and they really like to... "cause I notice when I'm going well, no-one's that happy and it's like no-one wants to give you a shot when you're hanging out but when you've been clean for six months everyone wants to give you a shot, it's things like that I've noticed, you know. (R67)"
>
> That's another big step because all my so-called friends are down here and to leave them is going to be hard, but they're not really friends anyway, they're just acquaintances through pubs and drugs, that's pretty much it. So, yeah, to leave them it's going to hurt them, but it's probably not going to hurt me as much as it's going to hurt them, but what can you do, you've got to get rid of the old people, you know what I mean? (R5)
>
> He's [his boss, who also has a drinking problem] always ringing up to come to work, even if I have a day off – "Are you going to come tomorrow? I'll even come and get you." "Yeah I'll be there, I'll be there." And he'd say "You got any beers in your bags?" and I say "No." I know I got beers in the bags; as soon as I get to work I'll open a beer, [and] by lunchtime he's looking at me going "fuck it," let's go and get a beer, and I've already had six by then and I'm thinking oh, I don't really need another one but I go with him and then I might have another six that afternoon. (R6)

Finally, and in response to the preceding considerations, it is common in philosophy and in common-sense, to distinguish between what people want and what they "really want" or value and the differential responses may in part reflect this distinction. Gary Watson describes a person's values as: "...that set of considerations which he – in a cool and non-deceptive moment – articulates as definitive of the good, fulfilling, and defensible life" [(6), p. 105]. However, as Watson points out, our valuational system and our motivational system may come apart. Another related distinction is between people's experiential interests and their critical interests [(7): p. 201]. The former are satisfied when a person's present inclination for certain kinds of felt experiences is met. Desiring a warm bath and lying in it, having a wish to smell roses and smelling them, having a yen to hear Bach and listening to it, all count as examples. Critical interests, by contrast, are not tied either to the present, or to any kind of feeling. That one's treasured antique violin is passed down to a grandchild, or that one's standing in the community as a decent citizen is recognized would count as examples of critical interests.

These distinctions provide an alternative explanation to self-deception or pressure to adopt socially acceptable narratives of addiction where there are instances of different content or emphasis in what is said to professionals and what is said to peers. When addicted persons are with their drug using peers, attention-grabbing drug cues abound. Their experiential interests or immediate urges dominate their attention and what they say about drug use then is much more likely to be, as it were, in the heat of the moment. In a more reflective moment when their critical interests come to the fore, such as when they are with a therapist or a researcher, they are likely to express a measured assessment of their drug use which encourages them to describe how it impacts on their life extended over a longer period than the time it takes to make the next score.

Foddy and Savulescu's reason for dismissing the possibility of reliable first hand reports is the taboo nature of drugs and pleasure that supposedly prevents the addict from delivering an honest appraisal of their drug-related activities to those outside their peer group. As we've shown there is reason to think that this assessment is unduly pessimistic – especially surely as applied to alcohol. If that is right then any claim that we should privilege what users say to their peers over what they say to professionals and others must turn on privileging experiential interests and synchronic desires for pleasure over critical interests and diachronic values, and this is a matter on which the Liberal view must remain agnostic. While both perspectives must be taken seriously, and are equally important in understanding addiction, in our view the persistence of grief, regret, and internal conflict in many of our subjects (including many alcoholics) provides at least a *prima facie* reason for privileging their critical interests.

THE DIACHRONIC VALUE OF PLEASURE IN ADDICTION

While the self-reports of those who are addicted cannot tell the whole story of the role of pleasure in addiction, self-report data provides a valuable insight into the changing role of pleasure over the course of addiction. In this section we will draw on material from qualitative interviews with 69 opioid and alcohol-dependent subjects in order to counter what we think is the overly narrow understanding of pleasure in addiction assumed in the choice accounts. As we have said, we agree that a life of pleasure could be autonomously preferred and that some user's lives may be autonomously structured around the pursuit of drug related pleasures. Most of our subjects did not characterize or experience their lives or their drug-seeking as autonomous in this way. However, our interviews revealed a nuanced and changing role for pleasure across the course of addiction.

On the basis of our interviews we can distinguish three sub-groups of users: the first group said that pleasure was their main motivation for using substances. On the Schwartz Value Questionnaire they scored "hedonism" as their most important value. But this simple nomination disguised an important aspect of their self-understanding in relation to the incentive pleasure gave them. Pleasure was, for them, intensely motivating, but they realized that in the long run the damage their drug use caused had the effect of hindering their goal of a hedonistic life. They were disposed to stop their consumption for hedonistic reasons, and yet found doing so beyond them. The Liberal account argues that even in these cases where pleasure is the only value at stake, there is no reason to think one's short term appetites must align with one's long-term hedonistic project to maximize the rewards of consumption over time. What they say is in line with the Choice model: at the moment of consumption, it is the appetitive reward the person most wants, and that although this may count as weak-willed it is not *prima facie* non-autonomous. Our view is that, on the contrary, the extraordinary difficulty some subjects face in orienting themselves toward the pleasure they both want and value most signifies an important loss of control – of self-authorship. We make good on this claim in a later section.

The second group consisted of people who cited pleasure as the initial reason for consuming; over time, however, after repeated use, the pleasurable effects of the substances they were taking faded out and pleasure was no longer their main motivation for use. The third group claimed to have never really experienced pleasure from using. For both the second and third group their ongoing motivation to use drugs was something of a mystery to them. They explained it by reference to addiction – which they seemed to experience as a motivating force distinct from any interest in or expectation of pleasure.

PLEASURE ALL THE WAY THROUGH, BUT A PLEASURABLE LIFE IS MORE THAN USING

We identified a sub-group of users who acknowledged they were motivated primarily by pleasure. Still, even for this group our data shows that the Choice model may be too simplistic. Those who valued hedonism did so based on an understanding of that notion that was broader than just the "instant pleasure" derivable from substance use; their sense of the value of pleasure was *diachronic* in nature.

A hedonistic lifestyle, as understood by many of those we interviewed, is not reducible to a narrowly focused pleasure-seeking or seen in terms of the aggregation of a set of pleasurable experiences. Only a minority of the respondents described themselves as pleasure seekers in this narrow sense, and even they were skeptical about the contribution of substance use to their hedonistic lifestyle in the long run. One person, who described himself as hedonistic, made clear that substance use was only part of a hedonistic life. Other users described how drug use can conflict with other primarily hedonistic values, such as holidays and material goods, which nevertheless require planning and a diachronic perspective at odds with the synchronic focus induced by substance use.

> I just enjoyed life and work but life more than work (...). I think I wanted to be successful. I was very hedonistic. You know I wanted the right clothes; I wanted to eat in the right restaurants and be with the right people, go to the right parties and that sort of thing. (MHE 001)
>
> When you're drinking you're just thinking of the moment, you're not thinking of anything else sort of thing, anyone or anything in particular you know, you're just thinking about having a good time and a laugh and a joke maybe with a couple of friends that you're with or something like that, but you're not... it's not as if you're sitting there talking about planning and buying a house or what are we going to do... plan a holiday to go overseas next year or something like that. (R32)

One young female alcoholic stated that although she was doing many nice things in her life (including a job she enjoyed, and frequently attending festivals), due to her excessive alcohol use, she was not able to remember many of those enjoyable things and that her alcohol use was also frequently spoiling enjoyable occasions. Another user described herself as a "willing addict"; she claimed that all she had ever wanted to become in life was an addict. However this seemed tightly connected with a kind of status she had within her using and dealing family gained by her ability to be able to get every prescribed medication she wanted from the time she was a minor, rather than from the pleasures of use itself.

Additionally most of our respondents were highly skeptical about the possibility of long-term use without significant negative consequences.

> Well don't get me wrong, I love using mate. If I could use successfully I would. I'd still be using. I love using; I just don't like the shit that comes with it. (R50)

Another respondent described it as follows:

> Heroin is an astonishing thing. I will never... regret taking heroin. In fact those two years I took heroin are actually one of the best two years of my life. (P1)

Yet this respondent did decide to stop because of the negative consequences of his use. He describes the experience of coming off heroin as an extra bill he had to pay for his use, an extra hard time. Adherents to the Choice model will say that such cases make their point. It shows that people *will* stop using when the costs become too high – and of course many of those costs are a result of the unjustified normative bias which stigmatizes drug use.

In response we agree that many people do stop using when the costs rise and this may be particularly true of this hedonistic sub-group.

But others don't even when, from their own point of view the costs are manifestly enormous – including impending death – and the hedonistic benefits are invisible. If the Choice and Liberal theorist's claim that addicts will stop when the costs become too high amounts to the truism that addicts will stop using when their momentary drives to use no longer outweigh competing motivations they have done no more than reiterate their own account of motivation. The important issue for us is *why* some individual's motivations are unresponsive to massively increasing costs and decreasing rewards and whether this calls into question the Liberal *prima facie* assumption of rationality or autonomy in these cases.

The assumption of the Liberal and Lay views that addicts freely choose to take addictive substances for their rewarding properties certainly has application *to a sub-group of addicted persons.* However we see that even in this group people are quite skeptical about the contribution of substances to a pleasurable lifestyle in the long run. Although they don't necessarily regret their use and still like the effects of the substance, they acknowledge the ways in which repeated consumption for instant pleasure ultimately undermines other diachronic values and reasons that they endorse. The Liberal view accepts this latter nuance, but insists that individuals among this group remain motivated by their appetite for the rewards of their preferred substance and that we have no special reason to suppose they lack autonomy. To do so is unjustifiably to privilege their reflective preferences over their first order preferences. We think that there is an important difference between the initial motivational profile of the hedonist drug user who smoothly translates her pleasure-oriented values into action and the same person later on, utterly disabused of the belief that drug use will promote her hedonistic ends, but who is nevertheless episodically motivated to consume drugs when the cues pressuring her to do so become overwhelming – a difference relevant to the assessment of autonomy.

INITIAL PLEASURE

This group of respondents said they used substances for their pleasurable effects, but only, or especially, at the start of their addiction. They described their initial use as a honeymoon period, until their lives began to fall apart, a period in which substance use ceased to be pleasurable:

> that's the love-hate thing I have with... when I first started, I liked the feeling but then once I got addicted I didn't like it. And I always wanted to quit because of that. (FHE 041)

This group, for whom drug use no longer produces pleasure and who want to quit, divides between those who end up using to ameliorate the negative effects of craving and withdrawal and those for whom pleasure or relief ceases to play a useful explanatory role.

> I mean some people will say oh, the drugs stopped working for me. I don't agree, you know, I don't believe that... I mean I think if they weren't working you wouldn't do them. They do. They make a person feel... (...) and then after a while, when I said it takes on a life of its own, what you get is the sort of relief that you get when you stop (...) running, you know (...) you're really punching that last couple of Ks out or whatever (...) 'cause you know that when (...) you get to that certain point and you get that needle into your arm and you get it you'll be able to breathe, you'll be able to go, oh, phew, it's ... that's all better, it's [like] bashing your head against a brick wall, it feels so good when you stop. (MHE 9)

While it sounds odd to portray those who use substances to relieve unpleasant sensations as living a hedonic existence, drug use for such individuals might still be the most rewarding option. The relief described by this user is indeed fully consistent with the choice model and can be accommodated by Foddy and Savulescu. Yet even where our users' stories are consistent with the claims of the choice account we think these accounts miss something important in the phenomenology of addiction. The idea of drug use "taking on a life of its own" recurs throughout our interviews. It is the point at which drug use ceases to serve its original hedonic function and becomes detached from the user's perceived interests, values, and desires.

We think that for a significant sub-group of users pleasure ceases to have the explanatory value attached to it by Foddy and Savalescu, and that at some point neurobiological models, such as that proposed by Robinson and Berridge (8); Berridge et al. (9), and Koob and Volkow (10), are a better fit with their reported experiences. The fit between the neurobiology, the phenomenology, and the behavior may be thought to constitute converging lines of evidence for the view we present. We do not suggest that the neurobiological evidence could be sufficient on its own.

These neurobiological models do however purport to provide an explanation of the *shifting* role of pleasure in different stages of addiction that our subjects and others describe. Although initial substance use can release a large amount of dopamine in the brain, causing intense feelings of pleasure, repeated substance use has quite a different effect. Because the brain is over-fueled with dopamine, neural changes in the reward pathways occur to restore the balance, such as the decrease of post-synaptic dopamine receptors, to overcome the effect of the substance. This results in tolerance for the substance (with less pleasure experienced), but also a higher threshold for experiencing those rewards obtained from normal rewarding activities, like food, sex, and social cooperation. Koob and Volkow (10) call this the "motivational withdrawal syndrome," roughly, the emergence of a negative emotional state – anhedonia – that occurs after abstinence [(10), p. 217]. This state can persist for months or even years after abstinence.

But that is not the only change caused by the huge surges in dopamine release by substance use. Dopamine's function is twofold: it primes us on the circumstances or cues in which the pleasurable event occurs, and it reinforces behavior that is directed to those goals. These effects occur because the intensity of a drug experience provides a learning signal that this reward was better than expected. On the next occasion when the same cues appear we will be more sensitive in our recognition of the type of activity generating what we have learnt, and we will be disposed to pay attention and direct our behavior accordingly (11, 12). The huge amount of dopamine release works as a Trojan horse that overtakes the reward-related learning process and creates long-term associative memory processes directing a person to further substance use [(13). p. 575]. Becoming hypersensitive for drug-associated cues then occurs mostly in the absence of subjective feelings of pleasure. Thus the increasingly addicted person continues to want a substance they no longer have a strong liking for. Repeated substance use increases compulsive wanting, or craving, and at the same time diminishes experienced pleasure. Normally we want what we like, and we like what we want, but Berridge (14) has shown that these systems operate through different neural pathways. It is not so much the pleasurable effect (the liking) that drives the addicted person, but the reinforcing, conditioned learning aspects of dopamine driving the behavior (15).

Summing up, there is a major strand of research that argues that the neurobiological effects of sustained drug use help to understand and characterize the function of pleasure for this group. This group learns to continue wanting a drug that has ceased to generate for them the pleasure it originally had. This is not just a "very strong appetite" for pleasure as this is normally understood. It has compulsive elements divorced from any person-level expectation of pleasure, in that it captures and monopolizes the addicted person's attention making it extremely difficult for them to focus on and pursue other more valued activities.

We acknowledge that the science is far from settled, so it pays to be cautious in recruiting data to support philosophical theorizing. Philosophers lack the expertise to adjudicate between positions within the neuroscience of addiction. But we do not in any case claim what Foddy and Savulescu are especially keen to deny – that this research establishes that addiction is a brain disease or that addictive action is somehow not intentional. We take no position here on whether addiction is a brain disease (We think that some of the common arguments against the disease claim are bad arguments, but that's another story.). We do not think that an argument that the autonomy of addicts is impaired depends on establishing a disease model or upon showing that addicts do not intend and choose those of their actions that are motivated by their drug-related urges.

While it is clearly true, as the choice model emphasizes, that the particular actions an addicted person undertakes in procuring and consuming drugs are responsive to a variety of contingencies, we think this flexibility is not as significant as proponents of such models have it. In particular it does not show that drug consumption is not in some sense compelled, or that it must be the most rewarding synchronic option available, at least on any ordinary understanding of the notion of reward [see (3) on this point]. On a view which sees wanting and liking as dissociable and dissociated in many long-term users, drug use ceases to be chosen in the sense proposed by the choice models, that is, as *rationally responsive*, either globally or locally, to an evaluation of the rewards on offer. The *means* taken to drug use may indeed be flexible and responsive to local contingencies and so drug use can be delayed or moderated in some circumstances, but the *goal* itself seems to be a stubborn feature of their psychology. In the hard core user it is relatively impervious to reflection, choice, and control, even when it is clearly highly dysfunctional. We think that this is an important feature of addiction. Drug use becomes, as one of our respondents put it, like a chore or an "obligation." It becomes something they have to do but that they no longer enjoy or understand themselves doing. Here is a representative sample capturing this idea:

> Yeah but now it's just... it's not even fun anymore really, it just sort of becomes a... I don't know, more or less like a chore I suppose but yeah I just... I want to get away from it. (R29)
>
> It's... there was reason, early part, until I came to understand why I was behaving the way I was behaving. So in... no, not now. No. There's no reason. (R39)
>
> [W]hen I was 20, 30, when I was 40 my drinking was good, I had good times on the drink, from when I was 50 to 60 just... I'm just drinking for nothing (...) I'm just drinking for drinking sake now. (R24)

Now Foddy and Savulescu may counter that we see the same phenomenon in the other kinds of cases they give. Perhaps repeated high consumption of sugar or repeated gambling has the same effects in some people and so they feel driven to consume or to gamble even though they say they no longer enjoy it, and even though it has disastrous consequences which they certainly do not enjoy. If this were to be the case we would not see it as reason either to reject those neurobiological or phenomenological accounts which accept the liking/wanting dissociation in addiction, or to become skeptical about the category of addiction. The relevant behavior is addictive even if it responds to substances or stimuli which do not usually pose a risk of addiction[2].

NEVER EXPERIENCED PLEASURE

Summing up, the groups we have described so far report that although the drug use fulfilled a certain role for a period of time, at some point this ceased to be the case. It ceased either because tolerance led to a loss of pleasure, or because, for more complicated reasons, their drug use could no longer be rationally or successfully incorporated as part of a more sophisticated hedonistically motivated lifestyle. They developed a love-hate relationship, or simply a hate relationship, with their drug of choice as the pleasure diminished and the costs became too high.

We can now distinguish a third group who don't describe any feelings of pleasure or hedonism when using drugs. Some within this group emphasized the strong physical dependency that came with their consumption:

> [A] lot of people talk about a honeymoon period on drugs. I can't remember a time like that, I can remember starting

---

[2]We think that behavioral evidence and phenomenological report strongly suggest both the dissociation between wanting and liking in human addicts that Berridge claims to have found in rats, and the monopolization of attention and cue-driven action in addiction. Certainly the claims about monopolization of attention, cue sensitization, and cue-driven behavior in addiction are uncontroversial and have been established in many psychological studies that do not rely on neuroscience. Addiction neuroscience aims to uncover the neural mechanisms that drive behavior. Perhaps the work we have cited – though it is certainly in the mainstream – does not successfully uncover those mechanisms and explain the observed phenomena. It might explain too little: there could be other relevant pathways that explain addictions not well explained by the dopamine theory. It might on the other hand explain too much. This seems to be the thrust of much of Foddy and Savulescu's discussion of the data. They say the same responses have been observed for a wide range of non-drug substances so either we must say that people may be addicted to all these other substances (a reductio) or the research simply describes normal responses to pleasure and does not serve to support the view that addicts are in any way impaired (qua addicted). Perhaps they are right; more work needs to be done to test this view. But there is at least a respectable body of opinion that people may form addictions to non-drug substances such as sugar and to activities such as gambling, with similar behavioral features and consequences (mutatis mutandis) to drug addictions. Whether this will extend to include such apparently innocent substances such as water and milk as Foddy and Savulescu suggest remains to be seen since the studies they refer to have not, to our knowledge, been replicated.

> drugs and pretty much straight away trying to stop all the time. Like I know people talk about that it was nice and exciting and it was a carnival at the beginning but I didn't find it like that (...). I hardly even remember starting drugs, I mostly remember trying to stop all the time. (R47)

Others within this group described the use of substances as a way to feel normal, as a painkiller, or self-medication for psychological problems. One young woman described how she always felt she didn't have a right to belong in the world the same way other people do, she would stare in the mirror for hours, trying to figure out who she was.

> [U]sing heroin made me feel normal, it took that away, so I didn't feel bad about it at all, I thought I'll do anything I can to get it, I don't mind if I have to work [in prostitution] and I thought that it was the only thing that would help but of course it's taken everything away from me now (...). Yeah I didn't use it to have fun I used it to feel normal, then it turned into just an addiction. (R22)

Addiction is seen by many of our subjects as a motivating force that is separate to and distinct from the desires for pleasure or relief or acceptance that originally motivated their drug use and as undermining both their pleasures and their plans. In the light of the costs their drug use imposes on them we think that, for at least a subset of users, pleasure, and reward do not explain continued use.

AUTONOMY AND ADDICTION

In light of the distinctions of the role of pleasure in addiction we think it appropriate to respond more fully to an argument from Foddy and Savulescu regarding addiction and autonomy. We would claim that the evidence of dissatisfaction and repeated failed attempts to quit calls into question the autonomy of the addict. We do not assert that it calls into question a *substantive* conception of autonomy, for we are not here making any normative claims about the irrationality of seeking pleasure through substances over more healthy activities. We agree with Foddy and Savulescu [(1): p. 8] that in testing whether addiction threatens autonomy the correct conception is a procedural account. Then the question of whether autonomy is threatened has nothing to do with the *content* of the desire one acts upon, yet fails to identify with or endorse. Whether autonomy is threatened is a matter of whether the machinery of the will – involving the interplay between the motivational and valuational systems – functions properly. Foddy and Savulescu claim that addiction does not diverge in any significant way from many other phenomena in which agents repeatedly regret past actions. They write (p8)

> Human beings make choices they regret, sometimes even repeatedly. There may be an ideal conception of autonomy, according to which making choices in the knowledge that one will regret them later, is non-autonomous. But telling us that addiction is non-autonomous in this sense is telling us very little: It is not distinguishing it from ordinary cases of weakness of will.

But, on the contrary, we think severe cases of addiction are not like the ordinary cases of weakness of will they have in mind. To explain this more fully we invoke a tripartite distinction between wanting, liking, and valuing. In ordinary cases of weakness of will wanting combines with liking in opposing the agent's best judgment. When I eat chocolate though I'm on a diet or snuggle up in bed instead of going for an early morning swim in accordance with my fitness regime I am doing what I both want to do and enjoy doing at that time though I think that all things considered I should be doing something else and even though I know I will regret it later. But I *like* chocolate and warm beds. If I did not, my actions would be puzzling indeed.

That we can describe these cases as weakly giving in to one's desires for chocolate or for comfort makes sense partly because the pleasure or reward competes against the value judgment[3]. Are cases of addiction just like this? If they are, then we do indeed have reason to be skeptical about the category of addiction, since in the story just given we have no reason to conclude that I am addicted to chocolates, warm beds, or whatever else.

However, if we take the self-report data from addicts seriously, as we have argued that we should, this is not true of at least a subset of addicts for whom even the immediate outcome of their consumption is dominated by pain and regret. For this group, pleasure (or reward) and the expectation of pleasure (or reward) – that is, what they *like* – has dropped out of the picture[4]. An appetite toward pleasure or reward does not explain their actions. Here the competition is between valuing and mere wanting. You may want something you neither like nor value; furthermore you may want it so strongly that you simply cannot stop thinking about or successfully inhibit the automatic action tendencies that arise in response to environmental cues, and any attempt you make at synchronic self-control will eventually fail. Both strength and persistence of wanting and the opposition of wanting to liking or valuing, are important elements of what distinguishes weakness of will – even persistent weakness of will – from compulsion. Autonomy comes in degrees and while there will be borderline cases we claim that at least some hard cases of addiction are clear cases of compulsion rather than weakness of will – even chronic weakness of will – or unthinking habit[5]. If the distinctions outlined here are correct they suggest that addiction cannot be as readily assimilated to everyday moral experience as proponents of the Liberal View suppose and places the onus back on them to explain, consistently with their view, what has gone wrong in such cases.

We see a significant problem with the Liberal position of neutrality between synchronic and diachronic perspectives in an

---

[3]This is not the full story of weakness of will. See Kennett (20) for a detailed account.

[4]That is, the expectation of pleasure at a personal level. Perhaps the system "expects" pleasure – in the sense laid out by the neurobiological accounts. If so the explanation of action is sub-personal and as argued elsewhere (3) this would be inconsistent with an important feature of choice accounts – that the addict's action is susceptible to a rationalizing explanation, in terms of their beliefs and expected reward.

[5]Note: this is *not* to suggest that addicts lack autonomy altogether or that it is impossible for the compelled addict to reduce or quit – since they may be able to avail themselves of techniques of diachronic self-control. Nor is to suggest that *chronically* weak-willed individuals are not also lacking autonomy. We think they are to the extent that they become synchronic, disunified agents – see discussion below and see also Levy (21) for an interpretation along these lines of the failure of autonomy in addiction. There is no space here to provide a complete description and defense of the distinction we have outlined between weakness of will and compulsion: for a book length treatment see Kennett (20), and for particular application to the case of addiction see Kennett (3, 22) and Kennett et al. (23).

account of autonomy. The Liberal position does not want to privilege the satisfaction of our reflective desires over the satisfaction of desires formed in the heat of the moment. We of course agree that the satisfaction of momentary desires for such things as food, sex, or drugs can often contribute value to someone's life, and that we should not automatically assume that a person who prioritizes synchronic pleasures lacks autonomy. A view which prioritizes reflective preferences can accommodate the endorsement of the satisfaction of synchronic desires as autonomous and can also describe when they become non-autonomous. But what, on the neutral Liberal view, could count as impaired autonomy at all? Foddy and Savulescu agree that it is possible some addicts lack autonomy. Which addicts, and what would they have to lack *qua addicts* for Foddy and Savulescu to count them as having impaired autonomy?

Let us briefly sketch a reason for thinking that the procedural account we favor is to be preferred over neutrality. Who or what can be autonomous? It seems to us that a condition of autonomy is diachronic agency. Purely synchronic agents, e.g., very young children or deeply amnesic patients, cannot be autonomous. You need to be capable of remembering the past and projecting yourself into the future – you need the capacity for mental time travel – in order to be autonomous. But of course mere access to your past and the capacity to predict the likely future is not enough for autonomous agency. As two of us have argued at length elsewhere both planning and diachronic self-control are fundamental to the construction of the kind of unified agent who can properly be held responsible for their actions (16–19). The importance of diachronic capacities and perspectives in the construction of an agent who is even so much as capable of autonomy or failures of autonomy does at least suggest a reason for privileging the reflective perspective in identifying when autonomy is impaired and to what degree. In severe cases of addiction the radical impairments to diachronic agency can be understand only when we see the individual as failing to unify their agency in accord with their reflective selves.

CONCLUSION

Pleasure seems to play a significant role in addiction though this diminishes across time and users become increasingly resentful of, or despairing of, the effects of their substance use on their capacity to realize other values. The Lay and Liberal Views are of course right that a desire for pleasure can play an important role in explaining consumption in first-stage substance use, though this excludes the category of users who self-medicate. But in the long run the influence of substance use on health and on social relationships seems, to many users, not to be worth the trouble, especially when the early pleasurable effects fade. Yet, for a significant number of users in this group, *the loss of pleasure does not result in a cessation of addictive use*. Even for the people who seemed to want to pursue a life of hedonism, substance use has only a temporary role in this. Although our respondents did not deny the pleasurable effects of substances during the early stages of their use, they were mostly quite skeptical about the pleasurable effects in the long run. This seems to us to present a problem for accounts that depend on an assumption that the desires for pleasurable rewards continue, more or less in the same form, throughout different phases of addiction. The Lay View seems particularly taken with this assumption. It also presents a problem for the idea that we should err on the side of assuming that those who are called addicts are rational choosers who value drugs for the pleasure they produce more than they value anything else.

Our interviews combined with other data call into question each of Foddy and Savulescu's three assumptions: First, while we do not know for certain whether any addict values anything more than the satisfaction of his addictive desires, the clear unhappiness of many of them with their drug-taking lifestyle and their repeated attempts to quit suggest that they do.

Second, the same evidence of unhappiness and failed attempts to quit also calls into question the autonomy of the addict. Many are no longer motivated by what they like about drugs and so cannot be characterized correctly as acting weakly in the way we might characterize someone who regrets eating too much chocolate (for pleasure) on some occasion. The addicted person is not weak of will in that sense. The stubborn resistance of their goals to their reflective judgments is not properly explained by assimilation to ordinary cases of temptation where for the most part we do manage to act in accordance with our judgments.

Third, addictive desires appear to shift from being, "just strong, regular appetitive desires" to desires which have lost the ordinary connection with reward. With or without any normative bias that may play a role in shaping an addicted person's preference structure, it is misleading to portray people struggling with addiction simply as motivated by strong appetites for pleasure. For the last group we identified it looks false. Those people never experienced the claimed rewards. Others struggle to quit despite extraordinarily heavy and increasing costs. Many of our respondents continued using in the face of costs which were not comfortably relegated to a distant and discounted future but were rather experienced by them daily, including at the point of use – such as pain, serious, and disabling health problems, and very credible risk of death. In our view it does not appear that such users are acting autonomously on the basis of a strong appetite for pleasure, or that their motivation conforms to the supposed universal principles underlying the choice model. If the choice view or the minimal Liberal view licenses agnosticism on the issue of whether such individuals suffer impaired autonomy or not it leaves us wondering what, if anything, a clear case of impaired autonomy could be.

As one of us has argued elsewhere, to insist either that such users *are* motivated by pleasure or reward or to make this the default assumption makes the Choice model stipulative rather than genuinely explanatory of a range of cases (3, 4). This is a pity since both the choice model and the Liberal view to which it gives rise have insightful things to say about addiction and the role of pleasure in establishing and maintaining it.

ACKNOWLEDGMENTS

We thank the editors and the referees, Owen Flanagan and Bennett Foddy for their very helpful comments on this piece. We also gratefully acknowledge the support of the Australian Research Council (DP1094144) for our research project on addiction and moral identity.

REFERENCES

1. Foddy B, Savulescu J. A liberal account of addiction. *Philos Psychi- atry Psychol* (2010) 17(1):1–22.
2. Monterosso J, Ainslie G. The picoeconomic approach to addic- tions: analyzing the conflict of suc- cessive motivational states. *Addict Res Theory* (2009) 17(2):115–34.
3. Kennett J. Addiction, choice, and disease: how voluntary is volun- tary action in addiction? In: Vin- cent N editor. *Neuroscience and Legal Responsibility*. New York: Oxford University Press (2013). p. 257–78.
4. Kennett J, McConnell D. Explain- ing addiction: how far does the reward account of moti- vation take us? *Inquiry* (2013) 56(5):470–89.
5. Dalrymple T. *Romancing Opiates: Pharmacological Lies and the Addic- tion Bureaucracy*. (1st ed.) New York: Encounter Books (2006).
6. Watson G. Free agency. In: Watson G editor. *Free Will*. New York: Oxford University Press (1982). p. 96–110.
7. Dworkin R. *Life's Dominion: An Argument about Abortion, Euthana- sia, and Individual Freedom*. New York: Knopf (1993).
8. Robinson TE, Berridge KC. The neural basis of drug craving: an incentive-sensitization theory of addiction. *Brain Res Brain Res Rev* (1993) 18(3):247–91. doi:10.1016/ 0165-0173(93)90013-P
9. Berridge KC, Robinson TE, Aldridge JW. Dissecting compo- nents of reward: 'liking', 'want- ing,' and learning. *Curr Opin Pharmacol* (2009) 9(1):65–73. doi:10.1016/j.coph.2008.12.014
10. Koob GF, Volkow ND. Neurocircuitry of addic- tion. *Neuropsychopharmacology* (2010) 35(1):217–38. doi:10.1038/npp.2009.110
11. Kalivas PW, Volkow ND. The neural basis of addiction: a pathology of motivation and choice. *Am J Psychi- atry* (2005) 162(8):1403–13. doi:10. 1176/appi.ajp.162.8.1403
12. EMCDDA. *Addiction Neurobiology: Ethical and Social Implications*. Luxembourg: EMCDDA (2009).
13. Hyman SE, Malenka RC, Nestler EJ. Neural mechanisms of addiction: the role of reward-related learning and memory. *Annu Rev Neurosci* (2006) 29:565–98. doi:10.1146/annurev.neuro.29.051605.113009
14. Berridge KC. Wanting and lik- ing: observations from the neuro- science and psychology laboratory. *Inquiry* (2009) 52(4):378. doi:10. 1080/00201740903087359
15. Volkow ND, Wang GJ, Fowler JS, Tomasi D, Telang F, Baler R. Addic- tion: decreased reward sensitivity and increased expectation sensi- tivity conspire to overwhelm the brain's control circuit. *Bioessays* (2010) 32(9):748–55. doi:10.1002/ bies.201000042
16. Kennett J, Matthews S. Identity, con- trol and responsibility: the case of dissociative identity disorder. *Philos Psychol* (2002) 15:509–26. doi:10. 1080/0951508021000042
17. Kennett J, Matthews S. The unity and disunity of agency. *Philos Psychiatry Psychol* (2003) 10(4):302–12.
18. Kennett J, Matthews S. Normative agency. In: MacKenzie C, Atkins K editors. *Practical Identity and Nar- rative Agency*. New York: Routledge (2008). p. 212–31.
19. Kennett J, Matthews S. Mental time travel, agency and responsibility. In: Matthew B, Lisa B editors. *Psy- chiatry as Cognitive Neuroscience: Philosophical Perspectives*. Oxford: Oxford University Press (2009). p. 327–50.
20. Kennett J. *Agency and Responsibil- ity: A Common-Sense Moral Psy- chology*. Oxford: Clarendon Press (2001).
21. Levy N. Autonomy and addiction. *Can J Philos* (2006) 36:427–48. doi: 10.1353/cjp.2006.0018
22. Kennett J. Just say no? Addiction and the elements of self-control. In: Neil L editor. *Addiction and Self- Control*. Oxford: Oxford University Press (2013). p. 144–64.
23. Kennett J, Vincent NA, Snoek A. Addiction, responsibility, crime and coercion. In: Clausen J, Levy N editors. *Handbook of Neuroethics*. Springer (Forthcoming).
24. Ainslie G. A Research-based Theory of Addictive Motivation. *Law Philos* (2000) 19(1):77–115.
25. Heyman GM. *Addiction: a disorder of choice*. Cambridge, MA: Harvard University Press (2009).

15

How many people have alcohol use disorders? Using the harmful dysfunction analysis to reconcile prevalence estimates in two community surveys

Jerome C. Wakefield*[1]* and Mark F. Schmitz*[2]

[1] *Silver School of Social Work and Department of Psychiatry, School of Medicine, New York University, New York, NY, USA*
[2] *School of Social Work, Temple University, Philadelphia, PA, USA*

Edited by:
Hanna Pickard, University of Oxford, UK

Reviewed by:
Giovanni Martinotti, Catholic University of Rome, Italy
Steve Sussman, University of Southern California, USA
Gene M. Heyman, Boston College and Harvard University, USA

****Correspondence:***
Jerome C. Wakefield, Silver School of Social Work, New York University, 1 Washington Square North, New York, NY 10003, USA
e-mail: jerome.wakefield@nyu.edu

Community prevalence rates of alcohol use disorders (AUDs) provided by epidemiological studies using DSM-based diagnostic criteria pose several challenges: the rates appear implausibly high to many epidemiologists; they do not converge across similar studies; and, due to low service utilization by those diagnosed as disordered, they yield estimates of unmet need for services so high that credibility for planning purposes is jeopardized. For example, two early community studies using DSM diagnostic criteria, the Epidemiologic Catchment Area Study (ECA) and the National Comorbidity Survey (NCS), yielded lifetime AUD prevalence rates of 14 and 24%, respectively, with NCS unmet need for services 19% of the entire population. Attempts to address these challenges by adding clinical significance requirements to diagnostic criteria have proven unsuccessful. Hypothesizing that these challenges are due to high rates of false-positive diagnoses of problem drinking as AUDs, we test an alternative approach. We use the harmful dysfunction (HD) analysis of the concept of mental disorder as a guide to construct more valid criteria within the framework of the standard out-of-control model of AUD. The proposed HD criteria require harm and dysfunction, where harm can be any negative social, personal, or physical outcome, and dysfunction requires either withdrawal symptoms or inability to stop drinking. Using HD criteria, ECA and NCS lifetime prevalences converge to much-reduced rates of 6 and 6.8%, respectively. Due to higher service utilization rates, NCS lifetime unmet need is reduced to 3.4%. Service use and duration comparisons suggest that HD criteria possess increased diagnostic validity. Moreover, HD criteria eliminate 90% of transient teenage drinking from disorder status. The HD version of the out-of-control model thus potentially resolves the three classic prevalence challenges while offering a more rigorous approach to distinguishing AUDs from problematic drinking.

Keywords: alcohol use disorder, alcohol dependence, addiction, validity of diagnosis, harmful dysfunction, diagnostic criteria, psychiatric epidemiology

INTRODUCTION AND CONCEPTUAL BACKGROUND

In this paper, we provide a novel reanalysis of prevalence rates for alcohol use disorder (AUD) in two major epidemiological surveys. First, in a lengthier-than-usual conceptual introduction, we offer a rationale for rethinking standard DSM-type AUD diagnostic criteria. Then, in "Materials and Methods," systematically applying the harmful dysfunction (HD) analysis of mental disorder (1) to AUD diagnosis for the first time, we use items available in the two surveys to formulate more conceptually valid AUD diagnostic criteria that better identify dysfunction and harm. We then use the HD-derived criteria to recalculate AUD prevalence rates in the surveys, comparing the results to the prevalences yielded by the DSM-based criteria originally used in the studies, and also to the prevalences yielded by the new DSM-5 criteria.

We evaluate the HD and DSM criteria sets using a variety of validity tests. Some of the validity tests use standard validators, such as episode duration and service use, whereas others are more novel. For example, we examine the degree to which each criteria set addresses the longstanding puzzle of divergent prevalence rates of AUD across surveys, a problem tackled in classic papers by Regier et al. (2) and Narrow et al. (3) but which they failed to resolve. We also examine whether the HD analysis might explain the puzzlingly high rate of spontaneous remission among adolescents with apparent AUD, a finding often cited by those who argue that addiction is not really a disorder at all but a normal choice process (4, 5). Additionally, we use the HD analysis to provide estimates of unmet need for treatment of AUD that are dramatically different from standard estimates and address the paradox of enormous rates of apparent AUD but without any felt need for treatment.

THE PUZZLE OF HIGH AND VARYING PREVALENCE RATES OF ALCOHOL USE DISORDERS IN COMMUNITY EPIDEMIOLOGICAL STUDIES

Epidemiological studies of community prevalence of AUDs attempt to answer the question: how many people suffer from an AUD during their lifetime (lifetime prevalence) or during a given year (1-year prevalence)? The answer to the prevalence question has major implications for theories of etiology, research, and public policy.

The usefulness of such prevalence estimates depends on how validly the diagnostic criteria identify AUD. However, AUD prevalence estimates yielded by major DSM-based epidemiological surveys indicate rates of untreated disorder that many epidemiologists find implausibly high and that reveal puzzling disparities across studies with broadly similar methodologies. In particular, the first two large DSM-based community epidemiological surveys, the epidemiologic catchment area study [ECA (6)] and National Comorbidity Survey [NCS (7)] used similar methods and collected data within a decade of each other in the early 1980s and early 1990s, yet yielded lifetime prevalence of AUDs in the American population of 14 and 24%, respectively.

The more recent National Epidemiologic Survey on Alcohol and Related Conditions [NESARC (8, 9)], the largest ($N = 43{,}098$) cross-sectional study to date, with data collected only a decade after the NCS, reported a lifetime DSM-IV (10) AUD rate of 30%, substantially higher than the previous studies. Edwards et al. (11) recently assessed lifetime DSM-IV and DSM-5 AUD prevalence in a different data set and found essentially the same prevalence rate of 31% for DSM-IV and 32% for DSM-5 AUD.

Moreover, the lifetime DSM AUD prevalences derived from such cross-sectional studies are likely substantial underestimates due to respondents' failure to recall symptoms. DSM AUD prevalence estimates increase dramatically in longitudinal studies in which respondents are assessed periodically for recent disorder. In the Dunedin longitudinal study of a representative New Zealand community sample, the prevalence of alcohol dependence alone (not including alcohol abuse) during one or more of four sampled 1-year periods between the ages of 18 and 32 was 32% (12). This estimate did not include those who had symptoms only during the other 11 1-year periods between ages 18 and 32, those who qualified for diagnosis only before age 18 or after age 32, and those who had alcohol abuse without dependence. Based on the abuse/dependence ratio in other studies, one can project that the Dunedin lifetime DSM-IV AUD prevalence including both dependence and abuse – or equivalently applying the new single DSM-5 AUD category – would be well over 50% of the population in just the four sampled 1-year periods. These rates are difficult to square with current claims that AUD is a brain disease (13–15).

An alternative view is that many of the diagnosed individuals in epidemiological studies do not in fact have a disorder of alcohol use at all but rather are heavy or problem drinkers for a period of time. Of NESARC AUDs, 72% reported just one lifetime episode, with a mean duration for single-episode cases of 2.7 years for abuse and 3.4 years for dependence. Other studies support high and rapid remission rates for AUDs rather than the chronic deteriorating course often predicted (16). Moreover, the rates at which diagnosed individuals seek help are extremely low. Lifetime NESARC dependence and abuse cases sought some form of service only 24 and 7% of the time, respectively. The revelation that, contrary to the "disease" model of alcoholism, large numbers of heavy drinkers manage to stop drinking heavily without therapeutic support (17) suggests a non-disorder interpretation, thus that many DSM diagnoses of AUD may be invalid if the diagnoses are intended to identify a psychiatric disorder of impaired deliberation or motivation in choosing to drink.

VALIDITY CONCERNS ABOUT DSM DIAGNOSTIC CRITERIA

The ECA, NCS, and NESARC used DSM-III, DSM-III-R, and DSM-IV diagnostic criteria, respectively. It is not difficult to see why DSM AUD criteria might be invalid and give rise to inflated AUD prevalence estimates. The DSM system through its various editions has included a confusing mélange of symptoms, conceptualizations, and categories for AUD, and the criteria for AUD have often consisted primarily of harmful or socially undesirable effects of alcohol use that can equally be present in non-disordered heavy use of alcohol. Moreover, some DSM indicators of dependence have been equally indicative of strong desire or habit within a drinking-accepting environmental context. The general problem with DSM criteria has been the use of criteria that lack adequate specificity for identifying cases in which it can be inferred that there is an underlying dysfunction of alcohol desire, as opposed to negative effects of alcohol or indicators of strong desire to drink alcohol. A systematic critique of DSM criteria is beyond the scope of this article, but detailed specifications of DSM-III (18), DSM-III-R (19), and DSM-5 (20) AUD diagnostic criteria and how they were translated into ECA and NCS diagnostic criteria are provided in the **Tables A1**, **A2**, and **A5** in Appendix, respectively.

Whereas DSM-III through to DSM-IV distinguished alcohol abuse and dependence, the abuse category was eliminated in DSM-5. Yet the abuse criteria (except for legal difficulties) were incorporated in DSM-5 into a generic AUD category along with dependence criteria and a new "craving" criterion, with a diagnostic threshold lowered to 2 symptoms out of 11 from the previous three symptoms out of seven. Thus, an individual can now be diagnosed with AUD on the basis of symptoms that are very weak indicators of dysfunction, such as the former abuse symptoms of arguing with family members over alcohol use and driving under the influence of alcohol.

FAILURE OF THE REGIER ET AL. (1998) AND NARROW ET AL. (2002) ATTEMPTS TO IMPROVE AUD DIAGNOSTIC VALIDITY

Based on the premise that implausibly high community disorder rates were due to the use of overly broad DSM diagnostic criteria, two now-classic epidemiological analyses by Regier et al. (2) and Narrow et al. (3) attempted to resolve the issue of high and divergent prevalence rates emerging from the ECA and NCS epidemiological surveys. Their reanalyses addressed a broad range of disorders, but we limit the present discussion to AUDs.

Regier et al. (2) considered only alcohol dependence, not alcohol abuse. After limiting the two studies to a common age range of 18–54 years old, the ECA and NCS 1-year prevalences (generally considered more valid than lifetime prevalences in cross-sectional studies relying on memory) were a divergent 4.1 and 7.4%, respectively, with lifetime prevalences similarly divergent at 8.6 and 14.9%, respectively. Regier et al. performed a series of corrections to the two studies' data sets to try to bring the divergent 1-year rates more into harmony. These included limiting both samples to those with certain race or geographic demographic characteristics that yielded adequate subsample sizes in both studies to minimize variance, weighting frequencies in both studies to match age and gender frequencies in the 1990 Census, and applying similar DSM-III-based diagnostic criteria with as closely similar wording as possible across studies. Despite these corrections, the ECA and NCS alcohol dependence prevalence rates remained high and divergent at 4.6 and 8.3%, respectively.

Regier et al. suggested that the problem could lie instead in inflated diagnostic rates due to invalid DSM criteria yielding false-positive diagnoses: "The obvious question is whether each of the final groups contains subjects with valid clinical diagnoses or if either or both have a high proportion of false-positive responses. ... Based on the high prevalence rates identified in both the ECA and the NCS, it is reasonable to hypothesize that some syndromes in the community ... do not represent true psychopathologic disorders" (pp. 112, 114). The implication was that changes in diagnostic criteria to improve validity were required.

Extending Regier et al.'s work, Narrow et al. (3) examined all AUD including dependence and abuse, but only 1-year disorder. They attempted to increase diagnostic validity by imposing a clinical significance criterion, requiring service use or interference with life a lot, on all ECA and NCS diagnoses. Noting that NCS prevalence rates are generally higher than ECA rates, Narrow et al. also used the questionable strategy of combining the primary ECA data with a second wave of ECA data collection a year after the first, in which newly emergent symptoms as well as newly recalled symptoms from the past were reported. They then compared the cumulative two-wave ECA data to the NCS one-wave data, thus increasing the overall ECA AUD prevalence rate to be closer to the higher NCS rate (9.1 versus 9.9%, respectively). However, when they applied the clinical significance requirement to increase validity, the resulting 1-year AUD rates diverged significantly, with final rates of 8.9 and 6.5%, respectively.

The Narrow et al. reanalyses thus failed to establish convergence for AUD. They also suffered from several problems. First, there was not a persuasive rationale for comparing two-wave ECA data to one-wave NCS data, except the *ad hoc* desire to force rates to converge. Second, the appropriateness of using service contact as a clinical significance diagnostic criterion is questionable, because it undermines the point of a community study (21). Third, clinical significance criteria generally have been found to have little power to distinguish disorder from non-disordered distress (22, 23). Finally, divergent lifetime estimates were not addressed.

The Narrow et al. results triggered a debate that continues to this day over whether cases eliminated from epidemiological disorder diagnoses by clinical significance criteria are mild disorders or not disorders at all (24–28). Kessler et al. (24) accused Narrow et al. (3) of "an attempt to declare that mild cases do not exist" (p. 1118). Regier et al. (28) responded that the goal is to increase homogeneity and therefore validity: "Our objective is to define increasingly homogenous diagnostic groups with greater predictive validity with respect to both prevention and treatment response" (p. 1059). Given that disorders can be mild and that non-disordered heavy drinking can be quite harmful, an approach to increasing validity and homogeneity other than by a clinical significance threshold appears desirable.

THE HARMFUL DYSFUNCTION ANALYSIS OF THE CONCEPT OF MENTAL DISORDER

The study reported here attempts to improve the conceptual validity (i.e., the disorder/non-disorder differentiation) of AUD criteria by directly altering the diagnostic criteria rather than by adding clinical significance criteria. Our attempt is guided by the HD analysis of the concept of mental disorder (1, 29–34). The DSM-5 definition of mental disorder asserts that a psychological disturbance and the consequent distress and role impairment is a disorder only when it "reflects a dysfunction in the psychological, biological, or developmental processes underlying mental functioning" [(20), p. 20]. The HD analysis elaborates the definition's concept of dysfunction as failure of some psychological mechanism to perform its naturally selected biological function. Dysfunction in this sense is *not* equivalent to "dysfunction" in the sense of failing to function effectively in various social roles such as in occupational or marital roles (as in a "dysfunctional marriage" or when one is "dysfunctional at work"). Such failures are a form of harm, but they often exist in non-disordered conditions and are not dysfunctions in the definition's intended sense of the failure of some underlying psychological mechanism. Given the frequent harmfulness of alcohol, the dysfunction requirement is critical to the distinction between disordered and non-disordered drinking.

The judgment that harm is being caused by a dysfunction is often highly inferential and fallible given our limited knowledge, yet nonetheless implicit in all disorder diagnoses. Often, inferences to underlying dysfunction are based on the context of the symptoms (35), yet contextual information is lacking in many AUD criteria (e.g., did you drink more than intended because of social pressure, because the drinking itself made you more relaxed about your goals, because you wanted a more intense high, or because you no longer felt in control of your choice?). The DSM-5's and HD analysis's dysfunction requirement underscores that social deviance and conflicts between the individual and society, although often warranting intervention, are not mental disorders unless they are due to underlying dysfunctions. This provides a conceptual "firewall" between sheer social control – such as intervention to stop people from driving while intoxicated or to prevent alcohol-facilitated foolish sexual choices – and medically necessitated psychiatric treatment for disorder, in an area in which moral and psychiatric judgments may easily get confusingly mixed together.

THE CONCEPT OF MENTAL DISORDER AND THE LOSS-OF-CONTROL MODEL OF ALCOHOL USE DYSFUNCTION

Given the lack of gold standards for dysfunction or, for that matter, significant harm, the application of the HD analysis to the domain of alcohol disorders depends on many decisions and judgments that are disputable. Thus, there is no one unique HD "solution" to how to diagnose alcohol disorders. Moreover, standard epidemiological studies do not necessarily ask questions in the way most favorable for an HD analysis, so any reanalysis has to be approximate and make conceptual compromises.

In this initial attempt to construct HD-inspired diagnostic criteria for AUD, we do not propose a new conception of the relevant dysfunction. Rather, we provisionally accept the standard view that the dysfunction in AUD involves a "dependence syndrome" in which there is impairment of deliberation or motivation that entails a pathological degree of loss-of-control over alcohol drinking (36–41). The loss-of-control account was the basis for both the ICD-10 and DSM-III-R and DSM-IV approaches (42, 43).

We attempt to be more rigorous about which criteria indicate harm, which indicate dysfunction, and which indicate neither. Edwards and Gross were explicit in their "biaxial" model that the dependence syndrome as dysfunction must be distinguished from all the many serious harms, which themselves of course may warrant medical attention, that alcohol use can cause: "A person may, for example, develop cirrhosis, lose his job, crash his car, or break up his marriage through his drinking without suffering from the dependence syndrome .... [T]he diagnosis of dependence ... should be made in relation to the primary symptoms ... and not by reference to the secondary damage" [(37), pp. 1060–1]. We believe that the most plausible interpretation of the biaxial conception was ignored when DSM separated dependence, a presumptive dysfunction, from abuse, a presumptive harm; as DSM-5's definition of mental disorder indicates, to be a disorder a condition must possess both dysfunction and harm, so neither is a disorder by itself. To this extent, the DSM-5's change to one AUD disorder combining dependence and abuse criteria makes sense. However, the DSM-5's threshold for diagnosis of any 2 out of 11 symptoms undermines the validity of diagnosis by not requiring that both dysfunction and harm are present. The power of the HD approach to limit false-positives and improve validity lies in distinguishing harm indicators from indicators of loss-of-control dysfunction.

An alternative option would be to abandon the loss-of-control view and embrace some alternative framework for understanding dysfunction in AUD. However, no competing conception of the possible dysfunction underlying AUDs conceived as psychiatric disorders is as well-developed as the out-of-control account at this time. Brain-disorder accounts of substance use disorders, while varying in the specific brain mechanisms that are proposed as dysfunctional, are largely aimed at providing a deeper explanation of the loss-of-control phenomenon and so fall within the same domain.

In the recent literature, there are many who reject the interpretation of alcoholism as a disorder caused by a psychological dysfunction of deliberation or motivation. They propose instead that behavior labeled addiction is the result of normal choice mechanisms. The account of addiction as disorder has been particularly challenged by empirical data on non-clinical community patterns of substance use showing high rates of spontaneous quitting even after prolonged heavy use among those qualifying for substance use disorder diagnoses (44–48). Moreover, in some psychiatric accounts, the "out-of-control" description of the hypothesized deliberative or motivational dysfunction has been implausibly exaggerated into a total lack of control rather than a degree of impairment and even, in some early descriptions, into an almost inevitable descent into madness and death, which does not at all fit the data and has garnered further skepticism. There has consequently been enormous interest in models of decision making that might explain apparent addictions as resulting from normal choice processes rather than dysfunction (5, 49–56). These authors point out that patterns of drinking that have been called compulsive are predicted by well-established choice models and that this approach is supported by much available data. These alternative approaches to alcoholism predict that many who meet the presumed criteria for loss-of-control (usually interpreted as dependence, not abuse) will be able to quit drinking without professional help, contrary to some standard "pathology" views.

We explore a different approach here to understanding the provocative finding that so many "out-of-control drinkers" don't seek help and manage to quit drinking. We suggest that the hypothesized loss-of-control AUD dysfunction has not been translated rigorously enough into diagnostic criteria, yielding high false-positive vulnerability. Thus, the true AUDs that do exist have been obscured in epidemiological data by a tidal wave of non-cases that, although they have various alcohol problems and symptoms, are misclassified as AUDs understood as alcohol addiction. According to this view, the "normal choice" accounts may well explain many or even most cases classified as AUDs in the community epidemiological literature, but these cases have been miscategorized as disorders due to invalid diagnostic criteria.

AIMS OF THE STUDY

The present study uses the HD analysis to reformulate AUD diagnostic criteria in an attempt to more validly capture the "out-of-control" model of AUD. In this initial test of the viability of this approach, we restrict our analysis to the ECA and NCS studies. In evaluating the results, we adopt the same four criteria as Narrow et al.: lower AUD prevalence; converging ECA and NCS AUD prevalence estimates; greater validity of criteria as indicated by AUD cases manifesting standard validators; and increased concordance between diagnosis and treatment, thus more meaningful estimates of unmet need for AUD services. We compare the HD analysis to traditional DSM criteria and to DSM-5 criteria.

MATERIALS AND METHODS

SAMPLE AND MEASURES

Two datasets were used in these analyses. The NCS (7) is a community-based epidemiological survey administered in face-to-face interviews between September 14, 1990 and February 6, 1992, to 8,098 persons aged 15–54-years who are representative of the US population. The sample used here consists of all adults aged 18–54 ($N = 7,599$). The ECA (6) interviewed respondents aged 18–98 ($N = 19,182$) at five sampled sites (Baltimore, MD, USA; Durham, NC, USA; Los Angeles, CA, USA; St. Louis, MO, USA; and New Haven, CT, USA) face-to-face between 1980 and 1985. Our analytic sample includes only adults aged 18–54 ($N = 11,092$). Data were weighted to account for selection and non-response effects, and to match age, sex, and race distributions in the US Census, in order to provide nationally representative estimates.

HD ALCOHOL USE DISORDER DIAGNOSTIC CRITERIA

For the purpose of our HD analysis of AUD, we assumed, consistent with the majority of the field's literature over the past half-century, that the psychiatric disorder category of AUD refers to a disorder in which something has gone wrong with the functioning of the individual's systems of deliberation, motivation, and decision making, when it comes to partaking of alcohol (57). We also accepted the standard view that this change in motivational structure can come about either due to physiological changes (e.g., withdrawal symptoms when one stops drinking, drinking to prevent withdrawal symptoms, inability to function normally without alcohol use) or psychological reasons (e.g., inability to stop or cut down drinking despite wanting to do so, craving for alcohol). We proceeded similarly to DSM-5, defining one disorder that includes all conditions deemed AUDs, rather than two (dependence and abuse) as in DSM-IV.

We created three versions of the diagnostic criteria for HD AUD. All were shaped by the HD conceptualization, but each drew on a different set of questions. The "HD/ECA" version is formulated within the constraints imposed by the questions available in the ECA, as shown in **Table A3** in Appendix. The "HD/NCS" version is formulated using the somewhat broader NCS question set, as shown in **Table A4** in Appendix. These HD formulations allowed us to test within each study for differences between standard and HD prevalence rates. The third "HD/NCS (ECA comparable)" version, also shown in **Table A4** in Appendix, was based on NCS questions but limited so as to be optimally comparable to the HD/ECA criteria. This formulation allowed us to test whether increasing the comparability of HD criteria across studies yielded more convergent ECA and NCS prevalence rates.

To create these HD criteria sets, we categorized a study's symptom questions into the two broad HD components of dysfunction and harm based on consensus after extensive discussion. Symptoms that fit neither category of dysfunction or harm (e.g., tolerance, habitual use of alcohol) are not shown and were ignored in our HD formulation. Because virtually all diagnostic criteria for AUD can have false-positive instances in which there is no disorder but only normal intense desire, judgments of how to categorize symptoms inevitably involved subjective judgments about optimally balancing the elimination of false-positive diagnoses against the avoidance of false negative diagnoses, and the judgments of others might diverge from ours.

We made the HD AUD as broad as possible by requiring that any one or more dysfunction criteria and any one or more harm criteria be met for diagnosis. The HD/ECA dysfunction questions included: withdrawal symptoms (shakes, fits, DTs, hallucinations); need a drink before breakfast; could not do your ordinary daily work well unless you had had something to drink; and wanted to stop drinking but couldn't. The HD/NCS dysfunction criteria included: withdrawal symptoms when stopping drinking; use of alcohol to make withdrawal symptoms go away; either persistently wanting to stop or cut down or actually trying to cut down or stop drinking alcohol, but being unable to do so; and feeling such a strong desire for alcohol that one could not resist it. The set of symptoms indicating harm were extensive in both studies (**Tables A3** and **A4** in Appendix).

We formulated the best HD criteria for each study, allowing criteria to differ across studies. The literature tends to emphasize that relatively small differences in criteria can sometimes cause rather large differences in prevalence rates. Consequently, previous attempts to achieve convergent AUD rates attempted to homogenize diagnostic criteria across studies (2, 3). In contrast, our HD-type criteria diverged considerably across studies in both content and wording of the specific dysfunction and harm items, as the appendix tables indicate. We hypothesized that if there is a cogent underlying AUD construct, and if diagnostic criteria selected from each study validly reflect this construct, then varying syndromal definitions should approximate to the same construct and yield convergent results.

A potentially controversial decision was not to include as a dysfunction indicator what is known as the "larger/longer" question, which asks whether the respondent drinks larger amounts or longer than intended. Larger/longer is sometimes labeled an "out-of-control" question (11) but we did not think this question as currently formulated indicates dysfunction with adequate specificity. The question overestimates the rationality of human agents by assuming that prior judgments about what is best, which may be shaped by social expectations, normally control later behavior. Drinking more than intended is commonly due to social pressure rather than compulsion; being the only one to stop drinking in a group can be quite difficult. Moreover, the larger/longer question refers to behavior that occurs during an episode of drinking, after one starts to drink. Thus, the disinhibiting effects of alcohol itself on one's resolve rather than a motivational disorder about needing to drink alcohol can be responsible for drinking more than intended. More specificity in the question might make it usable as a dysfunction indicator in the future.

Another controversial judgment was that continuing to use alcohol despite knowledge of negative consequences – for example, threats to health or family conflicts over use – does not constitute adequate evidence to infer a dysfunction. Many people drink against medical advice, and we concluded that this is a problem but not *prima facie* specifically a dysfunction. The fact that rats may continue to engage in alcohol use despite foot shocks has been cited as a dependence indicator (58), but this observation begs the question between strongly preferred use and loss-of-control. For example, the classic demonstration of the normal curiosity motive is that chimps will undergo electric shocks to look out of a window, but no one concludes they have a curiosity addiction.

The HD analysis maintains that a dysfunction is only a disorder if it causes harm. However, there can be disagreement about precisely what forms of harm should be allowable. For example, the DSM relies heavily on social role impairment to fulfill the "harm" criterion, whereas the ICD aspires to separate disorder diagnosis from evaluation of role impairment due to the heavy cultural loading of role impairment. Some argue that when a dysfunction's harm is due solely to social disapproval or stigma, labeling the condition as a disorder illegitimately pathologizes anomalous variation that would be benign in a context of social tolerance (59–62). However, in this initial test of the HD approach, we included all available harm items of whatever nature within our HD criteria for each data set. Given that we were predicting a substantial reduction in prevalence, we did not want to construct the "harm" criterion in a way that could be seen as biasing the result toward our predicted lower prevalence. We thus construed "harm" in the broadest possible terms, including such socially anchored harms as family arguments, to allow for the most challenging test of our prediction.

DIAGNOSTIC CRITERIA FOR COMPARISON RATES OF ALCOHOL USE DISORDER: ECA, NCS, DSM-5, AND NARROW ET AL.

We used the standard AUD variables from the NCS and ECA, which include both dependence and abuse (**Tables A3** and **A4** in

Appendix), to calculate standard lifetime and 1-year prevalence rates to compare to the HD rates.

Lifetime and 1-year disorder diagnoses in both the ECA and the NCS were calculated using a "broad" approach that required fulfilling diagnostic criteria with symptoms experienced at some point, but not necessarily during the same period of time as required by the DSM (1-year disorder required at least one symptom in the last year). To evaluate the effects of moving from broad to narrow 1-year definitions where all symptoms must occur in the last year, we also calculated the "narrow" version of NCS 1-year AUD.

We also created lifetime and 1-year NCS DSM-5 prevalence estimates based on an approximation to the new DSM-5 diagnostic criteria, requiring at least 2 out of 11 symptoms. (The ECA contained insufficient comparable questions to make an ECA DSM-5 version practical.) The NCS questions used for the DSM-5 AUD diagnostic criteria are indicated in **Table A5** in Appendix. One-year DSM-5 AUD was calculated using the narrow approach; at least two symptoms qualifying the individual for diagnosis must have occurred within the year prior to the interview. Finally, we also cite for comparative purposes the prevalence rates derived from Narrow et al.'s (3) reanalysis of the ECA and NCS, described above.

Use of DSM combined dependence and abuse versus dependence-only in AUD comparison rates

DSM-III inaugurated the distinction between dependence and abuse, which lasted through to DSM-IV and has been eliminated in DSM-5. We compare HD prevalence to standardly cited AUD prevalence rates, which in the ECA and NCS as well as most published studies of AUD, including all the major studies evaluating DSM-5 AUD criteria, are based on combined dependence and abuse. On its face, "abusing" alcohol does not appear to imply disorder, so one might wonder why we include abuse in the primary AUD analyses rather than just focusing on dependence cases which seem more tailored to the out-of-control model. There are three reasons. First, despite the seeming semantic inconsistency, DSM-III and subsequent DSM editions have classified abuse as an AUD, and all major epidemiological surveys have followed suit in reporting their results. To take one example, in Sussman et al.'s (63) attempt to estimate overall addiction rates, they note, "Both drug 'abuse' and 'dependence' were considered as 'addicted' in the table and in our calculations" (p. 5). The classification of abuse as a true AUD generally has been justified by claims that it is a mild form of dependence or that it is a prodromal condition increasing risk for dependence. Second, the new DSM-5 approach has eliminated the dependence/abuse distinction and reflects a "dimensional" view that there is no in-principle separation of abuse from dependence, which are interpreted to represent milder and more severe points on a continuum of disorder. To pursue legitimate comparisons to DSM-5, we needed to include DSM abuse cases from earlier criteria sets. Third, we needed to include DSM abuse within our primary comparisons because those with DSM abuse can in principle satisfy HD (as well as DSM-5) diagnostic criteria. This is because we define HD AUD to include any individual with one form of dysfunction and one harm. Thus, an individual might meet DSM abuse criteria based on one harm, and also have only one dependence symptom (e.g., an individual might have withdrawal symptoms and also drive under the influence but have no other symptoms), and thus not qualify for dependence diagnosis, and yet meet HD AUD based on a harm and a dysfunction (and also meet DSM-5 criteria based on 2 out of the 11 possible abuse and dependence symptoms). Thus, restricting the comparison to dependence would have foreclosed the empirical question of whether DSM abuse cases qualify as HD cases (or, for that matter, as DSM-5 cases).

However, we were cognizant of the possible objection that it is really the criteria for DSM dependence that represented the true out-of-control construct, thus that the HD analysis appeared to be an improvement only because it was compared to the broader category of combined dependence/abuse rather than the stricter category of dependence to which it is quite similar. To address this concern, we repeated all of our primary analyses, but this time comparing HD disorder to DSM dependence rather than combined dependence/abuse. We assess whether this change in comparison category changes our conclusions in important ways.

VALIDATOR VARIABLES

Several variables were used as validators in the analyses, all based on lifetime NCS reports. One validator was directly associated with alcohol use: mean duration of the AUD, calculated from age of onset and age of recency reports. Three validators assessed service use associated with the use of alcohol or drugs: percentage who ever saw a mental health professional about substance use; percentage who ever attended AA or NA meetings because of their substance use; percentage who ever went to a drug or alcohol outpatient clinic for help with emotions, nerves, or use of alcohol or drugs. Non-substance use comorbidity was assessed by the percentage of respondents having any lifetime mood or anxiety disorder, assessed with the standard NCS/DSM-III-R criteria based diagnostic variables.

Once we had the results of our primary analyses, we then performed several *post hoc* analyses to illuminate the meaning of our results. These included tests of HD specificity, HD sensitivity, HD item frequencies, and a comparison of HD and standard remission rates. These tests are described below in Results.

STATISTICAL ANALYSIS

All of the statistical analyses used Stata 12 survey estimation procedures (64), which calculate weighted coefficients (using the ECA and NCS weights) to yield national estimates, and use Taylor series linearization to calculate standard errors, adjusting for the complex sampling designs of the two surveys. Because of the overlapping nature of the different groups, independent sample *t*-tests were not performed, and significant differences are indicated by non-overlapping 95% confidence intervals presented in the results below.

RESULTS

Demographic characteristics of those with standard NCS AUD and those with the HD version of NCS AUD are presented in **Table 1**, for both lifetime and 1-year diagnoses. Differences are minimal, with 1-year HD disordered individuals tending to be slightly older and less educated than 1-year NCS AUD individuals.

Table 1 | Means and percentages (95% confidence intervals) for demographic variables of lifetime and 1-year alcohol disorders, ages 18–54, N = 7,599.

	Lifetime[a]		1-year[b]	
	NCS (*n* = 1,947)	HD/NCS (*n* = 550)	NCS (*n* = 793)	HD/NCS (*n* = 336)
Female (%)	31.5 (28.0, 34.9)	31.2 (25.3, 37.1)	27.8 (23.4, 32.3)	27.5 (19.3, 35.7)
Mean age	33.3 (32.6, 33.9)	34.6 (33.6, 35.6)	30.7 (29.7, 31.7)	34.1 (33.0, 35.3)
Mean years of education	12.8 (12.5, 13.0)	12.2 (11.9, 12.4)	12.4 (12.2, 12.7)	11.9 (11.6, 12.2)
White (%)	84.0 (79.6, 88.4)	80.9 (74.0, 87.7)	82.5 (76.5, 88.4)	79.8 (71.6, 88.0)

Weighted and corrected for sampling design.

NCS, National Comorbidity Survey; HD, harmful dysfunction. See "Appendix" for details of diagnostic criteria.

Significant differences between groups are indicated by non-overlapping 95% confidence intervals.

[a]For each lifetime diagnostic criteria set, the symptoms could occur at any time point in the respondent's lifetime; the symptoms did not need to occur together.

[b]For the 1-year NCS criteria set, at least one symptom had to appear in the year prior to the interview; in the 1-year HD diagnostic criteria set, all symptoms had to appear in the year prior to the interview.

Table 2 | Lifetime[a] prevalence (95% confidence intervals) for alcohol use disorder (AUD) in the ECA and NCS community studies, using standard versus harmful dysfunction (HD) diagnostic criteria, and limited to common age range of 18–54.

Community study	Diagnostic criteria used to calculate AUD prevalence rate			
	Standard ECA and NCS criteria	DSM-5 Criteria	HD/ECA and HD/NCS criteria	HD/ECA and HD/NCS (adjusted to be ECA comparable) criteria
ECA (*N* = 11,092)	15.4 (14.6, 16.1)		6.0 (5.4, 6.6)	6.0 (5.4, 6.6)
NCS (*N* = 7,599)	24.9 (23.1, 26.7)	19.5 (18.0, 21.0)	6.8 (5.9, 7.7)	5.5 (4.9, 6.1)

Weighted and corrected for sampling design.

ECA, epidemiologic catchment area study; NCS, National Comorbidity Survey; HD, harmful dysfunction. See "Appendix" for details of diagnostic criteria.

Significant differences between groups are indicated by non-overlapping 95% confidence intervals.

[a]For each diagnostic criteria set, the symptoms could occur at any time point in the respondent's lifetime; the symptoms did not need to occur together.

Lifetime ECA and NCS AUD prevalence estimates for ages 18–54 using various diagnostic criteria sets are presented in **Table 2**. Standard ECA and NCS criteria yield AUD prevalences of 15 and 25%, respectively. The DSM-5 criteria yield a lifetime prevalence estimate of 19.5%, significantly higher than the ECA's but significantly lower than the NCS's. The HD criteria yield dramatically lower lifetime prevalence estimates for both the ECA and the NCS of 6 and 6.8%, respectively, both significantly and very substantially lower than the ECA, NCS, or DSM-5 rates. This addresses the first challenge of the seemingly implausibly high prevalence rates.

For comparison purposes, we note that the reported ECA and NCS lifetime dependence prevalence rates, excluding abuse-only cases, as reported by Regier et al. (2), are 11.3 and 14.9% for the ECA and NCS, respectively. These dependence rates are still substantially above HD AUD rates.

To test whether ECA and NCS prevalences converge if similar criteria are used, we recalculated the HD/NCS criteria using the ECA comparable version. This yielded 6% for the ECA and 5.5% for the NCS, which were not significantly different. Indeed, even before this correction the ECA and NCS HD rates of 6% and 6.8%, respectively, were not different. This addressed the second challenge, of showing that with more valid diagnostic criteria, the rates across studies might converge.

Similar results were found for 1-year prevalence estimates (**Table 3**). The 1-year AUD estimates using the ECA and NCS standard criteria were 7.3 and 9.9%, respectively. These rates were significantly different from each other, and significantly higher than the corresponding HD analysis's estimates for the ECA and NCS of 3.3 and 4.3%, respectfully, which were not significantly different. Recalculating the NCS prevalence using a narrow approach that required clustering of criteria lowered the rate considerably (7.0%) but still left it significantly above the HD rate, demonstrating that the reduction resulting from the HD analysis was not due to the change to narrow criteria alone but to the differences in symptom criteria for disorder. The DSM-5 prevalence estimate (9.8%) is virtually identical with the standard NCS result.

Narrow et al. (3), in their unsuccessful attempt to reconcile the significant differences in the ECA and NCS 1-year prevalence estimates, arrived at ECA and NCS AUD rates of 8.9 and 6.5%, respectively. These adjusted rates are quite different from each other and in both cases significantly higher than the corresponding HD estimates. For comparative purposes (not reported in the table), the NESARC 1-year AUD rate was 8.5% (9), and the Dunedin study average 1-year rate for alcohol dependence alone for ages 18–32 was 12.7% (12).

As in the lifetime analysis, we recalculated the HD/NCS prevalence using HD/ECA comparable criteria to test for consistency

Table 3 | One-year [a]prevalence (95% confidence intervals) for alcohol use disorder (AUD) in the ECA and NCS community studies, using standard versus harmful dysfunction (HD) diagnostic criteria, and limited to common age range of 18–54.

Community study	Diagnostic criteria used to calculate AUD prevalence rate					
	Standard ECA and NCS criteria	NCS: narrow criteria	DSM-5 criteria	Narrow et al. (3), including clinical significance criteria	HD/ECA and HD/NCS criteria	HD/ECA and HD/NCS (adjusted to be ECA comparable) criteria
ECA ($N = 11,092$)	7.3 (6.7, 8.0)			8.9 (8.3, 9.5)	3.3 (2.8, 3.8)	3.3 (2.8, 3.8)
NCS ($N = 7,599$)	9.9 (8.9, 11.0)	7.0 (6.1, 7.9)	9.8 (8.9, 10.7)	6.5 (5.7, 7.3)	4.3 (3.7, 5.0)	3.6 (3.0, 4.2)

Weighted and corrected for sampling design.
ECA, epidemiologic catchment area study; NCS, National Comorbidity Survey; HD, harmful dysfunction. See "Appendix" for details of diagnostic criteria.
Significant differences between groups are indicated by non-overlapping 95% confidence intervals.
[a]*For the Standard ECA and NCS criteria sets, at least one symptom had to appear in the year prior to the interview; in the NCS, narrow criteria, DSM-5, Narrow et al. and HD diagnostic criteria sets, all symptoms had to appear in the year prior to the interview.*

Table 4 | Means and percentages (95% confidence intervals) for validators of NCS lifetime [a]alcohol use disorders, ages 18–54, $N = 7,599$.

	NCS ($n = 1,947$)	HD/NCS ($n = 550$)	DSM-5 ($n = 1,536$)
Mean duration, years	8.3 (7.6, 9.0)	12.1 (11.1, 13.1)	9.1 (8.3, 9.9)
% See mental health professional about substance use, ever[b]	11.8 (10.4, 13.3)	27.1 (22.1, 32.2)	14.9 (12.9, 16.8)
% Attended AA or NA meetings, ever[c]	18.4 (15.7, 21.1)	44.6 (38.3, 50.9)	22.6 (19.1, 26.0)
% Went to drug or alcohol outpatient clinic, ever[d]	6.0 (4.6, 7.3)	15.8 (11.7, 20.0)	7.2 (5.5, 8.8)
% Have any NCS mood or anxiety disorder, lifetime[e]	47.7 (44.0, 51.4)	62.4 (57.4, 67.4)	50.7 (47.0, 54.4)
% Of transient teen users with NCS AUD having the given disorder, ages 15–54[f]	100 ($n = 287$)	10.3 (5.5, 12.6) ($n = 29$)	65.2 (57.7, 72.6) ($n = 184$)

Weighted and corrected for sampling design.
NCS, National Comorbidity Survey; HD, harmful dysfunction.
Significant differences between groups are indicated by non-overlapping 95% confidence intervals.
[a]*For each diagnostic criteria set, the symptoms could occur at any point in the respondent's lifetime. They did not need to occur at the same time point.*
[b]*Did you ever see a mental health specialist about your substance use? (By mental health specialists we mean psychiatrists, psychologists, or social workers.)*
[c]*Did you ever go to a self-help group like Alcoholics Anonymous or Narcotics Anonymous because of your substance use?*
[d]*Have you ever gone to a drug or alcohol outpatient clinic for professional help with your emotions or nerves or your use of alcohol or drugs?*
[e]*% Any mood or anxiety disorder, lifetime, for the entire sample: 34.7 (32.6, 36.7).*
[f]*Teen transient users defined as having lifetime NCS alcohol disorder, but not having 1-year NCS alcohol disorder, age of onset at 19 years old or younger, alcohol disorder duration <5 years; uses full sample, N = 8098, for analyses. By the definition, all of the teen transient users have lifetime NCS alcohol disorder, giving the 100% result for that cell in the above table. The other cells in that row are based on those 287 cases as the base rate in the denominators.*

across studies, and found the ECA and NCS rates converging to 3.3 and 3.6%, respectively. These tests address the first two challenges for the 1-year rates; they show dramatically reduced rates relative to other studies, and rates that converge across the two target studies when comparable HD-based criteria are used.

Here, too, for comparative purposes, we note the standard 1-year dependence prevalence rates of 5.0 and 8.3% for the ECA and NCS, respectively, taken from Regier et al. (2). Like the lifetime dependence rates, these 1-year dependence rates are still substantially above those yielded by the HD analysis.

An additional finding is that DSM-5 criteria, at least in our approximation, does not substantially improve on previous criteria with regard to implausibly high rates (**Tables 2** and **3**). The lifetime rate of 19.5% is a bit lower than the NCS lifetime rate but higher than the ECA rate, and the 1-year DSM-5 rate of 9.8% is the same as the NCS rate and significantly higher than the ECA rate. This is to be expected; the changes to the criteria in DSM-5 were designed to leave overall AUD prevalence about the same as before. For comparison purposes, Edwards et al. (11) found a lifetime DSM-5 AUD prevalence rate of 32%, and Agrawal et al. (65) and Mewton et al. (66) found 1-year DSM-5 prevalence rates of 10.8 and 9.7%, respectively.

Reducing prevalence rates can be easily accomplished in a number of ways, but the achievement is meaningless if the resulting classification is not valid (21). The results of validator tests for lifetime disorder are presented in **Table 4**, and consistently support the validity of the HD criteria. The HD cases possess significantly greater duration – by about 3–4 years on average – than NCS and DSM-5 cases. For each of three service use indicators – saw a mental health professional, attended AA, and went to an alcohol outpatient clinic – the rates for the HD group are double or more the rates of the other two groups, and significantly higher in every case. Regarding comorbid mood and anxiety disorders, these disorders as defined by the DSM are quite common so all the rates are high, but the rate of comorbidity for the HD group is still significantly higher than for either of the other two groups.

Table 5 | Means and percentages (95% confidence intervals) for validators of NCS 1-year [a]alcohol use disorders, ages 18–54, *N* = 7,599.

	NCS: broad criteria (*n* = 793)	NCS: narrow criteria (*n* = 539)	HD/NCS (*n* = 336)	DSM-5 (*n* = 762)
Mean duration, years	10.4 (9.3, 11.4)	10.5 (9.3, 11.7)	13.0 (11.9, 14.1)	10.7 (9.6, 11.8)
% See mental health professional about substance use, ever[b]	11.9 (9.1, 14.8)	11.6 (8.7, 14.4)	31.5 (24.6, 38.4)	19.1 (15.3, 22.8)
% Attended AA or NA meetings, ever[c]	20.5 (16.1, 24.9)	23.3 (18.0, 28.6)	52.2 (44.7, 59.7)	29.4 (24.3, 34.5)
% Went to drug or alcohol outpatient clinic, ever[d]	7.8 (5.3, 10.4)	8.5 (5.1, 12.0)	20.4 (14.3, 26.5)	11.5 (8.4, 14.6)
% Have any NCS mood or anxiety disorder, lifetime[e]	50.1 (44.4, 55.8)	49.9 (43.2, 56.6)	62.8 (56.0, 69.7)	52.4 (47.1, 57.6)

Weighted and corrected for sampling design.

NCS, National Comorbidity Survey; HD, harmful dysfunction.

Significant differences between groups are indicated by non-overlapping 95% confidence intervals.

[a]*For the NCS: broad criteria set, at least one symptom had to appear in the year prior to the interview; in the NCS: narrow, HD and DSM-5 diagnostic criteria sets, all symptoms had to appear in the year prior to the interview.*

[b]*Did you ever see a mental health specialist about your substance use? (By mental health specialists we mean psychiatrists, psychologists, or social workers.)*

[c]*Did you ever go to a self-help group like Alcoholics Anonymous or Narcotics Anonymous because of your substance use?*

[d]*Have you ever gone to a drug or alcohol outpatient clinic for professional help with your emotions or nerves or your use of alcohol or drugs?*

[e] *% Any mood or anxiety disorder, lifetime for the entire sample: 34.7 (32.6, 36.7).*

Table 6 | Unmet need: percentages (95% confidence intervals) of the general population having lifetime and 1-year alcohol use disorders but no use of services, using NCS, HD, and DSM-5 diagnostic criteria, ages 18–54, *N* = 7,599.

	NCS	NCS: narrow criteria	HD/NCS	DSM-5
Percentage of the general population with lifetime alcohol use disorder but no service use[a]	19.2 (17.5, 20.9) (*n* = 1,475)		3.4 (2.7, 4.1) (*n* = 272)	14.0 (12.6, 15.5) (*n* = 1,088)
Percentage of the general population with 1-year alcohol use disorder but no service use[b]	7.4 (6.5, 8.4) (*n* = 577)	5.1 (4.4, 5.8) (*n* = 381)	1.8 (1.3, 2.2) (*n* = 144)	6.3 (5.5, 7.1) (*n* = 476)

Weighted and corrected for sampling design. The number of cases of unmet need for each cell is given in square brackets.

NCS, National Comorbidity Survey; HD, harmful dysfunction.

"No service use": respondent reported never having used any of the following three services: (1) seen a mental health professional about substance use, (2) gone to a self-help group like Alcoholics Anonymous or Narcotics Anonymous because of substance use, (3) gone to a drug or alcohol outpatient clinic for help with emotions, nerves, or use of alcohol or drugs.

[a]*For each diagnostic criteria set, the symptoms could occur at any point in the respondent's lifetime. They did not need to occur at the same time point. The baseline lifetime disorder prevalence estimates are NCS: 24.9; HD: 6.8; DSM-5: 19.5.*

[b]*For the NCS criteria set, at least one symptom had to appear in the year prior to the interview; in the NCS: narrow, HD/NCS, and DSM-5 diagnostic criteria sets, all symptoms had to appear in the year prior to the interview. The baseline 1-year disorder prevalence rates are NCS: 9.9; NCS: narrow: 7.0; HD: 4.3; DSM-5: 9.8.*

For the 1-year disorders, the validators tell a similar story (**Table 5**). Duration is on average about two and a half years longer for HD AUDs than for the others. Service use for all three service use validators is significantly greater for HD criteria than for NCS criteria, and as compared to the DSM-5 group is significantly greater for two of the service use validators (saw a mental health professional, attended AA) and marginally greater for the third (attended an outpatient alcohol clinic). The validator rates for the NCS 1-year narrow approach are no different from the rates for the standard approach and do not changes the pattern of results of the comparisons to the HD model, so the broad versus narrow approach is not determining the results. Comorbidity is significantly higher among HD-diagnosed than among NCS-diagnosed individuals, and higher but not quite significantly so in relation to DSM-5-diagnosed individuals.

Finally, the fourth challenge concerns the level of unmet need. We defined unmet need for services as anyone who satisfies diagnostic criteria for an AUD but answers "no" to all three questions regarding service use (saw a mental health professional, attended AA, went to an outpatient clinic). Obviously, there are many reasons for need for help with alcohol problems, some of which may qualify as medically necessary when the alcohol is threatening to exacerbate health problems. However, here we focus on unmet need based specifically on AUD diagnosis. The result for the NCS confirms the problem of unmanageable unmet need estimates, with 19.2% of the entire population having an unmet need for AUD services based on lifetime disorder, and 7.4% in a 1-year period (**Table 6**). The DSM-5 criteria reduce these estimates somewhat but still leave them enormously high, with 14.0% lifetime and 6.3% 1-year unmet need. Even the NCS 1-year narrowly defined group yields a rate of 5% of the entire population having unmet need in a given year. The HD criteria alter this unmanageably challenging landscape by reducing lifetime and 1-year AUD unmet need rates to 3.4 and 1.8%, respectively.

SPECIFICITY ANALYSIS

As noted earlier, in *post hoc* analyses we performed rough tests to examine diagnostic specificity and sensitivity. For testing specificity, the challenge was to identify a criterion group of respondents who exhibit drinking behaviors that might qualify for AUD diagnosis, but who likely are not genuinely disordered. The group we identified consists of respondents who participated in sufficiently heavy drinking during their teenage years to be classified by NCS criteria as having an AUD, but who were transient in their heavy usage and had remitted during young adulthood and no longer qualified for AUD. There has been much discussion recently of the possibility that such transient "teen bingers" are being misclassified as having AUD (67–70). We assumed that many members of this group are drinking as part of youthful social relationships and – if they quickly and enduringly gave up such behaviors as they matured – are most likely not suffering from a physical or psychological dysfunction. We operationalized this criterion group as any respondent who met lifetime NCS alcohol disorder criteria, had an age of onset of 19 years old or younger, had alcohol disorder duration <5 years, and remitted and did not have 1-year NCS alcohol disorder at the time of the NCS interview. We predicted that more valid HD diagnostic criteria should eliminate disproportionately many of this group from their classification as disordered by the NCS.

The result of the specificity test for HD AUD validity, using transient teen users classified by the NCS as disordered as the criterion group, is presented in **Table 4**. By definition, 100% of these individuals qualify for NCS lifetime disorder, yet given their overall history, it is plausible that most were not disordered. We found that DSM-5 criteria still classify 65% of these transient teen users as disordered. In contrast, the HD analysis essentially depathologizes this group, classifying only 10% of them as disordered. Notably, this is a disproportionate reduction; overall, the HD criteria classify about 25% of the NCS disorders as HD disorders.

SENSITIVITY ANALYSIS

Regarding sensitivity, a challenge facing the HD analysis is the fear of false negative diagnoses due to reduction in cases. To examine this issue, we used service use indicators to test for sensitivity of 1-year diagnosis. The idea was to see whether the HD analysis missed a large number of individuals who sought services. The test is approximate because the service use questions are lifetime rather than 1-year and they do not specify whether the individual sought help for alcohol or other substances. Moreover, many individuals seeking help with alcohol issues, or referred for such help, may not be disordered. However, if the rate of individuals seeking help but not HD disordered was extremely high, this might be a red flag that there are problematic levels of false negatives.

We calculated the absolute number of individuals (unweighted) with 1-year AUD who sought three kinds of measured service use, comparing rates among those diagnosed with standard NCS AUD versus HD/NCS AUD. For standard NCS 1-year disorder, the numbers who sought services from the three service venues of mental health professionals, AA or NA, and outpatient alcohol or drug clinics were 94, 163, and 62, respectively; and for HD/NCS the numbers were 106, 175, and 69, respectively. In other words, despite the fact that HD/NCS classified only 42% as many individuals as disordered as did the standard NCS criteria, HD/NCS AUD still included a larger number of individuals who sought services in each of the three service categories. By this test, it appears that despite the HD approach's lowering of prevalence, false negatives may be minimal.

ITEM-LEVEL ANALYSES

Our primary analysis was undertaken at the full syndromal level. Further studies will be necessary to explore the impact of each individual symptom criterion on HD diagnosis and validity. However, in *post hoc* analyses we calculated item-level prevalences in the NCS HD sample to check whether any particular criteria had a major role in the results.

For the four dysfunction indicators, the percentages of HD disorders having that dysfunction ranged from 38 to 58%, and the average number of dysfunctions was 1.9. Thus, in general if a dysfunction was present then more than one dysfunction was present. Regarding the nine harm items, in terms of percentages of HD cases manifesting each harm, the average was 40%, but there was a lower outlier (alcohol use often kept you from working, going to school, taking care of children, 4%) and two higher outliers (problems with your family, friends, at work, at school or with the police, 70%; under the effects of alcohol in situations that increased your chances of getting hurt, like driving a car, 77%). The average number of harms for HD cases was 3.6, so the two upper-end outliers were not responsible for our results; without them, there was still an average of more than two harms per HD case. Given the redundancy of both dysfunction and harm in many cases, membership in the HD AUD category appears to be a relativity robust feature not dependent on a particular item.

REMISSION RATES OF STANDARD VERSUS HD AUD

An issue that has become salient in recent discussions of AUD is whether individuals spontaneously remit from what is supposed to be a disorder lacking control. Although in fact lack of control during an episode of disorder is in principle conceptually distinct from whether one can or does remit from the disorder, critics of the out-of-control model have tended to link the two, suggesting that remission conflicts with the notion of being out-of-control and that the observed pattern of remission conflicts with the out-of-control model (54). Consequently, high rates of AUD remission reported in epidemiological surveys have fueled arguments that perhaps the entire conceptualization of AUD as a disorder is mistaken.

To examine the remission issue, we performed a *post hoc* analysis in which we compared NCS remission rates using standard criteria to NCS remission rates using the HD criteria. As the indicator of remission, we used the percentage of lifetime cases that were not 1-year cases. For the NCS study, the standard 1-year and lifetime rates were 9.9 and 24.9%, respectively, yielding a remission rate of 60%. For the HD analysis, the 1-year and lifetime NCS disorder rates were 4.3 and 6.8%, respectively, yielding a substantially lower remission rate of 37%. This result suggests the possibility that as criteria are made more valid for picking out AUD in the sense of disorder, remission rates may tend to drop substantially.

HD ANALYSIS VERSUS DSM DEPENDENCE

As noted in "Materials and Methods," one might object to the above analyses that HD AUD is basically like traditional dependence, and the improvements in convergence and validity that we found for the HD criteria are explained by the fact that we compared the HD criteria to the larger and less valid category of DSM combined dependence/abuse. We thus repeated our analyses of convergence of prevalence rates, validator rates, specificity and sensitivity tests, and unmet need rates, but this time comparing HD criteria to criteria for DSM dependence as defined in the ECA and NCS (**Tables A1** and **A2** in Appendix). These analyses do not include a comparison to DSM-5 criteria, because DSM-5 eliminated the dependence/abuse distinction.

First, was our striking finding of convergent prevalence rates across studies virtually guaranteed by the HD analysis's similarity to DSM dependence? The answer is that no such piggybacking on dependence can explain our convergence results. The results indicate, first, that DSM dependence is itself highly divergent across the ECA and NCS studies. Lifetime prevalence of DSM dependence in the ECA is 8.8% (8.1, 9.5), but in the NCS it is 14.9% (13.6, 16.3). Similarly, 1-year prevalence of DSM dependence in the ECA is 4.2% (3.8, 4.7), whereas in the NCS it is 7.4% (6.5, 8.4); with Regier et al.'s corrections to increase comparability, the 1-year prevalences are 4.6 and 8.3%, respectively. In both cases, the ECA/NCS differences are not only significant but substantial, in contrast to the convergence of HD prevalences.

When it comes to convergence of prevalence rates across studies, DSM dependence actually performs worse than combined dependence/abuse. Using the percentage change in prevalence from the ECA to the NCS as a measure of divergence (the larger the percentage change, the greater the divergence), the ECA-to-NCS percentage changes in both lifetime and 1-year prevalence is greater for dependence (lifetime, 69% change; 1-year, 76% change both without and with corrections) than for combined dependence/abuse (lifetime, 62% change; 1-year, 37% change). Therefore, no purported resemblance to dependence can explain the lower changes in HD prevalence rates (without corrections, lifetime, 13% change; 1-year, 30% change; with corrections to increase comparability, lifetime, 8% change; 1-year, 9% change).

We also duplicated our earlier validity analysis using the same five primary validators, but applied to NCS dependence rather than combined dependence/abuse. For four validators (duration, ever saw a mental health professional for substance use, ever attended AA or NA meetings, ever went to an outpatient drug or alcohol clinic), the percentage with HD disorder who had that validator was significantly and substantially higher than the percentage of those with NCS dependence disorder who had the validator (**Table 7**). Generally speaking, the average duration of HD disorder was about two and a half years longer than for DSM dependence (e.g., average lifetime duration was 9.7 years for DSM dependence, and 12.1 years for HD disorder), and the rates of service use for HD disorder were consistently about twice as high as for DSM dependence (e.g., percentages of 1-year DSM dependence cases using mental health professional and AA/NA services were 14.7 and 25.7%, respectively, whereas corresponding percentages for 1-year HD were 31.5 and 52.2%, respectively). For the one remaining validator (comorbid mood or anxiety disorder), HD disorder was higher on the validator but not significantly so (**Table 7**). These results support the greater validity of HD disorder over NCS dependence.

Table 7 | Means and percentages (95% confidence intervals) for validators of NCS lifetime and 1-year [a] alcohol dependence disorders versus HD AUD, ages 18–54, $N = 7{,}599$.

	NCS dependence: lifetime ($n = 1{,}182$)	NCS dependence: 1-year ($n = 597$)	HD lifetime ($n = 550$)	HD 1-year ($n = 336$)
Mean duration, years	9.7 (9.0, 10.5)	10.5 (9.3, 11.7)	12.1 (11.1, 13.1)	13.0 (11.9, 14.1)
% See mental health professional about substance use, ever[b]	16.9 (14.5, 19.4)	14.7 (11.2, 18.1)	27.1 (22.1, 32.2)	31.5 (24.6, 38.4)
% Attended AA or NA meetings, ever[c]	27.6 (23.6, 31.6)	25.7 (19.8, 31.7)	44.6 (38.3, 50.9)	52.2 (44.7, 59.7)
% Went to drug or alcohol outpatient clinic, ever[d]	8.8 (6.8, 10.8)	9.7 (6.6, 12.8)	15.8 (11.7, 20.0)	20.4 (14.3, 26.5)
% Have any NCS mood or anxiety disorder, lifetime[e]	53.1 (48.8, 57.4)	53.9 (48.0, 59.8)	62.4 (57.4, 67.4)	62.8 (56.0, 69.7)
% Of transient teen users with NCS AUD having the given disorder, ages 15–54	100 ($n = 88$)		17.8 (7.7, 27.9) ($n = 19$)	
% Of general population with given alcohol disorder but no service use	10.0 (8.9, 11.2) ($n = 777$)	5.1 (4.3, 5.9) ($n = 399$)	3.4 (2.7, 4.1) ($n = 272$)	1.8 (1.3, 2.2) ($n = 144$)

Weighted and corrected for sampling design.

[a] For the NCS at least one symptom had to appear in the year prior to the interview.

[b] Did you ever see a mental health specialist about your substance use? (By mental health specialists we mean psychiatrists, psychologists, or social workers.)

[c] Did you ever go to a self-help group like Alcoholics Anonymous or Narcotics Anonymous because of your substance use?

[d] Have you ever gone to a drug or alcohol outpatient clinic for professional help with your emotions or nerves or your use of alcohol or drugs?

[e] % Any mood or anxiety disorder, lifetime for the entire sample: 34.7 (32.6, 36.7).

NCS alcohol dependence lifetime prevalence: 14.9% (13.6, 16.3).

HD alcohol disorder lifetime prevalence: 6.8% (5.9, 7.7).

NCS alcohol dependence 1-year prevalence: 7.4% (6.5, 8.4).

HD alcohol disorder 1-year prevalence: 4.3% (3.7, 5.0).

Is NCS dependence more valid on our indicators than NCS combined dependence/abuse? Comparing **Table 7** to **Tables 4** and **5**, the increment in validity in moving from combined dependence/abuse to dependence, as indicated by increasing percentages of validators, is surprisingly modest. For 1-year disorder, there is a trend for dependence to be slightly higher on validator percentages, but the increases do not reach significance on any of the validators. Of particular interest is that the reported duration of dependence cases and combined dependence/abuse cases is virtually identical. Looking at lifetime validators, dependence is significantly higher than combined dependence/abuse on two out of the five validators (seeing a professional, attending AA or NA), and for the other three validators there is not a significant difference. A limitation is that these NCS analyses used DSM-III-R criteria, but these are quite similar in major respects to DSM-IV criteria (three out of nine symptoms, many having similar wording to that used in DSM-IV). Clearly, the validity results for the HD criteria cannot be explained by any parasitic relationship to dependence, which does only very modestly better than combined dependence/abuse.

In terms of unmet need (**Table 7**), dependence rates are lower than combined dependence/abuse, but still very high. The HD analysis reduces both lifetime and 1-year NCS dependence rates of unmet need by about two-thirds. For example, in a given year, instead of 5.1% of the entire adult population having unmet need for treatment according to the dependence criteria, only 1.8% of the population has unmet need for treatment by the HD analysis.

For the HD versus dependence comparison, we duplicated the specificity and sensitivity analyses we did for combined dependence/abuse. For specificity, of the individuals who reported transient adolescent drinking and who qualified for NCS dependence, only about 18% of them also qualified for HD disorder, so the HD criteria are still making a major difference (**Table 7**). This is a highly disproportionate reduction; overall, about 47% of those who qualified for NCS dependence also qualified for HD disorder. Thus, if one suspects that transient adolescent use of alcohol is being overdiagnosed, then the HD analysis appears to offer a more effective corrective than dependence.

The sensitivity analysis again used 1-year data, and we used the two most frequent service use indicators – ever seeing a professional about substance use and ever attending AA or NA meetings (again, these items were limited by not being specific to alcohol). For both validators, despite the fact that 1-year HD disorders occurred only 56% as frequently as NCS dependence, the absolute number of diagnosed individuals who reported service use was higher for HD disorder than for NCS dependence. For 1-year NCS dependence, 88 individuals reported seeing a mental health professional and 153 reported attending AA or NA; the comparable figures for 1-year HD disorder were 106 seeking professional help and 175 attending AA or NA. The HD criteria thus managed to pick out the service use seekers from among a much larger pool of NCS-dependent individuals, and even identified a considerable number of help-seeking individuals the NCS dependence criteria had missed.

The remission rate of NCS DSM dependence – that is, the percentage of those with lifetime dependence who did not have 1-year dependence – was 50%. This was lower than the remission rate for combined dependence/abuse (60%) but higher than the HD remission rate (37%).

These analyses disconfirm the idea that the success of the HD analysis in yielding prevalence convergence across studies and increasing validator levels is due to its being similar to dependence and our having used the broader dependence/abuse category for comparisons. Indeed, within the constraints of these analyses, these results cast doubt on the common belief that DSM dependence is a much more valid category than combined dependence/abuse. In any event, the incremental value of the HD approach over dependence is strongly affirmed.

DISCUSSION

The distinction between problem drinking and AUD is important both conceptually and pragmatically. Mixing together those who choose to drink heavily or suffer adverse effects of doing so with those who have a mental disorder of drinking motivation – thus yielding "false-positive" AUD diagnoses – undermines attempts to establish brain correlates of disorder, identify etiological pathways and risk factors for disorder, offer patients appropriate prognosis and informed consent for treatment, and test treatments aimed at ameliorating disorder (71). The standard view of the dysfunction that exists in AUD since about the mid-twentieth century, and the view underlying the DSM's approach to diagnosis of AUDs as well as the present analysis, is that some people who drink to excess suffer from a motivational dysfunction that leads to loss of normal-range deliberative control over drinking (57). The attempt to improve validity of AUD diagnosis in the present study took place within the framework of the loss-of-control model.

Alcohol use is an area of social ambivalence that warrants caution among nosologists lest they become agents of social control by labeling harmful or disapproved behavior as disordered when there is no evidence of dysfunction. Yet DSM AUD diagnostic criteria seem to inhabit an alternative conceptual universe in which problems common among the non-addicted, such as arguing with family members over alcohol use, strong preference for alcohol-related activities, and driving under the influence of alcohol are taken as *prima facie* evidence of a psychiatric disorder rather than simply harmful effects of drinking. Without valid criteria distinguishing AUD from non-disordered problems, in the long run it will be more difficult for research to unlock AUD etiology and to identify effective treatments, and in the short run treatment selection will be muddied by diagnostic mixing of very different conditions.

The present study attempted to approach the criteria with a strict focus on conceptual validity, especially in requiring indicators of dysfunction. Our central hypothesis was that the out-of-control model had not been given a fair test because of confusion in diagnostic criteria between motivational dysfunctions on the one hand and harmful effects of drinking and strong preferences for drinking on the other hand. We provided initial data on the validity of a possible HD translation of the loss-of-control model.

MAJOR NOVEL FINDINGS

Other researchers have noted the potential usefulness of conceptualizing AUDs in terms of the HD analysis (72,73), and some efforts to revise criteria have been along lines consistent with implicit HD thinking (74–76). However, this is the first study explicitly and systematically to formulate criteria for AUD based strictly on HD considerations, apply them to major epidemiological data sets, and evaluate the outcome in a systematic way. The evaluation offers the first three-way validator analysis comparing the validity of the approaches of traditional DSMs, the new DSM-5, and the HD analysis to defining AUD, using standard validators such as duration, service use, and comorbidity.

The results suggest that, in terms of the validators we were able to deploy from the NCS data set, the DSM-5 criteria generally yielded non-significant trends toward elevated validator levels relative to the NCS's DSM-III-R criteria while modestly reducing prevalence. Thus, the DSM-5 changes seem not to represent any great progress in terms of validity. In contrast, the HD analysis significantly and substantially increased validator rates over both DSM-III-R and DSM-5 while also significantly and substantially lowering prevalence rates relative to DSM-III-R and DSM-5 as well as yielding convergent rates across studies. The results suggest that continued exploration of a somewhat revised out-of-control model of addictive pathology is warranted. Substantively, the results indicate that a stricter approach to AUD diagnosis could yield a lifetime prevalence more in the 6% range than the 30% range.

This paper also presents the first attempt subsequent to Regier et al.'s (2) and Narrow et al.'s (3) classic papers to resolve the two-decade-old puzzle of divergent ECA and NCS prevalence rates. According to our findings, there is an underlying convergence once a more valid and narrower HD-derived definition of AUD is applied to the data. This finding of convergent prevalence rates across studies emerged despite somewhat divergent criteria, as we had hypothesized. These findings implicitly address broader doubts about the viability of community studies of psychiatric disorder. Of course, convergence can have many other explanations, and further research will be necessary to confirm that increased validity is responsible for the present convergence. However, the validator results reported here tend to support this explanation.

This is also the first successful attempt we know of to formulate and test an explanation of the much-discussed puzzle of high transient adolescent rates of AUD. The high rates of apparently spontaneously remitting adolescent AUD have been prominently featured in recent arguments that AUD is not really a disorder at all but a matter of normal-range choice (4, 5). Our analysis indicates that the vast majority of these cases do not satisfy HD requirements for disorder. This suggests that it might be misguided to rely on these cases to argue that there is no true AUD, because in fact the identification of these cases as AUDs in epidemiological surveys is likely due to invalid definitions of AUD yielding large numbers of false-positive cases during adolescence.

Hasin's (77) statement that "we still lack the ability to differentiate between young individuals in the general population who evidence the criteria and remit and those who go on to develop chronic, debilitating alcohol or other drug disorders" (p. 703) is no longer entirely true in light of the present results. Of those young individuals who satisfied NCS AUD criteria but remitted within 5 years and did not have a current disorder at the time of the NCS interview, 90% of them were eliminated from the disorder category by applying the HD analysis criteria, higher than the overall 72% reduction of prevalence. In contrast, of those young people who had at least a 10-year duration and had current 1-year disorder at the time of the NCS interview, only 42% were eliminated as non-disordered. Thus, HD criteria do offer some predictive power when it comes to likely transience of adolescent onset cases.

This paper's calculations of unmet need for treatment offer an estimate that, while still challengingly high at about 4.5 million U.S. adults with unmet need for AUD treatment per year, greatly diverges from standard unmet need rates of about 17 million individuals per year. Further research is needed to address whether these revised estimates represent an improved differentiation of those with unmet need for treatment of harmful compulsive use from those experiencing other alcohol-related issues, which they might or might not want treated. In evaluating these unmet need results, one must consider the remarkable statistics on unmet versus felt need from the 2012 National Survey on Drug Use and Health: "Among the 16.8 million persons aged 12 or older who needed but did not receive specialty treatment for an alcohol use problem in 2012, 665,000 persons (4.0%) felt they needed treatment for their alcohol use problem. . .. Of the 665,000, . . ., 490,000 did not make an effort to get treatment, and 174,000 made an effort but were unable to get treatment" (78). Thus, of those qualifying for AUD status under current criteria but who did not receive treatment, about 1% actually felt they needed treatment and made some effort to seek treatment but were unsuccessful. While there are many psychological, social, and institutional obstacles to seeking treatment for AUD, there is a *prima facie* implausibility to these extraordinary rates of unfelt need among those purportedly needing treatment for compulsive alcohol use. Our analysis suggests a possible resolution to this puzzle; a very large number of these individuals do not have a true AUD with deliberational or motivational dysfunction and the resulting harm, and they judge, perhaps correctly, that treatment for AUD is unwarranted.

A surprising finding of this study was that all of the major conclusions about validity arrived at from the above comparisons of HD disorder to combined dependence/abuse held just as strongly when the HD analysis was compared to DSM dependence. The present analyses suggest that DSM dependence may not be as conceptually valid as has sometimes been claimed.

LIMITATIONS

This study had all the limitations of the original cross-sectional ECA and NCS analyses, such as respondents' faulty memories and limitations of lay interviewers. Longitudinal analysis would no doubt increase HD estimates. We analyzed only psychiatric disorders of deliberative control over alcohol drinking, but there are many other medical conditions related to alcohol use warranting treatment so AUD "should therefore not monopolize medical and social concern" [(37), p. 1060]. Secondary analysis was limited by the need to use questions as originally worded, rather than wording that would be optimal for the HD approach (e.g., with more contextual exclusions to eliminate false-positives).

A conceptual limitation is that the HD analysis's concepts of "dysfunction" and "harm" that we used to conceptualize AUD, like other concepts currently used to conceptualize AUDs such as "compulsive," "dependent," or "out-of-control," are fuzzy concepts. They thus required difficult judgments to operationalize, which we reached by discussion and consensus. So, there remains room for dispute about HD criteria. However, our judgments resonated with concerns about validity of diagnostic criteria expressed by others (72, 74, 79–83). In aiming for plausible prevalence estimates, clearly one can decide within the range of one's guiding concepts to err on the side of avoiding false negatives and establishing relatively high AUD prevalence versus erring on the side of avoiding false-positives and establishing relatively low prevalence of alcoholism. However, validity considerations place limits on such flexibility if one is attempting to validly identify mental disorder. Future studies should explore alternative choices of HD-inspired criteria that can be justified theoretically.

Our translation of DSM-5 criteria into NCS questions also involved subjective judgment. Alternative translations with correspondingly altered results are possible. However, *post hoc* shadow analyses suggested that such alternative translations would not alter the primary findings of the analysis with regard to DSM-5 validators or comparisons of DSM-5 to other approaches.

We restricted our analysis to the ECA and NCS, the two data sets that were the target of Regier et al.'s (2) and Narrow et al.'s (3) early reanalyses. This provided a useful comparison point because they tried a variety of other strategies to increase validity and cross-study comparability, all of which failed to achieve the desired result. There are two other major epidemiological data sets available for public use, the National Comorbidity Survey Replication (NCS-R) (84) and the NESARC, and it might be asked why these were not included as well. The NCS-R reported substantially lower rates of dependence-only prevalence (5.4%) than other studies. However, it has emerged that the NCS-R used flawed methodology that generated artificially low dependence prevalence rates. Specifically, respondents were not asked dependence symptom questions unless they first responded positively to an abuse question, yet the abuse and dependence questions (taken from DSM-IV) do not overlap, so this procedure eliminated many dependence cases (9, 85–87). Kessler, the lead NCS-R researcher, admitted that this was an error and changed the procedure in later studies (88). These flaws render the NCS-R inappropriate for AUD prevalence studies, and its low reported dependence rate is meaningless. Regarding the NESARC, we report the NESARC's AUD prevalences for comparison purposes but we did not reanalyze the NESARC in detail for this report. This is because that survey provides a very different array of validators and analysis opportunities that are not available in the NCS and ECA. A detailed NESARC HD analysis that extends the present framework is a priority that requires a separate report and is currently underway.

A further limitation is that our lowered prevalence estimates are limited to AUD and ignore other alcohol-related pathologies and problems. Thus, for example, although the HD approach lowers AUD prevalence, the prevalence of other psychiatric disorders induced by heavy use of alcohol (89) and the possible coexistence of multiple substance abuse in alcoholics (90) remain unaccounted for in our prevalence rates.

Finally, it should be emphasized that diagnosis is not the same as treatment need (91), and it is not the same as risk of disorder despite often being confused with risk (92, 93). Some disorders are mild and need not be aggressively treated, whereas many alcohol-related problems, even if not AUDs, create risk or actual harm that demands intervention.

IMPLICATIONS REGARDING DSM-5

One of the primary findings of our analysis is that DSM-5's single AUD category is not much of a change from DSM-IV's dependence and abuse combined when it comes to prevalence and validator results. The prevalence result was expected because DSM-5 AUD criteria were designed to preserve overall DSM-IV dependence plus abuse prevalence. However, the lack of validator improvement is more concerning and may reflect an underlying validity problem. Based on "the lack of data to support an intermediate state between drug use and drug dependence" [(94), p. 867], and despite acknowledgment that "the dependence process and its consequences do seem conceptually distinct" [(77), p. 703], the DSM-5 criteria make no provision to differentiate AUD from problem drinking, and the dependence dimension essentially swallows up symptomatic problem drinking. In giving up the distinction between disorder and problem drinking and giving up the search for valid differentiating criteria, DSM-5 likely violates DSM-5's definition of mental disorder by classifying some alcohol problems as disorders even when there is no evidence of underlying dysfunction (e.g., when there are two abuse symptoms). The provisional positive evaluation of the HD analysis in this study suggests that the DSM-5 changes may have been premature and may obscure a potential alternative approach that has many advantages. It thus appears that the HD approach is worth further empirical exploration in seeking improved validity of AUD diagnostic criteria.

CONCLUSION

It remains an open question whether the loss-of-control model is a satisfactory model of a genuine AUD dysfunction. However, the results of this study suggest that a problem in testing the loss-of-control model has been its questionable translation into diagnostic criteria. Conceptually driven revisions to diagnostic criteria that particularly attend to dysfunction indicators could lead to cleaner tests of the model's validity. This paper's results argue for a renewed effort to construct such diagnostic criteria sets that more effectively distinguish AUDs from other alcohol-related problems and thus might reduce false-positive AUD diagnoses that lead to confusion in the scientific and clinical literature.

AUTHOR CONTRIBUTIONS

Both Jerome C. Wakefield and Mark F. Schmitz contributed substantially to the conceptualization, data analysis, first-drafting, and revising of this paper.

ACKNOWLEDGMENTS

We thank Lynn Warner and Judith Baer for helpful general discussions and material concerning the historical chronology of thinking about alcohol use disorders at the outset of our working on this topic.

REFERENCES

1. Wakefield JC. The concept of mental disorder: on the boundary between biological facts and social values. *Am Psychol* (1992) **47**:373–88. doi:10.1037/0003-066X.47.3.373
2. Regier DA, Kaelber CT, Rae DS, Farmer ME, Knauper B, Kessler RC, et al. Limitations of diagnostic criteria and assessment instruments for mental disorders: implications for research and policy. *Arch Gen Psychiatry* (1998) **55**:109–15. doi:10.1001/archpsyc.55.2.109

3. Narrow WE, Rae DS, Robins LN, Regier DA. Revised prevalence estimates of mental disorder in the United States: using a clinical significance criterion to reconcile 2 survey's estimates. *Arch Gen Psychiatry* (2002) **59**:115–23. doi:10.1001/archpsyc.59.2.115
4. Heyman GM. Addiction and choice: theory and new data. *Front Psychiatry* (2013) **4**:31. doi:10.3389/fpsyt.2013.00031
5. Pickard H. The purpose in chronic addiction. *AJOB Neurosci* (2012) **3**(2):40–9. doi:10.1080/21507740.2012.663058
6. Robins LN, Regier DA. *Psychiatric Disorders in America.* New York: Free Press (1991).
7. Kessler RC, McGonagle KA, Zhao S, Nelson CB, Eshelman S, Wittchen HU, et al. Lifetime and 12-month prevalence of DSM-III-R psychiatric disorders in the United States: results from the National Comorbidity Survey. *Arch Gen Psychiatry* (1994) **51**:8–19. doi:10.1001/archpsyc.1994.03950010008002
8. Grant BF, Goldstein RB, Chou SP, Huang B, Stinson FS, Dawson DA, et al. Sociodemographic and psychopathologic predictors of first incidence of DSM-IV substance use, mood and anxiety disorders: results from the wave 2 National Epidemiologic Survey on alcohol and related conditions. *Mol Psychiatry* (2009) **14**:1051–66. doi:10.1038/mp.2008.41
9. Hasin DS, Stinson FS, Ogburn E, Grant BF. Prevalence, correlates, disability, and comorbidity of DSM-IV alcohol abuse and dependence in the United States: results from the National Epidemiologic Survey on alcohol and related conditions. *Arch Gen Psychiatry* (2007) **64**(7):830–42. doi:10.1001/archpsyc.64.7.830
10. American Psychiatric Association. *Diagnostic and Statistical Manual of Mental Disorders.* 4th ed. Text rev. ed. Washington, DC: American Psychiatric Association (2000).
11. Edwards AC, Gillespie NA, Aggen SH, Kendler KS. Assessment of a modified DSM-5 diagnosis of alcohol use disorder in a genetically informative population. *Alcohol Clin Exp Res* (2013) **37**(3):443–51. doi:10.1111/j.1530-0277.2012.01954.x
12. Moffitt TE, Caspi A, Taylor A, Kokaua J, Milne BJ, Polanczyk G, et al. How common are common mental disorders? Evidence that lifetime prevalence rates are doubled by prospective versus retrospective ascertainment. *Psychol Med* (2010) **40**:899–909. doi:10.1017/S0033291709991036
13. Leshner AI. Addiction is a brain disease, and it matters. *Science* (1997) **278**:44–5. doi:10.1126/science.278.5335.45
14. O'Brien CP, Volkow N, Li TK. What's in a word? Addiction versus dependence in DSM-V. *Am J Psychiatry* (2006) **163**(5):764–5. doi:10.1176/appi.ajp.163.5.764
15. Volkow ND, Li TK. Drug addiction: the neurobiology of behavior gone awry. *Nat Rev Neurosci* (2004) **5**:963–70. doi:10.1038/nrn1539
16. de Bruijn C, van den Brink W, de Graaf R, Vollebergh WA. The three year course of alcohol use disorders in the general population: DSM-IV, ICD-10 and the Craving Withdrawal Model. *Addiction* (2006) **101**(3):385–92. doi:10.1111/j.1360-0443.2006.01327.x
17. Dawson DA, Grant BF, Stinson FS, Chou PS, Huang B, Ruan WJ. Recovery from DSM-IV alcohol dependence: United States, 2001-2002. *Addiction* (2005) **100**:281–2. doi:10.1111/j.1360-0443.2004.00964.x
18. American Psychiatric Association. *Diagnostic and Statistical Manual of Mental Disorders.* 3rd ed. Washington, DC: American Psychiatric Association (1980).
19. American Psychiatric Association. *Diagnostic and Statistical Manual of Mental Disorders.* 3rd ed. revised ed. Washington, DC: American Psychiatric Association (1987).
20. American Psychiatric Association. *Diagnostic and Statistical Manual of Mental Disorders: DSM-5.* 5th ed. Washington, DC: American Psychiatric Association (2013).
21. Wakefield JC, Spitzer RL. Lowered estimates – but of what? *Arch Gen Psychiatry* (2002) **59**:129–30. doi:10.1001/archpsyc.59.2.129
22. Spitzer RL, Wakefield JC. DSM-IV diagnostic criterion for clinical significance: does it help solve the false positives problem? *Am J Psychiatry* (1999) **156**:1856–64.
23. Wakefield JC, Schmitz MF, Baer JC. Does the DSM-IV clinical significance criterion for major depression reduce false positives? Evidence from the NCS-R. *Am J Psychiatry* (2010) **167**:298–304. doi:10.1176/appi.ajp.2009.09040553
24. Kessler RC, Merikangas KR, Berglund P, Eaton WW, Koretz DS, Walters EE. Mild disorders should not be eliminated from the DSM-V. *Arch Gen Psychiatry* (2003) **60**:1117–22. doi:10.1001/archpsyc.60.11.1117
25. Kessler RC, Merikangas KR, Berglund P, Eaton WW, Koretz DS, Walters EE. In reply. *Arch Gen Psychiatry* (2004) **61**:1051–2. doi:10.1001/archpsyc.61.10.1051-b
26. Mechanic D. Is the prevalence of mental disorders a good measure of the need for services? *Health Aff (Millwood)* (2003) **22**:8–20. doi:10.1377/hlthaff.22.5.8
27. Regier DA. Mental disorder diagnostic theory and practical reality: an evolutionary perspective. *Health Aff (Millwood)* (2003) **22**:21–7. doi:10.1377/hlthaff.22.5.21
28. Regier DA, Narrow WE, Rae DS. For DSM-V, it's the "disorder threshold," stupid. *Arch Gen Psychiatry* (2004) **61**:1051. doi:10.1001/archpsyc.61.10.1051-b
29. Wakefield JC. Disorder as harmful dysfunction: a conceptual critique of DSM-III-R's definition of mental disorder. *Psychol Rev* (1992) **99**:232–47. doi:10.1037/0033-295X.99.2.232
30. Wakefield JC. Limits of operationalization: a critique of Spitzer and Endicott's (1978) proposed operational criteria for mental disorder. *J Abnorm Psychol* (1993) **102**:160–72. doi:10.1037/0021-843X.102.1.160
31. Wakefield JC. Evolutionary versus prototype analyses of the concept of disorder. *J Abnorm Psychol* (1999) **108**:374–99. doi:10.1037/0021-843X.108.3.374
32. Wakefield JC. Disorder as a black box essentialist concept. *J Abnorm Psychol* (1999) **108**:465–72. doi:10.1037/0021-843X.108.3.465
33. Wakefield JC. The concept of mental disorder: diagnostic implications of the harmful dysfunction analysis. *World Psychiatry* (2006) **6**:149–56.
34. Wakefield JC, First MB. Clarifying the distinction between disorder and non-disorder: confronting the overdiagnosis ("false positives") problem in DSM-V. In: Phillips KA, First MB, Pincus HA, editors. *Advancing DSM: Dilemmas in Psychiatric Diagnosis.* Washington, DC: American Psychiatric Press (2003). p. 23–56.
35. Wakefield JC, First MB. Placing symptoms in context: the role of contextual criteria in reducing false positives in diagnostic and statistical manual of mental disorders diagnoses. *Compr Psychiatry* (2012) **53**:130–9. doi:10.1016/j.comppsych.2011.03.001
36. Edwards G. The alcohol dependence syndrome: a concept as stimulus to enquiry. *Br J Addict* (1986) **81**:171–83. doi:10.1111/j.1360-0443.1986.tb00313.x
37. Edwards G, Gross MM. Alcohol dependence: provisional description of a clinical syndrome. *Br Med J* (1976) **1**:1058–61. doi:10.1136/bmj.1.6017.1058
38. Edwards G, Arif A, Hodgson R. Nomenclature and classification of drug and alcohol related problems. *Bull World Health Organ* (1981) **59**:225–42.
39. Jellinek EM. The alcohol problem: formulations and attitudes. *Q J Stud Alcohol* (1943) **4**:446–61.
40. Jellinek EM. Phases of alcohol addiction. *Q J Stud Alcohol* (1952) **13**:673–84.
41. Jellinek EM. *The Disease Concept of Alcoholism.* New Haven, CT: College and University Press (1960).
42. Hasin D. Classification of alcohol use disorders. *Alcohol Res Health* (2003) **27**(1):5–17.
43. Rounsaville BJ, Spitzer RL, Williams JBW. Proposed changes in DSM-III substance use disorders: description and rationale. *Am J Psychiatry* (1986) **143**:463–8.
44. Biernacki P. *Pathways from Heroin Addiction: Recovery Without Treatment.* Philadelphia, PA: Temple University Press (1986).
45. Robins LN. Vietnam veterans' rapid recovery from heroin addiction: a fluke or normal expectation? *Addiction* (1993) **188**:1041–54. doi:10.1111/j.1360-0443.1993.tb02123.x
46. Robins LN, Murphy G. Drug use in a normal population of young Negro men. *Am J Public Health Nations Health* (1967) **57**:1580–96. doi:10.2105/AJPH.57.9.1580
47. Waldorf D. Natural recovery from opiate addiction: some social-psychological processes of untreated recovery. *J Drug Issues* (1983) **13**:237–79.
48. Waldorf D, Reinarmen C, Murphy S. *Cocaine Changes: The Experience of Using and Quitting.* Philadelphia, PA: Temple University Press (1991).
49. Ainslie G. *Picoeconomics: The Strategic Interaction of Successive Motivational States Within the Person.* Cambridge: Cambridge University Press (1992).
50. Becker GS, Murphy KM. A theory of rational addiction. *J Polit Econ* (1988) **96**:675–700. doi:10.1086/261558
51. Herrnstein RJ. On the law of effect. *J Exp Anal Behav* (1970) **13**:243–66. doi:10.1901/jeab.1970.13-243
52. Herrnstein RJ. Behavior, reinforcement, and utility. *Psychol Sci* (1990) **1**:217–24. doi:10.1111/j.1467-9280.1990.tb00203.x
53. Heyman GM. *Addiction: A Disorder of Choice.* Cambridge, MA: Harvard University Press (2009).
54. Heyman GM. Quitting drugs: quantitative and qualitative features. *Annu Rev Clin Psychol* (2013) **9**:29–59. doi:10.1146/annurev-clinpsy-032511-143041

55. Rachlin H. In what sense are addicts irrational? *Drug Alcohol Depend* (2007) **90**(Suppl):S92–9. doi:10.1016/j.drugalcdep.2006.07.011
56. Rachlin H, Green L. Commitment, choice, and self-control. *J Exp Anal Behav* (1972) **17**:15–22. doi:10.1901/jeab.1972.17-15
57. Wakefield JC. Mental disorder and moral responsibility: disorders of personhood as harmful dysfunctions, with special reference to alcoholism. *Philos Psychiatr Psychol* (2009) **16**:91–9. doi:10.1353/ppp.0.0220
58. Hasin D, Hatzenbuehler ML, Keyes K, Ogburn E. Substance use disorders: diagnostic and statistical manual of mental disorders, fourth edition (DSM-IV) and international classification of diseases, tenth edition (ICD-10). *Addiction* (2006) **101**(Suppl 1):59–75. doi:10.1111/j.1360-0443.2006.01584.x
59. Cooper RV. Avoiding false positives: zones of rarity, the threshold problem, and the DSM clinical significance criterion. *Can J Psychiatry* (2013) **58**(11):606–11.
60. Levy N. Addiction is not a brain disease (and it matters). *Front Psychiatry* (2013) **4**:24. doi:10.3389/fpsyt.2013.00024
61. Wakefield JC. Disability and diagnosis: should role impairment be eliminated from DSM/ICD diagnostic criteria? *World Psychiatry* (2009) **8**:87–8.
62. Wakefield JC. Addiction, the concept of disorder, and pathways to harm: comment on Levy. *Front Psychiatry* (2013) **4**:34. doi:10.3389/fpsyt.2013.00034
63. Sussman S, Lishas N, Griffiths M. Prevalence of the addictions: a problem of the majority or the minority? *Eval Health Prof* (2011) **34**(1):3–56. doi:10.1177/0163278710380124
64. Stata Corporation. *Stata Statistical Software, Release 12 (Version 12)*. College Station, TX: Stata Corporation (2011).
65. Agrawal A, Heath AC, Lynskey MT. DSM-IV to DSM-5: the impact of proposed revisions on diagnosis of alcohol use disorders. *Addiction* (2011) **106**:1935–43. doi:10.1111/j.1360-0443.2011.03517.x
66. Mewton L, Slade T, McBride O, Grove R, Teesson M. An evaluation of the proposed DSM-5 alcohol use disorder criteria using Australian national data. *Addiction* (2011) **106**:941–50. doi:10.1111/j.1360-0443.2010.03340.x
67. Caetano R, Babor TF. Diagnosis of alcohol dependence in epidemiological surveys: an epidemic of youthful alcohol dependence or a case of measurement error? *Addiction* (2006) **101**:111–4. doi:10.1111/j.1360-0443.2006.01599.x
68. Chung T, Martin CS. What were they thinking? Adolescents' interpretations of DSM-IV alcohol dependence symptom queries and implications for diagnostic validity. *Drug Alcohol Depend* (2005) **80**:191–200. doi:10.1016/j.drugalcdep.2005.03.023
69. Edwards G. "The evil genius of the habit": DSM-5 seen in historical context. *J Stud Alcohol Drugs* (2012) **73**:699–701.
70. Winters KC, Martin CS, Chung T. Substance use disorders in DSM-V when applied to adolescents. *Addiction* (2011) **106**:882–3. doi:10.1111/j.1360-0443.2010.03334.x
71. Wakefield JC. False positives in psychiatric diagnosis: implications for human freedom. *Theor Med Bioeth* (2010) **31**(1):5–17. doi:10.1007/s11017-010-9132-2
72. Martin CS, Chung T, Langenbucher JW. How should we revise diagnostic criteria for substance use disorders in the DSM-V? *J Abnorm Psychol* (2008) **117**(3):561–75. doi:10.1037/0021-843X.117.3.561
73. Vergés A, Steinley D, Trull TJ, Sher KJ. It's the algorithm! Why differential rates of chronicity and comorbidity are not evidence for the validity of the abuse-dependence distinction. *J Abnorm Psychol* (2010) **119**(4):650–61. doi:10.1037/a0020116
74. Babor TF, Caetano R. The trouble with alcohol abuse: what are we trying to measure, diagnose, count and prevent? *Addiction* (2008) **103**:1057–9. doi:10.1111/j.1360-0443.2008.02263.x
75. de Bruijn C, van den Brink W, de Graaf R, Vollebergh WAM. The craving withdrawal model for alcoholism: towards the DSM-V. Improving the discriminant validity of alcohol use disorder diagnosis. *Alcohol Alcohol* (2005) **40**:314–22. doi:10.1093/alcalc/agh166
76. Langenbucher J, Martin CS, Labouvie E, Sanjuan PM, Bavly L, Pollock NK. Toward the DSM-V: the Withdrawal-Gate Model versus the DSM-IV in the diagnosis of alcohol abuse and dependence. *J Consult Clin Psychol* (2000) **68**:799–809. doi:10.1037/0022-006X.68.5.799
77. Hasin DS. Combining abuse and dependence in DSM-5. *J Stud Alcohol Drugs* (2012) **73**:702–4.
78. Substance Abuse and Mental Health Services Administration. *Results from the 2012 National Survey on Drug Use and Health: Summary of National Findings*. Rockville (MD): Substance Abuse and Mental Health Services Administration (2013). NSDUH Series H-46, HHS Publication No. (SMA) 13-4795. Available from: http://www.samhsa.gov/data/NSDUH/2012SummNatFindDetTables/NationalFindings/NSDUHresults2012.htm#ch7.3
79. Drummond C. The end of the dependence syndrome as we know it? *Addiction* (2011) **106**:892–3. doi:10.1111/j.1360-0443.2010.03314.x
80. Hasin DS, Rossem RV, McCloud S, Endicott J. Differentiating DSM-IV alcohol dependence and abuse by course: community heavy drinkers. *J Subst Abuse* (1997) **9**:127–35. doi:10.1016/S0899-3289(97)90011-0
81. Hughes JR. Defining dependence: describing symptom clusters versus central constructs. *Addiction* (2007) **102**:1531–2. doi:10.1111/j.1360-0443.2007.01932.x
82. Jones KD, Gill C, Ray S. Review of the proposed DSM-5 substance use disorder. *J Addict Offender Couns* (2012) **33**:115–23. doi:10.1002/j.2161-1874.2012.00009.x
83. Martin CS, Steinley DL, Verges A, Sher KJ. Letter to the editor: the proposed 2/11 symptom algorithm for DSM-5 substance use disorders is too lenient. *Psychol Med* (2011) **41**:2008–10. doi:10.1017/S0033291711000717
84. Kessler RC, Berglund PA, Demler O, Jin R, Walters EE. Lifetime prevalence and age-of-onset distributions of DSM-IV disorders in the National Comorbidity Survey replication. *Arch Gen Psychiatry* (2005) **62**(6):593–602. doi:10.1001/archpsyc.62.6.617
85. Cotler LB. Drug use disorders in the National Comorbidity Survey: have we come a long way? [letter]. *Arch Gen Psychiatry* (2007) **64**(3):380–1. doi:10.1001/archpsyc.64.3.380
86. Grant BF, Compton WM, Crowley TJ, Hasin DS, Helzer JE, Li T-K, et al. Errors in assessing DSM-IV substance use disorders [letter]. *Arch Gen Psychiatry* (2007) **64**(3):379–80. doi:10.1001/archpsyc.64.3.379
87. Hasin DS, Grant BF. The co-occurrence of DSM-IV alcohol abuse in DSM-IV alcohol dependence: results of the National Epidemiologic Survey on alcohol and related conditions on heterogeneity that differ by population subgroup. *Arch Gen Psychiatry* (2004) **61**:891–6. doi:10.1001/archpsyc.61.9.891
88. Kessler RC, Merikangas KR. In reply [letter]. *Arch Gen Psychiatry* (2007) **64**(3):381–2. doi:10.1001/archpsyc.64.3.381
89. Mueser KT, Drake RE, Wallach MA. Dual diagnosis: a review of etiological theories. *Addict Behav* (1998) **23**(6):717–34. doi:10.1016/S0306-4603(98)00073-2
90. Martinotti G, Carli V, Tedeschi D, Di Giannantonio M, Roy A, Janiri L, et al. Mono- and polysubstance dependent subjects differ on social factors, childhood trauma, personality, suicidal behaviour, and comorbid Axis I diagnoses. *Addict Behav* (2009) **34**(9):790–3. doi:10.1016/j.addbeh.2009.04.012
91. Spitzer RL. Diagnosis and need for treatment are not the same. *Arch Gen Psychiatry* (1998) **55**:120. doi:10.1001/archpsyc.55.2.120
92. Li TK, Hewitt BG, Grant BF. The alcohol dependence syndrome, 30 years later: a commentary. The 2006 H. David Archibald lecture. *Addiction* (2007) **102**:1522–30. doi:10.1111/j.1360-0443.2007.01911.x
93. West R, Miller P. What is the purpose of diagnosing addiction or dependence and what does this mean for establishing diagnostic criteria? *Addiction* (2011) **106**(5):863–5. doi:10.1111/j.1360-0443.2011.03377.x
94. O'Brien C. Addiction and dependence in DSM-V. *Addiction* (2011) **106**:866–7. doi:10.1111/j.1360-0443.2010.03144.x

APPENDIX

Table A1 | DSM-III diagnostic criteria for alcohol use disorders and their translation using epidemiologic catchment area study (ECA) questions.

DSM-III diagnostic criteria for alcohol use disorders	Corresponding ECA questions used for the given DSM-III criteria
DIAGNOSTIC CRITERIA FOR ALCOHOL ABUSE (A, B, AND C)	
A. Pattern of pathological alcohol use: (any one of) need for daily use of alcohol for adequate functioning; inability to cut down or stop drinking; repeated efforts to control or reduce excess drinking by "going on the wagon" (periods of temporary abstinence) or restricting drinking to certain times of the day; binges (remaining intoxicated throughout the day for at least 2 days); occasional consumption of a fifth of spirits (or its equivalent in wine or beer); amnesic periods for events occurring while intoxicated (blackouts); continuation of drinking despite a serious physical disorder that the individual knows is exacerbated by alcohol use; drinking of non-beverage alcohol	Answer "yes" to any one or more of the following Have you ever wanted to stop drinking but couldn't? Some people promise themselves not to drink before 5 o'clock or never to drink alone, in order to control their drinking. Have you ever done anything like that? Have you ever drunk as much as a fifth of liquor in 1 day, that would be about 20 drinks, or three bottles of wine or as much as three six-packs of beer in 1 day? Have you ever had blackouts while drinking, that is, where you drank enough so that you couldn't remember the next day what you had said or done? Have you ever continued to drink when you knew you had a serious physical illness that might be made worse by drinking? Has there ever been a period in your life when you could not do your ordinary daily work well unless you had had something to drink? How many times have you gone on benders that lasted at least a couple of days? (two or more counted as symptom)
B. Impairment in social or occupational functioning due to alcohol use: e.g., (any one of) violence while intoxicated, absence from work, loss of job, legal difficulties (e.g., arrest for intoxicated behavior, traffic accidents while intoxicated), arguments, or difficulties with family or friends because of excessive alcohol use	Answer "yes" to any one or more of the following Has your family ever objected because you were drinking too much? Have friends, your doctor, your clergyman, or any other professional ever said you were drinking too much for your own good? Have you ever had job (or school) troubles because of drinking – like missing too much work or drinking on the job (or at school)? Did you ever lose a job (or get kicked out of school) on account of drinking? Have you ever gotten into trouble driving because of drinking – like having an accident or being arrested for drunk driving? Have you ever been arrested or held at the police station because of drinking or for disturbing the peace while drinking? Have you ever gotten into physical fights while drinking?
C. Duration of disturbance of at least 1 month	(Not measured)
DIAGNOSTIC CRITERIA FOR ALCOHOL DEPENDENCE (A AND B)	
A. Either a pattern of pathological alcohol use or impairment in social or occupational functioning due to alcohol use (i.e., any one symptom of either pathological use or impairment; see above Alcohol Abuse criteria for pathological use and for impairment in social or occupational functioning)	Answer "yes" to any one or more of the questions above for either pathological use or impairment in social or occupational functioning (see ECA questions used for alcohol abuse)
B. Either tolerance or withdrawal Tolerance: need for markedly increased amounts of alcohol to achieve the desired effect, or markedly diminished effect with regular use of the same amount	Answer "yes" to any one or more of the following Has there ever been a period of 2 weeks when every day you were drinking seven or more beers, seven or more drinks, or seven or more glasses of wine?
Withdrawal: development of alcohol withdrawal (e.g., morning "shakes" and malaise relieved by drinking) after cessation of or reduction in drinking	Did you ever need a drink just after you had gotten up (that is, before breakfast)? Have you ever had "the shakes" after stopping or cutting down on drinking (for example, your hands shake so that your coffee cup rattles in the saucer or you have trouble lighting a cigarette)?

Table A2 | DSM-III-R diagnostic criteria for alcohol use disorders and their translation using National Comorbidity Survey (NCS) questions.

DSM-III-R diagnostic criteria for alcohol use disorders	Corresponding NCS questions used for the given DSM-III-R criteria
DIAGNOSTIC CRITERIA FOR PSYCHOACTIVE ALCOHOL ABUSE (A, B, AND C)	
A. A maladaptive pattern of psychoactive substance use indicated by at least one of the following (1) Continued use despite knowledge of having a persistent or recurrent social, occupational, psychological, or physical problem that is caused or exacerbated by use of the psychoactive substance (2) Recurrent use in situations in which use is physically hazardous (e.g., driving while intoxicated)	Answer "yes" to any one or more of the following Did alcohol ever cause you problems with your family, friends, at work, at school or with the police? Did your use of alcohol ever cause you to be expelled from school, or to be demoted or fired from work? Have you often been under the effects of alcohol or feeling its after-effects in a situation which increased your chances of getting hurt – like when driving a car or boat, using knives or guns or machinery, crossing against traffic, climbing or swimming? Did you continue to use alcohol after it caused an accident (when you injured yourself while under the influence of alcohol – like had a bad fall or cut yourself badly, been hurt in a traffic accident, or anything like that)? Have you ever had any health problems as a result of using alcohol – such as liver disease, stomach disease, pancreatitis, feet tingling, numbness, memory problems, an accidental overdose, a persistent cough, a seizure of fit, hepatitis, or abscesses? Have you ever had any emotional or psychological problems from using alcohol – such as feeling uninterested in things, feeling depressed, suspicious of people, paranoid, or having strange ideas?
B. Some symptoms of the disturbance have persisted for at least 1 month, or have occurred repeatedly over a longer period of time	Built into the question responses in the NCS, emphasizing the word "often" in the symptom question, or coding symptom duration lasting at least 1-year within the diagnostic algorithm.
C. Never met the criteria for psychoactive substance dependence for this substance	Built into the hierarchy for NCS diagnosis; abuse can be diagnosed only if dependence is not diagnosed
DIAGNOSTIC CRITERIA FOR PSYCHOACTIVE ALCOHOL DEPENDENCE (A AND B)	
A. At least three of the following	At least three of the following (to satisfy a given DSM-III-R numbered criterion, answer "yes" to any one or more of the corresponding NCS questions)
(1) Substance often taken in larger amounts or over a longer period than the person intended	Did you often use larger amounts of alcohol than you intended to when you began, or did you use it for a longer period of time than you intended to? Did you often start using alcohol and find it difficult to stop before you became completely intoxicated or high?
(2) Persistent desire or one or more unsuccessful efforts to cut down or control substance use	Have you ever felt such a strong desire or urge to use alcohol that you could not resist it or could not think of anything else? Did your use of alcohol ever become so regular that you would not change when, or how much you took it, no matter what you were doing or where you were? Have you ever wanted or tried to stop or cut down on alcohol but found you could not?
(3) A great deal of time spent in activities necessary to get the substance (e.g., theft), taking the substance (e.g., chain smoking), or recovering from its effects	Did you ever have a period of a month or more when you spent a great deal of time using alcohol, getting it, or getting over its effects?
(4) Frequent intoxication or withdrawal symptoms when expected to fulfill major role obligations at work, school, or home (e.g., does not go to work because hung over, goes to school or work "high," intoxicated while taking care of his or her children), or when substance use is physically hazardous (e.g., drives while intoxicated)	Have you often been under the effects of alcohol or suffering its after-effects while at work or school or taking care of children? Has your use of alcohol often kept you from working, going to school, or taking care of children? Have you often been under the effects of alcohol or feeling its after-effects in a situation which increased your chances of getting hurt – like when driving a car or boat, using knives or guns or machinery, crossing against traffic, climbing or swimming?

(Continued)

Table A2 | Continued

DSM-III-R diagnostic criteria for alcohol use disorders	Corresponding NCS questions used for the given DSM-III-R criteria
(5) Important social, occupational, or recreational activities given up or reduced because of substance use	Have you ever given up or greatly reduced important activities in order to get, or to use alcohol – activities like sports, work, or seeing family and friends?
(6) Continued substance use despite knowledge of having a persistent or recurrent social, psychological, or physical problem that is caused or exacerbated by the use of the substance (e.g., keeps using heroin despite family arguments about it, cocaine-induced depression, or having an ulcer made worse by drinking)	Did alcohol ever cause you problems with your family, friends, at work, at school, or with the police? Did your use of alcohol ever cause you to be expelled from school, or to be demoted or fired from work? Did you continue to use alcohol after it caused an accident (when you injured yourself while under the influence of alcohol – like had a bad fall or cut yourself badly, been hurt in a traffic accident, or anything like that)? Have you ever had any health problems as a result of using alcohol – such as liver disease, stomach disease, pancreatitis, feet tingling, numbness, memory problems, an accidental overdose, a persistent cough, a seizure of fit, hepatitis, or abscesses? Have you ever had any emotional or psychological problems from using alcohol – such as feeling uninterested in things, feeling depressed, suspicious of people, paranoid, or having strange ideas?
(7) Marked tolerance: need for markedly increased amounts of the substance (i.e., at least a 50% increase) in order to achieve intoxication or desired effect, or markedly diminished effect with continued use of the same amount	Did you ever find that you had to use more alcohol than usual to get the same effect or that the same amount had less effect on you than before?
(8) Characteristic symptoms of withdrawal	Did stopping or cutting down on alcohol ever make you sick or cause you problems like those listed on page 17?
(9) Substance often taken to relieve or avoid withdrawal symptoms	Did you ever use alcohol to make these withdrawal symptoms go away or to keep from having them?
B. Some symptoms of the disturbance have persisted for at least 1 month, or have occurred repeatedly over a longer period of time	In the NCS at least two of the above nine symptoms had to occur often or persist for at least 1-year

Table A3 | Harmful dysfunction (HD) diagnostic categories of harm and dysfunction and how they were translated using epidemiologic catchment area study (ECA) questions.

HD/ECA	ECA alcohol question
Harm	Has your family ever objected because you were drinking too much?
Harm	Have friends, your doctor, your clergyman, or any other professional ever said you were drinking too much for your own good?
Harm	Have you ever had job (or school) troubles because of drinking – like missing too much work or drinking on the job (or at school)?
Harm	Did you ever lose a job (or get kicked out of school) on account of drinking?
Harm	Have you ever gotten into trouble driving because of drinking – like having an accident or being arrested for drunk driving?
Harm	Have you ever been arrested or held at the police station because of drinking or for disturbing the peace while driving?
Harm	Have you ever gotten into physical fights while drinking?
Harm	Have you ever had blackouts while driving, that is, where you drank enough so that you could not remember the next day what you had said or done?
Harm	Did drinking ever cause you to have liver disease or yellow jaundice?
Harm	Did drinking ever cause you to have vomiting blood or other stomach troubles?
Harm	Did drinking ever cause you to have trouble with tingling or numbness in your feet?
Harm	Did drinking ever cause you to have memory trouble when you haven't been drinking (not blackouts)
Harm	Did drinking ever cause you to have inflammation of your pancreas, or pancreatitis?
Harm	Have you ever continued to drink when you knew you had a serious physical illness that might be made worse by drinking?
Dysfunction	Have you ever had "the shakes" after stopping or cutting down on drinking (for example, your hands shake so that your coffee cup rattles in the saucer or you have trouble lighting a cigarette)?
Dysfunction	Have you ever had fits or seizures after stopping or cutting down on drinking?
Dysfunction	Have you ever had the DT's (Hallucinations and fever) when you quit drinking?
Dysfunction	Have you ever seen or heard things that weren't really there after cutting down on drinking?
Dysfunction	Did you ever need a drink just after you had gotten up (that is, before breakfast)?
Dysfunction	Has there ever been a period in your life when you could not do your ordinary daily work well unless you had had something to drink?
Dysfunction	Have you ever wanted to stop drinking but couldn't?

Table A4 | Harmful dysfunction (HD) diagnostic categories of harm and dysfunction and how they were translated using National Comorbidity Survey (NCS) questions.

HD/NCS	HD/NCS (ECA comparable)	NCS alcohol question
Harm	Not used	Has your use of alcohol often kept you from working, going to school, or taking care of children?
Harm	Harm	Did alcohol ever cause you problems with your family, friends, at work, at school, or with the police?
Harm	Harm	Did your use of alcohol ever cause you to be expelled from school, or to be demoted or fired from work?
Harm	Harm	Have you often been under the effects of alcohol or feeling its after-effects in a situation which increased your chances of getting hurt – like when driving a car or boat, using knives or guns or machinery, crossing against traffic, climbing or swimming?
Harm	Harm	Did you continue to use alcohol after it caused an accident (when you injured yourself while under the influence of alcohol – like had a bad fall or cut yourself badly, been hurt in a traffic accident, or anything like that)?
Harm	Harm	Have you ever had any health problems as a result of using alcohol – such as liver disease, stomach disease, pancreatitis, feet tingling, numbness, memory problems, an accidental overdose, a persistent cough, a seizure of fit, hepatitis, or abscesses?
Harm	Harm	Have you ever had any emotional or psychological problems from using alcohol – such as feeling uninterested in things, feeling depressed, suspicious of people, paranoid, or having strange ideas?
Harm	Harm	Did you ever continue to use alcohol while taking medication you knew was dangerous to mix with alcohol or drugs, or when you had a serious health problem that could be made worse by alcohol or drugs?
Harm	Harm	Have you ever given up or greatly reduced important activities in order to get, or to use alcohol – activities like sports, work, or seeing family and friends?
Dysfunction	Dysfunction	Did stopping or cutting down on alcohol ever make you sick or cause you problems like those listed on page 17?
Dysfunction	Dysfunction	Did you ever use alcohol to make these withdrawal symptoms go away or to keep from having them?
Dysfunction	Dysfunction	Have you ever wanted or tried to stop or cut down on alcohol but found you could not?
Dysfunction	Not used	Have you ever felt such a strong desire or urge to use alcohol that you could not resist it or could not think of anything else?

Table A5 | DSM-5 diagnostic criteria for alcohol use disorder and their translation using National Comorbidity Survey (NCS) questions.

DSM-5 Alcohol use disorder criteria	NCS questions used for the given criteria
A. A problematic pattern of alcohol use leading to clinically significant impairment or distress, as manifested by at least two of the following, occurring within a 12-month period	
1. Alcohol is often taken in larger amounts or over a longer period than was intended	Did you often use larger amounts of alcohol than you intended to when you began, or did you use it for a longer period of time than you intended to?
2. There is a persistent desire or unsuccessful efforts to cut down or control alcohol use	Have you ever wanted or tried to stop or cut down on alcohol but found you could not?
3. A great deal of time is spent in activities necessary to obtain alcohol, use alcohol, or recover from its effects	Did you ever have a period of a month or more when you spent a great deal of time using alcohol, getting it, or getting over its effects?
4. Craving, or a strong desire or urge to use alcohol	Have you ever felt such a strong desire or urge to use alcohol that you could not resist it or could not think of anything else?
5. Recurrent alcohol use resulting in a failure to fulfill major role obligations at work, school, or home	Has your use of alcohol often kept you from working, going to school, or taking care of children? Did your use of alcohol ever cause you to be expelled from school, or to be demoted or fired from work?
6. Continued alcohol use despite having persistent or recurrent social or interpersonal problems caused or exacerbated by the effects of alcohol	Did alcohol ever cause you problems with your family, friends, at work, at school or with the police? Did you continue to use alcohol after it caused an accident (when you injured yourself while under the influence of alcohol – like had a bad fall or cut yourself badly, been hurt in a traffic accident, or anything like that)?
7. Important social, occupational, or recreational activities are given up or reduced because of alcohol use	Have you ever given up or greatly reduced important activities in order to get, or to use alcohol – activities like sports, work, or seeing family and friends?
8. Recurrent alcohol use in situations in which it is physically hazardous	Have you often been under the effects of alcohol or feeling its after-effects in a situation which increased your chances of getting hurt – like when driving a car or boat, using knives or guns or machinery, crossing against traffic, climbing or swimming?
9. Alcohol use is continued despite knowledge of having a persistent or recurrent physical or psychological problem that is likely to have been caused or exacerbated by alcohol	Did you ever continue to use alcohol while taking medication you knew was dangerous to mix with alcohol or drugs, or when you had a serious health problem that could be made worse by alcohol or drugs?
10. Tolerance, as defined by either of the following: a. A need for markedly increased amounts of alcohol to achieve intoxication or desired effect b. Markedly diminished effect with continued use of the same amount of alcohol	Did you ever find that you had to use more alcohol than usual to get the same effect or that the same amount had less effect on you than before?
11. Withdrawal, as manifested by either of the following: a. The characteristic withdrawal syndrome for alcohol (refer to Criteria A and B of the criteria set for alcohol withdrawal) b. Alcohol (or a closely related substance, such as a benzodiazepine) is taken to relieve or avoid withdrawal symptoms	Did stopping or cutting down on alcohol ever make you sick or cause you problems like those listed on page 17? Did you ever use alcohol to make these withdrawal symptoms go away or to keep from having them?

16

Addiction is not a natural kind

Jeremy Michael Pober *

Department of Philosophy, San Francisco State University, San Francisco, CA, USA

Edited by:
Hanna Pickard, University of Oxford, UK

Reviewed by:
Serge H. Ahmed, CNRS, France
Bennett Foddy, University of Oxford, UK

***Correspondence:**
Jeremy Michael Pober, Department of Philosophy, San Francisco State University, 1600 Holloway Avenue, San Francisco, CA 94132, USA
e-mail: jeremy.pober@gmail.com

I argue that addiction is not an appropriate category to support generalizations for the purposes of scientific prediction. That is, addiction is not a natural kind. I discuss the Homeostatic Property Cluster (HPC) theory of kinds, according to which members of a kind share a cluster of properties generated by a common mechanism or set of mechanisms. Leading accounts of addiction in literature fail to offer a mechanism that explains addiction across substances. I discuss popular variants of the disease conception and demonstrate that at least one class of substances that fails to confirm a major prediction of each account. When no mechanism can be found to explain the occurrence of the relevant properties in members of a category, the HPC view suggests that we revise our categories. I discuss options offered by the HPC view, including category revision and category replacement. I then conclude that talk of addiction as a prediction-supporting category should be replaced with categories such as "S-addiction" and "T-addiction," where S and T are substances or sets of substances of abuse, as these categories are genuine natural kinds.

Keywords: addiction, natural kinds, theories of addiction, philosophy of neuroscience, philosophy of psychiatry

INTRODUCTION: ADDICTION AND GENERALIZATIONS

Addiction is discussed as a unified class or condition in philosophical and scientific literature (1). That is, addiction is treated as a category under which substantive generalizations can be subsumed. Basic scientists are concerned with generalizations for the purposes of prediction, clinical scientists for the purpose of diagnosis and treatment of symptoms – ideally on the basis of the knowledge generated by basic science – and philosophers are interested in attributions of responsibility to individuals and to which categories of individuals those attributions apply, as responsibility is an essential component of autonomy[1]. While this tendency to subsume generalizations under the category addiction is prevalent in many fields, it is especially explicit in the dominant paradigm in cognitive neuroscience, the disease paradigm [e.g., Ref. (2, 3)].

But are we justified in making these generalizations? In this discussion, I shall argue that we are not. We ought not treat all cases of addiction as a unified category for scientific, clinical, or philosophical purposes.

GENERALIZATIONS AND KIND TERMS

Categories in the sciences that support generalizations are referred to as *natural kinds*. To a first approximation, members of a kind share properties in virtue of something that makes them members of this category[2]. Members of a kind share these properties non-accidentally. If the kind is a natural kind, they share these properties in virtue of some scientific basis, be it a shared atomic structure in the physical sciences, or according to the Homeostatic Property Cluster (HPC) view of natural kinds, shared mechanisms in the life sciences.

Many have argued, both in philosophy [e.g., Ref. (4, 5)] and neuroscience [e.g., Ref. (6)] that addiction is a syndrome that varies greatly between individuals on a case by case basis. I agree that there is at least this level of variance, but such variance does not undermine the hypothesis that addiction is a natural kind.

As I'll discuss, categories or kind terms in the life sciences such as biology and psychology contain a high degree of inherent variation across members, and this variation is not a problem for their ability to count as generalization-subsuming categories. However, this variance among individual members of a kind is unproblematic only insofar as those members share whatever properties they do in virtue of a common mechanism or set of mechanisms.

The dominant paradigm contends that addiction constitutes a natural kind as different expressions of a single *disease*, hence the term (hereafter used) *disease paradigm*. The name suggests that the underlying mechanisms are bio/psychological in nature, thus, according to the disease paradigm, addiction is putatively a natural kind[3].

My argument is that addiction is not a natural kind because the properties shared by addicted individuals are not explained in virtue of underlying shared mechanisms across substances of addiction.

---

[1]While there are many practical uses of defining addiction, including legal and personal reasons (19), I focus on the three mentioned above as I understand them to be intimately related: clinical diagnosis and treatment for mental disorders depends on the underlying neurocognitive structure of the patient. And while the relationship between what psychology tells us about the mind/brain and how we attribute moral status such as moral responsibility is doubtless a complex issue, rather, I am simply saying that realist moral psychology requires that the attribution of moral properties be in some way influenced by how the mind actually works.

[2]These features are often referred to as essences, though I will avoid this term as it is loaded in implying something metaphysically special, i.e., Aristotelian essences (12), and I wish to avoid such confusion. However, essences need not be metaphysically special.

[3]There are two kinds of kinds, so to speak: natural and social. Very roughly, members of natural kinds share properties in virtue of something natural or physical and members of social kinds share their properties in virtue of something social (11).

Because kind term claims are warranted by the existence (or lack thereof) of mechanisms, they are dependent on current science. Thus, my argument more specifically is that the disease conception, as the dominant paradigm in current cognitive neuroscience, fails to provide evidence – and indeed provides disconfirming evidence – that the mechanisms of addiction apply across addictive substances.

Rather, the best suited natural kind terms to explain what we refer to as "addiction" are several subcategories, which, for lack of a better vocabulary, I will distinguish as "S-addiction" "T-addiction," etc., where S and T stand in for either particular addicting substances or sets of substances.

The argument proceeds as follows. In S 2, I sketch the popular HPC theory of kinds, and in S 3 I suggest how HPC kinds might map onto addiction.

Then, in S 4, I discuss how various models of addiction fail to identify a unified set of mechanisms that explain all cases. I review three mechanistic proposals popular within the disease paradigm. First, I discuss the aberrant learning hypothesis (7), which proposes that habitual behaviors out of the control of conscious/executive systems, realized in dopaminergic projections to and in the dorsal striatum is hypothesized to underlie drug-related behaviors. However, I present evidence that addiction to cannabis does not seem to involve such dopamine activity in the dorsal striatum. Second, I discuss the incentive sensitization hypothesis (8), which proposes that neuroadaptations to the mesolimbic dopamine system cause addicted individuals to consistently overvalue the extent to which they "want" drugs at the expense of other stimuli, including non-drug rewards. However, evidence suggests cannabis addiction seems to involve an increase in the "wanting" of non-drug rewards. Finally, I discuss the frontostriatal dysfunction model [e.g., Ref. (9, 10)]. On this view, multiple circuits realized at least in part in prefrontal cortical areas underlie various aspects of executive control and are inhibited in addiction. However, there is evidence that the neuroadaptations to certain prefrontal areas, including the medial PFC generally but especially the ventromedial and dorsomedial areas, differ between instances of addiction to cocaine and stimulants versus addiction to opiates.

In S 5 I discuss what categories might best explain the phenomena of addiction, and in S 6 I consider the scientific and philosophical implications of the disunity of addiction.

TERMINOLOGY AND STRATEGY

Before offering an account of natural kinds as well as one of addiction, I should make a note about my strategy in defining those terms. There is no one, uncontested theory of natural kinds, let alone addiction, nor do I wish to settle the dispute about which account is best[4]. I aim to give an account of natural kinds that is generous in what it counts as natural kinds and one of addiction that limits what it counts as addiction to clear cases. For if addiction is not a natural kind given a wide account of natural kinds and a narrow one of addiction, then it stands to reason that the same would be true of a narrower account of kinds – one that demanded more for a category to count as a kind – or a broader one of addiction, where more varied cases count as addiction.

I understand the HPC theory of kinds to be the broadest account available. Other theories allow far less variance within members of a kind, by requiring members of a kind to share either property sets rather than clusters or microstructural essences. In either case, addiction as a natural kind would be a non-starter in virtue of the variance in behaviors that count as addictive from case to case or the lack of a shared essence in life sciences kinds in the first place[5]. Similarly, I restrict my discussion to addiction to substances, rather than addiction to, e.g., gambling.

I should emphasize that this logic only holds for demarcating the *extensions* of addiction and natural kind. That is, it falls short at restricting the possible intensions, i.e., theories explaining in virtue of what the extension "addiction" applies to its instances[6]. And theories within the disease paradigm do not differ on what instances count as addiction so much as they do on how to explain the phenomena exhibited commonly by organisms that count as addicted. I restrict my discussion to theories within the disease paradigm because it is the paradigm investigating addiction at the level most salient for natural kinds, that of mechanisms underlying the property cluster.

NATURAL KINDS IN PSYCHOLOGY (AND BIOLOGY)

The HPC theory of natural kinds is designed to balance accounting for the inherent variability in biological and psychological kinds while at the same time preserving explanatory value in terms of prediction and induction (11, 12). This is an attractive model not only because it is gaining traction across the life sciences and being given credence by practicing experimental cognitive neuroscientists [e.g., Ref. (13)], but, more importantly for my purposes, because it is expressly designed to account for the variation inherent to categories such as addiction.

The two basic tenets of the HPC view are: (1) that kinds are defined by a cluster of properties that reliably occur in members of the kind and (2) that the properties co-occur in virtue of some shared causal or mechanistic structure[7] – the homeostatic in HPC refers to causally maintained co-occurrence. Species are paradigmatic HPC kinds in biology (11, 14).

The challenge for the HPC view is to articulate which categories count as kinds given the fact that members of a kind vary so much. There must be a way to determine: (a) what properties can count in the homeostatic cluster that defines the kind and (b) when a set of properties is truly a cluster and not just an arbitrary set. Both

[4] I am not critiquing any definition of addiction in favor of any other, rather, I am pointing out inadequacies with various definitions. My main point is that whatever definition of addiction one chooses, there are problems applying it to all cases of what we call addiction. Against the disease conception, I argue that no mechanism can account for the properties of an agent understood as "addiction" in all cases; for the purposive conception I argue that the definition itself has trouble explaining some cases of what we call addiction.

[5] For instance, Hacking (59) endorses family resemblances but not clusters (where the former must count as somehow co-sufficient and the latter, as I have explained, need not) as well as restricts natural kinds to human-independent categories. Yet stricter still are more "traditional" accounts of natural kinds which pose essences as necessary and sufficient conditions for kindhood [e.g., Ref. (60)] On such accounts, addiction would not be a natural kind: it has no metaphysically special essence, and it is a kind defined at least in part by human behaviors.

[6] I am thankful to Bennett Foddy for bringing up this point in review.

[7] More precisely, the members must have those properties generated by mechanisms/sets of mechanisms that are tokens of the same type.

questions are answered by trying to maximize the importance of causal influence: it is properties that are causally basic, as opposed to surface properties that are part of the cluster, and it is when causally basic properties co-occur in virtue of a mechanism or set of mechanisms that the set of properties is truly a cluster (12).

THE HPC VIEW: KEY CONCEPTS

Properties can be said to be superficial or causally basic: causally basic properties are those by which the other properties can be fully (perhaps reductively) explained. For instance, the causally basic properties of the kind "human" are things like the ability to interbreed and sharing a common ancestry. The superficial properties of the kind human are just those properties that humans share that other categories/kinds don't: having opposable thumbs isn't part of the surface property list of humans because it is shared by a higher taxa (primates), but having a complex grammar or a prefrontal cortex larger than other mammals are. The fact that humans have and share these properties can be explained by humans' shared ancestry and history of breeding.

But these causally basic properties are distinct from the mechanisms that cause them to co-occur in humans. Selection and reproduction might be what cause the surface properties to occur, but the mechanisms of evolution – such as invasive gene suppression and advantageous mutation – are what explain the co-occurrence of those causally basic properties themselves. The mechanisms make the set a cluster, or, better, they make the cluster a *homeostatic* cluster [example from Ref. (12)].

Note that the former causal relationship is stronger than the latter. Uniquely human surface properties can be largely if not entirely explained by the selective history and ancestral genotype of human conspecifics (arguably plus the environmental pressures on them), but no mechanism of gene flow can fully explain those abilities without an additional story being told about the particular historical facts of human reproduction.

Thus, a kind is defined by a cluster of causally basic properties whose clustering is the result of an underlying mechanism/set of mechanisms.

DELINEATING KINDS FROM MERE CATEGORIES

Consider an example from evolutionary biology. Squids have eyes much like humans (or whichever taxa our particular kind of visual system belongs to). However, the set of human and squid eyes is considered a homoplasy – a shared trait in virtue of distinct evolutionary histories and mechanisms – rather than an homology, or a shared trait in virtue of a shared ancestral history (14, 15). No putative natural kind to which human eyes belong (e.g., primate eyes, mammal eyes) includes squid eyes (16).

Yet, human and squid eyes have some of the same surface properties (the ability to detect objects, motion, light changes, etc.) and possibly in virtue of the same causally basic properties (a retina, a pupil, etc.). And we can subsume some basic generalizations under a category that includes human and squid eyes, such as that they will both detect an organism of sufficient size moving across their field of view and send this information to the brain. So why don't human and squid eyes count as a natural kind?

Griffiths refers to the causally basic properties whose co-occurrence is supported not by random chance (as in the case of homoplasy) but by mechanisms to be *maximally* predictive (14). This term is a little misleading in that one might expect maximally predictive categories to be the categories that currently possess the largest cluster of properties.

However, this notion of a maximally predictive category can be made clear by understanding that science is an ever-progressing discipline, and all entities studied by biology or psychology, be they organisms, parts of organisms, mental states, etc., will have properties that have yet to be identified, let alone understood, or explained scientifically. The question, then, is, what is the best way to predict which categories will explain clustering or co-occurrence of properties to be discovered or explained in the future? The answer provided by the HPC view is that the best way to predict future clustering is *not* by present clustering. Rather, the best way to predict future clustering is by reference to mechanisms that explain the co-occurrence of the properties in a cluster.

HPC KINDS AND REVISABILITY

The fact that natural kind claims are warranted on the basis of mechanisms, rather than on the basis of property clusters, is just one facet of the HPC view's commitment to the ongoing nature of scientific practice. Wilson and colleagues sum up this commitment well, claiming that "[t]he HPC view carries a commitment to a thoroughgoing naturalism, according to which philosophical reflection on science is continuous with and epistemically regulated by ongoing scientific practice" [Ref. (12), p. 202]. This view entails not only a commitment to categories that will be most useful for predictions in future scientific endeavors, but also a commitment to take seriously the results of those endeavors.

Because science is an ongoing practice, scientific claims are always falsifiable or empirically revisable. This means that all natural kind claims are understood as working hypotheses. In Boyd's words, they are all *a posteriori* claims (11). More simply, the content of a kind term is whatever the best current science tells us it is: to paraphrase Griffiths (14), addiction means whatever psychology tells us is going on in the mind/brains of addicted individuals.

The upshot of this reasoning is that when I make a claim that "addiction is not a natural kind," I am making a claim tantamount to a working hypothesis, up for revision if the best current science of addiction changes. But this does not mean the claim is unwarranted *at this time*, it just means it will never be immune from scrutiny in light of new evidence.

ADDICTION AS HPC KIND?

The surface properties of addiction are addictive behaviors or "the addictive phenotype" and the causally basic properties are the person-level functions that putatively explain the phenotype, including psychological factors like habitual desire and loss of control (17), as well as environmental factors captured at a high level of abstraction (e.g., opportunities for employment/advancement). I discuss the causally basic properties proposed by varieties of the disease paradigm in detail in the next section.

Which mechanisms underlie the co-occurrence of these causally basic properties is the primary question addressed in the cognitive neuroscience of addiction. When we discuss "a mechanism for addiction," what we mean is a mechanism that explains to co-occurrence of some or all of the causally basic properties in the cluster. Thus, according to Everitt and Robbins (7), behavioral control being shifted from prefrontal areas and the ventral striatum to the dorsal striatum is the mechanism responsible for the property of having behavior insensitive to the agent's conscious desire or executive control, which in turn explains the compulsive drug-taking behavior.

This kind of mechanism, realized in the brain of individuals, is described on a different level – one might say a different kind of mechanism altogether – than the mechanisms of evolution that fix the cluster of properties for the species human. Nonetheless, the important point for kind terms is that they both play the right causal role, that is, they explain the occurrence of the causally basic properties, but to which the causally basic properties cannot be reduced to them.

My argument is that, given the candidate mechanisms proposed in literature, at least one class of cases of addiction as delineated by substance, the proposed mechanism fails to underlie the causally basic properties. I contend, in essence, that the category "addiction" is like a category of eyes that includes both human and squid eyes, whereas the categories "S-addiction" and "T-addiction," etc., are like categories that include only human eyes (or some other category of eyes defined by homology and not homoplasy).

I should clarify that I am not claiming instances of addiction to different substances are themselves an example of convergent evolution. Rather, I am arguing that a category based on convergent evolution, i.e., one that includes both human and squid eyes, and a category "addiction" including addiction to all substances, stand in the same relation to categories that are genuine natural kinds. They are examples of categories that share a property cluster but not in virtue of a common mechanism.

ADDICTION AND LOSS OF CONTROL

The DSM defines addiction based on patterns of use, that is to say, behavioral criteria. But experimental models focus on something like loss of control. Why? When seeking a mechanism to explain the property cluster of addiction – something in virtue of which addiction applies as a property to individuals – we need to look for a mechanism *for something.* In this section, I'll discuss why loss of control is an appropriate candidate to be explained mechanistically. For it is the mechanisms that seek to explain loss of control with which I will take issue.

First, one cannot look for a mechanism responsible for a behavior on the neurocognitive level without a prior understanding of the psychological function that explains behavior: there is no brain area for aggression, rather, there are functions, realized neuroanatomically, that explain aggressive behaviors (18).

Second, a behavioral definition necessarily casts the net too widely, as it cannot distinguish between an addict and an enthusiast in the right conditions [Sinnott-Armstrong and Pickard (19), though, see Griffiths (66) for reasons why we might not want to make such a distinction]. By enthusiast I mean someone who has a strong desire for something but one that is completely within the agent's control. Sinnott-Armstrong and Pickard give the example of an avid golfer, though in theory this could apply to an avid drug user who is not addicted (be it from not being addicted yet, not having the predisposition, etc.). An enthusiast who needs to travel somewhere for business where he or she cannot obtain drugs has good reason not to use drugs, and, will subsequently abstain. However, suppose for the purposes of this thought experiment that the enthusiast never encountered such a situation as a matter of chance: what, behaviorally, would distinguish him from an addict? Sinnott-Armstrong and Pickard (19) therefore suggest that having a motivational structure that includes a loss of control is an essential part of addiction. Of course, having no control but no desire to use drugs also does not constitute addiction, so it must be both[8].

The HPC account need not entirely ignore behavior as a part of addiction. I suggest that the addictive phenotype, i.e., addiction-related behaviors as described in the DSM, are the surface properties, explained by the causally basic properties which can be loosely described at a coarse grain as the functions underlying having a strong and habitual desire and a loss of control.[9] Further, it is the causally basic properties that are supposed to be definitive of the kind, and thus these properties constitute a valid definition, whereas the behaviors are not causally basic. Finally, person-level properties such as loss of control stand in just the right relation to subpersonal functional mechanisms: the latter can account for the occurrence of the former without fully (reductively) explaining it (20).

I emphasize that the causally basic properties can be described – in the sense that they can be grouped together – as "loss of control," not that loss of control is itself a causally basic property. For loss of control, when understood at anything but the coarsest of grains, is far too heterogeneous to count as property, and thus a candidate to be causally basic[10]. First of all, loss of control itself is a broader category than loss of control in addiction, which refers to some specific sort (or sorts) of loss of control. Further, addiction theorists disagree on how to cash out loss of control in terms of the functions that generate behavior which can be described as not controlled (to some extent) by the agent.

Indeed, each theorist I discuss cashes out loss of control in a different way: for the aberrant learning hypothesis, the causally basic property is the habit-based behaviors that are not sensitive to executive control systems, whereas for the frontostriatal dysfunction model it is impaired activity in the executive systems themselves – understood at a fine grain to include multiple functional systems such as incentive salience attribution, emotion regulation, executive override functions, and others – that are the causally basic properties. Notably, some even propose different numbers of causally basic functions related to loss of control: the aberrant learning and incentive sensitization hypotheses give one functional neuroadaptation primacy[11] whereas the frontostriatal model suggests the equal contribution of several functions.

---

[8] Sinnott-Armstrong and Pickard (19) add a third criterion, that the addiction causes harm, though they also suggest that loss of control might be inherently harmful. This part of the definition is not necessary for the purposes of this discussion; my arguments do not turn on any explanation of harm.

[9] I should note that not all theorists endorse some form of loss of control as central [e.g., Ref. (61)]. However, the theorists discussed, that is, those in the disease paradigm of addiction, do. See my (62) for a discussion on the unity of addiction in Pickard's theory.

[10] I am thankful to Bennett Foddy for raising this point in review.

[11] Everitt and Robbins (7) do discuss the role of the prefrontal cortex distinct from the dorsal striatum, however, they also later suggest that prefrontal neuroadaptations may temporally precede addiction (63).

When I say loss of control in general, I mean to refer to those causally basic properties hypothesized by the respective theories discussed here that can be grouped together as underlying some sort of loss of control, and not some property itself.

The key point is that the way in which addiction according to the disease paradigm putatively maps to HPC kinds can now be stated more precisely. The surface properties are addictive behaviors, the causally basic properties are the functions suggested by the theorists related to loss of control, and the mechanisms are the neurocognitive adaptations proposed to be causally relevant to those functions.

THEORIES OF ADDICTION

The disease conception of addiction is close to the received view in cognitive neuroscience. Melis and colleagues sum up the view well:

> [N]ot different from traditional diseases, drug addiction bears with it a number of biological abnormalities. which justifies the label disease. Although repetitive use of drugs affects different organs. the primary target appears to be the brain – thus brain disease [Ref. (21), p. 102].

In this section, I'll discuss some various proposals for relevant mechanisms. I'll then detail how the suggested mechanisms in each theory fail to account for a class of substances.

Varieties of the disease conception suggest different mechanisms on the level of functional neurocircuits – that is, sets of brain areas with assigned functions – to explain the occurrence of the causally basic properties. I'll discuss a few prevalent models: (1) Everitt and Robbins (7) suggest that aberrant associative learning results in uncontrollable habits realized in dopaminergic projections to and within the dorsal striatum, and that addiction involves transfer of behavioral control from voluntary reward-based systems to these nearly reflexive habit learning systems via dopaminergic projections from the ventral to the dorsal striatum. (2) Robinson and Berridge (22–24) suggest that the mesolimbic dopamine (DA) system malfunctions in addiction. They suggest that the function of the system is to compute the "incentive salience" of a stimulus, or how much an organism "wants" (as opposed to "likes") that stimulus. They hypothesize that, in addiction, the system changes to habitually overvalue drug-related stimuli at the expense of other classes of stimuli. (3) Volkow and colleagues (6, 10, 25) suggest that several neurocircuits involving various prefrontal control regions underlie different aspects of loss of control in addiction, and that these circuits "conspire" to overwhelm cognitive control systems.

In each case, evidence shows that at least one substance of abuse violates a major prediction of the theory such that it is not obvious that the putative mechanism is operant in those cases. For the former two, cannabis is the exception; for the third, opiates are.

THEORY ONE: ABERRANT LEARNING AND THE DORSAL STRIATUM

Everitt, Robbins, and colleagues (7, 26) suggest that a dopaminergic neurocognitive circuit focused around the dorsal striatum plays a central role in the generation of addictive behaviors. Specifically, they suggest that behavioral control shifts from normal reward-based learning functions realized in the mesolimbic DA system[12] to habit-based learning functions realized in the dorsal striatum.

The dorsal striatum is involved in unmediated stimulus-response associations, as opposed to mediated S-R associations (27). A mediated S-R association is one that is related to some other mental factor. The relationship between food (S) and eating (R) is generally a mediated response: a rat will eat food if it's hungry, but not if it's full (under normal circumstances). Thus the food-stimulus/eating-behavior association is mediated by hunger levels. These associations are realized in a neurocognitive circuit involving the ventral striatum, ventral tegmental area (VTA), and OFC – essentially, the mesolimbic DA system (27).

An unmediated association is an automatic and involuntary association between stimulus and response, such as walking into a dark room and reaching for/moving a light switch.

Everitt and Robbins suggest that addiction occurs when drug-taking and drug-seeking behavior cease to be generated by mediated S-R mechanisms and begin to be generated by unmediated ones. In functional terms, drug-taking and drug-seeking become automatic, involuntary responses to drug-related stimuli (or conditioned cues) in addiction, whereas in drug use that is not addiction, they are mediated by some psychological factor. In an elaborate series of experiments, Everitt and Robbins have demonstrated that activation of the dorsal striatum is involved in the animal model of relapse: drug-seeking behavior after prolonged abstinence in response to conditioned stimuli.

A major prediction of this model is that these dopaminergic circuits in the dorsal striatum change over time in response to the influx of dopamine from the drug of choice. This can be measured experimentally in a few ways. First, dopamine type 2/type 3 (D2/3) receptor availability will decrease in the dorsal striatum in addicted individuals. This lowered receptor availability is the brain's response to repeated, externally induced dopaminergic innervations: rather than over-activating constantly, the brain raises the threshold for activation in terms of required D2/3 levels. To be clear, it is not the receptors themselves that are hypothesized to play a causal role in addiction, rather, measuring receptor levels is intended to indirectly measure the causally efficacious dopamine activity[13]. And this prediction is confirmed in many substances, including cocaine (28), alcohol (29), opiates (30), methamphetamine (31), and nicotine (32). Yet D2/3 receptor availability is not affected within statistically significant levels in either adolescents (33) or adults (34) recovering from cannabis addiction.

A second experimental model is to investigate the level of dopamine transporters in and around the dorsal striatum *in vivo*, which also decreases as a response to repeated, artificially induced influxes of dopamine. In a study by Leroy and colleagues (35), striatal and extrastriatal dopamine transporter levels were compared between three groups: healthy controls, individuals addicted to nicotine, and individuals addicted to nicotine and cannabis. The latter two groups showed no significant difference in dopamine

[12]The postulated function of the mesolimbic DA system differs between theories of addiction. For Everitt and Robbins, it is involved in the learning of reward value, whereas, for, e.g., Robinson and Berridge (22, 23), it is involved in the attribution of incentive salience.

[13]I am thankful to Serge Ahmed for raising this point in review.

transporter levels, but both demonstrated a significant difference compared to controls, suggesting that cannabis – unlike nicotine – does not decrease dopamine transporter levels in and around the dorsal striatum.

Therefore, the data available on dopamine activity in the dorsal striatum in cannabis addiction that has been collected thus far points to the conclusion that cannabis, in contrast to virtually every other drug of abuse, does not involve the neuroadaptation proposed to underlie addiction in this theory.

THEORY TWO: INCENTIVE SENSITIZATION

Robinson and Berridge (22–24) agree with Everitt and Robbins that regular drug use starts out affecting the mesolimbic DA system, but disagree on the function of that system as well as the location of the salient neuroadaptations for the transition to addiction. They suggest the mesolimbic DA circuit computes incentive salience, or the extent to which an organism "wants" a stimulus, as opposed to – and independent of – the extent to which the organism "likes" it, and this function itself is compromised in addiction.

All drugs of abuse produce a rush of dopamine to the VTA, which transmits more throughout the circuit (21, 36). According to the incentive sensitization theory, this causes the system to improperly compute the incentive salience value of the drug in terms of its objective benefit, significantly overvaluing the substance that caused the DA release. Over time, the brain builds up a tolerance to higher DA levels, and as a result, salience values of stimuli across the board, so to speak, are devalued – except for drug-related stimuli, which are re-overvalued each time the drug is consumed. In functional terms, addiction occurs when we automatically value drug-related stimuli as the stimuli with the highest incentive salience value (whether we consciously endorse this valuation or not). This process is referred to as *incentive sensitization.*

A major prediction of this theory, then, is that non-drug-related rewards such as food, water, and sex (though not money, presumably because it becomes associated in the brains of addicts with obtaining drugs) generate less activation in mesolimbic DA system areas, especially the ventral striatum, than in conspecifics, and drug-related stimuli generate greater activation. And this prediction has been confirmed in addiction to alcohol (37), cocaine (38), and nicotine (39). But again, this prediction is not borne out with cannabis: heavy cannabis users exhibit greater ventral striatum activation in response to cannabis-related stimuli more than non-users, but they also exhibit greater activation to non-drug-related stimuli (40)[14]! Further, Wolfing and colleagues (41) found that verbal reports as well as psychophysiological measurements (EEG and skin conductance resonance or SCR) showed that habitual cannabis users value valenced non-drug stimuli greater than do controls[15].

An experimental paradigm related to incentive sensitization at the neural level is behavioral sensitization. In this paradigm, animal models are noted to initially have increased spontaneous locomotor activity in response to drugs of abuse, and this activity decreases with repeated exposure, hence behavioral sensitization. And the process is hypothesized to mimic sensitization at the neural level [Varvel et al. (42); though, see Ref. (43) for a challenge to this connection]. Varvel and colleagues performed an elaborate series of experiments on comparisons between behavioral sensitization to methamphetamine and to cannabis. In all iterations in which there was evidence for behavioral sensitization to methamphetamine, there was no evidence for behavioral sensitization to cannabis.

Functionally, then, this theory runs into a problem explaining the occurrence of strong, habitual desire with loss of control in cannabis addiction. If drugs are the only thing of value to an agent (in the agent's unconscious valuation), then the agent will predictably keep taking drugs at the expense of other rewards. But, according to this data, cannabis use doesn't necessarily make one want cannabis at the expense of other things, it makes one want everything more. Thus it is not clear why the agent would prefer the drug over other non-drug rewards. In other words, it might explain the agent's becoming a hedonist in general, but not an addict to a particular substance.

THEORY THREE: THE FRONTOSTRIATAL DYSFUNCTION MODEL

Volkow and colleagues (9, 44) proposed a decade ago that prefrontal cortical areas, involved in executive control and inhibition (among other functions) in normal brain function also underlie the loss of control aspect of addiction. Specifically, the systems are compromised in terms of overall functional capacity, and, as a result, exhibit decreased activity via a variety of measures. In other words, an agent's normal self-control systems fail to block drug-taking and drug-seeking behavior, resulting in use that is out of the agent's control.

More recently (10, 25), they have expanded this model to discuss particular aspects of compromised inhibition which are each assigned to a specific neurocircuit involving distinct subregions of the PFC; in large part this move is simply a reflection of a better understanding of the heterogeneity of PFC function [Goldstein and Volkow (10); for a review of PFC areas and their respective functions, see Ref. (45)]. Many of these circuits involve projections between the PFC and ventral striatum, however, I focus on PFC related data here.

While the full details of this intricate model are beyond the scope of this discussion, a crucial point is that the various neurocircuits are postulated not to independently promote aspects of the

[14]The findings of Nestor and colleagues suggest cannabis is a problem for *any* theory of addiction that posits greater VS activation in response to drug-related stimuli in the face of decreased activation to non-drug-related "rewarding" stimuli. An influential theory of addiction that I have not discussed makes a similar prediction with a similar neural basis but with a different functional story. The "allostatic" theory of addiction [e.g., Ref. (64)] suggests that repeated, externally induced dopaminergic innervations and the resulting hypodopaminergic state generate an anhedonic affective/nocioceptive state in addicted individuals, who then use the drug of their preference to retain normal hedonic functioning. Similarly, addiction is supposed to result in reward-system driven overvaluation of drug-related and undervaluation of non-drug-related stimuli, except here the over/undervaluations are computed in terms of reward value rather than incentive salience. But the suggested physiological basis for this computation is still the mesolimbic DA system, and thus the evidence from cannabis is problematic.

[15]However, by this study's measurements – in contrast to the Gruber data – habitual cannabis users did not overvalue non-drug rewards to the same extent as they did drug rewards in comparison to controls.

addictive phenotype but rather to feed off of each other and "conspire" to produce the addictive phenotype (6). Thus, for addiction to be a natural kind on this account, the set of mechanisms must explain addiction across substances.

However, opiates cause a problem for predictions involving several of the proposed circuits. Indeed, there are myriad differences between opiate and either cocaine or stimulant addiction summarized by Badiani and colleagues (1). I will focus here on the data they discuss that is most relevant to the frontostriatal theory.

According to Volkow and colleagues (10, 25), the medial PFC as a whole is involved in several relevant neurocircuits, including one underlying the balancing of immediate gratification with the attainment of long-term goals, and this circuit's function is compromised in addiction. Because of the decreased activity in the area, the theory predicts that spiny neuron density will increase in the mPFC (as a homeostatic response to lowered neurotransmitter levels in virtue of decreased activity). And this result has been confirmed in cocaine, methamphetamine, and cannabis (46, 47). However, animal models of heroin addiction show the opposite: decreased spiny neuron density in the mPFC in abstinent rats (46). Further evidence regarding differences in mPFC morphology come from measuring long-term potentiation (LTP) in GABAergic synapses in animal models *in vivo.* Repeated cocaine exposure suppresses LTP in the mPFC, and, subsequently, abstinence facilitated LTP reformation (48, 49). Abstinence after repeated exposure to heroin, however, had no significant effect on LTP (50).

Moreover, distinct subregions of the medial PFC, especially the ventromedial PFC (vmPFC), are implicated independently of the mPFC as a whole in the function of other circuits relevant to self control in the PFC. Specifically, the vmPFC is involved in stimulus valuation and salience attribution as well as emotion regulation (10).

Yet evidence suggests that these subregions are differentially involved in addiction to cocaine and opiates. For heroin, context-induced reinstatement can be attenuated by inhibiting the vmPFC (51). This is plausible given the theoretical interpretation of the circuits in which the vmPFC is involved. For it would seem to be that the reason relapse can be cue induced in the first place is because the associated cues are given such a high valuation or attributed salience. However, for cocaine, context-induced reinstatement can be attenuated when the dorsal, but not the ventral mPFC is inhibited (52). Not only is this result functionally difficult to explain since the dmPFC is not implicated in valuation and salience attribution, but it demonstrates that the involvement of PFC neuroadaptations in addiction cannot be assumed to be the same across substances.

IMPLICATIONS FOR THE CATEGORY OF ADDICTION

At least according to the best neuroscientific theories of addiction available, there is no mechanism underlying loss of control in addiction across substances. I thus argue that, barring further evidence in the future to the contrary, addiction is not a natural kind. In this section, I'll discuss what ought to be done to find natural kinds in addiction science. First, however, I want to address the scope of the claim I'm making. Specifically, I want to address the possibility of what finding further evidence in the future to the contrary might mean for this claim.

NATURAL KINDS AND THE STATUS OF ADDICTION SCIENCE

Because the HPC view is committed to the best current science, its claims are always working hypotheses, up for revision in light of future empirical evidence. This means that when I claim "addiction is not a natural kind," I am making a statement tantamount to a working hypothesis, warranted by the state of science at this time. However, there are two ways the science could change such that the data would no longer support my contention, and I want to address both possibilities. First, a future theory of the mechanisms of addiction could be introduced that would meet the criteria I've discussed for natural kindhood, i.e., that would explain addiction across substances in terms of a common causal mechanism or set of mechanisms. Such a theory could be a reformulation or augmentation of a current theory, or a novel hypothesis. Second, the experimental findings that have warranted the theories already discussed may be invalidated. I discuss each of these possibilities in turn, and suggest reasons as to why I am still justified in making the claim that addiction is not a natural kind.

What if future research finds mechanisms of addiction that truly apply to addiction across substances? In that event, the basis for warranting kind claims would change to respect the new findings, and, subsequently my thesis would be unwarranted – barring research even further in the future to the contrary of *those* claims. However, such a possibility is in principle entirely consistent with making the claim at the current time that addiction is not a natural kind, since this sort of claim always entails a status as a working hypothesis.

Because mechanisms that unify kinds are what warrant the making of natural kind claims, and because these mechanistic findings are always themselves up for revision in light of new evidence, a kind theorist is left with two options: make no kind claims at all until the science is essentially static (e.g., it seems rather safe to assume that the unity of an element category in chemistry like gold will not be challenged), or make kind claims that are tantamount to working hypotheses. But it is the current generalizations that we make that enable science to progress: the claim that addiction is not a natural kind is based on past science, and aimed to help future science (and philosophy; see S 6). The empirical literature discussed here was generated because scientists were studying the nature of what they took to be a valid category, and this study has produced scientific progress. In other words, science is well served by making and augmenting working hypotheses about the unity/disunity of various categories.

A distinct possibility is that the theories that warrant my claims about the disunity of the category addiction themselves will be falsified by future science. And this possibility is at least *prima facie* plausible. For instance, Ahmed (53, 54) rightly questions the addiction status of animal models who have been given no choice but to repeatedly take the drug presented to them, which calls into question many of the experimental findings on which these theories are based. If a radical version of this claim were true such that none of the current theories proposed were valid enough to warrant any claims about natural kinds, what would that mean for my claim that addiction is not a natural kind? Samuels (55) suggests that when studying a putative category where no potential, reasonably supported mechanistic basis has been proposed, we take the working hypothesis that the category is a HPC kind based on similarity of surface properties. And addiction would seem, at least *prima facie*, to qualify as having similar surface properties (addiction-related behaviors) for instances of addiction across substances, though a more robust discussion of the behavioral and epidemiological patterns of addicts to various substances would need to happen before such a claim could be made with any amount of confidence.

However, I do not understand the possibility that the experimental basis for these theories may be invalidated to undermine my claim that addiction, as the science stands right now, is not a natural kind. For such an argument is a criticism of what is currently the dominant paradigm in addiction, and a distinct one from the point I am making. The dominant paradigm of addiction, as I understand it, suggests that: (1) results from the animal models of addiction used over the last half century or so project to instances of addiction in humans and (2) that mechanistic explanations of addiction to one substance project to instances of addiction to other substances[16]. Both of these claims are still part of the dominant paradigm; I am challenging the latter claim and arguments like Ahmed's are challenging the former. And while I am sympathetic to Ahmed's argument, I am not, in this discussion myself, challenging the projectability from animal models to humans. Rather, I am making a separate challenge to a dominant view that still largely accepts this tenet.

THE SEARCH FOR KIND TERMS

When investigation of a category previously thought to be a natural kind fails to reveal a mechanism underlying the property cluster, the natural kind theorist is committed to one of two alternatives to rectify the situation: category revision and category replacement (14, 56). The commitment to category replacement or revision in light of empirical evidence is part and parcel of the HPC view's commitment to scientific practice. A common mechanistic basis among members of a category is what warrants natural kind claims, and since the mechanistic claims are empirically revisable, so are the claims about which categories count as natural kinds.

To again paraphrase Griffiths (14), this is not to say that nothing is happening in individuals we refer to as addicted. It just means that classifying them as suffering from addiction might not be particularly illuminating as to what's going on in their brains. And the strategies of category replacement and/or revision are the next step in the search for categories that will be illuminating.

In this section, I'll go over how these two strategies might be used by an addiction scientist to find valid natural kinds. I shall also explain why I prefer the category replacement strategy, where we cease to discuss in terms of "addiction" simpliciter and come to discuss patients in terms of "S-addiction" or "T-addiction."

CATEGORY REVISION

Category revision means rethinking the extension of the category, i.e., the set of entities to which it refers. And there is a move available to the addiction theorist to salvage some category similar to addiction.

For whichever mechanistic account of addiction ends up being correct, addiction theorists might simply revise the extension of "addiction" to refer to cases of addiction caused by the right mechanisms. Thus, if the aberrant learning model is correct, it might be the case that there is a natural kind of disorder encompassing addiction to cocaine, nicotine, alcohol, etc., but not cannabis. When looking for the common mechanisms of addiction, researchers might just cease to demand that patients putatively addicted to cannabis display evidence of those specific neuroadaptations. (If the frontostriatal dysfunction account is correct, we'd have to jettison heroin addiction from the natural kind.)

CATEGORY REPLACEMENT

Another option is to replace addiction as a category with related categories that better track distinct mechanisms. Notably, the mechanisms underlying loss of control in addiction do not seem to vary across users of the same substance; minimally, I am not arguing here that they do. Thus, nothing I have suggested contradicts – and indeed, the evidence might be said to corroborate[17] – the idea that "cocaine addiction" and "cannabis addiction" for example, are natural kinds.

Moreover, under such a conception it might be the case that addiction to two (or more) substances end up using the same set of mechanisms. For instance, suppose cocaine and methamphetamine are found to have the same mechanism or set of mechanisms that end up being the consensus for underlying loss of control in addiction. Then patients addicted to either substance would be members of a category that counted as a single natural kind.

REASONS TO PREFER CATEGORY REPLACEMENT

While both category revision of addiction (to exclude cannabis or opiates) and category replacement of addiction with "S-addiction," "T-addiction," etc., are both equally valid strategies, I find the second option more attractive.

Whichever theory is correct, category replacement, at least utilizing the strategy I have suggested, might lead us to the same place as category revision. That is, it is possible that if the aberrant learning hypothesis is correct, and if this is the case, investigation would then determine that S-/T-addiction are the only two real kinds, where S is cannabis and T is all substances except cannabis, just as we would with category revision if the aberrant learning hypothesis were correct.

I argue that if this is the case, and we would arrive at the same conclusion either way, then the claim will be on far better theoretical standing if arrived at via the second strategy. For it would be reached as a conclusion of investigation rather than as a stipulated premise.

Fundamentally, the lesson I hope we would draw from the discrepancies between substances of addiction is that, given the current state of addiction science, assuming a unitary category of addiction is no longer justified. At the beginning stages of investigation – for instance, when it was discovered that all drugs of abuse

[16] I understand projection in this sense to roughly mean an inference from a pattern in a specific subset of samples to another, larger specific set or subset (65). See Boyd (11) for further discussion of projectability and natural kinds.

[17] I should note that this might be a relic of the experimental construct which tests a group of individuals in treatment for addiction to a particular substance against a control group of non-users or occasional users of the same drug.

target or act on the mesolimbic circuit with dopamine (36) – it might have been reasonable to infer as a working hypothesis the unity of addiction from the unity of acute use. But that was when our best evidence about long-term addiction was indirect, i.e., from short-term use, and the situation is now different.

One could object that perhaps addiction *per se* is analogous to a higher taxa category in species biology. That is, S-addiction is like the species human and addiction is, for example, the genus primates[18]. But this analogy does not work: in the case of taxa, the relevant mechanisms are evolutionary, and all taxa share some ancestry (indeed, biological categories only count as taxa if they do, otherwise the putative taxon is merely a homoplasy). However, in the case of addiction, the relevant mechanisms are physiological/neurocognitive, and these mechanisms either play a causally efficacious role in the drug-related behavior of addicts to a given substance, or they do not.

CONCLUSION: IMPLICATIONS FOR SCIENTISTS AND PHILOSOPHERS

I hope I have demonstrated in this paper that natural kinds are just a simple yet relatively precise way to capture the conceptual commitments of theoretical constructs such as "addiction" (or "emotion," or "species").

In this concluding section, I wish to discuss why various members of the scientific and philosophical community might benefit from replacing "addiction" with "S-addiction." All researchers make predictions or inferences on the basis of category membership. And in all cases, researchers benefit from using categories that are supported by underlying mechanisms.

BASIC SCIENCE

Basic scientists are concerned with making the most powerful explanations they can, and the relevance of natural kinds is thus direct. Natural kinds are categories that are maximally predictive, and categories that fail to be natural kinds *ipso facto* fail to be maximally predictive, no matter how much their members have in common.

Natural kinds *just are* the categories scientists ought to use for the basis of making predictions, and thus for the design of experiments. It is telling that experimental cohorts are rarely if ever composed of patients with addictions to distinct substances (that is, a patient with S-addiction and one with T-addiction in the same cohort, as opposed to comorbidity studies): conclusions would be very difficult to draw.

CLINICAL SCIENCE

Clinicians are most concerned with what ameliorates the condition of their patients. But again, mechanisms matter. Supposing that, say, the aberrant learning hypothesis is correct, and we begin to develop drugs that target the dorsal striatum. Those drugs wouldn't work for instances of cannabis addiction. Similarly, while behavioral measures might target higher-level phenomena seemingly independent of mechanism, the mechanism still matters. Therapies that work to create and reinforce new associations will work well for fixing maladaptive mediated associations but not unmediated ones (or, minimally, better for the former type than the latter). Thus if loss of control in addiction to various drugs of abuse is underwritten by distinct mechanisms, different therapies will be differentially effective.

Thus clinicians are best served by devising treatments for "S-addiction" and "T-addiction" rather than addiction *per se*[19]. Simply put, natural kinds form the best basis for diagnosis and treatment just as they do prediction and induction.

PHILOSOPHY

Moral psychologists are interested in attributions of moral properties like responsibility and autonomy based on an individual's mental composition (or psychology). The relationship between physical and moral properties – assuming that there is any – is a topic of great debate and by no means one I shall enter here.

Indeed, it is logically possible that the mechanisms underlying varieties of loss of control in addiction are irrelevant for the ascription of moral properties: it may be that the high level properties themselves are all that is needed. It might not be a knock against a naturalistic theory of moral psychology that the mechanistic level doesn't matter for moral purposes. And if the mechanistic level doesn't matter, then a category's being a natural kind doesn't matter for the purposes of generalizations to subsume moral ascriptions.

However, there is reason to think that it might. Pickard (5) suggests that addicts maintain a middle ground in ascriptions of moral autonomy between full responsibility and full blamelessness. Madva (under review) claims (primarily in regard to implicit bias) that having some but not full control over a behavior might be a good psychological basis on which to ascribe such partial responsibility. Indeed, he suggests, following Holton (57) that addicts might exhibit such partial control insofar as "raising the stakes," i.e., the rewards for quitting, has significant effects on who is able to abstain. In other words, if someone can quit in some circumstances and not others, then that is a good indicator of partial control.

Might the mechanisms underlying loss of control in addiction have relevance to the magnitude of control lost? It is at least *prima facie* an hypothesis worthy of empirical investigation. If Everitt and Robbins are correct, then, devolution of behavioral control from ventral to dorsal striatum corresponds with a higher degree of loss of control than before the "switch." And thus addictions not involving this morphological change would not entail the same magnitude of loss of control. Further, if Holton and colleagues are right that the ability to quit under a greater variety of circumstances indicates greater control, then it is also telling that cannabis users are statistically less likely to seek treatment than users of other substances (58).

---

[18] I am thankful to Alex Madva for raising this point in response to an earlier draft.

[19] This is a distinct point from the fact that addiction treatment must be individually tailored, although that point is certainly valid. However, even the greatest amount of variation in treatment for any disorder will contain some matter of commonality, and which categories we base those generalizations on will matter. In other words, person-to-person variation in treatment for addiction is still variation on the same theme. Combining my argument with the personal variation insight suggests that there should be person-to-person variation in "S-addiction" as well as "T-addiction" but that the addiction-related properties of individuals in group S are statistically far likelier to resemble each other more than any given individual in group T.

In other words, it is at least a hypothesis worth investigating empirically (and a theory worth investigating conceptually) that different addictions, in virtue of different mechanisms, differentially contribute to the ascription of moral properties.

ACKNOWLEDGMENTS

I'd like to thank several individuals for their contributions to this work. First, Matt Barker for a substantive correspondence on HPCs and natural kinds, as well as David Gard and Jim Sparrell for discussions on addiction. Additional thanks to Serge Ahmed and Bennett Foddy for insightful and helpful comments in review of this paper. Special thanks to Hanna Pickard for her assistance as editor in the various stages of preparation of this manuscript, and to Alex Madva, for numerous discussions and comments on multiple drafts.

REFERENCES

1. Badiani A, Belin D, Epstein D, Calu D, Shaham Y. Opiate versus psychostimulant addiction: the differences do matter. *Nat Neurosci Rev* (2011) 12:685–700. doi:10.1038/nrn3104
2. Feltenstein MW, See RE. The neuro- circuitry of addiction: an overview. *Br J Pharmacol* (2008) 154:261–74. doi:10.1038/bjp.2008.51
3. Nestler EJ. Is there a common mol- ecular pathway for addiction? *Nat Neurosci* (2005) 8:1445–9. doi:10. 1038/nn1578
4. Charland LC. Cynthia's dilemma: consenting to heroin prescription. *Am J Bioeth* (2002) 2(2):37–47. doi: 10.1162/152651602317533686
5. Pickard HA. The instrumental rationality of addiction. *Behav Brain Sci* (2011) 34:320–1. doi:10.1017/ S0140525X1100077X
6. Koob GF, Volkow ND. Neuro- circuitry of addiction. *Neuropsy- chopharmacology* (2010) 35:217–38. doi:10.1038/npp.2009.110
7. Everitt BJ, Robbins TW. Neural systems of reinforcement for drug addiction: from actions to habits to compulsion. *Nat Neurosci* (2005) 8:1481–8. doi:10.1038/nn1579
8. Robinson TE, Berridge KC. The neural basis of drug craving: an incentive sensitization theory of addiction. *Brain Res Brain Res Rev* (1993) 18:247–91. doi:10.1016/ 0165-0173(93)90013-P
9. Goldstein RZ, Volkow ND. Drug addiction and its underlying neuro- biological basis: neuroimaging evi- dence for the involvement of the frontal cortex. *Am J Psychiatry* (2002) 159:1642–52. doi:10.1176/ appi.ajp.159.10.1642
10. Goldstein RZ, Volkow ND. Dys- function of the prefrontal cortex in addiction: neuroimaging findings and clinical implications. *Nat Neu- rosci Rev* (2011) 12:652–69. doi:10. 1038/nrn3119
11. Boyd R. Realis, anti- foundationalism and the enthu- siasm for natural kinds. *Phi- los Stud* (1991) 61:127–48. doi:10.1007/BF00385837
12. Wilson RA, Barker MJ, Brigandt I. When traditional essentialism fails: biological natural kinds. *Philos Top- ics* (2010) 35:189–215. doi:10.5840/philtopics2007351/29
13. Barrett LF. Are emotions natural kinds? *Perspect Psychol Sci* (2006) 1:28–58. doi:10.1111/j.1745-6916. 2006.00003.x
14. Griffiths PE. *What Emotions Really Are: The Problem of Psychological Categories*. Chicago: University of Chicago Press (1997).
15. Brigandt I, Griffiths PE. The importance of homology for biol- ogy and philosophy. *Biol Phi- los* (2007) 22:633–41. doi:10.1007/ s10539-007-9094-6
16. Matthen M. Defining vision: what homology thinking contributes. *Biol Philos* (2007) 22:675–89. doi: 10.1007/s10539-007-9088-4
17. Foddy B, Savulescu J. Addiction and autonomy: can addicted peo- ple consent to the prescription of their drug of addiction? *Bioethics* (2006) 20:1–15. doi:10.1111/j.1467- 8519.2006.00470.x
18. Bechtel W, Richardson RC. Neu- roimaging as a tool for functionally decomposing cognitive processes. In: Hanson SJ, Bunzl M, editors. *Foundational Issues in Human Brain Mapping*. Cambridge, MA: MIT Press (2010). p. 241–62.
19. Sinnott-Armstrong W, Pickard HA. What is addiction? In: Fulford KWM, Davies M, Gipps R, Graham G, Sadler J, Stanghellini G, editors. *Oxford Handbook of Philosophy of Psychiatry*. (Chap. 50), New York: Oxford University Press (2013). p. 851–64.
20. Shea N. Neural mechanisms of decision-making and the personal level. In: Fulford KWM, Davies M, Gipps R, Graham G, Sadler J, Stanghellini G, editors. *Oxford Handbook of Philosophy of Psychia- try*. (Chap. 62), New York: Oxford University Press (2013). p. 1063–82.
21. Melis M, Spiga S, Diana M. The dopamine hypothesis of drug addiction: hypodopaminergic state. *Int Rev Neurobiol* (2005) 63:101–54. doi:10.1016/ S0074- 7742(05)63005-X
22. Robinson TE, Berridge KC. The neural basis of drug craving: an incentive-sensitization theory of addiction. *Addiction* (1993) 95:S91–117. doi:10.1046/j.1360-0443.95.8s2.19.x
23. Robinson TE, Berridge KC. The incentive sensitization theory of addiction: some current issues. *Phi- los Trans R Soc Lond B Biol Sci* (2008) 363:3137–46. doi:10.1098/ rstb.2008.0093
24. Berridge KC. The debate over dopamine's role in reward: the case for incentive salience. *Psychopharmacol- ogy (Berl)* (2007) 191:391–431. doi:10.1007/ s00213-006-0578-x
25. Volkow ND, Wang GJ, Tomasi D, Baler RD. Unbalanced neuronal cir- cuits in addiction. *Curr Opin Neu- robiol* (2013) 23(4):639–48. doi:10. 1016/j.conb.2013.01.002
26. Everitt BJ, Belin D, Economidou D, Pelloux Y, Dalley JW, Robbins TW. Neural mechanisms underlying the vulnerability to develop compul- sive drug-seeking habits and addic- tion. *Philos Trans R Soc Lond B Biol Sci* (2008) 363:3125–35. doi:10. 1098/rstb.2008.0089
27. White NM, McDonald RJ. Mul- tiple parallel memory systems in the brain of the rat. *Neurobiol Learn Mem* (2002) 77:125–84. doi: 10.1006/ nlme.2001.4008
28. Porrino LJ, Daunais JB, Smith HR, Nader MA. The expanding effects of cocaine: studies in a nonhu- man primate model of cocaine self- administration. *Neurosci Biobehav Rev* (2004) 27:813–20. doi:10.1016/ j.neubiorev.2003.11.013
29. Volkow ND, Wang GJ, Fowler JS, Logan J, Hitzemann R, Ding YS, et al. Decreases in dopamine recep- tors but not in dopamine trans- porters in alcoholics. *Alcohol Clin Exp Res* (1996) 20:1594–8. doi:10. 1111/j.1530-0277.1996.tb05936.x
30. Wang GJ, Volkow ND, Fowler JS, Logan J, Abumrad NN, Hitze- mann RJ, et al. Dopamine D2 receptor availability in opiate- dependent subjects before and after naloxone-precipitated withdrawal. *Neuropsychopharmacology* (1997) 16:174–82. doi:10.1016/S0893- 133X(96)00184-4
31. Volkow ND, Chang L, Wang GJ, Fowler JS, Ding YS, Sedler M, et al. Low level of brain dopamine D2 receptors in methampheta- mine abusers: association with metabolism in the orbitofrontal cortex. *Am J Psychiatry* (2001) 158:2015–21. doi:10.1176/appi.ajp. 158.12.2015
32. Fehr C, Yakushev I, Hohmann N, Buchholz HG, Landvogt C, Deck- ers H, et al. Association of low stri- atal dopamine D2 receptor avail- ability with nicotine dependence similar to that seen with other drugs of abuse. *Am J Psychia- try* (2008) 165:507–14. doi:10.1176/ appi.ajp.2007.07020352
33. Sevy S, Smith GS, Ma Y, Dhawan V, Chaly T, Kingsley PB, et al. Cerebral glucose metabolism and D2/D3 receptor availability in young adults with cannabis depen- dence measured with positron emis- sion tomography. *Psychopharmacol- ogy (Berl)* (2008) 197:549–56. doi: 10.1007/s00213-008-1075-1
34. Stokes PR, Egerton A, Watson B, Reid A, Lappin J, Howes OD, et al. History of cannabis use is not associated with alterations in striatal dopamine D2/ D3 recep- tor availability. *J Psychopharma- col* (2012) 26:144–9. doi:10.1177/ 0269881111414090
35. Leroy C, Karila L, Martinot JL, Lukasiewicz M, Duchesnay E, Com- tat C, et al. Striatal and extras- triatal dopamine transporter in cannabis and tobacco addiction: a high-resolution PET study. *Addict Biol* (2011) 17:981–90. doi:10.1111/ j.1369-1600.2011.00356.x
36. Di Chiara G, Imperato A. Drugs abused by humans preferentially increase synaptic dopamine con- centrations in the mesolimbic sys- tem of freely moving rats. *Proc Natl Acad Sci U S A* (1988) 85:5274–8. doi:10.1073/ pnas.85.14.5274
37. Wrase J, Schlagenhauf F, Kienast T, Wüstenberg T, Bermpohl F, Kahnt T, et al. Dysfunction of reward pro- cessing correlates with alcohol crav- ing in detoxified alcoholics. *Neu- roimage* (2007) 35:787–94. doi:10. 1016/j.neuroimage.2006.11.043
38. Bjork JM, Smith AR, Hommer DW. Striatal sensitivity to reward deliveries and omissions in sub- stance dependent patients. *Neu- roimage* (2008) 42:1609–21. doi:10. 1016/j.neuroimage.2008.06.035
39. Bühler M, Vollstädt-Klein S, Kobiella A, Budde H, Reed LJ, Braus DF, et al. Nicotine dependence is characterized by disordered reward processing in a network driving motiva- tion. *Biol Psychiatry* (2010) 67: 745–52. doi:10.1016/j.biopsych. 2009.10.029

40. Nestor L, Hester R, Garavan R. Increased ventral striatal BOLD activity during non-drug reward anticipation in cannabis users. *Neuroimage* (2010) 49:1133–43. doi:10.1016/j.neuroimage.2009.07. 022
41. Wolfing K, Flor H, Grusser SM. Psychophysiological responses to drug-associated stimuli in chronic heavy cannabis use. *Eur J Neurosci* (2008) 27:976–83. doi:10.1111/j. 1460-9568.2008.06051.x
42. Varvel SA, Martin BR, Lichtman AH. Lack of behavioral sensiti- zation after repeated exposure to THC in mice and comparison to methamphetamine. *Psychopharma- cology (Berl)* (2007) 193:511–9. doi: 10.1007/s00213-007-0811-2
43. Ahmed SH, Cador M. Dissoci- ation of psychomotor sensitiza- tion from compulsive cocaine con- sumption. *Neuropsychopharmacol- ogy* (2006) 31:563–71. doi:10.1038/ sj.npp.1300834
44. Volkow ND, Fowler JS. Addic- tion, a disease of compulsion and drive: involvement of the orbitofrontal cortex. *Cereb Cor- tex* (2000) 10:318–25. doi:10.1093/ cercor/10.3.318
45. Ray R, Zald DH. Anatomical insights into the interaction of emotion and cognition in the prefrontal cortex. *Neurosci Biobehav Rev* (2012) 36:479–501. doi:10. 1016/j.neubiorev.2011.08.005
46. Robinson TE, Kolb B. Structural plasticity associated with exposure to drugs of abuse. *Neuropharmacol- ogy* (2004) 47:33–46. doi:10.1016/j. neuropharm.2004.06.025
47. Kolb B, Gorny G, Limebeer CL, Parker LA. Chronic treatment with delta-9-tetrahydrocannabinol alters the structure of neurons in the nucleus accumbens shell and medial prefrontal cortex of rats. *Synapse* (2006) 60:429–36. doi:10.1002/syn. 20313
48. Huang CC, Lin HJ, Hsu KS. Repeated cocaine adminis- tration promotes long-term potentiation induction in rat medial prefrontal cortex. *Cereb Cortex* (2007) 17:1877–88. doi:10.1093/cercor/bhl096
49. Lu H, Cheng PL, Lim BK, Khosh- nevisrad N, Poo MM. Elevated BDNF after cocaine withdrawal facilitates LTP in medial prefrontal cortex by suppressing GABA inhi- bition. *Neuron* (2010) 67:821–33. doi:10.1016/j.neuron.2010.08.012
50. Van den Oever MC, Goriounova NA, Li KW, Van der Schors RC, Binnekade R, Schoffelmeer AN, et al. Prefrontal cortex AMPA recep- tor plasticity is crucial for cue- induced relapse to heroin-seeking. *Nat Neurosci* (2008) 11:1053–8. doi: 10.1038/nn.2165
51. Bossert JM, Stern AL, Theberge FR, Cifani C, Koya E, Hope BT, et al. Ventral medial prefrontal cor- tex neuronal ensembles mediate context-induced relapse to heroin. *Nat Neurosci* (2011) 14:420–2. doi: 10.1038/nn.2758
52. Fuchs RA, Evans KA, Ledford CC, Parker MP, Case JM, Mehta RH, et al. The role of the dorso- medial prefrontal cortex, baso- lateral amygdala, and dorsal hippocampus in contextual reinstatement of cocaine seeking in rats. *Neuropsychopharmacology* (2005) 30:296–309. doi:10.1038/sj.npp.1300579
53. Ahmed SH. Validation crisis in animal models of drug addiction: beyond non-disordered drug use toward drug addiction. *Neurosci Biobehav Rev* (2010) 35:172–84. doi:10.1016/j.neubiorev.2010.04. 005
54. Ahmed SH. The science of making drug-addicted ani- mals. *Neuroscience* (2012) 211: 107–25. doi:10.1016/j.neuroscience. 2011.08.014
55. Samuels R. Delusion as a natural kind. In: Broome M, Bortolotti L, editors. *Psychiatry as Cogni- tive Neuroscience: Philosophical Per- spectives.* (Chap. 3), New York: Oxford University Press (2009). p. 49–79.
56. Scarantino A. How to define emotions scientifically. *Emot Rev* (2012) 4:358–68. doi:10.1177/1754073912445810
57. Holton R. *Willing, Wanting, Waiting.* New York: Oxford University Press (2009).
58. Vandrey R, Haney M. How real is the risk of addiction? In: Holland J, editor. *The Pot Book: A Com- plete Guide to Cannabis: Its Role in Medicine, Politics, Science, and Cul- ture.* Rochester,VT: Park Street Press (2010). p. 187–95.
59. Hacking I. A tradition of nat- ural kinds. *Philos Stud* (1991) 61: 109–26. doi:10.1007/BF00385836
60. Dupre J. Natural kinds and biologi- cal taxa. *Philos Rev* (1981) 90:66–90. doi:10.2307/2184373
61. Pickard HA. The purpose in chronic addiction. *AJOB Neu- rosci* (2012) 3:40–9. doi:10.1080/ 21507740.2012.663058
62. Pober JM. Is addiction a heterogeneous condition? Reflections on Pickard's "the purpose in chronic addiction." *AJOB Neurosci* (2012) 3:52–4. doi:10.10 80/21507740.2012.666327
63. Belin D, Mar AC, Dalley JW, Rob- bins TW, Everitt BJ. High impul- sivity predicts the switch to com- pulsive cocaine seeking. *Science* (2008) 320:1352–5. doi:10.1126/ science.1158136
64. Koob GF, Le Moal M. Drug addiction, dysregulation of reward, and allostasis. *Neuropscyhopharma- cology* (2001) 24:318–25.
65. Godfrey-Smith P. *Theory and Real- ity.* Chicago: University of Chicago Press (2003).
66. Griffiths MD. Is loss of control always a consequence of addiction? *Front Psychiatry* (2013) 4:36. doi:10. 3389/fpsyt.2013.00036

17

Addiction: choice or compulsion?

Edmund Henden[1]*, Hans Olav Melberg[2] and Ole Jørgen Røgeberg[3]

[1] Centre for the Study of Professions, Oslo and Akershus University College of Applied Sciences, Oslo, Norway
[2] Department of Health Management and Health Economics, University of Oslo, Oslo, Norway
[3] Ragnar Frisch Centre for Economic Research, Oslo, Norway

Edited by:
Hanna Pickard, University of Oxford, UK

Reviewed by:
Serge H. Ahmed, CNRS, France
Gideon Yaffe, University of Southern California, USA
George Ainslie, Veterans Affairs Medical Center, USA

***Correspondence:**
Edmund Henden, Centre for the Study of Professions, Oslo and Akershus University College of Applied Sciences, PO Box 4, St. Olavs Plass, Oslo, Norway
e-mail: Edmund.Henden@hioa.no

Normative thinking about addiction has traditionally been divided between, on the one hand, a medical model which sees addiction as a disease characterized by compulsive and relapsing drug use over which the addict has little or no control and, on the other, a moral model which sees addiction as a choice characterized by voluntary behavior under the control of the addict. Proponents of the former appeal to evidence showing that regular consumption of drugs causes persistent changes in the brain structures and functions known to be involved in the motivation of behavior. On this evidence, it is often concluded that becoming addicted involves a transition from voluntary, chosen drug use to non-voluntary compulsive drug use. Against this view, proponents of the moral model provide ample evidence that addictive drug use involves voluntary chosen behavior. In this article we argue that although they are right about something, both views are mistaken. We present a third model that neither rules out the view of addictive drug use as compulsive, nor that it involves voluntary chosen behavior.

Keywords: addiction, compulsion, irresistible desires, choice, rationality

INTRODUCTION

The view of addiction as a neurobiological disease characterized by compulsive and relapsing drug use has come under renewed attack by several philosophers and psychologists (1–7).[1] Their critique is partly empirical, partly conceptual. According to the empirical criticism, the disease view is not supported by the empirical evidence appealed to by its proponents. This includes biological evidence of changes to the normal operation of the brain caused by regular consumption of drugs as well as observational evidence of addicts' repetitive self-destructive behavior. But this is insufficient, the critics claim, to warrant a conception of addiction as a disease. The biological evidence is of neurobiological correlates of drug use such as increased levels of the neurotransmitter dopamine, but these correlates are common to most forms of pleasurable experience (2, 3, 5). Sweet food, lottery prizes, sex, and exercise all create strong desires oriented toward some reward, and all essentially involve the same type of brain changes. There is nothing pathological about strong desires.

The second type of empirical evidence relates to the alleged compulsive patterns of self-destructive behavior often observed in addicts, and frequently accompanied by strong ambivalence: the addict expresses a desire not to consume drugs prior to, after, or even during the drug intake (8–11). The assumption is that this reveals the neurobiological effects of drug use to be significantly different from the seemingly similar effects of other desired activities or goods. Whereas strong desires ordinarily do not remove a person's ability to control her behavior, addictive desires do, so the argument goes. Against this, the critics point out, there is plenty of evidence that addictive behavior involves voluntary, intentional, even rational actions. Indeed, under close scrutiny the drug-oriented behavior of addicts is shown to be less unusual than it may appear: it is influenced by a variety of incentives such as financial concerns, fear of arrest, values regarding parenthood, etc.; studies of addictions in the general population find moreover that most addicts quit drugs by their mid-30s, often without assistance (2, 4). How drug users describe loss of control depends variously on the appearance and characteristics of the person surveying them (12), and if we are to believe the experimental evidence it is *the believed* alcohol content rather than *the actual* alcohol content that influences how much alcoholics drink. Such evidence, it is argued, shows both that addicts can be persuaded to exercise their capacity for self-control if they are given what appear to them to be sufficiently good reasons, and that statements regarding loss of control are – at least to some extent – factually inaccurate and motivated by a desire to shift attribution of behavior from choices to circumstances.

Of course, nobody denies that addicts tend to pursue behaviors associated with risk and self-harm. But so do people who eat junk food, drive over the speed limit, have a sedentary lifestyle or practice base jumping. It seems excessive to argue that all such instances of risky, potentially harmful behavior are involuntary. The reason people often engage in such behavior is because they consider the benefits outweigh the costs. The ambivalence of addicts toward their addictive behavior is less typical of those pursing these other risky behaviors, but this too might have another explanation: given the stigma of addiction, proclaiming a desire to quit and helplessness in the face of "addiction" could be a functional device – something addicts just *say*, either because they are self-deceived or because they wish to defer responsibility for their socially unacceptable behavior (2). Some critics of addiction as

[1]The disease view of addiction was also criticized as part of the earlier "anti-psychiatry" movement in the seventies [e.g., (49)], though this criticism seems to have had less impact on the general view of addictions in psychiatry and psychology.

disease believe that "addicts," as we tend to think of them, do not really exist; there are only people who make bad decisions (7).

The conceptual critique of the disease view questions what it means to say that addiction is a "disease" that is characterized by "compulsive" and relapsing drug use. How can we reconcile a view of addictive behavior as a disease with a view of behavior-in-general as a choice? How do they differ and why? Clearly, one difference is that addiction involves behavior which in some sense is "out of control." But in common usage, the notion of "out of control" ordinarily represents a continuum, ranging across cases of non-voluntary, non-intentional behavior, such as reflexive knee jerks, to cases of highly voluntary, intentional – even rational (in a welfare-maximizing sense) – actions involving self-harm due to ignorance or lack of foresight. Where along this continuum should addiction be placed?

Critics of the disease view assume that the notions of "disease" and "compulsion" commit its proponents to locating it closer to the non-voluntary end of the continuum, while the empirical evidence, they argue, in fact suggests a location closer to the rational end (2–4). They appear to have two main reasons for this contention. First, while symptoms of typical diseases such as Alzheimer's or cancer are biologically based and non-voluntary in the sense that they do not develop as the result of decision-making processes but are beyond the person's capacity to volitionally influence, this is not so in the case of the repetitive drug-oriented behavior of addicts. Although this behavior is the most prominent symptom of addiction, its development is clearly affected by decisions made and is volitionally influenced (4). It is flexible, adaptable, and involves elements of planning. Second, to claim that addictive behavior is compulsive means that it is caused by irresistible desires (2, 4–6). Irresistible desires, however, should not be affected by the presence of competing incentives. After all, the notion that "nothing else can compete" is a defining feature of irresistibility. Nevertheless, addictive behavior *is* clearly influenced by incentives.

In our opinion, these arguments show that a certain strong version of the disease view should be abandoned. However, we want to argue, another – weaker and more plausible – version of this view is still available. This view places addiction closer to the middle of the above-mentioned continuum. Our argument – and our article – has three parts. First, we argue that behavior can be *compulsive* even if it is not caused by *irresistible* desires. In support of this, we present evidence that demonstrates that behavior is commonly categorized as "compulsive" in clinical practice even if it is not caused by irresistible desires. Now, some critics of the disease view have taken the observation that addictive behavior is not caused by irresistible desires as a springboard to suggest that addictive behavior must in fact be ordinary rational behavior instead. The most systematic development of this view of addiction as ordinary rational behavior has taken place in the economics literature. In the second part of the article, we argue that the causal mechanism proposed by advocates of the so-called "rational addiction theories" in economics is both theoretically implausible and empirically false. Ambivalence is pervasive in addiction and irrationality appears to be the hallmark of addictive behavior. In the third part we return to the question of what constitutes addictive behavior as compulsive. If it is not the irresistible desire, what is it? We would like to present an alternative view, one based on a long tradition in philosophy and psychology. According to this view, addictive behavior is compulsive because it counterfactually depends on a motivational mechanism that systematically causes dissociation in the addict's decision-making machinery. While the mechanism does not remove the addict's ability to control her drug-oriented behavior, it sharply increases the effort she has to make to take advantage of alternatives to drugs compared to non-addicts. This view, which fits well with recent evidence in neuroscience, is not only consistent with the claim that addictive behavior is characterized by compulsive and relapsing drug use, it is also consistent with the claim that addiction involves voluntary, intentional behavior that is motivated by the addict's decision-making processes.

ADDICTION AND IRRESISTIBLE DESIRES

In a recently published book, Heyman argues that addiction is not a neurobiological disease because addictive behavior develops as the result of addicts' decision-making processes and thus is within their capacity to volitionally influence (4). Although Heyman is clearly correct in saying that addiction involves voluntary behavior, that does not rule out a view of addiction as a mental disorder – which is its current medical diagnosis (13). This is worth mentioning, not least because few would claim that the symptoms of mental disorders necessarily develop independently of the persons' decision-making processes and beyond their volitional influence. The whole point of psychological therapy depends on the ability in at least some of the victims of mental disorder to volitionally influence the symptoms of their disorder and learn how to exercise that capacity by attending psychological therapy. In other words, if addiction is a mental disorder, there is no obvious reason why we should be committed to the view that the symptoms of addiction – i.e., repetitive drug-oriented behavior – must be *non-voluntary* or unresponsive to incentives. Now, compulsion is clearly a symptom of mental disorder, but to what extent is it correct to view addictive behavior as compulsive? This, obviously, depends on how we define compulsive behavior.

The point of departure in most philosophical discussions of compulsive behavior is not diagnostic practice in psychiatry, but rather a concern with the metaphysics of free will. It has been commonly assumed that compulsive behavior involves a loss of freedom of the will.[2] Many philosophers have therefore tended to conceptualize compulsive behavior as analogous to instances of interpersonal compulsion where someone is forced by someone else to act against her will. They have therefore tended to treat the notion of "compulsive behavior" as analytically equivalent to "compelled behavior" (2, 14–17). In the interpersonal case, the "compelling agent" is another person, while in the intrapersonal case it is an irresistible desire. A reasonable question is whether this conceptualization is consistent with the defining features of compulsive behavior used as diagnostic signposts in clinical practice.[3] If it is not, metaphysical analysis will clearly be

[2]The notion of "free will" is, of course, notoriously difficult, and there is little agreement on how it should be analyzed. For present purposes, we assume that a person has free will with respect to a particular action at some time if she has the ability to refrain from that action at that time.

[3]In psychiatry the term "compulsion" is, of course, used to refer to a kind of symptom of many different disorders. When we use the terms "compulsion" and "compulsive"

of little use for understanding real world behavior categorized as compulsive (as opposed to behaviors in philosophical thought-experiments). Clinical descriptions of compulsive behavior tend to emphasize a number of features (18–20): first, compulsive behavior is strongly cue-dependent in the sense that it is regularly triggered by certain situations, places, or people associated with the type of behavior in question. Second, compulsive persons feel repetitively driven to perform the behavior, often in spite of themselves; reports of feelings of compulsion are therefore common. Third, if compulsive persons sincerely try to refrain from acting upon their compulsive motivation, achieving success becomes, they report, increasingly difficult over time. These factors are present in obsessive-compulsive disorder (OCD) and impulse-control disorders (ICD) such as kleptomania (compulsive stealing), trichotillomania (compulsive hair-pulling), and compulsive buying. But is this kind of compulsive behavior consistent with the philosophical view that equates compulsiveness with irresistible desires?

In order to answer the question, we need first to be clear about what it means for a desire to be "irresistible."[4] A desire is irresistible at some time *t* to a person *S* if *S* is unable at *t* to resist acting on that desire. Put differently: if a person's action was caused by an irresistible desire, it was *literally impossible* for her to *not* perform that action. However, there have been different accounts of precisely what kind of powerlessness this implies. Very generally, these accounts can be divided into two main groups. The first group covers what might be called "desire-centered accounts," accounts which seek to explicate powerlessness in terms of the abnormal strength of the desire to perform the compulsive action. This desire is presumably so strong that no other motives can realistically compete. The second group, includes what might be called "control-centered accounts," they seek to explicate powerlessness in terms of a loss of normal capacity for rational self-control. Let us quickly run through some examples of each of these account categories and see if they can adequately characterize the compulsive behaviors associated with clinical cases of compulsion.

Starting with the desire-centered accounts, they can be further divided into non-normative and normative versions. According to the non-normative desire-centered account, the compulsive person's powerlessness is seen as an inability to resist acting on a desire because this desire, in virtue of its abnormal physical strength, is the immediate cause of the bodily movements made by the person in performing the compulsive behavior; no choice or decision has been made to make these movements. As one writer puts it, the appropriate interpersonal analogy to compulsion according to this view, is the thug who literally tosses me out of the room; just as I cannot help the way my body moves, so the compulsive person cannot help the way her body moves (21). On this account, compulsive behavior is non-voluntary and non-intentional. Compulsive people are powerless because they are physically incapable of refraining from their compulsive behavior. This account seems at odds with what is standardly referred to as compulsive behavior in the clinical literature. Compulsive behavior in clinical cases seems intentional and related to active choice. As one researcher remarks, in typical cases of OCD the person often carries out her compulsive behavior quite deliberately, taking particular care to carry it out precisely as she feels it ought to be done. If, for some reason, the behavior is disrupted, she will experience it as invalidated and in need of being restarted (19, 20). This suggests that the behavior can easily be delayed, reshaped, or substituted. Furthermore, there seems to be a growing consensus in the clinical literature that persons with OCD engage in their compulsive behavior in order to temporarily reduce the distress or anxiety associated with some obsession (18, 22). Usually they report a fear of disastrous consequences if the behavior is not properly carried out. There is clearly then an element of both purpose and control in OCD behavior that is at odds with seeing the behavior as non-voluntary and non-intentional in the sense implied by the non-normative, desire-centered account.

In contrast to the non-normative, desire-centered account, under the normative desire-centered account, the compulsive person's powerlessness involves an inability to resist acting on a desire because the desire coerces her to *choose* the compulsive behavior (15, 23). This implies a normative notion of the strength of desire since what counts as "coercion" depends on what an individual can reasonably be expected to hold out against. The claim made by the normative desire-centered account is that the threat of unbearable psychological pain motivates the compulsive person in a way similar to how the threat of grievous bodily harm allows a robber to coerce his victims into handing over their money.

Though less starkly at odds with the clinical literature on compulsive behavior than the non-normative account, this account – too – fails to fit the facts. While compulsive persons clearly experiences distress in trying to refrain from compulsive behavior, there is little evidence to suggest that these feelings generally reach the level of "unbearable psychological pain." Many researchers appear to believe, for example, that typical ICD-s, such as compulsive buying, are carried out to provide temporary relief or escape from feelings of general tension, whether it be depression, boredom, frustration, or some other negative mood state, often generating in the process certain soothing or pleasurable sensations (18). Whether preventing a person, on these occasions, from experiencing relief and pleasure – while no doubt unpleasant – is sufficient to create "unbearable psychological pain," let alone a sense of "threat" similar to the robber's threat of bodily harm, does not seem plausible.

A consideration that might provide further evidence against the coercion view is that compliance in cases of compulsion seems, in general, much harder to justify than compliance in cases of robbery (24). To see this, imagine we increased the cost of compliance in both cases: if you comply with "the threat" – i.e., hand over your money to the robber or use your money to buy something you don't need in order to satisfy a compulsive desire – your child will go hungry for the next 2 weeks since you won't be able to buy her enough food. If the coercive threats in these two cases were no different, we would not expect to see any difference in their

in what follows, what we have in mind will be the sort of repetitive physical behavior performed in characteristic circumstances that is typically referred to as "compulsive" in the clinical literature. We do not mean to suggest that compulsive behavior in this sense is a symptom of *all* compulsive disorders, nor that there is one specific mechanism that explains all observed varieties of compulsive behavior.

[4]By "desire" we mean in what follows *cognitive* desire, i.e., a motivating state that involves some favorable representation of the state of affairs that one acts in a certain way (e.g., as desirable, pleasurable, enjoyable, or good).

respective justification of compliance. Arguably, though, there is such a difference. While it seems likely that most people would find it unreasonable to expect non-compliance on the part of the victim to the demands of the robber, it seems much less likely that they would find it equally unreasonable to expect non-compliance on the part of the compulsive buyer. If this is correct, people's reactive attitudes to the victims of robbers would appear to differ in important respects from their reactive attitudes to compulsive buyers.

Even if the desire-centered accounts fail to characterize what is standardly referred to as compulsive behavior in the clinical literature, what about the control-centered accounts? Whereas the desire-centered accounts see compulsion as explained by the overwhelming force of drug-oriented desires, the control-centered accounts see it explained by a loss of normal capacities for rational self-control (14, 17). The difference between the two accounts is this: the former does not necessarily imply that compulsive people have lost their normal capacity for rational self-control. Thus, someone who fails to resist acting on some desire because of its abnormal physical strength doesn't necessarily fail because she has lost her normal capacity to rational control herself – she may both possess this capacity and exercise it properly. The reason she fails is that she is overpowered by the superior force of her compulsive desire. Compare this with a case in which you are being tossed out a room by a thug: that you are being tossed out against your will doesn't necessarily mean there is anything wrong with your will, e.g., that you have lost this capacity altogether, or that you have failed to exercise it properly. It might simply mean that you are overpowered by your opponent's superior physical strength (21).

Depending on what is meant by "normal capacity for rational self-control," there might be different views of precisely what kind of powerlessness the control-centered accounts implicate. Perhaps the most common is a reasons-based view, according to which rational self-control is understood in terms of reasons-responsiveness, and its loss as a lack of susceptibility to countervailing reasons (25–27). That is, someone has lost her capacity at some time *t* if a certain sort of counterfactual is true of her: if she were presented with what she took to be good and sufficient reasons for not performing some compulsive action at *t*, she would still perform that action at *t*. Given standard interpretation of the truth-conditions of such counterfactuals, it would be literally impossible for her to successfully resist, no matter what sort of incentives she is presented with. Does this account succeed in characterizing what in the clinical literature is standardly referred to as compulsive behavior?

Once again, there seems to be little reason to assume that it does. Supportive evidence can be gleaned from the apparent success of response prevention therapy as a treatment modality for OCD. The aim of response prevention therapy is to break the relationship between the various trigger situations which provoke the compulsive urge, and the compulsive behavior, by repeatedly exposing the compulsive person to different trigger situations but encouraging her to refrain from the compulsive behavior (20). For example, a compulsive person whose washing rituals are a result of an obsession about being contaminated by dogs, may be instructed to pat a dog and then refrain from washing her hands or to take a bath only after a given period of time. As the sessions are repeated, the interval is extended. Research shows that if the pattern is followed in each of the trigger situations, the cumulative effect is progressively less discomfort and desire to engage in the compulsive behavior. On the assumption that compulsive behavior involves a complete loss of the normal capacity for rational self-control, it is difficult to see how compulsive persons could successfully engage in this kind of exposure therapy. Without that capacity, how could they possibly comply with instructions to delay their response to a trigger situation? Inference to the best explanation suggests that they retain their capacities. What response prevention therapy does is to give them an incentive to put more effort into exercising them.[5]

To sum up. If the arguments of this section are correct, the term "compulsive behavior" as used by the critics of the disease view is not co-extensional with the term "compulsive behavior" as it is standardly used in the clinical literature. There is no implicit or explicit assumption in the clinical literature that compulsive behavior must be caused by "irresistible desires." The term "compulsive behavior" simply refers to repetitive behavioral patterns performed in characteristic circumstances which the compulsive person finds it difficult to override by intentional effort. On this description, compulsive persons are not necessarily powerless with respect to their compulsive behavior. Neither does it rule out the possibility of this behavior being voluntary, intentional, and even motivated by the compulsive person's decision-making processes. This does not, of course, show that *addictive* behavior is compulsive. Some critics of the disease view who argue that addictive behavior is not caused by irresistible desires appear to take this to suggest that addictions must involve ordinary rational behavior instead. As we noted above, the latter view has perhaps been most systematically developed in the economics literature, where so-called "rational addiction theories" provide the dominant model of addiction. In the next section, we argue that these theories fail to explain what is distinctive about addiction.

THE THEORY OF RATIONAL ADDICTION

Viewing addiction merely as a specific pattern of rational choices obviates the need for a theory of addiction. Addictive behavior is nothing more than ordinary behavior, and needs no additional explanation. On the other hand, insofar as addictions typically involve a small set of substances and activities, these substances and activities must have something in common that makes an addictive form of behavior all the more likely. Then again, not everyone becomes an addict, and systematic differences have been found between high and low risk individuals. Such regularities require an explanation: if addictions are constituted by ordinary rational choices, why do they appear to be different from ordinary behavior?

One of the most extensively developed attempts to answer this question was proposed in the theory of rational addiction and its descendants [e.g., (28–30)]. According to this family of theories, the peculiar features of addictive behavior derive from the peculiar

[5] It is worth noting here that not all versions of the control-centered accounts of compulsivity need be vulnerable to this kind of objection. The version we criticize is the one that equates compulsivity with a failure of what Fisher and Ravizza refer to as "strong reasons-responsiveness" (50).

incentives that can arise when a good has lagged effects. It means in short that consumption of a good is consumption-for-enjoyment-now, but also crucially, an investment decision accommodating the lagged effects the individual expects to enjoy in the future. Given a particular pattern of short- and long-term effects, such as those produced by a drug, some consumers find that – for them – the best consumption plan is gradually to increase consumption to ever higher levels. These consumers display what the theory labels "addictions." On this view addictive behavior is neither paradoxical nor troublesome. Drug users may be unhappy, but "they would be even more unhappy if they were prevented from consuming the addictive goods" (28). Differences between people are due to differences in time preferences, available choice sets, or uncertainty: if drug effects differ across consumers and individuals are uncertain about which effects they should anticipate, they will make a rational choice under uncertainty which, in the event, may turn out to be the wrong one, creating a situation where high-level drug use becomes the optimal way forward (30). Provided the behavior does not harm others, as Becker and Murphy (28) write, there is no reason to intervene. An addiction as far as the economic approach is concerned is simply an unproblematic matter of choice.

This conception of addiction as rational choice must be clearly distinguished from the view of rational individuals dealing with addictions. A rational choice proponent need not necessarily see addictive behavior as rational. They could view addiction as a disease that hijacked our decision-making apparatus and reduced our autonomy, so that our rationality would be reduced *given* an addiction. However, rational choice would still be involved *before* the addiction took hold: the risk of "getting addicted," the rational choice proponent could argue, is a rational choice for some, involving a trade-off between the risk of losing autonomy on the one hand, and something else that is valued on the other – pleasure, respite from boredom, etc. This, however, would not be a theory of addiction as such, since it would not explain how or to what extent addiction reduced the individual's autonomy.

The theory of rational addiction, by contrast, is a *theory of addiction.* To quote Becker and Murphy again, their claim is that "rational choice theory can explain a wide variety of addictive behavior." In addition to intoxicants and cigarettes, they mention addictions to "work, eating, music, television, their standard of living, other people, religion, and many other activities." Their explanation of such behavior requires goods or activities to have lagged (i.e., delayed) effects on the user. Addictive goods can be both beneficial and harmful. Harmful addictions, which are the most interesting, require that the good or activity has two properties. First, current consumption reduces your future "baseline" welfare. A high sugar intake makes you fatter tomorrow, which you may dislike. Smoking today makes you cough up phlegm the next morning and feel a bothersome appetite for more cigarettes. Second, current consumption increases the future value of a unit of the addictive good itself. If your growing waistline makes you sad, it gives "comfort food" more sadness to work on. As your body's craving for nicotine increases, cigarettes can help satisfy this renewed urge in addition to giving you the benefits it already did. As a rational individual, you balance these effects and work out the plan for future consumption that would maximize your welfare.

An important but often ignored criticism of the theory of rational addiction as a theory of how people actually come to be addicted points to the incredible amount of intricacy all this planning involves. In deciding whether to smoke a cigarette here and now, you are actually designing and evaluating a plan on cigarette-smoking-starting-now-and-far-into-the-future. You take into account expected changes in smoking legislation, tobacco taxes, the way current use affects tomorrow's tastes, uncertainty regarding risks, etc. In this sense, the theory of rational addiction is much more elaborate than simply positing that individuals respond to incentives or rationally take into account the possibility of getting an "addiction-disease." Instead, according to adherents, addictive behavior can usefully be viewed as a highly intricate and sophisticated plan that optimally solves a complex decision problem featuring delayed effects and uncertainty. Whether we find this to be useful will depend essentially on what we want to use the theory for.

EVALUATING THE THEORY OF RATIONAL ADDICTION[6]

The above description of rational addiction theory may make it sound "unrealistic," especially to non-economists. However, as Mäki (31) warns, "[m]uch of the criticism of economics [. . .] is based on the mistaken belief that criticism is easy – such as when inferring from unrealistic assumptions to models being incorrect [. . .] it is not easy to reliably identify [the] flaws (of economics) almost regardless of how serious they are." The reason is that economic models can serve a multitude of different aims, and the criteria against which they should be judged – and the evidence relevant to judging them – will vary with the aim.

The reason we need to point this out is because economic models can be insulated from criticism by claiming they are merely explorations of formal frameworks or false-but-useful ways of summarizing stylized facts. When we discuss rational addiction theory, however, we are interested in the theory as an attempt to explain the underlying causal mechanisms which generate addictive behavior in the real world. This view of the theory is common both among contributors to the written literature and researchers working on them: a survey of researchers with peer-reviewed publications on rational addiction theory found 39% of them agreeing that the rational addiction literature "provides insights into how addicts choose that are relevant for psychologists and treatment professionals," while 56% agreed that the literature "contains insights on the welfare consequences of addictive goods and public policies toward these" (32).

This, in our view, is mistaken [see (33, 34) for details and supporting references]. The shortcomings of the theory in this respect may generalize to other attempts at explaining addictions as ordinary and rational behavior. At a broad level, the problem is that addictions are characterized by seemingly flip-flopping attitudes and ambivalence, self-control issues, regret, etc. The addicts fail to verbalize motives for their actions that would make them understandable, sensible, and time-consistent, and in the absence of simple and recognizable motives for the behavior, the rational choice believer is compelled to posit ever-subtler, sophisticated but ultimately non-credible motives and incentives to explain the

[6]The following discussion is largely based on Rogeberg and Melberg (34), to which we refer readers who want additional details.

behavior. Rational addiction theory and its variants exemplify this problem. They explain addictive behavior patterns as the result of optimal choices given a specific choice problem. The shape of the optimal consumption path is determined by the structure and strength of the lagged and immediate effects of the good, as well as the consumer's time preferences and other consumption opportunities. By varying these and the number of lagged effects we can generate a variety of consumption paths: rising, falling, cyclic, chaotic. In other words, the optimal consumption plan is sensitive to details in the choice problem facing the consumer. Empirically, it is hard to identify the actual decision problem facing any particular individual. The incentives consist of the "net" subjective valuation of a bundle of different effects on health, psyche, etc. In this sense, the theory "explains" behavior in terms of a detailed hypothesis about unobservable and non-measurable mental constructs. We could identify the lagged "effects" of the drugs with more objectively measurable effects, such as those on health, but this will not solve the problem. The actual lag structures of harmful effects are unlikely to match the assumptions that generate "typical" addictive patterns, and the effects on disease risk, the body and future tastes are not known to the required level of precision in the scientific literature. Since real addicts are supposed to face and have solved this decision problem, it is a further problem for the theory that surveyed individuals state beliefs about lagged effects that are in clear contradiction with the required assumptions, and it is a further problem that even educated experimental subjects generally fail to find the optimal solution to structurally identical investment problems in experiments where this could earn them actual money (35). Put differently: the choice problem that is claimed to generate addictive behaviors is neither the one individuals actually face, nor the one they believe themselves to be facing, nor indeed the one the average smoker or "junkie" is likely to recognize if it was explained to them, nor a choice problem they would be able to find the optimal solution to in practice. The "typical" addictive consumption pattern is more stable over time and across people than it "should be" according to the theory. The cross-sectional variation in beliefs about effects of drugs and the time-variation in knowledge about the effects of drugs should generate a variety of drug use patterns rather than the ones taken as a stylized fact by the theory. The theory says that factors X generate Y, but there is no evidence that X is present where Y is present, and no evidence that experimental manipulations that create factors X lead to behavior pattern Y. The theory, quite simply, is not credible as a description of the underlying choice processes generating addictions, and there are no plausible arguments showing why selection effects or simpler heuristics would allow most people to search for and implement these optimal paths in alternative ways.[7]

That addiction involves ordinary rational behavior is not a tenable proposition in our view. On the contrary, we believe there are good reasons to assume that addictive behavior is compulsive in the clinical sense of the DSM-IV. Yet what DSM-IV gives us is, of course, a purely descriptive sense of "compulsive." It does not explain what makes these behavioral patterns compulsive. If their compulsivity is not constituted by an irresistible desire for drugs, what does constitute them? And what kind of evidence would show that addictive behavior *is* compulsive? The key to answering these questions lies neither in the abnormal strength of addictive desires, we contend, nor in a loss of normal capacities for rational self-control, but rather in certain special features intrinsic to addicts' decision-making processes.

ADDICTION AND COMPULSIVE BEHAVIOR

Compulsion, somewhat paradoxically, seems to involve deliberate, goal-directed behavior caused by something that is external to the person and independent of practical deliberation. On the one hand, something seems to assail the person – as if from without. On the other hand, it is an essentially active phenomenon, a kind of intentional behavior aimed at altering mood states or regulating affect. There is, in other words, an appearance of control in a class of behaviors largely defined by loss of control. We believe that both these features need to be addressed by our notion of compulsion. Philosophers, often motivated by a concern with the metaphysics of free will, have focused exclusively on the apparent loss of control. However, their picture of compulsive behavior as motivationally compelled, and of addictive behavior as compulsive due to the *irresistibility* of its psychological antecedents, is difficult to reconcile with the intentionality and controlled nature of such actions and with how the term "compulsive behavior" is applied to clinical cases. Instead, we want to suggest that compulsive behavior can be understood in terms of persistent patterns of failed decision-making caused by a dissociation in the person's volitional control. This analysis does not entail that the person must have lost her capacity to resist. We also believe it fits better with the application of this notion to clinical cases. If we are on the right track, then there is good reason to say that one of the defining features of addiction is precisely its compulsive nature.

It has been common in much philosophy to treat volitional control as more or less the same as rational self-control, that is, a capacity persons have to bring their actions into line with what they judge to have most reason to do. Persons exercise rational self-control by directing (in various ways) their attention away from rebellious desires in order to form, retain, or execute intentions to do what they consider to be the most valuable course of action. On the assumption that all there is to volitional control is rational self-control, it follows that a failure of rational self-control necessarily is a failure of volitional control. This has the implication that when persons' behavior is "out of control," it can only be due to some force over which they have no control, a motivational element that is completely external to their volitional capacities, e.g., a desire that causes their behavior directly, independently of their decision-making system.

[7] In our view the most interesting work on addiction from economists comes from researchers who try to establish a middle ground between viewing addiction as a disease that completely removes the addict's ability to control his behavior and viewing it as nothing more than an extremely subtle and sophisticated form of maneuvering undertaken by the addict in the face of complex incentives. Bernheim and Rangel [(51, 52), see also (53)] have developed a theory, for instance, in which addiction is the outcome of processes that affect our expectation of pleasure or welfare derived from using the drug, as well as affecting the likelihood that we will make the consumption decision using a "cold," rational decision process. Their work can be seen as an attempt to examine how rational agents would deal with addictions when the addiction itself is a disturbance of the choice process.

This conflation of volitional control and rational self-control makes it hard to handle even standard cases of compulsive behavior. Compulsive persons sometimes make conscious and active efforts to do *the opposite* of what they take themselves to have most reason to do, in some cases by using attention-managing strategies to block out thoughts about these reasons (36).[8] Consider, for example, the sort of ritualistic compulsions typical of OCD. Persons with OCD tend not to want to be interrupted or distracted while engaged in these rituals. As we have seen, the clinical literature indicates that they serve a distinct function, namely to reduce negative feelings. Yet there is no logical connection between the description under which they intentionally engage in behavior of this sort (say, checking, hoarding, or washing) and the goal to which their actions are directed. So while they may make an active decision and spend considerable effort translating that decision into action, the behavioral pattern itself seems recruited through some associative or implicit learning process independent of practical deliberation and voluntary control. Consequently compulsive persons often regard their own action as excessive, unpleasant, and pointless. That is, they do not associate anything pleasurable or desirable with its performance. It does not seem plausible that they are driven by a strong cognitive desire to perform it. Nevertheless, they perform it intentionally. They even make an effort to do it "properly." Initiating and executing compulsive behavior of this sort clearly require considerable amounts of volitional control, even though it may involve a failure to pursue what the compulsive persons themselves consider the most valuable course of action.[9] Rather than being characterized by *a loss of volitional control*, therefore, we believe it is more plausible to say that compulsive behavior is characterized by *a dissociation in volitional control.* This view finds further support in the observation that compulsive persons often appear to recognize at the same time as they are deciding to perform the compulsive action that it is a mistake ("It is a pointless to wash my hands yet again"), yet go on to intentionally form and implement their decision to undertake that action in spite of these normative considerations. In fact, dissociative experiences, such as feelings of "standing outside oneself while acting," are frequently reported across a range of compulsive phenomena, including addiction to drugs (37). There seems, in other words, to be a disparity between compulsive persons' decisions and actions on the one hand, and their evaluative preferences (what course of action they judge most valuable) on the other, which can be explained neither in terms of a failure of volitional control nor in terms of the abnormal strength of their cognitive desire to engage in the behavior.[10]

We believe the possibility of this kind of failed decision-making – the irrationality of which is displayed in a form of incoherence in the person's attitudes – is an essential feature of compulsive behavior. One way of understanding this phenomenon is by distinguishing between two ways of making choices. Postulating the existence of a duality behind people's choices is, of course, not new. It has a long history in philosophy and psychology, reaching back to Aristotle's distinction between the rational and non-rational part of the soul.[11] While most early work on this duality was conceptual in nature and based on informal observations of human behavior and personal introspection, the development of what have become known as "dual-process theories" only started with the cognitive revolution in psychology in the 1960s and 1970s. Experimental studies of attention, learning, memory, and reasoning were important influences (38). Since then, a wide variety of evidence has converged on the conclusion that some sort of dual-process notion is needed to explain how the overall process of decision-making occurs (39, 40). Unlike before, we are now beginning to understand the biology and cognitive structure of the different parts (41). According to dual-process theory, decision-making can broadly be divided into two modes, one fast, intuitive, and effortless shaped by biology and implicit learning, the other slow, analytical, and effortful shaped by culture and formal tuition. While the former mode – in the dual-process literature often referred to as type-1 processes – depends on environmental cues, is associative, automatic, and can control behavior directly without need for controlled attention, the latter – often referred to as type-2 processes – depends on de-contextualization, is rule-based and requires controlled attention and effort. There is much disagreement about precisely how these processes should be characterized and distinguished (39, 42). We cannot enter into this debate here. For present purposes, what matters is that dual-process theory allows a closer scrutiny of the vulnerable aspects of the decision-making process by permitting focus on the important ways in which the different modes of decision-making interact.

To achieve rational decision-making the two modes have to work well together to reliably contribute to the person's goal achievement (43). This requires two things. First, that the person's type-2 process can exert an executive function and override the impulsive output of her type-1 process. For this to happen, her type-2 process must be able to generate a more considered response that is in line with her normative reasons, as well as involve inhibitory mechanisms to suppress the response tendencies of her type-1 process. Second, it requires that the person's

[8]This is, of course, not true of all cases of compulsive behavior. Often compulsive behavior becomes over-learned and automatized as a result of repetition and may require virtually no active efforts at all (54).

[9]We can specify the motivational economy in volitional vs. valuational conflicts by applying the four-type utility framework proposed by Kahneman and colleagues [see (55)]. In utility-maximizing terms, "volitional" could then be specified in terms of "decision utility," and "valuational" in terms of "predicted utility." See Berridge and Aldridge (56) for a practical illustration of how this framework can be used to explain irrational decision-making. Having said that, our general approach does not depend, we believe, on any specific view of the motivational economy involved.

[10]Although this conflicts with standard assumptions in economics, there are economic models of behavior that break the link between "optimal behavior" and "actual behavior" by including preferences or psychological quirks that are inconsistent with a pure rational choice model [see e.g., (51)]. In a pure rational choice model, the chosen action will always be optimal (or optimal by expectation), which "allows" the researcher to infer the welfare-determining preferences from the behavior (i.e., revealed preferences). With this link broken, the researcher has to provide a higher level of evidential support for the theoretical assumptions themselves, while welfare analyses need to distinguish between different concepts of welfare or "utility," for instance along the lines of Kahneman et al. (55).

[11]"For in the continent and the incontinent person we praise their reason, i.e., the [part] of the soul that has reason, because it exhorts them correctly and toward what is best; but they evidently also have in them some other [part] that is by nature something besides reason, conflicting and struggling with reason." (57), 1102b 15–20.

type-1 process selects adequate and relevant information about the practical situation that can provide input for her type-2 process (41). There is widespread agreement that some form of automatic, pre-conscious processing determines the person's locus of attention and what stored memories and beliefs are recalled for as relevant to her current situation. This suggests that the person's normative reasons (represented in her type-2 process) might be shaped, even to a significant degree, by type-1 encoding of information about which aspects of the situation need to be taken into account, and which can be ignored.[12]

Given this view of rational decision-making, *failed* decision-making can be seen to arise in two ways. One might be if the decision-making process of either type is internally biased. This could be the result of either an under or over appreciation of certain contextual cues, a failure to ignore distracting features, or a process for combining and processing information that uses simplified algorithms with potential biases. If a type-1 process fails to encode relevant information, or encodes irrelevant information that enters into the person's subsequent analytic type-2 process, it may cause blindness to special circumstances or to longer-range goals. In consequence the person's flexibility to be able to consider alternative reasons for acting is systematically undermined. Decision-making can also fail if a conflict arises between type-1 and type-2 processes. In the standard scenario, the person fails to suppress an intuitive but non-normative response generated by her type-1 process despite the fact that it conflicts with a considered normative response generated by her type-2 process. In contrast with cases of internally biased decision-making, the possibility of such executive failures implies that the person may be consciously aware while making her decision that it is mistaken. There seems to be no clear reason to assume that executive failures of this sort must presuppose that the person has any abnormally strong cognitive desire to respond in line with her type-1 process or has lost her ability to refrain from responding in this way. Rather, the failure is simply one of putting insufficient effort into overriding a type-1 process. That such failures occasionally occur should not surprise us given the cue-dependency, computational speed, and dissociated nature of type-1 processes. These decision processes plug more or less directly into the person's motor system and seem almost to have "actional" character. Type-2 processes, on the other hand, require an effort that tires the person and may make it harder to engage in type-2 reasoning and override type-1 processes resulting in so-called "decision-fatigue" (5, 44).

We believe it is plausible that compulsive behavior involves persistent patterns of failed decision-making in one or the other of these two senses.[13] In the former, a mis-contextualization of information enters into the person's subsequent analytic type-2 process and causes a biased response, and in the latter, there is an executive failure to appropriately engage type-2 processes or use their output to override the impulsive output of a type-1 process. In either case, when failed decision-making *occurs repetitively, leading to a maladaptive behavioral pattern* deserving of the label "compulsive," it is plausibly because some type-1 process has become fixed in inert dispositions and patterns of perception and response. Presumably, there is some underlying cue-triggered motivational mechanism which – perhaps due to repetition and reinforcement – has become deeply entrenched. In cases where there is subjective experience of conflict, this mechanism repeatedly pulls the person's decisions away from her evaluative preferences. In cases where there is no subjective experience of conflict, she may be led to consistently ignore special circumstances or longer-range goals and hence systematically undermine her ability to consider alternative reasons for acting.[14] Whether or not there is an experience of conflict in a particular case may be a matter of the psychological resources of the individual (e.g., insight vs. tendency to rationalize or confabulate reasons for actions generated by her type-1 process). In either case, the persons' maladaptive behavioral patterns may counterfactually depend on the same type of entrenched motivational mechanism.

If this general picture of compulsivity is on the right track, is there any reason to believe that *addiction* involves compulsive behavior?[15] The best reason is that addictive behavior appears to be strongly cue-dependent (9, 45), and that addicts regularly and systematically fail to take advantage of alternatives to drugs in spite of negative consequences for themselves, and often in spite of what they judge to be the most valuable course of action (11). There is a tendency for addicts to systematically ignore or downplay the costs of taking drugs while greatly exaggerating its benefits (4). As George Ainslie has argued, addicts often frame their decisions temporally as repeated, independent choices between alternatives one at a time on the basis of their immediate costs and benefits, rather than as single choices over series of similar alternatives across time on the basis of their summed costs and benefits (46). In such cases the addict's decision-making process is clearly biased since she concentrates too much on the immediate benefits of drugs and systematically ignores her longer-range goals. From a conceptual point of view, what could explain such biasing within a dual-process approach is that a drug-oriented type-1 process – due to

[12]A difficult philosophical issue concerns the account of the self and its rationality in face of the conflict described by dual-process theory. According to one influential view, we should identify the self with the "better" type-2 processes because only on this level do we notice and are bothered by a lack of rational integration (58). While we cannot address all the issues raised by this claim at this juncture [but see (43) for a discussion], for present purposes, we assume that in (at least) standard cases, the self is associated with type-2 processing.

[13]One important implication of a dual-process approach to decision-making is that each one of us is potentially vulnerable to developing compulsive behavioral patterns, including addictions. Redish and colleagues propose a variant of this approach as a unified framework for addiction where they distinguish between 10 different failure points in our decision-making system, each of which may be capable of driving a person to make addictive decision "mistakes." The reason some people go on to develop addictions while others do not depends on the specific "interaction between the genetics of the individual, the developmental environment (social and physical), the developmental stage of the individual, and the behavioral experience with the addictive substance" [(59), 430].

[14]In the social cognition literature, one variant of this phenomenon is referred to as "cognitive narrowing," which is a tendency to focus attention on an immediate, concrete, low-level task (e.g., shopping or buying) that prevents consideration of the longer term consequences of an action (36).

[15]One interesting issue concerns how this picture of compulsivity relates to the defects in action and agency discussed in the philosophical literature as "weakness of will" [see e.g., (60)]. Although we cannot address this issue here (the relevant literature is voluminous), one of the authors has argued elsewhere that there are some important differences between addiction/compulsion and weakness of will. See Henden (61).

the entrenchment of some underlying cue-triggered motivational mechanism – has become fixed in a pattern of perception and response that systematically fails to encode logically relevant information about drug-related situations. When such drug-oriented type-1 processes regularly shape the content and locus of attention of a person's subsequent analytic type-2 processes, they cause the rate at which she discounts the value of future rewards, such as, e.g., the benefits of abstinence, to increase drastically relative to the rate at which she discounts consumption. The result is that when opportunities for consumption arise, the person's estimate of their values has increased so much more relative to her estimate of the value of abstinence that her preference reverses. But in addition to such cases of so-called "hyperbolic discounting" we believe (more controversially) that there is also evidence of cases in which addicts fail to take advantage of alternatives to drugs in spite of judging, at the moment of choice, that the value of abstaining is higher than the value of consumption. In these cases the problem is not internal biasing of analytic type-2 processes, but rather a regular failure to override type-1 processes which systematically fail to encode relevant information about drug-related situations.

Evidence of such dual-process conflicts in addiction comes from the observation that many addicts appear to make conscious and strenuous efforts to exercise restraint at the same time as they are seeking or actually taking drugs. As addiction researcher Robert West puts it: "When the restraint fails, there is often (but not always) no sense of the addict having changed his mind and deciding to engage in the behavior as a positive step; rather the sense is of a failure to exert control followed by regret and a feeling of having let oneself down" (47). As neuroscientists Kent Berridge and Terry E. Robinson note in a similar vein, there is plenty of evidence that addicts often continue to seek and take drugs even when no pleasure can be obtained, even in the absence of withdrawal – even – in fact when they are convinced that taking drugs is a disastrous course of action for them (11). Addicts, this would suggest, will often continue to judge that abstaining is the most valuable course of action even as they are carrying out their drug-oriented behavior.

What explains these kinds of systematic errors in drug-oriented decision-making? Specifying the nature of the underlying mechanism(s) is an important component of the empirical explanation of the compulsive character of addictive behavior. Our aim in this article has not been to propose any such explanation, but to suggest how to make conceptually sense of the "compulsive character" of behavior in a way that does not depend on the notion of irresistible desire and, in addition, to provide evidence in support of the view that addictive behavior *is* compulsive in this sense. That being said, an example of a mechanism that seems to fit well with the dual-process analysis of compulsivity is that proposed by Berridge and Robinson in their influential work on incentive-sensitization. Incentive-sensitization is a mechanism whereby repeated drug use produces a dopaminergic response that becomes sensitized by causing certain regions in the brain involved in the motivation of behavior to be more easily activated by drugs or drug-related cues independent of the addict's cognitive desires, judgments, or "likings." In a series of papers Berridge and Robinson provide evidence that the psychological process and neural substrate responsible for determining cognitive-affective liking are separable from the psychological process and neural substrate responsible for determining incentive salience – the degree to which a goal or stimulus is action-driving – or what they call "wanting" (48). While normally "liking" and "wanting" go together so that we "want" the things we "like" (e.g., the hedonic value associated with some environmental cue or circumstance serves as a trigger to activate and direct "wanting"), in addiction they come apart, making addicts "want" things they do not "like." The reason incentive-sensitization might give us an empirical explanation of why addictive behavior is compulsive in the sense we have characterized compulsivity in this article is that it might explain why addicts' drug-oriented type-1 processes become fixed in inert dispositions and patterns of perception and response which lead to systematically biasing of their type-2 processes or to the creation of regular conflicts between their type-1 and type-2 processes. Continuous failures to override type-1 processes that are dependent on an entrenched motivational mechanism like incentive-sensitization arise since these processes are difficult to override by intentional effort due to their cue-dependency, computational speed and frequency, and because addicts simply put insufficient effort into overriding them (perhaps due to decision-fatigue, misjudgment, or some other reason).[16] This, of course, is perfectly consistent with the common observation that quitting drugs is hard if you are an addict, but without entailing that this is because addicts are driven by irresistible desires for drugs or have lost their powers of resistance. A dual-process analysis of the notion of compulsivity does not, therefore, rule out the intentionality of addictive behavior. However, nor does it rule out the possibility that some other psychological or neurological mechanism (or combination of mechanisms) than incentive-sensitization might in the end turn out to provide the best empirical explanation of the compulsive behavior of human addicts (or at least be part of such an explanation).[17] Ultimately, it is a matter for the sciences to decide the precise nature of the relevant mechanism(s) which create(s) persistent dissociations in addicts' decision-making machinery – or indeed of any of the various mechanisms that might be responsible for the different compulsive disorders.

CONCLUSION

The question posed in the title of this article would seem to necessitate an either/or answer: *either* addiction involves voluntary, chosen behavior and is therefore not compulsive *or* it involves

[16]It is worth noting that this view of compulsivity, in relying on the notion of "level of effort" rather than "motivational irresistibility," implies that compulsivity is a matter of degree. It is consistent, therefore, with the possibility of differences between forms of compulsive behavior in terms of how difficult they are to resist, e.g., between the kinds of behavior seen in, say, OCD and in the different addictions. For more on the conceptual connection between effort expenditure and compulsivity, see Henden (61).

[17]The incentive-sensitization theory of addiction remains controversial. Most of the data supporting it come from laboratory animal studies with little consideration of the social context in which the drugs were administered. This has caused some to criticize the theory for failing to generalize to human addicts [for a recent discussion, see (62)]. There is also evidence suggesting that incentive-sensitization by itself is not sufficient to create repetitive drug-oriented behavior in animals if they are given more options [see (63)]. For replies to some of these criticisms, see Robinson and Berridge (64); Robinson et al. (65).

compulsion and therefore is not voluntary, chosen behavior. The bone of contention over which the respective proponents of the medical and the moral model of addiction do battle seems to rely in large part on the assumed contradiction between these two answers. The normative implications are obviously deep and far-reaching. If addiction rules out voluntary behavior and choice, then addicts can only (at best) be indirectly responsible for their drug use. That widens the scope for public policy interventions. If, by contrast, addiction involves voluntary, chosen behavior, this scope for intervention will be correspondingly constrained. Our aim in this article has been to argue that a middle path is not only possible but actually quite plausible in the light of the evidence: behavior can be voluntary, chosen, and compulsive at the same time. One way of making conceptual sense of this is to assume that our decision-making system is divisible. If such divisions stabilize due to the entrenchment of some underlying motivational mechanism and cause regular and systematic failures in the person's decision-making with respect to actions of a certain type, they create compulsive behavioral patterns that may be very difficult for her to override by intentional effort alone. There are many good reasons, in our opinion, to believe that addictions essentially depend on such divisions in the decision-making system of addicts. However, this view does not mean that it is *literally impossible* for addicts to refrain from drugs. It only means it is much harder for them than it is for people who are not addicted. Even heavily addicted individuals have the capacity to abstain, although they may need help to learn how to exercise that capacity properly. We believe this mix of the "moral" and the "medical" model of addiction may open up for a more nuanced approach to many of the pressing normative issues raised by public policies, practices, and treatments in the addiction field.

ACKNOWLEDGMENTS

We would like to extend our thanks to the Research Council of Norway for providing financial support for the writing of this paper.

REFERENCES

1. Benn P. Disease, addiction and the freedom to resist. *Philos Pap* (2007) 3:465–81. doi:10.1080/05568640709485210
2. Foddy B, Savulescu J. Addiction and autonomy: can addicted peo- ple consent to the prescription of their drug of choice? *Bioethics* (2006) 20(1):1–15. doi:10.1111/j. 1467-8519.2006.00470.x
3. Foddy B, Savulescu J. A liberal account of addiction. *Philos Psychi- atr Psychol* (2010) 17(1):1–22. doi: 10.1353/ppp.0.0282
4. Heyman GM. *Addiction, a Disorder of Choice*. Cambridge: Harvard University Press (2009).
5. Levy N. Addiction, autonomy and ego-depletion: a response to Bennett Foddy and Julian Savulescu. *Bioethics* (2006) 20(1):16–20. doi: 10.1111/j.1467-8519.2006.00471.x
6. Pickard H. The purpose in chronic addiction. *AJOB Neurosci* (2012) 3(2):40–9. doi:10.1080/21507740. 2012.663058
7. Schaler JA. *Addiction is a Choice*. Chicago: Open Court Publishing Company (2000).
8. Charland LC. Cynthia's dilemma: consenting to heroin prescription. *Am J Bioeth* (2002) 2(2):37–47. doi: 10.1162/152651602317533686
9. Hyman SE. The neurobiology of addiction: implications for vol- un- tary control of behaviour. *Am J Bioeth* (2007) 7(1):8–11. doi:10. 1080/15265160601063969
10. Leshner AI. Addiction is a brain dis- ease, and it matters. *Science* (1997) 278:45–7. doi:10.1126/science.278. 5335.45
11. Robinson TE, Berridge KC. The neural basis of drug craving: an incentive-sensitization theory of addiction. *Brain Res Rev* (1993) 18:252–5. doi:10.1016/0165-0173(93)90013-P
12. Davies JB. *The Myth of Addiction*. London : Routledge (1997).
13. American Psychiatric Association. *Diagnostic and Statistical Manual of Mental Disorders*. 4th ed. Wash- ington, DC: American Psychiatric Association (1994).
14. Frankfurt H. Freedom of the will and the concept of a per- son. *The Importance of What We Care About*. New York: Cam- bridge University Press (1988). p. 11–26.
15. Greenspan P. Behavior control and freedom of action. *Philos Rev* (1978) 97:225–40.
16. Nielsen K. The compatibility of freedom and determinism. In: Kane R, editor. *Free Will*. New York: Wiley-Blackwell (2002). p. 39–46.
17. Watson G. *Skepticism about Weakness of the Will. In Agency and Answerability*. New York: Oxford University Press (2004). p. 33–58.
18. Abramowitz JS, Deacon BJ. Obsessive-compulsive disorder: essential phenomenology and over- lap with other anxiety disorders. In: Abramowitz JS, Houts AC, editors. *Concepts and Controversies in Obsessive-Compulsive Disorder*. New York: Springer (2005). p. 119–33.
19. de Silva P, Rachman S. *Obsessive- Compulsive Disorder: The Facts*. 3rd ed. Oxford: Oxford University Press (2004).
20. de Silva P. Obsessive-compulsive disorder. In: Carr A, McNulty M, editors. *The Handbook of Adult Clin- ical Psychology*. London: Routledge (2006). p. 509–10.
21. Watson G. Disordered appetites: addiction, compulsion, and dependence. *Agency and Answer- ability*. New York: Oxford University Press (2004). p. 59–87.
22. Rachman S, Hodgson RJ. *Obsessions and Compulsions*. Englewood Cliffs, NJ: Prentice Hall (1980).
23. Watson G. Excusing addiction. *Agency and Answerability*. New York: Oxford University Press (2004). p. 318–50.
24. Vihvelin K. Stop me before I kill again. *Philos Stud* (1994) 75:115–48. doi:10.1007/BF00989883
25. Glover J. *Responsibility*. London: Routledge and Kegan Paul (1970).
26. Gert B, Duggan T. Free will as abil- ity to will. *Noûs* (1979) 13:197–217. doi:10.2307/2214397
27. Fisher JM. *The Metaphysics of Free Will*. Cambridge, MA: Blackwell (1994).
28. Becker GS, Murphy KM. A theory of rational addiction. *J Polit Econ* (1988) 96(4):675–700. doi:10.1086/ 261558
29. Orphanides A, Zervos D. Rational addiction with learning and regret. *J Polit Econ* (1995) 103(4):739–58. doi:10.1086/262001
30. Orphanides A, Zervos D. Myopia and addictive behaviour. *Econ J* (1998) 108:75–91. doi:10.1111/ 1468-0297.00274
31. Mäki U. Realistic realism about unrealistic models. In: Kincaid H, Ross D, editors. *Oxford Handbook of the Philos- ophy of Economics*. New York: Oxford University Press (2009). p. 68–98.
32. Melberg HO, Rogeberg OJ. Ratio- nal addiction theory: a survey of opinions. *J Drug Policy Anal* (2010) 3(1):5. doi:10.2202/1941- 2851.1019
33. Rogeberg O. Taking absurd theories seriously: economics and the case of rational addiction theories. *Philos Sci* (2004) 71:263–85. doi:10.1086/ 421535
34. Rogeberg OJ, Melberg HO. Accep- tance of unsupported claims about reality: a blind spot in economics. *J Econ Methodol* (2011) 18:29– 52. doi:10.1080/1350178X.2011. 556817
35. Fehr E, Zych PK. Do addicts behave rationally? *Scand J Econ* (1998) 100(3):643–61. doi:10.1111/1467- 9442.00127
36. Heatherton TF, Baumeister RF. Binge eating as escape from self-awareness. *Psy- chol Bull* (1991) 110:86–108. doi:10.1037/0033-2909.110.1.86
37. Evans J, Coventry K. A dual-process approach to behavioral addiction: the case of gambling. In: Reinout W, Wiers RW, Stacy AW, editors. *Handbook of Implicit Cognition and Addiction*. Thousands Oaks, CA: Sage (2006). p. 29–44.
38. Frankish K, Evans JStBT. The duality of mind: an historical perspective. In: Evans JStBT, Frankish K, editors. *In Two Minds: Dual Processes and Beyond*. New York: Oxford (2009). p. 1–29.
39. Sloman SA. The empirical case for two systems of reasoning. *Psychol Bull* (1996) 119(1):3–22. doi:10. 1037/0033-2909.119.1.3
40. Frankish K. *Mind and Supermind*. Cambridge: Cambridge University Press (2004).
41. Stanovich KE. On the distinc- tion between rationality and intelli- gence: implications for understand- ing individual differences in rea- soning. In: Holyoak KJ, Morrison RG, editors. *The Oxford Handbookof Thinking and Reasoning*. New York: Oxford (2013). p. 343–65.

42. Stanovich KE. Distinguishing the reflective, algorithmic, and autonomous minds: is it time for a tri-process theory? In: Evans JStBT, Frankish K, editors. *In Two Minds: Dual Processes and Beyond*. New York: Oxford (2009). p. 55–88.
43. Saunders C, Over DE. In two minds about rationality. In: Evans JStBT, Frankish K, editors. *In Two Minds: Dual Processes and Beyond*. New York: Oxford (2009). p. 317–34.
44. Baumeister RF. The psychology of irrationality. In: Brocas I, Car- rillo JD, editors. *The Psychology of Economic Decisions: Rationality and Well-Being* New York: Oxford (2003). p. 3–16.
45. Loewenstein G. A visceral account of addiction. In: Elster J, Skog OJ, editors. *Getting Hooked: Rationality and Addiction*. Cambridge: The MIT Press (1999). p. 235–64.
46. Ainslie G. *Breakdown of Will*. Cam- bridge: Cambridge University Press (2001).
47. West R. *Theory of Addiction*. Oxford: Blackwell (2006).
48. Robinson TE, Berridge KC. What is the role of dopamine in reward: hedonic impact, reward learning, or incentive salience? *Brain Res Rev* (1998) 28:309–69. doi:10.1016/S0165-0173(98)00019-8
49. Szasz T. The ethics of addiction. *Am J Psychiatry* (1971) 128(5):541–6.
50. Fisher JM, Ravizza M. *Responsi- bility and Control: An Essay on Moral Responsibility*. Cambridge: Cambridge University Press (1998).
51. Bernheim BD, Rangel A. Addiction and cue-triggered decision processes. *Am Econ Rev* (2004) 94(5):1558–90. doi:10.1257/0002828043052222
52. Bernheim BD, Rangel A. From neu- roscience to public policy: a new economic view of addiction. *Swed Econ Policy Rev* (2005) 12:99.
53. Fehr E, Rangel A. Neuroeconomic foundations of economic choice – recent advances. *J Econ Perspect* (2011) 25:3–30. doi:10.1257/jep.25. 4.3
54. Tiffany ST. A cognitive model of drug urges and drug-use behav- ior: role of automatic and nonauto- matic processes. *Psychol Rev* (1990) 97:147–68. doi:10.1037/0033-295X. 97.2.147
55. Kahneman D, Wakker PP, Sarin R. Back to Bentham? Explorations of experienced utility. *Q J Econ* (1997) 112:375–405. doi:10.1162/ 003355397555235
56. Berridge KC, Aldridge JW. Decision utility, incentive salience, and cue-triggered "wanting." In: Morsella E, Bargh JA, Gollwitzer PM, edi- tors. *Handbook of Human Action*. New York: Oxford University Press (2009), p. 509–32.
57. Aristotle. *Nicomachean Ethics*. trans. T. Irwin. Indianapolis: Hackett Publishing Company, Inc. (1995).
58. Stanovich KE. *The Robot's Rebel- lion: Finding Meaning in the Age of Darwin*. Chicago: Chicago Univer- sity Press (2004).
59. Redish AD, Jensen S, John- son A. A unified framework for addiction: vulnerabilities in the decision process. *Behav Brain Sci* (2008) 31:415–87. doi:10.1017/S0140525X0800472X
60. Holton R. *Willing, Wanting, Waiting*. New York: Oxford University Press (2009).
61. Henden E. Addictive actions. *Philos Psychol* (Forthcoming 2012).
62. Ahmed SH, Lenoir M, Guillem K. Neurobiology of addiction ver- sus drug use driven by lack of choice. *Curr Opin Neurobiol* (2013) 23:1–7. doi:10.1016/j.conb.2013.01. 028
63. Lenoir M, Serre F, Cantin L, Ahmed SH. Intense sweetness sur- passes cocaine reward. *PLoS ONE* (2007) 8:e698. doi:10.1371/journal. pone.0000698
64. Robinson TE, Berridge KC. The incentive sensitization theory of addiction: some current issues. *Phi- los Trans R Soc Lond B Biol Sci* (2008) 363:3137–46. doi:10.1098/ rstb.2008.0093
65. Robinson MJF, Robinson TE, Berridge KC. Incentive salience and the transition to addiction. In: Miller P, editor. *Biological Research on Addiction*. Vol. 2. Academic Press (2013). p. 391–9.

18

The shame of addiction

Owen Flanagan*

Department of Philosophy, Duke University, Durham, NC, USA

Edited by:
Hanna Pickard, University of Oxford, UK

Reviewed by:
Serge H. Ahmed, CNRS, France
Neil Levy, Florey Institute of Neuroscience and Mental Health, Australia

***Correspondence:**
Owen Flanagan, Department of Philosophy, Duke University, 201 West Duke Building, Durham, NC 27708, USA
e-mail: ojf@duke.edu

Addiction is a person-level phenomenon that involves twin normative failures. A failure of normal rational effective agency or self-control with respect to the substance; and shame at both this failure, and the failure to live up to the standards for a good life that the addict himself acknowledges and aspires to. Feeling shame for addiction is not a mistake. It is part of the shape of addiction, part of the normal phenomenology of addiction, and often a source of motivation for the addict to heal. Like other recent attempts in the addiction literature to return normative concepts such as "choice" and "responsibility" to their rightful place in understanding and treating addiction, the twin normative failure model is fully compatible with investigation of genetic and neuroscientific causes of addiction. Furthermore, the model does not re-moralize addiction. There can be shame without blame.

Keywords: addiction, alcoholism, substance-related disorders, shame, blame, guilt, willing addicts, resigned addicts

"Dear friends, be men; let shame be in your hearts . . . Among men who feel shame, more are saved than die." Ajax to his troops in Homer's *Illiad*

THE TWIN NORMATIVE FAILURE MODEL OF ADDICTION

I propose a twin normative failure model of addiction in which the self-regarding reactive attitudes of bewilderment, disappointment, and shame play a constitutive role[1]. The addict cannot pass her own survey because she self-interprets, and self-interprets correctly, that she fails to execute normal powers of effective rational agency, she decides not to use and uses; she also fails to live up to the hopes, expectations, standards, and ideals she has for a good life for herself because of her addiction. It is possible and desirable to understand addiction as a normative failing in both these respects, one of rational effective agency, the second of moral quality broadly construed, without also moralizing addiction. Recognition of these twin normative failures is a powerful source of desperation and motivation to heal on the part of the addict and an immensely valuable tool for the therapeutic community to keep in view and use non-moralistically, as it tries help the addict to heal. In earlier times, it may have been that most addicts died for reasons related to addiction. Now, perhaps, with much deeper knowledge of the causes, components, effects, and nature of addiction we can make Ajax's maxim true for addicts: "Among men who feel shame, more are saved than die."

I intend the twin moral failure analysis to be true to the perspective of the addict, his close relations, as well as from the perspective of the professional and non-professional therapeutic communities that work and live with addicts. I also intend the analysis to describe normal and reliable features of addiction. The exceptions, the cases where there is no shame on the part of the addict descriptively, and where shame would be unwarranted normatively involve abnormal psychiatric conditions, e.g., schizoid personality disorder, or unusual social conditions where there are no choice-worthy options for a good human life, or where the addict has a certain social status, social permission (opiate addicts in hospice), and/or financial resources to be an addict with impunity.

To many, the view will seem too strong in two respects. First, some addicts are willing and not ashamed, so the view is descriptively false. Second, the view is reactionary: despite my claim that the twin normative failure model does not moralize addiction because it acknowledges shame without endorsing blame, it nonetheless returns us to the view that addiction is a moral failing. After spelling out the view more fully, I reply to these and several other objections.

ADDICTION IS A NORMATIVE DISORDER

In a seminal paper in philosophy and cognitive science, "Intentional Systems," Dennett (1) distinguished between three stances we commonly take toward ourselves and other human beings, the "intentional stance," the "design stance," and the "physical stance." From the perspective of the intentional stance we deploy psychological or mental vocabulary to describe, explain, and predict our own mental states and actions and those of others. We think of ourselves and our fellows as "intentional systems," as human individuals chock full of beliefs, desires, emotions, and goals. And we think of a particular integrated suite of embodied intentional states and dispositions as what makes an individual tick, what makes them who they are, what's behind the personality and character they display. The design stance goes below the intentional or person level and uses concepts related to normal or proper function: drinking a cup of coffee involves a perceptual system that registers that there is a cup of coffee, a system that computes desire and eventuates in a decision to drink it, which sends a signal to the motor system to move the hand in the right way, lift-to-lips, and drink. The physical stance goes lower still to the level of actual physical realization. The physical stance is especially useful when there is breakdown of proper function: Ann drinks coffee through a straw because in the bike accident she badly sprained both wrists.

[1] I mean the view to apply in the first instance to alcohol, cocaine, and opiate addiction.

Higher levels depend upon and are implemented by the lower levels. One could take the physical stance description lower: sprains are implemented on wrists, specifically on ligaments, which are made of flesh, which is eventually, like everything else, implemented on bosons and fermions[2]. But higher levels also have emergent properties in one perfectly natural sense. Wiffle balls are round, but the molecules that compose them are not. A hard hit wiffle ball can cause a bruise, but a hard hit polymer atom in a wiffle ball cannot cause a bruise. Wholes have properties that their parts don't. So too persons have properties that their parts, brain parts, and gene parts do not. Addiction is a person-level phenomenon. Neither brains nor genes are the sole cause of addiction; nor do brains or genes become addicted. That said genetic and neural malfunctions are clearly an important part of the explanation of how and why some people, some intentional systems, become addicts and suffer addiction.

At the intentional stance level, but not at lower levels, persons, whole persons, are normative creatures in two senses, one constituted by our power to assess or evaluate ourselves as rational or reason-responsive agents in a broad sense and to do what we decide is best to do all things considered; the other constituted by our power to assess or evaluate ourselves morally or from a moral point of view. Normative governance consists of two complex and highly interactive capacities, rational governance and moral governance. Rational governance refers to the capacity of persons to determine what we have reason to do, what makes sense to do given our aims, interests, and the way(s) the world is. Moral governance is the capacity to judge some of the things we do (or intend to do) as good or bad, right or wrong.

Our power to assess or evaluate ourselves as rational or reason-responsive agents is both episodic and diachronic. Episodically, at any one time or period in a life, there is always a set of possibly true answers to two sorts of questions. One set concerns what a person is doing here and now (at this time or within this period of time); the other set concerns why the person is doing it. As to the question of what I myself am doing, suppose what I am doing here and now is driving my car through the Holland Tunnel from Manhattan to New Jersey. As to why, the reason is that I believe that for someone in my physical position, in lower Manhattan, with a car, and wanting to get to Jersey, the best or most convenient way to get to Jersey is to take the Holland Tunnel. My physical position and my desire to get to Jersey give me good reason to drive through the Tunnel. I am responding to that reason in driving through the Tunnel. Normally, when a person has reason to Φ, she Φ's. Addicts are puzzling including to themselves. When it comes to their drug of choice (DOC), what David Foster Wallace types as "the Substance," they are performatively inconsistent (2). They resolve not to use and use. Many addicts report that the resolve and the action that undermines it occur at the same time, virtually in the same instant.

Our lives are also lived and led in diachronic psychological space and not just in the moment or in brief episodes. We experience ourselves as someone who was there in the past and we conceive ourselves as someone who will be there in the further future, short-term and long-term. We experience ourselves as not just being alive, but as having a life to lead, self-direct, or control, where a life is conceived as "the sum of one's aspirations, decisions, activities, projects, and human relationships" [(3), p. 5]. Most of us probably do not have a blueprint for our whole life, what Rawls (4) called a "life plan," but we do have for ourselves multifarious projects and plans nested together in various, possibly ever-adjusting, relations of priority and expansiveness. For many, most, perhaps all of us persons, we develop a narrative self-interpretation of ourselves as persons and perpetually evaluate how well we are doing in becoming who we aim to be and in accomplishing what we aim to accomplish. A basic way in which to understand the inter-relationships between our past, present, and future is to conceive of the lives we lead "as an unfolding story" (5, 6)[3]. There comes a time in every addict's life when he comes to see that his "self-represented identity" and his "actual full identity" are on divergent paths, likely far apart, possibly inconsistent (7)[4].

Finally, our lives are lived in social space as gregarious social animals. Most humans have natural desires for companionship and most of us recognize, even if only inchoately, that we cannot survive, develop ourselves as persons, or live good lives, that is, lives which are happy as well as meaningful and fulfilling, without situating ourselves in complex socio-moral relationships with other persons. And despite wide cultural variation in the exact norms governing social practices we all typically engage in normatively governed practices of "lending and borrowing, promising and consenting, buying and selling, making friends, entering into marriage, establishing a family, offering and accepting aid, and so forth" [(8), 20]. Reliably gaining the goods associated with these practices – security, self-esteem, self-respect, social trust, friendship – involve broadly moral evaluation diachronically by oneself and others[5].

---

[2]According to Dennett's pragmatic taxonomy, the "intentional stance" is person-level psychology; the "design stance" is computational cognitive psychology, and the "physical stance" is neuroscience. One could, for pragmatic reasons and perfectly in the spirit of his taxonomy go higher than the intentional stance – to sociology and then anthropology – and lower that his physical stance, to biochemistry and eventually to basic physics. One my view, but possibly not on Dennett's (he is well-known for his instrumentalist or eliminativist tendencies), the higher-level entities truly have properties that the lower levels don't have. There really are such things as beliefs and desires. People have beliefs and desires; people contain brains and brains contain neurons; but neurons don't have brains and brains aren't people, and probably brains do not have beliefs and desire, although people with brains do, and so on.

[3]I don't mean to overstate the degree to which people do or ought to examine and evaluate their lives from an articulate reflective pose (see Flanagan (33), for a critique of Charles Taylor for this intellectualist mistake). The point is that people have ideals, ends, goals, and purposes – many of which are socially scripted – and we are consciously or semi-consciously aware of how we are doing in relation to these ideals, ends, goals, and purposes. There are rational evaluations and adjustments of both ends and means along the way, as well as all the familiar kinds of rationalization and defensive denial that one really wanted to do such and so, or be such and so in the first place.

[4]"Self-represented identity" is the story from the first-person point of view; "actual full identity" is the true story of who one is, what one is like, the story that would be told by an ideal observer with the right theory of the human mind and action and knowledge of all the facts.

[5]I need to emphasize the idea that evaluation occurs "in broadly moral terms." Later, following Williams (34), I distinguish between "morality, the peculiar institution," which is roughly the kind picked out as "moral" inside the Abrahamic traditions and "the ethical," which is much broader and includes the aspirations to live well

This picture of levels of explanation and of persons as normative beings in the twin – rational self-interpretation and self-control sense, what I call, the "rational effective agency sense", and "the moral sense" – has implications for thinking realistically and humanely about addiction. Addiction is a person-level disorder – actually a person-in-a-particular-social-world disorder – in which there is failure of normative governance by rational norms of narrative or biographical integration and moral norms. The result is first bewilderment on the part of the agent that she has lost some of her normal capacities to direct her behavior by what she judges as her considered desires and reasons (for example, to drink like a normal person; not to drink to blackout), and eventually deep shame, as well as a host of other reactive attitudes, at the fact that she is not doing well by her own and often widely shared standards[6]. The model of addiction, the "twin normative failure model," and of the addict, I propose rejects reductive models of addiction that claim that addiction is a design or physical level disorder. Addiction occurs in creatures with brains and genes (and bosons and fermions) but it is not a disorder of brains and genes (or bosons and fermions). It might involve disorders of either or both (9–11)[7]. Persons are addicts. Addiction is a person-level disorder, a diachronic intra-personal and inter-personal disorder; it is a disorder of persons that involves normally and reliably shame in one's own eyes, and thus losses of self-respect and self-esteem, as well as social shame, a sense that even if one is not actually seen for who and how one is by others, one would be judged weak, weird, undisciplined, untrustworthy, and scary if one were seen for how one is as a person-in-the-grip of an addictive behavior pattern. Addiction fully engages the reactive attitudes of the addict, even if neither he, nor his community, judges him harshly or moralistically[8].

by achieving maximal intersection of the goods that comprise what is true, beautiful, and good. I intend what I am calling "moral" and what constitutes "the moral failing" of the addict to align with "the ethical" and not with "morality, the peculiar institution."

[6]The *Big Book of AA* describes the relevant first-person phenomenology as "incomprehensible demoralization (p. 30)."

[7]I am collaborating on a project with geneticists (31) who find that in mice, cocaine and opioid use activates genes associated with the salt and water instincts. The instincts to maximize salt and water intake when these are present and the organism needs them, are clearly adaptations, perhaps in exactly the form that leads some, but by no means all mice (29, 30) to become addicted mice. The addiction that piggybacks on these instincts is not an adaptation; it was not selected for in the original evolutionary environment or in recent ones to serve a fitness-enhancing effect. Liedtke thinks that this gene-level activity may be what at the genetic level subserves what some neuroscientists call the "midbrain mutiny" that involves the "hijacking" of normal reasons-responsiveness and control capacities by unusual schedules of reinforcement (35), or by an unwelcomed disassociation of the normally coordinated brain based "liking-wanting" systems (36), or by exhaustion of the brain's mental muscle, aka, "willpower" (37), or by stress hypersensitivity (38). This gene-level explanation of higher order brain level processes that subserve addiction, which itself rests on an evolutionary explanation of selection of genes that code for salt and water instinct, and (45) one of these higher order brain explanations can both be true as far as what happens at the gene level and the brain level without even the combined resources of both levels remotely describing or explaining addiction at the person level.

[8]"The reactive attitudes" according to Strawson (18) are the set of familiar sentiments, emotions, or attitudes such as anger, guilt, shame, forgiveness, resentment, happiness, and gratitude that regulate human interaction.

One consequence of my view of addiction and its relationship to the experience of being an addict is that it accepts rather than resists the idea that addiction really is, in the eyes of the addict, and those with whom she is in community, a normative problem. The addict has trouble with respect to her addiction putting her reasons, her best thinking, in reliable control of her actions, and she has trouble (perhaps for this reason) abiding by the moral norms upon which her sense of her own integrity and self-worth turns. It is disrespectful to the phenomenon of addiction, to addicts who experience their addiction as involving these twin normative failings, and to the wider community, which judges addiction as bewildering, sad, and shameful to deny that it is a straightforward normative disorder. It is equally extremely shortsighted and inhumane to think that the problem that an addict has is a straightforward problem that can be solved by a psychopharmacological intervention to stop the desire to use or the effects of using. What most don't see because of the meager dialectical offerings – addiction is either a moral or a brain/gene disorder – is the prospect that one can see addiction as involving biographically interpretative assessment of one's own reason responsiveness failings as well as moral failings without either the addict herself or her community moralizing and blaming her. The theory is that at the level of persons, social persons, addiction is a failure in two highly interactive normative systems at once. One can think this, just as one can think that addiction involves some choice and some responsibility without blaming the addict and moralizing addiction. Let me explain.

DSM 5 ON SUBSTANCE ABUSE AND ADDICTIVE DISORDERS

Technically DSM 5, (12) like its predecessors, is only a diagnostic manual. It offers a classificatory scheme. DSM 5 taxonomizes and conceptually disciplines disorder. It doesn't claim to explain (indeed it positively refuses to provide etiologies), or to offer treatment or therapeutic regimens. What DSM 5 is not agnostic about is that the symptom cluster it uses to diagnose substance-related disorders will yield to neuro-specification[9]. The manual is full of strong hints that it expects its symptom clusters to be filled in by neuro-specifics. We learn that all drugs of abuse have in common "direct activation of the brain reward system;" that people with "impairments of brain inhibitory mechanisms may be particularly predisposed to develop substance use disorders." The section on substance abuse disorders, like the rest of DSM 5, is filled with "maybes" about connections to genes and the brain. The facts are that there must be such connections; humans are genetically endowed animals and our nervous systems are involved in everything we do. But it is a mistake to think that all properties of persons reduce to properties of parts, even especially important parts. I could argue that all the winks and nods to neuroscience

[9]Insell (39) the head of NIMH is impatient about filling in the details, and wants to push on to the neuro-specifications of all bona fide mental disorders quickly. And he is willing to put the money he controls as head of NIMH where his mouth is Meanwhile, Frances (40) former head of the DSM IV taskforce laments the rush to neuroscientific reduction because neuroscience is immature, and because, like me, he is skeptical that all mental disorders are brain disorders, and third because he worries about the dominance of money in seeking neuro-pharmacological "cures" for problems that either are not in the brain at all or, even if they have a brain dysfunction component, are mostly psychosocial problems.

(and to a lesser extent, to genetics) is part of the mindless cultural spread of neuro-enthusiasm (and what Rob Wilson calls "smallism"), which although true, would distract from my aim to describe what addiction is in a way that is true to the phenomenon and that is also therapeutically useful, recognizing the many roles that shame and related reactive attitudes can and do play in healing from addiction.

It is also a mistake – a related one – to think that all the essential features of addiction are features that can be revealed in non-human animal models of addiction. The brain reward system of non-human animals has interesting similarities to the human reward system, but the social ecologies of mice and humans are entirely different, as are the capacities served by culture and an enormous prefrontal cortex. A rodent cannot consciously resolve, possibly in consultation with fellow mice, to refrain from consuming a drug because its life is not going well, because it is causing communal harm. A rodent cannot relapse, and then regret and feel ashamed or guilty for its failure to maintain abstinence. Animal models may teach us about how dangerous and imprudent it can be to suddenly reverse preferences over time, but the full character of human addiction is no mere preference reversal or oscillation. It normally involves an interpretation and evaluation of oneself as having let oneself down; of having broken promises to one's own self (and others). Non-human animals, at least the ones studied in addiction labs, are not self-interpretatively normed. They don't see themselves as leading a life. Nor are they moved by thoughts of what counts as a good person/rodent, nor puzzled or disturbed by feelings of guilt, shame, and embarrassment. The moral virtue or value of self-control and of responsibility for self is irrelevant to animal addiction. But with a human being, a person's social relationships, the effects of his actions on others, his loyalties and friendships, his trustworthiness, are deeply relevant to his being an addicted human being[10].

What is really interesting is that the DSM 5 criteria for substance-related and addictive disorders are very plausible and never mention, not once, the brain or genes. What they do mention, and rightly so, are normative impairments. Here is the list of diagnostic criteria for alcohol-related disorders [(12), pp. 490–491], which are representative of the substance abuses overall:

1. Alcohol is often taken in larger amounts or over a longer period than was intended.
2. There is a persistent desire or unsuccessful efforts to cut down or control alcohol use.
3. A great deal of time is spent in activities necessary to obtain alcohol, use alcohol, or recover from its effects.
4. Craving, or a strong desire or urge to use alcohol.
5. Recurrent alcohol use resulting in a failure to fulfill major role obligations at work, school, or home.
6. Continued alcohol use despite having persistent or recurrent social or inter-personal problems caused or exacerbated by the effects of alcohol.
7. Important social, occupational, or recreational activities are given up or reduced because of alcohol use.
8. Recurrent alcohol use in situations in which it is physically hazardous.
9. Alcohol use is continued despite knowledge of having a persistent or recurrent physical or psychological problem that is likely to have been caused or exacerbated by alcohol.
10. Tolerance, as defined by either of the following:
    a. A need for markedly increased amounts of alcohol to achieve intoxication or desired effect.
    b. A markedly diminished effect with continued use of the same amount of alcohol.
11. Withdrawal, as manifested by either of the following:
    a. The characteristic withdrawal symptoms for alcohol (refer to Criteria A and B of the criteria set for alcohol withdrawal, pp. 499–500).
    b. Alcohol (or a closely related substance, such as a benzodiazepine) is taken to relieve or avoid withdrawal symptoms.

THE PHENOMENOLOGY OF ADDICTION

DSM is wisely explicit, despite the thick vein of neuro-enthusiasm that courses through it, that substance abuse involves "*impaired control*" and "*social impairment.*" The language it uses to depict addiction is the language of the intentional stance. The addict has trouble carrying out his "intentions" (1); he "desires" to control using and makes "persistent efforts" to do so (2); he spends "a great deal of time in activities necessary to obtain alcohol" (3); he has "persistent and recurrent social and inter-personal problems" (4–7). Understood in this way, it looks as if DSM 5 embeds something in the vicinity of the twin normative failure model in its description of the typical cluster of features that define, characterize, or constitute addiction.

But, truth be told, DSM 5 is unclear about whether it considers these features merely symptomatic (often that seems the implication) the way fever is with a flu, or whether it understands these features as constitutive, as necessary, or as part of the typical psychological profile of addicts. For any mental disorder we can distinguish among its causes, its components or constituents, and its consequences. Because humans are self-interpreting animals, classifications, components, and consequences are absorbed, recorded, reflectively assessed, and they change the person being classified, who as a consequence of his disorder and his comprehension of it causes myriad further effects on himself and others. If one examines the vast literature comprised of memoirs of addiction (13) as well as writings by therapists who work with addicts, most every entry on the DSM 5 list will be familiar as constitutive of addiction. When the addict feels shame before his own eyes, when he observes his control failures, when he understands that he is an addict not living up to his own standards or best interests,

[10] Ahmed (29, 30) has done very important work inside the animal modeling tradition emphasizing that most rats offered cocaine do not get addicted and, more importantly for treating addiction, that compulsive cocaine use is lower in environments where there are multiple pleasure-producing and choice-worthy options besides the cocaine. My concern with animal models is not based on denial, not even skepticism, that there are genetic and/or neurobiological components of addiction, or on doubt that the brain might be the best place for interventionist strategies to short circuit the desire to use, the compulsion to use, the effects of use, and so on. It might be. The point is that even if the brain is an effective, even the most effective, site of intervention, this is not evidence that addiction is a brain disorder or that it is sensible or good to model it as such. Removing the battery of a car is an excellent way to immobilize it, but a running car is not a battery phenomenon and is not well modeled by the battery, what the battery is, does, and the ways it can malfunction. See below on Woodward's (32) model of causation for why this is so.

he changes, for better or worse. The story of who he is, what he is like, how well he is doing in the task of accomplishing what he intends, of living well, absorbs ever new material. There is narrative self-interpretative adjustment. Since narrative is partly constitutive of the self, he changes (7, 14). For the addict, along the descent depicted by DSM 5 steps 1–11, he is bewildering to himself, possibly terrifying – he can't get a grip – he's a disaster, a train wreck harming himself and those he loves. This first personal normative assessment does really capture the shape, the texture, and the phenomenology of addiction. Is there a mistake? No. Indeed, it is only by understanding these normative failings that the addict shows himself the self-respect he deserves as a person and leverages, normally with communal assistance, his remaining powers of agency to get back on track and repair himself as well as the situations and relations that have been damaged along the way.

Despite the fact that the DSM 5 list of symptoms includes failures in self-control and in reliability – in behavioral failures with respect to norms – it is missing any reference to normative feeling states, to reactive attitudes associated with these behavioral failures. The addict has "cravings," and greater "tolerance" involves changes in the "effects" of the DOC. He continues to use despite "knowledge" that using causes him problems, etc. But there is nothing in 1–11 about the way the addict experiences his failures to rationally effectively and morally guide his life through and past the allure of alcohol, which consistently undermines, possibly defeats his attempts to live well and to be well[11]. Interpreting the DSM 5 criteria to include these reactive attitudes or extending its criteria to include the feelings associated with the twin normative failures it almost always involves, would capture better the psychology of addiction than any purely behavioral, neuroscientific, or genetic model.

THE INTERPRETATIVE, REASONS-RESPONSIVENESS, EFFECTIVE AGENCY FAILURE

The twins that fail in addiction are fraternal, not identical. What I call the interpretive, reasons-responsiveness, effective agency failure is really a set of failures that include cognitive mistakes such as minimization (I don't drink too much; I just need to stop at *n*, where *n*> what a normal person would think is wise), and rationalization (you'd drink a lot too if you had my _____). One failure that is most familiar to both addicts and those in relation to them is a failure to execute rational control, to be able to execute rational plans, the failure to be in charge. The simplest way to put this point is in terms of the performative inconsistency mentioned earlier, which every addict understands as constitutive of his situation: I will/decide/pledge/promise to myself (possibly to others as well) that I will moderate or stop using; and then I use. P and not P. The failure is one of effective agency, of leading one's life and not just tagging along for the addicted ride. The addict like everyone else sees himself as a being with hopes, projects and plans, responsibilities and obligations, friendships, and loves, as an historical, enduring being, possessed of long-range interests. But his own defective agency gums up the works, the work of being and becoming the person he aims to be. He fails at reliably enacting in-charge selfhood. If his DOC, the Substance, is available he loses normal self-control against getting lost in a preference oscillating and the preference-reversing moment or episode. He is bewildered and ashamed.

According to DSM 5, this sort of complex failure begins in mild addiction at step 1, where the substance abuser uses more that he at first intends. And it gets worse as the problem becomes more severe. It is sometimes hard to tell from behavior where exactly a drinker is in terms of loss of the ability to stop in a normal reasons-responsive way, i.e., by making an all things/future me considered judgment that they should moderate or stop, and then doing so. The *Big Book of AA* written in 1939, not a scientific work, recognizes correctly a certain kind of "heavy drinker," who if he has reason to stop (the liver, the job, the spouse) stops. And much recent work confirms that many people who drink heavily, possibly in binges, possibly regularly, at some point, in their lives stop (15, 16, 43). But there is a type of drinker who seems not to be like this. They try to stop but can't. Caroline Knapp's, *Drinking: A*

[11] Contrast DSM 5 (12) with Graham's (9) – what I call "the ignoble eightfold path of addiction," especially, (iii), (iv), and (vii) which emphasize the self-directed reactive attitudes in addiction. DSM 5's 1–11 speak about ways the addict fails to exert various kinds of control despite his best efforts and it speaks about feelings toward alcohol (craving, tolerance). I am emphasizing the addict's feelings toward his SELF, possibly as a result of these failures and the harm he does to himself and others. And these reactive attitudes I claim, are part of what addiction is, and what needs treatment. TWO CAVEATS: first, in (vi–viii) Graham places I think too much stock in the belief that relapse is more or less inevitable. Second, I read (vi) as descriptive not prescriptive. It is true that relapse powerfully engages recognition of the twin normative failures including shame and its suite. Increased knowledge about addiction, of course, teaches that despite the shame, the addict may not in any robust sense be to blame or deserve blame.

(i) A person commences a behavior that is potentially harmful or deleterious. They consume a deleterious drug or other chemical substance or gamble.

(ii) The behavior eventually becomes an object of focal attention and periodically repeated or habitual activity. The focus is such that at times or in some cases it may be "the only tune or story in the addict's head, and nothing else drives it out".

(iii) The behavior produces consequences that are not just harmful or that seriously risk harm to self (and/or to others) but are perceived as harmful or destructive by the agent.

(iv) The perception or self-conscious experience of harmful consequences leads the person on certain lucid, critical or self-reflective occasions to negatively self-evaluate the behavior and attempt to refrain or quit. This does not mean the addict knows how to quit or how difficult it may be to quit or whether they can quit for any consistent period of time. But an attempt to refrain is made.

(v) The addict refrains, quits or inhibits the behavior during certain periods (perhaps without assistance, perhaps only with assistance – individual cases and occasions vary).

(vi) Quitting or cessation ultimately (timing and intervals vary) proves unsuccessful, however. The addict relapses. They "fall back" into the detrimental behavior after a period of temporary stoppage. The behavior returns together with its negative consequences or risks.

(vii) Relapse is interpreted by the agent as a form of personal disappointment or failure, not just as something destructive or risky, but as a source of shame, regret, self-blame, and embarrassment or as grounds for diminished self-confidence or self-esteem.

(viii) The steps or phases of harmful behavior, temporary abstention, and relapse cycle repeatedly. The recycling, in some cases, may cease permanently, perhaps without harmful long-term residue. And the person just plain quits. (Thousands of addicts just plain quit for good at some point. They "age out" of their addiction.) Or the addictive pattern may lead to an addict.s enduring exposure to harm or personal demise.

Love Story, Pete Hamill's, *A Drinking Life*, and Charles Jackson's, *The Lost Weekend* are powerful depiction of such lives.

The brain basis of addiction, according to animal studies, lies, in significant part, in the mesolimbic dopamine and brain reward system. It is possible that this area is compromised in humans, not only in opiate addiction, but in alcoholism as well. Suppose it is, and that therefore a compromised mesolimbic reward system is a necessary condition of human addiction. It does not follow that it is sufficient or that it is the only necessary condition (42, 44). In humans, addiction is constituted not only by craving, compulsive use, and "jonesing" for the Substance, which may be subserved primarily by the compromised mesolimbic reward system, it is also experienced and treated just in case the person experiences herself as unable to stop given that she has reason to (the personal and social costs mentioned in DSM 5); and that she is ashamed that she is not able to live as she judges to be good. This sort of self-regarding reactive attitude is I claim is a normal part of the phenomenology of addiction but not mentioned in DSM 5. It is implausible that human beings control against consumption impulsivity and imprudent preference reversal only by virtue of some sort of inhibitory mechanism in the brain reward system. If they did, then it might be plausible to say that addiction represents a disorder of that mechanism, and of nothing else. But human sources of inhibition and self-control are known to be many and various. Human powers of deliberation, self-assessment, and reason responsiveness are subserved by neural systems, especially in prefrontal cortex, that differ in organizational complexity from those of rodents. Furthermore, human linguistic capacities put us in unusual touch with communal norms and with communal reasons for abiding by those norms. To be sure, the addict has trouble making her reasons effective and this may have to do with damage to the circuitry in the mesolimbic areas or in the areas that connect prefrontal cortex to lower regions. But the facts are that addict has her reasons to stop, wishes to stop, but can't. And it is this experience of the failure to execute effective agency, according to my argument, that is also constitutive of human addiction, although almost certainly not of rodent addiction[12]. A human addict cannot in a situation in which he is considering if he can and should refrain from drug consumption, regard himself "as waiting to discover or to observe in which direction he will be moved" [(17), p. 51]. To be counted by him as a decision of whether or not to refrain, the state of deciding must be thought to conform to some standard of possessing a good reason. The question "Will I abstain?" is unavoidably indistinguishable from "should I abstain here and now?" The total situation I am in as an addict confronts me, and sets the problem. I may try to take account of things about myself that I believe are not in my power to change (because I lack the means or skill to change) and those things I believe I can change. The anxiety, felt need, impulse, the craving, the sudden passion to consume, when they occur, may feel like something that descends upon me. I may try to double back upon myself and think of myself as something more, or less, than I really am. "Can I, or can I not, free myself of this behavior?" "Perhaps I can." But the fact is: there are normative elements in states of mind and types of conduct relevant to being an addict, and these normative elements cannot be reframed in the descriptions of neural inhibitory mechanisms operating in independence of a person's own self-assessment and biographically reflective reason responsiveness. The key for the addict is to find some way – often with professional help or non-professional communal help – to leverage his remaining powers of agency, first and foremost in relation to his DOC, to stop using the Substance. Sometimes the first choice is to be tied like Ulysses to the mast for a time. But it is an important but underestimated fact that every addict who does not use any longer has done exactly that, moderated or stopped using (15, 16, 43). Such former addicts have rediscovered, reclaimed effective agency. And they are abundant.

THE MORAL FAILURE

Persons enter the world valuing certain things and not others and they exit the same way. We are creatures with ends. Some of these have to do with resource needs and acquisitive desires related to these needs – for food, clothing, and shelter; others have to do with social needs, with needs for company and affection. We are gregarious animals. No person, no matter what her conception of flourishing or well-being would choose a life without friends, says Aristotle[13]. When Strawson (18) calls attention to the reactive attitudes, the suite of emotions and sentiments that guide inter-personal commerce and that involve reactions to the good will, ill will, and indifference of others, he is careful to include affection, love, gratitude, and forgiveness, along with anger, resentment, and shame. According to Strawson, these emotional dispositions come with the equipment. He compares the reactive attitudes to induction. We cannot ask whether induction is rational. It is arational, part of our animal nature, not something we can give up. What we can do, however, in both the case of induction and the case of the suite of reactive attitudes is to adjust, moderate, modify, tune up and/or tune down as necessary both natural innate attitudes. We modify our original disposition to apply the straight rule of induction via feedback from its application. For example, when we apply the straight rule to small or unrepresentative samples we get poor predictions and we adjust the rule[14]. Eventually over world historical time, the methods of inductive logic, statistics, and probability theory develop. With respect to the reactive emotional attitudes, different social ecologies develop different norms for apt emotions (19).

A key idea in Strawson is that the reactive attitudes are not only essential to inter-personal relations, they are also essential to how we see, judge, and regulate our own mind and behavior; they are also intra-personal. I can experience, indeed I do experience, the reactive attitudes to my own mental states and actions. Anger at myself for what I did, as well as disappointment, pride, embarrassment, shame, and guilt are familiar components of a human life. Self-esteem is a general feeling that one is decent, worthy, doing well; self-respect involves knowing with some degree of confidence and proper humility that this feeling is warranted.

---

[12]One can, of course, make a rodent a psychological mess, extremely anxious, fearful, and so on, by mixing reinforcement schedules that both encourage and inhibit addiction.

[13]Psychopaths or people with schizoid personality disorder might be exceptions to Aristotle's surmise.

[14]The straight rule is crude and says this: if I observe that A's are B's to m/n, then I do/should infer that unobserved A's are B's to m/n.

It is commonplace for modern people to think that ancient and superficial peoples ran on shame whereas we run on guilt. Williams (20) has turned this idea on its head. The idea that, for example, the Greeks were a shame culture not a guilt culture is true but not a weakness or superficial characteristic. Shame is not simply a feeling caused by being seen, naked as it were, by others. It also involves not passing one's own survey. "Shame looks to what I am" [(20), p. 92]. Guilt, the modern emotion, is the narrow reactive attitude. It is largely internalized anger at certain actions and its roots are in what Williams calls "morality, the peculiar institution." Morality, the peculiar institution, is the narrow normative domain that encompasses all and only the domains that the God of Abraham is interested in assessing each person on come Judgment Day (its secular version comes in Kant). Ethics, in the broad sense, prized by the Greeks, by Nietzsche, and by Williams, is concerned with living a good human life more generally. It involves aspirations to flourish, which involves living at the intersections of what is good, true, and beautiful, whereas modern moral philosophy focuses primarily on the good, and even there it is narrowly conceived.

Here is how this relates to addiction. Almost all addicts experience failures of basic agent capacities, for example, in the first criteria of DSM 5 there is a failure to do what one reflectively intends. The non-addict will get that the addict might fail if a drink or drug is right in front of her (we relate from chocolate candy type experiences). But the addict will decide, indeed she will resolve not to purchase alcohol or cocaine and then find herself driving to the liquor store or crack house. This is shameful and is experienced as such both on the way to score, although in something of a blur, and afterward. I am ashamed of who I am, not simply for what I did. And it builds. An addict is someone, who like everyone else, has educational, career, and inter-personal aspirations, and he reliably fails to achieve them; or he achieves them to some degree, and then his addiction undermines these accomplishments. Every alcoholic and every addict in rooms of AA and NA and most every memoir of addiction (even if the author is not inculcated into 12-step ways of speaking) will speak of extreme feelings of shame for who one is, who one has become in one's own eyes, even if one has not yet been fully seen by others and even if objective failures are still in the "not-yet" category (2, 13, 21)[15].

The main point is that the ongoing epistemic-interpretative failure that involves: (1) the inability to draw normal inferences about the harms one is doing to oneself or others (caused by various classical defense mechanisms); and (2) the inability to get one's mind, body, and behavior to respond to decisions and resolutions in the normal ways; PLUS (3) the persistent failure to live as one expects oneself to live as a worthy human being undermine the basic goods of self-esteem and self-respect. One is ashamed of who one is. The alcoholic needs to put the "plug in the jug" (the crack addict needs to stop scoring eight balls; the smack addict to put down the needle). But the disease of addiction doesn't end there and then. And the reason is simple. Addiction is not a synchronic disorder that ends with the end of taking one's DOC. It is a diachronic molar person-level disorder and as such requires psychological, epistemic, moral, and narrative healing and reconstruction.

SOCIAL CAPITAL

A consistent finding in the literature on human well-being is that the best predictor of well-being – better that income, better than health even – is social capital (22). Almost all the variance between Northern Europeans and North Americans on the one hand, and citizens of sub-Sahara Africa on the other hand, in well-being measures has to do with the fact that almost half of informants in sub-Sahara Africa say that if they fell off a bar stool (here used only metaphorically), there would be no one they could count on to help, not a friend, not their mother, father, brother, or sister.

In his important book, *Bowling Alone*, Putnam (23) plots some of the causes and consequences of breakdowns in community and loss of social capital in America. There are insights for those concerned with addiction in these sorts of studies. First, addictions increase when there is socio-economic displacement, breakdown in community, and the availability of drugs and alcohol. Second, healing individuals typically involves reintegration into community, often a community whose other members have also experienced the bewildering twin normative failures and the self-degradation that results, and who get, at a minimum, that this sort of thing can happen to otherwise decent, worthy people, and who have experience, strength, and hope to share about how to regain control of one's self, one's life. Eventually, actually at the same time, there is reintegration into the wider social community, doing school or one's job as one is supposed to, being there for one's friends and family in the way a good person is, an end to actual or psychological isolation and concealment that is a common accompaniment of addiction (2, 13, 16, 21, 24, 25). Self-esteem and self-respect return and shame dissipates, possibly pride grows.

RESPONSIBILITY "WITHOUT THE STING"

Strawson (18) writes about the possibility of taking "the objective attitude" toward certain persons. The objective attitude is one that involves a surmise, possibly a conviction that the normal reactive attitudes are not deserved in certain cases and should be suspended. Children have temper tantrums and anger is not warranted. So we suspend, or try not to act on anger, even if we can't help to feel it to some degree. We also can and do suspend or try to suspend our normal reactions to the insane, to those who suffer from compulsions, who have no rational control over their actions.

Can and should we take an objective attitude toward the addicts in our midst? Probably. Can or should addicts take an objective attitude toward themselves? Probably. But there are psychological limits to our abilities to overcome natural dispositions. Furthermore, the addict feeling shame and the wider community thinking it is a shame that his life is going so badly is a humane reaction. It need not be taken to warrant blame. It signals that both the addict and we recognize that he could do better and be better. Understanding that he is an addict is a humane way of saying that we get that he is in a terrible fix and that we sympathize (46–48).

The more we learn about the complex socio-psycho-biological nature of addiction, about the ways various cultures encourage heavy drinking, about the effects of SES and drug availability,

[15]The 12-step community speaks of addiction as a medical, psychological, and spiritual disease. Amazingly, the medical aspect was once thought to be or to involve an allergy to alcohol. The psychological and spiritual aspects refer to a host of problems in the self-esteem, self-respect, shame, and self-degradation arena.

about genetic propensities, about the effects of weird reinforcement regimens, and of brain glitches, we have reason to adjust full normal subjective engagement to the addict. Williams makes this interesting point: "What arouses guilt in an agent is an act or omission of the sort that typically elicits from other people anger, resentment, or indignation. What the agent may offer in order to turn this away is reparation; he may also fear punishment or may inflict it on himself. What arouses shame, on the other hand, is something that typically elicits from others contempt or derision or avoidance" [(20), pp. 89–90]. This seems right; the life of the addict is a source of both guilt and shame. And thus he receives an odd admixture of reactions from others; in part, there are the normal reactive attitudes that full blown autonomous agents receive, anger and indignation; but there is also something else, a set of reactions that indicate that you have put me – us – off. You are puzzling, weird, to be avoided[16].

Williams goes on: "His (the person who is ashamed) reaction is a wish to hide or disappear, and this is one thing that links shame as, minimally, embarrassment with shame as social or personal reduction. More positively, shame may be expressed in attempts to reconstruct or improve oneself" [(20), p. 90].

CONCLUSION

All this seems about right. And in particular: shame is partly constitutive of addiction. The addict cannot pass his own survey. He is appalled by the twin normative failures from which he suffers, and shame is the appropriate, respectful, humane, first-person response to these failures. Shame begets using and more using begets more shame, and the vicious cycle is produced and maintains itself. Overcoming shame is part of overcoming addiction. Shame is also normally a crucial factor motivating the addict's attempt to reclaim, reconstruct, and improve himself. It motivates the addict to want to get a grip. That said, there are many reasons for the addict to forgive himself and engage in the difficult project of reconstruction and improvement with the knowledge that his agentic capacities in relation to the Substance are compromised, deficient; and, at the same time and for the same reasons, there are reasons for others to keep the addict in the realm of the very usual, the puzzling, the not-so-nice-to-be-around, but to also engage him with sympathy and compassion, maybe with forgiveness. The more we know about addiction the more this becomes both possible and sensible. At the same time, both the addict and the community that is asked to understand and treat him with compassion need to acknowledge that the addict is a person who suffers twin normative failure. He will need to heal to once again be treated as a full-fledged normal agent. He must regain his full normative agency and regain traction in his quest to live well.

FOUR OBJECTIONS AND REPLIES

THE WILLING ADDICT OBJECTION

The process or condition that you are calling addiction really includes matters characteristic of a certain kind of addict, a so-called unwilling addict. Some addicts, however, are willing, and do not feel shame or guilt over their addictive behavior patterns (26). Willing addicts don't double back on themselves and wish that their behavior was otherwise or that they should control their impulses to consume. Pickard (25) offers a powerful version of this objection in correspondence. Based on her clinical experience and standard DSM understanding, she writes that among addicts "are some people who are severely personality disordered, really genuinely don't want people or friends in their lives (this is part of having schizoid PD, diagnostically) and have a 'relationship' with drugs instead; some are so narcissistic and grandiose that the claim that they feel shame or look on their lives critically or think they could do wrong would require very deep, very inaccessible levels of the unconscious to make it true."

The objection is that there are certain individuals with schizoid personality disorder, perhaps there are others in the manic phase of bipolar disorder, who are addicts in the sense that they have lost rational effective control over using, but do not feel shame, and thus do not suffer the twin failures and who thus are not, according to me, addicts. But they really are addicts. So the twin normative criterion is descriptively false.

Before I respond to the objection, I can strengthen it as an objection, by pointing to two recent memoirs where the protagonists might be addicts in the sense of satisfying condition no. 1 of the twin normative failure model – he can't stop if or insofar as he tries – but he doesn't feel shame. *Narcopolis* by Thayil (27) and *The Wet and the Dry* by Osborne (28) brilliantly present two different types of character who don't seem to satisfy the shame condition. In Thayil's semi-fictional memoir, the 1970s opium dens of Mumbai, then known as Bombay, are a romantic haven for souls who have almost no other options, plus opium is really cheap. He and they are addicted and they don't give a shit. Even if Thayil is not proud to be an addict, he is not ashamed either. Osborne's story meanwhile is a hilarious romp through the Middle East by a man who is a "drinker" and who is hoping that laws and social mores of Muslim countries that disapprove of drinking will help him at least temporarily to moderate. They don't and he doesn't.

So now the strengthened objection is this: there are at least four types of addicts that do not satisfy the shame condition: (1) people with personality disorders such as schizoid PD; (2) people in full blown mania; (3) people that have easy access to the Substance, to their DOC, and no other choice-worthy options are available [see Ref. (29, 30)]; (4) "Drinkers," like Osborne – also think of Richard Burton, Richard Harris, Peter O'Toole, and Christopher Hitchens or a heroin user with resources to get reliably pure doses, a Keith Richards type. This latter may be an approved of life style among a certain mostly white elite in the UK, but probably not in the US.

Reply

No doubt cases of addiction are heterogeneous in many respects, and dimensional in depth, severity, and so on. Are there willing addicts?[17] Surely, there are people who minimize and rationalize,

[16] Pickard (25) argues that for individuals with both addictions and personality disorders, we can and should decouple (1) Holding a person responsible for what she did; (2) Holding her responsible for her future actions; (3) Blaming a person for failures on 1 or 2.

[17] Kennett (41) helpfully distinguishes four possible kinds of addicts: willing; unwilling; wanton; and resigned. She is skeptical about willing addicts. Wanton addicts, if there are any, are not reflective in ways that would allow noticing the twin normative failures or perhaps if they did, caring about them. Mice addicts are wanton addicts. I doubt that there are any person addicts who fit the bill since even wantons will need

and people who think they could stop if they decided to do so. Some of these probably do fall into the class of willing users, even willing abusers. They choose to use, but believe they could stop if they had sufficient reason to do so. They like using excessively, asocially, possibly even antisocially. Some of these people might be wrong that they could stop if they tried (in the normal reason-responsive way), in which case they would be wrong that they are not addicts because they do not satisfy the first normative condition, the effective agency condition. They do; they just don't know that they do. The *Big Book of AA* says if you think you are not an alcoholic, you may be right. There is a test: try some controlled drinking and if you can do so reliably and without always feeling overwhelming desire to use, then you were right – you were just a heavy drinker not an alcoholic. On my view, if a person could stop if they decide to do so, they do not suffer the first normative failure of effective agency (nor would they be self-deceived, etc.). And such an individual would not be an addict according to the view on offer.

But what about the memoir cases and Pickard's psychiatric case(s)? One thing to say about the two memoir cases is that in both cases some shame is experienced; Osborne, at least, is often embarrassed about the blackouts and some of the predicaments his drinking gets him in. The shame condition in the twin normative failure model does not specify how much shame needs to be experienced. This could also be said of people with bipolar disorder when they are not in the grandiose bullet-proof phase, during which down-times they do backtrack, second-guess, and so on.

But this doesn't solve the problems with the Pickard case of schizoid personality disorder where no shame is experienced diachronically; where possibly there is pride instead. A response specifically to these cases might distinguish addicts who satisfy the first condition (call them addicts type-1) and those who satisfy both (addicts type-2). Another is to claim that even the people who don't feel shame ought to, which concedes that the criterion is normative not descriptive. The option I am inclined to take is to restrict the twin normative failure model to people who do not have severe personality disorders (e.g., schizoid PD) and people who are not in the grandiose phases of bipolar disorder. This would still leave the model open to this objection: there are social environments that are so degraded that there is no shame in addiction descriptively – perhaps the addicts are literally and rightly hopeless – and in which shame, guilt, blame are normatively unwarranted. Shamelessly addicted is simply the way some people live. I accept this. In such environments the concept of addiction in my sense has at best only a weak grip, only the first condition of addiction would be met, and even that only in a weak sense: if the resigned or hopeless addicts in such worlds wanted to stop (they don't), they couldn't[18]. The twin normative failure model is a useful model in environments where there are multiple choice-worthy options, not otherwise.

to schedule desires and trying to do so will result in recognition of their inability to successfully schedule substance-related desires (unless supply is unlimited), and thus in recognition and bewilderment over their control capacities. This much will lead, even the amoralist, to frustration and anger at his failure to live as he wishes, to coordinate demand/need to supply, and to gain the satisfactions he seeks. There probably are resigned or hopeless addicts, but even they will normally experience themselves, and will be seen by others as suffering the twin normative failures of loss of effective agency and life standard failure, although the space of live options for such resigned individuals will have pretty much closed off. Resignation is normally a sad emotion constituted in part by the sense that things could have gone better. When an environment is really objectively hopeless, offering no decent options for a good human life, then there just may be no norms against which the addicts life is better or worse than any other. I accept that in such environments, the twin normative failure model starts to lose its grip; perhaps, it is irrelevant.

THE ESSENCE AND THE PERIPHERY OBJECTION

The twin normative failure model of addiction is swollen and inflated. There is too much that you are including as proper parts of addiction or of an addictive behavior pattern. The essence of addiction is at the brain level. The presence or absence of shame and negative self-evaluative attitudes, of various moral attitudes and emotions, the failures of reason responsiveness are sequelae of addiction, not part of addiction.

Reply

First, if an essence involves characterizing the set of properties that are invariant or at least highly reliable accompaniments of a kind, then the two normative failure model has at least as much credibility as any other model. I claim that you will find evidence of both normative failures in most every addict's first personal testimony and in the third personal testimony of professionals who work with addicts. The shame of addiction is shame that is directed to the content that [I cannot control my behavior in relation to the Substance] and that [because of my using the Substance I fail to live up to my ends, values, goals, and standards]. Those who favor only brain or genetic bases for the disease have yet to agree about what that single basis is, if there is one, or whether it is polyneural or polygenic, if there are several, and how exactly (and when) confirmation/disconfirmation might come for the various contender hypotheses. I claim that there is confirmation for the twin normative failure model right now. Second, although a less inclusive or thinner concept of addiction (a least common denominator conception, as it were) may work as an operational stipulation in the case of models of certain non-human animal behavior, it is without merit in the richer conceptual and normative world of human beings, at the person level. Third, and relatedly, the objection favors an unrealistic simplifying assumption requiring that we define the dysfunction of addiction synchronically rather than diachronically, and over some aspect that is hypothesized, but not yet shown to obtain over all creatures that can suffer addiction. But claiming that the hypothesized shared basis is the essence, and that all other features, especially ones that reliably appear in *Homo sapiens* are not, is to change the question. Fourth, the method of gaining insight into essences is unstable. We have already seen how some geneticists think they can reduce the neuroscientific base of addiction to a genetic one in DNA, and even RNA, that serve the salt or water instincts (31) [19]. For familiar reasons, this

[18]These sad cases are "resigned addicts" (41). It needn't be that a whole social world has no choice-worthy options; it can be that certain social groups are trapped by racism or sexism or terrible poverty to have no or very limited choice-worthy options in a world where there are abundant options for others.

[19]To be fair, since full blown reduction never occurs, the geneticist should not claim reduction, but something like the further specification of mechanisms at the lower level (genes) that explain partly why the brain is doing what it is doing. Similar humility on the part of those who work on the neuroscience of addiction would claim to provide insight into some of the mechanisms involved in addiction.

move opens the geneticists' account to a further reduction into the language of bosons and fermions or whatever is the language of fundamental physics. With each reduction we move further and further from the phenomenon we started and are providing a less ecologically valid account of that phenomenon. If we are speaking of addiction among humans and addiction constitutes any sort of well-behaved or unified kind, every bit of evidence indicates that it is a psychological or behavioral kind that is also a double-normed social kind. This is perfectly compatible with this kind also having certain common features at the level of the brain and genes since kinds defined at the higher level have all the properties that the lower levels have but the reserve is not true, and this matters.

THE INTERVENTION OBJECTION

The key to curing addiction is to arrest it, to stop the addict from using. Your view says that addicts fail to be able to exert normal self-control capacities and are ashamed of both this fact and the fact that they are failing to live a good human life. But you also acknowledge that knowing or experiencing this and also desiring to stop is normally not enough to stop. For this we are working toward pharmacological interventions that help addicts stop using, which is a necessary condition for any and all further healing. There are drugs that make the alcoholic sick if she uses, and others that mitigate the effects of cocaine and opiates. Eventually, work in genetics will yield simple interventions that adjust genes for those predisposed, and so on. If you think these interventions are already working, or might work, to arrest addiction, then you acknowledge that brain or genes cause of addiction.

Reply

The first part of the objection is not an objection to the view. I have said exactly nothing about opposing any and all therapeutic techniques that are helpful to the addict. If various kinds of psychopharmacological interventions can help without comparable costs, then, good, use them. But do not make the mistake of thinking that in locating an intervention site that one has identified the cause. Also beware the related mistake (sometimes made by psychoanalysis) that the root cause must be treated to arrest an ailment. First, many things are fixed without fixing what caused the breakdown. The weather caused the bicycle chain to rust. I clean the chain and oil it. I fix the bike but have done nothing to the weather. On the other side, we need to beware mono-causal thinking. The pragmatics of causal talk makes it sensible to say such things as the rock broke the window. But really the rock only broke the window because it, the window, had a certain density and brittleness (if it had been shatterproof, no breakage). And the window broke only because the boy threw the rock, and he threw it only because he was angry, and so on. No rock, no broken window; no angry boy, no broken window. The best analysis of causation in the philosophy of science says that the total cause of Θ is the set of events and processes ($\alpha, \beta, \gamma, \delta \ldots \omega$) such that if (counterfactually) anyone of them were different Θ would not have occurred as it is (32). And so it is with addiction. Take away the family that thinks adult drunkenness or drug use is amusing and some "addicts" never become one, take away the hopelessness of some urban environments and the rate of addiction will go down, and so on for genetic predispositions, etc. The first point is that many interventions do treat or require treating causes, and in so far as it is wise to treat a cause (or constituent or effect) of some disorder, and such intervention is effective, this should be applauded. But it is not at the same time any evidence at all that the cause has been found. It is rare for any phenomena that there is any such thing as the cause. Genes are causal factors in addiction, brains are causal factors, and families are causal factors. But invariably using a fair amount of some substance is a causal contributor to addiction, and this social practice – drinking, snorting, and mainlining – is not in the genes or the head.

OBJECTION: RE-MORALIZING ADDICTION

Fourth and finally, it will be objected that the appeal to the shame of addiction reintroduces the idea that addiction is a moral failing.

Reply

This is a simplistic and mistaken objection. Addiction is a normative disorder, a twin normative disorder that involves shame at one's own survey, first because one is not an effective agent in relation to the Substance and cannot reliably do what one judges best, and second, because one is messing up one's life because of one's relation to the Substance. These are normal responses by the addict to his own realistic assessment of his plight. It is an interesting and important question whether an addict can take or adopt an "objective attitude" toward himself. It seems often to occur to some imperfect extent, and insofar as it does happen it may well prepare the person for self-forgiveness, and for reclamation of self-esteem and self-respect. There can be shame without blame. We acknowledge this when we say of the addict or the way he lives that "it" is "a shame." Or to put the matter another way: guilt is anger turned inward and normally involves blame. Shame involves disappointment at self, but need not involve anger at self. Anger can immobilize; but shame can and often does motivate a change in direction, a search for a way to overcome his extraordinarily destructive relation to the Substance. As for others, knowledge is power, and the more that is know about the nature, causes, and multifarious trajectories of addiction, the more reasons others have to treat addicts as special cases, not as suffering an ordinary physical disease, but also not as fully effective agents, as worthy of sympathy and compassion because they suffer the shame of addiction. My recommendation is to accept that addiction just is a normative disorder, while at the same time not moralizing it.

ACKNOWLEDGMENTS

George Graham was helpful at every stage of writing this paper. George's thinking and writings on the nature of mental illness, and his suggestions, comments, and criticisms of this paper have contributed immeasurably to my thinking and writing about addiction. I am also grateful to Hanna Pickard, Serife Tekin, and Colin Klein, as well as Neil Levy and Serge Ahmed served initially anonymous referees and made extremely helpful critical comments on an earlier version.

REFERENCES

1. Dennett DC. Intentional systems. *J Philos* (1971) 68(4):87–106. doi:10. 2307/2025382
2. Flanagan O. What it is like to be an addict. In: Poland J, Graham G, editors. *Addiction and Responsibil- ity*. Cambridge: MIT Press (2011). p. 269–92.
3. Rachels J. *The End of Life: Euthana- sia and Morality*. Oxford: Oxford University Press (1986).
4. Rawls J. *The Theory of Justice*. Cam- bridge, MA: Harvard (1971).
5. Taylor C. Self-interpreting ani- mals. *Philosophy and the Human Sciences: Philosophical Papers. Volume 1*. Cambridge: Cam- bridge University Press (1985). p. 45–76.
6. Taylor C. The concept of a per- son. *Philosophy and the Human Sci- ences: Philosophical Papers. Volume 1 (Orig. 1981)*. Cambridge: Cam- bridge University Press (1985). p. 97–114.
7. Flanagan O. *Varieties of Moral Per-sonality: Ethics and Psychological Realism*. Cambridge, MA: Harvard (1991).
8. Deigh J. *An Introduction to Ethics*. Cambridge: Cambridge University Press (2010).
9. Graham G. *TheDisorderedMind:An Introduction to Philosophy of Mind and Mental Illness*. 2nd ed. New York: Routledge (2013).
10. Graham G, Flanagan O. *Psychiatry and the Brain*. Available from: http:// blog.oup.com/ 2013/08/psychiatry-brain-dsm-5- rdoc/
11. Levy N. Addiction is not a brain disease (and it matters). *Front Psychiatry* (2013) 4:24. doi:10.3389/fpsyt. 2013.00024.
12. DSM 5. 2013. Arlington, VA: American Psychiatric Association.
13. Flanagan O. Identity and addiction: what alcoholic memoirs teach. In: Fulford K, Davies M, Gipps R, Graham G, Sadler J, Strangellini G, et al., editors. *The Oxford Handbook of Philosophy and Psychiatry*. Oxford: Oxford University Press (2013). p. 865–88.
14. Tekin S. Self-concept through a diagnostic looking glass: narrative and mental disorder. *Phil Psychol* (2011) 24(3):357–80. doi:10.1080/09515089.2011. 559622
15. Vaillant GE. *The Natural History of Alcoholism Revisited*. Cambridge: Harvard (1995).
16. Heyman GM. *Addiction: A Disorder of Choice*. Cambridge, MA: Harvard University Press (2009).
17. Hampshire S. *Freedom of the Individual*. London: Chatto andWindus (1965).
18. Strawson PF. Freedom and resentment. *Proceedings of the British Academy*. (1960).
19. Gibbard *A. Wise Choices, Apt Feelings*. Cambridge: Harvard University Press (1990).
20. Williams BAO. *Shame and Necessity*. Berkeley: University of California Press (1993).
21. Flanagan O. Phenomenal authority: the epistemic authority of alcoholics anonymous. In: Levy N, editor. *Addiction and Self-Control*. Oxford: Oxford (2013). p. 67–93.
22. Helliwell J, Richard L, Jeffrey S, editors. *World Happiness Report. 2011*. NewYork: The Earth Institute, Columbia University (2011).
23. Robert P. *Bowling Alone: The Collapse and Revival of American Community*. New York: Simon & Schuster (2000).
24. Pearce S, Pickard H. How therapeutic communities work: specific factors related to positive outcomes. *Int J Soc Psychiatry* (2012) 58:1–10.
25. Pickard H. Responsibility without blame: philosophical reflections on clinical practice. In: Fulford K, Davies M, Gipps R, Graham G, Sadler J, Strangellini G, et al., editors. *The Oxford Handbook of Philosophy* and Psychiatry. Oxford: Oxford University Press (2013). p. 1134–54.
26. Foddy B, Savulescu J. A liberal account of addiction. *Philos Psychiatry Psychol* (2010) 17(1):1–22. doi:10.1353/ppp.0.0282
27. Thayil J. *Narcopolis: A Novel*. New York: Penguin (2012).
28. Osborne L. *The Wet and the Dry*. New York: Crown (2013).
29. Ahmed SH. Validation crisis in animal models of drug addiction: beyond non-disordered drug use toward drug addiction. *Neurosci Biobehav Rev* (2010) 35(2):172–84. doi:10.1016/j.neubiorev.2010.04. 005
30. Ahmed SH. The science of making drug-addicted animals. *Neuroscience* (2012) 1(211):107–25. doi:10.1016/j.neuroscience.2011. 08.014
31. Liedtke W, McKinley MJ, Walker L, Zhang H, Pfenning A, Drago J, et al. Relation of addiction genes to hypothalamic gene changes subserving genesis and gratification of a classic instinct, sodium appetite. *PNAS* (2011) 108:12509–14. doi:10.1073/pnas.1109199108
32. Woodward J. *Making Things Happen: A Theory of Causal Explanation*. New York: Oxford (2003).
33. FlanaganO. Identity and strong and weak evaluation. In: Flanagan O, Rorty AO, editors. *Identity, Character, and Morality*. Cambridge MA: MIT Press (1990). p. 37–66.
34. Williams BAO. *Ethics and the Limits of Philosophy*. London: Fontana (1985).
35. Ainsle G. *Breakdown of Will*. Cambridge: Cambridge University Press (2001).
36. Berridge K, Robinson TE. Parsing reward. *Trends Neurosci* (2003) 26(9):507–13. doi:10.1016/S0166- 2236(03)00233-9
37. Baumeister RF,Tierney J. *Willpower: Rediscovering the Greatest Human Strength*. New York: Penguin (2012).
38. Koob GF, Le Moal M. *Neurobiology of Addiction*. London: Academic Press (2006). 2006 p.
39. Thomas I. *Director's Blog*. (2013). Available from: http://www.nimh. nih. gov/about/director/2013/ transforming-diagnosis.shtml
40. Frances A. *Saving Normal*. New York:William Morrow (2013).
41. Kennett J. Just say no?Addiction and elements of self-control. In: Levy N, editor. *Addiction and Self-Control*. Oxford: Oxford (2013).
42. Bayne T, Levy N. The feeling of doing: deconstructing the phenomenology of agency. In: Sebanz N, Prinz W, editors. *Disorders of Volition*. Cambridge: MIT Press (2006). p. 49–68.
43. Fingarette H. *Heavy Drinking: The Myth of Alcoholism as a Disease*. Berkeley: University of California (1988).
44. Graham G. Ordering disorder: mental disorder, brain disorder, and therapeutic intervention. In: Fulford K, Davies M, Gipps R, Graham G, Sadler J, Strangellini G, et al., editors. *The Oxford Handbook of Philosophy and Psychiatry*. Oxford: Oxford University Press (2013). p. 512–30.
45. Hochendoner S, Hilton D, Lawrence AJ, Denton DA. Relation of addiction genes to hypothalamic gene changes subserving genesis and gratification of a classic instinct, sodium appetite. *Proc Natl Acad Sci U S A* (2011) 108:12509–14. doi:10. 1073/pnas.1109199108
46. Wallace RJ. Addiction as defect of the will: some philosophical reflections. Addiction and responsibility: part I. *Law Philos* (1999) 18:621–54.
47. Yaffe G. Recent work on addiction and responsible agency. *Philoso Public Aff* (2001) 30(Spring, 2001):178–221. doi:10.1111/j.1088-4963.2001.00178.x
48. Holton R. Willing, Wanting, Waiting. Oxford: Oxford University Press (2009).

19

MicroRNAs and drug addiction

Purva Bali*[1,2] *and Paul J. Kenny*[1,2]

[1] *Laboratory of Behavioral and Molecular Neuroscience, Department of Molecular Therapeutics, The Scripps Research Institute – Florida, Jupiter, FL, USA*
[2] *Laboratory of Behavioral and Molecular Neuroscience, Department of Neuroscience, The Scripps Research Institute – Florida, Jupiter, FL, USA*

Edited by:
Andre Pietrzykowski, Rutgers University, USA

Reviewed by:
Marissa A. Ehringer, University of Colorado, USA
Hironori Kawahara, University of Pennsylvania School of Medicine, USA

****Correspondence:***
Paul J. Kenny, Laboratory of Behavioral and Molecular Neuroscience, Department of Molecular Therapeutics, The Scripps Research Institute – Florida, 130 Scripps Way, Jupiter, FL 33458, USA.
e-mail: pjkenny@scripps.edu

Drug addiction is considered a disorder of neuroplasticity in brain reward and cognition systems resulting from aberrant activation of gene expression programs in response to prolonged drug consumption. Non-coding RNAs (ncRNAs) are key regulators of almost all aspects of cellular physiology. MicroRNAs (miRNAs) are small (~21–23 nucleotides) ncRNAs transcripts that regulate gene expression at the post-transcriptional level. Recently, miRNAs were shown to play key roles in the drug-induced remodeling of brain reward systems that likely drives the emergence of addiction. Here, we review evidence suggesting that one particular miRNA, miR-212, plays a particularly prominent role in vulnerability to cocaine addiction. We review evidence showing that miR-212 expression is increased in the dorsal striatum of rats that show compulsive-like cocaine-taking behaviors. Increases in miR-212 expression appear to protect against cocaine addiction, as virus-mediated striatal miR-212 overexpression decreases cocaine consumption in rats. Conversely, disruption of striatal miR-212 signaling using an antisense oligonucleotide increases cocaine intake. We also review data that identify two mechanisms by which miR-212 may regulate cocaine intake. First, miR-212 has been shown to amplify striatal cAMP response element binding protein (CREB) signaling through a mechanism involving activation of Raf1 kinase. Second, miR-212 was also shown to regulate cocaine intake by repressing striatal expression of methyl CpG binding protein 2 (MeCP2), consequently decreasing protein levels of brain-derived neurotrophic factor (BDNF). The concerted actions of miR-212 on striatal CREB and MeCP2/BDNF activity greatly attenuate the motivational effects of cocaine. These findings highlight the unique role for miRNAs in simultaneously controlling multiple signaling cascades implicated in addiction.

Keywords: miRNA, miR-212, MeCP2, cocaine

INTRODUCTION

Non-coding RNAs (ncRNAs) can be defined as biologically functional RNAs that do not encode proteins. This class of transcripts is characterized by the presence of an increased density of stop codons and lack of extensive open reading frames (ORFs). For decades, work on ncRNAs focused almost exclusively on transport RNAs (tRNAs) and ribosomal RNAs (rRNAs), which are key regulators of mRNA translation into encoded proteins. However, recent advances in high throughput sequencing technologies have revealed tremendous diversity in ncRNAs. Moreover, ncRNAs are playing an increasingly more recognized role in key aspects of cellular function, including the regulation of gene expression, often through novel mechanisms of action. ncRNAs have also been implicated in key cellular process such as DNA imprinting, RNA splicing, editing, transcription, mRNA degradation, and translational repression. Interestingly, analysis of ncRNA complexity through evolution reveals that the proportion of non-coding sequences in eukaryotic genomes correlates closely with the complexity of the organism, even when proportion of the protein coding genes remains relatively static across organisms (Heimberg et al., 2008).

It is currently thought that only about 2% of the human genome codes for functional proteins, yet more than 80% of transcripts encoded in the genome may have some biochemical activity. In a recent study, Djebali et al. (2012) used ultra-deep sequencing of RNAs from different cell lines and concluded that ~75% of the genome is transcribed at some point during the cellular life cycle. These extensive studies using sequencing and sophisticated ncRNA prediction algorithms have led to the identification of thousands of ncRNAs in the human genome, and perhaps many more remain to be discovered (Majer and Booth, 2010; Yang et al., 2010).

On the basis of their length and function this heterogeneous group of transcripts can be further categorized into short ncRNAs and long ncRNAs. The short ncRNAs include microRNAs (miRNAs) and short-interfering RNAs (siRNAs), which are generally 18–25 nucleotides in length. Small RNAs (smRNAs) such as the small nucleolar RNAs (snoRNAs), smRNAs, piwi-interacting RNA (piRNAs) are between 20 and 300 nucleotides in length. The long ncRNAs (>200 nucleotides) can further be grouped into different categories on the basis of their origin (Orom and Shiekhattar, 2011) and have a broader spectrum of functions including chromatin modulation, recruitment of transcription factors, and nuclear-cytoplasmic transport (Mattick and Makunin, 2006). Indeed, there is now compelling computational and experimental evidence that many previously uncharacterized ncRNAs of unknown function, considered largely "transcriptional noise," have key functional roles in almost all aspects of cellular physiology.

Using the high throughput *in situ* expression data from Allen Brain Atlas, Mercer et al. have recently shown that more than 800 different ncRNAs are widely expressed in the adult brain (Mercer et al., 2008). In another study, Landgraf et al. created a miRNA expression atlas by sequencing and analyzing multiple smRNAs libraries (Landgraf et al., 2007). Their data also reveals a tissue/cell specific expression of these RNAs, which correlates with *in situ* expression data. Hence, it is likely that ncRNAs play an important role in basic aspects of brain function and behavior.

MicroRNAs IN BRAIN

Amongst the different classes of ncRNAs, miRNAs are perhaps the best characterized. Since their discovery in *C. elegans* in 1993 (Lee et al., 1993), hundreds of miRNAs have been identified in different species. Initial studies demonstrated that these short (~22 nucleotide) RNAs are mainly involved in binding to the 3′ untranslated region (3′UTR) of mRNA transcripts that share complementarity with nucleotides in their so-called seed sequence (nucleotides 2–7). Binding of miRNAs to mRNA transcripts results in post-transcription silencing of the target mRNA *via* RNA-induced silencing complex (RISC)-induced translational repression or sequestering them for storage or degradation (Bartel, 2004). However, emerging new evidence suggests that the non-seed region of miRNAs may bind to the 5′UTR or the coding sequence of target transcripts and thereby influence translation processes (Orom et al., 2008; Elcheva et al., 2009). To add further complexity, recent reports show that miRNAs can also positively regulate gene expression in some cellular contexts (Vasudevan et al., 2007; Place et al., 2008). Computational sequence analysis predicts that each miRNA can target 10–100s of mRNA transcripts (Esteller, 2011). In addition, each gene transcript can itself be targeted by potentially hundreds of miRNAs.

The brain may be a particularly prominent organ within which miRNAs play an important role in controlling gene expression and neuronal activity. In a study by Miska et al. it was established that there was considerable abundance of miRNAs in rodent and primate brain (Miska et al., 2004). Further, they developed a microarray-based method to monitor the spatiotemporal expression of miRNAs during mouse brain development and found that there was a dynamic change in miRNA expression levels during development. As a result of these new methodologies there have been more than 300 miRNAs identified in adult mouse brain. Of these brain-enriched miRNAs some are present ubiquitously whereas others are expressed in a cell specific manner (Bak et al., 2008).

Another powerful tool that improved our understanding of the functional relevance of miRNAs in neuronal tissues was the development of mice with genetic manipulations in the genes encoding Dicer and Arognaute2 (Ago2). Both of these proteins are important components of the miRNA biogenesis pathway. Dicer is an endoribonuclease that catalyzes the processing of precursor miRNA into its mature form. Characterization of Dicer1 mutants in *C. elegans* suggested that this protein plays a critical role in brain development (Grishok et al., 2001). To assess its role in mammalian brain development Bernstein et al. disrupted Dicer in mice and observed embryonic lethality with depleted number of stem cells, suggesting that this enzyme is important for development in general (Bernstein et al., 2003). Subsequently a number of groups knocked down Dicer *via* conditional gene targeting, with the findings consistent in demonstrating that ablation of dicer results in decreased miRNA expression and defects in neuronal cell differentiation and survival (Kanellopoulou et al., 2005; Murchison et al., 2005; Schaefer et al., 2007). These phenotypes could be rescued by re-expression of the gene (Kanellopoulou et al., 2005), highlighting the importance for Dicer and the smRNAs species processed by this endoribonuclease in neuronal development and function. More recently, conditional deletion of Dicer established that miRNAs expressed during neurogenesis play a role in the maintenance of neural progenitor cells, with disruption in this action contributing to defects in neuronal migration and subsequently in cortical lamination (De Pietri Tonelli et al., 2008; Kawase-Koga et al., 2009; Clovis et al., 2012).

Arognaute2, a member of the argonaute family of proteins, is the catalytically active component of the RISC that not only facilitates miRNA processing but also their regulatory actions on target mRNA transcripts (Hock and Meister, 2008). In a study by Diederichs and Haber, it was shown that overexpression of Ago2 results in increased miRNA biogenesis (Diederichs and Haber, 2007). Similar to genetic disruption of Dicer, Ago2 deletion results in embryonic lethality in mice, but conditional knock down of Ago2 reveals defects in neural tube closure and mispatterning of the anterior structure of the brain. Mouse embryonic fibroblast (MEFs) isolated from these mutant mice have reduced miRNA expression, which can be reversed by Ago2 expression (Morita et al., 2007). These findings highlight the importance of Ago2 in neuronal differentiation, brain morphogenesis, and development (Liu et al., 2004; Morita et al., 2007).

Schratt et al. found that the brain-specific miRNA, miR-134, is localized to the synaptodendritic compartment and negatively regulates the size of dendritic spines (Schratt et al., 2006). This action of miR-134 occurs through its inhibitory action on lim1 kinase expression. Another brain-enriched miRNA, miR-124, has been shown to play a critical role in the transition of progenitor neuronal cells to adult neurons by inhibiting networks of non-neuronal genes, thereby facilitating the expression of the neuronal identity (Conaco et al., 2006; Makeyev et al., 2007). Aizawa and colleagues examined the effects of double deletion of miR-9-2 and miR-9-3 on brain development in mice (Shibata et al., 2008, 2011). They found that these miR-9 family members regulate the proliferation and differentiation of neural progenitor cells in telencephalon through inhibitory actions on regulator proteins important for neurogenesis, including the homeobox protein Meis2 and the transcription factor Forkhead box protein G1 (FOXG1) (Shibata et al., 2008, 2011). Other miRNAs shown to regulate neuronal lineage commitment include members of the let-7 family and miR-125b (Leucht et al., 2008; Rybak et al., 2008). More recently, hippocampus-expressed miRNAs such as miR-134 and miR-34 have been shown to target the deacetylase sirtuin-1 (SIRT1) and thereby influence learning and memory processes (Gao et al., 2010; Zovoilis et al., 2011). In addition to their role in neuronal development and function, miRNAs may also play key role in neuronal dysfunction associated neurodegenerative diseases. For example, miR-34c has been implicated in the cognitive impairment associated with dementia. As discussed below, miRNAs have also been implicated in drug addiction, considered by many to be an aberrant form of learning and memory.

DRUG ADDICTION AND MicroRNAs

Addiction can be defined as compulsive drug use despite negative consequences. During the last decade, multiple cellular and molecular studies have revealed significant convergence between the actions of drugs of abuse in the brain that drive the development of addiction and the molecular processes involved in learning and memory. Indeed, addiction is often conceptualized as a disorder of synaptic plasticity, and hence the cellular and molecular mechanisms involved in learning-associated synaptic plasticity and concomitant remodeling of neuronal circuits may provide an important heuristic framework to investigate the addiction process.

In a study by Schaefer et al. it was shown that cocaine-induced robust alterations in the expression of a wide-range of miRNAs in the striatum, a key brain site involved in addiction. Indeed, a subset of these miRNAs whose expression was impacted by cocaine were shown to regulate the expression levels of a wide-range of genes known to influence the motivational properties of cocaine, including *Bdnf*, *FosB* (*FBJ murine osteosarcoma viral oncogene homolog B*), and *Cdk5r1* (cyclin-dependent kinase 5 activator 1). In the same study, the effects on cocaine reinforcement of selectively ablating Ago2, the catalytic component of RISC involved in transducing the inhibitory actions of miRNAs on their target transcripts, was assessed. Specifically, Schaefer et al. investigated the effects knocking down Ago2 in medium spiny neurons (MSNs) of the striatum that express the dopamine D2 receptor (D2R) (Schaefer et al., 2010). Disruption of Ago2 in D2R MSNs resulted in dramatically reduced conditioned rewarding effects of cocaine in mice, reflected in attenuated cocaine-induced conditioned place preference (CPP). More importantly, the Ago2-D2R mutant mice also demonstrated reduced intravenous cocaine self-administration behavior across a wide-range of cocaine doses (Schaefer et al., 2010). Such downward shifts in the cocaine dose-response curve are interpreted as reduced motivation to consume the drug. Finally, Ago2 ablation in D2R MSNs dramatically decreased miRNA expression and activity in striatum. Hence, as cocaine self-administration behavior is considered the most direct measure of drug reinforcement in laboratory animals, these data provide compelling support for a key role for Ago2, and by extension miRNAs, in striatal MSNs in regulating the reinforcing properties of cocaine that drive the development of addiction (Schaefer et al., 2010).

Another interesting study performed by Eipper-Mains et al. (2011) links cocaine exposure to Ago2 induction (Eipper-Mains et al., 2011). Characterization of the subcellular fractions of the striatum shows that Ago2 is localized in synapses and is cocaine-responsive. Specifically, chronic cocaine exposure resulted in increased Ago2 mRNA and protein in the striatum, and concomitantly altered miRNA expression levels. This increase in Ago2 protein was associated with postsynaptic densities (PSDs) in striatum but not in medial prefrontal cortex (mPFC). Intriguingly, a large number of cocaine-responsive miRNAs identified so far (miR-8 family, miR-145, miR-451) can putatively target genes implicated in addiction, including TrkB receptor, which transduces the actions of BDNF in brain and play a crucial role in activity-dependent synaptic plasticity.

Chandrasekar and Dreyer identified another set of miRNAs (miR-181a, let-7d, and miR-124) whose expression is sensitive to cocaine (Chandrasekar and Dreyer, 2009). They found that chronic cocaine administration suppressed the expression of miR-124 and let-7d, but induced miR-181a in the mesolimbic dopaminergic system. The critical role of the mesolimbic dopaminergic system in addiction is well established (Koob and Volkow, 2010). *In situ* hybridization confirmed that the alterations in the expression of these miRNAs occurred in brain regions related to reward and memory. Further, *in vitro* overexpression of these miRNAs modulated the expression levels of proteins like BDNF and the dopamine D3 receptor, which have been heavily implicated in drug addiction (Heidbreder et al., 2005; Ghitza et al., 2010). In a subsequent study the same group also showed that *in vivo* modulation of these miRNAs in ventral striatum (nucleus accumbens) affects cocaine-induced place conditioning (Chandrasekar and Dreyer, 2011). These data show that cocaine can impact the expression of a range of different miRNAs depending on treatment and testing context, and support an important role for such miRNAs and their targeted mRNA transcripts in the development of drug addiction.

Alterations in dopamine signaling can lead to long-lasting neuronal adaptations that result in decreased or increased propensity for drug use. One of the proposed mechanism by which this can occur is dopamine transmission-induced alterations in the expression and subunit composition of AMPA receptors (Wolf, 2010). AMPA receptors are postsynaptic glutamate gated ion channels that mediate excitatory neurotransmission in the central nervous system. As such, AMPA receptors are core regulators of synaptic plasticity and activity-dependent remodeling of brain circuitries (Du et al., 2004; Haas et al., 2006). In a recent study by Saba et al. it was found that miR-181a expression in nucleus accumbens was increased by dopamine-mediated transmission and by the psychomotor stimulant drugs cocaine and amphetamines (Saba et al., 2012). Moreover, miR-181a was shown to repress GluA2-AMPA receptor subunit expression, and thereby modulate the magnitude of AMPA receptor clustering. Hence, miR-181a may be a key miRNA involved in drug-induced remodeling of the nucleus accumbens and greater striatal complex in response to drug exposure, thereby driving regulating the emergence of addiction. Recent evidence suggests that miRNAs also play a key role in the actions of other classes of addictive drugs, including nicotine, alcohol, and opiates; for recent review and detailed table describing specific miRNAs see Im and Kenny (2012).

THE miR-212/132 CLUSTER

The miR-132/miR-212 family of miRNAs was first identified in a genome wide search for genes responsive to the transcription factor cAMP response element binding protein (CREB) using an approach termed Serial Analysis of chromatin occupancy (SACO) (Impey et al., 2004). This family of miRNAs is highly conserved in vertebrates, is transcribed as a polycistronic primary transcript, and is highly enriched in the mature neurons of the forebrain (Marson et al., 2008; Hansen et al., 2010). Analysis of the promoter for this miRNA gene cluster reveals the presence of multiple

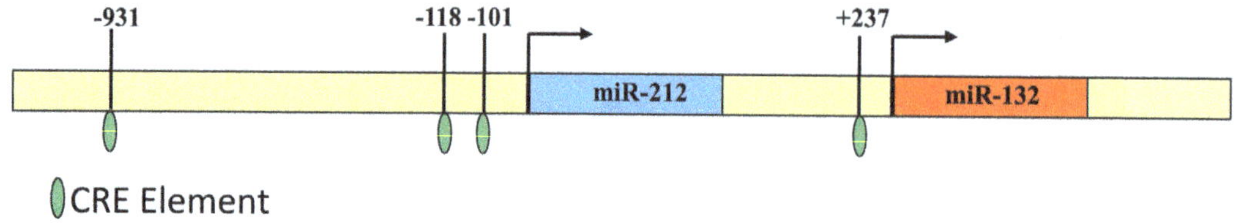

FIGURE 1 | The miR-212/132 gene cluster is located on chromosome 17 in humans, 10 in rats, and 11 in mouse. Shown are mouse/human miR-212 and miR-132 genes, with locations of CRE elements through which CREB can stimulate miR-212 and miR-132 transcription.

cAMP response element (CRE) sites and experimental evidence verifies that these miRNAs are indeed CREB inducible (Vo et al., 2005); (see **Figure 1**) Recent studies from Remenyi et al. have shown that this gene cluster in fact produces four mature miRNAs, namely miR-132, miR-132*, miR-212, and miR-212*, where miR-132* and miR-212* are encoded by the same primary transcript, but on the opposite strand, as the miR-132 and miR-212 miRNAs, respectively (Remenyi et al., 2010). Moreover, each of these four miRNAs likely have their own unique set of target mRNA transcripts. Intriguingly, even though these four miRNAs are transcribed in equal measure (by virtue of all being encoded in the same primary transcript), their relative abundance varies dramatically within various cell types including neurons, with miR-132 being far more abundant than the other three transcripts (Remenyi et al., 2010). Hence, it is likely that as yet uncharacterized mechanisms are involved in preferentially stabilizing miR-132 levels, and/or destabilizing miR-132*, miR-212, and miR-212*.

A series of studies in the last few years have demonstrated the importance of miR-132 cluster in neuronal morphogenesis and in regulating synaptic plasticity. In particular, miR-132 has been shown to increase dendritic spine complexity in both immature cortical and hippocampal neurons in part by translational inhibition of p250GAP. As p250GAP is a Rho-Rac family GTPase activating protein, this finding highlights a role for Rho, and also transducers downstream of Rac-GTPases such as PAK, in the effects of miR-132 on activity-dependent neuronal remodeling (Wayman et al., 2008; Hansen et al., 2010; Magill et al., 2010).

COCAINE INTAKE AND miR-212

Two recent studies from our group have identified a key role for miR-212, also encoded by the miR-212/132 gene cluster, in regulating compulsive-like cocaine intake in rats (Hollander et al., 2010; Im et al., 2010). As described above, the striatum is a key brain region that regulates compulsive cocaine use. The first study showed that in rats with extended access to cocaine (6 h per day) there is a ~1.75-fold increase in both striatal miR-212 and miR-132 levels (Hollander et al., 2010). Similar increases in expression were not detected in rats that received non-contingent cocaine infusions time-locked to rats that volitionally consumed cocaine, or in rats with restricted access to cocaine (1 h per day). Further, lentivirus-mediated overexpression of miR-212 in the dorsal striatum resulted in a remarkable decrease in cocaine intake in the extended access rats compared to vector control, but overexpression did not alter cocaine intake in rats with restricted drug access (**Figure 2**). The decreased cocaine intake is related to a profound decrease in the motivational properties of the drug, as reflected by a large downward shift in the cocaine dose-response curve in the same animals. Conversely, inhibition of miR-212 signaling in the striatum, achieved by infusion of an antisense oligonucleotide, dramatically increased the motivational properties of cocaine in rats with extended, but not restricted, access to the drug (**Figure 2**). These data suggest that intrinsic or drug-induce alterations in the expression or activity of striatal miR-212 may influence vulnerability to addiction in human cocaine users.

miR-212 REGULATES COCAINE INTAKE THROUGH STRIATAL CREB SIGNALING

As noted above, expression of miR-212 is regulated by CREB. In many cases, miRNAs have been shown to influence signaling cascades that increase their expression and further modify the activity those cascades through positive or negative feedback mechanisms (Tsang et al., 2007). As CREB overexpression in ventral striatum is known to diminish the motivational properties of cocaine (Carlezon et al., 1998), we tested the hypothesis that miR-212 may regulate cocaine intake in extended access rats by amplifying striatal CREB activity through positive feedback mechanisms. Consistent with a profound stimulatory effect of miR-212 on CREB in cultured cells *in vitro*, we found that levels of CREB that was phosphorylated at serine 133 (i.e., activated CREB) was significantly increased (Hollander et al., 2010). Furthermore, forskolin-stimulated expression of the CREB-responsive gene *fos* was also increased by miR-212, as was the activity of a luciferase-based CREB reporter construct (CRE-containing element from promoter of EVX-1). Dominant negative or phosphorylation-deficient mutant forms of CREB attenuated these stimulatory effects of miR-212 on CREB signaling. More importantly, we also found that miR-212 amplified CREB signaling in the striatum *in vivo*. Specifically, we found that rats with extended access to cocaine showed increased expression of the CREB-responsive gene *Nurr1*, and that expression levels were greatly increased by miR-212 overexpression in striatum (Hollander et al., 2010).

These findings identify miR-212 as a novel cocaine-responsive gene that is up regulated in the striatum in response to cocaine overconsumption that serves to promote CREB activity through positive feedback and thereby attenuate the motivational properties of the drug. Based on these findings, we next investigated the mechanisms by which miR-212 may amplify CREB signaling. We found that miR-212 increases activity-dependent production of cAMP by sensitizing adenylyl cyclase activity. This stimulatory

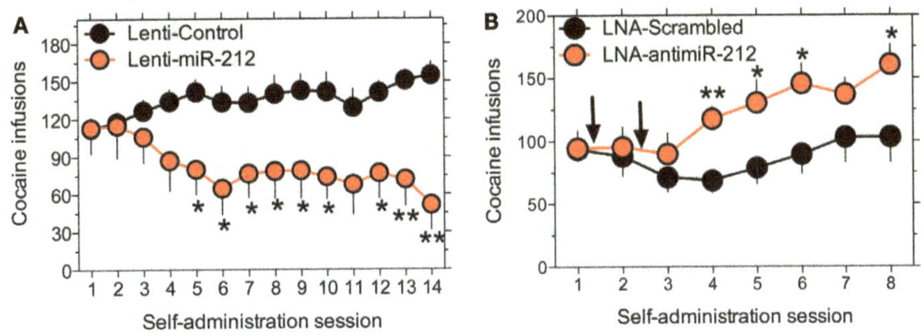

FIGURE 2 | Overexpression of miR-212 in striatum reverses the motivational properties of cocaine in rats with extended but not restricted access to cocaine. (A) Striatal miR-212 overexpression reverses the long-term trajectory of cocaine-taking behavior in rats with extended access. **(B)** Disruption of miR-212 signaling in striatum, achieved by local infusion of a locked nucleic acid (LNA) modified antisense oligonucleotide against miR-212 (LNA-antimiR-212) increases cocaine intake in extended access. Reproduced with permission from (Hollander et al., 2010).

action on adenylyl cyclase results in accumulation of phosphorylated CREB and increased activity of the core CREB co-activators CREB-regulated transcription co-activator-1 and -2 (CRTC1 and CRTC2), also known as TORC1 and TORC2. Further investigation of the mechanism by which miR-212 enhances CREB signaling revealed that the kinase Raf1 was activated by miR-212, and was found to play a key role in sensitizing adenylyl cyclase activity. Finally, computational and biochemical analysis showed that Sprouty-related EVH1 domain-containing protein 1 (SPRED1), a known negative regulator of Raf1 signaling, is a miR-212 target mRNA transcript and SPRED1 repression by miR-212 contributes to its stimulatory effects on Raf1 and CREB activity (Hollander et al., 2010).

To investigate the functional relevance of miR-212-induced amplification of CREB activity *in vivo* on the suppressive effects of this miRNA on cocaine intake, we examined the effects of overexpressing the CREB co-activator CRTC1 (TORC1) on cocaine intake in rats with restricted or extended cocaine access. It is known that CRTC overexpression increases CREB activity and that miR-212 increases CRTC1 expression (Hollander et al., 2010). Consistent with an important role for striatal CREB signaling in attenuating the motivational properties of cocaine, we found that striatal TORC1 overexpression decreased cocaine intake in extended but not restricted access rats. These findings support the hypothesis that miR-212 controls cocaine intake at least in part by amplifying the CREB-TORC signaling axis in striatum. Moreover, these findings provide compelling support for a key role for miR-212 in regulating the development of compulsive drug taking in rats, and perhaps in influencing vulnerability to cocaine addiction in human drug users.

miR-212 ALSO REGULATES COCAINE INTAKE THROUGH STRIATAL MeCP2

Considering that miR-212 expression levels may play a key role in regulating vulnerability to cocaine addiction, we next investigated the mechanisms by which baseline and cocaine-induced increases in striatal miR-212 levels are regulated. Interestingly, sequence analysis of the miR-212/132 gene cluster reveals that it is located in a CpG enriched region, which can serve as substrate for DNA methylation and gene regulation. Methyl CpG binding protein 2 (MeCP2) is known to bind to methylated DNA and can act as a gene repressor by recruiting other chromatin remodeling proteins that combine to form the so-called repressor complex (Guy et al., 2011). Based on these observations, we hypothesized that MeCP2 may regulate baseline and cocaine-induced changes in miR-212 expression in striatum and thereby influence cocaine-taking behavior. Consistent with this hypothesis, *in vitro* studies showed that knockdown of MeCP2 increased miR-212 (and miR-132) expression in cultured cells (Im et al., 2010). Similarly, pharmacologically induced disruption of DNA methyltransferase activity, which would be expected to attenuate the inhibitory activity of MeCP2 on gene expression, also increased miR-212/132 levels. Furthermore, we found that knockdown of striatal MeCP2 expression, achieved by virus-mediated delivery of a short hairpin interfering RNA (shRNA) against MeCP2, resulted in profoundly decreased cocaine intake in rats with extended but not restricted access to cocaine (**Figure 3**). Knockdown of striatal MeCP2 dramatically increased the stimulatory effects of self-administered cocaine on striatal miR-212 expression in rats with extended but not restricted access to the drug. More importantly, disruption of striatal miR-212 signaling, achieved by striatal infusion of an antisense oligonucleotide, reversed the inhibitory effects of MeCP2 knockdown on cocaine intake in extended access rats (Im et al., 2010). These findings are consistent with an inhibitory effect of MeCP2 on miR-212 expression, suggesting that MeCP2 acts as a pro-addiction transcriptional repressor that, by attenuating miR-212 expression in response to cocaine, increases vulnerability to addiction.

Intriguingly, miR-132 was previously shown to repress the expression of MeCP2 through direct interaction with the transcript 3′UTR (Klein et al., 2007). Moreover, as miR-132 and miR-212 share the same seed region, this suggests that miR-212 may similarly repress MeCP2. Based on these observations, we hypothesized that in addition to the inhibitory effects of MeCP2 on miR-212 expression described above, MeCP2 levels in turn may be repressed by miR-212. In other words, miR-212 and MeCP2 may be locked in a homeostatic relationship that serves to control miR-212 expression level and thereby

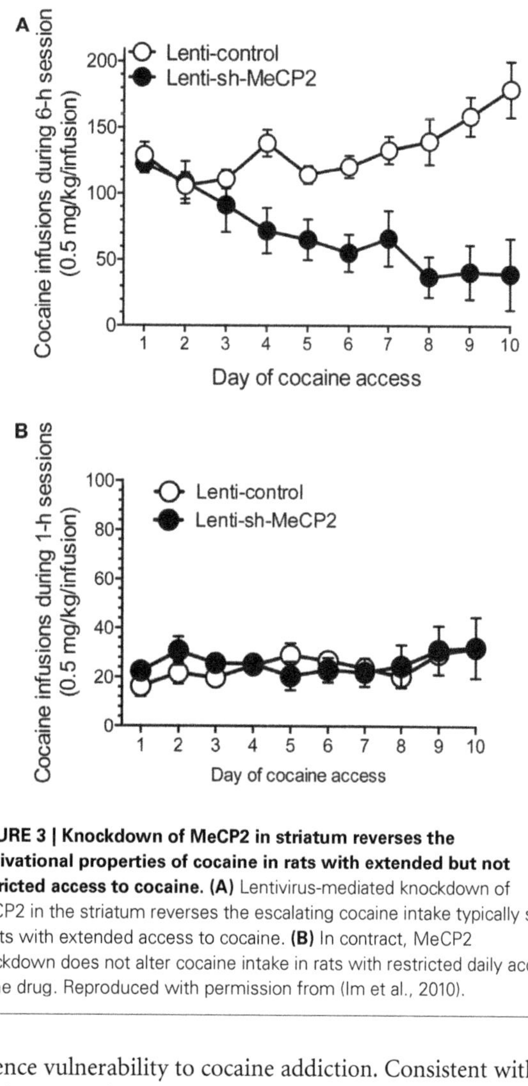

FIGURE 3 | Knockdown of MeCP2 in striatum reverses the motivational properties of cocaine in rats with extended but not restricted access to cocaine. (A) Lentivirus-mediated knockdown of MeCP2 in the striatum reverses the escalating cocaine intake typically seen in rats with extended access to cocaine. **(B)** In contract, MeCP2 knockdown does not alter cocaine intake in rats with restricted daily access to the drug. Reproduced with permission from (Im et al., 2010).

influence vulnerability to cocaine addiction. Consistent with this hypothesis, we found that miR-212 overexpression profoundly decreased MeCP2 expression in cultured cells and in the striatum *in vivo* (Im et al., 2010). Hence, homeostatic interactions between miR-212 and MeCP2 may determine vulnerability to cocaine addiction.

ROLE FOR BDNF IN REGULATING THE ACTIONS OF STRIATAL miR-212 ON COCAINE INTAKE

It has been reported that the levels of MeCP2 are closely related to those of, BDNF (Chang et al., 2006). However, the complex mechanisms by which MeCP2 regulates BDNF levels remain unclear. BDNF in the striatum is known to increase the motivational properties of cocaine (Horger et al., 1999; Schoenbaum et al., 2007). We therefore hypothesized that miR-212-MeCP2 interactions may regulate cocaine intake by influencing levels of BDNF in striatum. We observed that virus-mediated MeCP2 knockdown or miR-212 expression (which decreases MeCP2 levels) in striatum reduced BDNF expression. Moreover, virus-mediated increases in BDNF expression in striatum increased cocaine intake in rats with extended but not restricted access. Conversely, disruption of striatal BDNF signaling using a neutralizing antibody reduced cocaine intake in extended but restricted access rats (Im et al., 2010). These findings suggest that miR-212-MeCP2 interactions may determine expression levels of BDNF in striatum, which in turn regulates the motivational properties of cocaine.

NON-NEURONAL ROLES OF miR-212

Besides playing a critical role in drug-induced neuroplasticity relevant to addiction, there is emerging evidence that miR-212 is also involved in a host of other biological and pathophysiological processes. Indeed, miR-212 expression is deregulated in various cancers and its expression has been correlated to disease progression. In pancreatic carcinomas it has been shown that miR-212 targets the tumor suppressor retinoblastoma (Rb1) (Park et al., 2011), whereas the methyl binding protein (MeCP2) seems to be the main target in some of the gastric tumors (Wada et al., 2010). Incoronato et al. showed that miR-212 targets phosphoprotein enriched in diabetes (PED), a wide spectrum anti-apoptotic protein, and thereby plays an important role in tumor suppression (Incoronato et al., 2010). In a follow up study the same group also demonstrated that the expression on miR-212 in lung carcinomas is regulated by histone modifications (Incoronato et al., 2011). This suggests that epigenetic mechanisms may play an important role in regulating miRNA expression in different cancers and other biological processes.

Besides cancer, miR-212 has also been implicated in regulating organogenesis by playing a key role in modulating epithelial stromal interactions (Ucar et al., 2010). In addition, miR-212 expression can be regulated by various hormones, adding another layer of complexity to their regulation and role in development and disease (Godoy et al., 2011). Studies from Turrini et al. reveal that miR-212 may mediate drug resistance by targeting the ABC efflux transporter (Turrini et al., 2012). Two recent reports implicate the importance of the miR-132/212 family in cardiovascular development and disorders. In the first study, smRNAs deep sequencing analysis in vascular smooth muscle cells show that the miR-132/miR-212 cluster is induced by the hormone angiotensin II and by targeting PTEN, increases the expression of the gene MCP1 (Monocyte chemotactic protein 1), a key regulator of cardiovascular disorders (Jin et al., 2012). In the other study, Ucar et al. demonstrate that these miRNAs activate calcineurin signaling in cardiomyocytes by targeting the transcription factor Foxo3, and thus play an important role in cardiac hypertrophy (Ucar et al., 2012).

CONCLUSION

Taken together, these studies highlight the fact that miR-212 plays a critical role in fine-tuning transcriptional and neuroplastic responses to drugs of abuse. Specifically, we found that miR-212 can control cocaine intake through two complementary mechanisms: amplifying CREB signaling and reducing MeCP2/BDNF transmission in striatum.

Since miR-212 and miR-132 share the same seed region it is widely believed that they target the same mRNAs. However, only a few putative miR-212/132 targets have been verified experimentally, which include MeCP2, Rb1and HB-EGF. There is increasing evidence available now showing that the 5′ and 3′ regions of the miRNAs can form the basis of differential target recognition despite having the identical seed region (Brennecke et al., 2005; Jalvy-Delvaille et al., 2012). There is also a possibility that differential expression or availability of these members can also regulate gene expression in a differential manner. Future studies in this respect could further help in improving our understanding of how miR-212 and miR-132 regulate different neuronal and non-neuronal functions or if these two miRNAs are functionally redundant? More generally, these findings highlight the novel role for miRNAs in addiction, and suggest that other ncRNAs may also play important roles in the disorder.

ACKNOWLEDGMENTS

Supported by a grant from the National Institute on Drug Abuse (DA025983 to Paul J. Kenny). This is manuscript number 21989 from The Scripps Research Institute.

REFERENCES

1. Bak, M., Silahtaroglu, A., Moller, M., Christensen, M., Rath, M. F., Skryabin, B., et al. (2008). MicroRNA expression in the adult mouse central nervous system. *RNA* 14, 432–444.
2. Bartel, D. P. (2004). MicroRNAs: genomics, biogenesis, mechanism, and function. *Cell* 116, 281–297.
3. Bernstein, E., Kim, S. Y., Carmell, M. A., Murchison, E. P., Alcorn, H., Li, M. Z., et al. (2003). Dicer is essential for mouse development. *Nat. Genet.* 35, 215–217.
4. Brennecke, J., Stark, A., Russell, R. B., and Cohen, S. M. (2005). Principles of microRNA-target recognition. *PLoS Biol.* 3:e85. doi:10.1371/journal.pbio.0030085
5. Carlezon, W. A. Jr., Thome, J., Olson, V. G., Lane-Ladd, S. B., Brodkin, E. S., Hiroi, N., et al. (1998). Regulation of cocaine reward by CREB. *Science* 282, 2272–2275.
6. Chandrasekar, V., and Dreyer, J. L. (2009). microRNAs miR-124, let- 7d and miR-181a regulate cocaine- induced plasticity. *Mol. Cell. Neu- rosci.* 42, 350–362.
7. Chandrasekar, V., and Dreyer, J. L. (2011). Regulation of MiR-124, Let- 7d, and MiR-181a in the accum- bens affects the expression, extinc- tion, and reinstatement of cocaine- induced conditioned place prefer- ence. *Neuropsychopharmacology* 36, 1149–1164.
8. Chang, Q., Khare, G., Dani, V., Nelson, S., and Jaenisch, R. (2006). The disease progression of Mecp2 mutant mice is affected by the level of BDNF expression. *Neuron* 49, 341–348.
9. Clovis, Y. M., Enard, W., Marinaro, F., Huttner, W. B., and De Pietri Tonelli, D. (2012). Convergent repression of Foxp2 31 UTR by miR-9 and miR- 132 in embryonic mouse neocor- tex: implications for radial migra- tion of neurons. *Development* 139, 3332–3342.
10. Conaco, C., Otto, S., Han, J. J., and Mandel, G. (2006). Recip- rocal actions of REST and a microRNA promote neuronal iden- tity. *Proc. Natl. Acad. Sci. U.S.A.* 103, 2422–2427.
11. De Pietri Tonelli, D., Pulvers, J. N., Haffner, C., Murchison, E. P., Han- non, G. J., and Huttner, W. B. (2008). miRNAs are essential for survival and differentiation of newborn neu- rons but not for expansion of neural progenitors during early neurogene- sis in the mouse embryonic neocor- tex. *Development* 135, 3911–3921.
12. Diederichs, S., and Haber, D. A. (2007). Dual role for argonautes in microRNA processing and posttranscriptional regulation of microRNA expression. *Cell* 131, 1097–1108.
13. Djebali, S., Davis, C. A., Merkel, A., Dobin, A., Lassmann, T., Mortazavi, A., et al. (2012). Landscape of tran- scription in human cells. *Nature* 489, 101–108.
14. Du, J., Gray, N. A., Falke, C. A., Chen, W., Yuan, P., Szabo, S. T., et al. (2004). Modulation of synaptic plas- ticity by antimanic agents: the role of AMPA glutamate receptor subunit 1 synaptic expression. *J. Neurosci.* 24, 6578–6589.
15. Eipper-Mains, J. E., Kiraly, D. D., Palakodeti, D., Mains, R. E., Eipper, B. A., and Graveley, B. R. (2011). microRNA-Seq reveals cocaine- regulated expression of striatal microRNAs. *RNA* 17, 1529–1543.
16. Elcheva, I., Goswami, S., Noubissi, F. K., and Spiegelman, V. S. (2009). CRD-BP protects the coding region of betaTrCP1 mRNA from miR-183- mediated degradation. *Mol. Cell* 35, 240–246.
17. Esteller, M. (2011). Non-coding RNAs in human disease. *Nat. Rev. Genet.* 12, 861–874.
18. Gao, J., Wang, W. Y., Mao, Y. W., Graff, J., Guan, J. S., Pan, L., et al. (2010). A novel pathway regulates mem- ory and plasticity via SIRT1 and miR-134. *Nature* 466, 1105–1109.
19. Ghitza, U. E., Zhai, H., Wu, P., Airavaara, M., Shaham, Y., and Lu, L. (2010). Role of BDNF and GDNF in drug reward and relapse: a review. *Neu- rosci. Biobehav. Rev.* 35, 157–171.
20. Godoy, J., Nishimura, M., and Webster, N. J. (2011). Gonadotropin-releasing hormone induces miR-132 and miR-212 to regulate cellular morphology and migration in immortalized LbetaT2 pituitary gonadotrope cells. *Mol. Endocrinol.* 25, 810–820.
21. Grishok, A., Pasquinelli, A. E., Conte, D., Li, N., Parrish, S., Ha, I., et al. (2001). Genes and mechanisms related to RNA interference regulate expression of the small temporal RNAs that control *C. elegans* developmen- tal timing. *Cell* 106, 23–34.
22. Guy, J., Cheval, H., Selfridge, J., and Bird, A. (2011). The role of MeCP2 in the brain. *Annu. Rev. Cell Dev. Biol.* 27, 631–652.
23. Haas, K., Li, J., and Cline, H. T. (2006). AMPA receptors regu- late experience-dependent dendritic arbor growth in vivo. *Proc. Natl. Acad. Sci. U.S.A.* 103, 12127–12131.
24. Hansen, K. F., Sakamoto, K., Way- man, G. A., Impey, S., and Obri- etan, K. (2010). Transgenic miR132 alters neuronal spine density and impairs novel object recognition memory. *PLoS ONE* 5:e15497. doi:10.1371/journal.pone.0015497
25. Heidbreder, C. A., Gardner, E. L., Xi, Z. X., Thanos, P. K., Mugnaini, M., Hagan, J. J., et al. (2005). The role of central dopamine D3 receptors in drug addiction: a review of pharma- cological evidence. *Brain Res. Brain Res. Rev.* 49, 77–105.
26. Heimberg, A. M., Sempere, L. F., Moy, V. N., Donoghue, P. C., and Peterson, K. J. (2008). MicroRNAs and the advent of vertebrate morpholog- ical complexity. *Proc. Natl. Acad. Sci. U.S.A.* 105, 2946–2950.
27. Hock, J., and Meister, G. (2008). The Argonaute protein family. *Genome Biol.* 9, 210.
28. Hollander, J. A., Im, H. I., Amelio, A. L., Kocerha, J., Bali, P., Lu, Q., et al. (2010). Striatal microRNA controls cocaine intake through CREB signalling. *Nature* 466, 197–202.
29. Horger, B. A., Iyasere, C. A., Berhow, M. T., Messer, C. J., Nestler, E. J., and Taylor, J. R. (1999). Enhancement of locomotor activity and conditioned reward to cocaine by brain-derived neurotrophic factor. *J. Neurosci.* 19, 4110–4122.
30. Im, H. I., Hollander, J. A., Bali, P., and Kenny, P. J. (2010). MeCP2 controls BDNF expression and cocaine intake through homeostatic interactions with microRNA-212. *Nat. Neurosci.* 13, 1120–1127.
31. Im, H. I., and Kenny, P. J. (2012). MicroRNAs in neuronal function and dysfunction. *Trends Neurosci.* 35, 325–334.
32. Impey, S., Mccorkle, S. R., Cha-Molstad, H., Dwyer, J. M., Yochum, G. S., Boss, J. M., et al. (2004). Defin- ing the CREB regulon: a genome- wide analysis of transcription fac- tor regulatory regions. *Cell* 119, 1041–1054.
33. Incoronato, M., Garofalo, M., Urso, L., Romano, G., Quintavalle, C., Zanca, C., et al. (2010). miR-212 increases tumor necrosis factor- related apoptosis-inducing ligand sensitivity in non-small cell lung cancer by targeting the antiapop- totic protein PED. *Cancer Res.* 70, 3638–3646.
34. Incoronato, M., Urso, L., Portela, A., Laukkanen, M. O., Soini, Y., Quin- tavalle, C., et al. (2011). Epigenetic regulation of miR-212 expression in lung cancer. *PLoS ONE* 6:e27722. doi:10.1371/journal.pone.0027722
35. Jalvy-Delvaille, S., Maurel, M., Majo, V., Pierre, N., Chabas, S., Combe, C., et al. (2012). Molecular basis of differential target regulation by miR-96 and miR-182: the Glypican- 3 as a model. *Nucleic Acids Res.* 40, 1356–1365.
36. Jin, W., Reddy, M. A., Chen, Z., Putta, S., Lanting, L., Kato, M., et al. (2012). Small RNA sequencing reveals microRNAs that modulate angiotensin II effects in vascular smooth muscle cells. *J. Biol. Chem.* 287, 15672–15683.
37. Kanellopoulou, C., Muljo, S. A., Kung, A. L., Ganesan, S., Drapkin, R., Jenuwein, T., et al. (2005). Dicer- deficient mouse embryonic stem cells are defective in differentiation and centromeric silencing. *Genes Dev.* 19, 489–501.
38. Kawase-Koga, Y., Otaegi, G., and Sun, T. (2009). Different timings of Dicer deletion affect neurogenesis and gli- ogenesis in the developing mouse central nervous system. *Dev. Dyn.* 238, 2800–2812.
39. Klein, M. E., Lioy, D. T., Ma, L., Impey, S., Mandel, G., and Goodman, R. H. (2007). Homeostatic regulation of MeCP2 expression by a CREB- induced microRNA. *Nat. Neurosci.* 10, 1513–1514.
40. Koob, G. F., and Volkow, N. D. (2010). Neurocircuitry of addic- tion. *Neuropsychopharmacology* 35, 217–238.

41. Landgraf, P., Rusu, M., Sheridan, R., Sewer, A., Iovino, N., Aravin, A., et al. (2007). A mammalian microRNA expression atlas based on small RNA library sequencing. *Cell* 129, 1401–1414.
42. Lee, R. C., Feinbaum, R. L., and Ambros, V. (1993). The *C. elegans* heterochronic gene lin-4 encodes small RNAs with antisense complementar- ity to lin-14. *Cell* 75, 843–854.
43. Leucht, C., Stigloher, C., Wizenmann, A., Klafke, R., Folchert, A., and Bally-Cuif, L. (2008). MicroRNA-9 directs late organizer activity of the midbrain-hindbrain boundary. *Nat. Neurosci.* 11, 641–648.
44. Liu, J., Carmell, M. A., Rivas, F. V., Mars- den, C. G., Thomson, J. M., Song, J. J., et al. (2004). Argonaute2 is the cat- alytic engine of mammalian RNAi. *Science* 305, 1437–1441.
45. Magill, S. T., Cambronne, X. A., Luikart, B. W., Lioy, D. T., Leighton, B. H., Westbrook, G. L., et al. (2010). microRNA-132 regulates dendritic growth and arborization of newborn neurons in the adult hippocampus. *Proc. Natl. Acad. Sci. U.S.A.* 107, 20382–20387.
46. Majer, A., and Booth, S. A. (2010). Computational methodologies for studying non-coding RNAs relevant to central nervous system function and dysfunction. *Brain Res.* 1338, 131–145.
47. Makeyev, E. V., Zhang, J., Carrasco, M. A., and Maniatis, T. (2007). The MicroRNA miR-124 promotes neuronal differentiation by trigger- ing brain-specific alternative pre- mRNA splicing. *Mol. Cell* 27, 435–448.
48. Marson, A., Levine, S. S., Cole, M. F., Frampton, G. M., Brambrink, T., Johnstone, S., et al. (2008). Con- necting microRNA genes to the core transcriptional regulatory circuitry of embryonic stem cells. *Cell* 134, 521–533.
49. Mattick, J. S., and Makunin, I. V. (2006). Non-coding RNA. *Hum. Mol. Genet.* 15, R17–R29.
50. Mercer, T. R., Dinger, M. E., Sunkin, S. M., Mehler, M. F., and Mattick, J. S. (2008). Specific expression of long noncoding RNAs in the mouse brain. *Proc. Natl. Acad. Sci. U.S.A.* 105, 716–721.
51. Miska, E. A., Alvarez-Saavedra, E., Townsend, M., Yoshii, A., Sestan, N., Rakic, P., et al. (2004). Microarray analysis of microRNA expression in the developing mammalian brain. *Genome Biol.* 5, R68.
52. Morita, S., Horii, T., Kimura, M., Goto, Y., Ochiya, T., and Hatada, I. (2007). One Argonaute fam- ily member, Eif2c2 (Ago2), is essential for development and appears not to be involved in DNA methylation. *Genomics* 89, 687–696.
53. Murchison, E. P., Partridge, J. F., Tam, O. H., Cheloufi, S., and Hannon, G. J. (2005). Characterization of Dicer- deficient murine embryonic stem cells. *Proc. Natl. Acad. Sci. U.S.A.* 102, 12135–12140.
54. Orom, U. A., Nielsen, F. C., and Lund, A. H. (2008). MicroRNA-10a binds the 51 UTR of ribosomal protein mRNAs and enhances their translation. *Mol. Cell* 30, 460–471.
55. Orom, U. A., and Shiekhattar, R. (2011). Long non-coding RNAs and enhancers. *Curr. Opin. Genet. Dev.* 21, 194–198.
56. Park, J. K., Henry, J. C., Jiang, J., Esau, C., Gusev, Y., Lerner, M. R., et al. (2011). miR-132 and miR-212 are increased in pancreatic cancer and target the retinoblastoma tumor suppressor. *Biochem. Biophys. Res. Commun.* 406, 518–523.
57. Place, R. F., Li, L. C., Pookot, D., Noonan, E. J., and Dahiya, R. (2008). MicroRNA-373 induces expression of genes with com- plementary promoter sequences. *Proc. Natl. Acad. Sci. U.S.A.* 105, 1608–1613.
58. Remenyi, J., Hunter, C. J., Cole, C., Ando, H., Impey, S., Monk, C. E., et al. (2010). Regulation of the miR- 212/132 locus by MSK1 and CREB in response to neurotrophins. *Biochem. J.* 428, 281–291.
59. Rybak, A., Fuchs, H., Smirnova, L., Brandt, C., Pohl, E. E., Nitsch, R., et al. (2008). A feedback loop compris- ing lin-28 and let-7 controls pre-let- 7 maturation during neural stem- cell commitment. *Nat. Cell Biol.* 10, 987–993.
60. Saba, R., Storchel, P. H., Aksoy-Aksel, A., Kepura, F., Lippi, G., Plant, T. D., et al. (2012). Dopamine- regulated microRNA MiR-181a con- trols GluA2 surface expression in hippocampal neurons. *Mol. Cell. Biol.* 32, 619–632.
61. Schaefer, A., Im, H. I., Veno, M. T., Fowler, C. D., Min, A., Intra- tor, A., et al. (2010). Argonaute 2 in dopamine 2 receptor- expressing neurons regulates cocaine addiction. *J. Exp. Med.* 207, 1843–1851.
62. Schaefer, A., O'Carroll, D., Tan, C. L., Hillman, D., Sugimori, M., Llinas, R., et al. (2007). Cerebellar neurode- generation in the absence of microR- NAs. *J. Exp. Med.* 204, 1553–1558.
63. Schoenbaum, G., Stalnaker, T. A., and Shaham, Y. (2007). A role for BDNF in cocaine reward and relapse. *Nat. Neurosci.* 10, 935–936.
64. Schratt, G. M., Tuebing, F., Nigh, E. A., Kane, C. G., Sabatini, M. E., Kiebler, M., et al. (2006). A brain-specific microRNA regulates dendritic spine development. *Nature* 439, 283–289.
65. Shibata, M., Kurokawa, D., Nakao, H., Ohmura, T., and Aizawa, S. (2008). MicroRNA-9 modulates Cajal-Retzius cell differentiation by suppressing Foxg1 expression in mouse medial pallium. *J. Neurosci.* 28, 10415–10421.
66. Shibata, M., Nakao, H., Kiyonari, H., Abe, T., and Aizawa, S. (2011). MicroRNA-9 regulates neurogenesis in mouse telencephalon by target- ing multiple transcription factors. *J. Neurosci.* 31, 3407–3422.
67. Tsang, J., Zhu, J., and Van Oudenaar- den, A. (2007). MicroRNA-mediated feedback and feedforward loops are recurrent network motifs in mammals. *Mol. Cell* 26, 753–767.
68. Turrini, E., Haenisch, S., Laechelt, S., Diewock, T., Bruhn, O., and Cascorbi, I. (2012). MicroRNA pro- filing in K-562 cells under ima- tinib treatment: influence of miR- 212 and miR-328 on ABCG2 expres- sion. *Pharmacogenet. Genomics* 22, 198–205.
69. Ucar, A., Gupta, S. K., Fiedler, J., Erikci, E., Kardasinski, M., Batkai, S., et al. (2012). The miRNA-212/132 family regulates both cardiac hypertrophy and cardiomyocyte autophagy. *Nat. Commun.* 3, 1078.
70. Ucar, A.,Vafaizadeh,V., Jarry, H., Fiedler, J., Klemmt, P. A., Thum, T., et al. (2010). miR-212 and miR-132 are required for epithelial stromal interactions necessary for mouse mammary gland development. *Nat. Genet.* 42, 1101–1108.
71. Vasudevan, S., Tong, Y., and Steitz, J. A. (2007). Switching from repres- sion to activation: microRNAs can up-regulate translation. *Science* 318, 1931–1934.
72. Vo, N., Klein, M. E., Varlamova, O., Keller, D. M., Yamamoto, T., Goodman, R. H., et al. (2005). A cAMP-response element binding protein-induced microRNA reg- ulates neuronal morphogenesis. *Proc. Natl. Acad. Sci. U.S.A.* 102, 16426–16431.
73. Wada, R., Akiyama, Y., Hashimoto, Y., Fukamachi, H., and Yuasa, Y. (2010). miR-212 is downregu- lated and suppresses methyl-CpG- binding protein MeCP2 in human gastric cancer. *Int. J. Cancer* 127, 1106–1114.
74. Wayman, G. A., Davare, M., Ando, H., Fortin, D., Varlamova, O., Cheng, H. Y., et al. (2008). An activity-regulated microRNA controls dendritic plas- ticity by down-regulating p250GAP. *Proc. Natl. Acad. Sci. U.S.A.* 105, 9093–9098.
75. Wolf, M. E. (2010). The Bermuda Triangle of cocaine-induced neu- roadaptations. *Trends Neurosci.* 33, 391–398.
76. Yang, J. H., Shao, P., Zhou, H., Chen, Y. Q., and Qu, L. H. (2010). deepBase: a database for deeply annotating and mining deep sequencing data. *Nucleic Acids Res.* 38, D123–D130.
77. Zovoilis, A., Agbemenyah, H. Y., Agis- Balboa, R. C., Stilling, R. M., Edbauer, D., Rao, P., et al. (2011). microRNA-34c is a novel target to treat dementias. *EMBO J.* 30, 4299–4308.

20

Dyadic social interaction as an alternative reward to cocaine

Gerald Zernig[1,2]*, Kai K. Kummer[1] and Janine M. Prast[1]

[1] Experimental Psychiatry Unit, Department of General Psychiatry and Social Psychiatry, Innsbruck Medical University, Innsbruck, Austria
[2] Department of Psychology, Leopold-Franzens University of Innsbruck, Innsbruck, Austria

Edited by:
Hanna Pickard, University of Oxford, UK

Reviewed by:
Elio Acquas, Università degli Studi di Cagliari, Italy
Mark Andrew Smith, Davidson College, USA

***Correspondence:**
Gerald Zernig, Experimental Psychiatry Unit, Department of General Psychiatry and Social Psychiatry, Innsbruck Medical University, Innrain 66 a, Room 35-G1-010, A-6020 Innsbruck, Austria
e-mail: gerald.zernig@i-med.ac.at

Individuals suffering from substance use disorders often show severely impaired social interaction, preferring drugs of abuse to the contact with others. Their impaired social interaction is doubly harmful for them as (1) therapy itself is based and dependent on social interaction and as (2) social interaction is not available to them as an "alternative", i.e., non-drug reward, decreasing their motivation to stop drug use. We therefore developed an animal experimental model to investigate the neurobiology of dyadic social interaction- vs. cocaine reward. We took care to avoid: (a) engaging sexual attraction-related aspects of such a social interaction and (b) hierarchical difference as confounding stimuli. The cocaine- or social interaction stimulus was offered – in a mutually exclusive setting – within the confines of a conditioned place preference (CPP) apparatus. In our paradigm, only four 15-min episodes of social interaction proved sufficient to (i) switch the rats' preference from cocaine-associated contextual stimuli to social interaction CPP and (ii) inhibit the subsequent reacquisition/reexpression of cocaine CPP. This behavioral effect was paralleled by a reversal of brain activation (i.e., EGR1 expression) in the nucleus accumbens, the central and basolateral amygdala, and the ventral tegmental area. Of relevance for the psychotherapy of addictive disorders, the most rewarding sensory component of the composite stimulus "social interaction" was touch. To test our hypothesis that motivation is encoded in neuron ensembles dedicated to specific reward scenarios, we are currently (1) mapping the neural circuits involved in cocaine- vs. social-interaction reward and (2) adapting our paradigm for C57BL/6 mice to make use of the plethora of transgenic models available in this species.

Keywords: social interaction, cocaine, conditioned place preference, Sprague-Dawley rat, C57BL/6 mouse, substance use disorder

INTRODUCTION

Individuals suffering from substance use disorders often show severely impaired social interaction, preferring drugs of abuse to the contact with others. Their impaired social interaction is doubly harmful for them as (1) therapy itself is based and dependent on social interaction with their psychotherapist (1, 2), physician, case manager, etc., and as (2) social interaction is not available to them as an "alternative", i.e., non-drug reward, decreasing their motivation to stop drug use. We therefore developed an animal experimental model to investigate the neurobiology of dyadic social interaction (DSI)- vs. cocaine-reward. The results were very encouraging, robust, and have so far been demonstrated by three generations of experimenters comprising a total of seven individual experimenters (3–6): just four episodes of 15-min DSI with a weight- and sex-matched male conspecific were not only able to countercondition place preference from cocaine to this form of social interaction but, following a subsequent cocaine exposure, were able to inhibit the reacquisition of cocaine conditioned place preference (CPP) that regularly occurred if the rats' cocaine CPP was simply extinguished without social interaction counterconditioning (SIC). After the four DSI episodes, many animals even fully defended their DSI preference against the cocaine challenge (3). The behavioral reversal was paralleled by a DSI-mediated reversal in the cocaine CPP-induced activation (quantified by EGR1 expression) of several brain regions implicated in reward/reinforcement: the nucleus accumbens shell (AcbSh) and core (AcbC), the central (CeA) and basolateral (BLA) amygdala, and the ventral tegmental area (VTA). We are currently investigating which neuron type(s) in the accumbens mediate this effect and are validating our paradigm in C57BL/6 mice to benefit from transgenic methods for the neurobiological investigation of this therapeutically promising effect. Of note, impaired social interaction is also a hallmark of several other psychiatric disorders such as major depression, dysthymia, and autism spectrum disorders. We initially focused on cocaine as a prototypical drug of abuse and opine that our findings may well generalize to ethanol (alcohol) and opioids. In fact, time allowing, we intend to expand our paradigm to ethanol vs. social interaction. To conclude, a number of patients suffering from a variety of psychiatric disorders would profit from the societally beneficial investigation of the neurobiological basis of the shift of one's preference from a harmful stimulus to social interaction.

METHODS: OVERVIEW OF OUR BEHAVIORAL PARADIGM

In the operationalization of the beneficial effect of social interaction on drug craving, we took care (a) to avoid engaging sexual attraction-related aspects of such a social interaction by allowing only same-sex interaction between male conspecifics and (b) to avoid hierarchical difference as a confounding stimulus by allowing DSI only between weight-matched males. The cocaine- or social-interaction stimulus was offered – in a mutually exclusive setting – within the confines of a CPP apparatus. CPP (3–12) is a plausible measure of what humans may be able to report as "drug craving" (13), one of the most important determinants of drug lapse and relapse (14). Of note, CPP has also been demonstrated in humans (15).

In our paradigm, the animals receive an intraperitoneal (i.p.) injection of saline and are placed in the conditioning chamber, either alone (saline control, sal) or with another conspecific of the same-sex and weight (DSI) or receive an i.p. injection of 15 mg/kg cocaine (concentration refers to pure base) and are placed in the conditioning chamber alone (coc). Training- and test session length is always 900 s. Our paradigm comprises three different experimental approaches, ranked according to decreasing experimenter time requirement:

(1) **SIC effect on the reacquisition/reexpression of cocaine CPP**
This is the experiment in our paradigm that in our opinion has the highest face validity and translational promise for the human situation. It is also by far the most time consuming, requiring 24 days for completion [see fig. 1 of (3)]. Animals are first trained to acquire CPP for cocaine (coc) in an alternate-day design with four exposures to coc or saline (sal) each, with cocaine assigned to the initially non-preferred compartment. After the animal has acquired coc CPP, the preference for coc is extinguished by pairing the previously coc-associated compartment with sal too. Extinction is obtained and tested in four cycles, each consisting of sal conditioning – sal conditioning – CPP test (T1–T4). After T4, the animal is exposed to one more coc training session (arguably modeling a "freebie" in the human situation) and tested for reacquisition/reexpression of coc CPP 24 h later, i.e., in a cocaine-free state. In the SIC condition, after CPP for coc is established, the previously coc-paired compartment is paired with sal, and the previously sal-paired compartment is now paired with the usual i.p. sal injection followed by a DSI with a sex- and weight-matched male conspecific through cycles T1–T4, each cycle consisting of sal – DSI – CPP test. The final coc challenge (i.e., coc training) and the test of the reacquisition/rexpression of coc CPP is performed as described for the coc CPP extinction protocol.
In one special application of this experimental approach (10), we performed the experiment only to the end of the first reconditioning cycle, i.e., T1. At T1, the animal usually has lost its preference for coc, spending equal amounts of time in the previously coc-paired chamber (now sal-paired), and the DSI-paired chamber (previously paired with sal alone). We hypothesized that any compound that enhances this beneficial reversal from coc CPP to DSI CPP would produce an increased time in the DSI-associated chamber. The sigma1 receptor antagonist BD1047 did (10).

(2) **Concurrent CPP for social interaction vs. cocaine: a choice paradigm**
In a much less time-consuming experiment [total experiment time, 10 days, see fig. 1 of Ref. (3)], CPP for DSI and cocaine is acquired concurrently in an alternate-day stimulus exposure paradigm (9). It turned out that at a coc dose of 15 mg/kg i.p., CPP for coc and DSI is the same, resulting in no overall preference for either stimulus (9). By lesioning different brain regions, we could tip the CPP balance as if on a seesaw: lesioning the AcbC or BLA shifted net CPP toward social interaction, whereas lesioning the AcbSh shifted net CPP toward cocaine (9). As even the anatomically crude lesioning of whole brain regions produced such a dramatic effect on the net CPP preference, we expect this paradigm to yield data of extreme interest when applying double immunohistochemical methods (see Outlook, below). By manipulating the cocaine training dose, this paradigm also allows for a fully quantitative analysis of the preference shift. Our concurrent drug- vs. social-interaction paradigm has been confirmed and further validated with amphetamine by Bardo and colleagues (16).

(3) **CPP for either social interaction or cocaine**
The purest experimental approach with respect to the neurobiological investigation of the CPP induced by coc vs. DSI is, of course, to train and test the animals separately for the coc- or the DSI stimulus (12). The time requirement is 10 days [see fig. 1 of Ref. (3)], i.e., the same as for the concurrent CPP paradigm described under item 2, above. Bardo and coworkers have further validated our paradigm and have found that the length of exposure to DSI and the age of the animals are of great importance for successfully establishing DSI as a reward (16).
Thus, each of our three different experimental approaches yields answers to different questions as detailed below.

RESULTS: DYADIC SOCIAL INTERACTION vs. COCAINE: CHANGES IN CONDITIONED PLACE PREFERENCE AND REGIONAL BRAIN ACTIVITY AS QUANTIFIED BY EGR1 MAPPING

In our paradigm, just four 15-min episodes of social interaction with a weight- and sex-matched male rat not only reversed CPP from cocaine to this form of social interaction and inhibited the subsequent reacquisition/reexpression of cocaine CPP (3), but also reversed the cocaine-conditioning-induced activation, i.e., protein expression of the immediate early gene EGR1 (early growth response 1; also known as zif268), in the AcbSh and AcbC, the VTA, and the BLA and CeA (3, 6). The cocaine CPP-associated EGR1 expression reversal by social interaction was paralleled by an increase in pCREB (the phosphorylated form of cAMP response element binding protein) and a decrease in FosB/deltaFosB expression (5), echoing opposing roles of pCREB vs. deltaFosB in drug reward (17, 18). In a rat concurrent CPP paradigm, lesioning the AcbC, or the BLA tipped the balance toward the acquisition/expression of social interaction CPP, whereas AcbSh lesioning shifted the balance toward cocaine CPP (9), suggesting that the core is more important for acquisition/expression of drug reward and the shell for acquisition/expression of social interaction reward. Differential activation during acquisition/expression of CPP was also demonstrated (12) for the AcbC and prelimbic cortex (DSI CPP) and the granular and dorsal agranular insular cortex (cocaine CPP). The sensory component of the composite stimulus "social interaction" that contributed most to its rewarding effects was touch (taction), whereas crowding diminished social interaction reward (4). When we limited touch by separating the rats by "prison-type" steel bars, it still proved rewarding (4). Our findings were confirmed by Neisewander and colleagues using a steel mesh barrier (19). Increasing the weight of the social interaction partner (thus most likely increasing his physical dominance/hierarchical superiority) systematically decreased the rewarding effect of social interaction, more predictably for the smaller rat than for the bigger rat (4).

OUTLOOK: IDENTIFICATION OF THE INVOLVED NEURON ENSEMBLES BY DOUBLE IMMUNOCHEMISTRY

In our paradigm (3), DSI had the most pronounced effect on AcbSh and AcbC activation and on the activation of brain regions containing projection neurons to the accumbens. We therefore want to focus on the accumbens. The major output neurons of the nucleus accumbens, just like of the more dorsal parts of the striatum, are dynorphin/D1-dopamine-receptor-expressing medium spiny neurons (D1-MSNs, i.e., GABAergic projection neurons) and enkephalin/D2-expressing MSNs (D2-MSNs). The activity of these D1- and D2-MSNs is not only regulated by dopaminergic afferents from the VTA but also, directly and indirectly, by a number of different GABAergic interneurons (GAIs), i.e., parvalbumin-positive (PV-GAIs), NPY-positive GAIs (NPY-GAIs), calretinin-positive GAIs (CR-GAIs), by cholinergic interneurons (ChIs) (20–24), and by glutamatergic terminals from the medial prefrontal and orbital cortex and the amygdala (25–31). We intend to quantify the contribution of each of the neuron types described above by double immunohistochemistry for EGR1 and either dynorphin for D1-MSNs, enkephalin or the D2 dopamine receptor (D2DR) for D2-MSNs, parvalbumin (PV-GAIs; fast-spiking), neuropeptide Y (NPY-GAIs; prolonged plateau potential low threshold spiking GAIs, PLTS), calretinin (CR-GAIs), or choline acetyltransferase (ChAT; ChIs).

In order to make use of the plethora of transgenic models available in the mouse, we also intend to validate and optimize our behavioral paradigm in this species, i.e., in C57BL/6 mice. Experiments are ongoing and promising.

DISCUSSION

Our findings are part of an emerging wealth of data on social interaction and animal experimental measures of substance use disorders, generated by a number of independent groups over the last 6 years (16, 19, 32–34). In contrast to Neisewander and colleagues (32) who showed that social interaction, if offered together with the drug stimulus, actually enhanced drug reward, we demonstrated that social interaction, if offered in a mutually exclusive setting, decreased it. While Izenwasser and colleagues (34) or Ribeiro Do Couto and coworkers (33) studied the effect of dyadic and group social interaction offered in the home cage, we focused on DSI offered as a non-drug stimulus within the confines of the CPP apparatus itself. Independently from us, Neisewander and colleagues demonstrated the rewarding effect of limited physical contact through a mesh barrier (19), in accordance with our observation that physical contact through "prison-type" steel bars was sufficient to produce reward, albeit to a lesser degree than full physical contact (4). Bardo and coworkers have taken great care to further validate our paradigm and have found that the length of exposure to DSI and the age of the animals is of great importance for successfully establishing DSI as a reward (16).

Our choice of EGR1 as a brain activation marker was based on the seminal paper by Everitt and colleagues (35) who showed that infusion of EGR1 antisense oligodeoxynucleotides into the BLA prior to the reactivation of a well-learned memory for a conditioned stimulus-cocaine association, abolished the acquired conditioned reinforcing properties of the drug-associated stimulus and thus its impact on the learning of a new cocaine-seeking response and that reconsolidation of CS-fear memories also required EGR1 in the amygdala.

A great deal of time can be spent on discussing the merits and shortcomings of using a biased approach in CPP, i.e., assigning the to-be conditioned stimulus to the initially non-preferred chamber – as opposed to, say, counterbalancing the animals according to their pretest preference to obtain an across-group equality in pretest times [please, see the excellent reviews of Ref. (7, 8)]. From the translational perspective, it does not matter: substance use disorders are defined by one stimulus, i.e., the drug of abuse, channeling, and limiting the individual's behavior toward this drug of abuse, regardless of where and how broad the interests of this individuals lay before the drug of abuse took control of the individual's behavior (36, 37).

With respect to other limitations of our paradigm, our findings, obtained in "young adult" rats, may not be generalizable to "old adult" rats, as the findings of Bardo and colleagues (16) suggest. In our paradigm, we have also tried to increase the attractiveness of DSI by single-housing the animals, another issue addressed in Ref. (16). It also turned out that limiting the time of exposure to social interaction to 15 min may have proved to be favorable to obtain a rewarding effect of this non-drug stimulus (16). We chose to investigate males; applying our paradigm to females is an obvious avenue to explore.

The development of our experimental paradigm was based on the intention of one of us (G.Z.) to operationalize in an animal model what he thinks to be one of the core aspects of the beneficial effects of religious experience, i.e., an idealized dyadic relationship, in recovering addicts (38, 39). While we indeed did find that DSI proved beneficial with respect to the reorientation away from cocaine (as a prototypical drug of abuse) toward social interaction as a non-drug stimulus, there is no agreement that our paradigm indeed operationalizes any aspect of religious experience. Thus, a disputed premise may have led to what we opine is an important experimental finding.

Finally, our findings present a challenge to a view holding that drugs of abuse control an individual to a degree that precludes any choice. Similar to our findings with DSI, Ahmed and coworkers could demonstrate in rats that intense sweetness can surpass cocaine reward, even in drug-sensitized and -addicted individuals

(40). The findings of Ahmed and colleagues and our group offer hope for the psychotherapy of drug dependent individuals in that a behavioral change may still be possible, even if an individual initially shows a seemingly exclusive preference for a drug of abuse.

ACKNOWLEDGMENTS

This work was supported by the graduate program Signal Processing in Neurons (www.neurospin.at, Austrian Science Fund grant FWF W1206-B18) and the Verein fuer Experimentelle Psychiatrie, Psychotherapie und Pharmakologie (VEPPP).

REFERENCES

1. Grawe K, Donati R, Bernauer F. *Psy- chotherapie im Wandel. Von der Konfession zur Profession*. Goettingen: Hogrefe (1995).
2. Leichsenring F, Leibing E. The efficacy of short-term psychdy- namic psychotherapy in specific psychiatric disorders. A meta- analysis. *Arch Gen Psychiatry* (2004) 61:1208–16. doi:10.1001/archpsyc. 61.12.1208
3. Fritz M, El Rawas R, Salti A, Klement S, Bardo MT, Kemm- ler G, et al. Reversal of cocaine- conditioned place preference and mesocorticolimbic Zif268 expres- sion by social interaction in rats. *Addict Biol* (2011) 16:273–84. doi: 10.1111/j.1369-1600.2010.00285.x
4. Kummer K, Klement S, Eggart V, Mayr MJ, Saria A, Zernig G. Con- ditioned place preference for social interaction in rats: contribution of sensory components. *Front Behav Neurosci* (2011) 5:80. doi:10.3389/ fnbeh.2011.00080
5. El Rawas R, Klement S, Salti A, Fritz M, Dechant G, Saria A, et al. Preventive role of social interaction for cocaine conditioned place preference: correlation with FosB/DeltaFosB and pCREB expres- sion in rat mesocorticolimbic areas. *Front Behav Neurosci* (2012) 6:8. doi:10.3389/fnbeh.2012.00008
6. Prast JM, Kummer KK, Barwitz CM, Humpel C, Dechant G, Zernig G. Acetylcholine, drug reward and substance use disorder treatment: intra- and interindividual striatal and accumbal neuron ensemble heterogeneity may explain appar- ent discrepant findings. *Pharmacol- ogy* (2012) 90:264–73. doi:10.1159/ 000342636
7. Bardo MT, Bevins RA. Conditioned place preference: what does it add to our preclinical understanding of drug reward? *Psychopharmacol- ogy (Berl)* (2000) 153:31–43. doi:10. 1007/s002130000569
8. Tzschentke TM. Measuring reward with the conditioned place preference (CPP) paradigm: update of the last decade. *Addict Biol* (2007) 12(3–4):227–462. doi:10.1111/j.1369-1600.2007. 00070.x
9. Fritz M, El Rawas R, Klement S, Kummer K, Mayr MJ, Eggart V, et al. Differential effects of accumbens core vs shell lesion in a rat concurrent conditioned place preference paradigm for cocaine vs social interaction. *PLoS One* (2011) 6:e26761. doi:10.1371/ journal.pone.0026761
10. Fritz M, Klement S, El Rawas R, Saria A, Zernig G. Sigma1 receptor antagonist BD1047 enhances rever- sal of conditioned place preference from cocaine to social interaction. *Pharmacology* (2011) 87:45–8. doi: 10.1159/000322534
11. Zernig G, Fritz M, Klement S, El Rawas R, Saria A. Social interaction- vs cocaine conditioned place pref- erence is associated with a differen- tial activation of nucleus accumbens core cholinergic interneurons. *Drug Alcohol Depend* (2011) 16:273.
12. El Rawas R, Klement S, Kummer KK, Fritz M, Dechant G, Saria A, et al. Brain regions associated with the acquisition of conditioned place preference for cocaine ver- sus social interaction. *Front Behav Neurosci* (2012) 6:63. doi:10.3389/ fnbeh.2012.00063
13. Epstein DH, Willner-Reid J, Vahabzadeh M, Mezghanni M, Lin JL, Preston KL. Real-time electronic diary reports of cue exposure and mood in the hours before cocaine and heroin craving and use. *Arch Gen Psychiatry* (2009) 66:88–94. doi:10.1001/archgenpsychiatry. 2008.509
14. Preston KL, Vahabzadeh M, Schmit- tner J, Lin JL, Gorelick DA, Epstein DH. Cocaine craving and use dur- ing daily life. *Psychopharmacology (Berl)* (2009) 207:291–301. doi:10. 1007/s00213-009-1655-8
15. Childs E, de Wit H. Amphetamine-induced place preference in humans. *Biol Psychiatry* (2009) 65:900–4. doi:10.1016/j.biopsych.2008.11.016
16. Yates JR, Beckmann JS, Meyer AC, Bardo MT. Concurrent choice for social interaction and ampheta- mine using conditioned place pref- erence in rats: Effects of age and housing condition. *Drug Alcohol Depend* (2013) 129:240–6. doi:10. 1016/j.drugalcdep.2013.02.024
17. Hope B, Kosofsky B, Hyman SE, Nestler EJ. Regulation of immedi- ate early gene expression and AP-1 binding in the rat nucleus accum- bens by chronic cocaine. *Proc Natl Acad Sci USA* (1992) 89:5764–8. doi:10.1073/ pnas.89.13.5764
18. McClung CA, Nestler EJ. Regula- tion of gene expression and cocaine reward by CREB and DeltaFosB. *Nat Neurosci* (2003) 6:1208–15. doi:10. 1038/nn1143
19. Peartree NA, Hood LE, Thiel KJ, Sanabria F, Pentkowski NS, Chan- dler KN, et al. Limited physi- cal contact through a mesh bar- rier is sufficient for social reward- conditioned place preference in adolescent male rats. *Physiol Behav* (2012) 105:749–56. doi:10.1016/j. physbeh.2011.10.001
20. Pratt WE, Kelley AE. Nucleus accumbens acetylcholine regulates appetitive learning and motivation for food via activation of muscarinic receptors. *Behav Neurosci* (2004) 118:730–9. doi:10.1037/0735-7044. 118.4.730
21. Crespo JA, Sturm K, Saria A, Zernig G. Activation of muscarinic and nicotinic acetylcholine recep- tors in the nucleus accumbens core is necessary for the acquis- tion of drug reinforcement. *J Neu- rosci* (2006) 26:6004–10. doi:10. 1523/JNEUROSCI.4494-05.2006
22. Crespo JA, Stoeckl P, Zorn K, Saria A, Zernig G. Nucleus accumbens core acetylcholine is preferentially activated dur- ing drug- vs food-reinforcement acquisition. *Neuropsychophar- macology* (2008) 33:3213–20. doi:10.1038/npp.2008.48
23. Witten IB, Lin SC, Brodsky M, Diester I, Anikeeva P, Prakash R, et al. Cholinergic interneu- rons control local circuit activity and cocaine conditioning. *Science* (2010) 330:1677–81. doi:10.1126/ science.1193771
24. Crespo JA, Stöckl P, Ueberall F, Jenny M, Saria A, Zernig G. Activation of PKCzeta and PKMzeta in the nucleus accumbens core is neces- sary for the retrieval, consolidation and reconsolidation of drug mem- ory. *PLoS One* (2012) 7:e30502. doi: 10.1371/journal.pone.0030502
25. Kreitzer AC. Physiology and phar- macology of striatal neurons. *Annu Rev Neurosci* (2009) 32:127–47. doi:10.1146/annurev.neuro.051508. 135422
26. Tepper JM, Tecuapetla F, Koos T, Ibanez-Sandoval O. Heterogeneity and diversity of striatal GABAer- gic interneurons. *Front Neuroanat* (2010) 4:150. doi:10.3389/fnana. 2010.00150
27. English DF, Ibanez-Sandoval O, Stark E, Tecuapetla F, Buzsaki G, Deisseroth K, et al. GABAergic cir- cuits mediate the reinforcement- related signals of striatal cholinergic interneurons. *Nat Neurosci* (2011) 15:123–30. doi:10.1038/nn.2984
28. Cachope R, Mateo Y, Mathur BN, Irving J, Wang HL, Morales M, et al. Selective activation of choliner- gic interneurons enhances accum- bal phasic dopamine release: setting the tone for reward processing. *Cell Rep* (2012) 2:33–41. doi:10.1016/j. celrep.2012.05.011
29. Gittis AH, Kreitzer AC. Striatal microcircuitry and movement dis- orders. *Trends Neurosci* (2012) 35:557–64. doi:10.1016/j.tins.2012. 06.008
30. Surmeier DJ, Graybiel AM. A feud that wasn't: acetylcholine evokes dopamine release in the striatum. *Neuron* (2012) 75:1–3. doi:10.1016/ j.neuron.2012.06.028
31. Threlfell S, Lalic T, Platt NJ, Jen- nings KA, Deisseroth K, Cragg SJ. Striatal dopamine release is triggered by synchronized activity in cholinergic interneurons. *Neu- ron* (2012) 75:58–64. doi:10.1016/j. neuron.2012.04.038
32. Thiel KJ, Okun AC, Neisewander JL. Social reward-conditioned place preference: a model revealing an interaction between cocaine and social context rewards in rats. *Drug Alcohol Depend* (2008) 96:202–12. doi:10.1016/j.drugalcdep.2008.02. 013
33. Ribeiro Do Couto B, Aguilar MA, Lluch J, Rodriguez-Arias M, Minarro J. Social experi- ences affect reinstatement of cocaine-induced place preference in mice. *Psychopharmacol- ogy (Berl)* (2009) 207:485–98. doi:10.1007/ s00213-009-1678-1
34. Zakharova E, Miller J, Unterwald E, Wade D, Izenwasser S. Social and physical environment alter cocaine conditioned place prefer- ence and dopaminergic markers in adolescent male rats. *Neuro- science* (2009) 163:890–7. doi:10. 1016/j.neuroscience.2009.06.068
35. Lee JL, Diciano P, Thomas KL, Everitt BJ. Disrupting reconsoli- dation of drug memories reduces cocaine-seeking behavior. *Neuron* (2005) 47:795–801. doi:10.1016/j. neuron.2005.08.007

36. Zernig G, Ahmed SH, Cardinal RN, Morgan D, Acquas E, Foltin RW, et al. Explaining the escalation of drug use in substance dependence: models and appropriate animal laboratory tests. *Pharmacology* (2007) 80:65–119. doi:10.1159/000103923

37. Zernig G, Saria A, Kurz M, O'malley SS. *Handbook of alcoholism*. Boca Raton: CRC Press (2000).

38. Zernig G. Replication and further scientific investigations will tell the truth. *Addiction* (2008) 103:2033–4. doi:10.1111/j.1360-0443.2008. 02397.x

39. Zernig G, Wallner R, Grohs U, Kriechbaum N, Kemmler G, Saria A randomized trial of short psychotherapy vs sustained-release bupropion for smoking cessation. *Addiction* (2008) 103:2024–31. doi:10.1111/j.1360-0443.2008. 02348.x

40. Lenoir M, Serre F, Cantin L, Ahmed SH. Intense sweetness sur- passes cocaine reward. *PLoS One* (2007) 2:e698. doi:10.1371/journal. pone.0000698

Permissions

All chapters in this book were first published in AMA, by Frontiers; hereby published with permission under the Creative Commons Attribution License or equivalent. Every chapter published in this book has been scrutinized by our experts. Their significance has been extensively debated. The topics covered herein carry significant findings which will fuel the growth of the discipline. They may even be implemented as practical applications or may be referred to as a beginning point for another development.

The contributors of this book come from diverse backgrounds, making this book a truly international effort. This book will bring forth new frontiers with its revolutionizing research information and detailed analysis of the nascent developments around the world.

We would like to thank all the contributing authors for lending their expertise to make the book truly unique. They have played a crucial role in the development of this book. Without their invaluable contributions this book wouldn't have been possible. They have made vital efforts to compile up to date information on the varied aspects of this subject to make this book a valuable addition to the collection of many professionals and students.

This book was conceptualized with the vision of imparting up-to-date information and advanced data in this field. To ensure the same, a matchless editorial board was set up. Every individual on the board went through rigorous rounds of assessment to prove their worth. After which they invested a large part of their time researching and compiling the most relevant data for our readers.

The editorial board has been involved in producing this book since its inception. They have spent rigorous hours researching and exploring the diverse topics which have resulted in the successful publishing of this book. They have passed on their knowledge of decades through this book. To expedite this challenging task, the publisher supported the team at every step. A small team of assistant editors was also appointed to further simplify the editing procedure and attain best results for the readers.

Apart from the editorial board, the designing team has also invested a significant amount of their time in understanding the subject and creating the most relevant covers. They scrutinized every image to scout for the most suitable representation of the subject and create an appropriate cover for the book.

The publishing team has been an ardent support to the editorial, designing and production team. Their endless efforts to recruit the best for this project, has resulted in the accomplishment of this book. They are a veteran in the field of academics and their pool of knowledge is as vast as their experience in printing. Their expertise and guidance has proved useful at every step. Their uncompromising quality standards have made this book an exceptional effort. Their encouragement from time to time has been an inspiration for everyone.

The publisher and the editorial board hope that this book will prove to be a valuable piece of knowledge for researchers, students, practitioners and scholars across the globe.

List of Contributors

Sally Satel
Yale University School of Medicine, New Haven, CT, USA

Scott O. Lilienfeld
Department of Psychology, Emory University, Atlanta, GA, USA

Neil Levy
Florey Institute of Neuroscience and Mental Health, The University of Melbourne, Parkville, VIC, Australia

Brendan Dill
Department of Linguistics and Philosophy, Massachusetts Institute of Technology, Cambridge, MA, USA

Richard Holton
Department of Philosophy, University of Cambridge, Cambridge, UK

Gregory C. Sartor and Claes Wahlestedt
Hussman Institute for Human Genomics, University of Miami Miller School of Medicine, Miami, FL, USA

Georges St. Laurent III
St. Laurent Institute, Cambridge, MA, USA
Immunovirology - Biogenisis Group, University of Antioquia, Medellin, Colombia

Robert J. MacCoun
Goldman School of Public Policy and Berkeley Law, University of California at Berkeley, Berkeley, CA, USA

Nienke Liebregts and Dirk J. Korf
Law Faculty, Bonger Institute of Criminology, University of Amsterdam, Amsterdam, Netherlands

Peggy van der Pol, Margriet Van Laar and Ron de Graaf
Trimbos Institute, Netherlands Institute of Mental Health and Addiction, Utrecht, Netherlands

Wim van den Brink
Department of Psychiatry, Academic Medical Centre, University of Amsterdam, Amsterdam, Netherlands

George Ainslie
School of Economics, University of Cape Town, Cape Town, South Africa
Department of Veterans Affairs, Coatesville, PA, USA

Gene M. Heyman
Department of Psychology, Boston College, Chestnut Hill, MA, USA

Brian J. Dunn
Department of Psychology, Center for Studies in Behavioral Neurobiology, Concordia University, Montreal, QC, Canada

Jason Mignone
Prime, Buchholz & Associates, Inc., Portsmouth, NH, USA

Caroline Davis
Kinesiology and Health Science, York University, Toronto, ON, Canada

Robert D. Levitan, Allan S. Kaplan and James L. Kennedy
Centre for Addiction and Mental Health, Toronto, ON, Canada

Jacqueline C. Carter
Department of Psychology, Memorial University of Newfoundland, St. John's, NL, Canada

Edward H. Hagen and Casey J. Roulette
Department of Anthropology, Washington State University, Vancouver, WA, USA

Roger J. Sullivan
Department of Anthropology, California State University, Sacramento, CA, USA

Brian Johnson
Department of Psychiatry, State University of New York Upstate Medical University, Syracuse, NY, USA

Stéphanie Olière and Antoine Jolette-Riopel
Addiction Psychiatry Research Unit, Research Center, Centre Hospitalier de l'Université de Montréal (CRCHUM), Montreal, QC, Canada

Stéphane Potvin
Department of Psychiatry, University of Montreal, Montreal, QC, Canada
Research Center, Institut Universitaire en Santé Mentale de Montréal, Montreal, QC, Canada

Jeanette Kennett and Anke Snoek
Department of Philosophy, Macquarie University, Sydney, NSW, Australia

Didier Jutras-Aswad
Addiction Psychiatry Research Unit, Research Center, Centre Hospitalier de l'Université de Montréal (CRCHUM), Montreal, QC, Canada
Department of Psychiatry, University of Montreal, Montreal, QC, Canada

Steve Matthews
Australian Catholic University, Sydney, NSW, Australia

Jerome C. Wakefield
Silver School of Social Work and Department of Psychiatry, School of Medicine, New York University, New York, NY, USA

Mark F. Schmitz
School of Social Work, Temple University, Philadelphia, PA, USA

Jeremy Michael Pober
Department of Philosophy, San Francisco State University, San Francisco, CA, USA

Edmund Henden
Centre for the Study of Professions, Oslo and Akershus University College of Applied Sciences, Oslo, Norway

Hans Olav Melberg
Department of Health Management and Health Economics, University of Oslo, Oslo, Norway

Ole Jørgen Røgeberg
Ragnar Frisch Centre for Economic Research, Oslo, Norway

Owen Flanagan
Department of Philosophy, Duke University, Durham, NC, USA

Purva Bali and Paul J. Kenny
Laboratory of Behavioral and Molecular Neuroscience, Department of Molecular Therapeutics, The Scripps Research Institute - Florida, Jupiter, FL, USA
Laboratory of Behavioral and Molecular Neuroscience, Department of Neuroscience, The Scripps Research Institute - Florida, Jupiter, FL, USA

Gerald Zernig
Experimental Psychiatry Unit, Department of General Psychiatry and Social Psychiatry, Innsbruck Medical University, Innsbruck, Austria
Department of Psychology, Leopold-Franzens University of Innsbruck, Innsbruck, Austria

Kai K. Kummer and Janine M. Prast
Experimental Psychiatry Unit, Department of General Psychiatry and Social Psychiatry, Innsbruck Medical University, Innsbruck, Austria

Index

www.ingramcontent.com/pod-product-compliance
Lightning Source LLC
LaVergne TN
LVHW060550210926
848485LV00005B/1293
* 9 7 8 1 6 3 9 8 7 0 0 9 7 *